Americans With Disabilities Act Handbook

This book was originally published by the U.S. Equal Employment Opportunity Commission. The pages were unbound and three-hole punched for use in a three-ring binder. This reprint includes all the content of the original but is available as one perfect bound volume.

from

©1993, JIST Works, Inc. Reorder #2037

Printed on acid-free paper in the United States of America

JIST Works, Inc.
720 North Park Avenue
Indianapolis, IN 46202-3431
Phone: **1-317-264-3720**
FAX: **1-317-264-3709** or toll free **1-800-JIST- FAX**

ISBN: 1-56370-080-8

Table of Contents

Preamble

When President Bush signed into law the Americans with Disabilities Act--the world's first comprehensive civil rights law for people with disabilities--in front of 3,000 people on the White House lawn on July 26, 1990, the event represented an historical benchmark and a milestone in America's commitment to full and equal opportunity for all of its citizens.

The President's emphatic directive on that day--"Let the shameful walls of exclusion finally come tumbling down"--neatly encapsulated the simple yet long overdue message of the ADA: that 43 million Americans with disabilities are full-fledged citizens and as such are entitled to legal protections that ensure them equal opportunity and access to the mainstream of American life.

Enactment of the ADA reflects deeply held American ideals which treasure the contributions which individuals can make when free from arbitrary, unjust, or outmoded societal attitudes and practices that prevent the realization of their potential. The ADA reflects a recognition that the surest path to America's continued vitality, strength and vibrancy is through the full realization of the contributions of all of its citizens.

Introduction

This *ADA Handbook* represents one part of the overall effort by the Equal Employment Opportunity Commission(EEOC) and the Department of Justice(DOJ) to provide information and assistance on the ADA to people with disabilities, businesses, and the affected public. It is intended to serve as a basic resource document on the ADA. EEOC and DOJ are scheduled to publish ADA technical assistance manuals, containing more specific information on how to comply with the law, in early 1992. Further technical assistance will be provided through training, videotapes, information hotlines, media outreach, speaking presentations, and other publications. EEOC has responsibility for providing technical assistance for title I, dealing with employment. DOJ has responsibility for providing technical assistance for titles II and III, addressing public services and public accommodations, respectively. Many businesses with 15 or more employees will be covered by both title I and title III of the Act.

The *Handbook* contains annotated regulations for titles I, II, and III, resources for obtaining additional assistance, and an appendix which contains supplementary information related to the implementation of the ADA.

Duplication of all or parts of the *Handbook* is encouraged.

This document is available in the following alternate formats:

- Braille
- Large Print
- Audiotape
- Electronic file on computer disk and electronic bulletin board
  (202) 514-6193

To order additional copies of this document call:

At EEOC:
800-669-EEOC (Voice)
800-800-3302 (TDD)

At DOJ:
(202) 514-0301 (Voice)
(202) 514-0383 (TDD)

TITLE I

EQUAL EMPLOYMENT OPPORTUNITY FOR INDIVIDUALS WITH DISABILITIES

1. Background

The ADA is a federal antidiscrimination statute designed to remove barriers which prevent qualified individuals with disabilities from enjoying the same employment opportunities that are available to persons without disabilities.

Like the Civil Rights Act of 1964 that prohibits discrimination on the bases of race, color, religion, national origin, and sex, the ADA seeks to ensure access to equal employment opportunities based on merit. It does not guarantee equal results, establish quotas, or require preferences favoring individuals with disabilities over those without disabilities.

However, while the Civil Rights Act of 1964 prohibits any consideration of personal characteristics such as race or national origin, the ADA necessarily takes a different approach. When an individual's disability creates a barrier to employment opportunities, the ADA requires employers to consider whether reasonable accommodation could remove the barrier.

The ADA thus establishes a process in which the employer must assess a disabled individual's ability to perform the essential functions of the specific job held or desired. While the ADA focuses on eradicating barriers, the ADA does not relieve a disabled employee or applicant from the obligation to perform the essential functions of the job. To the contrary, the ADA is intended to enable disabled persons to compete in the workplace based on the same performance standards and requirements that employers expect of persons who are not disabled.

However, where that individual's functional limitation impedes such job performance, an employer must take steps to reasonably accommodate, and thus help overcome the particular impediment, unless to do so would impose an undue hardship. Such accommodations usually take the form of adjustments to the way a job customarily is performed, or to the work environment itself.

This process of identifying whether, and to what extent, a reasonable accommodation is required should be flexible and involve both the employer and the individual with a disability. Of course, the determination of whether an individual is qualified for a particular position must necessarily be made on a case-by-case basis. No specific form of accommodation is guaranteed for all individuals with a particular disability. Rather, an accommodation must be tailored to match the needs of the disabled individual with the needs of the job's essential functions.

This case-by-case approach is essential if qualified individuals of varying abilities are to receive equal opportunities to compete for an infinitely diverse range of jobs. For this reason, neither the ADA nor this regulation can supply the "correct" answer in advance for each employment decision concerning an individual with a disability. Instead, the ADA simply establishes parameters to guide employers in how to consider, and take into account, the disabling condition involved.

2. Introduction

The Equal Employment Opportunity Commission (the Commission or EEOC) is responsible for enforcement of title I of the Americans with Disabilities Act (ADA), 42 U.S.C. 12101 et seq. (1990), which prohibits employment discrimination on the basis of disability. The Commission believes that it is essential to issue interpretive guidance concurrently with the issuance of this part in order to ensure that qualified individuals with disabilities understand their rights under this part and to facilitate and encourage compliance by covered entities. This Appendix represents the

Commission's interpretation of the issues discussed, and the Commission will be guided by it when resolving charges of employment discrimination. The Appendix addresses the major provisions of this part and explains the major concepts of disability rights.

The terms "employer" or "employer or other covered entity" are used interchangeably throughout the Appendix to refer to all covered entities subject to the employment provisions of the ADA.

3. Summary

On July 26, 1990, the Americans with Disabilities Act (ADA) was signed into law. Section 106 of the ADA requires that the Equal Employment Opportunity Commission (EEOC) issue substantive regulations implementing title I (Employment) within one year of the date of enactment of the Act. Pursuant to this mandate, the Commission is publishing a new part 1630 to its regulations to implement title I and sections 3(2), 3(3), 501, 503, 506(e), 508, 510, and 511 of the ADA as those sections pertain to employment. New part 1630 prohibits discrimination against qualified individuals with disabilities in all aspects of employment.

EFFECTIVE DATE: July 26, 1992.

FOR FURTHER INFORMATION CONTACT: Elizabeth M. Thornton, Deputy Legal Counsel, (202) 663-4638 (voice), (202) 663-7026 (TDD) or Christopher G. Bell, Acting Associate Legal Counsel for Americans with Disabilities Act Services, (202) 663-4679 (voice), (202) 663-7026.

Copies of this final rule and interpretive appendix may be obtained by calling the Office of Communications and Legislative Affairs at (202) 663-4900. Copies in alternate formats may be obtained from the Office of Equal Employment Opportunity by calling (202) 663-4398 or (202) 663-4395 (voice) or (202) 663-4399 (TDD). The alternate formats available are: large print, braille, electronic file on computer disk, and audio-tape.

SUPPLEMENTARY INFORMATION:

4. Rulemaking History

The Commission actively solicited and considered public comment in the development of part 1630. On August 1, 1990, the Commission published an advance notice of proposed rulemaking (ANPRM), 55 FR 31192, informing the public that the Commission had begun the process of developing substantive regulations pursuant to title I of the ADA and inviting comment from interested groups and individuals. The comment period ended on August 31, 1990. In response to the ANPRM, the Commission received 138 comments from various disability rights organizations, employer groups, and individuals. Comments were also solicited at 62 ADA input meetings conducted by Commission field offices throughout the country. More than 2400 representatives from disability rights organizations and employer groups participated in these meetings.

On February 28, 1991, the Commission published a notice of proposed rulemaking (NPRM), 56 FR 8578, setting forth proposed part 1630 for public comment. The comment period ended April 29, 1991. In response to the NPRM, the Commission received 697 timely comments from interested groups and individuals. In many instances, a comment was submitted on behalf of several parties and represented the views of numerous groups, employers, or individuals with disabilities. The comments have been analyzed and considered in the development of this final rule.

5. Overview of Regulations

The format of part 1630 reflects congressional intent, as expressed in the legislative history, that the regulations implementing the employment provisions of the ADA be modeled on the regulations implementing Section 504 of the Rehabilitation Act of 1973, as amended, 34 CFR part 104. Accordingly, in developing part 1630, the Commission has been guided by the Section 504 regulations and the case law interpreting those regulations.

It is the intent of Congress that the regulations implementing the ADA be comprehensive and easily understood. Part 1630, therefore, defines terms not previously defined in the regulations implementing Section 504 of the Rehabilitation Act, such as "substantially limits," "essential functions," and "reasonable accommodation." Of necessity, many of the determinations that may be required by this part must be made on a case-by-case basis. Where possible, part 1630 establishes parameters to serve as guidelines in such inquiries.

The Commission is also issuing interpretive guidance concurrently with the issuance of part 1630 in order to ensure that qualified individuals with disabilities understand their rights under this part and to facilitate and encourage compliance by covered entities. Therefore, part 1630 is accompanied by an Appendix. This Appendix represents the Commission's interpretation of the issues discussed, and the Commission will be guided by it when resolving charges of employment discrimination. The Appendix addresses the major provisions of part 1630 and explains the major concepts of disability rights. Further, the Appendix cites to the authority, such as the legislative history of the ADA and case law interpreting Section 504 of the Rehabilitation Act, that provides the basis and purpose of the rule and interpretative guidance.

More detailed guidance on specific issues will be forthcoming in the Commission's Compliance Manual. Several Compliance Manual sections and policy guidances on ADA issues are currently under development and are expected to be issued prior to the effective date of the Act. Among the issues to be addressed in depth are the theories of discrimination; definitions of disability and of qualified individual with a disability; reasonable accommodation and undue hardship, including the scope of reassignment; and pre-employment inquiries.

To assist us in the development of this guidance, the Commission requested comment in the NPRM from disability rights organizations, employers, unions, state agencies concerned with employment or workers compensation practices, and interested individuals on specific questions about insurance, workers' compensation, and collective bargaining agreements. Many commenters responded to these questions, and several commenters addressed other matters pertinent to these areas. The Commission has considered these comments in the development of the final rule and will continue to consider them as it develops further ADA guidance.

In the NPRM, the Commission raised questions about a number of insurance-related matters. Specifically, the Commission asked commenters to discuss risk assessment and classification, the relationship between "risk" and "cost," and whether employers should consider the effects that changes in insurance coverage will have on individuals with disabilities before making those changes. Many commenters provided information about insurance practices and explained some of the considerations that affect insurance decisions. In addition, some commenters discussed their experiences with insurance plans and coverage. The commenters presented a wide range of opinions on insurance-related matters, and the Commission will consider the comments as it continues to analyze these complex matters.

The Commission received a large number of comments concerning inquiries about an individual's workers' compensation history. Many employers asserted that such inquiries are job related and consistent with business necessity. Several individuals with disabilities and disability rights organizations, however, argued that such inquiries are prohibited pre-employment inquiries and are not job related and consistent with business necessity. The Commission has addressed this issue in the interpretive guidance accompanying section 1630.14(a) and will discuss the matter further in future guidance.

There was little controversy about the submission of medical information to workers' compensation offices. A number of employers and employer groups pointed out that the workers' compensation offices of many states request medical information in connection with the administration of second-injury funds. Further, they noted that the disclosure of medical information may be necessary to the defense of a workers' compensation claim. The Commission has responded to these comments by amending the interpretive guidance accompanying section 1630.14(b). This amendment, discussed below, notes that the submission of medical information to workers' compensation offices in accordance with state workers' compensation laws is not inconsistent with section 1630.14(b). The Commission will address this area in greater detail and will discuss other issues concerning workers' compensation matters in future guidances, including the policy guidance on pre-employment inquiries.

With respect to collective bargaining agreements, the Commission asked commenters to discuss the relationship between collective bargaining agreements and such matters as undue hardship, reassignment to a vacant position, the determination of what constitutes a "vacant" position, and the confidentiality requirements of the ADA. The comments that we received reflected a wide variety of views. For example, some commenters argued that it would always be an undue hardship for an employer to provide a reasonable accommodation that conflicted with the provisions of a collective bargaining agreement. Other commenters, however, argued that an accommodation's effect on an agreement should not be considered when assessing undue hardship. Similarly, some commenters stated that the appropriateness of reassignment to a vacant position should depend upon the provisions of a collective bargaining agreement while others asserted that an agreement cannot limit the right to reassignment. Many commenters discussed the relationship between an agreement's seniority provisions and an employer's reasonable accommodation obligations.

In response to comments, the Commission has amended section 1630.2(n)(3) to include "the terms of a collective bargaining agreement" in the types of evidence relevant to determining the essential functions of a position. The Commission has made a corresponding change to the interpretive guidance on section 1630.2(n)(3). In addition, the Commission has amended the interpretive guidance on section 1630.15(d) to note that the terms of a collective bargaining agreement may be relevant to determining whether an accommodation would pose an undue hardship on the operation of a covered entity's business.

The divergent views expressed in the public comments demonstrate the complexity of employment-related issues concerning insurance, workers' compensation, and collective bargaining agreement matters. These highly complex issues require extensive research and analysis and warrant further consideration. Accordingly, the Commission has decided to address the issues in depth in future

Compliance Manual sections and policy guidances. The Commission will consider the public comments that it received in response to the NPRM as it develops further guidance on the application of title I of the ADA to these matters.

The Commission has also decided to address burdens-of-proof issues in future guidance documents, including the Compliance Manual section on the theories of discrimination. Many commenters discussed the allocation of the various burdens of proof under title I of the ADA and asked the Commission to clarify those burdens. The comments in this area addressed such matters as determining whether a person is a qualified individual with a disability, job relatedness and business necessity, and undue hardship. The Commission will consider these comments as it prepares further guidance in this area.

A discussion of other significant comments and an explanation of the changes made in part 1630 since publication of the NPRM follows.

6. Section-by-Section Analysis of Comments and Revisions

Section 1630.1 Purpose, applicability, and construction

The Commission has made a technical correction to section 1630.1(a) by adding section 506(e) to the list of statutory provisions implemented by this part. Section 506(e) of the ADA provides that the failure to receive technical assistance from the federal agencies that administer the ADA is not a defense to failing to meet the obligations of title I.

Some commenters asked the Commission to note that the ADA does not preempt state claims, such as state tort claims, that confer greater remedies than are available under the ADA. The Commission has added a paragraph to that effect in the Appendix discussion of sections 1630.1(b) and (c). This interpretation is consistent with the legislative history of the Act. See H.R. Rep. No. 485 Part 3, 101st Cong., 2d Sess. 69-70 (1990) [hereinafter referred to as House Judiciary Report].

In addition, the Commission has made a technical amendment to the Appendix discussion to note that the ADA does not automatically preempt medical standards or safety requirements established by Federal law or regulations. The Commission has also amended the discussion to refer to a direct threat that cannot be eliminated "or reduced" through reasonable accommodation. This language is consistent with the regulatory definition of direct threat. (See section 1630.2(r), below.)

Section 1630.2 Definitions

Section 1630.2(h) Physical or mental impairment

The Commission has amended the interpretive guidance accompanying section 1630.2(h) to note that the definition of the term "impairment" does not include characteristic predisposition to illness or disease.

In addition, the Commission has specifically noted in the interpretive guidance that pregnancy is not an impairment. This change responds to the numerous questions that the Commission has received concerning whether pregnancy is a disability covered by the ADA. Pregnancy, by itself, is not an impairment and is therefore not a disability.

Section 1630.2(j) Substantially limits

The Commission has revised the interpretive guidance accompanying section 1630.2(j) to make clear that the determination of whether an impairment substantially limits one or more major life activities is to be made without regard to the availability of medicines, assistive devices, or other mitigating measures. This interpretation is consistent with the legislative history of the ADA. See S. Rep. No. 116, 101st Cong., 1st Sess. 23 (1989) [hereinafter referred to as Senate Report]; H.R. Rep. No. 485 Part 2, 101st Cong., 2d Sess. 52 (1990) [hereinafter referred to as House Labor Report]; House Judiciary Report at 28. The Commission has also revised the examples in the third paragraph of this section's guidance. The examples now focus on the individual's capacity to perform major life activities rather than on the presence or absence of mitigating measures. These revisions respond to comments from disability rights groups, which were concerned that the discussion could be misconstrued to exclude from ADA coverage of individuals with disabilities who function well because of assistive devices or other mitigating measures.

In an amendment to the paragraph concerning the factors to consider when determining whether an impairment is substantially limiting, the Commission has provided a second example of an impairment's "impact." This example notes that a traumatic head injury's affect on cognitive functions is the "impact" of that impairment.

Many commenters addressed the provisions concerning the definition of "substantially limits" with respect to the major life activity of working (section 1630.2(j)(3)). Some employers generally supported the definition but argued that it should be applied narrowly. Other employers argued that the definition is too broad. Disability rights groups and individuals with disabilities, on the other hand, argued that the definition is too narrow, unduly limits coverage, and places an onerous burden on individuals seeking to establish that they are covered by the ADA. The Commission has responded to these comments by making a number of clarifications in this area.

The Commission has revised section 1630.2(j)(3)(ii) and the accompanying interpretive guidance to note that the listed factors "may" be considered when determining whether an individual is substantially limited in working. This revision clarifies that the factors are relevant to, but are not required elements of, a showing of a substantial limitation in working.

Disability rights groups asked the Commission to clarify that "substantially limited in working" applies only when an individual is not substantially limited in any other major life activity. In addition, several other commenters indicated confusion about whether and when the ability to work should be considered when assessing if an individual has a disability. In response to these comments, the Commission has amended the interpretive guidance by adding a new paragraph clarifying the circumstances under which one should determine whether an individual is substantially limited in the major life activity of working. This paragraph makes clear that a determination of whether an individual is substantially limited in the ability to work should be made only when the individual is not disabled in any other major life activity. Thus, individuals need not establish that they are substantially limited in working if they already have established that they are, have a record of, or are regarded as being substantially limited in another major life activity.

The proposed interpretive guidance in this area provided an example concerning a surgeon with a slight hand impairment. Several commenters expressed concern about this example. Many of these comments indicated that the example confused, rather than clarified, the matter. The Commission, therefore, has deleted this example. To explain further the application of the "substantially limited in working" concept, the Commission has provided another example (concerning a commercial airline pilot) in the interpretive guidance.

In addition, the Commission has clarified that the terms "numbers and types of jobs" (see section 1630.2(j)(3)(ii)(B)) and "numbers and types of other jobs" (see section 1630.2(j)(3)(ii)(C)) do not require an onerous evidentiary showing.

In the proposed Appendix, after the interpretive guidance accompanying section 1630.2(l), the Commission included a discussion entitled "Frequently Disabling Impairments." Many commenters expressed concern about this discussion. In response to these comments, and to avoid confusion, the Commission has revised the discussion and has deleted the list of frequently disabling impairments. The revised discussion now appears in the interpretive guidance accompanying section 1630.2(j).

Section 1630.2(l) Is regarded as having such an impairment

Section 1630.2(l)(3) has been changed to refer to "a substantially limiting impairment" rather than "such an impairment." This change clarifies that an individual meets the definition of the term "disability" when a covered entity treats the individual as having a substantially limiting impairment. That is, section 1630.2(l)(3) refers to any substantially limiting impairment, rather than just to one of the impairments described in sections 1630.2(l)(1) or (2).

The proposed interpretive guidance on section 1630.2(l) stated that, when determining whether an individual is regarded as substantially limited in working, "it should be assumed that all similar employers would apply the same exclusionary qualification standard that the employer charged with discrimination has used." The Commission specifically requested comment on this proposal, and many commenters addressed this issue. The Commission has decided to eliminate this assumption and to revise the interpretive guidance. The guidance now explains that an individual meets the "regarded as" part of the definition of disability if he or she can show that a covered entity made an employment decision because of a perception of a disability based on "myth, fear, or stereotype." This is consistent with the legislative history of the ADA. See House Judiciary Report at 30.

Section 1630.2(m) Qualified individual with a disability

Under the proposed part 1630, the first step in determining whether an individual with a disability is a qualified individual with a disability was to determine whether the individual "satisfies the requisite skill, experience and education requirements of the employment position" the individual holds or desires. Many employers and employer groups asserted that the proposed regulation unduly limited job prerequisites to skill, experience, and education requirements and did not permit employers to consider other job-related qualifications. To clarify that the reference to skill, experience, and education requirements was not intended to be an exhaustive list of permissible qualification requirements, the Commission has revised the phrase to include "skill, experience, education, and other job-related requirements." This revision recognizes that other types of job-related requirements may be relevant to determining whether an individual is qualified for a position.

Many individuals with disabilities and disability rights groups asked the Commission to emphasize that the determination of whether a person is a qualified individual with a disability must be made at the time of the employment action in question and cannot be based on speculation that the individual will become unable to perform the job in the future or may cause increased health insurance or workers' compensation costs. The Commission has amended the interpretive guidance on section 1630.2(m) to reflect this point. This guidance is consistent with the legislative history of the Act. See Senate Report at 26, House Labor Report at 55, 136; House Judiciary Report at 34, 71.

Section 1630.2(n) Essential functions

Many employers and employer groups objected to the use of the terms "primary" and "intrinsic" in the definition of essential functions. To avoid confusion about the meanings of "primary" and "intrinsic," the Commission has deleted these terms from the definition. The final regulation defines essential functions as "fundamental job duties" and notes that essential functions do not include the marginal functions of a position.

The proposed interpretive guidance accompanying section 1630.2(n)(2)(ii) noted that one of the factors in determining whether a function is essential is the number of employees available to perform a job function or among whom the performance of that function can be distributed. The proposed guidance explained that "[t]his may be a factor either because the total number of employees is low, or because of the fluctuating demands of the business operations." Some employers and employer groups expressed concern that this language could be interpreted as requiring an assessment of whether a job function could be distributed among all employees in any job at any level. The Commission has amended the interpretive guidance on this factor to clarify that the factor refers only to distribution among "available" employees.

Section 1630.2(n)(3) lists several kinds of evidence that are relevant to determining whether a particular job function is essential. Some employers and unions asked the Commission to recognize that collective bargaining agreements may help to identify a position's essential functions. In response to these comments, the Commission has added "[t]he terms of a collective bargaining agreement" to the list. In addition, the Commission has amended the interpretive guidance to note specifically that this type of evidence is relevant to the determination of essential functions. This addition is consistent with the legislative history of the Act. See Senate Report at 32; House Labor Report at 63.

Proposed section 1630.2(n)(3) referred to the evidence on the list as evidence "that may be considered in determining whether a particular function is essential." The Commission has revised this section to refer to evidence "of" whether a particular function is essential. The Commission made this revision in response to concerns about the meaning of the phrase "may be considered." In that regard, some commenters questioned whether the phrase meant that some of the listed evidence might not be considered when determining whether a function is essential to a position. This revision clarifies that all of the types of evidence on the list, when available, are relevant to the determination of a position's essential functions. As the final rule and interpretive guidance make clear, the list is not an exhaustive list of all types of relevant evidence. Other types of available evidence may also be relevant to the determination.

The Commission has amended the interpretive guidance concerning section 1630.2(n)(3)(ii) to make clear that covered entities are not required to develop and maintain written job descriptions. Such job descriptions are relevant to a determination of a position's essential functions, but they are not required by part 1630.

Several commenters suggested that the Commission establish a rebuttable presumption in favor of the employer's judgment concerning what functions are essential. The Commission has not done so. On that point, the Commission notes that the House Committee on the Judiciary specifically rejected an amendment that would have created such a presumption. See House Judiciary Report at 33-34.

The last paragraph of the interpretive guidance on section 1630.2(n) notes that the inquiry into what constitutes a position's essential functions is not intended to second guess an employer's business judgment regarding production standards, whether qualitative or quantitative. In response to several comments, the Commission has revised this paragraph to incorporate examples of qualitative production standards.

Section 1630.2(o) Reasonable accommodation

The Commission has deleted the reference to undue hardship from the definition of reasonable accommodation. This is a technical change reflecting that undue hardship is a defense to, rather than an aspect of, reasonable accommodation. As some commenters have noted, a defense to a term should not be part of the term's definition. Accordingly, we have separated the concept of undue hardship from the definition of reasonable accommodation. This change does not affect the obligations of employers or the rights of individuals with disabilities. Accordingly, a covered entity remains obligated to make reasonable accommodation to the known physical or mental limitations of an otherwise qualified individual with a disability unless to do so would impose an undue hardship on the operation of the covered entity's business. See section 1630.9.

With respect to section 1630.2(o)(1)(i), some commenters expressed confusion about the use of the phrase "qualified individual with a disability." In that regard, they noted that the phrase has a specific definition under this part (see section 1630.2(m)) and questioned whether an individual must meet that definition to request an accommodation with regard to the application process. The Commission has substituted the phrase "qualified applicant with a disability" for "qualified individual with a disability." This change clarifies that an individual with a disability who requests a reasonable accommodation to participate in the application process must be eligible only with respect to the application process.

The Commission has modified section 1630.2(o)(1)(iii) to state that reasonable accommodation includes modifications or adjustments that enable employees with disabilities to enjoy benefits and privileges that are "equal" to (rather than "the same" as) the benefits and privileges that are enjoyed by other employees. This change clarifies that such modifications or adjustments must ensure that individuals with disabilities receive equal access to the benefits and privileges afforded to other employees but may not be able to ensure that the individuals receive the same results of those benefits and privileges or precisely the same benefits and privileges.

Many commenters discussed whether the provision of daily attendant care is a form of reasonable accommodation. Employers and employer groups asserted that reasonable accommodation does not include such assistance. Disability rights groups and individuals with disabilities, however, asserted that such assistance is a form of reasonable accommodation but that this part did not make that clear. To clarify the extent of the reasonable accommodation obligation with respect to daily attendant care, the Commission has amended the interpretive guidance on section 1630.2(o) to make clear that it may be a reasonable accommodation to provide personal assistants to help with specified duties related to the job.

The Commission also has amended the interpretive guidance to note that allowing an individual with a disability to provide and use equipment, aids, or services that an employer is not required to provide may also be a form of reasonable accommodation. Some individuals with disabilities and disability rights groups asked the Commission to make this clear.

The interpretive guidance points out that reasonable accommodation may include making non-work areas accessible to individuals with disabilities. Many commenters asked the Commission to include rest rooms in the examples of accessible areas that may be required as reasonable accommodations. In response to those comments, the Commission has added rest rooms to the examples.

In response to other comments, the Commission has added a paragraph to the guidance concerning job restructuring as a form of reasonable accommodation. The new paragraph notes that job restructuring may involve changing when or how an essential function is performed.

Several commenters asked the Commission to provide additional guidance concerning the reasonable accommodation of reassignment to a vacant position. Specifically, commenters asked the Commission to clarify how long an employer must wait for a vacancy to arise when considering reassignment and to explain whether the employer is required to maintain the salary of an individual who is reassigned from a higher-paying position to a lower-paying one. The Commission has amended the discussion of reassignment to refer to reassignment to a position that is vacant "within a reasonable amount of time ... in light of the totality of the circumstances." In addition, the Commission has noted that an employer is not required to maintain the salaries of reassigned individuals with disabilities if it does not maintain the salaries of individuals who are not disabled.

Section 1630.2(p) Undue hardship

The Commission has substituted "facility" or "facilities" for "site" or "sites" in section 1630.2(p)(2) and has deleted the definition of the term "site." Many employers and employer groups expressed concern about the use and meaning of the term "site." The final regulation's use of the terms "facility" and "facilities" is consistent with the language of the statute.

The Commission has amended the last paragraph of the interpretive guidance accompanying section 1630.2(p) to note that, when the cost of a requested accommodation would result in an undue hardship and outside funding is not available, an individual with a disability should be given the option of paying the portion of the cost that constitutes an undue hardship. This amendment is consistent with the legislative history of the Act. See Senate Report at 36; House Labor Report at 69.

Several employers and employer groups asked the Commission to expand the list of factors to be considered when determining if an accommodation would impose an undue hardship on a covered entity by adding another factor: the relationship of an accommodation's cost to the value of the position at issue, as measured by the compensation paid to the holder of the position. Congress, however, specifically rejected this type of factor. See House Judiciary Report at 41 (noting that the House Judiciary Committee rejected an amendment proposing that an accommodation costing more than ten percent of the employee's salary be treated as an undue hardship). The Commission, therefore, has not added this to the list.

Section 1630.2(q) Qualification standards

The Commission has deleted the reference to direct threat from the definition of qualification standards. This revision is consistent with the revisions the Commission has made to sections 1630.10 and 1630.15(b). (See discussion below).

Section 1630.2(r) Direct threat

Many disability rights groups and individuals with disabilities asserted that the definition of direct threat should not include a reference to the health or safety of the individual with a disability. They expressed concern that the reference to "risk to self" would result in direct threat determinations that are based on negative stereotypes and paternalistic views about what is best for individuals with disabilities. Alternatively, the commenters asked the Commission to clarify that any assessment of risk must be based on the individual's present condition and not on speculation about the individual's future condition. They also asked the Commission to specify evidence other than medical knowledge that may be relevant to the determination of direct threat.

The final regulation retains the reference to the health or safety of the individual with a disability. As the Appendix notes, this is consistent with the legislative history of the ADA and the case law interpreting section 504 of the Rehabilitation Act.

To clarify the direct threat standard, the Commission has made four revisions to section 1630.2(r). First, the Commission has amended the first sentence of the definition of direct threat to refer to a significant risk of substantial harm that cannot be eliminated "or reduced" by reasonable accommodation. This amendment clarifies that the risk need not be eliminated entirely to fall below the direct threat definition; instead, the risk need only be reduced to the level at which there no longer exists a significant risk of substantial harm. In addition, the Commission has rephrased the second sentence of section 1630.2(r) to clarify that an employer's direct threat standard must apply to all individuals, not just to individuals with disabilities. Further, the Commission has made clear that a direct threat determination must be based on "an individualized assessment of the individual's present ability to safely perform the essential functions of the job." This clarifies that a determination that employment of an individual would pose a direct threat must involve an individualized inquiry and must be based on the individual's current condition. In addition, the Commission has added "the imminence of the potential harm" to the list of factors to be considered when determining whether employment of an individual would pose a direct threat. This change clarifies that both the probability of harm and the imminence of harm are relevant to direct threat determinations. This definition of direct threat is consistent with the legislative history of the Act. See Senate Report at 27, House Labor Report at 56-57, 73-75, House Judiciary Report at 45-46.

Further, the Commission has amended the interpretive guidance on section 1630.2(r) to highlight the individualized nature of the direct threat assessment. In addition, the Commission has cited examples of evidence other than medical knowledge that may be relevant to determining whether employment of an individual would pose a direct threat.

Section 1630.3 Exceptions to the definitions of "Disability" and "Qualified Individual with a Disability"

Many commenters asked the Commission to clarify that the term "rehabilitation program" includes self-help groups. In response to these comments, the Commission has amended the interpretive guidance in this area to include a reference to professionally recognized self-help programs.

The Commission has added a paragraph to the guidance on section 1630.3 to note that individuals who are not excluded under this provision from the definitions of the terms "disability" and "qualified individual with a disability" must still establish that they meet those definitions to be protected by part 1630. Several employers and employer groups asked the Commission to clarify that individuals are not automatically covered by the ADA simply because they do not fall into one of the exclusions listed in this section.

The proposed interpretive guidance on section 1630.3 noted that employers are entitled to seek reasonable assurances that an individual is not currently engaging in the illegal use of drugs. In that regard, the guidance stated, "It is essential that the individual offer evidence, such as a drug test, to prove that he or she is not currently engaging" in such use. Many commenters interpreted this guidance to require individuals to come forward with evidence even in the absence of a request by the employer. The Commission has revised the interpretive guidance to clarify that such evidence is required only upon request.

1630.6 Contractual or other arrangements

The Commission has added a sentence to the first paragraph of the interpretive guidance on section 1630.6 to clarify that this section has no impact on whether one is a covered entity or employer as defined by section 1630.2.

The proposed interpretive guidance on contractual or other relationships noted that section 1630.6 applied to parties on either side of the relationship. To illustrate this point, the guidance stated that "a copier company would be required to ensure the provision of any reasonable accommodation necessary to enable its copier service representative with a disability to service a client's machine." Several employers objected to this example. In that respect, the commenters argued that the language of the example was too broad and could be interpreted as requiring employers to make all customers' premises accessible. The Commission has revised this example to provide a clearer, more concrete indication of the scope of the reasonable accommodation obligation in this area.

In addition, the Commission has clarified the interpretive guidance by noting that the existence of a contractual relationship adds no new obligations "under this part."

1630.8 Relationship or association with an individual with a disability

The Commission has added the phrase "or otherwise discriminate against" to section 1630.8. This change clarifies that harassment or any other form of discrimination against a qualified individual because of the known disability of a person with whom the individual has a relationship or an association is also a prohibited form of discrimination.

The Commission has revised the first sentence of the interpretive guidance to refer to a person's relationship or association with an individual who has a "known" disability. This revision makes the language of the interpretive guidance consistent with the language of the regulation. In addition, to reflect current, preferred terminology, the Commission has substituted the term "people who have AIDS" for the term "AIDS patients." Finally, the Commission has added a paragraph to clarify that this provision applies to discrimination in other employment privileges and benefits, such as health insurance benefits.

1630.9 Not making reasonable accommodation

Section 1630.9(c) provides that "[a] covered entity shall not be excused from the requirements of this part because of any failure to receive technical assistance...." Some employers asked the Commission to revise this section and to state that the failure to receive technical assistance is a defense to not providing reasonable accommodation. The Commission has not made the requested revision. Section 1630.9(c) is consistent with section 506(e) of the ADA, which states that the failure to receive technical assistance from the federal agencies that administer the ADA does not excuse a covered entity from compliance with the requirements of the Act.

The first paragraph of the interpretive guidance accompanying section 1630.9 notes that the reasonable accommodation obligation does not require employers to provide adjustments or modifications that are primarily for the personal use of the individual with a disability. The Commission has amended this guidance to clarify that employers may be required to provide items that are customarily personal-use items where the items are specifically designed or required to meet job-related needs.

In addition, the Commission has amended the interpretive guidance to clarify that there must be a nexus between an individual's disability and the need for accommodation. Thus, the guidance notes that an individual with a disability is "otherwise qualified" if he or she is qualified for the job except that, "because of the disability," the individual needs reasonable accommodation to perform the essential functions of the job. Similarly, the guidance notes that employers are required to accommodate only the physical or mental limitations "resulting from the disability" that are known to the employer.

In response to commenters' requests for clarification, the Commission has noted that employers may require individuals with disabilities to provide documentation of the need for reasonable accommodation when the need for a requested accommodation is not obvious.

In addition, the Commission has amended the last paragraph of the interpretive guidance on the "Process of Determining the Appropriate Reasonable Accommodation." This amendment clarifies that an employer must consider allowing an individual with a disability to provide his or her own accommodation if the individual wishes to do so. The employer, however, may not require the individual to provide the accommodation.

1630.10 Qualification standards, tests, and other selection criteria

The Commission has added the phrase "on the basis of disability" to section 1630.10(a) to clarify that a selection criterion that is not job related and consistent with business necessity violates this section only when it screens out an individual with a disability (or a class of individuals with disabilities) on the basis of disability. That is, there must be a nexus between the exclusion and the disability. A selection criterion that screens out an individual with a disability for reasons that are not related to the disability does not violate this section. The Commission has made similar changes to the interpretive guidance on this section.

Proposed section 1630.10(b) stated that a covered entity could use as a qualification standard the requirement that an individual not pose a direct threat to the health or safety of the individual or others. Many individuals with disabilities objected to the inclusion of the direct threat reference in this section and asked the Commission to clarify that the direct threat standard must be raised by the covered entity as a defense. In that regard, they specifically asked the Commission to move the direct threat provision from section 1630.10 (qualification standards) to section 1630.15 (defenses). The Commission has deleted the direct threat provision from section 1630.10 and has moved it to section 1630.15. This is consistent with section 103 of the ADA, which refers to defenses and states (in section 103(b)) that the term "qualification standards" may include a requirement that an individual not pose a direct threat.

1630.11 Administration of tests

The Commission has revised the interpretive guidance concerning section 1630.11 to clarify that a request for an alternative test format or other testing accommodation generally should be made prior to the administration of the test or as soon as the individual with a disability becomes aware of the need for accommodation. In addition, the Commission has amended the last paragraph of the guidance on this section to note that an employer can require a written test of an applicant with dyslexia if the ability to read is "the skill the test is designed to measure." This language is consistent with the regulatory language, which refers to the skills a test purports to measure.

Some commenters noted that certain tests are designed to measure the speed with which an applicant performs a function. In response to these comments, the Commission has amended the interpretive guidance to state that an employer may require an applicant to complete a test within a specified time frame if speed is one of the skills being tested.

In response to comments, the Commission has amended the interpretive guidance accompanying section 1630.14(a) to clarify that employers may invite applicants to request accommodations for taking tests. (See section 1630.14(a), below)

1630.12 Retaliation and coercion

The Commission has amended section 1630.12 to clarify that this section also prohibits harassment.

1630.13 Prohibited medical examinations and inquiries

In response to the Commission's request for comment on certain workers' compensation matters, many commenters addressed whether a covered entity may ask applicants about their history of workers' compensation claims. Many employers and employer groups argued that an inquiry about an individual's workers' compensation history is job related and consistent with business necessity. Disability rights groups and individuals with disabilities, however, asserted that such an inquiry could disclose the existence of a disability. In response to comments and to clarify this matter, the Commission has amended the interpretive guidance accompanying section 1630.13(a). The amendment states that an employer may not inquire about an individual's workers' compensation history at the pre-offer stage.

The Commission has made a technical change to section 1630.13(b) by deleting the phrase "unless the examination or inquiry is shown to be job-related and consistent with business necessity" from the section. This change does not affect the substantive provisions of section 1630.13(b). The Commission has incorporated the job-relatedness and business-necessity requirement into a new section 1630.14(c), which clarifies the scope of permissible examinations or inquiries of employees. (See section 1630.14(c), below.)

1630.14 Medical examinations and inquiries specifically permitted

Section 1630.14(a) Acceptable pre-employment inquiry

Proposed section 1630.14(a) stated that a covered entity may make pre-employment inquiries into an applicant's ability to perform job-related functions. The interpretive guidance accompanying this section noted that an employer may ask an individual whether he or she can perform a job function with or without reasonable accommodation.

Many employers asked the Commission to provide additional guidance in this area. Specifically, the commenters asked whether an employer may ask how an individual will perform a job function when the individual's known disability appears to interfere with or prevent performance of job-related functions. To clarify this matter, the Commission has amended section 1630.14(a) to state that a covered entity "may ask an applicant to describe or to demonstrate how, with or without reasonable accommodation, the applicant will be able to perform job-related functions." The Commission has amended the interpretive guidance accompanying section 1630.14(a) to reflect this change.

Many commenters asked the Commission to state that employers may inquire, before tests are taken, whether candidates will require any reasonable accommodations to take the tests. They asked the Commission to acknowledge that such inquiries constitute permissible pre-employment inquiries. In response to these comments, the Commission has added a new paragraph to the interpretive guidance on section 1630.14(a). This paragraph clarifies that employers may ask candidates to inform them of the need for reasonable accommodation within a reasonable time before the administration of the test and may request documentation verifying the need for accommodation.

The Commission has received many comments from law enforcement and other public safety agencies concerning the administration of physical agility tests. In response to those comments, the Commission has added a new paragraph clarifying that such tests are not medical examinations.

Many employers and employer groups have asked the Commission to discuss whether employers may invite applicants to self-identify as individuals with disabilities. In that regard, many of the commenters noted that Section 503 of the Rehabilitation Act imposes certain obligations on government contractors. The interpretive guidance accompanying sections 1630.1(b) and (c) notes that "title I of the ADA would not be a defense to failing to collect information required to satisfy the affirmative action requirements of Section 503 of the Rehabilitation Act." To reiterate this point, the Commission has amended the interpretive guidance accompanying section 1630.14(a) to note specifically that this section does not restrict employers from collecting information and inviting individuals to identify themselves as individuals with disabilities as required to satisfy the affirmative action requirements of Section 503 of the Rehabilitation Act.

Section 1630.14(b) Employment entrance examinations

Section 1630.14(b) has been amended to include the phrase "(and/or inquiry)" after references to medical examinations. Some commenters were concerned that the regulation as drafted prohibited covered entities from making any medical inquiries or administering questionnaires that did not constitute examinations. This change clarifies that the term "employment entrance examinations" includes medical inquiries as well as medical examinations.

Section 1630.14(b)(2) has been revised to state that the results of employment entrance examinations "shall not be used for any purpose inconsistent with this part." This language is consistent with the language used in section 1630.14(c)(2).

The second paragraph of the proposed interpretive guidance on this section referred to "relevant" physical and psychological criteria. Some commenters questioned the use of the term "relevant" and expressed concern about its meaning. The Commission has deleted this term from the paragraph.

Many commenters addressed the confidentiality provisions of this section. They noted that it may be necessary to disclose medical information in defense of workers' compensation claims or during the course of other legal proceedings. In addition, they pointed out that the workers' compensation offices of many states request such information for the administration of second-injury funds or for other administrative purposes.

The Commission has revised the last paragraph of the interpretive guidance on section 1630.14(b) to reflect that the information obtained during a permitted employment entrance examination or inquiry may be used only "in a manner not inconsistent with this part." In addition, the Commission has added language clarifying that it is permissible to submit the information to state workers' compensation offices.

Several commenters asked the Commission to clarify whether information obtained from employment entrance examinations and inquiries may be used for insurance purposes. In response to these comments, the Commission has noted in the interpretive guidance that such information may be used for insurance purposes described in section 1630.16(f).

Section 1630.14(c) Examination of employees

The Commission has added a new section 1630.14(c), Examination of employees, that clarifies the scope of permissible medical examinations and inquiries. Several employers and employer groups expressed concern that the proposed version of part 1630 did not make it clear that covered entities may require employee medical examinations, such as fitness-for-duty examinations, that are job related and consistent with business necessity. New section 1630.14(c) clarifies this by expressly permitting covered entities to require employee medical examinations and inquiries that are job related and consistent with business necessity. The information obtained from such examinations or inquiries must be treated as a confidential medical record. This section also incorporates the last sentence of proposed section 1630.14(c). The remainder of proposed section 1630.14(c) has become section 1630.14(d).

To comport with this technical change in the regulation, the Commission has made corresponding changes in the interpretive guidance. Thus, the Commission has moved the second paragraph of the proposed guidance on section 1630.13(b) to the guidance on section 1630.14(c). In addition, the Commission has reworded the paragraph to note that this provision permits (rather than does not prohibit) certain medical examinations and inquiries.

Some commenters asked the Commission to clarify whether employers may make inquiries or require medical examinations in connection with the reasonable accommodation process. The Commission has noted in the interpretive guidance that such inquiries and examinations are permissible when they are necessary to the reasonable accommodation process described in this part.

1630.15 Defenses

The Commission has added a sentence to the interpretive guidance on section 1630.15(a) to clarify that the assertion that an insurance plan does not cover an individual's disability or that the disability would cause increased insurance or workers' compensation costs does not constitute a legitimate, nondiscriminatory reason for disparate treatment of an individual with a disability. This clarification, made in response to many comments from individuals with disabilities and disability rights groups, is consistent with the legislative history of the ADA. See Senate Report at 85; House Labor Report at 136; House Judiciary Report at 71.

The Commission has amended section 1630.15(b) by stating that the term "qualification standard" may include a requirement that an individual not pose a direct threat. As noted above, this is consistent with section 103 of the ADA and responds to many comments from individuals with disabilities.

The Commission has made a technical correction to section 1630.15(c) by changing the phrase "an individual or class of individuals with disabilities" to "an individual with a disability or a class of individuals with disabilities."

Several employers and employer groups asked the Commission to acknowledge that undue hardship considerations about reasonable accommodations at temporary work sites may be different from the considerations relevant to permanent work sites. In response to these comments, the Commission has amended the interpretive guidance on section 1630.15(d) to note that an accommodation that poses an undue hardship in a particular job setting, such as a temporary construction site, may not pose an undue hardship in another setting. This guidance is consistent with the legislative history of the ADA. See House Labor Report at 69-70; House Judiciary Report at 41-42.

The Commission also has amended the interpretive guidance to note that the terms of a collective bargaining agreement may be relevant to the determination of whether a requested accommodation would pose an undue hardship on the operation of a covered entity's business. This amendment, which responds to commenters' requests that the Commission recognize the relevancy of collective bargaining agreements, is consistent with the legislative history of the Act. See Senate Report at 32; House Labor Report at 63.

Section 1630.2(p)(2)(v) provides that the impact of an accommodation on the ability of other employees to perform their duties is one of the factors to be considered when determining whether the accommodation would impose an undue hardship on a covered entity. Many commenters addressed whether an accommodation's impact on the morale of other employees may be relevant to a determination of undue hardship. Some employers and employer groups asserted that a negative impact on employee morale should be considered an undue hardship. Disability rights groups and individuals with disabilities, however, argued that undue hardship determinations must not be based on the morale of other employees. It is the Commission's view that a negative effect on morale, by itself, is not sufficient to meet the undue hardship standard. Accordingly, the Commission has noted in the guidance on section 1630.15(d) that an employer cannot establish undue hardship by showing only that an accommodation would have a negative impact on employee morale.

1630.16 Specific activities permitted

The Commission has revised the second sentence of the interpretive guidance on section 1630.16(b) to state that an employer may hold individuals with alcoholism and individuals who engage in the illegal use of drugs to the same performance and conduct standards to which it holds "all of its" other employees. In addition, the Commission has deleted the term "otherwise" from the third sentence of the guidance. These revisions clarify that employers may hold all employees, disabled (including those disabled by alcoholism or drug addiction) and nondisabled, to the same performance and conduct standards.

Many commenters asked the Commission to clarify that the drug testing provisions of section 1630.16(c) pertain only to tests to determine the illegal use of drugs. Accordingly, the Commission has amended section 1630.16(c)(1) to refer to the administration of "such" drug tests and section 1630.16(c)(3) to refer to information obtained from a "test to determine the illegal use of drugs." We have also made a change in the grammatical structure of the last sentence of section 1630.16(c)(1). We have made similar changes to the corresponding section of the interpretive guidance. In addition, the Commission has amended the interpretive guidance to state that such tests are neither encouraged, "authorized," nor prohibited. This amendment conforms the language of the guidance to the language of section 1630.16(c)(1).

The Commission has revised section 1630.16(e)(1) to refer to communicable diseases that "are" (rather than "may be") transmitted through the handling of food. Several commenters asked the Commission to make this technical change, which adopts the statutory language.

Several commenters also asked the Commission to conform the language of proposed sections 1630.16(f)(1) and (2) to the language of sections 501(c)(1) and (2) of the Act. The Commission has made this change. Thus, sections 1630.16(f)(1) and (2) now refer to risks that are "not inconsistent with State law."

7. Executive Order 12291 and Regulatory Flexibility Act

The Commission published a Preliminary Regulatory Impact Analysis on February 28, 1991 (56 FR 8578). Based on the Preliminary Regulatory Impact Analysis, the Commission certifies that this final rule will not have a significant economic impact on a substantial number of small business entities. The Commission is issuing this final rule at this time in the absence of a Final Regulatory Impact Analysis in order to meet the statutory deadline. The Commission's Preliminary Regulatory Impact Analysis was based upon existing data on the costs of reasonable accommodation. The Commission received few comments on this aspect of its rulemaking. Because of the complexity inherent in assessing the economic costs and benefits of this rule and the relative paucity of data on this issue, the Commission will further study the economic impact of the regulation and intends to issue a Final Regulatory Impact Analysis prior to January 1, 1992. As indicated above, the Preliminary Regulatory Impact Analysis was published on February 28, 1991 (56 F.R. 8578) for comment. The Commission will also provide a copy to the public upon request by calling the Commission's Office of Communications and Legislative Affairs at (202) 663-4900. Commenters are urged to provide additional information as to the costs and benefits associated with this rule. This will further facilitate the development of a Final Regulatory Impact Analysis. Comments must be received by September 26, 1991. Written comments should be submitted to Frances M. Hart, Executive Officer, Executive Secretariat, Equal Employment Opportunity Commission, 1801 "L" Street, NW, Washington, D.C. 20507.

As a convenience to commenters, the Executive Secretariat will accept public comments transmitted by facsimile ("FAX") machine. The telephone number of the FAX receiver is (202) 663-4114. (This is not a toll-free number). Only public comments of six or fewer pages will be accepted via FAX transmittal. This limitation is necessary in order to assure access to the equipment. Comments sent by FAX in excess of six pages will not be accepted. Receipt of FAX transmittals will not be acknowledged, except that the sender may request confirmation of receipt by calling the Executive Secretariat Staff at (202) 663-4078. (This is not a toll-free number).

Comments received will be available for public inspection in the EEOC Library, room 6502, by appointment only, from 9 a.m. to 5 p.m., Monday through Friday except legal holidays from October 15, 1991, until the Final Regulatory Impact Analysis is published. Persons who need assistance to review the comments will be provided with appropriate aids such as readers or print magnifiers. To schedule an appointment call (202) 663-4630 (voice), (202) 663-4630 (TDD).

List of Subjects in 29 CFR Part 1630
>   Equal employment opportunity, Handicapped, Individuals with disabilities.
>   For the Commission,

>   (Signed)
>   Evan J. Kemp, Jr.
>   Chairman.

---

8. Annotated Regulations

Accordingly, 29 CFR Chapter XIV is amended by adding part 1630 to read as follows:

PART 1630-- REGULATIONS TO IMPLEMENT THE EQUAL EMPLOYMENT PROVISIONS OF THE AMERICANS WITH DISABILITIES ACT

Sec.

Authority: 42 U.S.C. 12116.

REGULATION

1630.1 Purpose, applicability, and construction.

(a) <u>Purpose</u>. The purpose of this part is to implement title I of the Americans with Disabilities Act (42 U.S.C. 12101, <u>et seq.</u>) (ADA), requiring equal employment opportunities for qualified individuals with disabilities, and sections 3(2), 3(3), 501, 503, 506(e), 508, 510, and 511 of the ADA as those sections pertain to the employment of qualified individuals with disabilities.

(b) <u>Applicability</u>. This part applies to "covered entities" as defined at section 1630.2(b).

(c) <u>Construction</u>. -- (1) <u>In general</u>. Except as otherwise provided in this part, this part does not apply a lesser standard than the standards applied under title V of the Rehabilitation Act of 1973

INTERPRETIVE GUIDANCE

Section 1630.1 Purpose, Applicability and Construction

Section 1630.1(a) Purpose

The Americans with Disabilities Act was signed into law on July 26, 1990. It is an antidiscrimination statute that requires that individuals with disabilities be given the same consideration for employment that individuals without disabilities are given. An individual who is qualified for an employment opportunity cannot be denied that opportunity because of the fact that the individual is disabled. The purpose of title I and this part is to ensure that qualified individuals with disabilities are protected from discrimination on the basis of disability.

The ADA uses the term "disabilities" rather than the term "handicaps" used in the Rehabilitation Act of 1973, 29 U.S.C. 701-796. Substantively, these terms are equivalent. As noted by the House Committee on the Judiciary, "[t]he use of the term 'disabilities' instead of the term 'handicaps' reflects the desire of the Committee to use the most current terminology. It reflects the preference of persons with disabilities to use that term rather than 'handicapped' as used in previous laws, such as the Rehabilitation Act of 1973 ...." H.R. Rep. No. 485 Part 3, 101st Cong., 2d Sess. 26-27 (1990) [hereinafter House Judiciary Report]; <u>see also</u> S. Rep. No. 116, 101st Cong., 1st Sess. 21 (1989) [hereinafter Senate Report]; H.R. Rep. No. 485 Part 2, 101st Cong., 2d Sess. 50-51 (1990) [hereinafter House Labor Report].

The use of the term "Americans" in the title of the ADA is not intended to imply that the Act only applies to United States citizens. Rather, the ADA protects all qualified individuals with disabilities, regardless of their citizenship status or nationality.

Section 1630.1(b) and (c) Applicability and Construction
Unless expressly stated otherwise, the standards applied in the ADA are not intended to be lesser than the standards applied under the Rehabilitation Act of 1973.

The ADA does not preempt any Federal law, or any state or local law, that grants to individuals with disabilities protection greater than or equivalent to that provided by the ADA. This means that the existence of a lesser standard of protection to individuals with disabilities under the ADA will not provide a defense to failing to meet a higher standard under another law. Thus, for example, title I of the ADA would not be a defense

REGULATION

(29 U.S.C. 790 - 794a), or the regulations issued by Federal agencies pursuant to that title.

(2) Relationship to other laws. This part does not invalidate or limit the remedies, rights, and procedures of any Federal law or law of any State or political subdivision of any State or jurisdiction that provides greater or equal protection for the rights of individuals with disabilities than are afforded by this part.

INTERPRETIVE GUIDANCE

to failing to collect information required to satisfy the affirmative action requirements of Section 503 of the Rehabilitation Act. On the other hand, the existence of a lesser standard under another law will not provide a defense to failing to meet a higher standard under the ADA. See House Labor Report at 135; House Judiciary Report at 69-70.

This also means that an individual with a disability could choose to pursue claims under a state discrimination or tort law that does not confer greater substantive rights, or even confers fewer substantive rights, if the potential available remedies would be greater than those available under the ADA and this part. The ADA does not restrict an individual with a disability from pursuing such claims in addition to charges brought under this part. House Judiciary at 69-70.

The ADA does not automatically preempt medical standards or safety requirements established by Federal law or regulations. It does not preempt State, county, or local laws, ordinances or regulations that are consistent with this part, and are designed to protect the public health from individuals who pose a direct threat, that cannot be eliminated or reduced by reasonable accommodation, to the health or safety of others. However, the ADA does preempt inconsistent requirements established by state or local law for safety or security sensitive positions. See Senate Report at 27; House Labor Report at 57.

An employer allegedly in violation of this part cannot successfully defend its actions by relying on the obligation to comply with the requirements of any state or local law that imposes prohibitions or limitations on the eligibility of qualified individuals with disabilities to practice any occupation or profession. For example, suppose a municipality has an ordinance that prohibits individuals with tuberculosis from teaching school children. If an individual with dormant tuberculosis challenges a private school's refusal to hire him or her because of the tuberculosis, the private school would not be able to rely on the city ordinance as a defense under the ADA.

REGULATION

1630.2 Definitions.

(a) <u>Commission</u> means the Equal Employment Opportunity Commission established by Section 705 of the Civil Rights Act of 1964 (42 U.S.C. 2000e-4).

(b) <u>Covered Entity</u> means an employer, employment agency, labor organization, or joint labor management committee.

(c) <u>Person, labor organization, employment agency, commerce and industry affecting commerce</u> shall have the same meaning given those terms in Section 701 of the Civil Rights Act of 1964 (42 U.S.C. 2000e).

(d) <u>State</u> means each of the several States, the District of Columbia, the Commonwealth of Puerto Rico, Guam, American Samoa, the Virgin Islands, the Trust Territory of the Pacific Islands, and the Commonwealth of the Northern Mariana Islands.

(e) <u>Employer</u>. -- (1) <u>In general</u>. The term "employer" means a person engaged in an industry affecting commerce who has 15 or more employees for each working day in each of 20 or more calendar weeks in the current or preceding calendar year, and any agent of such person, except that, from July 26, 1992 through July 25, 1994, an employer

INTERPRETIVE GUIDANCE

Sections 1630.2(a)-(f) Commission, Covered Entity, etc.

The definitions section of part 1630 includes several terms that are identical, or almost identical, to the terms found in title VII of the Civil Rights Act of 1964. Among these terms are "Commission," "Person," "State," and "Employer." These terms are to be given the same meaning under the ADA that they are given under title VII.

In general, the term "employee" has the same meaning that it is given under title VII. However, the ADA's definition of "employee" does not contain an exception, as does title VII, for elected officials and their personal staffs. It should be further noted that all state and local governments are covered by title II of the ADA whether or not they are also covered by this part. Title II, which is enforced by the Department of Justice, becomes effective on January 26, 1992. <u>See</u> 28 CFR part 35.

The term "covered entity" is not found in title VII. However, the title VII definitions of the entities included in the term "covered entity" (<u>e.g.</u>, employer, employment agency, <u>etc.</u>) are applicable to the ADA.

REGULATION

means a person engaged in an industry affecting commerce who has 25 or more employees for each working day in each of 20 or more calendar weeks in the current or preceding year and any agent of such person.

(2) Exceptions. The term employer does not include --

(i) the United States, a corporation wholly owned by the government of the United States, or an Indian tribe; or

(ii) a bona fide private membership club (other than a labor organization) that is exempt from taxation under Section 501(c) of the Internal Revenue Code of 1986.

(f) Employee means an individual employed by an employer.

REGULATION

(g) Disability means, with respect to an individual --

(1) a physical or mental impairment that substantially limits one or more of the major life activities of such individual;

(2) a record of such an impairment; or

(3) being regarded as having such an impairment. (See section 1630.3 for exceptions to this definition).

INTERPRETIVE GUIDANCE

Section 1630.2(g) Disability

In addition to the term "covered entity," there are several other terms that are unique to the ADA. The first of these is the term "disability." Congress adopted the definition of this term from the Rehabilitation Act definition of the term "individual with handicaps." By so doing, Congress intended that the relevant caselaw developed under the Rehabilitation Act be generally applicable to the term "disability" as used in the ADA. Senate Report at 21; House Labor Report at 50; House Judiciary Report at 27.

The definition of the term "disability" is divided into three parts. An individual must satisfy at least one of these parts in order to be considered an individual with a disability for purposes of this part. An individual is considered to have a "disability" if that individual either (1) has a physical or mental impairment which substantially limits one or more of that person's major life activities, (2) has a record of such an impairment, or, (3) is regarded by the covered entity as having such an impairment.

To understand the meaning of the term "disability," it is necessary to understand, as a preliminary matter, what is meant by the terms "physical or mental impairment," "major life activity," and "substantially limits." Each of these terms is discussed below.

REGULATION

(h) <u>Physical or mental impairment</u> means:

(1) Any physiological disorder, or condition, cosmetic disfigurement, or anatomical loss affecting one or more of the following body systems: neurological, musculoskeletal, special sense organs, respiratory (including speech organs), cardiovascular, reproductive, digestive, genito-urinary, hemic and lymphatic, skin, and endocrine; or

(2) Any mental or psychological disorder, such as mental retardation, organic brain syndrome, emotional or mental illness, and specific learning disabilities.

INTERPRETIVE GUIDANCE

Section 1630.2(h) Physical or Mental Impairment

This term adopts the definition of the term "physical or mental impairment" found in the regulations implementing Section 504 of the Rehabilitation Act at 34 CFR part 104. It defines physical or mental impairment as any physiological disorder or condition, cosmetic disfigurement, or anatomical loss affecting one or more of several body systems, or any mental or psychological disorder.

The existence of an impairment is to be determined without regard to mitigating measures such as medicines, or assistive or prosthetic devices. <u>See</u> Senate Report at 23; House Labor Report at 52; House Judiciary Report at 28. For example, an individual with epilepsy would be considered to have an impairment even if the symptoms of the disorder were completely controlled by medicine. Similarly, an individual with hearing loss would be considered to have an impairment even if the condition were correctable through the use of a hearing aid.

It is important to distinguish between conditions that are impairments and physical, psychological, environmental, cultural and economic characteristics that are not impairments. The definition of the term "impairment" does not include physical characteristics such as eye color, hair color, left-handedness, or height, weight or muscle tone that are within "normal" range and are not the result of a physiological disorder. The definition, likewise, does not include characteristic predisposition to illness or disease. Other conditions, such as pregnancy, that are not the result of a physiological disorder are also not impairments. Similarly, the definition does not include common personality traits such as poor judgment or a quick temper where these are not symptoms of a mental or psychological disorder. Environmental, cultural, or economic disadvantages such as poverty, lack of education or a prison record are not impairments. Advanced age, in and of itself, is also not an impairment. However, various medical conditions commonly associated with age, such as hearing loss, osteoporosis, or arthritis would constitute impairments within the meaning of this part. <u>See</u> Senate Report at 22-23; House Labor Report at 51-52; House Judiciary Report at 28-29.

REGULATION

(i) Major Life Activities means functions such as caring for oneself, performing manual tasks, walking, seeing, hearing, speaking, breathing, learning, and working.

INTERPRETIVE GUIDANCE

Section 1630.2(i) Major Life Activities

This term adopts the definition of the term "major life activities" found in the regulations implementing Section 504 of the Rehabilitation Act at 34 CFR part 104. "Major life activities" are those basic activities that the average person in the general population can perform with little or no difficulty. Major life activities include caring for oneself, performing manual tasks, walking, seeing, hearing, speaking, breathing, learning, and working. This list is not exhaustive. For example, other major life activities include, but are not limited to, sitting, standing, lifting, reaching. See Senate Report at 22; House Labor Report at 52; House Judiciary Report at 28.

REGULATION

(j) Substantially limits. -- (1) The term "substantially limits" means:

(i) Unable to perform a major life activity that the average person in the general population can perform; or

(ii) Significantly restricted as to the condition, manner or duration under which an individual can perform a particular major life activity as compared to the condition, manner, or duration under which the average person in the general population can perform that same major life activity.

(2) The following factors should be considered in determining whether an individual is substantially limited in a major life activity:

(i) The nature and severity of the impairment;

(ii) The duration or expected duration of the impairment; and

(iii) The permanent or long term impact, or the expected permanent or long term impact of or resulting from the impairment.

(3) With respect to the major life activity of "working" --

(i) The term "substan-

INTERPRETIVE GUIDANCE

Section 1630.2(j) Substantially Limits

Determining whether a physical or mental impairment exists is only the first step in determining whether or not an individual is disabled. Many impairments do not impact an individual's life to the degree that they constitute disabling impairments. An impairment rises to the level of disability if the impairment substantially limits one or more of the individual's major life activities. Multiple impairments that combine to substantially limit one or more of an individual's major life activities also constitute a disability.

The ADA and this part, like the Rehabilitation Act of 1973, do not attempt a "laundry list" of impairments that are "disabilities." The determination of whether an individual has a disability is not necessarily based on the name or diagnosis of the impairment the person has, but rather on the effect of that impairment on the life of the individual. Some impairments may be disabling for particular individuals but not for others, depending on the stage of the disease or disorder, the presence of other impairments that combine to make the impairment disabling or any number of other factors. Other impairments, however, such as HIV infection, are inherently substantially limiting.

On the other hand, temporary, non-chronic impairments of short duration, with little or no long term or permanent impact, are usually not disabilities. Such impairments may include, but are not limited to, broken limbs, sprained joints, concussions, appendicitis, and influenza. Similarly, except in rare circumstances, obesity is not considered a disabling impairment.

An impairment that prevents an individual from performing a major life activity substantially limits that major life activity. For example, an individual whose legs are paralyzed is substantially limited in the major life activity of walking because he or she is unable, due to the impairment, to perform that major life activity.

Alternatively, an impairment is substantially limiting if it significantly restricts the duration, manner or condition under which an individual can perform a particular major life activity as compared to the average person in the general population's ability to perform that same major life activity. Thus, for example, an individual who, because of an impairment, can only walk for very brief periods of time would be

REGULATION

tially limits" means significantly restricted in the ability to perform either a class of jobs or a broad range of jobs in various classes as compared to the average person having comparable training, skills and abilities. The inability to perform a single, particular job does not constitute a substantial limitation in the major life activity of working.

(ii) In addition to the factors listed in paragraph (j)(2) of this section, the following factors may be considered in determining whether an individual is substantially limited in the major life activity of "working":

(A) The geographical area to which the individual has reasonable access;

(B) The job from which the individual has been disqualified because of an impairment, and the number and types of jobs utilizing similar training, knowledge, skills or abilities, within that geographical area, from which the individual is also disqualified because of the impairment (class of jobs); and/or

(C) The job from which the individual has been disqualified because of an impairment, and the number and types of other jobs not

INTERPRETIVE GUIDANCE

substantially limited in the major life activity of walking. An individual who uses artificial legs would likewise be substantially limited in the major life activity of walking because the individual is unable to walk without the aid of prosthetic devices. Similarly, a diabetic who without insulin would lapse into a coma would be substantially limited because the individual cannot perform major life activities without the aid of medication. See Senate Report at 23; House Labor Report at 52. It should be noted that the term "average person" is not intended to imply a precise mathematical "average."

Part 1630 notes several factors that should be considered in making the determination of whether an impairment is substantially limiting. These factors are (1) the nature and severity of the impairment, (2) the duration or expected duration of the impairment, and (3) the permanent or long term impact, or the expected permanent or long term impact of, or resulting from, the impairment. The term "duration," as used in this context, refers to the length of time an impairment persists, while the term "impact" refers to the residual effects of an impairment. Thus, for example, a broken leg that takes eight weeks to heal is an impairment of fairly brief duration. However, if the broken leg heals improperly, the "impact" of the impairment would be the resulting permanent limp. Likewise, the effect on cognitive functions resulting from traumatic head injury would be the "impact" of that impairment.

The determination of whether an individual is substantially limited in a major life activity must be made on a case by case basis, without regard to mitigating measures such as medicines, or assistive or prosthetic devices. An individual is not substantially limited in a major life activity if the limitation, when viewed in light of the factors noted above, does not amount to a significant restriction when compared with the abilities of the average person. For example, an individual who had once been able to walk at an extraordinary speed would not be substantially limited in the major life activity of walking if, as a result of a physical impairment, he or she were only able to walk at an average speed, or even at moderately below average speed.

It is important to remember that the restriction on the performance of the major life activity must be the result of a condition that is an impairment. As noted earlier, advanced age, physical or personality characteristics, and environmental, cultural, and economic disadvantages are not impairments.

REGULATION

utilizing similar training, knowledge, skills or abilities, within that geographical area, from which the individual is also disqualified because of the impairment (broad range of jobs in various classes).

INTERPRETIVE GUIDANCE

Consequently, even if such factors substantially limit an individual's ability to perform a major life activity, this limitation will not constitute a disability. For example, an individual who is unable to read because he or she was never taught to read would not be an individual with a disability because lack of education is not an impairment. However, an individual who is unable to read because of dyslexia would be an individual with a disability because dyslexia, a learning disability, is an impairment.

If an individual is not substantially limited with respect to any other major life activity, the individual's ability to perform the major life activity of working should be considered. If an individual is substantially limited in any other major life activity, no determination should be made as to whether the individual is substantially limited in working. For example, if an individual is blind, i.e. substantially limited in the major life activity of seeing, there is no need to determine whether the individual is also substantially limited in the major life activity of working. The determination of whether an individual is substantially limited in working must also be made on a case by case basis.

This part lists specific factors that may be used in making the determination of whether the limitation in working is "substantial." These factors are:

(1) the geographical area to which the individual has reasonable access;

(2) the job from which the individual has been disqualified because of an impairment, and the number and types of jobs utilizing similar training, knowledge, skills or abilities, within that geographical area, from which the individual is also disqualified because of the impairment (class of jobs); and/or

(3) the job from which the individual has been disqualified because of an impairment, and the number and types of other jobs not utilizing similar training, knowledge, skills or abilities, within that geographical area, from which the individual is also disqualified because of the impairment (broad range of jobs in various classes).

Thus, an individual is not substantially limited in working just because he or she is unable to perform a particular job for one employer, or because he or she is unable to perform a special-

REGULATION

ized job or profession requiring extraordinary skill, prowess or talent. For example, an individual who cannot be a commercial airline pilot because of a minor vision impairment, but who can be a commercial airline co-pilot or a pilot for a courier service, would not be substantially limited in the major life activity of working. Nor would a professional baseball pitcher who develops a bad elbow and can no longer throw a baseball be considered substantially limited in the major life activity of working. In both of these examples, the individuals are not substantially limited in the ability to perform any other major life activity and, with regard to the major life activity of working, are only unable to perform either a particular specialized job or a narrow range of jobs. See Forrisi v. Bowen, 794 F.2d 931 (4th Cir. 1986); Jasany v. U.S. Postal Service, 755 F.2d 1244 (6th Cir. 1985); E.E Black, Ltd. v. Marshall, 497 F. Supp. 1088 (D. Hawaii 1980).

On the other hand, an individual does not have to be totally unable to work in order to be considered substantially limited in the major life activity of working. An individual is substantially limited in working if the individual is significantly restricted in the ability to perform a class of jobs or a broad range of jobs in various classes, when compared with the ability of the average person with comparable qualifications to perform those same jobs. For example, an individual who has a back condition that prevents the individual from performing any heavy labor job would be substantially limited in the major life activity of working because the individual's impairment eliminates his or her ability to perform a class of jobs. This would be so even if the individual were able to perform jobs in another class, e.g., the class of semi-skilled jobs. Similarly, suppose an individual has an allergy to a substance found in most high rise office buildings, but seldom found elsewhere, that makes breathing extremely difficult. Since this individual would be substantially limited in the ability to perform the broad range of jobs in various classes that are conducted in high rise office buildings within the geographical area to which he or she has reasonable access, he or she would be substantially limited in working.

The terms "number and types of jobs" and "number and types of other jobs," as used in the factors discussed above, are not intended to require an onerous evidentiary showing. Rather, the terms only require the presentation of evidence of general employment demographics and/or of recognized occupational classifications that indicate the approximate number of jobs

REGULATION

(e.g., "few," "many," "most") from which an individual would be excluded because of an impairment.

If an individual has a "mental or physical impairment" that "substantially limits" his or her ability to perform one or more "major life activities," that individual will satisfy the first part of the regulatory definition of "disability" and will be considered an individual with a disability. An individual who satisfies this first part of the definition of the term "disability" is not required to demonstrate that he or she satisfies either of the other parts of the definition. However, if an individual is unable to satisfy this part of the definition, he or she may be able to satisfy one of the other parts of the definition.

REGULATION

(k) Has a record of such impairment means has a history of, or has been misclassified as having, a mental or physical impairment that substantially limits one or more major life activities.

INTERPRETIVE GUIDANCE

Section 1630.2(k) Record of a Substantially Limiting Condition

The second part of the definition provides that an individual with a record of an impairment that substantially limits a major life activity is an individual with a disability. The intent of this provision, in part, is to ensure that people are not discriminated against because of a history of disability. For example, this provision protects former cancer patients from discrimination based on their prior medical history. This provision also ensures that individuals are not discriminated against because they have been misclassified as disabled. For example, individuals misclassified as learning disabled are protected from discrimination on the basis of that erroneous classification. Senate Report at 23; House Labor Report at 52-53; House Judiciary Report at 29.

This part of the definition is satisfied if a record relied on by an employer indicates that the individual has or has had a substantially limiting impairment. The impairment indicated in the record must be an impairment that would substantially limit one or more of the individual's major life activities. There are many types of records that could potentially contain this information, including but not limited to, education, medical, or employment records.

The fact that an individual has a record of being a disabled veteran, or of disability retirement, or is classified as disabled for other purposes does not guarantee that the individual will satisfy the definition of "disability" under part 1630. Other statutes, regulations and programs may have a definition of "disability" that is not the same as the definition set forth in the ADA and contained in part 1630. Accordingly, in order for an individual who has been classified in a record as "disabled" for some other purpose to be considered disabled for purposes of part 1630, the impairment indicated in the record must be a physical or mental impairment that substantially limits one or more of the individual's major life activities.

REGULATION

(l) <u>Is regarded as having such an impairment</u> means:

(1) Has a physical or mental impairment that does not substantially limit major life activities but is treated by a covered entity as constituting such limitation;

(2) Has a physical or mental impairment that substantially limits major life activities only as a result of the attitudes of others toward such impairment; or

(3) Has none of the impairments defined in paragraphs (h)(1) or (2) of this section but is treated by a covered entity as having a substantially limiting impairment.

INTERPRETIVE GUIDANCE

Section 1630.2(l) Regarded as Substantially Limited in a Major Life Activity

If an individual cannot satisfy either the first part of the definition of "disability" or the second "record of" part of the definition, he or she may be able to satisfy the third part of the definition. The third part of the definition provides that an individual who is regarded by an employer or other covered entity as having an impairment that substantially limits a major life activity is an individual with a disability.

There are three different ways in which an individual may satisfy the definition of "being regarded as having a disability":

(1) The individual may have an impairment which is not substantially limiting but is perceived by the employer or other covered entity as constituting a substantially limiting impairment;

(2) the individual may have an impairment which is only substantially limiting because of the attitudes of others toward the impairment; or

(3) the individual may have no impairment at all but is regarded by the employer or other covered entity as having a substantially limiting impairment.
Senate Report at 23; House Labor Report at 53; House Judiciary Report at 29.

An individual satisfies the first part of this definition if the individual has an impairment that is not substantially limiting, but the covered entity perceives the impairment as being substantially limiting. For example, suppose an employee has controlled high blood pressure that is not substantially limiting. If an employer reassigns the individual to less strenuous work because of unsubstantiated fears that the individual will suffer a heart attack if he or she continues to perform strenuous work, the employer would be regarding the individual as disabled.

An individual satisfies the second part of the "regarded as" definition if the individual has an impairment that is only substantially limiting because of the attitudes of others toward the condition. For example, an individual may have a prominent facial scar or disfigurement, or may have a condition that periodically causes an involuntary jerk of the head but does

REGULATION

not limit the individual's major life activities. If an employer discriminates against such an individual because of the negative reactions of customers, the employer would be regarding the individual as disabled and acting on the basis of that perceived disability. See Senate Report at 24; House Labor Report at 53; House Judiciary Report at 30-31.

An individual satisfies the third part of the "regarded as" definition of "disability" if the employer or other covered entity erroneously believes the individual has a substantially limiting impairment that the individual actually does not have. This situation could occur, for example, if an employer discharged an employee in response to a rumor that the employee is infected with Human Immunodeficiency Virus (HIV). Even though the rumor is totally unfounded and the individual has no impairment at all, the individual is considered an individual with a disability because the employer perceived of this individual as being disabled. Thus, in this example, the employer, by discharging this employee, is discriminating on the basis of disability.

The rationale for the "regarded as" part of the definition of disability was articulated by the Supreme Court in the context of the Rehabilitation Act of 1973 in School Board of Nassau County v. Arline, 480 U.S. 273 (1987). The Court noted that, although an individual may have an impairment that does not in fact substantially limit a major life activity, the reaction of others may prove just as disabling. "Such an impairment might not diminish a person's physical or mental capabilities, but could nevertheless substantially limit that person's ability to work as a result of the negative reactions of others to the impairment." 480 U.S. at 283. The Court concluded that by including "regarded as" in the Rehabilitation Act's definition, "Congress acknowledged that society's accumulated myths and fears about disability and diseases are as handicapping as are the physical limitations that flow from actual impairment." 480 U.S. at 284.

An individual rejected from a job because of the "myths, fears and sterotypes" associated with disabilities would be covered under this part of the definition of disability, whether or not the employer's or other covered entity's perception were shared by others in the field and whether or not the individual's actual physical or mental condition would be considered a disability under the first or second part of this definition. As the legislative history notes, sociologists have

REGULATION

identified common attitudinal barriers that frequently result in employers excluding individuals with disabilities. These include concerns regarding productivity, safety, insurance, liability, attendance, cost of accommodation and accessibility, workers' compensation costs, and acceptance by coworkers and customers.

Therefore, if an individual can show that an employer or other covered entity made an employment decision because of a perception of disability based on "myth, fear or stereotype," the individual will satisfy the "regarded as" part of the definition of disability. If the employer cannot articulate a nondiscriminatory reason for the employment action, an inference that the employer is acting on the basis of "myth, fear or stereotype" can be drawn.

REGULATION

(m)<u>Qualified individual with a disability</u> means an individual with a disability who satisfies the requisite skill, experience, education and other job-related requirements of the employment position such individual holds or desires, and who, with or without reasonable accommodation, can perform the essential functions of such position. (See section 1630.3 for exceptions to this definition).

INTERPRETIVE GUIDANCE

Section 1630.2(m) Qualified Individual with a Disability

The ADA prohibits discrimination on the basis of disability against qualified individuals with disabilities. The determination of whether an individual with a disability is "qualified" should be made in two steps. The first step is to determine if the individual satisfies the prerequisites for the position, such as possessing the appropriate educational background, employment experience, skills, licenses, etc. For example, the first step in determining whether an accountant who is paraplegic is qualified for a certified public accountant (CPA) position is to examine the individual's credentials to determine whether the individual is a licensed CPA. This is sometimes referred to in the Rehabilitation Act caselaw as determining whether the individual is "otherwise qualified" for the position. See Senate Report at 33; House Labor Report at 64-65. (See section 1630.9 Not Making Reasonable Accommodation).

The second step is to determine whether or not the individual can perform the essential functions of the position held or desired, with or without reasonable accommodation. The purpose of this second step is to ensure that individuals with disabilities who can perform the essential functions of the position held or desired are not denied employment opportunities because they are not able to perform marginal functions of the position. House Labor Report at 55.

The determination of whether an individual with a disability is qualified is to be made at the time of the employment decision. This determination should be based on the capabilities of the individual with a disability at the time of the employment decision, and should not be based on speculation that the employee may become unable in the future or may cause increased health insurance premiums or workers' compensation costs.

REGULATION

(n) Essential functions. -

(1) In general. The term "essential functions" means the fundamental job duties of the employment position the individual with a disability holds or desires. The term "essential functions" does not include the marginal functions of the position.

(2) A job function may be considered essential for any of several reasons, including but not limited to the following:

(i) The function may be essential because the reason the position exists is to perform that function;

(ii) The function may be essential because of the limited number of employees available among whom the performance of that job function can be distributed; and/or

(iii) The function may be highly specialized so that the incumbent in the position is hired for his or her expertise or ability to perform the particular function.

(3) Evidence of whether a particular function is essential includes, but is not limited to:

(i) The employer's judgment as to which functions are essential;

INTERPRETIVE GUIDANCE
Section 1630.2(n) Essential Functions

The determination of which functions are essential may be critical to the determination of whether or not the individual with a disability is qualified. The essential functions are those functions that the individual who holds the position must be able to perform unaided or with the assistance of a reasonable accommodation.

The inquiry into whether a particular function is essential initially focuses on whether the employer actually requires employees in the position to perform the functions that the employer asserts are essential. For example, an employer may state that typing is an essential function of a position. If, in fact, the employer has never required any employee in that particular position to type, this will be evidence that typing is not actually an essential function of the position.

If the individual who holds the position is actually required to perform the function the employer asserts is an essential function, the inquiry will then center around whether removing the function would fundamentally alter that position. This determination of whether or not a particular function is essential will generally include one or more of the following factors listed in part 1630.

The first factor is whether the position exists to perform a particular function. For example, an individual may be hired to proofread documents. The ability to proofread the documents would then be an essential function, since this is the only reason the position exists.

The second factor in determining whether a function is essential is the number of other employees available to perform that job function or among whom the performance of that job function can be distributed. This may be a factor either because the total number of available employees is low, or because of the fluctuating demands of the business operation. For example, if an employer has a relatively small number of available employees for the volume of work to be performed, it may be necessary that each employee perform a multitude of different functions. Therefore, the performance of those functions by each employee becomes more critical and the options for reorganizing the work become more limited. In such a situation, functions that might not be essential if there were a larger staff may become essential because the staff size is small compared to the volume of work that has to be done.

REGULATION

(ii) Written job descriptions prepared before advertising or interviewing applicants for the job;

(iii) The amount of time spent on the job performing the function;

(iv) The consequences of not requiring the incumbent to perform the function;

(v) The terms of a collective bargaining agreement;

(vi) The work experience of past incumbents in the job; and/or

(vii) The current work experience of incumbents in similar jobs.

INTERPRETIVE GUIDANCE

See Treadwell v. Alexander, 707 F.2d 473 (11th Cir. 1983).

A similar situation might occur in a larger work force if the workflow follows a cycle of heavy demand for labor intensive work followed by low demand periods. This type of workflow might also make the performance of each function during the peak periods more critical and might limit the employer's flexibility in reorganizing operating procedures. See Dexler v. Tisch, 660 F. Supp. 1418 (D. Conn. 1987).

The third factor is the degree of expertise or skill required to perform the function. In certain professions and highly skilled positions the employee is hired for his or her expertise or ability to perform the particular function. In such a situation, the performance of that specialized task would be an essential function.

Whether a particular function is essential is a factual determination that must be made on a case by case basis. In determining whether or not a particular function is essential, all relevant evidence should be considered. Part 1630 lists various types of evidence, such as an established job description, that should be considered in determining whether a particular function is essential. Since the list is not exhaustive, other relevant evidence may also be presented. Greater weight will not be granted to the types of evidence included on the list than to the types of evidence not listed.

Although part 1630 does not require employers to develop or maintain job descriptions, written job descriptions prepared before advertising or interviewing applicants for the job, as well as the employer's judgment as to what functions are essential are among the relevant evidence to be considered in determining whether a particular function is essential. The terms of a collective bargaining agreement are also relevant to the determination of whether a particular function is essential. The work experience of past employees in the job or of current employees in similar jobs is likewise relevant to the determination of whether a particular function is essential. See H.R. Conf. Rep. No. 101-596, 101st Cong., 2d Sess. 58 (1990) [hereinafter Conference Report]; House Judiciary Report at 33-34. See also Hall v. U.S. Postal Service, 857 F.2d 1073 (6th Cir. 1988).

The time spent performing the particular function may also be an indicator of whether that function is essential. For example,

REGULATION

if an employee spends the vast majority of his or her time working at a cash register, this would be evidence that operating the cash register is an essential function. The consequences of failing to require the employee to perform the function may be another indicator of whether a particular function is essential. For example, although a firefighter may not regularly have to carry an unconscious adult out of a burning building, the consequence of failing to require the firefighter to be able to perform this function would be serious.

It is important to note that the inquiry into essential functions is not intended to second guess an employer's business judgment with regard to production standards, whether qualitative or quantitative, nor to require employers to lower such standards. (See section 1630.10 Qualification Standards, Tests and Other Selection Criteria). If an employer requires its typists to be able to accurately type 75 words per minute, it will not be called upon to explain why an inaccurate work product, or a typing speed of 65 words per minute, would not be adequate. Similarly, if a hotel requires its service workers to thoroughly clean 16 rooms per day, it will not have to explain why it requires thorough cleaning, or why it chose a 16 room rather than a 10 room requirement. However, if an employer does require accurate 75 word per minute typing or the thorough cleaning of 16 rooms, it will have to show that it actually imposes such requirements on its employees in fact, and not simply on paper. It should also be noted that, if it is alleged that the employer intentionally selected the particular level of production to exclude individuals with disabilities, the employer may have to offer a legitimate, nondiscriminatory reason for its selection.

REGULATION

(o) Reasonable accommodation. -- (1) The term "reasonable accommodation" means:

(i) Modifications or adjustments to a job application process that enable a qualified applicant with a disability to be considered for the position such qualified applicant desires; or

(ii) Modifications or adjustments to the work environment, or to the manner or circumstances under which the position held or desired is customarily performed, that enable a qualified individual with a disability to perform the essential functions of that position; or

(iii) Modifications or adjustments that enable a covered entity's employee with a disability to enjoy equal benefits and privileges of employment as are enjoyed by its other similarly situated employees without disabilities.

(2) Reasonable accommodation may include but is not limited to:

(i) Making existing facilities used by employees readily accessible to and usable by individuals with disabilities; and

(ii) Job restructuring; part-time or modified work

INTERPRETIVE GUIDANCE

Section 1630.2(o) Reasonable Accommodation

An individual is considered a "qualified individual with a disability" if the individual can perform the essential functions of the position held or desired with or without reasonable accommodation. In general, an accommodation is any change in the work environment or in the way things are customarily done that enables an individual with a disability to enjoy equal employment opportunities. There are three categories of reasonable accommodation. These are (1) accommodations that are required to ensure equal opportunity in the application process; (2) accommodations that enable the employer's employees with disabilities to perform the essential functions of the position held or desired; and (3) accommodations that enable the employer's employees with disabilities to enjoy equal benefits and privileges of employment as are enjoyed by employees without disabilities. It should be noted that nothing in this part prohibits employers or other covered entities from providing accommodations beyond those required by this part.

Part 1630 lists the examples, specified in title I of the ADA, of the most common types of accommodation that an employer or other covered entity may be required to provide. There are any number of other specific accommodations that may be appropriate for particular situations but are not specifically mentioned in this listing. This listing is not intended to be exhaustive of accommodation possibilities. For example, other accommodations could include permitting the use of accrued paid leave or providing additional unpaid leave for necessary treatment, making employer provided transportation accessible, and providing reserved parking spaces. Providing personal assistants, such as a page turner for an employee with no hands or a travel attendant to act as a sighted guide to assist a blind employee on occasional business trips, may also be a reasonable accommodation. Senate Report at 31; House Labor Report at 62; House Judiciary Report at 39.

It may also be a reasonable accommodation to permit an individual with a disability the opportunity to provide and utilize equipment, aids or services that an employer is not required to provide as a reasonable accommodation. For example, it would be a reasonable accommodation for an employer to permit an individual who is blind to use a guide dog at work, even though the employer would not be required to provide a guide dog for the employee.

The accommodations included on the list of reasonable ac-

REGULATION

schedules; reassignment to a
vacant position; acquisition
or modifications of equipment or devices; appropriate
adjustment or modifications
of examinations, training
materials, or policies; the
provision of qualified readers
or interpreters; and other
similar accommodations for
individuals with disabilities.

(3) To determine the
appropriate reasonable
accommodation it may be
necessary for the covered
entity to initiate an informal,
interactive process with the
qualified individual with a
disability in need of the
accommodation. This process
should identify the precise
limitations resulting from the
disability and potential
reasonable accommodations
that could overcome those
limitations.

INTERPRETIVE GUIDANCE

commodations are generally self explanatory. However, there
are a few that require further explanation. One of these is the
accommodation of making existing facilities used by employees readily accessible to, and usable by, individuals with
disabilities. This accommodation includes both those areas that
must be accessible for the employee to perform essential job
functions, as well as non-work areas used by the employer's
employees for other purposes. For example, accessible break
rooms, lunch rooms, training rooms, restrooms, etc., may be
required as reasonable accommodations.

Another of the potential accommodations listed is "job restructuring." An employer or other covered entity may restructure
a job by reallocating or redistributing nonessential, marginal
job functions. For example, an employer may have two jobs,
each of which entails the performance of a number of marginal functions. The employer hires a qualified individual with
a disability who is able to perform some of the marginal
functions of each job but not all of the marginal functions of
either job. As an accommodation, the employer may redistrib-
ute the marginal functions so that all of the marginal functions
that the qualified individual with a disability can perform are
made a part of the position to be filled by the qualified individual with a disability. The remaining marginal functions that
the individual with a disability cannot perform would then be
transferred to the other position. See Senate Report at 31;
House Labor Report at 62.

An employer or other covered entity is not required to reallo-
cate essential functions. The essential functions are by definition those that the individual who holds the job would have to
perform, with or without reasonable accommodation, in order
to be considered qualified for the position. For example,
suppose a security guard position requires the individual who
holds the job to inspect identification cards. An employer
would not have to provide an individual who is legally blind
with an assistant to look at the identification cards for the
legally blind employee. In this situation the assistant would be
performing the job for the individual with a disability rather
than assisting the individual to perform the job. See Coleman
v. Darden, 595 F.2d 533 (10th Cir. 1979).

An employer or other covered entity may also restructure a job
by altering when and/or how an essential function is performed. For example, an essential function customarily performed in the early morning hours may be rescheduled until

REGULATION

later in the day as a reasonable accommodation to a disability that precludes performance of the function at the customary hour. Likewise, as a reasonable accommodation, an employee with a disability that inhibits the ability to write, may be permitted to computerize records that were customarily maintained manually.

Reassignment to a vacant position is also listed as a potential reasonable accommodation. In general, reassignment should be considered only when accommodation within the individual's current position would pose an undue hardship. Reassignment is not available to applicants. An applicant for a position must be qualified for, and be able to perform the essential functions of, the position sought with or without reasonable accommodation.

Reassignment may not be used to limit, segregate, or otherwise discriminate against employees with disabilities by forcing reassignments to undesirable positions or to designated offices or facilities. Employers should reassign the individual to an equivalent position, in terms of pay, status, etc., if the individual is qualified, and if the position is vacant within a reasonable amount of time. A "reasonable amount of time" should be determined in light of the totality of the circumstances. As an example, suppose there is no vacant position available at the time that an individual with a disability requests reassignment as a reasonable accommodation. The employer, however, knows that an equivalent position for which the individual is qualified, will become vacant next week. Under these circumstances, the employer should reassign the individual to the position when it becomes available.

An employer may reassign an individual to a lower graded position if there are no accommodations that would enable the employee to remain in the current position and there are no vacant equivalent positions for which the individual is qualified with or without reasonable accommodation. An employer, however, is not required to maintain the reassigned individual with a disability at the salary of the higher graded position if it does not so maintain reassigned employees who are not disabled. It should also be noted that an employer is not required to promote an individual with a disability as an accommodation. See Senate Report at 31-32; House Labor Report at 63.

The determination of which accommodation is appropriate in a particular situation involves a process in which the employer and employee identify the precise limitations imposed by the disability and explore potential accommodations that would overcome those limitations. This process is discussed more fully in section 1630.9 Not Making Reasonable Accommodation.

REGULATION

(p) Underline hardship. --

(1) In general. "Undue hardship" means, with respect to the provision of an accommodation, significant difficulty or expense incurred by a covered entity, when considered in light of the factors set forth in paragraph (p)(2) of this section.

(2) Factors to be considered. In determining whether an accommodation would impose an undue hardship on a covered entity, factors to be considered include:

(i) The nature and net cost of the accommodation needed under this part, taking into consideration the availability of tax credits and deductions, and/or outside funding;

(ii) The overall financial resources of the facility or facilities involved in the provision of the reasonable accommodation, the number of persons employed at such facility, and the effect on expenses and resources;

(iii) The overall financial resources of the covered entity, the overall size of the business of the covered entity with respect to the number of its employees, and the number, type and location of its facilities;

(iv) The type of operation

INTERPRETIVE GUIDANCE

Section 1630.2(p) Undue Hardship

An employer or other covered entity is not required to provide an accommodation that will impose an undue hardship on the operation of the employer's or other covered entity's business. The term "undue hardship" means significant difficulty or expense in, or resulting from, the provision of the accommodation. The "undue hardship" provision takes into account the financial realities of the particular employer or other covered entity. However, the concept of undue hardship is not limited to financial difficulty. "Undue hardship" refers to any accommodation that would be unduly costly, extensive, substantial, or disruptive, or that would fundamentally alter the nature or operation of the business. See Senate Report at 35; House Labor Report at 67.

For example, suppose an individual with a disabling visual impairment that makes it extremely difficult to see in dim lighting applies for a position as a waiter in a nightclub and requests that the club be brightly lit as a reasonable accommodation. Although the individual may be able to perform the job in bright lighting, the nightclub will probably be able to demonstrate that that particular accommodation, though inexpensive, would impose an undue hardship if the bright lighting would destroy the ambience of the nightclub and/or make it difficult for the customers to see the stage show. The fact that that particular accommodation poses an undue hardship, however, only means that the employer is not required to provide that accommodation. If there is another accommodation that will not create an undue hardship, the employer would be required to provide the alternative accommodation.

An employer's claim that the cost of a particular accommodation will impose an undue hardship will be analyzed in light of the factors outlined in part 1630. In part, this analysis requires a determination of whose financial resources should be considered in deciding whether the accommodation is unduly costly. In some cases the financial resources of the employer or other covered entity in its entirety should be considered in determining whether the cost of an accommodation poses an undue hardship. In other cases, consideration of the financial resources of the employer or other covered entity as a whole may be inappropriate because it may not give an accurate picture of the financial resources available to the particular facility that will actually be required to provide the accommodation. See House Labor Report at 68-69; House Judiciary Report at 40-41; see also Conference Report at 56-57.

REGULATION

or operations of the covered entity, including the composition, structure and functions of the workforce of such entity, and the geographic separateness and administrative or fiscal relationship of the facility or facilities in question to the covered entity; and

(v) The impact of the accommodation upon the operation of the facility, including the impact on the ability of other employees to perform their duties and the impact on the facility's ability to conduct business.

INTERPRETIVE GUIDANCE

If the employer or other covered entity asserts that only the financial resources of the facility where the individual will be employed should be considered, part 1630 requires a factual determination of the relationship between the employer or other covered entity and the facility that will provide the accommodation. As an example, suppose that an independently owned fast food franchise that receives no money from the franchisor refuses to hire an individual with a hearing impairment because it asserts that it would be an undue hardship to provide an interpreter to enable the individual to participate in monthly staff meetings. Since the financial relationship between the franchisor and the franchise is limited to payment of an annual franchise fee, only the financial resources of the franchise would be considered in determining whether or not providing the accommodation would be an undue hardship. See House Labor Report at 68; House Judiciary Report at 40.

If the employer or other covered entity can show that the cost of the accommodation would impose an undue hardship, it would still be required to provide the accommodation if the funding is available from another source, e.g., a State vocational rehabilitation agency, or if Federal, State or local tax deductions or tax credits are available to offset the cost of the accommodation. If the employer or other covered entity receives, or is eligible to receive, monies from an external source that would pay the entire cost of the accommodation, it cannot claim cost as an undue hardship. In the absence of such funding, the individual with a disability requesting the accommodation should be given the option of providing the accommodation or of paying that portion of the cost which constitutes the undue hardship on the operation of the business. To the extent that such monies pay or would pay for only part of the cost of the accommodation, only that portion of the cost of the accommodation that could not be recovered - the final net cost to the entity - may be considered in determining undue hardship. (See section 1630.9 Not Making Reasonable Accommodation). See Senate Report at 36; House Labor Report at 69.

REGULATION

(q) Qualification standards means the personal and professional attributes including the skill, experience, education, physical, medical, safety and other requirements established by a covered entity as requirements which an individual must meet in order to be eligible for the position held or desired.

REGULATION

(r) Direct Threat means a significant risk of substantial harm to the health or safety of the individual or others that cannot be eliminated or reduced by reasonable accommodation. The determination that an individual poses a "direct threat" shall be based on an individualized assessment of the individual's present ability to safely perform the essential functions of the job. This assessment shall be based on a reasonable medical judgment that relies on the most current medical knowledge and/or on the best available objective evidence. In determining whether an individual would pose a direct threat, the factors to be considered include:

(1) The duration of the risk;

(2) The nature and severity of the potential harm;

(3) The likelihood that the potential harm will occur; and

(4) The imminence of the potential harm.

INTERPRETIVE GUIDANCE
Section 1630.2(r) Direct Threat

An employer may require, as a qualification standard, that an individual not pose a direct threat to the health or safety of himself/herself or others. Like any other qualification standard, such a standard must apply to all applicants or employees and not just to individuals with disabilities. If, however, an individual poses a direct threat as a result of a disability, the employer must determine whether a reasonable accommodation would either eliminate the risk or reduce it to an acceptable level. If no accommodation exists that would either eliminate or reduce the risk, the employer may refuse to hire an applicant or may discharge an employee who poses a direct threat.

An employer, however, is not permitted to deny an employment opportunity to an individual with a disability merely because of a slightly increased risk. The risk can only be considered when it poses a significant risk, i.e., high probability, of substantial harm; a speculative or remote risk is insufficient. See Senate Report at 27; House Labor Report at 56-57; House Judiciary Report at 45.

Determining whether an individual poses a significant risk of substantial harm to others must be made on a case by case basis. The employer should identify the specific risk posed by the individual. For individuals with mental or emotional disabilities, the employer must identify the specific behavior on the part of the individual that would pose the direct threat. For individuals with physical disabilities, the employer must identify the aspect of the disability that would pose the direct threat. The employer should then consider the four factors listed in part 1630:

(1) the duration of the risk;
(2) the nature and severity of the potential harm;
(3) the likelihood that the potential harm will occur; and
(4) the imminence of the potential harm.

Such consideration must rely on objective, factual evidence - - not on subjective perceptions, irrational fears, patronizing attitudes, or stereotypes - - about the nature or effect of a particular disability, or of disability generally. See Senate Report at 27; House Labor Report at 56-57; House Judiciary Report at 45-46. See also Strathie v. Department of Transportation, 716 F.2d 227 (3d Cir. 1983). Relevant evidence may include input from the individual with a disability, the experi-

REGULATION

INTERPRETIVE GUIDANCE

ence of the individual with a disability in previous similar positions, and opinions of medical doctors, rehabilitation counselors, or physical therapists who have expertise in the disability involved and/or direct knowledge of the individual with the disability.

An employer is also permitted to require that an individual not pose a direct threat of harm to his or her own safety or health. If performing the particular functions of a job would result in a high probability of substantial harm to the individual, the employer could reject or discharge the individual unless a reasonable accommodation that would not cause an undue hardship would avert the harm. For example, an employer would not be required to hire an individual, disabled by narcolepsy, who frequently and unexpectedly loses consciousness for a carpentry job the essential functions of which require the use of power saws and other dangerous equipment, where no accommodation exists that will reduce or eliminate the risk.

The assessment that there exists a high probability of substantial harm to the individual, like the assessment that there exists a high probability of substantial harm to others, must be strictly based on valid medical analyses and/or on other objective evidence. This determination must be based on individualized factual data, using the factors discussed above, rather than on stereotypic or patronizing assumptions and must consider potential reasonable accommodations. Generalized fears about risks from the employment environment, such as exacerbation of the disability caused by stress, cannot be used by an employer to disqualify an individual with a disability. For example, a law firm could not reject an applicant with a history of disabling mental illness based on a generalized fear that the stress of trying to make partner might trigger a relapse of the individual's mental illness. Nor can general risks to individuals disqualify an individual with a disability. See Senate Report at 56; House Labor Report at 73-74; House Judiciary Report at 45. See also Mantolete v. Bolger, 767 F.2d 1416 (9th Cir. 1985); Bentivegna v. U.S. Department of Labor, 694 F.2d 619 (9th Cir. 1982).

REGULATION

1630.3 Exceptions to the definitions of "Disability" and "Qualified Individual with a Disability."

(a) The terms disability and qualified individual with a disability do not include individuals currently engaging in the illegal use of drugs, when the covered entity acts on the basis of such use.

(1) Drug means a controlled substance, as defined in schedules I through V of Section 202 of the Controlled Substances Act (21 U.S.C 812).

(2) Illegal use of drugs means the use of drugs the possession or distribution of which is unlawful under the Controlled Substances Act, as periodically updated by the Food and Drug Administration. This term does not include the use of a drug taken under the supervision of a licensed health care professional, or other uses authorized by the Controlled Substances Act or other provisions of Federal law.

(b) However, the terms "disability" and "qualified" individual with a disability may not exclude an individual who:

(1) Has successfully completed a supervised drug rehabilitation program and is no longer engaging in the illegal use of drugs, or has otherwise been rehabilitated successfully and is no longer engaging in the illegal use of drugs; or

INTERPRETIVE GUIDANCE

Section 1630.3 Exceptions to the Definitions of "Disability" and "Qualified Individual with a Disability"

Section 1630.3 (a) through (c) Illegal Use of Drugs
Part 1630 provides that an individual currently engaging in the illegal use of drugs is not an individual with a disability for purposes of this part when the employer or other covered entity acts on the basis of such use. Illegal use of drugs refers both to the use of unlawful drugs, such as cocaine, and to the unlawful use of prescription drugs.

Employers, for example, may discharge or deny employment to persons who illegally use drugs, on the basis of such use, without fear of being held liable for discrimination. The term "currently engaging" is not intended to be limited to the use of drugs on the day of, or within a matter of days or weeks before, the employment action in question. Rather, the provision is intended to apply to the illegal use of drugs that has occurred recently enough to indicate that the individual is actively engaged in such conduct. See Conference Report at 64.

Individuals who are erroneously perceived as engaging in the illegal use of drugs, but are not in fact illegally using drugs are not excluded from the definitions of the terms "disability" and "qualified individual with a disability." Individuals who are no longer illegally using drugs and who have either been rehabilitated successfully or are in the process of completing a rehabilitation program are, likewise, not excluded from the definitions of those terms. The term "rehabilitation program" refers to both in-patient and out-patient programs, as well as to appropriate employee assistance programs, professionally recognized self-help programs, such as Narcotics Anonymous, or other programs that provide professional (not necessarily medical) assistance and counseling for individuals who illegally use drugs. See Conference Report at 64; see also House Labor Report at 77; House Judiciary Report at 47.

It should be noted that this provision simply provides that certain individuals are not excluded from the definitions of "disability" and "qualified individual with a disability." Consequently, such individuals are still required to establish that they satisfy the requirements of these definitions in order to be protected by the ADA and this part. An individual erroneously regarded as illegally using drugs, for example, would have to show that he or she was regarded as a drug addict in order to

REGULATION

(2) Is participating in a supervised rehabilitation program and is no longer engaging in such use; or

(3) Is erroneously regarded as engaging in such use, but is not engaging in such use.

(c) It shall not be a violation of this part for a covered entity to adopt or administer reasonable policies or procedures, including but not limited to drug testing, designed to ensure that an individual described in paragraph (b)(1) or (2) of this section is no longer engaging in the illegal use of drugs. (See section 1630.16(c) Drug testing).

(d) Disability does not include:

(1) Transvestism, transsexualism, pedophilia, exhibitionism, voyeurism, gender identity disorders not resulting from physical impairments, or other sexual behavior disorders;

(2) Compulsive gambling, kleptomania, or pyromania; or

(3) Psychoactive substance use disorders resulting from current illegal use of drugs.

(e) Homosexuality and bisexuality are not impairments and so are not disabilities as defined in this part.

INTERPRETIVE GUIDANCE

demonstrate that he or she meets the definition of "disability" as defined in this part.

Employers are entitled to seek reasonable assurances that no illegal use of drugs is occurring or has occurred recently enough so that continuing use is a real and ongoing problem. The reasonable assurances that employers may ask applicants or employees to provide include evidence that the individual is participating in a drug treatment program and/or evidence, such as drug test results, to show that the individual is not currently engaging in the illegal use of drugs. An employer, such as a law enforcement agency, may also be able to impose a qualification standard that excludes individuals with a history of illegal use of drugs if it can show that the standard is job-related and consistent with business necessity. (See section 1630.10 Qualification Standards, Tests and Other Selection Criteria) See Conference Report at 64.

REGULATION
1630.4 Discrimination prohibited.

It is unlawful for a covered entity to discriminate on the basis of disability against a qualified individual with a disability in regard to:

(a) Recruitment, advertising, and job application procedures;

(b) Hiring, upgrading, promotion, award of tenure, demotion, transfer, layoff, termination, right of return from layoff, and rehiring;

(c) Rates of pay or any other form of compensation and changes in compensation;

(d) Job assignments, job classifications, organizational structures, position descriptions, lines of progression, and seniority lists;

(e) Leaves of absence, sick leave, or any other leave;

(f) Fringe benefits available by virtue of employment, whether or not administered by the covered entity;

(g) Selection and financial support for training, including: apprenticeships, professional meetings, conferences and other related activities, and selection for leaves of absence to pursue training;

INTERPRETIVE GUIDANCE
Section 1630.4 Discrimination Prohibited

This provision prohibits discrimination against a qualified individual with a disability in all aspects of the employment relationship. The range of employment decisions covered by this nondiscrimination mandate is to be construed in a manner consistent with the regulations implementing Section 504 of the Rehabilitation Act of 1973.

Part 1630 is not intended to limit the ability of covered entities to choose and maintain a qualified workforce. Employers can continue to use job-related criteria to select qualified employees, and can continue to hire employees who can perform the essential functions of the job.

REGULATION

(h) Activities sponsored by a covered entity including social and recreational programs; and

(i) Any other term, condition, or privilege of employment.

The term "discrimination" includes, but is not limited to, the acts described in sections 1630.5 through 1630.13 of this part.

INTERPRETIVE GUIDANCE

REGULATION

1630.5 Limiting, segregating, and classifying.

It is unlawful for a covered entity to limit, segregate, or classify a job applicant or employee in a way that adversely affects his or her employment opportunities or status on the basis of disability.

INTERPRETIVE GUIDANCE

Section 1630.5 Limiting, Segregating and Classifying

This provision and the several provisions that follow describe various specific forms of discrimination that are included within the general prohibition of section 1630.4. Covered entities are prohibited from restricting the employment opportunities of qualified individuals with disabilities on the basis of stereotypes and myths about the individual's disability. Rather, the capabilities of qualified individuals with disabilities must be determined on an individualized, case by case basis. Covered entities are also prohibited from segregating qualified employees with disabilities into separate work areas or into separate lines of advancement.

Thus, for example, it would be a violation of this part for an employer to limit the duties of an employee with a disability based on a presumption of what is best for an individual with such a disability, or on a presumption about the abilities of an individual with such a disability. It would be a violation of this part for an employer to adopt a separate track of job promotion or progression for employees with disabilities based on a presumption that employees with disabilities are uninterested in, or incapable of, performing particular jobs. Similarly, it would be a violation for an employer to assign or reassign (as a reasonable accommodation) employees with disabilities to one particular office or installation, or to require that employees with disabilities only use particular employer provided non-work facilities such as segregated break-rooms, lunch rooms, or lounges. It would also be a violation of this part to deny employment to an applicant or employee with a disability based on generalized fears about the safety of an individual with such a disability, or based on generalized assumptions about the absenteeism rate of an individual with such a disability.

In addition, it should also be noted that this part is intended to require that employees with disabilities be accorded equal access to whatever health insurance coverage the employer provides to other employees. This part does not, however, affect pre-existing condition clauses included in health insurance policies offered by employers. Consequently, employers may continue to offer policies that contain such clauses, even if they adversely affect individuals with disabilities, so long as the clauses are not used as a subterfuge to evade the purposes of this part.

So, for example, it would be permissible for an employer to

REGULATION

offer an insurance policy that limits coverage for certain procedures or treatments to a specified number per year. Thus, if a health insurance plan provided coverage for five blood transfusions a year to all covered employees, it would not be discriminatory to offer this plan simply because a hemophiliac employee may require more than five blood transfusions annually. However, it would not be permissible to limit or deny the hemophiliac employee coverage for other procedures, such as heart surgery or the setting of a broken leg, even though the plan would not have to provide coverage for the additional blood transfusions that may be involved in these procedures. Likewise, limits may be placed on reimbursements for certain procedures or on the types of drugs or procedures covered (e.g. limits on the number of permitted X-rays or non-coverage of experimental drugs or procedures), but that limitation must be applied equally to individuals with and without disabilities. See Senate Report at 28-29; House Labor Report at 58-59; House Judiciary Report at 36.

Leave policies or benefit plans that are uniformly applied do not violate this part simply because they do not address the special needs of every individual with a disability. Thus, for example, an employer that reduces the number of paid sick leave days that it will provide to all employees, or reduces the amount of medical insurance coverage that it will provide to all employees, is not in violation of this part, even if the benefits reduction has an impact on employees with disabilities in need of greater sick leave and medical coverage. Benefits reductions adopted for discriminatory reasons are in violation of this part. See Alexander v. Choate, 469 U.S. 287 (1985). See Senate Report at 85; House Labor Report at 137. (See also, the discussion at section 1630.16(f) Health Insurance, Life Insurance, and Other Benefit Plans).

REGULATION

1630.6 Contractual or other arrangements.

(a) In general. It is unlawful for a covered entity to participate in a contractual or other arrangement or relationship that has the effect of subjecting the covered entity's own qualified applicant or employee with a disability to the discrimination prohibited by this part.

(b) Contractual or other arrangement defined. The phrase "contractual or other arrangement or relationship" includes, but is not limited to, a relationship with an employment or referral agency; labor union, including collective bargaining agreements; an organization providing fringe benefits to an employee of the covered entity; or an organization providing training and apprenticeship programs.

(c) Application. This section applies to a covered entity, with respect to its own applicants or employees, whether the entity offered the contract or initiated the relationship, or whether the entity accepted the contract or acceded to the relationship. A covered entity is not liable for the actions of the other party or parties to the contract which only affect that other party's employees or applicants.

INTERPRETIVE GUIDANCE

Section 1630.6 Contractual or Other Arrangements

An employer or other covered entity may not do through a contractual or other relationship what it is prohibited from doing directly. This provision does not affect the determination of whether or not one is a "covered entity" or "employer" as defined in section 1630.2.

This provision only applies to situations where an employer or other covered entity has entered into a contractual relationship that has the effect of discriminating against its own employees or applicants with disabilities. Accordingly, it would be a violation for an employer to participate in a contractual relationship that results in discrimination against the employer's employees with disabilities in hiring, training, promotion, or in any other aspect of the employment relationship. This provision applies whether or not the employer or other covered entity intended for the contractual relationship to have the discriminatory effect.

Part 1630 notes that this provision applies to parties on either side of the contractual or other relationship. This is intended to highlight that an employer whose employees provide services to others, like an employer whose employees receive services, must ensure that those employees are not discriminated against on the basis of disability. For example, a copier company whose service representative is a dwarf could be required to provide a stepstool, as a reasonable accommodation, to enable him to perform the necessary repairs. However, the employer would not be required, as a reasonable accommodation, to make structural changes to its customer's inaccessible premises.

The existence of the contractual relationship adds no new obligations under part 1630. The employer, therefore, is not liable through the contractual arrangement for any discrimination by the contractor against the contractor's own employees or applicants, although the contractor, as an employer, may be liable for such discrimination.

An employer or other covered entity, on the other hand, cannot evade the obligations imposed by this part by engaging in a contractual or other relationship. For example, an employer cannot avoid its responsibility to make reasonable accommodation subject to the undue hardship limitation through a contractual arrangement. See Conference Report at 59; House Labor Report at 59-61; House Judiciary Report at 36-37.

REGULATION

INTERPRETIVE GUIDANCE

To illustrate, assume that an employer is seeking to contract with a company to provide training for its employees. Any responsibilities of reasonable accommodation applicable to the employer in providing the training remain with that employer even if it contracts with another company for this service. Thus, if the training company were planning to conduct the training at an inaccessible location, thereby making it impossible for an employee who uses a wheelchair to attend, the employer would have a duty to make reasonable accommodation unless to do so would impose an undue hardship. Under these circumstances, appropriate accommodations might include (1) having the training company identify accessible training sites and relocate the training program; (2) having the training company make the training site accessible; (3) directly making the training site accessible or providing the training company with the means by which to make the site accessible; (4) identifying and contracting with another training company that uses accessible sites; or (5) any other accommodation that would result in making the training available to the employee.

As another illustration, assume that instead of contracting with a training company, the employer contracts with a hotel to host a conference for its employees. The employer will have a duty to ascertain and ensure the accessibility of the hotel and its conference facilities. To fulfill this obligation the employer could, for example, inspect the hotel first-hand or ask a local disability group to inspect the hotel. Alternatively, the employer could ensure that the contract with the hotel specifies it will provide accessible guest rooms for those who need them and that all rooms to be used for the conference, including exhibit and meeting rooms, are accessible. If the hotel breaches this accessibility provision, the hotel may be liable to the employer, under a non-ADA breach of contract theory, for the cost of any accommodation needed to provide access to the hotel and conference, and for any other costs accrued by the employer. (In addition, the hotel may also be independently liable under title III of the ADA). However, this would not relieve the employer of its responsibility under this part nor shield it from charges of discrimination by its own employees. See House Labor Report at 40; House Judiciary Report at 37.

REGULATION

1630.7 Standards, criteria, or methods of administration.

It is unlawful for a covered entity to use standards, criteria, or methods of administration, which are not job-related and consistent with business necessity, and:

(a) That have the effect of discriminating on the basis of disability; or

(b) That perpetuate the discrimination of others who are subject to common administrative control.

INTERPRETIVE GUIDANCE

REGULATION

1630.8 Relationship or association with an individual with a disability.

It is unlawful for a covered entity to exclude or deny equal jobs or benefits to, or otherwise discriminate against, a qualified individual because of the known disability of an individual with whom the qualified individual is known to have a family, business, social or other relationship or association.

INTERPRETIVE GUIDANCE

Section 1630.8 Relationship or Association with an Individual with a Disability

This provision is intended to protect any qualified individual, whether or not that individual has a disability, from discrimination because that person is known to have an association or relationship with an individual who has a known disability. This protection is not limited to those who have a familial relationship with an individual with a disability.

To illustrate the scope of this provision, assume that a qualified applicant without a disability applies for a job and discloses to the employer that his or her spouse has a disability. The employer thereupon declines to hire the applicant because the employer believes that the applicant would have to miss work or frequently leave work early in order to care for the spouse. Such a refusal to hire would be prohibited by this provision. Similarly, this provision would prohibit an employer from discharging an employee because the employee does volunteer work with people who have AIDS, and the employer fears that the employee may contract the disease.

This provision also applies to other benefits and privileges of employment. For example, an employer that provides health insurance benefits to its employees for their dependents may not reduce the level of those benefits to an employee simply because that employee has a dependent with a disability. This is true even if the provision of such benefits would result in increased health insurance costs for the employer.

It should be noted, however, that an employer need not provide the applicant or employee without a disability with a reasonable accommodation because that duty only applies to qualified applicants or employees with disabilities. Thus, for example, an employee would not be entitled to a modified work schedule as an accommodation to enable the employee to care for a spouse with a disability. See Senate Report at 30; House Labor Report at 61-62; House Judiciary Report at 38-39.

REGULATION
1630.9 Not making reasonable accommodation.

(a) It is unlawful for a covered entity not to make reasonable accommodation to the known physical or mental limitations of an otherwise qualified applicant or employee with a disability, unless such covered entity can demonstrate that the accommodation would impose an undue hardship on the operation of its business.

INTERPRETIVE GUIDANCE
Section 1630.9 Not Making Reasonable Accommodation

The obligation to make reasonable accommodation is a form of non-discrimination. It applies to all employment decisions and to the job application process. This obligation does not extend to the provision of adjustments or modifications that are primarily for the personal benefit of the individual with a disability. Thus, if an adjustment or modification is job-related, e.g., specifically assists the individual in performing the duties of a particular job, it will be considered a type of reasonable accommodation. On the other hand, if an adjustment or modification assists the individual throughout his or her daily activities, on and off the job, it will be considered a personal item that the employer is not required to provide. Accordingly, an employer would generally not be required to provide an employee with a disability with a prosthetic limb, wheelchair, or eyeglasses. Nor would an employer have to provide as an accommodation any amenity or convenience that is not job-related, such as a private hot plate, hot pot or refrigerator that is not provided to employees without disabilities. See Senate Report at 31; House Labor Report at 62.

It should be noted, however, that the provision of such items may be required as a reasonable accommodation where such items are specifically designed or required to meet job-related rather than personal needs. An employer, for example, may have to provide an individual with a disabling visual impairment with eyeglasses specifically designed to enable the individual to use the office computer monitors, but that are not otherwise needed by the individual outside of the office.

The term "supported employment," which has been applied to a wide variety of programs to assist individuals with severe disabilities in both competitive and non-competitive employment, is not synonymous with reasonable accommodation. Examples of supported employment include modified training materials, restructuring essential functions to enable an individual to perform a job, or hiring an outside professional ("job coach") to assist in job training. Whether a particular form of assistance would be required as a reasonable accommodation must be determined on an individualized, case by case basis without regard to whether that assistance is referred to as "supported employment." For example, an employer, under certain circumstances, may be required to provide modified training materials or a temporary "job coach" to assist in the training of a qualified individual with a disability as a reasonable accommodation. However, an employer would not be

REGULATION

required to restructure the essential functions of a position to fit the skills of an individual with a disability who is not otherwise qualified to perform the position, as is done in certain supported employment programs. See 34 CFR part 363. It should be noted that it would not be a violation of this part for an employer to provide any of these personal modifications or adjustments, or to engage in supported employment or similar rehabilitative programs.

The obligation to make reasonable accommodation applies to all services and programs provided in connection with employment, and to all non-work facilities provided or maintained by an employer for use by its employees. Accordingly, the obligation to accommodate is applicable to employer sponsored placement or counseling services, and to employer provided cafeterias, lounges, gymnasiums, auditoriums, transportation and the like.

The reasonable accommodation requirement is best understood as a means by which barriers to the equal employment opportunity of an individual with a disability are removed or alleviated. These barriers may, for example, be physical or structural obstacles that inhibit or prevent the access of an individual with a disability to job sites, facilities or equipment. Or they may be rigid work schedules that permit no flexibility as to when work is performed or when breaks may be taken, or inflexible job procedures that unduly limit the modes of communication that are used on the job, or the way in which particular tasks are accomplished.

The term "otherwise qualified" is intended to make clear that the obligation to make reasonable accommodation is owed only to an individual with a disability who is qualified within the meaning of section 1630.2(m) in that he or she satisfies all the skill, experience, education and other job-related selection criteria. An individual with a disability is "otherwise qualified," in other words, if he or she is qualified for a job, except that, because of the disability, he or she needs a reasonable accommodation to be able to perform the job's essential functions.

For example, if a law firm requires that all incoming lawyers have graduated from an accredited law school and have passed the bar examination, the law firm need not provide an accommodation to an individual with a visual impairment who has not met these selection criteria. That individual is not entitled to a reasonable accommodation because the individual is not "otherwise qualified" for the position.

REGULATION

On the other hand, if the individual has graduated from an accredited law school and passed the bar examination, the individual would be "otherwise qualified." The law firm would thus be required to provide a reasonable accommodation, such as a machine that magnifies print, to enable the individual to perform the essential functions of the attorney position, unless the necessary accommodation would impose an undue hardship on the law firm. See Senate Report at 33-34; House Labor Report at 64-65.

The reasonable accommodation that is required by this part should provide the qualified individual with a disability with an equal employment opportunity. Equal employment opportunity means an opportunity to attain the same level of performance, or to enjoy the same level of benefits and privileges of employment as are available to the average similarly situated employee without a disability. Thus, for example, an accommodation made to assist an employee with a disability in the performance of his or her job must be adequate to enable the individual to perform the essential functions of the relevant position. The accommodation, however, does not have to be the "best" accommodation possible, so long as it is sufficient to meet the job-related needs of the individual being accommodated. Accordingly, an employer would not have to provide an employee disabled by a back impairment with a state-of-the art mechanical lifting device if it provided the employee with a less expensive or more readily available device that enabled the employee to perform the essential functions of the job. See Senate Report at 35; House Labor Report at 66; see also Carter v. Bennett, 840 F.2d 63 (D.C. Cir. 1988).

Employers are obligated to make reasonable accommodation only to the physical or mental limitations resulting from the disability of a qualified individual with a disability that are known to the employer. Thus, an employer would not be expected to accommodate disabilities of which it is unaware. If an employee with a known disability is having difficulty performing his or her job, an employer may inquire whether the employee is in need of a reasonable accommodation. In general, however, it is the responsibility of the individual with a disability to inform the employer that an accommodation is needed. When the need for an accommodation is not obvious, an employer, before providing a reasonable accommodation, may require that the individual with a disability provide documentation of the need for accommodation. See Senate Report at 34; House Labor Report at 65.

REGULATION

Process of Determining the Appropriate Reasonable Accommodation

Once a qualified individual with a disability has requested provision of a reasonable accommodation, the employer must make a reasonable effort to determine the appropriate accommodation. The appropriate reasonable accommodation is best determined through a flexible, interactive process that involves both the employer and the qualified individual with a disability. Although this process is described below in terms of accommodations that enable the individual with a disability to perform the essential functions of the position held or desired, it is equally applicable to accommodations involving the job application process, and to accommodations that enable the individual with a disability to enjoy equal benefits and privileges of employment. See Senate Report at 34-35; House Labor Report at 65-67.

When a qualified individual with a disability has requested a reasonable accommodation to assist in the performance of a job, the employer, using a problem solving approach, should:

(1) analyze the particular job involved and determine its purpose and essential functions;

(2) consult with the individual with a disability to ascertain the precise job-related limitations imposed by the individual's disability and how those limitations could be overcome with a reasonable accommodation;

(3) in consultation with the individual to be accommodated, identify potential accommodations and assess the effectiveness each would have in enabling the individual to perform the essential functions of the position; and

(4) consider the preference of the individual to be accommodated and select and implement the accommodation that is most appropriate for both the employee and the employer.

In many instances, the appropriate reasonable accommodation may be so obvious to either or both the employer and the qualified individual with a disability that it may not be necessary to proceed in this step-by-step fashion. For example, if an employee who uses a wheelchair requests that his or her desk be placed on blocks to elevate the desktop above the arms of the wheelchair and the employer complies, an appropriate

| REGULATION | INTERPRETIVE GUIDANCE |

accommodation has been requested, identified, and provided without either the employee or employer being aware of having engaged in any sort of "reasonable accommodation process."

However, in some instances neither the individual requesting the accommodation nor the employer can readily identify the appropriate accommodation. For example, the individual needing the accommodation may not know enough about the equipment used by the employer or the exact nature of the work site to suggest an appropriate accommodation. Likewise, the employer may not know enough about the individual's disability or the limitations that disability would impose on the performance of the job to suggest an appropriate accommodation. Under such circumstances, it may be necessary for the employer to initiate a more defined problem solving process, such as the step-by-step process described above, as part of its reasonable effort to identify the appropriate reasonable accommodation.

This process requires the individual assessment of both the particular job at issue, and the specific physical or mental limitations of the particular individual in need of reasonable accommodation. With regard to assessment of the job, "individual assessment" means analyzing the actual job duties and determining the true purpose or object of the job. Such an assessment is necessary to ascertain which job functions are the essential functions that an accommodation must enable an individual with a disability to perform.

After assessing the relevant job, the employer, in consultation with the individual requesting the accommodation, should make an assessment of the specific limitations imposed by the disability on the individual's performance of the job's essential functions. This assessment will make it possible to ascertain the precise barrier to the employment opportunity which, in turn, will make it possible to determine the accommodation(s) that could alleviate or remove that barrier.

If consultation with the individual in need of the accommodation still does not reveal potential appropriate accommodations, then the employer, as part of this process, may find that technical assistance is helpful in determining how to accommodate the particular individual in the specific situation. Such assistance could be sought from the Commission, from state or local rehabilitation agencies, or from disability constituent organizations. It should be noted, however, that, as provided in section 1630.9(c) of this part, the failure to obtain or receive technical assistance from the federal agencies that administer the ADA will not excuse

REGULATION

(b) It is unlawful for a covered entity to deny employment opportunities to an otherwise qualified job applicant or employee with a disability based on the need of such covered entity to make reasonable accommodation to such individual's physical or mental impairments.

(c) A covered entity shall not be excused from the requirements of this part because of any failure to receive technical assistance authorized by section 506 of the ADA, including any failure in the development or dissemination of any technical assistance manual authorized by that Act.

(d) A qualified individual with a disability is not required to accept an accommodation, aid, service, opportunity or benefit which such qualified individual chooses not to accept. However, if such individual rejects a reasonable accommodation, aid, service, opportunity or benefit that is necessary to enable the individual to perform the essential functions of the position held or desired, and cannot, as a result of that rejection, perform the essential functions of the position, the individual will not be considered a qualified individual with a disability.

INTERPRETIVE GUIDANCE

the employer from its reasonable accommodation obligation. Once potential accommodations have been identified, the employer should assess the effectiveness of each potential accommodation in assisting the individual in need of the accommodation in the performance of the essential functions of the position. If more than one of these accommodations will enable the individual to perform the essential functions or if the individual would prefer to provide his or her own accommodation, the preference of the individual with a disability should be given primary consideration. However, the employer providing the accommodation has the ultimate discretion to choose between effective accommodations, and may choose the less expensive accommodation or the accommodation that is easier for it to provide. It should also be noted that the individual's willingness to provide his or her own accommodation does not relieve the employer of the duty to provide the accommodation should the individual for any reason be unable or unwilling to continue to provide the accommodation.

Reasonable Accommodation Process Illustrated

The following example illustrates the informal reasonable accommodation process. Suppose a Sack Handler position requires that the employee pick up fifty pound sacks and carry them from the company loading dock to the storage room, and that a sack handler who is disabled by a back impairment requests a reasonable accommodation. Upon receiving the request, the employer analyzes the Sack Handler job and determines that the essential function and purpose of the job is not the requirement that the job holder physically lift and carry the sacks, but the requirement that the job holder cause the sack to move from the loading dock to the storage room.

The employer then meets with the sack handler to ascertain precisely the barrier posed by the individual's specific disability to the performance of the job's essential function of relocating the sacks. At this meeting the employer learns that the individual can, in fact, lift the sacks to waist level, but is prevented by his or her disability from carrying the sacks from the loading dock to the storage room. The employer and the individual agree that any of a number of potential accommodations, such as the provision of a dolly, hand truck, or cart, could enable the individual to transport the sacks that he or she has lifted.

REGULATION

Upon further consideration, however, it is determined that the provision of a cart is not a feasible effective option. No carts are currently available at the company, and those that can be purchased by the company are the wrong shape to hold many of the bulky and irregularly shaped sacks that must be moved. Both the dolly and the hand truck, on the other hand, appear to be effective options. Both are readily available to the company, and either will enable the individual to relocate the sacks that he or she has lifted. The sack handler indicates his or her preference for the dolly. In consideration of this expressed preference, and because the employer feels that the dolly will allow the individual to move more sacks at a time and so be more efficient than would a hand truck, the employer ultimately provides the sack handler with a dolly in fulfillment of the obligation to make reasonable accommodation.

Section 1630.9(b).

This provision states that an employer or other covered entity cannot prefer or select a qualified individual without a disability over an equally qualified individual with a disability merely because the individual with a disability will require a reasonable accommodation. In other words, an individual's need for an accommodation cannot enter into the employer's or other covered entity's decision regarding hiring, discharge, promotion, or other similar employment decisions, unless the accommodation would impose an undue hardship on the employer. See House Labor Report at 70.

Section 1630.9(d).

The purpose of this provision is to clarify that an employer or other covered entity may not compel a qualified individual with a disability to accept an accommodation, where that accommodation is neither requested nor needed by the individual. However, if a necessary reasonable accommodation is refused, the individual may not be considered qualified. For example, an individual with a visual impairment that restricts his or her field of vision but who is able to read unaided would not be required to accept a reader as an accommodation. However, if the individual were not able to read unaided and reading was an essential function of the job, the individual would not be qualified for the job if he or she refused a reasonable accommodation that would enable him or her to read. See Senate Report at 34; House Labor Report at 65; House Judiciary Report at 71-72.

REGULATION
1630.10 Qualification standards, tests, and other selection criteria.

It is unlawful for a covered entity to use qualification standards, employment tests or other selection criteria that screen out or tend to screen out an individual with a disability or a class of individuals with disabilities, on the basis of disability, unless the standard, test or other selection criteria, as used by the covered entity, is shown to be job-related for the position in question and is consistent with business necessity.

INTERPRETIVE GUIDANCE
Section 1630.10 Qualification Standards, Tests, and Other Selection Criteria

The purpose of this provision is to ensure that individuals with disabilities are not excluded from job opportunities unless they are actually unable to do the job. It is to ensure that there is a fit between job criteria and an applicant's (or employee's) actual ability to do the job. Accordingly, job criteria that even unintentionally screen out, or tend to screen out, an individual with a disability or a class of individuals with disabilities because of their disability may not be used unless the employer demonstrates that that criteria, as used by the employer, are job-related to the position to which they are being applied and are consistent with business necessity. The concept of "business necessity" has the same meaning as the concept of "business necessity" under Section 504 of the Rehabilitation Act of 1973.

Selection criteria that exclude, or tend to exclude, an individual with a disability or a class of individuals with disabilities because of their disability but do not concern an essential function of the job would not be consistent with business necessity.

The use of selection criteria that are related to an essential function of the job may be consistent with business necessity. However, selection criteria that are related to an essential function of the job may not be used to exclude an individual with a disability if that individual could satisfy the criteria with the provision of a reasonable accommodation. Experience under a similar provision of the regulations implementing Section 504 of the Rehabilitation Act indicates that challenges to selection criteria are, in fact, most often resolved by reasonable accommodation. It is therefore anticipated that challenges to selection criteria brought under this part will generally be resolved in a like manner.

This provision is applicable to all types of selection criteria, including safety requirements, vision or hearing requirements, walking requirements, lifting requirements, and employment tests. See Senate Report at 37-39; House Labor Report at 70-72; House Judiciary Report at 42. As previously noted, however, it is not the intent of this part to second guess an employer's business judgment with regard to production standards. (See section 1630.2(n) Essential Functions). Consequently, production standards will generally not be subject to a challenge under this provision.

The Uniform Guidelines on Employee Selection Procedures (UGESP) 29 CFR part 1607 do not apply to the Rehabilitation Act and are similarly inapplicable to this part.

REGULATION

1630.11 Administration of tests.

It is unlawful for a covered entity to fail to select and administer tests concerning employment in the most effective manner to ensure that, when a test is administered to a job applicant or employee who has a disability that impairs sensory, manual or speaking skills, the test results accurately reflect the skills, aptitude, or whatever other factor of the applicant or employee that the test purports to measure, rather than reflecting the impaired sensory, manual, or speaking skills of such employee or applicant (except where such skills are the factors that the test purports to measure).

INTERPRETIVE GUIDANCE

Section 1630.11 Administration of Tests

The intent of this provision is to further emphasize that individuals with disabilities are not to be excluded from jobs that they can actually perform merely because a disability prevents them from taking a test, or negatively influences the results of a test, that is a prerequisite to the job. Read together with the reasonable accommodation requirement of section 1630.9, this provision requires that employment tests be administered to eligible applicants or employees with disabilities that impair sensory, manual, or speaking skills in formats that do not require the use of the impaired skill.

The employer or other covered entity is, generally, only required to provide such reasonable accommodation if it knows, prior to the administration of the test, that the individual is disabled and that the disability impairs sensory, manual or speaking skills. Thus, for example, it would be unlawful to administer a written employment test to an individual who has informed the employer, prior to the administration of the test, that he is disabled with dyslexia and unable to read. In such a case, as a reasonable accommodation and in accordance with this provision, an alternative oral test should be administered to that individual. By the same token, a written test may need to be substituted for an oral test if the applicant taking the test is an individual with a disability that impairs speaking skills or impairs the processing of auditory information.

Occasionally, an individual with a disability may not realize, prior to the administration of a test, that he or she will need an accommodation to take that particular test. In such a situation, the individual with a disability, upon becoming aware of the need for an accommodation, must so inform the employer or other covered entity. For example, suppose an individual with a disabling visual impairment does not request an accommodation for a written examination because he or she is usually able to take written tests with the aid of his or her own specially designed lens. If, when the test is distributed, the individual with a disability discovers that the lens is insufficient to distinguish the words of the test because of the unusually low color contrast between the paper and the ink, the individual would be entitled, at that point, to request an accommodation. The employer or other covered entity would, thereupon, have to provide a test with higher contrast, schedule a retest, or provide any other effective accommodation unless to do so would impose an undue hardship.

Other alternative or accessible test modes or formats include the administration of tests in large print or braille, or via a reader or sign interpreter. Where it is not possible to test in an alternative format, the employer may be required, as a reasonable accommodation, to evaluate the skill to be tested in another manner (e.g., through an interview, or through education, license, or work experience requirements). An employer may also be required, as a reasonable accommodation, to allow more time to complete the test. In addition, the employer's obligation to make reasonable accommodation extends to ensuring that the test site is accessible. (See section 1630.9 Not Making Reasonable Accommodation) See Senate Report at 37-38; House Labor Report at 70-72; House Judiciary Report at 42; see also Stutts v. Freeman, 694 F.2d 666 (11th Cir. 1983); Crane v. Dole, 617 F. Supp. 156 (D.D.C. 1985).

This provision does not require that an employer offer every applicant his or her choice of test format. Rather, this provision only requires that an employer provide, upon advance request, alternative, accessible tests to individuals with disabilities that impair sensory, manual, or speaking skills needed to take the test.

This provision does not apply to employment tests that require the use of sensory, manual, or speaking skills where the tests are intended to measure those skills. Thus, an employer could require that an applicant with dyslexia take a written test for a particular position if the ability to read is the skill the test is designed to measure. Similarly, an employer could require that an applicant complete a test within established time frames if speed were one of the skills for which the applicant was being tested. However, the results of such a test could not be used to exclude an individual with a disability unless the skill was necessary to perform an essential function of the position and no reasonable accommodation was available to enable the individual to perform that function, or the necessary accommodation would impose an undue hardship.

REGULATION

1630.12 Retaliation and coercion.

(a) <u>Retaliation</u>. It is unlawful to discriminate against any individual because that individual has opposed any act or practice made unlawful by this part or because that individual made a charge, testified, assisted, or participated in any manner in an investigation, proceeding, or hearing to enforce any provision contained in this part.

(b) <u>Coercion, interference or intimidation</u>. It is unlawful to coerce, intimidate, threaten, harass or interfere with any individual in the exercise or enjoyment of, or because that individual aided or encouraged any other individual in the exercise of, any right granted or protected by this part.

REGULATION

1630.13 Prohibited medical examinations and inquiries.

(a) <u>Pre-employment examination or inquiry</u>. Except as permitted by section 1630.14, it is unlawful for a covered entity to conduct a medical examination of an applicant or to make inquiries as to whether an applicant is an individual with a disability or as to the nature or severity of such disability.

(b) <u>Examination or inquiry of employees</u>. Except as permitted by section 1630.14, it is unlawful for a covered entity to require a medical examination of an employee or to make inquiries as to whether an employee is an individual with a disability or as to the nature or severity of such disability.

INTERPRETIVE GUIDANCE

Section 1630.13 Prohibited Medical Examinations and Inquiries
Section 1630.13(a) Pre-employment Examination or Inquiry

This provision makes clear that an employer cannot inquire as to whether an individual has a disability at the pre-offer stage of the selection process. Nor can an employer inquire at the pre-offer stage about an applicant's workers' compensation history.

Employers may ask questions that relate to the applicant's ability to perform job-related functions. However, these questions should not be phrased in terms of disability. An employer, for example, may ask whether the applicant has a driver's license, if driving is a job function, but may not ask whether the applicant has a visual disability. Employers may ask about an applicant's ability to perform both essential and marginal job functions. Employers, though, may not refuse to hire an applicant with a disability because the applicant's disability prevents him or her from performing marginal functions. <u>See</u> Senate Report at 39; House Labor Report at 72-73; House Judiciary Report at 42-43.

Section 1630.13(b) Examination or Inquiry of Employees

The purpose of this provision is to prevent the administration to employees of medical tests or inquiries that do not serve a legitimate business purpose. For example, if an employee suddenly starts to use increased amounts of sick leave or starts to appear sickly, an employer could not require that employee to be tested for AIDS, HIV infection, or cancer unless the employer can demonstrate that such testing is job-related and consistent with business necessity. <u>See</u> Senate Report at 39; House Labor Report at 75; House Judiciary Report at 44.

REGULATION

1630.14 Medical examinations and inquiries specifically permitted.

(a) Acceptable pre-employment inquiry. A covered entity may make pre-employment inquiries into the ability of an applicant to perform job-related functions, and/or may ask an applicant to describe or to demonstrate how, with or without reasonable accommodation, the applicant will be able to perform job-related functions.

INTERPRETIVE GUIDANCE

Section 1630.14 Medical Examinations and Inquiries Specifically Permitted

Section 1630.14(a) Pre-employment Inquiry

Employers are permitted to make pre-employment inquiries into the ability of an applicant to perform job-related functions. This inquiry must be narrowly tailored. The employer may describe or demonstrate the job function and inquire whether or not the applicant can perform that function with or without reasonable accommodation. For example, an employer may explain that the job requires assembling small parts and ask if the individual will be able to perform that function, with or without reasonable accommodation. See Senate Report at 39; House Labor Report at 73; House Judiciary Report at 43.

An employer may also ask an applicant to describe or to demonstrate how, with or without reasonable accommodation, the applicant will be able to perform job-related functions. Such a request may be made of all applicants in the same job category regardless of disability. Such a request may also be made of an applicant whose known disability may interfere with or prevent the performance of a job-related function, whether or not the employer routinely makes such a request of all applicants in the job category. For example, an employer may ask an individual with one leg who applies for a position as a home washing machine repairman to demonstrate or to explain how, with or without reasonable accommodation, he would be able to transport himself and his tools down basement stairs. However, the employer may not inquire as to the nature or severity of the disability. Therefore, for example, the employer cannot ask how the individual lost the leg or whether the loss of the leg is indicative of an underlying impairment.

On the other hand, if the known disability of an applicant will not interfere with or prevent the performance of a job-related function, the employer may only request a description or demonstration by the applicant if it routinely makes such a request of all applicants in the same job category. So, for example, it would not be permitted for an employer to request that an applicant with one leg demonstrate his ability to assemble small parts while seated at a table, if the employer does not routinely request that all applicants provide such a demonstration.

An employer that requires an applicant with a disability to demonstrate how he or she will perform a job-related function must either provide the reasonable accommodation the appli-cant needs to perform the function or permit the applicant to explain how, with the accommodation, he or she will perform the function. If the job-related function is not an essential function, the employer may not exclude the applicant with a disability because of the applicant's inability to perform that function. Rather, the employer must, as a reasonable accom-modation, either provide an accommodation that will enable the individual to perform the function, transfer the function to another position, or exchange the function for one the appli-cant is able to perform.

An employer may not use an application form that lists a number of potentially disabling impairments and ask the applicant to check any of the impairments he or she may have. In addition, as noted above, an employer may not ask how a particular individual became disabled or the prognosis of the individual's disability. The employer is also prohibited from asking how often the individual will require leave for treat-ment or use leave as a result of incapacitation because of the disability. However, the employer may state the attendance requirements of the job and inquire whether the applicant can meet them.

An employer is permitted to ask, on a test announcement or application form, that individuals with disabilities who will require a reasonable accommodation in order to take the test so inform the employer within a reasonable established time period prior to the administration of the test. The employer may also request that documentation of the need for the accommodation accompany the request. Requested accommo-dations may include accessible testing sites, modified testing conditions and accessible test formats. (See section 1630.11 Administration of Tests).

Physical agility tests are not medical examinations and so may be given at any point in the application or employment pro-cess. Such tests must be given to all similarly situated appli-cants or employees regardless of disability. If such tests screen out or tend to screen out an individual with a disability or a class of individuals with disabilities, the employer would have to demonstrate that the test is job-related and consistent with business necessity and that performance cannot be achieved with reasonable accommodation. (See section 1630.9 Not Making Reasonable Accommodation: Process of Determining the Appropriate Reasonable Accommodation).

REGULATION

As previously noted, collecting information and inviting individuals to identify themselves as individuals with disabilities as required to satisfy the affirmative action requirements of Section 503 of the Rehabilitation Act is not restricted by this part. (See section 1630.1(b) and (c) Applicability and Construction).

Section 1630.14(b) Employment Entrance Examination

(b) Employment entrance examination. A covered entity may require a medical examination (and/or inquiry) after making an offer of employment to a job applicant and before the applicant begins his or her employment duties, and may condition an offer of employment on the results of such examination (and/or inquiry), if all entering employees in the same job category are subjected to such an examination (and/or inquiry) regardless of disability.

An employer is permitted to require post-offer medical examinations before the employee actually starts working. The employer may condition the offer of employment on the results of the examination, provided that all entering employees in the same job category are subjected to such an examination, regardless of disability, and that the confidentiality requirements specified in this part are met.

This provision recognizes that in many industries, such as air transportation or construction, applicants for certain positions are chosen on the basis of many factors including physical and psychological criteria, some of which may be identified as a result of post-offer medical examinations given prior to entry on duty. Only those employees who meet the employer's physical and psychological criteria for the job, with or without reasonable accommodation, will be qualified to receive confirmed offers of employment and begin working.

(1) Information obtained under paragraph (b) of this section regarding the medical condition or history of the applicant shall be collected and maintained on separate forms and in separate medical files and be treated as a confidential medical record, except that:

Medical examinations permitted by this section are not required to be job-related and consistent with business necessity. However, if an employer withdraws an offer of employment because the medical examination reveals that the employee does not satisfy certain employment criteria, either the exclusionary criteria must not screen out or tend to screen out an individual with a disability or a class of individuals with disabilities, or they must be job-related and consistent with business necessity. As part of the showing that an exclusionary criteria is job-related and consistent with business necessity, the employer must also demonstrate that there is no reasonable accommodation that will enable the individual with a disability to perform the essential functions of the job. See Conference Report at 59-60; Senate Report at 39; House Labor Report at 73-74; House Judiciary Report at 43.

(i) Supervisors and managers may be informed regarding necessary restrictions on the work or duties of the employee and necessary accommodations;

(ii) First aid and safety personnel may be informed, when appropriate, if the disability might require

As an example, suppose an employer makes a conditional offer of employment to an applicant, and it is an essential function of the job that the incumbent be available to work every day for the next three months. An employment entrance

REGULATION

emergency treatment; and

(iii) Government officials investigating compliance with this part shall be provided relevant information on request.

(2) The results of such examination shall not be used for any purpose inconsistent with this part.

(3) Medical examinations conducted in accordance with this section do not have to be job-related and consistent with business necessity. However, if certain criteria are used to screen out an employee or employees with disabilities as a result of such an examination or inquiry, the exclusionary criteria must be job-related and consistent with business necessity, and performance of the essential job functions cannot be accomplished with reasonable accommodation as required in this part. (See section 1630.15(b) Defenses to charges of discriminatory application of selection criteria).

(c) Examination of employees. A covered entity may require a medical examination (and/or inquiry) of an employee that is job-related and consistent with business necessity. A covered entity may make inquiries into the ability of an employee to perform job-related functions.

INTERPRETIVE GUIDANCE

examination then reveals that the applicant has a disabling impairment that, according to reasonable medical judgment that relies on the most current medical knowledge, will require treatment that will render the applicant unable to work for a portion of the three month period. Under these circumstances, the employer would be able to withdraw the employment offer without violating this part.

The information obtained in the course of a permitted entrance examination or inquiry is to be treated as a confidential medical record and may only be used in a manner not inconsistent with this part. State workers' compensation laws are not preempted by the ADA or this part. These laws require the collection of information from individuals for state administrative purposes that do not conflict with the ADA or this part. Consequently, employers or other covered entities may submit information to state workers' compensation offices or second injury funds in accordance with state workers' compensation laws without violating this part.

Consistent with this section and with section 1630.16(f) of this part, information obtained in the course of a permitted entrance examination or inquiry may be used for insurance purposes described in section 1630.16(f).

Section 1630.14(c) Examination of employees
This provision permits employers to make inquiries or require medical examinations (fitness for duty exams) when there is a need to determine whether an employee is still able to perform the essential functions of his or her job. The provision permits employers or other covered entities to make inquiries or require medical examinations necessary to the reasonable accommodation process described in this part. This provision also permits periodic physicals to determine fitness for duty or other medical monitoring if such physicals or monitoring are

REGULATION

(1) Information obtained under paragraph (c) of this section regarding the medical condition or history of any employee shall be collected and maintained on separate forms and in separate medical files and be treated as a confidential medical record, except that:

(i) Supervisors and managers may be informed regarding necessary restrictions on the work or duties of the employee and necessary accommodations;

(ii) First aid and safety personnel may be informed, when appropriate, if the disability might require emergency treatment; and

(iii) Government officials investigating compliance with this part shall be provided relevant information on request.

(2) Information obtained under paragraph (c) of this section regarding the medical condition or history of any employee shall not be used for any purpose inconsistent with this part.

(d) Other acceptable examinations and inquiries. A covered entity may conduct voluntary medical examinations and activities, including voluntary medical histories, which are part of an employee health program

INTERPRETIVE GUIDANCE

required by medical standards or requirements established by Federal, state, or local law that are consistent with the ADA and this part (or in the case of a federal standard, with Section 504 of the Rehabilitation Act) in that they are job-related and consistent with business necessity.

Such standards may include federal safety regulations that regulate bus and truck driver qualifications, as well as laws establishing medical requirements for pilots or other air transportation personnel. These standards also include health standards promulgated pursuant to the Occupational Safety and Health Act of 1970, the Federal Coal Mine Health and Safety Act of 1969, or other similar statutes that require that employees exposed to certain toxic and hazardous substances be medically monitored at specific intervals. See House Labor Report at 74-75.

The information obtained in the course of such examination or inquiries is to be treated as a confidential medical record and may only be used in a manner not inconsistent with this part.

Section 1630.14(d) Other Acceptable Examinations and Inquiries

Part 1630 permits voluntary medical examinations, including voluntary medical histories, as part of employee health programs. These programs often include, for example, medical screening for high blood pressure, weight control counseling, and cancer detection. Voluntary activities, such as blood pressure monitoring and the administering of prescription

REGULATION

available to employees at the work site.

(1) Information obtained under paragraph (d) of this section regarding the medical condition or history of any employee shall be collected and maintained on separate forms and in separate medical files and be treated as a confidential medical record, except that:

(i) Supervisors and managers may be informed regarding necessary restrictions on the work or duties of the employee and necessary accommodations;

(ii) First aid and safety personnel may be informed, when appropriate, if the disability might require emergency treatment; and

(iii) Government officials investigating compliance with this part shall be provided relevant information on request.

(2) Information obtained under paragraph (d) of this section regarding the medical condition or history of any employee shall not be used for any purpose inconsistent with this part.

INTERPRETIVE GUIDANCE

drugs, such as insulin, are also permitted. It should be noted, however, that the medical records developed in the course of such activities must be maintained in the confidential manner required by this part and must not be used for any purpose in violation of this part, such as limiting health insurance eligibility. House Labor Report at 75; House Judiciary Report at 43-44.

REGULATION
1630.15 Defenses.

Defenses to an allegation of discrimination under this part may include, but are not limited to, the following:

(a)Disparate treatment charges. It may be a defense to a charge of disparate treatment brought under sections 1630.4 through 1630.8 and 1630.11 through 1630.12 that the challenged action is justified by a legitimate, nondiscriminatory reason.

(b) Charges of discriminatory application of selection criteria. -- (1) In general. It may be a defense to a charge of discrimination, as described in section 1630.10, that an alleged application of

INTERPRETIVE GUIDANCE
Section 1630.15 Defenses

The section on defenses in part 1630 is not intended to be exhaustive. However, it is intended to inform employers of some of the potential defenses available to a charge of discrimination under the ADA and this part.

Section 1630.15(a) Disparate Treatment Defenses

The "traditional" defense to a charge of disparate treatment under title VII, as expressed in McDonnell Douglas Corp. v. Green, 411 U.S. 792 (1973), Texas Department of Community Affairs v. Burdine, 450 U.S. 248 (1981), and their progeny, may be applicable to charges of disparate treatment brought under the ADA. See Prewitt v. U.S. Postal Service, 662 F.2d 292 (5th Cir. 1981). Disparate treatment means, with respect to title I of the ADA, that an individual was treated differently on the basis of his or her disability. For example, disparate treatment has occurred where an employer excludes an employee with a severe facial disfigurement from staff meetings because the employer does not like to look at the employee. The individual is being treated differently because of the employer's attitude towards his or her perceived disability. Disparate treatment has also occurred where an employer has a policy of not hiring individuals with AIDS regardless of the individuals' qualifications.

The crux of the defense to this type of charge is that the individual was treated differently not because of his or her disability but for a legitimate nondiscriminatory reason such as poor performance unrelated to the individual's disability. The fact that the individual's disability is not covered by the employer's current insurance plan or would cause the employer's insurance premiums or workers' compensation costs to increase, would not be a legitimate nondiscriminatory reason justifying disparate treatment of a individual with a disability. Senate Report at 85; House Labor Report at 136 and House Judiciary Report at 70. The defense of a legitimate nondiscriminatory reason is rebutted if the alleged nondiscriminatory reason is shown to be pretextual.

Section 1630.15(b) and (c) Disparate Impact Defenses

Disparate impact means, with respect to title I of the ADA and this part, that uniformly applied criteria have an adverse impact on an individual with a disability or a disproportionately negative impact on a class of individuals with disabilities. Section 1630.15(b) clarifies that an employer may use selection criteria that have such a disparate impact, i.e., that

REGULATION

qualification standards, tests, or selection criteria that screens out or tends to screen out or otherwise denies a job or benefit to an individual with a disability has been shown to be job-related and consistent with business necessity, and such performance cannot be accomplished with reasonable accommodation, as required in this part.

(2) Direct threat as a qualification standard. The term "qualification standard" may include a requirement that an individual shall not pose a direct threat to the health or safety of the individual or others in the workplace. (See section 1630.2(r) defining direct threat).

(c) Other disparate impact charges. It may be a defense to a charge of discrimination brought under this part that a uniformly applied standard, criterion, or policy has a disparate impact on an individual with a disability or a class of individuals with disabilities that the challenged standard, criterion or policy has been shown to be job-related and consistent with business necessity, and such performance cannot be accomplished with reasonable accommodation, as required in this part.

INTERPRETIVE GUIDANCE

screen out or tend to screen out an individual with a disability or a class of individuals with disabilities only when they are job-related and consistent with business necessity.

For example, an employer interviews two candidates for a position, one of whom is blind. Both are equally qualified. The employer decides that while it is not essential to the job it would be convenient to have an employee who has a driver's license and so could occasionally be asked to run errands by car. The employer hires the individual who is sighted because this individual has a driver's license. This is an example of a uniformly applied criterion, having a driver's permit, that screens out an individual who has a disability that makes it impossible to obtain a driver's permit. The employer would, thus, have to show that this criterion is job-related and consistent with business necessity. See House Labor Report at 55.

However, even if the criterion is job-related and consistent with business necessity, an employer could not exclude an individual with a disability if the criterion could be met or job performance accomplished with a reasonable accommodation. For example, suppose an employer requires, as part of its application process, an interview that is job-related and consistent with business necessity. The employer would not be able to refuse to hire a hearing impaired applicant because he or she could not be interviewed. This is so because an interpreter could be provided as a reasonable accommodation that would allow the individual to be interviewed, and thus satisfy the selection criterion.

With regard to safety requirements that screen out or tend to screen out an individual with a disability or a class of individuals with disabilities, an employer must demonstrate that the requirement, as applied to the individual, satisfies the "direct threat" standard in section 1630.2(r) in order to show that the requirement is job related and consistent with business necessity.

Section 1630.15(c) clarifies that there may be uniformly applied standards, criteria and policies not relating to selection that may also screen out or tend to screen out an individual with a disability or a class of individuals with disabilities. Like selection criteria that have a disparate impact, non-selection criteria having such an impact may also have to be job-related and consistent with business necessity, subject to consideration of reasonable accommodation.

ADA Handbook

REGULATION

INTERPRETIVE GUIDANCE

It should be noted, however, that some uniformly applied employment policies or practices, such as leave policies, are not subject to challenge under the adverse impact theory. "No-leave" policies (e.g., no leave during the first six months of employment) are likewise not subject to challenge under the adverse impact theory. However, an employer, in spite of its "no-leave" policy, may, in appropriate circumstances, have to consider the provision of leave to an employee with a disability as a reasonable accommodation, unless the provision of leave would impose an undue hardship. See discussion at section 1630.5 Limiting, Segregating and Classifying, and section 1630.10 Qualification Standards, Tests, and Other Selection Criteria.

(d) Charges of not making reasonable accommodation. It may be a defense to a charge of discrimination, as described in section 1630.9, that a requested or necessary accommodation would impose an undue hardship on the operation of the covered entity's business.

Section 1630.15(d) Defense to Not Making Reasonable Accommodation

An employer or other covered entity alleged to have discriminated because it did not make a reasonable accommodation, as required by this part, may offer as a defense that it would have been an undue hardship to make the accommodation.

It should be noted, however, that an employer cannot simply assert that a needed accommodation will cause it undue hardship, as defined in section 1630.2(p), and thereupon be relieved of the duty to provide accommodation. Rather, an employer will have to present evidence and demonstrate that the accommodation will, in fact, cause it undue hardship. Whether a particular accommodation will impose an undue hardship for a particular employer is determined on a case by case basis. Consequently, an accommodation that poses an undue hardship for one employer at a particular time may not pose an undue hardship for another employer, or even for the same employer at another time. Likewise, an accommodation that poses an undue hardship for one employer in a particular job setting, such as a temporary construction worksite, may not pose an undue hardship for another employer, or even for the same employer at a permanent worksite. See House Judiciary Report at 42.

The concept of undue hardship that has evolved under Section 504 of the Rehabilitation Act and is embodied in this part is unlike the "undue hardship" defense associated with the provision of religious accommodation under title VII of the Civil Rights Act of 1964. To demonstrate undue hardship pursuant to the ADA and this part, an employer must show substantially more difficulty or expense than would be needed

REGULATION

to satisfy the "de minimis" title VII standard of undue hardship. For example, to demonstrate that the cost of an accommodation poses an undue hardship, an employer would have to show that the cost is undue as compared to the employer's budget. Simply comparing the cost of the accommodation to the salary of the individual with a disability in need of the accommodation will not suffice. Moreover, even if it is determined that the cost of an accommodation would unduly burden an employer, the employer cannot avoid making the accommodation if the individual with a disability can arrange to cover that portion of the cost that rises to the undue hardship level, or can otherwise arrange to provide the accommodation. Under such circumstances, the necessary accommodation would no longer pose an undue hardship. See Senate Report at 36; House Labor Report at 68-69; House Judiciary Report at 40-41.

Excessive cost is only one of several possible bases upon which an employer might be able to demonstrate undue hardship. Alternatively, for example, an employer could demonstrate that the provision of a particular accommodation would be unduly disruptive to its other employees or to the functioning of its business. The terms of a collective bargaining agreement may be relevant to this determination. By way of illustration, an employer would likely be able to show undue hardship if the employer could show that the requested accommodation of the upward adjustment of the business' thermostat would result in it becoming unduly hot for its other employees, or for its patrons or customers. The employer would thus not have to provide this accommodation. However, if there were an alternate accommodation that would not result in undue hardship, the employer would have to provide that accommodation.

It should be noted, moreover, that the employer would not be able to show undue hardship if the disruption to its employees were the result of those employees' fears or prejudices toward the individual's disability and not the result of the provision of the accommodation. Nor would the employer be able to demonstrate undue hardship by showing that the provision of the accommodation has a negative impact on the morale of its other employees but not on the ability of these employees to perform their jobs.

REGULATION

(e) <u>Conflict with other federal laws</u>. It may be a defense to a charge of discrimination under this part that a challenged action is required or necessitated by another Federal law or regulation, or that another Federal law or regulation prohibits an action (including the provision of a particular reasonable accommodation) that would otherwise be required by this part.

(f) <u>Additional defenses</u>. It may be a defense to a charge of discrimination under this part that the alleged discriminatory action is specifically permitted by sections 1630.14 or 1630.16.

INTERPRETIVE GUIDANCE

Section 1630.15(e) Defense - Conflicting Federal Laws and Regulations

There are several Federal laws and regulations that address medical standards and safety requirements. If the alleged discriminatory action was taken in compliance with another Federal law or regulation, the employer may offer its obligation to comply with the conflicting standard as a defense. The employer's defense of a conflicting Federal requirement or regulation may be rebutted by a showing of pretext, or by showing that the Federal standard did not require the discriminatory action, or that there was a non-exclusionary means to comply with the standard that would not conflict with this part. <u>See</u> House Labor Report at 74.

REGULATION

1630.16 Specific activities permitted.

(a) Religious entities. A religious corporation, association, educational institution, or society is permitted to give preference in employment to individuals of a particular religion to perform work connected with the carrying on by that corporation, association, educational institution, or society of its activities. A religious entity may require that all applicants and employees conform to the religious tenets of such organization. However, a religious entity may not discriminate against a qualified individual, who satisfies the permitted religious criteria, because of his or her disability.

(b) Regulation of alcohol and drugs. A covered entity:

(1) May prohibit the illegal use of drugs and the use of alcohol at the workplace by all employees;

(2) May require that employees not be under the influence of alcohol or be engaging in the illegal use of drugs at the workplace;

(3) May require that all employees behave in conformance with the requirements established under the Drug-Free Workplace Act of 1988 (41 U.S.C. 701 et seq.);

INTERPRETIVE GUIDANCE

Section 1630.16 Specific Activities Permitted

Section 1630.16(a) Religious Entities

Religious organizations are not exempt from title I of the ADA or this part. A religious corporation, association, educational institution, or society may give a preference in employment to individuals of the particular religion, and may require that applicants and employees conform to the religious tenets of the organization. However, a religious organization may not discriminate against an individual who satisfies the permitted religious criteria because that individual is disabled. The religious entity, in other words, is required to consider qualified individuals with disabilities who satisfy the permitted religious criteria on an equal basis with qualified individuals without disabilities who similarly satisfy the religious criteria. See Senate Report at 42; House Labor Report at 76-77; House Judiciary Report at 46.

Section 1630.16(b) Regulation of Alcohol and Drugs

This provision permits employers to establish or comply with certain standards regulating the use of drugs and alcohol in the workplace. It also allows employers to hold alcoholics and persons who engage in the illegal use of drugs to the same performance and conduct standards to which it holds all of its other employees. Individuals disabled by alcoholism are entitled to the same protections accorded other individuals with disabilities under this part. As noted above, individuals currently engaging in the illegal use of drugs are not individuals with disabilities for purposes of part 1630 when the employer acts on the basis of such use.

REGULATION

(4) May hold an employee who engages in the illegal use of drugs or who is an alcoholic to the same qualification standards for employment or job performance and behavior to which the entity holds its other employees, even if any unsatisfactory performance or behavior is related to the employee's drug use or alcoholism;

(5) May require that its employees employed in an industry subject to such regulations comply with the standards established in the regulations (if any) of the Departments of Defense and Transportation, and of the Nuclear Regulatory Commission, regarding alcohol and the illegal use of drugs; and

(6) May require that employees employed in sensitive positions comply with the regulations (if any) of the Departments of Defense and Transportation and of the Nuclear Regulatory Commission that apply to employment in sensitive positions subject to such regulations.

(c) Drug testing. -- (1) General policy. For purposes of this part, a test to determine the illegal use of drugs is not considered a medical examination. Thus, the administration of such drug tests by a covered entity to its

INTERPRETIVE GUIDANCE

Section 1630.16(c) Drug Testing
This provision reflects title I's neutrality toward testing for the illegal use of drugs. Such drug tests are neither encouraged, authorized nor prohibited. The results of such drug tests may be used as a basis for disciplinary action. Tests for the illegal use of drugs are not considered medical examinations for purposes of this part. If the results reveal information about an individual's medical condition beyond whether the individual

REGULATION

job applicants or employees is not a violation of section 1630.13 of this part. However, this part does not encourage, prohibit, or authorize a covered entity to conduct drug tests of job applicants or employees to determine the illegal use of drugs or to make employment decisions based on such test results.

(2) Transportation Employees. This part does not encourage, prohibit, or authorize the otherwise lawful exercise by entities subject to the jurisdiction of the Department of Transportation of authority to:

(i) Test employees of entities in, and applicants for, positions involving safety sensitive duties for the illegal use of drugs or for on-duty impairment by alcohol; and

(ii) Remove from safety-sensitive positions persons who test positive for illegal use of drugs or on-duty impairment by alcohol pursuant to paragraph (c)(2)(i) of this section.

(3) Confidentiality. Any information regarding the medical condition or history of any employee or applicant obtained from a test to determine the illegal use of drugs, except information regarding the illegal use of drugs, is subject to the requirements of

INTERPRETIVE GUIDANCE

is currently engaging in the illegal use of drugs, this additional information is to be treated as a confidential medical record. For example, if a test for the illegal use of drugs reveals the presence of a controlled substance that has been lawfully prescribed for a particular medical condition, this information is to be treated as a confidential medical record. See House Labor Report at 79; House Judiciary Report at 47.

REGULATION

section 1630.14(b)(2) and (3) of this part.

(d) Regulation of smoking. A covered entity may prohibit or impose restrictions on smoking in places of employment. Such restrictions do not violate any provision of this part.

(e) Infectious and communicable diseases: food handling jobs. -- (1) In general. Under title I of the ADA, section 103(d)(1), the Secretary of Health and Human Services is to prepare a list, to be updated annually, of infectious and communicable diseases which are transmitted through the handling of food. If an individual with a disability is disabled by one of the infectious or communicable diseases included on this list, and if the risk of transmitting the disease associated with the handling of food cannot be eliminated by reasonable accommodation, a covered entity may refuse to assign or continue to assign such individual to a job involving food handling. However, if the individual with a disability is a current employee, the employer must consider whether he or she can be accommodated by reassignment to a vacant position not involving food handling.

(2) Effect on state or other laws. This part does not

INTERPRETIVE GUIDANCE

Section 1630.16(e) Infectious and Communicable Diseases; Food Handling Jobs

This provision addressing food handling jobs applies the "direct threat" analysis to the particular situation of accommodating individuals with infectious or communicable diseases that are transmitted through the handling of food. The Department of Health and Human Services is to prepare a list of infectious and communicable diseases that are transmitted through the handling of food. (Copies may be obtained from Center for Infectious Diseases, Centers for Disease Control, 1600 Clifton Road NE., Mailstop C09, Atlanta, GA 30333.) If an individual with a disability has one of the listed diseases and works in or applies for a position in food handling, the employer must determine whether there is a reasonable accommodation that will eliminate the risk of transmitting the disease through the handling of food. If there is an accommodation that will not pose an undue hardship, and that will prevent the transmission of the disease through the handling of food, the employer must provide the accommodation to the individual. The employer, under these circumstances, would not be permitted to discriminate against the individual because of the need to provide the reasonable accommodation and would be required to maintain the individual in the food handling job.

If no such reasonable accommodation is possible, the employer may refuse to assign, or to continue to assign the individual to a position involving food handling. This means that if such an individual is an applicant for a food handling position the employer is not required to hire the individual. However, if the individual is a current employee, the employer would be required to consider the accommodation of reassignment to a vacant position not involving food handling for which the individual is qualified. Conference Report at 61-63. (See section 1630.2(r) Direct Threat).

REGULATION

preempt, modify, or amend any State, county, or local law, ordinance or regulation applicable to food handling which:

(i) Is in accordance with the list, referred to in paragraph (e)(1) of this section, of infectious or communicable diseases and the modes of transmissibility published by the Secretary of Health and Human Services; and

(ii) Is designed to protect the public health from individuals who pose a significant risk to the health or safety of others, where that risk cannot be eliminated by reasonable accommodation.

(f) Health insurance, life insurance, and other benefit plans. --(1) An insurer, hospital, or medical service company, health maintenance organization, or any agent or entity that administers benefit plans, or similar organizations may underwrite risks, classify risks, or administer such risks that are based on or not inconsistent with State law.

(2) A covered entity may establish, sponsor, observe or administer the terms of a bona fide benefit plan that are based on underwriting risks, classifying risks, or administering such risks that are based on or not inconsistent with State law.

INTERPRETIVE GUIDANCE

Section 1630.16(f) Health Insurance, Life Insurance, and Other Benefit Plans

This provision is a limited exemption that is only applicable to those who establish, sponsor, observe or administer benefit plans, such as health and life insurance plans. It does not apply to those who establish, sponsor, observe or administer plans not involving benefits, such as liability insurance plans.

The purpose of this provision is to permit the development and administration of benefit plans in accordance with accepted principles of risk assessment. This provision is not intended to disrupt the current regulatory structure for self-insured employers. These employers may establish, sponsor, observe, or administer the terms of a bona fide benefit plan not subject to state laws that regulate insurance. This provision is also not intended to disrupt the current nature of insurance underwriting, or current insurance industry practices in sales, underwriting, pricing, administrative and other services, claims and similar insurance related activities based on classification of risks as regulated by the States.

The activities permitted by this provision do not violate part 1630 even if they result in limitations on individuals with

REGULATION

(3) A covered entity may establish, sponsor, observe, or administer the terms of a bona fide benefit plan that is not subject to State laws that regulate insurance.

(4) The activities described in paragraphs (f)(1),(2), and (3) of this section are permitted unless these activities are being used as a subterfuge to evade the purposes of this part.

INTERPRETIVE GUIDANCE

disabilities, provided that these activities are not used as a subterfuge to evade the purposes of this part. Whether or not these activities are being used as a subterfuge is to be determined without regard to the date the insurance plan or employee benefit plan was adopted.

However, an employer or other covered entity cannot deny a qualified individual with a disability equal access to insurance or subject a qualified individual with a disability to different terms or conditions of insurance based on disability alone, if the disability does not pose increased risks. Part 1630 requires that decisions not based on risk classification be made in conformity with non-discrimination requirements. See Senate Report at 84-86; House Labor Report at 136-138; House Judiciary Report at 70-71. See the discussion of section 1630.5 Limiting, Segregating and Classifying.

TITLE II

NONDISCRIMINATION ON THE BASIS OF DISABILITY IN STATE AND LOCAL GOVERNMENT SERVICES

Title II - Nondiscrimination on the Basis of Disability
in State and Local Government Services

1. Summary

This rule implements subtitle A of title II of the Americans with Disabilities Act, Pub. L. 101-336, which prohibits discrimination on the basis of disability by public entities. Subtitle A protects qualified individuals with disabilities from discrimination on the basis of disability in the services, programs, or activities of all State and local governments. It extends the prohibition of discrimination in federally assisted programs established by section 504 of the Rehabilitation Act of 1973 to all activities of State and local governments, including those that do not receive Federal financial assistance, and incorporates specific prohibitions of discrimination on the basis of disability from titles I, III, and V of the Americans with Disabilities Act. This rule, therefore, adopts the general prohibitions of discrimination established under section 504, as well as the requirements for making programs accessible to individuals with disabilities and for providing equally effective communications. It also sets forth standards for what constitutes discrimination on the basis of mental or physical disability, provides a definition of disability and qualified individual with a disability, and establishes a complaint mechanism for resolving allegations of discrimination.

The effective date of this rule is January 26, 1992.

For further information about this rule contact the Office on the Americans with Disabilities Act, Civil Rights Division, U.S. Department of Justice, Washington, D.C. 20530. (202) 514-0301 (Voice), (202) 514-0381 (TDD). These telephone numbers are not toll-free numbers.

2. Background

The landmark Americans with Disabilities Act ("ADA" or "the Act"), enacted on July 26, 1990, provides comprehensive civil rights protections to individuals with disabilities in the areas of employment, public accommodations, State and local government services, and telecommunications.

This regulation implements subtitle A of title II of the ADA, which applies to State and local governments. Most programs and activities of State and local governments are recipients of Federal financial assistance from one or more Federal funding agencies and, therefore, are already covered by section 504 of the Rehabilitation Act of 1973, as amended (29 U.S.C. 794) ("section 504"), which prohibits discrimination on the basis of handicap in federally assisted programs and activities. Because title II of the ADA essentially extends the nondiscrimination mandate of section 504 to those State and local governments that do not receive Federal financial assistance, this rule hews closely to the provisions of existing section 504 regulations. This approach is also based on section 204 of the ADA, which provides that the regulations issued by the Attorney General to implement title II shall be consistent with the ADA and with the Department of Health, Education, and Welfare's coordination regulation, now codified at 28 CFR Part 41, and, with respect to "program accessibility, existing facilities," and "communications," with the Department of Justice's regulation for its federally conducted programs and activities, codified at 28 CFR Part 39.

The first regulation implementing section 504 was issued in 1977 by the Department of Health, Education, and Welfare (HEW) for the programs and activities to which it provided Federal financial assistance. The following year, pursuant to Executive Order 11914, HEW issued its coordination regulation for federally assisted programs, which served as the model for regulations issued by the other Federal agencies that administer grant programs. HEW's coordination authority, and the coordination regulation issued under that authority, were transferred to the Department of Justice by Executive Order 12250 in 1980.

In 1978, Congress extended application of section 504 to programs and activities conducted by Federal Executive agencies and the United States Postal Service. Pursuant to Executive Order 12250, the Department of Justice developed a prototype regulation to implement the 1978 amendment for federally conducted programs and activities. More than 80 Federal agencies have now issued final regulations based on that prototype, prohibiting discrimination based on handicap in the programs and activities they conduct.

Despite the large number of regulations implementing section 504 for federally assisted and federally conducted programs and activities, there is very little variation in their substantive requirements, or even in their language. Major portions of this regulation, therefore, are taken directly from the existing regulations.

In addition, section 204(b) of the ADA requires that the Department's regulation implementing subtitle A of title II be consistent with the ADA. Thus, the Department's final regulation includes provisions and concepts from titles I and III of the ADA.

3. Rulemaking History

On February 22, 1991, the Department of Justice published a notice of proposed rulemaking (NPRM) implementing title III of the ADA in the Federal Register. 56 FR 7452. On February 28, 1991, the Department published a notice of proposed rulemaking implementing subtitle A of title II of the ADA in the Federal Register. 56 FR 8538. Each NPRM solicited comments on the definitions, standards, and procedures of the proposed rules. By the April 29, 1991, close of the comment period of the NPRM for title II, the Department had received 2,718 comments. Following the close of the comment period, the Department received an additional 222 comments.

In order to encourage public participation in the development of the Department's rules under the ADA, the Department held four public hearings. Hearings were held in Dallas, Texas on March 4-5, 1991, in Washington, D.C. on March 13-15, 1991, in San Francisco, California on March 18-19, 1991, and in Chicago, Illinois on March 27-28, 1991. At these hearings, 329 persons testified and 1,567 pages of testimony were compiled. Transcripts of the hearings were included in the Department's rulemaking docket.

The comments that the Department received occupy almost six feet of shelf space and contain over 10,000 pages. The Department received comments from individuals from all fifty States and the District of Columbia. Nearly 75% of the comments that the Department received came from individuals and from organizations representing the interests of persons with disabilities. The Department received 292 comments from entities covered by the ADA and trade associations representing businesses in the private sector, and 67 from government units, such as mayors' offices, public school districts, and various State agencies working with individuals with disabilities.

The Department received one comment from a consortium of 540 organizations representing a broad spectrum of persons with disabilities. In addition, at least another 25 commenters endorsed the position expressed by this consortium, or submitted identical comments on one or both proposed regulations.

An organization representing persons with hearing impairments submitted a large number of comments. This organization presented the Department with 479 individual comments, each providing in chart form a detailed representation of what type of auxiliary aid or service would be useful in the various categories of places of public accommodation.

The Department received a number of comments based on almost ten different form letters. For example, individuals who have a heightened sensitivity to a variety of chemical substances submitted 266 post cards detailing how exposure to various environmental conditions restricts their access to public and commercial buildings. Another large group of form letters came from groups affiliated with independent living centers.

The vast majority of the comments addressed the Department's proposal implementing title III. Slightly more than 100 comments addressed only issues presented in the proposed title II regulation.

The Department read and analyzed each comment that was submitted in a timely fashion. Transcripts of the four hearings were analyzed along with the written comments. The decisions that the Department has made in response to these comments, however, were not made on the basis of the number of commenters addressing any one point but on a thorough consideration of the merits of the points of view expressed in the comments. Copies of the written comments, including transcripts of the four hearings, will remain available for public inspection in Room 854 of the HOLC Building, 320 First Street, N.W., Washington, D.C. from 10:00 a.m. to 5:00 p.m., Monday through Friday, except for legal holidays, until August 30, 1991.

4. Overview of the Rule

The rule is organized into seven subparts. Subpart A, "General," includes the purpose and application sections, describes the relationship of the Act to other laws, and defines key terms used in the regulation. It also includes administrative requirements adapted from section 504 regulations for self-evaluations, notices, designation of responsible employees, and adoption of grievance procedures by public entities.

Subpart B, "General Requirements," contains the general prohibitions of discrimination based on the Act and the section 504 regulations. It also contains certain "miscellaneous" provisions derived from title V of the Act that involve issues such as retaliation and coercion against those asserting ADA rights, illegal use of drugs, and restrictions on smoking. These provisions are also included in the Department's proposed title III regulation, as is the general provision on maintenance of accessible features.

Subpart C addresses employment by public entities, which is also covered by title I of the Act. Subpart D, which is also based on the section 504 regulations, sets out the requirements for program accessibility in existing facilities and for new construction and alterations. Subpart E contains specific requirements relating to communications.

Subpart F establishes administrative procedures for enforcement of title II. As provided by section 203 of the Act, these are based on the procedures for enforcement of section 504, which, in turn, are based on the enforcement procedures for title VI of the Civil Rights Act of 1964 (42 U.S.C. 2000d to 2000d-4a). Subpart F also restates the provisions of title V of the ADA on attorneys fees, alternative means of dispute resolution, the effect of unavailability of technical assistance, and State immunity.

Subpart G designates the Federal agencies responsible for investigation of complaints under this part. It assigns enforcement responsibility for particular public entities, on the basis of their major functions, to eight Federal agencies that currently have substantial responsibilities for enforcing section 504. It provides that the Department of Justice would have enforcement responsibility for all State and local government entities not specifically assigned to other designated agencies, but that the Department may further assign specific functions to other agencies. The part would not, however, displace the existing enforcement authorities of the Federal funding agencies under section 504.

5. Regulatory Process Matters

This final rule has been reviewed by the Office of Management and Budget under Executive Order 12291. The Department is preparing a final regulatory impact analysis (RIA) of this rule and the Architectural and Transportation Barriers Compliance Board is preparing an RIA for its Americans with Disabilities Act Accessibility Guidelines for Buildings and Facilities (ADAAG) that are incorporated in Appendix A of the Department's final rule implementing title III of the ADA. Draft copies of both preliminary RIAs are available for comment; the Department will provide copies of these documents to the public upon request. Commenters are urged to provide additional information as to the costs and benefits associated with this rule. This will facilitate the development of a final RIA by January 1, 1992.

The Department's RIA will evaluate the economic impact of the final rule. Included among those title II provisions that are likely to result in significant economic impact are the requirements for auxiliary aids, barrier removal in existing facilities, and readily accessible new construction and alterations. An analysis of these costs will be included in the RIA.

The Preliminary RIA prepared for the notice of proposed rulemaking contained all of the available information that would have been included in a preliminary regulatory flexibility analysis, had one been prepared under the Regulatory Flexibility Act, concerning the rule's impact on small entities. The final RIA will contain all of the information that is required in a final regulatory flexibility analysis and will serve as such an analysis. Moreover, the extensive notice and comment procedure followed by the Department in the promulgation of this rule, which included public hearings, dissemination of materials, and provision of speakers to affected groups, clearly provided any interested small entities with the notice and opportunity for comment provided for under the Regulatory Flexibility Act procedures.

The Department is preparing a statement of the federalism impact of the rule under Executive Order 12612 and will provide copies of this statement on request.

The reporting and recordkeeping requirements described in the rule are considered to be information collection requirements as that term is defined by the Office of Management and Budget in 5 CFR Part 1320. Accordingly, those information collection requirements have been submitted to OMB for review pursuant to the Paperwork Reduction Act.

Part 35 - NONDISCRIMINATION ON THE BASIS OF DISABILITY IN STATE AND LOCAL GOVERNMENT SERVICES

Subpart A -- General

Authority: 5 U.S.C. 301; 28 U.S.C. 509, 510; Title II, Pub. L. 101-336 (42 U.S.C. 12134).

REGULATION

Subpart A -- General
§35.101 Purpose.

The purpose of this part is to effectuate subtitle A of title II of the Americans with Disabilities Act of 1990, (42 U.S.C. 12131) which prohibits discrimination on the basis of disability by public entities.

ANALYSIS

Subpart A -- General
§35.101 Purpose.

Section 35.101 states the purpose of the rule, which is to effectuate subtitle A of title II of the Americans with Disabilities Act of 1990 (the Act), which prohibits discrimination on the basis of disability by public entities. This part does not, however, apply to matters within the scope of the authority of the Secretary of Transportation under subtitle B of title II of the Act.

REGULATION
§35.102 Application.

(a) Except as provided in paragraph (b) of this section, this part applies to all services, programs, and activities provided or made available by public entities.

(b) To the extent that public transportation services, programs, and activities of public entities are covered by subtitle B of title II (42 U.S.C. 12141), of the ADA, they are not subject to the requirements of this part.

ANALYSIS
§35.102 Application.

This provision specifies that, except as provided in paragraph (b), the regulation applies to all services, programs, and activities provided or made available by public entities, as that term is defined in §35.104. Section 504 of the Rehabilitation Act of 1973 (29 U.S.C. 794), which prohibits discrimination on the basis of handicap in federally assisted programs and activities, already covers those programs and activities of public entities that receive Federal financial assistance. Title II of the ADA extends this prohibition of discrimination to include all services, programs, and activities provided or made available by State and local governments or any of their instrumentalities or agencies, regardless of the receipt of Federal financial assistance. Except as provided in §35.134, this part does not apply to private entities.

The scope of title II's coverage of public entities is comparable to the coverage of Federal Executive agencies under the 1978 amendment to section 504, which extended section 504's application to all programs and activities "conducted by" Federal Executive agencies, in that title II applies to anything a public entity does. Title II coverage, however, is not limited to "Executive" agencies, but includes activities of the legislative and judicial branches of State and local governments. All governmental activities of public entities are covered, even if they are carried out by contractors. For example, a State is obligated by title II to ensure that the services, programs, and activities of a State park inn operated under contract by a private entity are in compliance with title II's requirements. The private entity operating the inn would also be subject to the obligations of public accommodations under title III of the Act and the Department's title III regulations at 28 CFR Part 36.

Aside from employment, which is also covered by title I of the Act, there are two major categories of programs or activities covered by this regulation: those involving general public contact as part of ongoing operations of the entity and those directly administered by the entities for program beneficiaries and participants. Activities in the first category include communication with the public (telephone contacts, office walk-ins, or interviews) and the public's use of the entity's facilities. Activities in the second category include programs that provide State or local government services or benefits.

REGULATION

Paragraph (b) of §35.102 explains that to the extent that the public transportation services, programs, and activities of public entities are covered by subtitle B of title II of the Act, they are subject to the regulation of the Department of Transportation (DOT) at 49 CFR Part 37, and are not covered by this part. The Department of Transportation's ADA regulation establishes specific requirements for construction of transportation facilities and acquisition of vehicles. Matters not covered by subtitle B, such as the provision of auxiliary aids, are covered by this rule. For example, activities that are covered by the Department of Transportation's regulation implementing subtitle B are not required to be included in the self-evaluation required by §35.105. In addition, activities not specifically addressed by DOT's ADA regulation may be covered by DOT's regulation implementing section 504 for its federally assisted programs and activities at 49 CFR Part 27. Like other programs of public entities that are also recipients of Federal financial assistance, those programs would be covered by both the section 504 regulation and this part. Although airports operated by public entities are not subject to DOT's ADA regulation, they are subject to subpart A of title II and to this rule.

Some commenters asked for clarification about the responsibilities of public school systems under section 504 and the ADA with respect to programs, services, and activities that are not covered by the Individuals with Disabilities Education Act (IDEA), including, for example, programs open to parents or to the public, graduation ceremonies, parent-teacher organization meetings, plays and other events open to the public, and adult education classes. Public school systems must comply with the ADA in all of their services, programs, or activities, including those that are open to parents or to the public. For instance, public school systems must provide program accessibility to parents and guardians with disabilities to these programs, activities, or services, and appropriate auxiliary aids and services whenever necessary to ensure effective communication, as long as the provision of the auxiliary aids results neither in an undue burden or in a fundamental alteration of the program.

REGULATION

§35.103 Relationship to other laws.

(a) _Rule of interpretation_. Except as otherwise provided in this part, this part shall not be construed to apply a lesser standard than the standards applied under title V of the Rehabilitation Act of 1973 (29 U.S.C. 791) or the regulations issued by Federal agencies pursuant to that title.

(b) _Other laws_. This part does not invalidate or limit the remedies, rights, and procedures of any other Federal laws, or State or local laws (including State common law) that provide greater or equal protection for the rights of individuals with disabilities or individuals associated with them.

ANALYSIS

§35.103 Relationship to other laws.

Section 35.103 is derived from sections 501(a) and (b) of the ADA. Paragraph (a) of this section provides that, except as otherwise specifically provided by this part, title II of the ADA is not intended to apply lesser standards than are required under title V of the Rehabilitation Act of 1973, as amended (29 U.S.C. 790-94), or the regulations implementing that title. The standards of title V of the Rehabilitation Act apply for purposes of the ADA to the extent that the ADA has not explicitly adopted a different standard than title V. Because title II of the ADA essentially extends the antidiscrimination prohibition embodied in section 504 to all actions of State and local governments, the standards adopted in this part are generally the same as those required under section 504 for federally assisted programs. Title II, however, also incorporates those provisions of titles I and III of the ADA that are not inconsistent with the regulations implementing section 504. Judiciary Committee report, H.R. Rep. No. 485, 101st Cong., 2d Sess., pt.3, at 51 (1990) [hereinafter "Judiciary report"]; Education and Labor Committee report, H.R. Rep. No. 485, 101st Cong., 2d Sess., pt. 2, at 84 (1990) [hereinafter "Education and Labor report"]. Therefore, this part also includes appropriate provisions derived from the regulations implementing those titles. The inclusion of specific language in this part, however, should not be interpreted as an indication that a requirement is not included under a regulation implementing section 504.

Paragraph (b) makes clear that Congress did not intend to displace any of the rights or remedies provided by other Federal laws (including section 504) or other State laws (including State common law) that provide greater or equal protection to individuals with disabilities. As discussed above, the standards adopted by title II of the ADA for State and local government services are generally the same as those required under section 504 for federally assisted programs and activities. Subpart F of the regulation establishes compliance procedures for processing complaints covered by both this part and section 504.

With respect to State law, a plaintiff may choose to pursue claims under a State law that does not confer greater substantive rights, or even confers fewer substantive rights, if the alleged violation is protected under the alternative law and the remedies are greater. For example, a person with a physical disability could seek damages under a State law that

ANALYSIS

allows compensatory and punitive damages for discrimination on the basis of physical disability, but not on the basis of mental disability. In that situation, the State law would provide narrower coverage, by excluding mental disabilities, but broader remedies, and an individual covered by both laws could choose to bring an action under both laws. Moreover, State tort claims confer greater remedies and are not pre-empted by the ADA. A plaintiff may join a State tort claim to a case brought under the ADA. In such a case, the plaintiff must, of course, prove all the elements of the State tort claim in order to prevail under that cause of action.

REGULATION

§35.104 Definitions.

For purposes of this part, the term --

Act means the Americans with Disabilities Act (Pub. L. 101-336, 104 Stat. 327, 42 U.S.C. 12101-12213 and 47 U.S.C. 225 and 611).

Assistant Attorney General means the Assistant Attorney General, Civil Rights Division, United States Department of Justice.

Auxiliary aids and services includes--

(1) Qualified interpreters, notetakers, transcription services, written materials, telephone handset amplifiers, assistive listening devices, assistive listening systems, telephones compatible with hearing aids, closed caption decoders, open and closed captioning, telecommunications devices for deaf persons (TDD's), videotext displays, or other effective methods of making aurally delivered materials available to individuals with hearing impairments;

(2) Qualified readers, taped texts, audio recordings, Brailled materials, large print materials, or other effective methods of making visually delivered materials available to

ANALYSIS

§35.104 Definitions.

"Act." The word "Act" is used in this part to refer to the Americans with Disabilities Act of 1990, Pub. L. 101-336, which is also referred to as the "ADA."

"Assistant Attorney General." The term "Assistant Attorney General" refers to the Assistant Attorney General of the Civil Rights Division of the Department of Justice.

"Auxiliary aids and services." Auxiliary aids and services include a wide range of services and devices for ensuring effective communication. The proposed definition in §35.104 provided a list of examples of auxiliary aids and services that was taken from the definition of auxiliary aids and services in section 3(1) of the ADA and was supplemented by examples from regulations implementing section 504 in federally conducted programs (see 28 CFR 39.103).

A substantial number of commenters suggested that additional examples be added to this list. The Department has added several items to this list but wishes to clarify that the list is not an all-inclusive or exhaustive catalogue of possible or available auxiliary aids or services. It is not possible to provide an exhaustive list, and an attempt to do so would omit the new devices that will become available with emerging technology.

Subparagraph (1) lists several examples, which would be considered auxiliary aids and services to make aurally delivered materials available to individuals with hearing impairments. The Department has changed the phrase used in the proposed rules, "orally delivered materials," to the statutory phrase, "aurally delivered materials," to track section 3 of the ADA and to include non-verbal sounds and alarms, and computer generated speech.

The Department has added videotext displays, transcrip-

REGULATION

individuals with visual
impairments;

(3) Acquisition or
modification of equipment
or devices; and

(4) Other similar
services and actions.

ANALYSIS

tion services, and closed and open captioning to the list of
examples. Videotext displays have become an important
means of accessing auditory communications through a public
address system. Transcription services are used to relay
aurally delivered material almost simultaneously in written
form to persons who are deaf or hearing-impaired. This
technology is often used at conferences, conventions, and
hearings. While the proposed rule expressly included television decoder equipment as an auxiliary aid or service, it did
not mention captioning itself. The final rule rectifies this
omission by mentioning both closed and open captioning.

Several persons and organizations requested that the
Department replace the term "telecommunications devices for
deaf persons" or "TDD's" with the term "text telephone."
The Department has declined to do so. The Department is
aware that the Architectural and Transportation Barriers
Compliance Board (ATBCB) has used the phrase "text telephone" in lieu of the statutory term "TDD" in its final accessibility guidelines. Title IV of the ADA, however, uses the
term "Telecommunications Device for the Deaf" and the
Department believes it would be inappropriate to abandon this
statutory term at this time.

Several commenters urged the Department to include in
the definition of "auxiliary aids and services" devices that are
now available or that may become available with emerging
technology. The Department declines to do so in the rule.
The Department, however, emphasizes that, although the
definition would include "state of the art" devices, public
entities are not required to use the newest or most advanced
technologies as long as the auxiliary aid or service that is
selected affords effective communication.

Subparagraph (2) lists examples of aids and services for
making visually delivered materials accessible to persons with
visual impairments. Many commenters proposed additional
examples, such as signage or mapping, audio description
services, secondary auditory programs, telebraillers, and
reading machines. While the Department declines to add
these items to the list, they are auxiliary aids and services and
may be appropriate depending on the circumstances.

Subparagraph (3) refers to acquisition or modification of
equipment or devices. Several commenters suggested the
addition of current technological innovations in microelec-

REGULATION

ANALYSIS

tronics and computerized control systems (e.g., voice recognition systems, automatic dialing telephones, and infrared elevator and light control systems) to the list of auxiliary aids. The Department interprets auxiliary aids and services as those aids and services designed to provide effective communications, i.e., making aurally and visually delivered information available to persons with hearing, speech, and vision impairments. Methods of making services, programs, or activities accessible to, or usable by, individuals with mobility or manual dexterity impairments are addressed by other sections of this part, including the provision for modifications in policies, practices, or procedures (§35.130(b)(7)).

Paragraph (b)(4) deals with other similar services and actions. Several commenters asked for clarification that "similar services and actions" include retrieving items from shelves, assistance in reaching a marginally accessible seat, pushing a barrier aside in order to provide an accessible route, or assistance in removing a sweater or coat. While retrieving an item from a shelf might be an "auxiliary aid or service" for a blind person who could not locate the item without assistance, it might be a method of providing program access for a person using a wheelchair who could not reach the shelf, or a reasonable modification to a self-service policy for an individual who lacked the ability to grasp the item. As explained above, auxiliary aids and services are those aids and services required to provide effective communications. Other forms of assistance are more appropriately addressed by other provisions of the final rule.

Complete complaint means a written statement that contains the complainant's name and address and describes the public entity's alleged discriminatory action in sufficient detail to inform the agency of the nature and date of the alleged violation of this part. It shall be signed by the complainant or by someone authorized to do so on his or her behalf. Complaints filed on behalf of classes or third parties

"Complete complaint." "Complete complaint" is defined to include all the information necessary to enable the Federal agency designated under subpart G as responsible for investigation of a complaint to initiate its investigation.

REGULATION

shall describe or identify (by name, if possible) the alleged victims of discrimination.

Current illegal use of drugs means illegal use of drugs that occurred recently enough to justify a reasonable belief that a person's drug use is current or that continuing use is a real and ongoing problem.

Designated agency means the Federal agency designated under subpart G of this part to oversee compliance activities under this part for particular components of State and local governments.

Disability means, with respect to an individual, a physical or mental impairment that substantially limits one or more of the major life activities of such individual; a record of such an impairment; or being regarded as having such an impairment.

ANALYSIS

"Current illegal use of drugs." The phrase "current illegal use of drugs" is used in §35.131. Its meaning is discussed in the preamble for that section.

"Designated agency." The term "designated agency" is used to refer to the Federal agency designated under subpart G of this rule as responsible for carrying out the administrative enforcement responsibilities established by subpart F of the rule.

"Disability." The definition of the term "disability" is the same as the definition in the title III regulation codified at 28 CFR Part 36. It is comparable to the definition of the term "individual with handicaps" in section 7(8) of the Rehabilitation Act and section 802(h) of the Fair Housing Act. The Education and Labor Committee report makes clear that the analysis of the term "individual with handicaps" by the Department of Health, Education, and Welfare (HEW) in its regulations implementing section 504 (42 FR 22685 (May 4, 1977)) and the analysis by the Department of Housing and Urban Development in its regulation implementing the Fair Housing Amendments Act of 1988 (54 FR 3232 (Jan. 23, 1989)) should also apply fully to the term "disability" (Education and Labor report at 50).

The use of the term "disability" instead of "handicap" and the term "individual with a disability" instead of "individual with handicaps" represents an effort by Congress to make use of up-to-date, currently accepted terminology. As with racial and ethnic epithets, the choice of terms to apply to a person with a disability is overlaid with stereotypes, patronizing attitudes, and other emotional connotations. Many individuals with disabilities, and organizations repre-

REGULATION

ANALYSIS

senting such individuals, object to the use of such terms as "handicapped person" or "the handicapped." In other recent legislation, Congress also recognized this shift in terminology, e.g., by changing the name of the National Council on the Handicapped to the National Council on Disability (Pub. L. 100-630).

In enacting the Americans with Disabilities Act, Congress concluded that it was important for the current legislation to use terminology most in line with the sensibilities of most Americans with disabilities. No change in definition or substance is intended nor should one be attributed to this change in phraseology.

The term "disability" means, with respect to an individual -

(A) A physical or mental impairment that substantially limits one or more of the major life activities of such individual;

(B) A record of such an impairment; or

(C) Being regarded as having such an impairment.

If an individual meets any one of these three tests, he or she is considered to be an individual with a disability for purposes of coverage under the Americans with Disabilities Act.

Congress adopted this same basic definition of "disability," first used in the Rehabilitation Act of 1973 and in the Fair Housing Amendments Act of 1988, for a number of reasons. First, it has worked well since it was adopted in 1974. Second, it would not be possible to guarantee comprehensiveness by providing a list of specific disabilities, especially because new disorders may be recognized in the future, as they have since the definition was first established in 1974.

(1)(i) The phrase physical or mental impairment means --

Test A -- A physical or mental impairment that substantially limits one or more of the major life activities of such individual

(A) Any physiological disorder or condition, cos-

Physical or mental impairment. Under the first test, an individual must have a physical or mental impairment. As

REGULATION

metic disfigurement, or anatomical loss affecting one or more of the following body systems: neurological, musculoskeletal, special sense organs, respiratory (including speech organs), cardiovascular, reproductive, digestive, genitourinary, hemic and lymphatic, skin, and endocrine;

(B) Any mental or psychological disorder such as mental retardation, organic brain syndrome, emotional or mental illness, and specific learning disabilities.

(ii) The phrase physical or mental impairment includes, but is not limited to, such contagious and noncontagious diseases and conditions as orthopedic, visual, speech and hearing impairments, cerebral palsy, epilepsy, muscular dystrophy, multiple sclerosis, cancer, heart disease, diabetes, mental retardation, emotional illness, specific learning disabilities, HIV disease (whether symptomatic or asymptomatic), tuberculosis, drug addiction, and alcoholism.

(iii) The phrase physical or mental impairment does not include homosexuality or bisexuality.

(2) The phrase major life activities means func-

ANALYSIS

explained in paragraph (1)(i) of the definition, "impairment" means any physiological disorder or condition, cosmetic disfigurement, or anatomical loss affecting one or more of the following body systems: neurological; musculoskeletal; special sense organs (which would include speech organs that are not respiratory such as vocal cords, soft palate, tongue, etc.); respiratory, including speech organs; cardiovascular; reproductive; digestive; genitourinary; hemic and lymphatic; skin; and endocrine. It also means any mental or psychological disorder, such as mental retardation, organic brain syndrome, emotional or mental illness, and specific learning disabilities. This list closely tracks the one used in the regulations for section 504 of the Rehabilitation Act of 1973 (see, e.g., 45 CFR 84.3(j)(2)(i)).

Many commenters asked that "traumatic brain injury" be added to the list in paragraph (1)(i). Traumatic brain injury is already included because it is a physiological condition affecting one of the listed body systems, i.e., "neurological." Therefore, it was unnecessary to add the term to the regulation, which only provides representative examples of physiological disorders.

It is not possible to include a list of all the specific conditions, contagious and noncontagious diseases, or infections that would constitute physical or mental impairments because of the difficulty of ensuring the comprehensiveness of such a list, particularly in light of the fact that other conditions or disorders may be identified in the future. However, the list of examples in paragraph (1)(ii) of the definition includes: orthopedic, visual, speech and hearing impairments, cerebral palsy, epilepsy, muscular dystrophy, multiple sclerosis, cancer, heart disease, diabetes, mental retardation, emotional illness, specific learning disabilities, HIV disease (symptomatic or asymptomatic), tuberculosis, drug addiction, and alcoholism. The phrase "symptomatic or asymptomatic" was inserted in the final rule after "HIV disease" in response to commenters who suggested the clarification was necessary.

The examples of "physical or mental impairments" in paragraph (1)(ii) are the same as those contained in many section 504 regulations, except for the addition of the phrase "contagious and noncontagious" to describe the types of diseases and conditions included, and the addition of "HIV disease (symptomatic or asymptomatic)" and "tuberculosis" to the list of examples. These additions are based on the com-

REGULATION

tions such as caring for one's self, performing manual tasks, walking, seeing, hearing, speaking, breathing, learning, and working.

ANALYSIS

mittee reports, caselaw, and official legal opinions interpreting section 504. In School Board of Nassau County v. Arline, 480 U.S. 273 (1987), a case involving an individual with tuberculosis, the Supreme Court held that people with contagious diseases are entitled to the protections afforded by section 504. Following the Arline decision, this Department's Office of Legal Counsel issued a legal opinion that concluded that symptomatic HIV disease is an impairment that substantially limits a major life activity; therefore it has been included in the definition of disability under this part. The opinion also concluded that asymptomatic HIV disease is an impairment that substantially limits a major life activity, either because of its actual effect on the individual with HIV disease or because the reactions of other people to individuals with HIV disease cause such individuals to be treated as though they are disabled. See Memorandum from Douglas W. Kmiec, Acting Assistant Attorney General, Office of Legal Counsel, Department of Justice, to Arthur B. Culvahouse, Jr., Counsel to the President (Sept. 27, 1988), reprinted in Hearings on S. 933, the Americans with Disabilities Act, Before the Subcomm. on the Handicapped of the Senate Comm. on Labor and Human Resources, 101st. Cong., 1st Sess. 346 (1989).

Paragraph (1)(iii) states that the phrase "physical or mental impairment" does not include homosexuality or bisexuality. These conditions were never considered impairments under other Federal disability laws. Section 511(a) of the statute makes clear that they are likewise not to be considered impairments under the Americans with Disabilities Act.

Physical or mental impairment does not include simple physical characteristics, such as blue eyes or black hair. Nor does it include environmental, cultural, economic, or other disadvantages, such as having a prison record, or being poor. Nor is age a disability. Similarly, the definition does not include common personality traits such as poor judgment or a quick temper where these are not symptoms of a mental or psychological disorder. However, a person who has these characteristics and also has a physical or mental impairment may be considered as having a disability for purposes of the Americans with Disabilities Act based on the impairment.

REGULATION

ANALYSIS

Substantial Limitation of a Major Life Activity. Under Test A, the impairment must be one that "substantially limits a major life activity." Major life activities include such things as caring for one's self, performing manual tasks, walking, seeing, hearing, speaking, breathing, learning, and working.

For example, a person who is paraplegic is substantially limited in the major life activity of walking, a person who is blind is substantially limited in the major life activity of seeing, and a person who is mentally retarded is substantially limited in the major life activity of learning. A person with traumatic brain injury is substantially limited in the major life activities of caring for one's self, learning, and working because of memory deficit, confusion, contextual difficulties, and inability to reason appropriately.

A person is considered an individual with a disability for purposes of Test A, the first prong of the definition, when the individual's important life activities are restricted as to the conditions, manner, or duration under which they can be performed in comparison to most people. A person with a minor, trivial impairment, such as a simple infected finger, is not impaired in a major life activity. A person who can walk for 10 miles continuously is not substantially limited in walking merely because, on the eleventh mile, he or she begins to experience pain, because most people would not be able to walk eleven miles without experiencing some discomfort.

The Department received many comments on the proposed rule's inclusion of the word "temporary" in the definition of "disability." The preamble indicated that impairments are not necessarily excluded from the definition of "disability" simply because they are temporary, but that the duration, or expected duration, of an impairment is one factor that may properly be considered in determining whether the impairment substantially limits a major life activity. The preamble recognized, however, that temporary impairments, such as a broken leg, are not commonly regarded as disabilities, and only in rare circumstances would the degree of the limitation and its expected duration be substantial. Nevertheless, many commenters objected to inclusion of the word "temporary" both because it is not in the statute and because it is not contained in the definition of "disability" set forth in the title I regulations of the Equal Employment Opportunity Commission (EEOC). The word "temporary" has been deleted from the final rule to conform with the statutory language.

REGULATION

ANALYSIS

The question of whether a temporary impairment is a disability must be resolved on a case-by-case basis, taking into consideration both the duration (or expected duration) of the impairment and the extent to which it actually limits a major life activity of the affected individual.

The question of whether a person has a disability should be assessed without regard to the availability of mitigating measures, such as reasonable modifications or auxiliary aids and services. For example, a person with hearing loss is substantially limited in the major life activity of hearing, even though the loss may be improved through the use of a hearing aid. Likewise, persons with impairments, such as epilepsy or diabetes, that substantially limit a major life activity, are covered under the first prong of the definition of disability, even if the effects of the impairment are controlled by medication.

Many commenters asked that environmental illness (also known as multiple chemical sensitivity) as well as allergy to cigarette smoke be recognized as disabilities. The Department, however, declines to state categorically that these types of allergies or sensitivities are disabilities, because the determination as to whether an impairment is a disability depends on whether, given the particular circumstances at issue, the impairment substantially limits one or more major life activities (or has a history of, or is regarded as having such an effect).

Sometimes respiratory or neurological functioning is so severely affected that an individual will satisfy the requirements to be considered disabled under the regulation. Such an individual would be entitled to all of the protections afforded by the Act and this part. In other cases, individuals may be sensitive to environmental elements or to smoke but their sensitivity will not rise to the level needed to constitute a disability. For example, their major life activity of breathing may be somewhat, but not substantially, impaired. In such circumstances, the individuals are not disabled and are not entitled to the protections of the statute despite their sensitivity to environmental agents.

In sum, the determination as to whether allergies to cigarette smoke, or allergies or sensitivities characterized by the commenters as environmental illness are disabilities covered by the regulation must be made using the same case-

REGULATION

ANALYSIS

by-case analysis that is applied to all other physical or mental impairments. Moreover, the addition of specific regulatory provisions relating to environmental illness in the final rule would be inappropriate at this time pending future consideration of the issue by the Architectural and Transportation Barriers Compliance Board, the Environmental Protection Agency, and the Occupational Safety and Health Administration of the Department of Labor.

Test B -- A record of such an impairment

(3) The phrase has a record of such an impairment means has a history of, or has been misclassified as having, a mental or physical impairment that substantially limits one or more major life activities.

This test is intended to cover those who have a record of an impairment. As explained in paragraph (3) of the rule's definition of disability, this includes a person who has a history of an impairment that substantially limited a major life activity, such as someone who has recovered from an impairment. It also includes persons who have been misclassified as having an impairment.

This provision is included in the definition in part to protect individuals who have recovered from a physical or mental impairment that previously substantially limited them in a major life activity. Discrimination on the basis of such a past impairment is prohibited. Frequently occurring examples of the first group (those who have a history of an impairment) are persons with histories of mental or emotional illness, heart disease, or cancer; examples of the second group (those who have been misclassified as having an impairment) are persons who have been misclassified as having mental retardation or mental illness.

(4) The phrase is regarded as having an impairment means-

Test C -- Being regarded as having such an impairment

(i) Has a physical or mental impairment that does not substantially limit major life activities but that is treated by a public entity as constituting such a limitation;

This test, as contained in paragraph (4) of the definition, is intended to cover persons who are treated by a public entity as having a physical or mental impairment that substantially limits a major life activity. It applies when a person is treated as if he or she has an impairment that substantially limits a major life activity, regardless of whether that person has an impairment.

(ii) Has a physical or mental impairment that substantially limits major life

The Americans with Disabilities Act uses the same "regarded as" test set forth in the regulations implementing section 504 of the Rehabilitation Act. See, e.g., 28 CFR 42.540(k)(2)(iv), which provides:

REGULATION

activities only as a result of the attitudes of others toward such impairment; or

(iii) Has none of the impairments defined in paragraph (1) of this definition but is treated by a public entity as having such an impairment.

(5) The term disability does not include --

(i) Transvestism, transsexualism, pedophilia, exhibitionism, voyeurism, gender identity disorders not resulting from physical impairments, or other sexual behavior disorders;

(ii) Compulsive gambling, kleptomania, or pyromania; or

(iii) Psychoactive substance use disorders resulting from current illegal use of drugs.

ANALYSIS

(iv) "Is regarded as having an impairment" means (A) Has a physical or mental impairment that does not substantially limit major life activities but that is treated by a recipient as constituting such a limitation; (B) Has a physical or mental impairment that substantially limits major life activities only as a result of the attitudes of others toward such impairment; or (C) Has none of the impairments defined in paragraph (k)(2)(i) of this section but is treated by a recipient as having such an impairment.

The perception of the covered entity is a key element of this test. A person who perceives himself or herself to have an impairment, but does not have an impairment, and is not treated as if he or she has an impairment, is not protected under this test.

A person would be covered under this test if a public entity refused to serve the person because it perceived that the person had an impairment that limited his or her enjoyment of the goods or services being offered.

For example, persons with severe burns often encounter discrimination in community activities, resulting in substantial limitation of major life activities. These persons would be covered under this test based on the attitudes of others towards the impairment, even if they did not view themselves as "impaired."

The rationale for this third test, as used in the Rehabilitation Act of 1973, was articulated by the Supreme Court in Arline, 480 U.S. 273 (1987). The Court noted that although an individual may have an impairment that does not in fact substantially limit a major life activity, the reaction of others may prove just as disabling. "Such an impairment might not diminish a person's physical or mental capabilities, but could nevertheless substantially limit that person's ability to work as a result of the negative reactions of others to the impairment." Id. at 283. The Court concluded that, by including this test in the Rehabilitation Act's definition, "Congress acknowledged that society's accumulated myths and fears about disability and diseases are as handicapping as are the physical limitations that flow from actual impairment." Id. at 284.

Thus, a person who is denied services or benefits by a public entity because of myths, fears, and stereotypes associ-

REGULATION

ANALYSIS

ated with disabilities would be covered under this third test whether or not the person's physical or mental condition would be considered a disability under the first or second test in the definition.

If a person is refused admittance on the basis of an actual or perceived physical or mental condition, and the public entity can articulate no legitimate reason for the refusal (such as failure to meet eligibility criteria), a perceived concern about admitting persons with disabilities could be inferred and the individual would qualify for coverage under the "regarded as" test. A person who is covered because of being regarded as having an impairment is not required to show that the public entity's perception is inaccurate (e.g., that he will be accepted by others) in order to receive benefits from the public entity.

Paragraph (5) of the definition lists certain conditions that are not included within the definition of "disability." The excluded conditions are: transvestism, transsexualism, pedophilia, exhibitionism, voyeurism, gender identity disorders not resulting from physical impairments, other sexual behavior disorders, compulsive gambling, kleptomania, pyromania, and psychoactive substance use disorders resulting from current illegal use of drugs. Unlike homosexuality and bisexuality, which are not considered impairments under either section 504 or the Americans with Disabilities Act (see the definition of "disability," paragraph (1)(iv)), the conditions listed in paragraph (5), except for transvestism, are not necessarily excluded as impairments under section 504. (Transvestism was excluded from the definition of disability for section 504 by the Fair Housing Amendments Act of 1988, Pub. L. 100-430, section 6(b)).

Drug means a controlled substance, as defined in schedules I through V of section 202 of the Controlled Substances Act (21 U.S.C. 812).

"Drug." The definition of the term "drug" is taken from section 510(d)(2) of the ADA.

Facility means all or any portion of buildings, structures, sites, complexes, equipment, rolling stock or other conveyances, roads,

"Facility." "Facility" means all or any portion of buildings, structures, sites, complexes, equipment, rolling stock or other conveyances, roads, walks, passageways, parking lots, or other real or personal property, including the site where the building, property, structure, or equipment is located. It

REGULATION

walks, passageways, parking lots, or other real or personal property, including the site where the building, property, structure, or equipment is located.

Historic preservation programs means programs conducted by a public entity that have preservation of historic properties as a primary purpose.

Historic properties means those properties that are listed or eligible for listing in the National Register of Historic Places or properties designated as historic under State or local law.

Illegal use of drugs means the use of one or more drugs, the possession or distribution of which is unlawful under the Controlled Substances Act (21 U.S.C. 812). The term illegal use of drugs does not include the use of a drug taken under supervision by a licensed health care professional, or other uses authorized by the Controlled Substances Act or other provisions of Federal law.

ANALYSIS

includes both indoor and outdoor areas where human-constructed improvements, structures, equipment, or property have been added to the natural environment.

Commenters raised questions about the applicability of this part to activities operated in mobile facilities, such as bookmobiles or mobile health screening units. Such activities would be covered by the requirement for program accessibility in §35.150, and would be included in the definition of "facility" as "other real or personal property," although standards for new construction and alterations of such facilities are not yet included in the accessibility standards adopted by §35.151. Sections 35.150 and 35.151 specifically address the obligations of public entities to ensure accessibility by providing curb ramps at pedestrian walkways.

"Historic preservation programs" and "Historic properties" are defined in order to aid in the interpretation of §§35.150(a)(2) and (b)(2), which relate to accessibility of historic preservation programs, and §35.151(d), which relates to the alteration of historic properties.

"Illegal use of drugs." The definition of "illegal use of drugs" is taken from section 510(d)(1) of the Act and clarifies that the term includes the illegal use of one or more drugs.

REGULATION

Individual with a disability means a person who has a disability. The term individual with a disability does not include an individual who is currently engaging in the illegal use of drugs, when the public entity acts on the basis of such use.

Public entity means —

(1) Any State or local government;

(2) Any department, agency, special purpose district, or other instrumentality of a State or States or local government; and

(3) The National Railroad Passenger Corporation, and any commuter authority (as defined in section 103(8) of the Rail Passenger Service Act).

Qualified individual with a disability means an individual with a disability who, with or without reasonable modifications to rules, policies, or practices, the removal of architectural, communication, or transportation barriers, or the provision of auxiliary aids and services, meets the essential eligibility requirements for the receipt of services or the participation in programs or activities provided by a public entity.

ANALYSIS

"Individual with a disability" means a person who has a disability but does not include an individual who is currently illegally using drugs, when the public entity acts on the basis of such use. The phrase "current illegal use of drugs" is explained in §35.131.

"Public entity." The term "public entity" is defined in accordance with section 201(1) of the ADA as any State or local government; any department, agency, special purpose district, or other instrumentality of a State or States or local government; or the National Railroad Passenger Corporation, and any commuter authority (as defined in section 103(8) of the Rail Passenger Service Act).

"Qualified individual with a disability." The definition of "qualified individual with a disability" is taken from section 201(2) of the Act, which is derived from the definition of "qualified handicapped person" in the Department of Health and Human Services' regulation implementing section 504 (45 CFR §84.3(k)). It combines the definition at 45 CFR 84.3(k)(1) for employment ("a handicapped person who, with reasonable accommodation, can perform the essential functions of the job in question") with the definition for other services at 45 CFR 84.3(k)(4) ("a handicapped person who meets the essential eligibility requirements for the receipt of such services").

Some commenters requested clarification of the term "essential eligibility requirements." Because of the variety of situations in which an individual's qualifications will be at issue, it is not possible to include more specific criteria in the definition. The "essential eligibility requirements" for partici-

REGULATION

pation in some activities covered under this part may be minimal. For example, most public entities provide information about their operations as a public service to anyone who requests it. In such situations, the only "eligibility requirement" for receipt of such information would be the request for it. Where such information is provided by telephone, even the ability to use a voice telephone is not an "essential eligibility requirement," because §35.161 requires a public entity to provide equally effective telecommunication systems for individuals with impaired hearing or speech.

For other activities, identification of the "essential eligibility requirements" may be more complex. Where questions of safety are involved, the principles established in §36.208 of the Department's regulation implementing title III of the ADA, to be codified at 28 CFR Part 36, will be applicable. That section implements section 302(b)(3) of the Act, which provides that a public accommodation is not required to permit an individual to participate in or benefit from the goods, services, facilities, privileges, advantages and accommodations of the public accommodation, if that individual poses a direct threat to the health or safety of others.

A "direct threat" is a significant risk to the health or safety of others that cannot be eliminated by a modification of policies, practices, or procedures, or by the provision of auxiliary aids or services. In School Board of Nassau County v. Arline, 480 U.S. 273 (1987), the Supreme Court recognized that there is a need to balance the interests of people with disabilities against legitimate concerns for public safety. Although persons with disabilities are generally entitled to the protection of this part, a person who poses a significant risk to others will not be "qualified," if reasonable modifications to the public entity's policies, practices, or procedures will not eliminate that risk.

The determination that a person poses a direct threat to the health or safety of others may not be based on generalizations or stereotypes about the effects of a particular disability. It must be based on an individualized assessment, based on reasonable judgment that relies on current medical evidence or on the best available objective evidence, to determine: the nature, duration, and severity of the risk; the probability that the potential injury will actually occur; and whether reasonable modifications of policies, practices, or procedures will mitigate the risk. This is the test established

REGULATION

by the Supreme Court in <u>Arline</u>. Such an inquiry is essential if the law is to achieve its goal of protecting disabled individuals from discrimination based on prejudice, stereotypes, or unfounded fear, while giving appropriate weight to legitimate concerns, such as the need to avoid exposing others to significant health and safety risks. Making this assessment will not usually require the services of a physician. Sources for medical knowledge include guidance from public health authorities, such as the U.S. Public Health Service, the Centers for Disease Control, and the National Institutes of Health, including the National Institute of Mental Health.

<u>Qualified interpreter</u> means an interpreter who is able to interpret effectively, accurately, and impartially both receptively and expressively, using any necessary specialized vocabulary.

"Qualified interpreter." The Department received substantial comment regarding the lack of a definition of "qualified interpreter." The proposed rule defined auxiliary aids and services to include the statutory term, "qualified interpreters" (§35.104), but did not define it. Section 35.160 requires the use of auxiliary aids including qualified interpreters and commenters stated that a lack of guidance on what the term means would create confusion among those trying to secure interpreting services and often result in less than effective communication.

Many commenters were concerned that, without clear guidance on the issue of "qualified" interpreter, the rule would be interpreted to mean "available, rather than qualified" interpreters. Some claimed that few public entities would understand the difference between a qualified interpreter and a person who simply knows a few signs or how to fingerspell.

In order to clarify what is meant by "qualified interpreter" the Department has added a definition of the term to the final rule. A qualified interpreter means an interpreter who is able to interpret effectively, accurately, and impartially both receptively and expressively, using any necessary specialized vocabulary. This definition focuses on the actual ability of the interpreter in a particular interpreting context to facilitate effective communication between the public entity and the individual with disabilities.

Public comment also revealed that public entities have at times asked persons who are deaf to provide family members or friends to interpret. In certain circumstances, notwithstanding that the family member of friend is able to interpret or is a certified interpreter, the family member or friend may not be

REGULATION

ANALYSIS

qualified to render the necessary interpretation because of factors such as emotional or personal involvement or considerations of confidentiality that may adversely affect the ability to interpret "effectively, accurately, and impartially."

The definition of "qualified interpreter" in this rule does not invalidate or limit standards for interpreting services of any State or local law that are equal to or more stringent than those imposed by this definition. For instance, the definition would not supersede any requirement of State law for use of a certified interpreter in court proceedings.

Section 504 means section 504 of the Rehabilitation Act of 1973 (Pub. L. 93-112, 87 Stat. 394 (29 U.S.C. 794)), as amended.

"Section 504." The Department added a definition of "section 504" because the term is used extensively in subpart F of this part.

State means each of the several States, the District of Columbia, the Commonwealth of Puerto Rico, Guam, American Samoa, the Virgin Islands, the Trust Territory of the Pacific Islands, and the Commonwealth of the Northern Mariana Islands.

"State." The definition of "State" is identical to the statutory definition in section 3(3) of the ADA.

REGULATION

§35.105 Self-evaluation.

(a) A public entity shall, within one year of the effective date of this part, evaluate its current services, policies, and practices, and the effects thereof, that do not or may not meet the requirements of this part and, to the extent modification of any such services, policies, and practices is required, the public entity shall proceed to make the necessary modifications.

(b) A public entity shall provide an opportunity to interested persons, including individuals with disabilities or organizations representing individuals with disabilities, to participate in the self-evaluation process by submitting comments.

(c) A public entity that employs 50 or more persons shall, for at least three years following completion of the self-evaluation, maintain on file and make available for public inspection:

(1) A list of the interested persons consulted;

(2) A description of areas examined and any problems identified; and

(3) A description of any modifications made.

(d) If a public entity has already complied with the

ANALYSIS

§35.105 Self-evaluation.

Section 35.105 establishes a requirement, based on the section 504 regulations for federally assisted and federally conducted programs, that a public entity evaluate its current policies and practices to identify and correct any that are not consistent with the requirements of this part. As noted in the discussion of §35.102, activities covered by the Department of Transportation's regulation implementing subtitle B of title II are not required to be included in the self-evaluation required by this section.

Experience has demonstrated the self-evaluation process to be a valuable means of establishing a working relationship with individuals with disabilities, which has promoted both effective and efficient implementation of section 504. The Department expects that it will likewise be useful to public entities newly covered by the ADA.

All public entities are required to do a self-evaluation. However, only those that employ 50 or more persons are required to maintain the self-evaluation on file and make it available for public inspection for three years. The number 50 was derived from the Department of Justice's section 504 regulations for federally assisted programs, 28 CFR 42.505(c). The Department received comments critical of this limitation, some suggesting the requirement apply to all public entities and others suggesting that the number be changed from 50 to 15. The final rule has not been changed. Although many regulations implementing section 504 for federally assisted programs do use 15 employees as the cut-off for this record-keeping requirement, the Department believes that it would be inappropriate to extend it to those smaller public entities covered by this regulation that do not receive Federal financial assistance. This approach has the benefit of minimizing paperwork burdens on small entities.

Paragraph (d) provides that the self-evaluation required by this section shall apply only to programs not subject to section 504 or those policies and practices, such as those involving communications access, that have not already been included in a self-evaluation required under an existing regulation implementing section 504. Because most self-evaluations were done from five to twelve years ago, however, the Department expects that a great many public entities will be reexamining all of their policies and programs. Programs and functions may have changed, and actions that were supposed

REGULATION

self-evaluation requirement of a regulation implementing section 504 of the Rehabilitation Act of 1973, then the requirements of this section shall apply only to those policies and practices that were not included in the previous self-evaluation.

ANALYSIS

to have been taken to comply with section 504 may not have been fully implemented or may no longer be effective. In addition, there have been statutory amendments to section 504 which have changed the coverage of section 504, particularly the Civil Rights Restoration Act of 1987, Pub. L. No. 100-259, 102 Stat. 28 (1988), which broadened the definition of a covered "program or activity."

Several commenters suggested that the Department clarify public entities' liability during the one-year period for compliance with the self-evaluation requirement. The self-evaluation requirement does not stay the effective date of the statute nor of this part. Public entities are, therefore, not shielded from discrimination claims during that time.

Other commenters suggested that the rule require that every self-evaluation include an examination of training efforts to assure that individuals with disabilities are not subjected to discrimination because of insensitivity, particularly in the law enforcement area. Although the Department has not added such a specific requirement to the rule, it would be appropriate for public entities to evaluate training efforts because, in many cases, lack of training leads to discriminatory practices, even when the policies in place are nondiscriminatory.

REGULATION
§35.106 Notice.

A public entity shall make available to applicants, participants, beneficiaries, and other interested persons information regarding the provisions of this part and its applicability to the services, programs, or activities of the public entity, and make such information available to them in such manner as the head of the entity finds necessary to apprise such persons of the protections against discrimination assured them by the Act and this part.

ANALYSIS
§35.106 Notice.

Section 35.106 requires a public entity to disseminate sufficient information to applicants, participants, beneficiaries, and other interested persons to inform them of the rights and protections afforded by the ADA and this regulation. Methods of providing this information include, for example, the publication of information in handbooks, manuals, and pamphlets that are distributed to the public to describe a public entity's programs and activities; the display of informative posters in service centers and other public places; or the broadcast of information by television or radio. In providing the notice, a public entity must comply with the requirements for effective communication in §35.160. The preamble to that section gives guidance on how to effectively communicate with individuals with disabilities.

REGULATION
§35.107 Designation of responsible employee and adoption of grievance procedures.

(a) <u>Designation of responsible employee</u>. A public entity that employs 50 or more persons shall designate at least one employee to coordinate its efforts to comply with and carry out its responsibilities under this part, including any investigation of any complaint communicated to it alleging its noncompliance with this part or alleging any actions that would be prohibited by this part. The public entity shall make available to all interested individuals the name, office address, and telephone number of the employee or employees designated pursuant to this paragraph.

(b) <u>Complaint procedure</u>. A public entity that employs 50 or more persons shall adopt and publish grievance procedures providing for prompt and equitable resolution of complaints alleging any action that would be prohibited by this part.

ANALYSIS
§35.107 Designation of responsible employee and adoption of grievance procedures.

Consistent with §35.105, Self-evaluation, the final rule requires that public entities with 50 or more employees designate a responsible employee and adopt grievance procedures. Most of the commenters who suggested that the requirement that self-evaluation be maintained on file for three years not be limited to those employing 50 or more persons made a similar suggestion concerning §35.107. Commenters recommended either that all public entities be subject to section 35.107, or that "50 or more persons" be changed to "15 or more persons." As explained in the discussion of §35.105, the Department has not adopted this suggestion.

The requirement for designation of an employee responsible for coordination of efforts to carry out responsibilities under this part is derived from the HEW regulation implementing section 504 in federally assisted programs. The requirement for designation of a particular employee and dissemination of information about how to locate that employee helps to ensure that individuals dealing with large agencies are able to easily find a responsible person who is familiar with the requirements of the Act and this part and can communicate those requirements to other individuals in the agency who may be unaware of their responsibilities. This paragraph in no way limits a public entity's obligation to ensure that all of its employees comply with the requirements of this part, but it ensures that any failure by individual employees can be promptly corrected by the designated employee.

Section 35.107(b) requires public entities with 50 or more employees to establish grievance procedures for resolving complaints of violations of this part. Similar requirements are found in the section 504 regulations for federally assisted programs (see, e.g., 45 CFR 84.7(b)). The rule, like the regulations for federally assisted programs, provides for investigation and resolution of complaints by a Federal enforcement agency. It is the view of the Department that public entities subject to this part should be required to establish a mechanism for resolution of complaints at the local level without requiring the complainant to resort to the Federal complaint procedures established under subpart F. Complainants would not, however, be required to exhaust the public entity's grievance procedures before filing a com-

REGULATION

ANALYSIS

plaint under subpart F. Delay in filing the complaint at the Federal level caused by pursuit of the remedies available under the grievance procedure would generally be considered good cause for extending the time allowed for filing under §35.170(b).

REGULATION
Subpart B -- General Requirements

§35.130 General prohibitions against discrimination.

(a) No qualified individual with a disability shall, on the basis of disability, be excluded from participation in or be denied the benefits of the services, programs, or activities of a public entity, or be subjected to discrimination by any public entity.

(b)(1) A public entity, in providing any aid, benefit, or service, may not, directly or through contractual, licensing, or other arrangements, on the basis of disability --

(i) Deny a qualified individual with a disability the opportunity to participate in or benefit from the aid, benefit, or service;

(ii) Afford a qualified individual with a disability an opportunity to participate in or benefit from the aid, benefit, or service that is not equal to that afforded others;

(iii) Provide a qualified individual with a disability with an aid, benefit, or service that is not as effective in affording equal opportunity to obtain the same result, to gain the same benefit, or to reach the same level of achievement as that provided to others;

ANALYSIS
Subpart B -- General Requirements

§35.130 General prohibitions against discrimination.

The general prohibitions against discrimination in the rule are generally based on the prohibitions in existing regulations implementing section 504 and, therefore, are already familiar to State and local entities covered by section 504. In addition, §35.130 includes a number of provisions derived from title III of the Act that are implicit to a certain degree in the requirements of regulations implementing section 504.

Several commenters suggested that this part should include the section of the proposed title III regulation that implemented section 309 of the Act, which requires that courses and examinations related to applications, licensing, certification, or credentialing be provided in an accessible place and manner or that alternative accessible arrangements be made. The Department has not adopted this suggestion. The requirements of this part, including the general prohibitions of discrimination in this section, the program access requirements of subpart D, and the communications requirements of subpart E, apply to courses and examinations provided by public entities. The Department considers these requirements to be sufficient to ensure that courses and examinations administered by public entities meet the requirements of section 309. For example, a public entity offering an examination must ensure that modifications of policies, practices, or procedures or the provision of auxiliary aids and services furnish the individual with a disability an equal opportunity to demonstrate his or her knowledge or ability. Also, any examination specially designed for individuals with disabilities must be offered as often and in as timely a manner as are other examinations. Further, under this part, courses and examinations must be offered in the most integrated setting appropriate. The analysis of §35.130(d) is relevant to this determination.

A number of commenters asked that the regulation be amended to require training of law enforcement personnel to recognize the difference between criminal activity and the effects of seizures or other disabilities such as mental retardation, cerebral palsy, traumatic brain injury, mental illness, or deafness. Several disabled commenters gave personal statements about the abuse they had received at the hands of law enforcement personnel. Two organizations that commented

REGULATION

ANALYSIS

(iv) Provide different or separate aids, benefits, or services to individuals with disabilities or to any class of individuals with disabilities than is provided to others unless such action is necessary to provide qualified individuals with disabilities with aids, benefits, or services that are as effective as those provided to others;

(v) Aid or perpetuate discrimination against a qualified individual with a disability by providing significant assistance to an agency, organization, or person that discriminates on the basis of disability in providing any aid, benefit, or service to beneficiaries of the public entity's program;

(vi) Deny a qualified individual with a disability the opportunity to participate as a member of planning or advisory boards;

(vii) Otherwise limit a qualified individual with a disability in the enjoyment of any right, privilege, advantage, or opportunity enjoyed by others receiving the aid, benefit, or service.

(2) A public entity may not deny a qualified individual with a disability the opportunity to participate in services, programs, or activities that are not separate or different, despite the

cited the Judiciary report at 50 as authority to require law enforcement training.

The Department has not added such a training requirement to the regulation. Discriminatory arrests and brutal treatment are already unlawful police activities. The general regulatory obligation to modify policies, practices, or procedures requires law enforcement to make changes in policies that result in discriminatory arrests or abuse of individuals with disabilities. Under this section law enforcement personnel would be required to make appropriate efforts to determine whether perceived strange or disruptive behavior or unconsciousness is the result of a disability. The Department notes that a number of States have attempted to address the problem of arresting disabled persons for noncriminal conduct resulting from their disability through adoption of the Uniform Duties to Disabled Persons Act, and encourages other jurisdictions to consider that approach.

Paragraph (a) restates the nondiscrimination mandate of section 202 of the ADA. The remaining paragraphs in §35.130 establish the general principles for analyzing whether any particular action of the public entity violates this mandate.

Paragraph (b) prohibits overt denials of equal treatment of individuals with disabilities. A public entity may not refuse to provide an individual with a disability with an equal opportunity to participate in or benefit from its program simply because the person has a disability.

Paragraph (b)(1)(i) provides that it is discriminatory to deny a person with a disability the right to participate in or benefit from the aid, benefit, or service provided by a public entity. Paragraph (b)(1)(ii) provides that the aids, benefits, and services provided to persons with disabilities must be equal to those provided to others, and paragraph (b)(1)(iii) requires that the aids, benefits, or services provided to individuals with disabilities must be as effective in affording equal opportunity to obtain the same result, to gain the same benefit, or to reach the same level of achievement as those provided to others. These paragraphs are taken from the regulations implementing section 504 and simply restate principles long established under section 504.

Paragraph (b)(1)(iv) permits the public entity to develop separate or different aids, benefits, or services when necessary

REGULATION

existence of permissibly separate or different programs or activities.

(3) A public entity may not, directly or through contractual or other arrangements, utilize criteria or methods of administration:

(i) That have the effect of subjecting qualified individuals with disabilities to discrimination on the basis of disability;

(ii) That have the purpose or effect of defeating or substantially impairing accomplishment of the objectives of the public entity's program with respect to individuals with disabilities; or

(iii) That perpetuate the discrimination of another public entity if both public entities are subject to common administrative control or are agencies of the same State.

(4) A public entity may not, in determining the site or location of a facility, make selections --

(i) That have the effect of excluding individuals with disabilities from, denying them the benefits of, or otherwise subjecting them to discrimination; or

(ii) That have the pur-

ANALYSIS

to provide individuals with disabilities with an equal opportunity to participate in or benefit from the public entity's programs or activities, but only when necessary to ensure that the aids, benefits, or services are as effective as those provided to others. Paragraph (b)(1)(iv) must be read in conjunction with paragraphs (b)(2), (d), and (e). Even when separate or different aids, benefits, or services would be more effective, paragraph (b)(2) provides that a qualified individual with a disability still has the right to choose to participate in the program that is not designed to accommodate individuals with disabilities. Paragraph (d) requires that a public entity administer services, programs, and activities in the most integrated setting appropriate to the needs of qualified individuals with disabilities.

Paragraph (b)(2) specifies that, notwithstanding the existence of separate or different programs or activities provided in accordance with this section, an individual with a disability shall not be denied the opportunity to participate in such programs or activities that are not separate or different. Paragraph (e), which is derived from section 501(d) of the Americans with Disabilities Act, states that nothing in this part shall be construed to require an individual with a disability to accept an accommodation, aid, service, opportunity, or benefit that he or she chooses not to accept.

Taken together, these provisions are intended to prohibit exclusion and segregation of individuals with disabilities and the denial of equal opportunities enjoyed by others, based on, among other things, presumptions, patronizing attitudes, fears, and stereotypes about individuals with disabilities. Consistent with these standards, public entities are required to ensure that their actions are based on facts applicable to individuals and not on presumptions as to what a class of individuals with disabilities can or cannot do.

Integration is fundamental to the purposes of the Americans with Disabilities Act. Provision of segregated accommodations and services relegates persons with disabilities to second-class status. For example, it would be a violation of this provision to require persons with disabilities to eat in the back room of a government cafeteria or to refuse to allow a person with a disability the full use of recreation or exercise facilities because of stereotypes about the person's ability to participate.

REGULATION

pose or effect of defeating or substantially impairing the accomplishment of the objectives of the service, program, or activity with respect to individuals with disabilities.

(5) A public entity, in the selection of procurement contractors, may not use criteria that subject qualified individuals with disabilities to discrimination on the basis of disability.

(6) A public entity may not administer a licensing or certification program in a manner that subjects qualified individuals with disabilities to discrimination on the basis of disability, nor may a public entity establish requirements for the programs or activities of licensees or certified entities that subject qualified individuals with disabilities to discrimination on the basis of disability. The programs or activities of entities that are licensed or certified by a public entity are not, themselves, covered by this part.

(7) A public entity shall make reasonable modifications in policies, practices, or procedures when the modifications are necessary to avoid discrimination on the basis of disability, unless the public entity can demonstrate that making the modifications would fundamen-

ANALYSIS

Many commenters objected to proposed paragraphs (b)(1)(iv) and (d) as allowing continued segregation of individuals with disabilities. The Department recognizes that promoting integration of individuals with disabilities into the mainstream of society is an important objective of the ADA and agrees that, in most instances, separate programs for individuals with disabilities will not be permitted. Nevertheless, section 504 does permit separate programs in limited circumstances, and Congress clearly intended the regulations issued under title II to adopt the standards of section 504. Furthermore, Congress included authority for separate programs in the specific requirements of title III of the Act. Section 302(b)(1)(A)(iii) of the Act provides for separate benefits in language similar to that in 35.130(b)(1)(iv), and section 302(b)(1)(B) includes the same requirement for "the most integrated setting appropriate" as in §35.130(d).

Even when separate programs are permitted, individuals with disabilities cannot be denied the opportunity to participate in programs that are not separate or different. This is an important and overarching principle of the Americans with Disabilities Act. Separate, special, or different programs that are designed to provide a benefit to persons with disabilities cannot be used to restrict the participation of persons with disabilities in general, integrated activities.

For example, a person who is blind may wish to decline participating in a special museum tour that allows persons to touch sculptures in an exhibit and instead tour the exhibit at his or her own pace with the museum's recorded tour. It is not the intent of this section to require the person who is blind to avail himself or herself of the special tour. Modified participation for persons with disabilities must be a choice, not a requirement.

In addition, it would not be a violation of this section for a public entity to offer recreational programs specially designed for children with mobility impairments. However, it would be a violation of this section if the entity then excluded these children from other recreational services for which they are qualified to participate when these services are made available to nondisabled children, or if the entity required children with disabilities to attend only designated programs.

Many commenters asked that the Department clarify a public entity's obligations within the integrated program when

REGULATION

tally alter the nature of the service, program, or activity.

(8) A public entity shall not impose or apply eligibility criteria that screen out or tend to screen out an individual with a disability or any class of individuals with disabilities from fully and equally enjoying any service, program, or activity, unless such criteria can be shown to be necessary for the provision of the service, program, or activity being offered.

(c) Nothing in this part prohibits a public entity from providing benefits, services, or advantages to individuals with disabilities, or to a particular class of individuals with disabilities beyond those required by this part.

(d) A public entity shall administer services, programs, and activities in the most integrated setting appropriate to the needs of qualified individuals with disabilities.

(e)(1) Nothing in this part shall be construed to require an individual with a disability to accept an accommodation, aid, service, opportunity, or benefit provided under the ADA or this part which such individual chooses not to accept.

(2) Nothing in the Act or this part authorizes the

ANALYSIS

it offers a separate program but an individual with a disability chooses not to participate in the separate program. It is impossible to make a blanket statement as to what level of auxiliary aids or modifications would be required in the integrated program. Rather, each situation must be assessed individually. The starting point is to question whether the separate program is in fact necessary or appropriate for the individual. Assuming the separate program would be appropriate for a particular individual, the extent to which that individual must be provided with modifications in the integrated program will depend not only on what the individual needs but also on the limitations and defenses of this part. For example, it may constitute an undue burden for a public accommodation, which provides a full-time interpreter in its special guided tour for individuals with hearing impairments, to hire an additional interpreter for those individuals who choose to attend the integrated program. The Department cannot identify categorically the level of assistance or aid required in the integrated program.

Paragraph (b)(1)(v) provides that a public entity may not aid or perpetuate discrimination against a qualified individual with a disability by providing significant assistance to an agency, organization, or person that discriminates on the basis of disability in providing any aid, benefit, or service to beneficiaries of the public entity's program. This paragraph is taken from the regulations implementing section 504 for federally assisted programs.

Paragraph (b)(1)(vi) prohibits the public entity from denying a qualified individual with a disability the opportunity to participate as a member of a planning or advisory board.

Paragraph (b)(1)(vii) prohibits the public entity from limiting a qualified individual with a disability in the enjoyment of any right, privilege, advantage, or opportunity enjoyed by others receiving any aid, benefit, or service.

Paragraph (b)(3) prohibits the public entity from utilizing criteria or methods of administration that deny individuals with disabilities access to the public entity's services, programs, and activities or that perpetuate the discrimination of another public entity, if both public entities are subject to common administrative control or are agencies of the same State. The phrase "criteria or methods of administration"

REGULATION

representative or guardian of an individual with a disability to decline food, water, medical treatment, or medical services for that individual.

(f) A public entity may not place a surcharge on a particular individual with a disability or any group of individuals with disabilities to cover the costs of measures, such as the provision of auxiliary aids or program accessibility, that are required to provide that individual or group with the nondiscriminatory treatment required by the Act or this part.

(g) A public entity shall not exclude or otherwise deny equal services, programs, or activities to an individual or entity because of the known disability of an individual with whom the individual or entity is known to have a relationship or association.

ANALYSIS

refers to official written policies of the public entity and to the actual practices of the public entity. This paragraph prohibits both blatantly exclusionary policies or practices and nonessential policies and practices that are neutral on their face, but deny individuals with disabilities an effective opportunity to participate. This standard is consistent with the interpretation of section 504 by the U.S. Supreme Court in Alexander v. Choate, 469 U.S. 287 (1985). The Court in Choate explained that members of Congress made numerous statements during passage of section 504 regarding eliminating architectural barriers, providing access to transportation, and eliminating discriminatory effects of job qualification procedures. The Court then noted: "These statements would ring hollow if the resulting legislation could not rectify the harms resulting from action that discriminated by effect as well as by design." Id. at 297 (footnote omitted).

Paragraph (b)(4) specifically applies the prohibition enunciated in §35.130(b)(3) to the process of selecting sites for construction of new facilities or selecting existing facilities to be used by the public entity. Paragraph (b)(4) does not apply to construction of additional buildings at an existing site.

Paragraph (b)(5) prohibits the public entity, in the selection of procurement contractors, from using criteria that subject qualified individuals with disabilities to discrimination on the basis of disability.

Paragraph (b)(6) prohibits the public entity from discriminating against qualified individuals with disabilities on the basis of disability in the granting of licenses or certification. A person is a "qualified individual with a disability" with respect to licensing or certification if he or she can meet the essential eligibility requirements for receiving the license or certification (see §35.104).

A number of commenters were troubled by the phrase "essential eligibility requirements" as applied to State licensing requirements, especially those for health care professions. Because of the variety of types of programs to which the definition of "qualified individual with a disability" applies, it is not possible to use more specific language in the definition. The phrase "essential eligibility requirements," however, is taken from the definitions in the regulations implementing section 504, so caselaw under section 504 will

REGULATION

be applicable to its interpretation. In Southeastern Community College v. Davis, 442 U.S. 397, for example, the Supreme Court held that section 504 does not require an institution to "lower or effect substantial modifications of standards to accommodate a handicapped person," 442 U.S. at 413, and that the school had established that the plaintiff was not "qualified" because she was not able to "serve the nursing profession in all customary ways," id. Whether a particular requirement is "essential" will, of course, depend on the facts of the particular case.

In addition, the public entity may not establish requirements for the programs or activities of licensees or certified entities that subject qualified individuals with disabilities to discrimination on the basis of disability. For example, the public entity must comply with this requirement when establishing safety standards for the operations of licensees. In that case the public entity must ensure that standards that it promulgates do not discriminate against the employment of qualified individuals with disabilities in an impermissible manner.

Paragraph (b)(6) does not extend the requirements of the Act or this part directly to the programs or activities of licensees or certified entities themselves. The programs or activities of licensees or certified entities are not themselves programs or activities of the public entity merely by virtue of the license or certificate.

Paragraph (b)(7) is a specific application of the requirement under the general prohibitions of discrimination that public entities make reasonable modifications in policies, practices, or procedures where necessary to avoid discrimination on the basis of disability. Section 302(b)(2)(A)(ii) of the ADA sets out this requirement specifically for public accommodations covered by title III of the Act, and the House Judiciary Committee Report directs the Attorney General to include those specific requirements in the title II regulation to the extent that they do not conflict with the regulations implementing section 504. Judiciary report at 52.

Paragraph (b)(8), a new paragraph not contained in the proposed rule, prohibits the imposition or application of eligibility criteria that screen out or tend to screen out an individual with a disability or any class of individuals with disabilities from fully and equally enjoying any service,

REGULATION

program, or activity, unless such criteria can be shown to be necessary for the provision of the service, program, or activity being offered. This prohibition is also a specific application of the general prohibitions of discrimination and is based on section 302(b)(2)(A)(i) of the ADA. It prohibits overt denials of equal treatment of individuals with disabilities, or establishment of exclusive or segregative criteria that would bar individuals with disabilities from participation in services, benefits, or activities.

Paragraph (b)(8) also prohibits policies that unnecessarily impose requirements or burdens on individuals with disabilities that are not placed on others. For example, public entities may not require that a qualified individual with a disability be accompanied by an attendant. A public entity is not, however, required to provide attendant care, or assistance in toileting, eating, or dressing to individuals with disabilities, except in special circumstances, such as where the individual is an inmate of a custodial or correctional institution.

In addition, paragraph (b)(8) prohibits the imposition of criteria that "tend to" screen out an individual with a disability. This concept, which is derived from current regulations under section 504 (see, e.g., 45 CFR 84.13), makes it discriminatory to impose policies or criteria that, while not creating a direct bar to individuals with disabilities, indirectly prevent or limit their ability to participate. For example, requiring presentation of a driver's license as the sole means of identification for purposes of paying by check would violate this section in situations where, for example, individuals with severe vision impairments or developmental disabilities or epilepsy are ineligible to receive a driver's license and the use of an alternative means of identification, such as another photo I.D. or credit card, is feasible.

A public entity may, however, impose neutral rules and criteria that screen out, or tend to screen out, individuals with disabilities if the criteria are necessary for the safe operation of the program in question. Examples of safety qualifications that would be justifiable in appropriate circumstances would include eligibility requirements for drivers' licenses, or a requirement that all participants in a recreational rafting expedition be able to meet a necessary level of swimming proficiency. Safety requirements must be based on actual risks and not on speculation, stereotypes, or generalizations about individuals with disabilities.

REGULATION

ANALYSIS

Paragraph (c) provides that nothing in this part prohibits a public entity from providing benefits, services, or advantages to individuals with disabilities, or to a particular class of individuals with disabilities, beyond those required by this part. It is derived from a provision in the section 504 regulations that permits programs conducted pursuant to Federal statute or Executive order that are designed to benefit only individuals with disabilities or a given class of individuals with disabilities to be limited to those individuals with disabilities. Section 504 ensures that federally assisted programs are made available to all individuals, without regard to disabilities, unless the Federal program under which the assistance is provided is specifically limited to individuals with disabilities or a particular class of individuals with disabilities. Because coverage under this part is not limited to federally assisted programs, paragraph (c) has been revised to clarify that State and local governments may provide special benefits, beyond those required by the non-discrimination requirements of this part, that are limited to individuals with disabilities or a particular class of individuals with disabilities, without thereby incurring additional obligations to persons without disabilities or to other classes of individuals with disabilities.

Paragraphs (d) and (e), previously referred to in the discussion of paragraph (b)(1)(iv), provide that the public entity must administer services, programs, and activities in the most integrated setting appropriate to the needs of qualified individuals with disabilities, i.e., in a setting that enables individuals with disabilities to interact with nondisabled persons to the fullest extent possible, and that persons with disabilities must be provided the option of declining to accept a particular accommodation.

Some commenters expressed concern that §35.130(e), which states that nothing in the rule requires an individual with a disability to accept special accommodations and services provided under the ADA, could be interpreted to allow guardians of infants or older people with disabilities to refuse medical treatment for their wards. Section 35.130(e) has been revised to make it clear that paragraph (e) is inapplicable to the concern of the commenters. A new paragraph (e)(2) has been added stating that nothing in the regulation authorizes the representative or guardian of an individual with a disability to decline food, water, medical treatment, or medical services for that individual. New paragraph (e)

REGULATION

clarifies that neither the ADA nor the regulation alters current Federal law ensuring the rights of incompetent individuals with disabilities to receive food, water, and medical treatment. See, e.g., Child Abuse Amendments of 1984 (42 U.S.C. 5106a(b)(10), 5106g(10)); Rehabilitation Act of 1973, as amended (29 U.S.C. 794); the Developmentally Disabled Assistance and Bill of Rights Act (42 U.S.C. 6042).

Sections 35.130(e)(1) and (2) are based on section 501(d) of the ADA. Section 501(d) was designed to clarify that nothing in the ADA requires individuals with disabilities to accept special accommodations and services for individuals with disabilities that may segregate them:

The Committee added this section [501(d)] to clarify that nothing in the ADA is intended to permit discriminatory treatment on the basis of disability, even when such treatment is rendered under the guise of providing an accommodation, service, aid or benefit to the individual with disability. For example, a blind individual may choose not to avail himself or herself of the right to go to the front of a line, even if a particular public accommodation has chosen to offer such a modification of a policy for blind individuals. Or, a blind individual may choose to decline to participate in a special museum tour that allows persons to touch sculptures in an exhibit and instead tour the exhibits at his or her own pace with the museum's recorded tour.

Judiciary report at 71-72. The Act is not to be construed to mean that an individual with disabilities must accept special accommodations and services for individuals with disabilities when that individual can participate in the regular services already offered. Because medical treatment, including treatment for particular conditions, is not a special accommodation or service for individuals with disabilities under section 501(d), neither the Act nor this part provides affirmative authority to suspend such treatment. Section 501(d) is intended to clarify that the Act is not designed to foster discrimination through mandatory acceptance of special services when other alternatives are provided; this concern does not reach to the provision of medical treatment for the disabling condition itself.

Paragraph (f) provides that a public entity may not place a surcharge on a particular individual with a disability, or any group of individuals with disabilities, to cover any costs of

REGULATION

measures required to provide that individual or group with the nondiscriminatory treatment required by the Act or this part. Such measures may include the provision of auxiliary aids or of modifications required to provide program accessibility.

Several commenters asked for clarification that the costs of interpreter services may not be assessed as an element of "court costs." The Department has already recognized that imposition of the cost of courtroom interpreter services is impermissible under section 504. The preamble to the Department's section 504 regulation for its federally assisted programs states that where a court system has an obligation to provide qualified interpreters, "it has the corresponding responsibility to pay for the services of the interpreters." (45 FR 37630 (June 3, 1980)). Accordingly, recouping the costs of interpreter services by assessing them as part of court costs would also be prohibited.

Paragraph (g), which prohibits discrimination on the basis of an individual's or entity's known relationship or association with an individual with a disability, is based on sections 102(b)(4) and 302(b)(1)(E) of the ADA. This paragraph was not contained in the proposed rule. The individuals covered under this paragraph are any individuals who are discriminated against because of their known association with an individual with a disability. For example, it would be a violation of this paragraph for a local government to refuse to allow a theater company to use a school auditorium on the grounds that the company had recently performed for an audience of individuals with HIV disease.

This protection is not limited to those who have a familial relationship with the individual who has a disability. Congress considered, and rejected, amendments that would have limited the scope of this provision to specific associations and relationships. Therefore, if a public entity refuses admission to a person with cerebral palsy and his or her companions, the companions have an independent right of action under the ADA and this section.

During the legislative process, the term "entity" was added to section 302(b)(1)(E) to clarify that the scope of the provision is intended to encompass not only persons who have a known association with a person with a disability, but also entities that provide services to or are otherwise associated with such individuals. This provision was intended to ensure

REGULATION

ANALYSIS

that entities such as health care providers, employees of social service agencies, and others who provide professional services to persons with disabilities are not subjected to discrimination because of their professional association with persons with disabilities.

REGULATION

§35.131 Illegal use of drugs.

(a) General. (1) Except as provided in paragraph (b) of this section, this part does not prohibit discrimination against an individual based on that individual's current illegal use of drugs.

(2) A public entity shall not discriminate on the basis of illegal use of drugs against an individual who is not engaging in current illegal use of drugs and who--

(i) Has successfully completed a supervised drug rehabilitation program or has otherwise been rehabilitated successfully;

(ii) Is participating in a supervised rehabilitation program; or

(iii) Is erroneously regarded as engaging in such use.

(b) Health and drug rehabilitation services. (1) A public entity shall not deny health services, or services provided in connection with drug rehabilitation, to an individual on the basis of that individual's current illegal use of drugs, if the individual is otherwise entitled to such services.

(2) A drug rehabilitation or treatment program may

ANALYSIS

§35.131 Illegal use of drugs.

Section 35.131 effectuates section 510 of the ADA, which clarifies the Act's application to people who use drugs illegally. Paragraph (a) provides that this part does not prohibit discrimination based on an individual's current illegal use of drugs.

The Act and the regulation distinguish between illegal use of drugs and the legal use of substances, whether or not those substances are "controlled substances," as defined in the Controlled Substances Act (21 U.S.C. 812). Some controlled substances are prescription drugs that have legitimate medical uses. Section 35.131 does not affect use of controlled substances pursuant to a valid prescription under supervision by a licensed health care professional, or other use that is authorized by the Controlled Substances Act or any other provision of Federal law. It does apply to illegal use of those substances, as well as to illegal use of controlled substances that are not prescription drugs. The key question is whether the individual's use of the substance is illegal, not whether the substance has recognized legal uses. Alcohol is not a controlled substance, so use of alcohol is not addressed by §35.131 (although alcoholics are individuals with disabilities, subject to the protections of the statute).

A distinction is also made between the use of a substance and the status of being addicted to that substance. Addiction is a disability, and addicts are individuals with disabilities protected by the Act. The protection, however, does not extend to actions based on the illegal use of the substance. In other words, an addict cannot use the fact of his or her addiction as a defense to an action based on illegal use of drugs. This distinction is not artificial. Congress intended to deny protection to people who engage in the illegal use of drugs, whether or not they are addicted, but to provide protection to addicts so long as they are not currently using drugs.

A third distinction is the difficult one between current use and former use. The definition of "current illegal use of drugs" in §35.104, which is based on the report of the Conference Committee, H.R. Conf. Rep. No. 596, 101st Cong., 2d Sess. 64 (1990) [hereinafter "Conference report"], is "illegal use of drugs that occurred recently enough to justify a reasonable belief that a person's drug use is current or that continuing use is a real and ongoing problem."

REGULATION

deny participation to individuals who engage in illegal use of drugs while they are in the program.

(c) Drug testing. (1) This part does not prohibit a public entity from adopting or administering reasonable policies or procedures, including but not limited to drug testing, designed to ensure that an individual who formerly engaged in the illegal use of drugs is not now engaging in current illegal use of drugs.

(2) Nothing in paragraph (c) of this section shall be construed to encourage, prohibit, restrict, or authorize the conduct of testing for the illegal use of drugs.

ANALYSIS

Paragraph (a)(2)(i) specifies that an individual who has successfully completed a supervised drug rehabilitation program or has otherwise been rehabilitated successfully and who is not engaging in current illegal use of drugs is protected. Paragraph (a)(2)(ii) clarifies that an individual who is currently participating in a supervised rehabilitation program and is not engaging in current illegal use of drugs is protected. Paragraph (a)(2)(iii) provides that a person who is erroneously regarded as engaging in current illegal use of drugs, but who is not engaging in such use, is protected.

Paragraph (b) provides a limited exception to the exclusion of current illegal users of drugs from the protections of the Act. It prohibits denial of health services, or services provided in connection with drug rehabilitation to an individual on the basis of current illegal use of drugs, if the individual is otherwise entitled to such services. A health care facility, such as a hospital or clinic, may not refuse treatment to an individual in need of the services it provides on the grounds that the individual is illegally using drugs, but it is not required by this section to provide services that it does not ordinarily provide. For example, a health care facility that specializes in a particular type of treatment, such as care of burn victims, is not required to provide drug rehabilitation services, but it cannot refuse to treat a individual's burns on the grounds that the individual is illegally using drugs.

Some commenters pointed out that abstention from the use of drugs is an essential condition of participation in some drug rehabilitation programs, and may be a necessary requirement in inpatient or residential settings. The Department believes that this comment is well-founded. Congress clearly intended to prohibit exclusion from drug treatment programs of the very individuals who need such programs because of their use of drugs, but, once an individual has been admitted to a program, abstention may be a necessary and appropriate condition to continued participation. The final rule therefore provides that a drug rehabilitation or treatment program may prohibit illegal use of drugs by individuals while they are participating in the program.

Paragraph (c) expresses Congress' intention that the Act be neutral with respect to testing for illegal use of drugs. This paragraph implements the provision in section 510(b) of the Act that allows entities "to adopt or administer reasonable policies or procedures, including but not limited to drug

REGULATION

testing," that ensure that an individual who is participating in a supervised rehabilitation program, or who has completed such a program or otherwise been rehabilitated successfully is no longer engaging in the illegal use of drugs. The section is not to be "construed to encourage, prohibit, restrict, or authorize the conducting of testing for the illegal use of drugs."

Paragraph 35.131(c) clarifies that it is not a violation of this part to adopt or administer reasonable policies or procedures to ensure that an individual who formerly engaged in the illegal use of drugs is not currently engaging in illegal use of drugs. Any such policies or procedures must, of course, be reasonable, and must be designed to identify accurately the illegal use of drugs. This paragraph does not authorize inquiries, tests, or other procedures that would disclose use of substances that are not controlled substances or are taken under supervision by a licensed health care professional, or other uses authorized by the Controlled Substances Act or other provisions of Federal law, because such uses are not included in the definition of "illegal use of drugs." A commenter argued that the rule should permit testing for lawful use of prescription drugs, but most commenters preferred that tests must be limited to unlawful use in order to avoid revealing the lawful use of prescription medicine used to treat disabilities.

REGULATION

§35.132 Smoking.

This part does not preclude the prohibition of, or the imposition of restrictions on, smoking in transportation covered by this part.

ANALYSIS

§35.132 Smoking.

Section 35.132 restates the clarification in section 501(b) of the Act that the Act does not preclude the prohibition of, or imposition of restrictions on, smoking in transportation covered by title II. Some commenters argued that this section is too limited in scope, and that the regulation should prohibit smoking in all facilities used by public entities. The reference to smoking in section 501, however, merely clarifies that the Act does not require public entities to accommodate smokers by permitting them to smoke in transportation facilities.

REGULATION

§35.133 Maintenance of accessible features.

(a) A public accommodation shall maintain in operable working condition those features of facilities and equipment that are required to be readily accessible to and usable by persons with disabilities by the Act or this part.

(b) This section does not prohibit isolated or temporary interruptions in service or access due to maintenance or repairs.

ANALYSIS

§35.133 Maintenance of accessible features.

Section 35.133 provides that a public entity shall maintain in operable working condition those features of facilities and equipment that are required to be readily accessible to and usable by persons with disabilities by the Act or this part. The Act requires that, to the maximum extent feasible, facilities must be accessible to, and usable by, individuals with disabilities. This section recognizes that it is not sufficient to provide features such as accessible routes, elevators, or ramps, if those features are not maintained in a manner that enables individuals with disabilities to use them. Inoperable elevators, locked accessible doors, or "accessible" routes that are obstructed by furniture, filing cabinets, or potted plants are neither "accessible to" nor "usable by" individuals with disabilities.

Some commenters objected that this section appeared to establish an absolute requirement and suggested that language from the preamble be included in the text of the regulation. It is, of course, impossible to guarantee that mechanical devices will never fail to operate. Paragraph (b) of the final regulation provides that this section does not prohibit isolated or temporary interruptions in service or access due to maintenance or repairs. This paragraph is intended to clarify that temporary obstructions or isolated instances of mechanical failure would not be considered violations of the Act or this part. However, allowing obstructions or "out of service" equipment to persist beyond a reasonable period of time would violate this part, as would repeated mechanical failures due to improper or inadequate maintenance. Failure of the public entity to ensure that accessible routes are properly maintained and free of obstructions, or failure to arrange prompt repair of inoperable elevators or other equipment intended to provide access would also violate this part.

Other commenters requested that this section be expanded to include specific requirements for inspection and maintenance of equipment, for training staff in the proper operation of equipment, and for maintenance of specific items. The Department believes that this section properly establishes the general requirement for maintaining access and that further details are not necessary.

REGULATION
§35.134 Retaliation or coercion.

(a) No private or public entity shall discriminate against any individual because that individual has opposed any act or practice made unlawful by this part, or because that individual made a charge, testified, assisted, or participated in any manner in an investigation, proceeding, or hearing under the Act or this part.

(b) No private or public entity shall coerce, intimidate, threaten, or interfere with any individual in the exercise or enjoyment of, or on account of his or her having exercised or enjoyed, or on account of his or her having aided or encouraged any other individual in the exercise or enjoyment of, any right granted or protected by the Act or this part.

ANALYSIS
§35.134 Retaliation or coercion.

Section 35.134 implements section 503 of the ADA, which prohibits retaliation against any individual who exercises his or her rights under the Act. This section is unchanged from the proposed rule. Paragraph (a) of §35.134 provides that no private or public entity shall discriminate against any individual because that individual has exercised his or her right to oppose any act or practice made unlawful by this part, or because that individual made a charge, testified, assisted, or participated in any manner in an investigation, proceeding, or hearing under the Act or this part.

Paragraph (b) provides that no private or public entity shall coerce, intimidate, threaten, or interfere with any individual in the exercise of his or her rights under this part or because that individual aided or encouraged any other individual in the exercise or enjoyment of any right granted or protected by the Act or this part.

This section protects not only individuals who allege a violation of the Act or this part, but also any individuals who support or assist them. This section applies to all investigations or proceedings initiated under the Act or this part without regard to the ultimate resolution of the underlying allegations. Because this section prohibits any act of retaliation or coercion in response to an individual's effort to exercise rights established by the Act and this part (or to support the efforts of another individual), the section applies not only to public entities subject to this part, but also to persons acting in an individual capacity or to private entities. For example, it would be a violation of the Act and this part for a private individual to harass or intimidate an individual with a disability in an effort to prevent that individual from attending a concert in a State-owned park. It would, likewise, be a violation of the Act and this part for a private entity to take adverse action against an employee who appeared as a witness on behalf of an individual who sought to enforce the Act.

REGULATION

§35.135 Personal devices and services.

This part does not require a public entity to provide to individuals with disabilities personal devices, such as wheelchairs; individually prescribed devices, such as prescription eyeglasses or hearing aids; readers for personal use or study; or services of a personal nature including assistance in eating, toileting, or dressing.

§§35.136-35.139 [Reserved]

ANALYSIS

§35.135 Personal devices and services.

The final rule includes a new §35.135, entitles "Personal devices and services," which states that the provision of personal devices and services is not required by title II. This new section, which serves as a limitation on all of the requirements of the regulation, replaces §35.160(b)(2) of the proposed rule, which addressed the issue of personal devices and services explicitly only in the context of communications. The personal devices and services limitation was intended to have general application in the proposed rule in all contexts where it was relevant. The final rule, therefore, clarifies this point by including a general provision that will explicitly apply not only to auxiliary aids and services but across-the-board to include other relevant areas such as, for example, modifications in policies, practices, and procedures (§35.130(b)(7)). The language of §35.135 parallels an analogous provision in the Department's title III regulations (28 CFR §36.306) but preserves the explicit reference to "readers for personal use or study" in §35.160(b)(2) of the proposed rule. This section does not preclude the short-term loan of personal receivers that are part of an assistive listening system.

REGULATION
Subpart C -- Employment

§35.140 Employment discrimination prohibited.

(a) No qualified individual with a disability shall, on the basis of disability, be subjected to discrimination in employment under any service, program, or activity conducted by a public entity.

(b)(1) For purposes of this part, the requirements of title I of the Act, as established by the regulations of the Equal Employment Opportunity Commission in 29 CFR part 1630, apply to employment in any service, program, or activity conducted by a public entity if that public entity is also subject to the jurisdiction of title I.

(2) For the purposes of this part, the requirements of section 504 of the Rehabilitation Act of 1973, as established by the regulations of the Department of Justice in 28 CFR part 41, as those requirements pertain to employment, apply to em-

ANALYSIS
Subpart C -- Employment

§35.140 Employment discrimination prohibited.

Title II of the ADA applies to all activities of public entities, including their employment practices. The proposed rule cross-referenced the definitions, requirements, and procedures of title I of the ADA, as established by the Equal Employment Opportunity Commission in 29 CFR Part 1630. This proposal would have resulted in use, under §35.140, of the title I definition of "employer," so that a public entity with 25 or more employees would have become subject to the requirements of §35.140 on July 26, 1992, one with 15 to 24 employees on July 26, 1994, and one with fewer than 15 employees would have been excluded completely.

The Department received comments objecting to this approach. The commenters asserted that Congress intended to establish nondiscrimination requirements for employment by all public entities, including those that employ fewer than 15 employees; and that Congress intended the employment requirements of title II to become effective at the same time that the other requirements of this regulation become effective, January 26, 1992. The Department has reexamined the statutory language and legislative history of the ADA on this issue and has concluded that Congress intended to cover the employment practices of all public entities and that the applicable effective date is that of title II.

The statutory language of section 204(b) of the ADA requires the Department to issue a regulation that is consistent with the ADA and the Department's coordination regulation under section 504, 28 CFR part 41. The coordination regulation specifically requires nondiscrimination in employment, 28 CFR §§41.52-41.55, and does not limit coverage based on size of employer. Moreover, under all section 504 implementing regulations issued in accordance with the Department's coordination regulation, employment coverage under section 504 extends to all employers with federally assisted programs or activities, regardless of size, and the effective date for those employment requirements has always been the same as the effective date for nonemployment requirements established in the same regulations. The Department therefore concludes that §35.140 must apply to all public entities upon the effective date of this regulation.

In the proposed regulation the Department cross-refer-

REGULATION

ployment in any service, program, or activity conducted by a public entity if that public entity is not also subject to the jurisdiction of title I.

§§35.141-35.148 [Reserved]

ANALYSIS

enced the regulations implementing title I of the ADA, issued by the Equal Employment Opportunity Commission at 29 CFR part 1630, as a compliance standard for §35.140 because, as proposed, the scope of coverage and effective date of coverage under title II would have been coextensive with title I. In the final regulation this language is modified slightly. Subparagraph (1) of new paragraph (b) makes it clear that the standards established by the Equal Employment Opportunity Commission in 29 CFR part 1630 will be the applicable compliance standards if the public entity is subject to title I. If the public entity is not covered by title I, or until it is covered by title I, subparagraph (b)(2) cross-references section 504 standards for what constitutes employment discrimination, as established by the Department of Justice in 28 CFR part 41. Standards for title I of the ADA and section 504 of the Rehabilitation Act are for the most part identical because title I of the ADA was based on requirements set forth in regulations implementing section 504.

The Department, together with the other Federal agencies responsible for the enforcement of Federal laws prohibiting employment discrimination on the basis of disability, recognizes the potential for jurisdictional overlap that exists with respect to coverage of public entities and the need to avoid problems related to overlapping coverage. The other Federal agencies include the Equal Employment Opportunity Commission, which is the agency primarily responsible for enforcement of title I of the ADA, the Department of Labor, which is the agency responsible for enforcement of section 503 of the Rehabilitation Act of 1973, and 26 Federal agencies with programs of Federal financial assistance, which are responsible for enforcing section 504 in those programs. Section 107 of the ADA requires that coordination mechanisms be developed in connection with the administrative enforcement of complaints alleging discrimination under title I and complaints alleging discrimination in employment in violation of the Rehabilitation Act. Although the ADA does not specifically require inclusion of employment complaints under title II in the coordinating mechanisms required by title I, Federal investigations of title II employment complaints will be coordinated on a government-wide basis also. The Department is currently working with the EEOC and other affected Federal agencies to develop effective coordinating mechanisms, and final regulations on this issue will be issued on or before January 26, 1992.

REGULATION
Subpart D -- Program Accessibility

§35.149 Discrimination prohibited.

Except as otherwise provided in §35.150, no qualified individual with a disability shall, because a public entity's facilities are inaccessible to or unusable by individuals with disabilities, be excluded from participation in, or be denied the benefits of the services, programs, or activities of a public entity, or be subjected to discrimination by any public entity.

ANALYSIS
Subpart D -- Program Accessibility

§35.149 Discrimination prohibited.

Section 35.149 states the general nondiscrimination principle underlying the program accessibility requirements of §§35.150 and 35.151.

REGULATION

§35.150 Existing facilities.

(a) <u>General</u>. A public entity shall operate each service, program, or activity so that the service, program, or activity, when viewed in its entirety, is readily accessible to and usable by individuals with disabilities. This paragraph does not --

(1) Necessarily require a public entity to make each of its existing facilities accessible to and usable by individuals with disabilities;

(2) Require a public entity to take any action that would threaten or destroy the historic significance of an historic property; or

(3) Require a public entity to take any action that it can demonstrate would result in a fundamental alteration in the nature of a service, program, or activity or in undue financial and administrative burdens. In those circumstances where personnel of the public entity believe that the proposed action would fundamentally alter the service, program, or activity or would result in undue financial and administrative burdens, a public entity has the burden of proving that compliance with §35.150(a) of this part would result in such alteration or burdens. The decision that compliance would result in such alteration or burdens

ANALYSIS

§35.150 Existing facilities.

Consistent with section 204(b) of the Act, this regulation adopts the program accessibility concept found in the section 504 regulations for federally conducted programs or activities (e.g., 28 CFR Part 39). The concept of "program accessibility" was first used in the section 504 regulation adopted by the Department of Health, Education, and Welfare for its federally assisted programs and activities in 1977. It allowed recipients to make their federally assisted programs and activities available to individuals with disabilities without extensive retrofitting of their existing buildings and facilities, by offering those programs through alternative methods. Program accessibility has proven to be a useful approach and was adopted in the regulations issued for programs and activities conducted by Federal Executive agencies. The Act provides that the concept of program access will continue to apply with respect to facilities now in existence, because the cost of retrofitting existing facilities is often prohibitive.

Section 35.150 requires that each service, program, or activity conducted by a public entity, when viewed in its entirety, be readily accessible to and usable by individuals with disabilities. The regulation makes clear, however, that a public entity is not required to make each of its existing facilities accessible (§35.150(a)(1)). Unlike title III of the Act, which requires public accommodations to remove architectural barriers where such removal is "readily achievable," or to provide goods and services through alternative methods, where those methods are "readily achievable," title II requires a public entity to make its programs accessible in all cases, except where to do so would result in a fundamental alteration in the nature of the program or in undue financial and administrative burdens. Congress intended the "undue burden" standard in title II to be significantly higher than the "readily achievable" standard in title III. Thus, although title II may not require removal of barriers in some cases where removal would be required under title III, the program access requirement of title II should enable individuals with disabilities to participate in and benefit from the services, programs, or activities of public entities in all but the most unusual cases.

Paragraph (a)(2), which establishes a special limitation on the obligation to ensure program accessibility in historic preservation programs, is discussed below in connection with paragraph (b).

REGULATION

must be made by the head of a public entity or his or her designee after considering all resources available for use in the funding and operation of the service, program, or activity, and must be accompanied by a written statement of the reasons for reaching that conclusion. If an action would result in such an alteration or such burdens, a public entity shall take any other action that would not result in such an alteration or such burdens but would nevertheless ensure that individuals with disabilities receive the benefits or services provided by the public entity.

(b) Methods. (1) General. A public entity may comply with the requirements of this section through such means as redesign of equipment, reassignment of services to accessible buildings, assignment of aides to beneficiaries, home visits, delivery of services at alternate accessible sites, alteration of existing facilities and construction of new facilities, use of accessible rolling stock or other conveyances, or any other methods that result in making its services, programs, or activities readily accessible to and usable by individuals with disabilities. A public entity is not required to make structural changes in existing facilities where other meth-

ANALYSIS

Paragraph (a)(3), which is taken from the section 504 regulations for federally conducted programs, generally codifies case law that defines the scope of the public entity's obligation to ensure program accessibility. This paragraph provides that, in meeting the program accessibility requirement, a public entity is not required to take any action that would result in a fundamental alteration in the nature of its service, program, or activity or in undue financial and administrative burdens. A similar limitation is provided in §35.164.

This paragraph does not establish an absolute defense; it does not relieve a public entity of all obligations to individuals with disabilities. Although a public entity is not required to take actions that would result in a fundamental alteration in the nature of a service, program, or activity or in undue financial and administrative burdens, it nevertheless must take any other steps necessary to ensure that individuals with disabilities receive the benefits or services provided by the public entity.

It is the Department's view that compliance with §35.150(a), like compliance with the corresponding provisions of the section 504 regulations for federally conducted programs, would in most cases not result in undue financial and administrative burdens on a public entity. In determining whether financial and administrative burdens are undue, all public entity resources available for use in the funding and operation of the service, program, or activity should be considered. The burden of proving that compliance with paragraph (a) of §35.150 would fundamentally alter the nature of a service, program, or activity or would result in undue financial and administrative burdens rests with the public entity.

The decision that compliance would result in such alteration or burdens must be made by the head of the public entity or his or her designee and must be accompanied by a written statement of the reasons for reaching that conclusion. The Department recognizes the difficulty of identifying the official responsible for this determination, given the variety of organizational forms that may be taken by public entities and their components. The intention of this paragraph is that the determination must be made by a high level official, no lower than a Department head, having budgetary authority and responsibility for making spending decisions.

REGULATION

ods are effective in achieving compliance with this section. A public entity, in making alterations to existing buildings, shall meet the accessibility requirements of §35.151. In choosing among available methods for meeting the requirements of this section, a public entity shall give priority to those methods that offer services, programs, and activities to qualified individuals with disabilities in the most integrated setting appropriate.

(2) Historic preservation programs. In meeting the requirements of §35.150(a) in historic preservation programs, a public entity shall give priority to methods that provide physical access to individuals with disabilities. In cases where a physical alteration to an historic property is not required because of paragraph (a)(2) or (a)(3) of this section, alternative methods of achieving program accessibility include --

(i) Using audio-visual materials and devices to depict those portions of an historic property that cannot otherwise be made accessible;

(ii) Assigning persons to guide individuals with handicaps into or through portions of historic proper-

ANALYSIS

Any person who believes that he or she or any specific class of persons has been injured by the public entity head's decision or failure to make a decision may file a complaint under the compliance procedures established in subpart F.

Paragraph (b)(1) sets forth a number of means by which program accessibility may be achieved, including redesign of equipment, reassignment of services to accessible buildings, and provision of aides.

The Department wishes to clarify that, consistent with longstanding interpretation of section 504, carrying an individual with a disability is considered an ineffective and therefore an unacceptable method for achieving program accessibility. Department of Health, Education, and Welfare, Office of Civil Rights, Policy Interpretation No. 4, 43 Fed. Reg. 36035 (August 14, 1978). Carrying will be permitted only in manifestly exceptional cases, and only if all personnel who are permitted to participate in carrying an individual with a disability are formally instructed on the safest and least humiliating means of carrying. "Manifestly exceptional" cases in which carrying would be permitted might include, for example, programs conducted in unique facilities, such as an oceanographic vessel, for which structural changes and devices necessary to adapt the facility for use by individuals with mobility impairments are unavailable or prohibitively expensive. Carrying is not permitted as an alternative to structural modifications such as installation of a ramp or a chairlift.

In choosing among methods, the public entity shall give priority consideration to those that will be consistent with provision of services in the most integrated setting appropriate to the needs of individuals with disabilities. Structural changes in existing facilities are required only when there is no other feasible way to make the public entity's program accessible. (It should be noted that "structural changes" include all physical changes to a facility; the term does not refer only to changes to structural features, such as removal of or alteration to a load-bearing structural member.) The requirements of §35.151 for alterations apply to structural changes undertaken to comply with this section. The public entity may comply with the program accessibility requirement by delivering services at alternate accessible sites or making home visits as appropriate.

REGULATION

ties that cannot otherwise be made accessible; or

(iii) Adopting other innovative methods.

(c) Time period for compliance. Where structural changes in facilities are undertaken to comply with the obligations established under this section, such changes shall be made within three years of January 26, 1992, but in any event as expeditiously as possible.

(d) Transition plan. (1) In the event that structural changes to facilities will be undertaken to achieve program accessibility, a public entity that employs 50 or more persons shall develop, within six months of January 26, 1992, a transition plan setting forth the steps necessary to complete such changes. A public entity shall provide an opportunity to interested persons, including individuals with disabilities or organizations representing individuals with disabilities, to participate in the development of the transition plan by submitting comments. A copy of the transition plan shall be made available for public inspection.

(2) If a public entity has responsibility or authority over streets, roads, or walkways, its transition plan shall

ANALYSIS

Historic preservation programs. In order to avoid possible conflict between the congressional mandates to preserve historic properties, on the one hand, and to eliminate discrimination against individuals with disabilities on the other, paragraph (a)(2) provides that a public entity is not required to take any action that would threaten or destroy the historic significance of an historic property. The special limitation on program accessibility set forth in paragraph (a)(2) is applicable only to historic preservation programs, as defined in §35.104, that is, programs that have preservation of historic properties as a primary purpose. Narrow application of the special limitation is justified because of the inherent flexibility of the program accessibility requirement. Where historic preservation is not a primary purpose of the program, the public entity is not required to use a particular facility. It can relocate all or part of its program to an accessible facility, make home visits, or use other standard methods of achieving program accessibility without making structural alterations that might threaten or destroy significant historic features of the historic property. Thus, government programs located in historic properties, such as an historic State capitol, are not excused from the requirement for program access.

Paragraph (a)(2), therefore, will apply only to those programs that uniquely concern the preservation and experience of the historic property itself. Because the primary benefit of an historic preservation program is the experience of the historic property, paragraph (b)(2) requires the public entity to give priority to methods of providing program accessibility that permit individuals with disabilities to have physical access to the historic property. This priority on physical access may also be viewed as a specific application of the general requirement that the public entity administer programs in the most integrated setting appropriate to the needs of qualified individuals with disabilities (§35.130(d)). Only when providing physical access would threaten or destroy the historic significance of an historic property, or would result in a fundamental alteration in the nature of the program or in undue financial and administrative burdens, may the public entity adopt alternative methods for providing program accessibility that do not ensure physical access. Examples of some alternative methods are provided in paragraph (b)(2).

Time periods. Paragraphs (c) and (d) establish time periods for complying with the program accessibility require-

REGULATION

include a schedule for
providing curb ramps or
other sloped areas where
pedestrian walks cross curbs,
giving priority to walkways
serving entities covered by
the Act, including State and
local government offices and
facilities, transportation,
places of public accommodation, and employers, fol-
lowed by walkways serving
other areas.

(3) The plan shall, at a
minimum --

(i) Identify physical
obstacles in the public
entity's facilities that limit
the accessibility of its programs or activities to individuals with disabilities;

(ii) Describe in detail the
methods that will be used to
make the facilities accessible;

(iii) Specify the sched-
ule for taking the steps
necessary to achieve compliance with this section and, if
the time period of the transition plan is longer than one
year, identify steps that will
be taken during each year of
the transition period; and

(iv) Indicate the official
responsible for implementation of the plan.

(4) If a public entity has
already complied with the
transition plan requirement

ANALYSIS

ment. Like the regulations for federally assisted programs
(e.g., 28 CFR 41.57(b)), paragraph (c) requires the public
entity to make any necessary structural changes in facilities
as soon as practicable, but in no event later than three years
after the effective date of this regulation.

The proposed rule provided that, aside from structural
changes, all other necessary steps to achieve compliance with
this part must be taken within sixty days. The sixty day
period was taken from regulations implementing section 504,
which generally were effective no more than thirty days after
publication. Because this regulation will not be effective
until January 26, 1992, the Department has concluded that no
additional transition period for non-structural changes is
necessary, so the sixty day period has been omitted in the
final rule. Of course, this section does not reduce or eliminate any obligations that are already applicable to a public
entity under section 504.

Where structural modifications are required, paragraph
(d) requires that a transition plan be developed by an entity
that employs 50 or more persons, within six months of the
effective date of this regulation. The legislative history of
title II of the ADA makes it clear that, under title II, "local
and state governments are required to provide curb cuts on
public streets." Education and Labor report at 84. As the
rationale for the provision of curb cuts, the House report
explains, "The employment, transportation, and public
accommodation sections of . . . [the ADA] would be meaningless if people who use wheelchairs were not afforded the
opportunity to travel on and between the streets." Id. Section 35.151(e), which establishes accessibility requirements
for new construction and alterations, requires that all newly
constructed or altered streets, roads, or highways must
contain curb ramps or other sloped areas at any intersection
having curbs or other barriers to entry from a street level
pedestrian walkway, and all newly constructed or altered
street level pedestrian walkways must have curb ramps or
other sloped areas at intersections to streets, roads, or highways. A new paragraph (d)(2) has been added to the final
rule to clarify the application of the general requirement for
program accessibility to the provision of curb cuts at existing crosswalks. This paragraph requires that the transition
plan include a schedule for providing curb ramps or other
sloped areas at existing pedestrian walkways, giving priority
to walkways serving entities covered by the Act, including

REGULATION

of a Federal agency regulation implementing section 504 of the Rehabilitation Act of 1973, then the requirements of this paragraph (d) shall apply only to those policies and practices that were not included in the previous transition plan.

ANALYSIS

State and local government offices and facilities, transportation, public accommodations, and employers, followed by walkways serving other areas. Pedestrian "walkways" include locations where access is required for use of public transportation, such as bus stops that are not located at intersections or crosswalks.

Similarly, a public entity should provide an adequate number of accessible parking spaces in existing parking lots or garages over which it has jurisdiction.

Paragraph (d)(3) provides that, if a public entity has already completed a transition plan required by a regulation implementing section 504, the transition plan required by this part will apply only to those policies and practices that were not covered by the previous transition plan. Some commenters suggested that the transition plan should include all aspects of the public entity's operations, including those that may have been covered by a previous transition plan under section 504. The Department believes that such a duplicative requirement would be inappropriate. Many public entities may find, however, that it will be simpler to include all of their operations in the transition plan than to attempt to identify and exclude specifically those that were addressed in a previous plan. Of course, entities covered under section 504 are not shielded from their obligations under that statute merely because they are included under the transition plan developed under this section.

REGULATION

§35.151 New construction and alterations.

(a) <u>Design and construction</u>. Each facility or part of a facility constructed by, on behalf of, or for the use of a public entity shall be designed and constructed in such manner that the facility or part of the facility is readily accessible to and usable by individuals with disabilities, if the construction was commenced after January 26, 1992.

(b) <u>Alteration</u>. Each facility or part of a facility altered by, on behalf of, or for the use of a public entity in a manner that affects or could affect the usability of the facility or part of the facility shall, to the maximum extent feasible, be altered in such manner that the altered portion of the facility is readily accessible to and usable by individuals with disabilities, if the alteration was commenced after January 26, 1992.

(c) <u>Accessibility standards</u>. Design, construction, or alteration of facilities in conformance with the Uniform Federal Accessibility Standards (UFAS) (Appendix A to 41 CFR part 101-19.6) or with the Americans with Disabilities Act Accessibility Guidelines for Buildings and Facilities (ADAAG) (Appendix A to 28 CFR part 36 shall be

ANALYSIS

§35.151 New construction and alterations.

Section 35.151 provides that those buildings that are constructed or altered by, on behalf of, or for the use of a public entity shall be designed, constructed, or altered to be readily accessible to and usable by individuals with disabilities if the construction was commenced after the effective date of this part. Facilities under design on that date will be governed by this section if the date that bids were invited falls after the effective date. This interpretation is consistent with Federal practice under section 504.

Section 35.151(c) establishes two standards for accessible new construction and alteration. Under paragraph (c), design, construction, or alteration of facilities in conformance with the Uniform Federal Accessibility Standards (UFAS) or with the Americans with Disabilities Act Accessibility Guidelines for Buildings and Facilities (hereinafter ADAAG) shall be deemed to comply with the requirements of this section with respect to those facilities except that, if ADAAG is chosen, the elevator exemption contained at §§36.401(d) and 36.404 does not apply. ADAAG is the standard for private buildings and was issued as guidelines by the Architectural and Transportation Barriers Compliance Board (ATBCB) under title III of the ADA. It has been adopted by the Department of Justice and is published as Appendix A to the Department's title III rule in today's <u>Federal Register</u>. Departures from particular requirements of these standards by the use of other methods shall be permitted when it is clearly evident that equivalent access to the facility or part of the facility is thereby provided. Use of two standards is a departure from the proposed rule.

The proposed rule adopted UFAS as the only interim accessibility standard because that standard was referenced by the regulations implementing section 504 of the Rehabilitation Act promulgated by most Federal funding agencies. It is, therefore, familiar to many State and local government entities subject to this rule. The Department, however, received many comments objecting to the adoption of UFAS. Commenters pointed out that, except for the elevator exemption, UFAS is not as stringent as ADAAG. Others suggested that the standard should be the same to lessen confusion.

Section 204(b) of the Act states that title II regulations must be consistent not only with section 504 regulations but also with "this Act." Based on this provision, the Depart-

REGULATION

deemed to comply with the
requirements of this section
with respect to those facilities, except that the elevator
exemption contained at
§4.1.3(5) and §4.1.6(1)(j) of
ADAAG shall not apply.
Departures from particular
requirements of either
standard by the use of other
methods shall be permitted
when it is clearly evident
that equivalent access to the
facility or part of the facility
is thereby provided.

(d) Alterations: Historic
properties. (1) Alterations
to historic properties shall
comply, to the maximum
extent feasible, with §4.1.7 of
UFAS or §4.1.7 of ADAAG.

(2) If it is not feasible to
provide physical access to an
historic property in a manner
that will not threaten or
destroy the historic significance of the building or
facility, alternative methods
of access shall be provided
pursuant to the requirements
of §35.150.

(e) Curb ramps. (1)
Newly constructed or altered
streets, roads, and highways
must contain curb ramps or
other sloped areas at any
intersection having curbs or
other barriers to entry from a
street level pedestrian walkway.

(2) Newly constructed
or altered street level pedes-

ANALYSIS

ment has determined that a public entity should be entitled to
choose to comply either with ADAAG or UFAS.

Public entities who choose to follow ADAAG, however, are
not entitled to the elevator exemption contained in title III of the
Act and implemented in the title III regulation at §36.401(d) for
new construction and §36.404 for alterations. Section 303(b) of
title III states that, with some exceptions, elevators are not
required in facilities that are less than three stories or have less
than 3000 square feet per story. The section 504 standard,
UFAS, contains no such exemption. Section 501 of the ADA
makes clear that nothing in the Act may be construed to apply a
lesser standard to public entities than the standards applied
under section 504. Because permitting the elevator exemption
would clearly result in application of a lesser standard than that
applied under section 504, paragraph (c) states that the elevator
exemption does not apply when public entities choose to follow
ADAAG. Thus, a two-story courthouse, whether built according to UFAS or ADAAG, must be constructed with an elevator.
It should be noted that Congress did not include an elevator
exemption for public transit facilities covered by subtitle B of
title II, which covers public transportation provided by public
entities, providing further evidence that Congress intended that
public buildings have elevators.

Section 504 of the ADA requires the ATBCB to issue
supplemental Minimum Guidelines and Requirements for
Accessible Design of buildings and facilities subject to the
Act, including title II. Section 204(c) of the ADA provides
that the Attorney General shall promulgate regulations implementing title II that are consistent with the ATBCB's ADA
guidelines. The ATBCB has announced its intention to issue
title II guidelines in the future. The Department anticipates
that, after the ATBCB's title II guidelines have been published, this rule will be amended to adopt new accessibility
standards consistent with the ATBCB's rulemaking. Until
that time, however, public entities will have a choice of
following UFAS or ADAAG, without the elevator exemption.

Existing buildings leased by the public entity after the
effective date of this part are not required by the regulation to
meet accessibility standards simply by virtue of being leased.
They are subject, however, to the program accessibility standard
for existing facilities in §35.150. To the extent the buildings are
newly constructed or altered, they must also meet the new
construction and alteration requirements of §35.151.

REGULATION

trian walkways must contain
curb ramps or other sloped
areas at intersections to
streets, roads, or highways.

§§35.152-35.159 [Reserved]

ANALYSIS

The Department received many comments urging that the Department require that public entities lease only accessible buildings. Federal practice under section 504 has always treated newly leased buildings as subject to the existing facility program accessibility standard. Section 204(b) of the Act states that, in the area of "program accessibility, existing facilities," the title II regulations must be consistent with section 504 regulations. Thus, the Department has adopted the section 504 principles for these types of leased buildings. Unlike the construction of new buildings where architectural barriers can be avoided at little or no cost, the application of new construction standards to an existing building being leased raises the same prospect of retrofitting buildings as the use of an existing Federal facility, and the same program accessibility standard should apply to both owned and leased existing buildings. Similarly, requiring that public entities only lease accessible space would significantly restrict the options of State and local governments in seeking leased space, which would be particularly burdensome in rural or sparsely populated areas.

On the other hand, the more accessible the leased space is, the fewer structural modifications will be required in the future for particular employees whose disabilities may necessitate barrier removal as a reasonable accommodation. Pursuant to the requirements for leased buildings contained in the Minimum Guidelines and Requirements for Accessible Design published under the Architectural Barriers Act by the ATBCB, 36 CFR 1190.34, the Federal Government may not lease a building unless it contains (1) one accessible route from an accessible entrance to those areas in which the principal activities for which the building is leased are conducted, (2) accessible toilet facilities, and (3) accessible parking facilities, if a parking area is included within the lease (36 CFR 1190.34). Although these requirements are not applicable to buildings leased by public entities covered by this regulation, such entities are encouraged to look for the most accessible space available to lease and to attempt to find space complying at least with these minimum Federal requirements.

Section 35.151(d) gives effect to the intent of Congress, expressed in section 504(c) of the Act, that this part recognize the national interest in preserving significant historic structures. Commenters criticized the Department's use of descriptive terms in the proposed rule that are different from those used in the ADA to describe eligible historic properties.

REGULATION

In addition, some commenters criticized the Department's decision to use the concept of "substantially impairing" the historic features of a property, which is a concept employed in regulations implementing section 504 of the Rehabilitation Act of 1973. Those commenters recommended that the Department adopt the criteria of "adverse effect" published by the Advisory Council on Historic Preservation under the National Historic Preservation Act, 36 CFR 800.9, as the standard for determining whether an historic property may be altered.

The Department agrees with these comments to the extent that they suggest that the language of the rule should conform to the language employed by Congress in the ADA. A definition of "historic property," drawn from section 504 of the ADA, has been added to §35.104 to clarify that the term applies to those properties listed or eligible for listing in the National Register of Historic Places, or properties designated as historic under State or local law.

The Department intends that the exception created by this section be applied only in those very rare situations in which it is not possible to provide access to an historic property using the special access provisions established by UFAS and ADAAG. Therefore, paragraph (d)(1) of §35.151 has been revised to clearly state that alterations to historic properties shall comply, to the maximum extent feasible, with section 4.1.7 of UFAS or section 4.1.7 of ADAAG. Paragraph (d)(2) has been revised to provide that, if it has been determined under the procedures established in UFAS and ADAAG that it is not feasible to provide physical access to an historic property in a manner that will not threaten or destroy the historic significance of the property, alternative methods of access shall be provided pursuant to the requirements of §35.150.

In response to comments, the Department has added to the final rule a new paragraph (e) setting out the requirements of §36.151 as applied to curb ramps. Paragraph (e) is taken from the statement contained in the preamble to the proposed rule that all newly constructed or altered streets, roads, and highways must contain curb ramps at any intersection having curbs or other barriers to entry from a street level pedestrian walkway, and that all newly constructed or altered street level pedestrian walkways must have curb ramps at intersections to streets, roads, or highways.

REGULATION
Subpart E -- Communications

§35.160 General.

(a) A public entity shall take appropriate steps to ensure that communications with applicants, participants, and members of the public with disabilities are as effective as communications with others.

(b)(1) A public entity shall furnish appropriate auxiliary aids and services where necessary to afford an individual with a disability an equal opportunity to participate in, and enjoy the benefits of, a service, program, or activity conducted by a public entity.

(2) In determining what type of auxiliary aid and service is necessary, a public entity shall give primary consideration to the requests of the individual with disabilities.

ANALYSIS
Subpart E -- Communications

§35.160 General.

Section 35.160 requires the public entity to take such steps as may be necessary to ensure that communications with applicants, participants, and members of the public with disabilities are as effective as communications with others.

Paragraph (b)(1) requires the public entity to furnish appropriate auxiliary aids and services when necessary to afford an individual with a disability an equal opportunity to participate in, and enjoy the benefits of, the public entity's service, program, or activity. The public entity must provide an opportunity for individuals with disabilities to request the auxiliary aids and services of their choice. This expressed choice shall be given primary consideration by the public entity (§35.160(b)(2)). The public entity shall honor the choice unless it can demonstrate that another effective means of communication exists or that use of the means chosen would not be required under §35.164.

Deference to the request of the individual with a disability is desirable because of the range of disabilities, the variety of auxiliary aids and services, and different circumstances requiring effective communication. For instance, some courtrooms are now equipped for "computer-assisted transcripts," which allow virtually instantaneous transcripts of courtroom argument and testimony to appear on displays. Such a system might be an effective auxiliary aid or service for a person who is deaf or has a hearing loss who uses speech to communicate, but may be useless for someone who uses sign language.

Although in some circumstances a notepad and written materials may be sufficient to permit effective communication, in other circumstances they may not be sufficient. For example, a qualified interpreter may be necessary when the information being communicated is complex, or is exchanged for a lengthy period of time. Generally, factors to be considered in determining whether an interpreter is required include the context in which the communication is taking place, the number of people involved, and the importance of the communication.

Several commenters asked that the rule clarify that the

REGULATION

provision of readers is sometimes necessary to ensure access to a public entity's services, programs, or activities. Reading devices or readers should be provided when necessary for equal participation and opportunity to benefit from any governmental service, program, or activity, such as reviewing public documents, examining demonstrative evidence, and filling out voter registration forms or forms needed to receive public benefits. The importance of providing qualified readers for examinations administered by public entities is discussed under §35.130. Reading devices and readers are appropriate auxiliary aids and services where necessary to permit an individual with a disability to participate in or benefit from a service, program, or activity.

Section 35.160(b)(2) of the proposed rule, which provided that a public entity need not furnish individually prescribed devices, readers for personal use or study, or other devices of a personal nature, has been deleted in favor of a new section in the final rule on personal devices and services (see §35.135).

In response to comments, the term "auxiliary aids and services" is used in place of "auxiliary aids" in the final rule. This phrase better reflects the range of aids and services that may be required under this section.

A number of comments raised questions about the extent of a public entity's obligation to provide access to television programming for persons with hearing impairments. Television and videotape programming produced by public entities are covered by this section. Access to audio portions of such programming may be provided by closed captioning.

REGULATION

§35.161 Telecommunication devices for the deaf (TDD's).

Where a public entity communicates by telephone with applicants and beneficiaries, TDD's or equally effective telecommunication systems shall be used to communicate with individuals with impaired hearing or speech.

ANALYSIS

§ 35.161 Telecommunication devices for the deaf (TDD's).

Section 35.161 requires that, where a public entity communicates with applicants and beneficiaries by telephone, TDD's or equally effective telecommunication systems be used to communicate with individuals with impaired speech or hearing.

Problems arise when a public entity which does not have a TDD needs to communicate with an individual who uses a TDD or vice versa. Title IV of the ADA addresses this problem by requiring establishment of telephone relay services to permit communications between individuals who communicate by TDD and individuals who communicate by the telephone alone. The relay services required by title IV would involve a relay operator using both a standard telephone and a TDD to type the voice messages to the TDD user and read the TDD messages to the standard telephone user.

Section 204(b) of the ADA requires that the regulation implementing title II with respect to communications be consistent with the Department's regulation implementing section 504 for its federally conducted programs and activities at 28 CFR pt. 39. Section 35.161, which is taken from §39.160(a)(2) of that regulation, requires the use of TDD's or equally effective telecommunication systems for communication with people who use TDD's. Of course, where relay services, such as those required by title IV of the ADA are available, a public entity may use those services to meet the requirements of this section.

Many commenters were concerned that public entities should not rely heavily on the establishment of relay services. The commenters explained that while relay services would be of vast benefit to both public entities and individuals who use TDD's, the services are not sufficient to provide access to all telephone services. First, relay systems do not provide effective access to the increasingly popular automated systems that require the caller to respond by pushing a button on a touch tone phone. Second, relay systems cannot operate fast enough to convey messages on answering machines, or to permit a TDD user to leave a recorded message. Third, communication through relay systems may not be appropriate in cases of crisis lines pertaining to rape, domestic violence, child abuse, and drugs. The Department believes that it is more appropriate for the Federal Communications Commission to address these issues in its rulemaking under title IV.

REGULATION

Some commenters requested that those entities with frequent contacts with clients who use TDD's have on-site TDD's to provide for direct communication between the entity and the individual. The Department encourages those entities that have extensive telephone contact with the public such as city halls, public libraries, and public aid offices, to have TDD's to insure more immediate access. Where the provision of telephone service is a major function of the entity, TDD's should be available.

REGULATION

§35.162 Telephone emergency services.

Telephone emergency services, including 911 services, shall provide direct access to individuals who use TDD's and computer modems.

ANALYSIS

Section 35.162 Telephone emergency services.

Many public entities provide telephone emergency services by which individuals can seek immediate assistance from police, fire, ambulance, and other emergency services. These telephone emergency services--including "911" services--are clearly an important public service whose reliability can be a matter of life or death. The legislative history of title II specifically reflects congressional intent that public entities must ensure that telephone emergency services, including 911 services, be accessible to persons with impaired hearing and speech through telecommunication technology (Conference report at 67; Education and Labor report at 84-85).

Proposed §35.162 mandated that public entities provide emergency telephone services to persons with disabilities that are "functionally equivalent" to voice services provided to others. Many commenters urged the Department to revise the section to make clear that direct access to telephone emergency services is required by title II of the ADA as indicated by the legislative history (Conference report at 67-68; Education and Labor report at 85). In response, the final rule mandates "direct access," instead of "access that is functionally equivalent" to that provided to all other telephone users. Telephone emergency access through a third party or through a relay service would not satisfy the requirement for direct access.

Several commenters asked about a separate seven-digit emergency call number for the 911 services. The requirement for direct access disallows the use of a separate seven-digit number where 911 service is available. Separate seven-digit emergency call numbers would be unfamiliar to many individuals and also more burdensome to use. A standard emergency 911 number is easier to remember and would save valuable time spent in searching in telephone books for a local seven-digit emergency number.

Many commenters requested the establishment of minimum standards of service (e.g., the quantity and location of TDD's and computer modems needed in a given emergency center). Instead of establishing these scoping requirements, the Department has established a performance standard through the mandate for direct access.

Section 35.162 requires public entities to take appropriate steps, including equipping their emergency systems with

REGULATION

modern technology, as may be necessary to promptly receive and respond to a call from users of TDD's and computer modems. Entities are allowed the flexibility to determine what is the appropriate technology for their particular needs. In order to avoid mandating use of particular technologies that may become outdated, the Department has eliminated the references to the Baudot and ASCII formats in the proposed rule.

Some commenters requested that the section require the installation of a voice amplification device on the handset of the dispatcher's telephone to amplify the dispatcher's voice. In an emergency, a person who has a hearing loss may be using a telephone that does not have an amplification device. Installation of speech amplification devices on the handsets of the dispatchers' telephones would respond to that situation. The Department encourages their use.

Several commenters emphasized the need for proper maintenance of TDD's used in telephone emergency services. Section 35.133, which mandates maintenance of accessible features, requires public entities to maintain in operable working condition TDD's and other devices that provide direct access to the emergency system.

REGULATION

§35.163 Information and signage.

(a) A public entity shall ensure that interested persons, including persons with impaired vision or hearing, can obtain information as to the existence and location of accessible services, activities, and facilities.

(b) A public entity shall provide signage at all inaccessible entrances to each of its facilities, directing users to an accessible entrance or to a location at which they can obtain information about accessible facilities. The international symbol for accessibility shall be used at each accessible entrance of a facility.

ANALYSIS

§35.163 Information and signage.

Section 35.163(a) requires the public entity to provide information to individuals with disabilities concerning accessible services, activities, and facilities. Paragraph (b) requires the public entity to provide signage at all inaccessible entrances to each of its facilities that directs users to an accessible entrance or to a location with information about accessible facilities.

Several commenters requested that, where TDD-equipped pay phones or portable TDD's exist, clear signage should be posted indicating the location of the TDD. The Department believes that this is required by paragraph (a). In addition, the Department recommends that, in large buildings that house TDD's, directional signage indicating the location of available TDD's should be placed adjacent to banks of telephones that do not contain a TDD.

REGULATION
§35.164 Duties.

This subpart does not require a public entity to take any action that it can demonstrate would result in a fundamental alteration in the nature of a service, program, or activity or in undue financial and administrative burdens. In those circumstances where personnel of the public entity believe that the proposed action would fundamentally alter the service, program, or activity or would result in undue financial and administrative burdens, a public entity has the burden of proving that compliance with this subpart would result in such alteration or burdens. The decision that compliance would result in such alteration or burdens must be made by the head of the public entity or his or her designee after considering all resources available for use in the funding and operation of the service, program, or activity and must be accompanied by a written statement of the reasons for reaching that conclusion. If an action required to comply with this subpart would result in such an alteration or such burdens, a public entity shall take any other action that would not result in such an alteration or such burdens but would nevertheless ensure that, to the maximum extent possible, individuals with disabilities receive the benefits or services provided by the public entity.

ANALYSIS
§35.164 Duties.

Section 35.164, like paragraph (a)(3) of §35.150, is taken from the section 504 regulations for federally conducted programs. Like paragraph (a)(3), it limits the obligation of the public entity to ensure effective communication in accordance with Davis and the circuit court opinions interpreting it. It also includes specific requirements for determining the existence of undue financial and administrative burdens. The preamble discussion of §35.150(a) regarding that determination is applicable to this section and further explains the public entity's obligation to comply with §§35.160-35.164. Because of the essential nature of the services provided by telephone emergency systems, the Department assumes that §35.164 will rarely be applied to §35.162.

REGULATION
Subpart F -- Compliance Procedures

ANALYSIS
Subpart F -- Compliance Procedures

Subpart F sets out the procedures for administrative enforcement of this part. Section 203 of the Act provides that the remedies, procedures, and rights set forth in section 505 of the Rehabilitation Act of 1973 (29 U.S.C. 794a) for enforcement of section 504 of the Rehabilitation Act, which prohibits discrimination on the basis of handicap in programs and activities that receive Federal financial assistance, shall be the remedies, procedures, and rights for enforcement of title II. Section 505, in turn, incorporates by reference the remedies, procedures, and rights set forth in title VI of the Civil Rights Act of 1964 (42 U.S.C. 2000d to 2000d-4a). Title VI, which prohibits discrimination on the basis of race, color, or national origin in federally assisted programs, is enforced by the Federal agencies that provide the Federal financial assistance to the covered programs and activities in question. If voluntary compliance cannot be achieved, Federal agencies enforce title VI either by the termination of Federal funds to a program that is found to discriminate, following an administrative hearing, or by a referral to this Department for judicial enforcement.

Title II of the ADA extended the requirements of section 504 to all services, programs, and activities of State and local governments, not only those that receive Federal financial assistance. The House Committee on Education and Labor explained the enforcement provisions as follows:

It is the Committee's intent that administrative enforcement of section 202 of the legislation should closely parallel the Federal government's experience with section 504 of the Rehabilitation Act of 1973. The Attorney General should use section 504 enforcement procedures and the Department's coordination role under Executive Order 12250 as models for regulation in this area.

The Committee envisions that the Department of Justice will identify appropriate Federal agencies to oversee compliance activities for State and local governments. As with section 504, these Federal agencies, including the Department of Justice, will receive, investigate, and where possible, resolve complaints of discrimination. If a Federal agency is unable to resolve a complaint by voluntary means, . . . the major enforcement sanction for the Federal government will be referral of cases by these Federal agencies to the Department of Justice.

REGULATION

The Department of Justice may then proceed to file suits in Federal district court. As with section 504, there is also a private right of action for persons with disabilities, which includes the full panoply of remedies. Again, consistent with section 504, it is not the Committee's intent that persons with disabilities need to exhaust Federal administrative remedies before exercising their private right of action.

Education & Labor report at 98. See also S. Rep. No. 116, 101st Cong., 1st Sess., at 57-58 (1989).

Subpart F effectuates the congressional intent by deferring to section 504 procedures where those procedures are applicable, that is, where a Federal agency has jurisdiction under section 504 by virtue of its provision of Federal financial assistance to the program or activity in which the discrimination is alleged to have occurred. Deferral to the 504 procedures also makes the sanction of fund termination available where necessary to achieve compliance. Because the Civil Rights Restoration Act (Pub. L. 100-259) extended the application of section 504 to all of the operations of the public entity receiving the Federal financial assistance, many activities of State and local governments are already covered by section 504. The procedures in subpart F apply to complaints concerning services, programs, and activities of public entities that are covered by the ADA.

Subpart G designates the Federal agencies responsible for enforcing the ADA with respect to specific components of State and local government. It does not, however, displace existing jurisdiction under section 504 of the various funding agencies. Individuals may still file discrimination complaints against recipients of Federal financial assistance with the agencies that provide that assistance, and the funding agencies will continue to process those complaints under their existing procedures for enforcing section 504. The substantive standards adopted in this part for title II of the ADA are generally the same as those required under section 504 for federally assisted programs, and public entities covered by the ADA are also covered by the requirements of section 504 to the extent that they receive Federal financial assistance. To the extent that title II provides greater protection to the rights of individuals with disabilities, however, the funding agencies will also apply the substantive requirements established under title II and this part in processing complaints covered by both this part and section 504, except that fund

REGULATION

termination procedures may be used only for violations of section 504.

Subpart F establishes the procedures to be followed by the agencies designated in subpart G for processing complaints against State and local government entities when the designated agency does not have jurisdiction under section 504.

REGULATION

§35.170 Complaints.

(a) Who may file. An individual who believes that he or she or a specific class of individuals has been subjected to discrimination on the basis of disability by a public entity may, by himself or herself or by an authorized representative, file a complaint under this part.

(b) Time for filing. A complaint must be filed not later than 180 days from the date of the alleged discrimination, unless the time for filing is extended by the designated agency for good cause shown. A complaint is deemed to be filed under this section on the date it is first filed with any Federal agency.

(c) Where to file. An individual may file a complaint with any agency that he or she believes to be the appropriate agency designated under subpart G of this part, or with any agency that provides funding to the public entity that is the subject of the complaint, or with the Department of Justice for referral as provided in §35.171(a)(2).

ANALYSIS

§35.170 Complaints.

Section 35.170 provides that any individual who believes that he or she or a specific class of individuals has been subjected to discrimination on the basis of disability by a public entity may, by himself or herself or by an authorized representative, file a complaint under this part within 180 days of the date of the alleged discrimination, unless the time for filing is extended by the agency for good cause. Although §35.107 requires public entities that employ 50 or more persons to establish grievance procedures for resolution of complaints, exhaustion of those procedures is not a prerequisite to filing a complaint under this section. If a complainant chooses to follow the public entity's grievance procedures, however, any resulting delay may be considered good cause for extending the time allowed for filing a complaint under this part.

Filing the complaint with any Federal agency will satisfy the requirement for timely filing. As explained below, a complaint filed with an agency that has jurisdiction under section 504 will be processed under the agency's procedures for enforcing section 504.

Some commenters objected to the complexity of allowing complaints to be filed with different agencies. The multiplicity of enforcement jurisdiction is the result of following the statutorily mandated enforcement scheme. The Department has, however, attempted to simplify procedures for complainants by making the Federal agency that receives the complaint responsible for referring it to an appropriate agency.

The Department has also added a new paragraph (c) to this section providing that a complaint may be filed with any agency designated under subpart G of this part, or with any agency that provides funding to the public entity that is the subject of the complaint, or with the Department of Justice. Under §35.171(a)(2), the Department of Justice will refer complaints for which it does not have jurisdiction under section 504 to an agency that does have jurisdiction under section 504, or to the agency designated under subpart G as responsible for complaints filed against the public entity that is the subject of the complaint or in the case of an employment complaint that is also subject to title I of the Act, to the Equal Employment Opportunity Commission. Complaints filed with the Department of Justice may be sent to the Coordination and Review Section, P.O. Box 66118, Civil Rights Division, U.S. Department of Justice, Washington, D.C. 20035-6118.

REGULATION

§35.171 Acceptance of complaints.

(a) Receipt of complaints. (1)(i) Any Federal agency that receives a complaint of discrimination on the basis of disability by a public entity shall promptly review the complaint to determine whether it has jurisdiction over the complaint under section 504.

(ii) If the agency does not have section 504 jurisdiction, it shall promptly determine whether it is the designated agency under subpart G of this part responsible for complaints filed against that public entity.

(2)(i) If an agency other than the Department of Justice determines that it does not have section 504 jurisdiction and is not the designated agency, it shall promptly refer the complaint, and notify the complainant that it is referring the complaint to the Department of Justice.

(ii) When the Department of Justice receives a complaint for which it does not have jurisdiction under section 504 and is not the designated agency, it shall refer the complaint to an agency that does have jurisdiction under section 504 or to the appropriate agency designated in subpart G of this part or, in the case of an

ANALYSIS

§35.171 Acceptance of complaints.

Section 35.171 establishes procedures for determining jurisdiction and responsibility for processing complaints against public entities. The final rule provides complainants an opportunity to file with the Federal funding agency of their choice. If that agency does not have jurisdiction under section 504, however, and is not the agency designated under subpart G as responsible for that public entity, the agency must refer the complaint to the Department of Justice, which will be responsible for referring it either to an agency that does have jurisdiction under section 504 or to the appropriate designated agency, or in the case of an employment complaint that is also subject to title I of the Act, to the Equal Employment Opportunity Commission.

Whenever an agency receives a complaint over which it has jurisdiction under section 504, it will process the complaint under its section 504 procedures. When the agency designated under subpart G receives a complaint for which it does not have jurisdiction under section 504, it will treat the complaint as an ADA complaint under the procedures established in this subpart.

Section 35.171 also describes agency responsibilities for the processing of employment complaints. As described in connection with §35.140, additional procedures regarding the coordination of employment complaints will be established in a coordination regulation issued by DOJ and EEOC. Agencies with jurisdiction under section 504 for complaints alleging employment discrimination also covered by title I will follow the procedures established by the coordination regulation for those complaints. Complaints covered by title I but not section 504 will be referred to the EEOC, and complaints covered by this part but not title I will be processed under the procedures in this part.

REGULATION

ANALYSIS

employment complaint that is also subject to title I of the Act, to the Equal Employment Opportunity Commission.

(3)(i) If the agency that receives a complaint has section 504 jurisdiction, it shall process the complaint according to its procedures for enforcing section 504.

(ii) If the agency that receives a complaint does not have section 504 jurisdiction, but is the designated agency, it shall process the complaint according to the procedures established by this subpart.

(b) Employment complaints. (1) If a complaint alleges employment discrimination subject to title I of the Act, and the agency has section 504 jurisdiction, the agency shall follow the procedures issued by the Department of Justice and the Equal Employment Opportunity Commission under section 107(b) of the Act.

(2) If a complaint alleges employment discrimination subject to title I of the Act, and the designated agency does not have section 504 jurisdiction, the agency shall refer the complaint to the Equal Employment Opportunity Commission for processing under title I of the Act.

REGULATION

ANALYSIS

(3) Complaints alleging employment discrimination subject to this part, but not to title I of the Act shall be processed in accordance with the procedures established by this subpart.

(c) Complete complaints. (1) A designated agency shall accept all complete complaints under this section and shall promptly notify the complainant and the public entity of the receipt and acceptance of the complaint.

(2) If the designated agency receives a complaint that is not complete, it shall notify the complainant and specify the additional information that is needed to make the complaint a complete complaint. If the complainant fails to complete the complaint, the designated agency shall close the complaint without prejudice.

REGULATION

§35.172 Resolution of complaints.

(a) The designated agency shall investigate each complete complaint, attempt informal resolution, and, if resolution is not achieved, issue to the complainant and the public entity a Letter of Findings that shall include --

(1) Findings of fact and conclusions of law;

(2) A description of a remedy for each violation found; and

(3) Notice of the rights available under paragraph (b) of this section.

(b) If the designated agency finds noncompliance, the procedures in §§35.173 and 35.174 shall be followed. At any time, the complainant may file a private suit pursuant to section 203 of the Act, whether or not the designated agency finds a violation.

ANALYSIS

§35.172 Resolution of complaints.

Section 35.172 requires the designated agency to either resolve the complaint or issue to the complainant and the public entity a Letter of Findings containing findings of fact and conclusions of law and a description of a remedy for each violation found.

The Act requires the Department of Justice to establish administrative procedures for resolution of complaints, but does not require complainants to exhaust these administrative remedies. The Committee Reports make clear that Congress intended to provide a private right of action with the full panoply of remedies for individual victims of discrimination. Because the Act does not require exhaustion of administrative remedies, the complainant may elect to proceed with a private suit at any time.

REGULATION

§35.173 Voluntary compliance agreements.

(a) When the designated agency issues a noncompliance Letter of Findings, the designated agency shall--

(1) Notify the Assistant Attorney General by forwarding a copy of the Letter of Findings to the Assistant Attorney General; and

(2) Initiate negotiations with the public entity to secure compliance by voluntary means.

(b) Where the designated agency is able to secure voluntary compliance, the voluntary compliance agreement shall --

(1) Be in writing and signed by the parties;

(2) Address each cited violation;

(3) Specify the corrective or remedial action to be taken, within a stated period of time, to come into compliance;

(4) Provide assurance that discrimination will not recur; and

(5) Provide for enforcement by the Attorney General.

ANALYSIS

§35.173 Voluntary compliance agreements.

Section 35.173 requires the agency to attempt to resolve all complaints in which it finds noncompliance through voluntary compliance agreements enforceable by the Attorney General.

REGULATION

§35.174 Referral.

If the public entity declines to enter into voluntary compliance negotiations or if negotiations are unsuccessful, the designated agency shall refer the matter to the Attorney General with a recommendation for appropriate action.

ANALYSIS

§35.174 Referral.

Section 35.174 provides for referral of the matter to the Department of Justice if the agency is unable to obtain voluntary compliance.

REGULATION

§35.175 Attorney's fees.

In any action or administrative proceeding commenced pursuant to the Act or this part, the court or agency, in its discretion, may allow the prevailing party, other than the United States, a reasonable attorney's fee, including litigation expenses, and costs, and the United States shall be liable for the foregoing the same as a private individual.

ANALYSIS

§35.175 Attorney's fees.

Section 35.175 states that courts are authorized to award attorneys fees, including litigation expenses and costs, as provided in section 505 of the Act. Litigation expenses include items such as expert witness fees, travel expenses, etc. The Judiciary Committee Report specifies that such items are included under the rubric of "attorneys fees" and not "costs" so that such expenses will be assessed against a plaintiff only under the standard set forth in Christiansburg Garment Co. v. Equal Employment Opportunity Commission, 434 U.S. 412 (1978). (Judiciary report at 73.)

REGULATION

§35.176 Alternative means of dispute resolution.

Where appropriate and to the extent authorized by law, the use of alternative means of dispute resolution, including settlement negotiations, conciliation, facilitation, mediation, factfinding, minitrials, and arbitration, is encouraged to resolve disputes arising under the Act and this part.

ANALYSIS

§35.176 Alternative means of dispute resolution.

Section 35.176 restates section 513 of the Act, which encourages use of alternative means of dispute resolution.

REGULATION

§35.177 Effect of unavailability of technical assistance.

A public entity shall not be excused from compliance with the requirements of this part because of any failure to receive technical assistance, including any failure in the development or dissemination of any technical assistance manual authorized by the Act.

ANALYSIS

§35.177 Effect of unavailability of technical assistance.

Section 35.177 explains that, as provided in section 506(e) of the Act, a public entity is not excused from compliance with the requirements of this part because of any failure to receive technical assistance.

REGULATION

§35.178 State immunity.

A State shall not be immune under the eleventh amendment to the Constitution of the United States from an action in Federal or State court of competent jurisdiction for a violation of this Act. In any action against a State for a violation of the requirements of this Act, remedies (including remedies both at law and in equity) are available for such a violation to the same extent as such remedies are available for such a violation in an action against any public or private entity other than a State.

§§35.179-35.189 [Reserved]

ANALYSIS

§35.178 State immunity.

Section 35.178 restates the provision of section 502 of the Act that a State is not immune under the eleventh amendment to the Constitution of the United States from an action in Federal or State court for violations of the Act, and that the same remedies are available for any such violations as are available in an action against an entity other than a State.

REGULATION
Subpart G -- Designated Agencies

§35.190 Designated agencies.

(a) The Assistant Attorney General shall coordinate the compliance activities of Federal agencies with respect to State and local government components, and shall provide policy guidance and interpretations to designated agencies to ensure the consistent and effective implementation of the requirements of this part.

(b) The Federal agencies listed in paragraph (b)(1)-(8) of this section shall have responsibility for the implementation of subpart F of this part for components of State and local governments that exercise responsibilities, regulate, or administer services, programs, or activities in the following functional areas.

(1) Department of Agriculture: all programs, services, and regulatory activities relating to farming and the raising of livestock, including extension services.

(2) Department of Education: all programs, services, and regulatory activities relating to the operation of elementary and secondary education systems and institutions, institutions of higher education and voca-

ANALYSIS
Subpart G -- Designated Agencies

§35.190 Designated agencies.

Subpart G designates the Federal agencies responsible for investigating complaints under this part. At least 26 agencies currently administer programs of Federal financial assistance that are subject to the nondiscrimination requirements of section 504 as well as other civil rights statutes. A majority of these agencies administer modest programs of Federal financial assistance and/or devote minimal resources exclusively to "external" civil rights enforcement activities. Under Executive Order 12250, the Department of Justice has encouraged the use of delegation agreements under which certain civil rights compliance responsibilities for a class of recipients funded by more than one agency are delegated by an agency or agencies to a "lead" agency. For example, many agencies that fund institutions of higher education have signed agreements that designate the Department of Education as the "lead" agency for this class of recipients.

The use of delegation agreements reduces overlap and duplication of effort, and thereby strengthens overall civil rights enforcement. However, the use of these agreements to date generally has been limited to education and health care recipients. These classes of recipients are funded by numerous agencies and the logical connection to a lead agency is clear (e.g., the Department of Education for colleges and universities, and the Department of Health and Human Services for hospitals).

The ADA's expanded coverage of State and local government operations further complicates the process of establishing Federal agency jurisdiction for the purpose of investigating complaints of discrimination on the basis of disability. Because all operations of public entities now are covered irrespective of the presence or absence of Federal financial assistance, many additional State and local government functions and organizations now are subject to Federal jurisdiction. In some cases, there is no historical or single clear-cut subject matter relationship with a Federal agency as was the case in the education example described above. Further, the 33,000 governmental jurisdictions subject to the ADA differ greatly in their organization, making a detailed and workable division of Federal agency jurisdiction by individual State, county, or municipal entity unrealistic.

REGULATION

tional education (other than schools of medicine, dentistry, nursing, and other health-related schools), and libraries.

(3) Department of Health and Human Services: all programs, services, and regulatory activities relating to the provision of health care and social services, including schools of medicine, dentistry, nursing, and other health-related schools, the operation of health care and social service providers and institutions, including "grass-roots" and community services organizations and programs, and preschool and daycare programs.

(4) Department of Housing and Urban Development: all programs, services, and regulatory activities relating to state and local public housing, and housing assistance and referral.

(5) Department of Interior: all programs, services, and regulatory activities relating to lands and natural resources, including parks and recreation, water and waste management, environmental protection, energy, historic and cultural preservation, and museums.

(6) Department of Justice: all programs, services, and regulatory activities relating to law enforcement,

ANALYSIS

This regulation applies the delegation concept to the investigation of complaints of discrimination on the basis of disability by public entities under the ADA. It designates eight agencies, rather than all agencies currently administering programs of Federal financial assistance, as responsible for investigating complaints under this part. These "designated agencies" generally have the largest civil rights compliance staffs, the most experience in complaint investigations and disability issues, and broad yet clear subject area responsibilities. This division of responsibilities is made functionally rather than by public entity type or name designation. For example, all entities (regardless of their title) that exercise responsibilities, regulate, or administer services or programs relating to lands and natural resources fall within the jurisdiction of the Department of Interior.

Complaints under this part will be investigated by the designated agency most closely related to the functions exercised by the governmental component against which the complaint is lodged. For example, a complaint against a State medical board, where such a board is a recognizable entity, will be investigated by the Department of Health and Human Services (the designated agency for regulatory activities relating to the provision of health care), even if the board is part of a general umbrella department of planning and regulation (for which the Department of Justice is the designated agency). If two or more agencies have apparent responsibility over a complaint, section 35.190(c) provides that the Assistant Attorney General shall determine which one of the agencies shall be the designated agency for purposes of that complaint.

Thirteen commenters, including four proposed designated agencies, addressed the Department of Justice's identification in the proposed regulation of nine "designated agencies" to investigate complaints under this part. Most comments addressed the proposed specific delegations to the various individual agencies. The Department of Justice agrees with several commenters who pointed out that responsibility for "historic and cultural preservation" functions appropriately belongs with the Department of Interior rather than the Department of Education. The Department of Justice also agrees with the Department of Education that "museums" more appropriately should be delegated to the Department of Interior, and that "preschool and daycare programs" more appropriately should be assigned to the Department of Health and Human Services, rather than to the Department of Education. The final rule reflects these decisions.

REGULATION

public safety, and the administration of justice, including
courts and correctional
institutions; commerce and
industry, including general
economic development,
banking and finance, con-
sumer protection, insurance,
and small business; planning,
development, and regulation
(unless assigned to other
designated agencies); state
and local government sup-
port services (e.g., audit,
personnel, comptroller,
administrative services); all
other government functions
not assigned to other designated agencies.

(7) Department of Labor:
all programs, services, and
regulatory activities relating
to labor and the work force.

(8) Department of Trans-
portation: all programs,
services, and regulatory
activities relating to transportation, including highways, public transportation,
traffic management (non-law
enforcement), automobile
licensing and inspection, and
driver licensing.

(c) Responsibility for
the implementation of
subpart F of this part for
components of State or local
governments that exercise
responsibilities, regulate, or
administer services, pro-
grams, or activities relating
to functions not assigned to
specific designated agencies

ANALYSIS

The Department of Commerce opposed its listing as the designated agency for "commerce and industry, including general economic development, banking and finance, consumer protection, insurance, and small business". The Department of Commerce cited its lack of a substantial existing section 504 enforcement program and experience with many of the specific functions to be delegated. The Department of Justice accedes to the Department of Commerce's position, and has assigned itself as the designated agency for these functions.

In response to a comment from the Department of Health and Human Services, the regulation's category of "medical and nursing schools" has been clarified to read "schools of medicine, dentistry, nursing, and other health-related fields". Also in response to a comment from the Department of Health and Human Services, "correctional institutions" have been specifically added to the public safety and administration of justice functions assigned to the Department of Justice.

The regulation also assigns the Department of Justice as the designated agency responsible for all State and local government functions not assigned to other designated agencies. The Department of Justice, under an agreement with the Department of the Treasury, continues to receive and coordinate the investigation of complaints filed under the Revenue Sharing Act. This entitlement program, which was terminated in 1986, provided civil rights compliance jurisdiction for a wide variety of complaints regarding the use of Federal funds to support various general activities of local governments. In the absence of any similar program of Federal financial assistance administered by another Federal agency, placement of designated agency responsibilities for miscellaneous and otherwise undesignated functions with the Department of Justice is an appropriate continuation of current practice.

The Department of Education objected to the proposed rule's inclusion of the functional area of "arts and humanities" within its responsibilities, and the Department of Housing and Urban Development objected to its proposed designation as responsible for activities relating to rent control, the real estate industry, and housing code enforcement. The Department has deleted these areas from the lists assigned to the Departments of Education and Housing and Urban

REGULATION

by paragraph (b) of this section may be assigned to other specific agencies by the Department of Justice.

(d) If two or more agencies have apparent responsibility over a complaint, the Assistant Attorney General shall determine which one of the agencies shall be the designated agency for purposes of that complaint.

§§35.191-5.999 [Reserved]

ANALYSIS

Development, respectively, and has added a new paragraph (c) to section 35.190, which provides that the Department of Justice may assign responsibility for components of State or local governments that exercise responsibilities, regulate, or administer services, programs, or activities relating to functions not assigned to specific designated agencies by paragraph (b) of this section to other appropriate agencies. The Department believes that this approach will provide more flexibility in determining the appropriate agency for investigation of complaints involving those components of State and local governments not specifically addressed by the listings in paragraph (b). As provided in §§35.170 and 35.171, complaints filed with the Department of Justice will be referred to the apropriate agency.

Several commenters proposed a stronger role for the Department of Justice, especially with respect to the receipt and assignment of complaints, and the overall monitoring of the effectiveness of the enforcement activities of Federal agencies. As discussed above, §§35.170 and 35.171 have been revised to provide for referral of complaints by the Department of Justice to appropriate enforcement agencies. Also, language has been added to §35.190(a) of the final regulation stating that the Assistant Attorney General shall provide policy guidance and interpretations to designated agencies to ensure the consistent and effective implementation of this part.

TITLE III

NONDISCRIMINATION ON THE BASIS OF DISABILITY BY PUBLIC ACCOMMODATIONS AND IN COMMERCIAL FACILITIES

Nondiscrimination On The Basis Of Disability by
Public Accommodations and in Commercial Facilities

1. Summary

This rule implements title III of the Americans with Disabilities Act, Public Law 101-336, which prohibits discrimination on the basis of disability by private entities in places of public accommodation, requires that all new places of public accommodation and commercial facilities be designed and constructed so as to be readily accessible to and usable by persons with disabilities, and requires that examinations or courses related to licensing or certification for professional and trade purposes be accessible to persons with disabilities.

The effective date of this rule is January 26, 1992.

For further information about this rule contact the Office on the Americans with Disabilities Act, Civil Rights Division; all of the U.S. Department of Justice, Washington, DC 20530. (202)514-0301 (Voice), (202)514-0383 (TDD). These telephone numbers are not toll-free numbers.

Copies of this rule are available in the following alternate formats: large print, Braille, electronic file on computer disk, and audio-tape. Copies may be obtained from the Office on the Americans with Disabilities Act at (202)514-0301 (Voice) or (202)514-0381 (TDD). The rule is also available on electronic bulletin board at (202)514-6193. These telephone numbers are not toll-free numbers.

2. Background

The landmark Americans with Disabilities Act ("ADA" or "the Act"), enacted on July 26, 1990, provides comprehensive civil rights protections to individuals with disabilities in the areas of employment, public accommodations, State and local government services, and telecommunications.

The legislation was originally developed by the National Council on Disability, an independent Federal agency that reviews and makes recommendations concerning Federal laws, programs, and policies affecting individuals with disabilities. In its 1986 study, "Toward Independence," the National Council on Disability recognized the inadequacy of the existing, limited patchwork of protections for individuals with disabilities, and recommended the enactment of a comprehensive civil rights law requiring equal opportunity for individuals with disabilities throughout American life. Although the 100th Congress did not act on the legislation, which was first introduced in 1988, then-Vice-President George Bush endorsed the concept of comprehensive disability rights legislation during his presidential campaign and became a dedicated advocate of the ADA.

The ADA was reintroduced in modified form in May 1989 for consideration by the 101st Congress. In June 1989, Attorney General Dick Thornburgh, in testimony before the Senate Committee on Labor and Human Resources, reiterated the Bush Administration's support for the ADA and suggested changes in the proposed legislation. After extensive negotiations between Senate sponsors and the Administration, the Senate passed an amended version of the ADA on September 7, 1989, by a vote of 76-8.

In the House, jurisdiction over the ADA was divided among four committees, each of which conducted extensive hearings and issued detailed committee reports: the Committee on Education and Labor, the Committee on the Judiciary, the Committee on Public Works and Transportation, and the Committee on Energy and Commerce. On October 12, 1989, the Attorney General testified in favor of the legislation before the Committee on the Judiciary. The Civil Rights Division, on February 22, 1990, provided testimony to the Committee on Small Business, which although technically without jurisdiction over the bill, conducted hearings on the legislation's impact on small business.

After extensive committee consideration and floor debate, the House of Representatives passed an amended version of the Senate bill on May 22, 1990, by a vote of 403-20. After resolving their differences in conference, the Senate and House took final action on the bill -- the House passing it by a vote of 377-28 on July 12, 1990, and the Senate, a day later, by a vote of 91-6. The ADA was enacted into law with the President's signature at a White House ceremony on July 26, 1990.

3. Rulemaking History

On February 22, 1991, the Department of Justice published a notice of proposed rulemaking (NPRM) implementing title III of the ADA in the Federal Register (56 FR 7452). On February 28, 1991, the Department published a notice of proposed rulemaking implementing subtitle A of title II of the ADA in the Federal Register (56 FR 8538). Each NPRM solicited comments on the definitions, standards, and procedures of the proposed rules. By the April 29, 1991, close of the comment period of the NPRM for title II, the Department had received 2,718 comments on the two proposed rules. Following the close of the comment period, the Department received an additional 222 comments.

In order to encourage public participation in the development of the Department's rules under the ADA, the Department held four public hearings. Hearings were held in Dallas, Texas on March 4-5, 1991; in Washington, DC on March 13-14-15, 1991; in San Francisco, California on March 18-19, 1991; and in Chicago, Illinois on March 27-28, 1991. At these hearings, 329 persons testified and 1,567 pages of testimony were compiled. Transcripts of the hearings were included in the Department's rulemaking docket.

The comments that the Department received occupy almost six feet of shelf space and contain over 10,000 pages. The Department received comments from individuals from all fifty States and the District of Columbia. Nearly 75% of the comments came from individuals and from organizations representing the interests of persons with disabilities. The Department received 292 comments from entities covered by the ADA and trade associations representing businesses in the private sector, and 67 from government units, such as mayors' offices, public school districts, and various State agencies working with individuals with disabilities.

The Department received one comment from a consortium of 511 organizations representing a broad spectrum of persons with disabilities. In addition, at least another 25 commenters endorsed the position expressed by this consortium or submitted identical comments on one or both proposed regulations.

An organization representing persons with hearing impairments submitted a large number of comments. This organization presented the Department with 479 individual comments, each providing in chart form a detailed representation of what type of auxiliary aid or service would be useful in the various categories of places of public accommodation.

The Department received a number of comments based on almost ten different form letters. For example, individuals who have a heightened sensitivity to a variety of chemical substances submitted 266 post cards detailing how exposure to various environmental conditions restricts their access to places of public accommodation and to commercial facilities. Another large group of form letters came from groups affiliated with independent living centers.

The vast majority of the comments addressed the Department's proposal implementing title III. Just over 100 comments addressed only issues presented in the proposed title II regulation.

The Department read and analyzed each comment that was submitted in a timely fashion. Transcripts of the four hearings were analyzed along with the written comments. The decisions that the Department has made in response to these comments, however, were not made on the basis of the number of commenters addressing any one point but on a thorough consideration of the merits of the points of view expressed in the comments. Copies of the written comments, including transcripts of the four hearings, will remain available for public inspection in Room 854 of the HOLC Building, 320 First Street, N.W., Washington, D.C. from 10:00 a.m. to 5:00 p.m., Monday through Friday, except for legal holidays, until August 30, 1991.

The Americans with Disabilities Act gives to individuals with disabilities civil rights protections with respect to discrimination that are parallel to those provided to individuals on the basis of race, color, national origin, sex, and religion. It combines in its own unique formula elements drawn principally from two key civil rights statutes -- the Civil Rights Act of 1964 and title V of the Rehabilitation Act of 1973. The ADA generally employs the framework of titles II (42 U.S.C. 2000a to 2000a-6) and VII (42 U.S.C. 2000e to 2000e-16) of the Civil Rights Act of 1964 for coverage and enforcement and the terms and concepts of section 504 of the Rehabilitation Act of 1973 (29 U.S.C. 794) for what constitutes discrimination.

Other recently enacted legislation will facilitate compliance with the ADA. As amended in 1990, the Internal Revenue Code allows a deduction of up to $15,000 per year for expenses associated with the removal of qualified architectural and transportation barriers. The 1990 amendment also permits eligible small businesses to receive a tax credit for certain costs of compliance with the ADA. An eligible small business is one whose gross receipts do not exceed $1,000,000 or whose workforce does not consist of more than 30 full-time workers. Qualifying businesses may claim a credit of up to 50 percent of eligible access expenditures that exceed $250 but do not exceed $10,250. Examples of eligible access expenditures include the necessary and reasonable costs of removing barriers, providing auxiliary aids, and acquiring or modifying equipment or devices.

In addition, the Communications Act of 1934 has been amended by the Television Decoder Circuitry Act of 1990, Public Law 101-431, to require as of July 1, 1993, that all televisions with screens of 13 inches or wider have built-in decoder circuitry for displaying closed captions. This new law will eventually lessen dependence on the use of portable decoders in achieving compliance with the auxiliary aids and services requirements of the rule.

4. Overview of the Rule

The final rule establishes standards and procedures for the implementation of title III of the Act, which addresses discrimination by private entities in places of public accommodation, commercial facilities, and certain examinations and courses. The careful consideration Congress gave title III is reflected in the detailed statutory provisions and the expansive reports of the Senate Committee on Labor and Human Resources and the House Committees on the Judiciary, and Education and Labor. The final rule follows closely the language of the Act and supplements it, where appropriate, with interpretive material found in the committee reports.

The rule is organized into six subparts. Subpart A, "General," includes the purpose and application sections, describes the relationship of the Act to other laws, and defines key terms used in the regulation.

Subpart B, "General Requirements," contains material derived from what the statute calls the "General Rule," and the "General Prohibition," in sections 302(a) and 302(b)(1), respectively, of the Act. Topics addressed by this subpart include discriminatory denials of access or participation, landlord and tenant obligations, the provision of unequal benefits, indirect discrimination through contracting, the participation of individuals with disabilities in the most integrated setting appropriate to their needs, and discrimination based on association with individuals with disabilities. Subpart B also contains a number of "miscellaneous" provisions derived from title V of the Act that involve issues such as retaliation and coercion for asserting ADA rights, illegal drug use, insurance, and restrictions on smoking in places of public accommodation. Finally, subpart B contains additional general provisions regarding direct threats to health or safety, maintenance of accessible features of facilities and equipment, and the coverage of places of public accommodation located in private residences.

Subpart C, "Specific Requirements," addresses the "Specific Prohibitions" in section 302(b)(2) of the Act. Included in this subpart are topics such as discriminatory eligibility criteria; reasonable modifications in policies, practices or procedures; auxiliary aids and services; the readily achievable removal of barriers and alternatives to barrier removal; the extent to which inventories of accessible or special goods are required; seating in assembly areas; personal devices and services; and transportation provided by public accommodations. Subpart C also incorporates the requirements of section 309 of title III relating to examinations and courses.

Subpart D, "New Construction and Alterations," sets forth the requirements for new construction and alterations based on section 303 of the Act. It addresses such issues as what facilities are covered by the new construction requirements, what an alteration is, the application of the elevator exception, the path of travel obligations resulting from an alteration to a primary function area, requirements for commercial facilities located in private residences, and the application of alterations requirements to historic buildings and facilities.

Subpart E, "Enforcement," describes the Act's title III enforcement procedures, including private actions, as well as investigations and litigation conducted by the Attorney General. These provisions are based on sections 308 and 310(b) of the Act.

Subpart F, "Certification of State Laws or Local Building Codes," establishes procedures for the certification of State or local building accessibility ordinances that meet or exceed the new construction and alterations requirements of the ADA. These provisions are based on section 308(b)(1)(A)(ii) of the Act.

The section-by-section analysis of the rule explains in detail the provisions of each of these subparts.

The Department is also today publishing a final rule for the implementation and enforcement of subtitle A of title II of the Act. This rule prohibits discrimination on the basis of disability against qualified individuals with disabilities in all services, programs, or activities of State and local government.

5. Regulatory Process Matters

This final rule has been reviewed by the Office of Management and Budget (OMB) under Executive Order 12291. The Department is preparing a regulatory impact analysis (RIA) of this rule, and the Architectural and Transportation Barriers Compliance Board is preparing an RIA for its Americans with Disabilities Act Accessibility Guidelines for Buildings and Facilities (ADAAG) that are incorporated in Appendix A of the Department's final rule. Draft copies of both preliminary RIAs are available for comment; the Department will provide copies of these documents to the public upon request. Commenters are urged to provide additional information as to the costs and benefits associated with this rule. This will facilitate the development of a final RIA by January 1, 1992.

The Department's RIA will evaluate the economic impact of the final rule. Included among those title III provisions that are likely to result in significant economic impact are the requirements for auxiliary aids, barrier removal in existing facilities, and readily accessible new construction and alterations. An analysis of the costs of these provision will be included in the RIA.

The preliminary RIA prepared for the notice of proposed rulemaking contained all of the available information that would have been included in a preliminary regulatory flexibility analysis, had one been prepared under the Regulatory Flexibility Act, concerning the rule's impact on small entities. The final RIA will contain all of the information that is required in a final regulatory flexibility analysis, and will serve as such an analysis. Moreover, the extensive notice and comment procedure followed by the Department in the promulgation of this rule, which included public hearings, dissemination of materials, and provision of speakers to affected groups, clearly provided any interested small entities with the notice and opportunity for comment provided for under the Regulatory Flexibility Act procedures.

This final rule will preempt State laws affecting entities subject to the ADA only to the extent that those laws directly conflict with the statutory requirements of the ADA. Therefore, this rule is not subject to Executive Order 12612, and a Federalism Assessment is not required.

The reporting and recordkeeping requirements described in subpart F of the rule are considered to be information collection requirements as that term is defined by the Office of Management and Budget in 5 CFR part 1320. Accordingly, those information collection requirements have been submitted to OMB for review pursuant to the Paperwork Reduction Act.

6. Outline of the Rule

Part 36 -- NONDISCRIMINATION ON THE BASIS OF DISABILITY BY PUBLIC AC-COMMODATIONS AND IN COMMERCIAL FACILITIES

Authority: 5 U.S.C. 301; 28 U.S.C. 509, 510; Pub. L. 101-336, 42 U.S.C. 12186.

REGULATION
Subpart A -- General

§36.101 Purpose.

The purpose of this part is to implement title III of the Americans with Disabilities Act of 1990 (42 U.S.C. 12181), which prohibits discrimination on the basis of disability by public accommodations and requires places of public accommodation and commercial facilities to be designed, constructed, and altered in compliance with the accessibility standards established by this part.

ANALYSIS
Subpart A -- General

Section 36.101 Purpose.

Section 36.101 states the purpose of the rule, which is to effectuate title III of the Americans with Disabilities Act of 1990. This title prohibits discrimination on the basis of disability by public accommodations, requires places of public accommodation and commercial facilities to be designed, constructed, and altered in compliance with the accessibility standards established by this part, and requires that examinations or courses related to licensing or certification for professional or trade purposes be accessible to persons with disabilities.

REGULATION

§36.102 Application.

(a) <u>General</u>. This part applies to any--

(1) Public accommodation;

(2) Commercial facility; or

(3) Private entity that offers examinations or courses related to applications, licensing, certification, or credentialing for secondary or postsecondary education, professional, or trade purposes.

(b) <u>Public accommodations</u>.

(1) The requirements of this part applicable to public accommodations are set forth in subparts B, C, and D of this part.

(2) The requirements of subparts B and C of this part obligate a public accommodation only with respect to the operations of a place of public accommodation.

(3) The requirements of subpart D of this part obligate a public accommodation only with respect to--

(i) A facility used as, or designed or constructed for use as, a place of public accommodation; or

(ii) A facility used as, or

ANALYSIS

Section 36.102 Application.

Section 36.102 specifies the range of entities and facilities that have obligations under the final rule. The rule applies to any public accommodation or commercial facility as those terms are defined in §36.104. It also applies, in accordance with section 309 of the ADA, to private entities that offer examinations or courses related to applications, licensing, certification, or credentialing for secondary or postsecondary education, professional, or trade purposes. Except as provided in §36.206, "Retaliation or coercion," this part does not apply to individuals other than public accommodations or to public entities. Coverage of private individuals and public entities is discussed in the preamble to §36.206.

As defined in §36.104, a public accommodation is a private entity that owns, leases or leases to, or operates a place of public accommodation. Section 36.102(b)(2) emphasizes that the general and specific public accommodations requirements of subparts B and C obligate a public accommodation only with respect to the operations of a place of public accommodation. This distinction is drawn in recognition of the fact that a private entity that meets the regulatory definition of public accommodation could also own, lease or lease to, or operate facilities that are not places of public accommodation. The rule would exceed the reach of the ADA if it were to apply the public accommodations requirements of subparts B and C to the operations of a private entity that do not involve a place of public accommodation. Similarly, §36.102(b)(3) provides that the new construction and alterations requirements of subpart D obligate a public accommodation only with respect to facilities used as, or designed or constructed for use as, places of public accommodation or commercial facilities.

On the other hand, as mandated by the ADA and reflected in §36.102(c), the new construction and alterations requirements of subpart D apply to a commercial facility whether or not the facility is a place of public accommodation, or is owned, leased, leased to, or operated by a public accommodation.

Section 36.102(e) states that the rule does not apply to any private club, religious entity, or public entity. Each of these terms is defined in §36.104. The exclusion of private clubs and religious entities is derived from section 307 of the ADA; and the exclusion of public entities is based on the

REGULATION

designed and constructed for
use as, a commercial facility.

(c) Commercial facili-
ties. The requirements of
this part applicable to commercial facilities are set forth
in subpart D of this part.

(d) Examinations and
courses. The requirements
of this part applicable to
private entities that offer
examinations or courses as
specified in paragraph (a) of
this section are set forth in
§36.309.

(e) Exemptions and
exclusions. This part does
not apply to any private club
(except to the extent that the
facilities of the private club
are made available to customers or patrons of a place
of public accommodation),
or to any religious entity or
public entity.

ANALYSIS

statutory definition of public accommodation in section 301(7)
of the ADA, which excludes entities other than private entities
from coverage under title III of the ADA.

REGULATION

§36.103 Relationship to other laws.

(a) <u>Rule of interpretation</u>. Except as otherwise provided in this part, this part shall not be construed to apply a lesser standard than the standards applied under title V of the Rehabilitation Act of 1973 (29 U.S.C. 791) or the regulations issued by Federal agencies pursuant to that title.

(b) <u>Section 504</u>. This part does not affect the obligations of a recipient of Federal financial assistance to comply with the requirements of section 504 of the Rehabilitation Act of 1973 (29 U.S.C. 794) and regulations issued by Federal agencies implementing section 504.

(c) <u>Other laws</u>. This part does not invalidate or limit the remedies, rights, and procedures of any other Federal laws, or State or local laws (including State common law) that provide greater or equal protection for the rights of individuals with disabilities or individuals associated with them.

ANALYSIS

Section 36.103 Relationship to other laws.

Section 36.103 is derived from sections 501 (a) and (b) of the ADA. Paragraph (a) provides that, except as otherwise specifically provided by this part, the ADA is not intended to apply lesser standards than are required under title V of the Rehabilitation Act of 1973, as amended (29 U.S.C. 790-794), or the regulations implementing that title. The standards of title V of the Rehabilitation Act apply for purposes of the ADA to the extent that the ADA has not explicitly adopted a different standard from title V. Where the ADA explicitly provides a different standard from section 504, the ADA standard applies to the ADA, but not to section 504. For example, section 504 requires that all federally assisted programs and activities be readily accessible to and usable by individuals with handicaps, even if major structural alterations are necessary to make a program accessible. Title III of the ADA, in contrast, only requires alterations to existing facilities if the modifications are "readily achievable," that is, able to be accomplished easily and without much difficulty or expense. A public accommodation that is covered under both section 504 and the ADA is still required to meet the "program accessibility" standard in order to comply with section 504, but would not be in violation of the ADA unless it failed to make "readily achievable" modifications. On the other hand, an entity covered by the ADA is required to make "readily achievable" modifications, even if the program can be made accessible without any architectural modifications. Thus, an entity covered by both section 504 and title III of the ADA must meet both the "program accessibility" requirement and the "readily achievable" requirement.

Paragraph (b) makes explicit that the rule does not affect the obligation of recipients of Federal financial assistance to comply with the requirements imposed under section 504 of the Rehabilitation Act of 1973.

Paragraph (c) makes clear that Congress did not intend to displace any of the rights or remedies provided by other Federal laws or other State or local laws (including State common law) that provide greater or equal protection to individuals with disabilities. A plaintiff may choose to pursue claims under a State law that does not confer greater substantive rights, or even confers fewer substantive rights, if the alleged violation is protected under the alternative law and the remedies are greater. For example, assume that a person with a physical disability seeks damages under a State

REGULATION

ANALYSIS

law that allows compensatory and punitive damages for discrimination on the basis of physical disability, but does not allow them on the basis of mental disability. In that situation, the State law would provide narrower coverage, by excluding mental disabilities, but broader remedies, and an individual covered by both laws could choose to bring an action under both laws. Moreover, State tort claims confer greater remedies and are not preempted by the ADA. A plaintiff may join a State tort claim to a case brought under the ADA. In such a case, the plaintiff must, of course, prove all the elements of the State tort claim in order to prevail under that cause of action.

A commenter had concerns about privacy requirements for banking transactions using telephone relay services. Title IV of the Act provides adequate protections for ensuring the confidentiality of communications using the relay services. This issue is more appropriately addressed by the Federal Communications Commission in its regulation implementing title IV of the Act.

REGULATION
§36.104 Definitions.

For purposes of this part, the term--

Act means the Americans with Disabilities Act of 1990 (Pub. L. 101-336, 104 Stat. 327, 42 U.S.C. 12101-12213 and 47 U.S.C. 225 and 611).

Commerce means travel, trade, traffic, commerce, transportation, or communication--

(1) Among the several States;

(2) Between any foreign country or any territory or possession and any State; or

(3) Between points in the same State but through another State or foreign country.

Commercial facilities means facilities --

(1) Whose operations will affect commerce;

ANALYSIS
Section 36.104 Definitions.

"Act." The word "Act" is used in the regulation to refer to the Americans with Disabilities Act of 1990, Pub. L. 101-336, which is also referred to as the "ADA."

"Commerce." The definition of "commerce" is identical to the statutory definition provided in section 301(1) of the ADA. It means travel, trade, traffic, commerce, transportation, or communication among the several States, between any foreign country or any territory or possession and any State, or between points in the same State but through another State or foreign country. Commerce is defined in the same manner as in title II of the Civil Rights Act of 1964, which prohibits racial discrimination in public accommodations.

The term "commerce" is used in the definition of "place of public accommodation." According to that definition, one of the criteria that an entity must meet before it can be considered a place of public accommodation is that its operations affect commerce. The term "commerce" is similarly used in the definition of "commercial facility."

The use of the phrase "operations affect commerce" applies the full scope of coverage of the Commerce Clause of the Constitution in enforcing the ADA. The Constitution gives Congress broad authority to regulate interstate commerce, including the activities of local business enterprises (e.g., a physician's office, a neighborhood restaurant, a laundromat, or a bakery) that affect interstate commerce through the purchase or sale of products manufactured in other States, or by providing services to individuals from other States. Because of the integrated nature of the national economy, the ADA and this final rule will have extremely broad application.

"Commercial facilities" are those facilities that are intended for nonresidential use by a private entity and whose operations affect commerce. As explained under §36.401, "New construction," the new construction and alteration requirements of subpart D of the rule apply to all commercial facilities, whether or not they are places of public accommo-

REGULATION

(2) That are intended for nonresidential use by a private entity; and

(3) That are not --

(i) Facilities that are covered or expressly exempted from coverage under the Fair Housing Act of 1968, as amended (42 U.S.C. 3601-3631);

(ii) Aircraft; or

(iii) Railroad locomotives, railroad freight cars, railroad cabooses, commuter or intercity passenger rail cars (including coaches, dining cars, sleeping cars, lounge cars, and food service cars), any other railroad cars described in section 242 of the Act or covered under title II of the Act, or railroad rights-of-way. For purposes of this definition, "rail" and "railroad" have the meaning given the term "railroad" in section 202(e) of the Federal Railroad Safety Act of 1970 (45 U.S.C. 431(e)).

ANALYSIS

dation. Those commercial facilities that are not places of public accommodation are not subject to the requirements of subparts B and C (e.g., those requirements concerning auxiliary aids and general nondiscrimination provisions).

Congress recognized that the employees within commercial facilities would generally be protected under title I (employment) of the Act. However, as the House Committee on Education and Labor pointed out, "[t]o the extent that new facilities are built in a manner that make[s] them accessible to all individuals, including potential employees, there will be less of a need for individual employers to engage in reasonable accommodations for particular employees." H.R. Rep. No. 485, 101st Cong., 2d Sess., pt. 2, at 117 (1990) [hereinafter "Education and Labor report"]. While employers of fewer than 15 employees are not covered by title I's employment discrimination provisions, there is no such limitation with respect to new construction covered under title III. Congress chose not to so limit the new construction provisions because of its desire for a uniform requirement of accessibility in new construction, because accessibility can be accomplished easily in the design and construction stage, and because future expansion of a business or sale or lease of the property to a larger employer or to a business that is a place of public accommodation is always a possibility.

The term "commercial facilities" is not intended to be defined by dictionary or common industry definitions. Included in this category are factories, warehouses, office buildings, and other buildings in which employment may occur. The phrase, "whose operations affect commerce," is to be read broadly, to include all types of activities reached under the commerce clause of the Constitution.

Privately operated airports are also included in the category of commercial facilities. They are not, however, places of public accommodation because they are not terminals used for "specified public transportation." (Transportation by aircraft is specifically excluded from the statutory definition of "specified public transportation.") Thus, privately operated airports are subject to the new construction and alteration requirements of this rule (subpart D) but not to subparts B and C. (Airports operated by public entities are covered by title II of the Act.) Places of public accommodation located within airports, such as restaurants, shops, lounges, or conference centers, however, are covered by subparts B and C of this part.

REGULATION

The statute's definition of "commercial facilities" specifically includes only facilities "that are intended for nonresidential use" and specifically exempts those facilities that are covered or expressly exempted from coverage under the Fair Housing Act of 1968, as amended (42 U.S.C. 3601-3631). The interplay between the Fair Housing Act and the ADA with respect to those facilities that are "places of public accommodation" was the subject of many comments and is addressed in the preamble discussion of the definition of "place of public accommodation."

Current illegal use of drugs means illegal use of drugs that occurred recently enough to justify a reasonable belief that a person's drug use is current or that continuing use is a real and ongoing problem.

"Current illegal use of drugs." The phrase "current illegal use of drugs" is used in §36.209. Its meaning is discussed in the preamble for that section.

Disability means, with respect to an individual, a physical or mental impairment that substantially limits one or more of the major life activities of such individual; a record of such an impairment; or being regarded as having such an impairment.

"Disability." The definition of the term "disability" is comparable to the definition of the term "individual with handicaps" in section 7(8)(B) of the Rehabilitation Act and section 802(h) of the Fair Housing Act. The Education and Labor Committee report makes clear that the analysis of the term "individual with handicaps" by the Department of Health, Education, and Welfare in its regulations implementing section 504 (42 FR 22685 (May 4, 1977)) and the analysis by the Department of Housing and Urban Development in its regulation implementing the Fair Housing Amendments Act of 1988 (54 FR 3232 (Jan. 23, 1989)) should also apply fully to the term "disability" (Education and Labor report at 50).

The use of the term "disability" instead of "handicap" and the term "individual with a disability" instead of "individual with handicaps" represents an effort by the Congress to make use of up-to-date, currently accepted terminology. The terminology applied to individuals with disabilities is a very significant and sensitive issue. As with racial and ethnic terms, the choice of words to describe a person with a disability is overlaid with stereotypes, patronizing attitudes, and other emotional connotations. Many individuals with disabilities, and organizations representing such individuals, object to the use of such terms as "handicapped person" or "the handicapped." In other recent legislation, Congress also recognized this shift in terminology, e.g., by changing the

REGULATION

name of the National Council on the Handicapped to the National Council on Disability (Pub. L. 100-630).

In enacting the Americans with Disabilities Act, Congress concluded that it was important for the current legislation to use terminology most in line with the sensibilities of most Americans with disabilities. No change in definition or substance is intended nor should be attributed to this change in phraseology.

The term "disability" means, with respect to an individual-

(A) a physical or mental impairment that substantially limits one or more of the major life activities of such individual;

(B) a record of such an impairment; or

(C) being regarded as having such an impairment.

If an individual meets any one of these three tests, he or she is considered to be an individual with a disability for purposes of coverage under the Americans with Disabilities Act.

Congress adopted this same basic definition of "disability," first used in the Rehabilitation Act of 1973 and in the Fair Housing Amendments Act of 1988, for a number of reasons. It has worked well since it was adopted in 1974. There is a substantial body of administrative interpretation and judicial precedent on this definition. Finally, it would not be possible to guarantee comprehensiveness by providing a list of specific disabilities, especially because new disorders may be recognized in the future, as they have since the definition was first established in 1974.

(1) The phrase physical or mental impairment means --

(i) Any physiological disorder or condition, cosmetic disfigurement, or anatomical loss affecting one or more of the following body systems: neurological; musculoskeletal; special

Test A -- A Physical or Mental Impairment That Substantially Limits One or More of the Major Life Activities of Such Individual

Physical or mental impairment. Under the first test, an individual must have a physical or mental impairment. As explained in paragraph (1)(i) of the definition, "impairment" means any physiological disorder or condition, cosmetic disfigurement, or anatomical loss affecting one or more of the following body systems: neurological; musculoskeletal;

REGULATION

sense organs; respiratory, including speech organs; cardiovascular; reproductive; digestive; genitourinary; hemic and lymphatic; skin; and endocrine;

(ii) Any mental or psychological disorder such as mental retardation, organic brain syndrome, emotional or mental illness, and specific learning disabilities;

(iii) The phrase physical or mental impairment includes, but is not limited to, such contagious and noncontagious diseases and conditions as orthopedic, visual, speech, and hearing impairments, cerebral palsy, epilepsy, muscular dystrophy, multiple sclerosis, cancer, heart disease, diabetes, mental retardation, emotional illness, specific learning disabilities, HIV disease (whether symptomatic or asymptomatic), tuberculosis, drug addiction, and alcoholism;

(iv) The phrase physical or mental impairment does not include homosexuality or bisexuality.

(2) The phrase major life activities means functions such as caring for one's self, performing manual tasks, walking, seeing, hearing, speaking, breathing, learning, and working.

ANALYSIS

special sense organs (including speech organs that are not respiratory, such as vocal cords, soft palate, and tongue); respiratory, including speech organs; cardiovascular; reproductive; digestive; genitourinary; hemic and lymphatic; skin; and endocrine. It also means any mental or psychological disorder, such as mental retardation, organic brain syndrome, emotional or mental illness, and specific learning disabilities. This list closely tracks the one used in the regulations for section 504 of the Rehabilitation Act of 1973 (see, e.g., 45 CFR 84.3(j)(2)(i)).

Many commenters asked that "traumatic brain injury" be added to the list in paragraph (1)(i). Traumatic brain injury is already included because it is a physiological condition affecting one of the listed body systems, i.e., "neurological." Therefore, it was unnecessary for the Department to add the term to the regulation.

It is not possible to include a list of all the specific conditions, contagious and noncontagious diseases, or infections that would constitute physical or mental impairments because of the difficulty of ensuring the comprehensiveness of such a list, particularly in light of the fact that other conditions or disorders may be identified in the future. However, the list of examples in paragraph (1)(iii) of the definition includes: orthopedic, visual, speech and hearing impairments; cerebral palsy; epilepsy, muscular dystrophy, multiple sclerosis, cancer, heart disease, diabetes, mental retardation, emotional illness, specific learning disabilities, HIV disease (symptomatic or asymptomatic), tuberculosis, drug addiction, and alcoholism.

The examples of "physical or mental impairments" in paragraph (1)(iii) are the same as those contained in many section 504 regulations, except for the addition of the phrase "contagious and noncontagious" to describe the types of diseases and conditions included, and the addition of "HIV disease (symptomatic or asymptomatic)" and "tuberculosis" to the list of examples. These additions are based on the ADA committee reports, caselaw, and official legal opinions interpreting section 504. In School Board of Nassau County v. Arline, 480 U.S. 273 (1987), a case involving an individual with tuberculosis, the Supreme Court held that people with contagious diseases are entitled to the protections afforded by section 504. Following the Arline decision, this Department's Office of Legal Counsel issued a legal opinion

REGULATION

ANALYSIS

(3) The phrase <u>has a record of such an impairment</u> means has a history of, or has been misclassified as having, a mental or physical impairment that substantially limits one or more major life activities.

(4) The phrase <u>is regarded as having an impairment</u> means --

(i) Has a physical or mental impairment that does not substantially limit major life activities but that is treated by a private entity as constituting such a limitation;

(ii) Has a physical or mental impairment that substantially limits major life activities only as a result of the attitudes of others toward such impairment; or

(iii) Has none of the impairments defined in paragraph (1) of this definition but is treated by a private entity as having such an impairment.

(5) The term <u>disability</u> does not include --

(i) Transvestism, transsexualism, pedophilia, exhibitionism, voyeurism, gender identity disorders not resulting from physical impairments, or other sexual behavior disorders;

that concluded that symptomatic HIV disease is an impairment that substantially limits a major life activity; therefore it has been included in the definition of disability under this part. The opinion also concluded that asymptomatic HIV disease is an impairment that substantially limits a major life activity, either because of its actual effect on the individual with HIV disease or because the reactions of other people to individuals with HIV disease cause such individuals to be treated as though they are disabled. <u>See</u> Memorandum from Douglas W. Kmiec, Acting Assistant Attorney General, Office of Legal Counsel, Department of Justice, to Arthur B. Culvahouse, Jr., Counsel to the President (Sept. 27, 1988), <u>reprinted</u> in Hearings on S. 933, the Americans with Disabilities Act, Before the Subcomm. on the Handicapped of the Senate Comm. on Labor and Human Resources, 101st Cong., 1st Sess. 346 (1989). The phrase "symptomatic or asymptomatic" was inserted in the final rule after "HIV disease" in response to commenters who suggested that the clarification was necessary to give full meaning to the Department's opinion.

Paragraph (1)(iv) of the definition states that the phrase "physical or mental impairment" does not include homosexuality or bisexuality. These conditions were never considered impairments under other Federal disability laws. Section 511(a) of the statute makes clear that they are likewise not to be considered impairments under the Americans with Disabilities Act.

Physical or mental impairment does not include simple physical characteristics, such as blue eyes or black hair. Nor does it include environmental, cultural, economic, or other disadvantages, such as having a prison record, or being poor. Nor is age a disability. Similarly, the definition does not include common personality traits such as poor judgment or a quick temper where these are not symptoms of a mental or psychological disorder. However, a person who has these characteristics and also has a physical or mental impairment may be considered as having a disability for purposes of the Americans with Disabilities Act based on the impairment.

<u>Substantial limitation of a major life activity</u>. Under Test A, the impairment must be one that "substantially limits a major life activity." Major life activities include such things as caring for one's self, performing manual tasks, walking, seeing, hearing, speaking, breathing, learning, and working. For example, a person who is paraplegic is substantially

REGULATION

(ii) Compulsive gambling, kleptomania, or pyromania; or

(iii) Psychoactive substance use disorders resulting from current illegal use of drugs.

ANALYSIS

limited in the major life activity of walking, a person who is blind is substantially limited in the major life activity of seeing, and a person who is mentally retarded is substantially limited in the major life activity of learning. A person with traumatic brain injury is substantially limited in the major life activities of caring for one's self, learning, and working because of memory deficit, confusion, contextual difficulties, and inability to reason appropriately.

A person is considered an individual with a disability for purposes of Test A, the first prong of the definition, when the individual's important life activities are restricted as to the conditions, manner, or duration under which they can be performed in comparison to most people. A person with a minor, trivial impairment, such as a simple infected finger, is not impaired in a major life activity. A person who can walk for 10 miles continuously is not substantially limited in walking merely because, on the eleventh mile, he or she begins to experience pain, because most people would not be able to walk eleven miles without experiencing some discomfort.

The Department received many comments on the proposed rule's inclusion of the word "temporary" in the definition of "disability." The preamble indicated that impairments are not necessarily excluded from the definition of "disability" simply because they are temporary, but that the duration, or expected duration, of an impairment is one factor that may properly be considered in determining whether the impairment substantially limits a major life activity. The preamble recognized, however, that temporary impairments, such as a broken leg, are not commonly regarded as disabilities, and only in rare circumstances would the degree of the limitation and its expected duration be substantial. Nevertheless, many commenters objected to inclusion of the word "temporary" both because it is not in the statute and because it is not contained in the definition of "disability" set forth in the title I regulations of the Equal Employment Opportunity Commission (EEOC). The word "temporary" has been deleted from the final rule to conform with the statutory language. The question of whether a temporary impairment is a disability must be resolved on a case-by-case basis, taking into consideration both the duration (or expected duration) of the impairment and the extent to which it actually limits a major life activity of the affected individual.

The question of whether a person has a disability should

REGULATION

ANALYSIS

be assessed without regard to the availability of mitigating measures, such as reasonable modifications or auxiliary aids and services. For example, a person with hearing loss is substantially limited in the major life activity of hearing, even though the loss may be improved through the use of a hearing aid. Likewise, persons with impairments, such as epilepsy or diabetes, that substantially limit a major life activity, are covered under the first prong of the definition of disability, even if the effects of the impairment are controlled by medication.

Many commenters asked that environmental illness (also known as multiple chemical sensitivity) as well as allergy to cigarette smoke be recognized as disabilities. The Department, however, declines to state categorically that these types of allergies or sensitivities are disabilities, because the determination as to whether an impairment is a disability depends on whether, given the particular circumstances at issue, the impairment substantially limits one or more major life activities (or has a history of, or is regarded as having such an effect).

Sometimes respiratory or neurological functioning is so severely affected that an individual will satisfy the requirements to be considered disabled under the regulation. Such an individual would be entitled to all of the protections afforded by the Act and this part. In other cases, individuals may be sensitive to environmental elements or to smoke but their sensitivity will not rise to the level needed to constitute a disability. For example, their major life activity of breathing may be somewhat, but not substantially, impaired. In such circumstances, the individuals are not disabled and are not entitled to the protections of the statute despite their sensitivity to environmental agents.

In sum, the determination as to whether allergies to cigarette smoke, or allergies or sensitivities characterized by the commenters as environmental illness are disabilities covered by the regulation must be made using the same case-by-case analysis that is applied to all other physical or mental impairments. Moreover, the addition of specific regulatory provisions relating to environmental illness in the final rule would be inappropriate at this time pending future consideration of the issue by the Architectural and Transportation Barriers Compliance Board, the Environmental Protection Agency, and the Occupational Safety and Health Administration of the

REGULATION

ANALYSIS
Department of Labor.

Test B -- A Record of Such an Impairment

This test is intended to cover those who have a record of an impairment. As explained in paragraph (3) of the rule's definition of disability, this includes a person who has a history of an impairment that substantially limited a major life activity, such as someone who has recovered from an impairment. It also includes persons who have been misclassified as having an impairment.

This provision is included in the definition in part to protect individuals who have recovered from a physical or mental impairment that previously substantially limited them in a major life activity. Discrimination on the basis of such a past impairment is prohibited. Frequently occurring examples of the first group (those who have a history of an impairment) are persons with histories of mental or emotional illness, heart disease, or cancer; examples of the second group (those who have been misclassified as having an impairment) are persons who have been misclassified as having mental retardation or mental illness.

Test C -- Being Regarded as Having Such an Impairment

This test, as contained in paragraph (4) of the definition, is intended to cover persons who are treated by a private entity or public accommodation as having a physical or mental impairment that substantially limits a major life activity. It applies when a person is treated as if he or she has an impairment that substantially limits a major life activity, regardless of whether that person has an impairment.

The Americans with Disabilities Act uses the same "regarded as" test set forth in the regulations implementing section 504 of the Rehabilitation Act. See, e.g., 28 CFR 42.540(k)(2)(iv), which provides:

(iv) "Is regarded as having an impairment" means (A) Has a physical or mental impairment that does not substantially limit major life activities but that is treated by a recipient as constituting such a limitation; (B) Has a physical or mental impairment that substantially limits major life activities only as a result of the attitudes of others toward such impairment; or (C) Has none of the impairments defined in paragraph

REGULATION

(k)(2)(i) of this section but is treated by a recipient as having such an impairment.

The perception of the private entity or public accommodation is a key element of this test. A person who perceives himself or herself to have an impairment, but does not have an impairment, and is not treated as if he or she has an impairment, is not protected under this test. A person would be covered under this test if a restaurant refused to serve that person because of a fear of "negative reactions" of others to that person. A person would also be covered if a public accommodation refused to serve a patron because it perceived that the patron had an impairment that limited his or her enjoyment of the goods or services being offered.

For example, persons with severe burns often encounter discrimination in community activities, resulting in substantial limitation of major life activities. These persons would be covered under this test based on the attitudes of others towards the impairment, even if they did not view themselves as "impaired."

The rationale for this third test, as used in the Rehabilitation Act of 1973, was articulated by the Supreme Court in Arline, 480 U.S. 273 (1987). The Court noted that, although an individual may have an impairment that does not in fact substantially limit a major life activity, the reaction of others may prove just as disabling. "Such an impairment might not diminish a person's physical or mental capabilities, but could nevertheless substantially limit that person's ability to work as a result of the negative reactions of others to the impairment." Id. at 283. The Court concluded that, by including this test in the Rehabilitation Act's definition, "Congress acknowledged that society's accumulated myths and fears about disability and disease are as handicapping as are the physical limitations that flow from actual impairment." Id. at 284.

Thus, a person who is not allowed into a public accommodation because of the myths, fears, and stereotypes associated with disabilities would be covered under this third test whether or not the person's physical or mental condition would be considered a disability under the first or second test in the definition.

If a person is refused admittance on the basis of an actual or perceived physical or mental condition, and the public

REGULATION

ANALYSIS

accommodation can articulate no legitimate reason for the refusal (such as failure to meet eligibility criteria), a perceived concern about admitting persons with disabilities could be inferred and the individual would qualify for coverage under the "regarded as" test. A person who is covered because of being regarded as having an impairment is not required to show that the public accommodation's perception is inaccurate (e.g., that he will be accepted by others, or that insurance rates will not increase) in order to be admitted to the public accommodation.

Paragraph (5) of the definition lists certain conditions that are not included within the definition of "disability." The excluded conditions are: transvestism, transsexualism, pedophilia, exhibitionism, voyeurism, gender identity disorders not resulting from physical impairments, other sexual behavior disorders, compulsive gambling, kleptomania, pyromania, and psychoactive substance use disorders resulting from current illegal use of drugs. Unlike homosexuality and bisexuality, which are not considered impairments under either the Americans with Disabilities Act (see the definition of "disability," paragraph (1)(iv)) or section 504, the conditions listed in paragraph (5), except for transvestism, are not necessarily excluded as impairments under section 504. (Transvestism was excluded from the definition of disability for section 504 by the Fair Housing Amendments Act of 1988, Pub. L. 100-430, §6(b).) The phrase "current illegal use of drugs" used in this definition is explained in the preamble to §36.209.

<u>Drug</u> means a controlled substance, as defined in schedules I through V of section 202 of the Controlled Substances Act (21 U.S.C. 812).

"Drug." The definition of the term "drug" is taken from section 510(d)(2) of the ADA.

<u>Facility</u> means all or any portion of buildings, structures, sites, complexes, equipment, rolling stock or other conveyances, roads, walks, passageways, parking lots, or other real or personal property, including the site where the building, property,

"Facility." "Facility" means all or any portion of buildings, structures, sites, complexes, equipment, rolling stock or other conveyances, roads, walks, passageways, parking lots, or other real or personal property, including the site where the building, property, structure, or equipment is located. Committee reports made clear that the definition of facility was drawn from the definition of facility in current Federal regulations (<u>see, e.g.</u>, Education and Labor report at 114). It includes both indoor and outdoor areas where human-con-

REGULATION
structure, or equipment is
located.

ANALYSIS
structed improvements, structures, equipment, or property
have been added to the natural environment.

The term "rolling stock or other conveyances" was not
included in the definition of facility in the proposed rule.
However, commenters raised questions about the applicability
of this part to places of public accommodation operated in
mobile facilities (such as cruise ships, floating restaurants, or
mobile health units). Those places of public accommodation
are covered under this part, and would be included in the
definition of "facility." Thus the requirements of subparts B
and C would apply to those places of public accommodation.
For example, a covered entity could not discriminate on the
basis of disability in the full and equal enjoyment of the
facilities (§36.201). Similarly, a cruise line could not apply
eligibility criteria to potential passengers in a manner that
would screen out individuals with disabilities, unless the
criteria are "necessary," as provided in §36.301.

However, standards for new construction and alterations of
such facilities are not yet included in the Americans with
Disabilities Act Accessibility Guidelines for Buildings and
Facilities (ADAAG) adopted by §36.406 and incorporated in
Appendix A. The Department therefore will not interpret the
new construction and alterations provisions of subpart D to
apply to the types of facilities discussed here, pending further
development of specific requirements.

Requirements pertaining to accessible transportation
services provided by public accommodations are included in
§36.310 of this part; standards pertaining to accessible vehicles will be issued by the Secretary of Transportation pursuant to section 306 of the Act, and will be codified at 49 CFR
Part 37.

A public accommodation has obligations under this rule
with respect to a cruise ship to the extent that its operations are
subject to the laws of the United States.

The definition of "facility" only includes the site over
which the private entity may exercise control or on which a
place of public accommodation or a commercial facility is
located. It does not include, for example, adjacent roads or
walks controlled by a public entity that is not subject to this
part. Public entities are subject to the requirements of title II
of the Act. The Department's regulation implementing title II,

REGULATION

ANALYSIS

which will be codified at 28 CFR part 35, addresses the obligations of public entities to ensure accessibility by providing curb ramps at pedestrian walkways.

Illegal use of drugs means the use of one or more drugs, the possession or distribution of which is unlawful under the Controlled Substances Act (21 U.S.C. 812). The term "illegal use of drugs" does not include the use of a drug taken under supervision by a licensed health care professional, or other uses authorized by the Controlled Substances Act or other provisions of Federal law.

"Illegal use of drugs." The definition of "illegal use of drugs" is taken from section 510(d)(1) of the Act and clarifies that the term includes the illegal use of one or more drugs.

Individual with a disability means a person who has a disability. The term "individual with a disability" does not include an individual who is currently engaging in the illegal use of drugs, when the private entity acts on the basis of such use.

"Individual with a disability" means a person who has a disability but does not include an individual who is currently illegally using drugs, when the public accommodation acts on the basis of such use. The phrase "current illegal use of drugs" is explained in the preamble to §36.209.

Place of public accommodation means a facility, operated by a private entity, whose operations affect commerce and fall within at least one of the following categories--

(1) An inn, hotel, motel, or other place of lodging, except for an establishment located within a building that contains not more than five rooms for rent or hire and that is actually occupied by the proprietor of the estab-

"Place of public accommodation." The term "place of public accommodation" is an adaptation of the statutory definition of "public accommodation" in section 301(7) of the ADA and appears as an element of the regulatory definition of public accommodation. The final rule defines "place of public accommodation" as a facility, operated by a private entity, whose operations affect commerce and fall within at least one of 12 specified categories. The term "public accommodation," on the other hand, is reserved by the final rule for the private entity that owns, leases (or leases to), or operates a place of public accommodation. It is the public accommodation, and not the place of public accommodation, that is subject to the regulation's nondiscrimination requirements. Placing the obligation not to discriminate on the public accommodation, as defined in the rule, is consistent with section 302(a) of the ADA, which places the obligation not to

REGULATION

lishment as the residence of the proprietor;

(2) A restaurant, bar, or other establishment serving food or drink;

(3) A motion picture house, theater, concert hall, stadium, or other place of exhibition or entertainment;

(4) An auditorium, convention center, lecture hall, or other place of public gathering;

(5) A bakery, grocery store, clothing store, hardware store, shopping center, or other sales or rental establishment;

(6) A laundromat, drycleaner, bank, barber shop, beauty shop, travel service, shoe repair service, funeral parlor, gas station, office of an accountant or lawyer, pharmacy, insurance office, professional office of a health care provider, hospital, or other service establishment;

(7) A terminal, depot, or other station used for specified public transportation;

(8) A museum, library, gallery, or other place of public display or collection;

(9) A park, zoo, amusement park, or other place of recreation;

ANALYSIS

discriminate on any person who owns, leases (or leases to), or operates a place of public accommodation.

Facilities operated by government agencies or other public entities as defined in this section do not qualify as places of public accommodation. The actions of public entities are governed by title II of the ADA and will be subject to regulations issued by the Department of Justice under that title. The receipt of government assistance by a private entity does not by itself preclude a facility from being considered as a place of public accommodation.

The definition of place of public accommodation incorporates the 12 categories of facilities represented in the statutory definition of public accommodation in section 301(7) of the ADA:

1. Places of lodging.

2. Establishments serving food or drink.

3. Places of exhibition or entertainment.

4. Places of public gathering.

5. Sales or rental establishments.

6. Service establishments.

7. Stations used for specified public transportation.

8. Places of public display or collection.

9. Places of recreation.

10. Places of education.

11. Social service center establishments.

12. Places of exercise or recreation.

In order to be a place of public accommodation, a facility must be operated by a private entity, its operations must affect commerce, and it must fall within one of these 12 categories. While the list of categories is exhaustive, the representative examples of facilities within each category are not. Within

REGULATION

(10) A nursery, elementary, secondary, undergraduate, or postgraduate private school, or other place of education;

(11) A day care center, senior citizen center, homeless shelter, food bank, adoption agency, or other social service center establishment; and

(12) A gymnasium, health spa, bowling alley, golf course, or other place of exercise or recreation.

ANALYSIS

each category only a few examples are given. The category of social service center establishments would include not only the types of establishments listed, day care centers, senior citizen centers, homeless shelters, food banks, adoption agencies, but also establishments such as substance abuse treatment centers, rape crisis centers, and halfway houses. As another example, the category of sales or rental establishments would include an innumerable array of facilities that would sweep far beyond the few examples given in the regulation. For example, other retail or wholesale establishments selling or renting items, such as bookstores, videotape rental stores, car rental establishments, pet stores, and jewelry stores would also be covered under this category, even though they are not specifically listed.

Several commenters requested clarification as to the coverage of wholesale establishments under the category of "sales or rental establishments." The Department intends for wholesale establishments to be covered under this category as places of public accommodation except in cases where they sell exclusively to other businesses and not to individuals. For example, a company that grows food produce and supplies its crops exclusively to food processing corporations on a wholesale basis does not become a public accommodation because of these transactions. If this company operates a road side stand where its crops are sold to the public, the road side stand would be a sales establishment covered by the ADA. Conversely, a sales establishment that markets its goods as "wholesale to the public" and sells to individuals would not be exempt from ADA coverage despite its use of the word "wholesale" as a marketing technique.

Of course, a company that operates a place of public accommodation is subject to this part only in the operation of that place of public accommodation. In the example given above, the wholesale produce company that operates a road side stand would be a public accommodation only for the purposes of the operation of that stand. The company would be prohibited from discriminating on the basis of disability in the operation of the road side stand, and it would be required to remove barriers to physical access to the extent that it is readily achievable to do so (see §36.304); however, in the event that it is not readily achievable to remove barriers, for example, by replacing a gravel surface or regrading the area around the stand to permit access by persons with mobility impairments, the company could meet its obligations through

REGULATION

ANALYSIS

alternative methods of making its goods available, such as delivering produce to a customer in his or her car (see §36.305). The concepts of readily achievable barrier removal and alternatives to barrier removal are discussed further in the preamble discussion of §§36.304 and 36.305.

Even if a facility does not fall within one of the 12 categories, and therefore does not qualify as a place of public accommodation, it still may be a commercial facility as defined in §36.104 and be subject to the new construction and alterations requirements of subpart D.

A number of commenters questioned the treatment of residential hotels and other residential facilities in the Department's proposed rule. These commenters were essentially seeking resolution of the relationship between the Fair Housing Act and the ADA concerning facilities that are both residential in nature and engage in activities that would cause them to be classified as "places of public accommodation" under the ADA. The ADA's express exemption relating to the Fair Housing Act applies only to "commercial facilities" and not to "places of public accommodation."

A facility whose operations affect interstate commerce is a place of public accommodation for purposes of the ADA to the extent that its operations include those types of activities engaged in or services provided by the facilities contained on the list of 12 categories in section 301(7) of the ADA. Thus, a facility that provides social services would be considered a "social service center establishment." Similarly, the category "places of lodging" would exclude solely residential facilities because the nature of a place of lodging contemplates the use of the facility for short-term stays.

Many facilities, however, are mixed use facilities. For example, in a large hotel that has a separate residential apartment wing, the residential wing would not be covered by the ADA because of the nature of the occupancy of that part of the facility. This residential wing would, however, be covered by the Fair Housing Act. The separate nonresidential accommodations in the rest of the hotel would be a place of lodging, and thus a public accommodation subject to the requirements of this final rule. If a hotel allows both residential and short-term stays, but does not allocate space for these different uses in separate, discrete units, both the ADA and the Fair Housing Act may apply to the facility. Such determinations will need

REGULATION

ANALYSIS

to be made on a case-by-case basis. Any place of lodging of the type described in paragraph (1) of the definition of place of public accommodation and that is an establishment located within a building that contains not more than five rooms for rent or hire and is actually occupied by the proprietor of the establishment as his or her residence is not covered by the ADA. (This exclusion from coverage does not apply to other categories of public accommodations, for example, professional offices or homeless shelters, that are located in a building that is also occupied as a private residence.)

A number of commenters noted that the term "residential hotel" may also apply to a type of hotel commonly known as a "single room occupancy hotel." Although such hotels or portions of such hotels may fall under the Fair Housing Act when operated or used as long-term residences, they are also considered "places of lodging" under the ADA when guests of such hotels are free to use them on a short-term basis. In addition, "single room occupancy hotels" may provide social services to their guests, often through the operation of Federal or State grant programs. In such a situation, the facility would be considered a "social service center establishment" and thus covered by the ADA as a place of public accommodation, regardless of the length of stay of the occupants.

A similar analysis would also be applied to other residential facilities that provide social services, including homeless shelters, shelters for people seeking refuge from domestic violence, nursing homes, residential care facilities, and other facilities where persons may reside for varying lengths of time. Such facilities should be analyzed under the Fair Housing Act to determine the application of that statute. The ADA, however, requires a separate and independent analysis. For example, if the facility, or a portion of the facility, is intended for or permits short-term stays, or if it can appropriately be categorized as a service establishment or as a social service establishment, then the facility or that portion of the facility used for the covered purpose is a place of public accommodation under the ADA. For example, a homeless shelter that is intended and used only for long-term residential stays and that does not provide social services to its residents would not be covered as a place of public accommodation. However, if this facility permitted short-term stays or provided social services to its residents, it would be covered under the ADA either as a "place of lodging" or as a "social service center establishment," or as both.

REGULATION

A private home, by itself, does not fall within any of the 12 categories. However, it can be covered as a place of public accommodation to the extent that it is used as a facility that would fall within one of the 12 categories. For example, if a professional office of a dentist, doctor, or psychologist is located in a private home, the portion of the home dedicated to office use (including areas used both for the residence and the office, e.g., the entrance to the home that is also used as the entrance to the professional office) would be considered a place of public accommodation. Places of public accommodation located in residential facilities are specifically addressed in §36.207.

If a tour of a commercial facility that is not otherwise a place of public accommodation, such as, for example, a factory or a movie studio production set, is open to the general public, the route followed by the tour is a place of public accommodation and the tour must be operated in accordance with the rule's requirements for public accommodations. The place of public accommodation defined by the tour does not include those portions of the commercial facility that are merely viewed from the tour route. Hence, the barrier removal requirements of §36.304 only apply to the physical route followed by the tour participants and not to work stations or other areas that are merely adjacent to, or within view of, the tour route. If the tour is not open to the general public, but rather is conducted, for example, for selected business colleagues, partners, customers, or consultants, the tour route is not a place of public accommodation and the tour is not subject to the requirements for public accommodations.

Public accommodations that receive Federal financial assistance are subject to the requirements of section 504 of the Rehabilitation Act as well as the requirements of the ADA.

Private schools, including elementary and secondary schools, are covered by the rule as places of public accommodation. The rule itself, however, does not require a private school to provide a free appropriate education or develop an individualized education program in accordance with regulations of the Department of Education implementing section 504 of the Rehabilitation Act of 1973, as amended (34 CFR part 104), and regulations implementing the Individuals with Disabilities Education Act (34 CFR part 300). The receipt of Federal assistance by a private school, however, would trigger application of the Department of Education's regulations to

REGULATION

ANALYSIS

the extent mandated by the particular type of assistance received.

Private club means a private club or establishment exempted from coverage under title II of the Civil Rights Act of 1964 (42 U.S.C. 2000a(e)).

"Private club." The term "private club" is defined in accordance with section 307 of the ADA as a private club or establishment exempted from coverage under title II of the Civil Rights Act of 1964. Title II of the 1964 Act exempts any "private club or other establishment not in fact open to the public, except to the extent that the facilities of such establishment are made available to the customers or patrons of [a place of public accommodation as defined in title II]." The rule, therefore, as reflected in §36.102(e) of the application section, limits the coverage of private clubs accordingly. The obligations of a private club that rents space to any other private entity for the operation of a place of public accommodation are discussed further in connection with §36.201.

In determining whether a private entity qualifies as a private club under title II, courts have considered such factors as the degree of member control of club operations, the selectivity of the membership selection process, whether substantial membership fees are charged, whether the entity is operated on a nonprofit basis, the extent to which the facilities are open to the public, the degree of public funding, and whether the club was created specifically to avoid compliance with the Civil Rights Act. See, e.g., Tillman v. Wheaton-Haven Recreation Ass'n, 410 U.S. 431 (1973); Daniel v. Paul, 395 U.S. 298 (1969); Olzman v. Lake Hills Swim Club, Inc., 495 F.2d 1333 (2d Cir. 1974); Anderson v. Pass Christian Isles Golf Club, Inc., 488 F.2d 855 (5th Cir. 1974); Smith v. YMCA, 462 F.2d 634 (5th Cir. 1972); Stout v. YMCA, 404 F.2d 687 (5th Cir. 1968); United States v. Richberg, 398 F.2d 523 (5th Cir. 1968); Nesmith v. YMCA, 397 F.2d 96 (4th Cir. 1968); United States v. Lansdowne Swim Club, 713 F. Supp. 785 (E.D. Pa. 1989); Durham v. Red Lake Fishing and Hunting Club, Inc., 666 F. Supp. 954 (W.D. Tex. 1987); New York v. Ocean Club, Inc., 602 F. Supp. 489 (E.D.N.Y. 1984); Brown v. Loudoun Golf and Country Club, Inc., 573 F. Supp. 399 (E.D. Va. 1983); United States v. Trustees of Fraternal Order of Eagles, 472 F. Supp. 1174 (E.D. Wis. 1979); Cornelius v. Benevolent Protective Order of Elks, 382 F. Supp. 1182 (D. Conn. 1974).

Private entity means a person or entity other than a public entity.

"Private entity." The term "private entity" is defined as any individual or entity other than a public entity. It is used as part of the definition of "public accommodation" in this section.

REGULATION

Public accommodation means a private entity that owns, leases (or leases to), or operates a place of public accommodation.

Public entity means --

(1) Any State or local government;

(2) Any department, agency, special purpose district, or other instrumentality of a State or States or local government; and

(3) The National Railroad Passenger Corporation, and any commuter authority (as defined in section 103(8) of the Rail Passenger Service Act (45 U.S.C. 541)).

ANALYSIS

The definition adds "individual" to the statutory definition of private entity (see section 301(6) of the ADA). This addition clarifies that an individual may be a private entity and, therefore, may be considered a public accommodation if he or she owns, leases (or leases to), or operates a place of public accommodation. The explicit inclusion of individuals under the definition of private entity is consistent with section 302(a) of the ADA, which broadly prohibits discrimination on the basis of disability by any person who owns, leases (or leases to), or operates a place of public accommodation.

"Public accommodation." The term "public accommodation" means a private entity that owns, leases (or leases to), or operates a place of public accommodation. The regulatory term, "public accommodation," corresponds to the statutory term, "person," in section 302(a) of the ADA. The ADA prohibits discrimination "by any person who owns, leases (or leases to), or operates a place of public accommodation." The text of the regulation consequently places the ADA's nondiscrimination obligations on "public accommodations" rather than on "persons" or on "places of public accommodation."

As stated in §36.102(b)(2), the requirements of subparts B and C obligate a public accommodation only with respect to the operations of a place of public accommodation. A public accommodation must also meet the requirements of subpart D with respect to facilities used as, or designed or constructed for use as, places of public accommodation or commercial facilities.

"Public entity." The term "public entity" is defined in accordance with section 201(1) of the ADA as any State or local government; any department, agency, special purpose district, or other instrumentality of a State or States or local government; and the National Railroad Passenger Corporation, and any commuter authority (as defined in section 103(8) of the Rail Passenger Service Act). It is used in the definition of "private entity" in §36.104. Public entities are excluded from the definition of private entity and therefore cannot qualify as public accommodations under this regulation. However, the actions of public entities are covered by title II of the ADA and by the Department's title II regulations codified at 28 CFR part 35.

REGULATION

Qualified interpreter means an interpreter who is able to interpret effectively, accurately and impartially both receptively and expressively, using any necessary specialized vocabulary.

ANALYSIS

"Qualified interpreter." The Department received substantial comment regarding the lack of a definition of "qualified interpreter." The proposed rule defined auxiliary aids and services to include the statutory term, "qualified interpreters" (§36.303(b)), but did not define that term. Section 36.303 requires the use of a qualified interpreter where necessary to achieve effective communication, unless an undue burden or fundamental alteration would result. Commenters stated that a lack of guidance on what the term means would create confusion among those trying to secure interpreting services and often result in less than effective communication.

Many commenters were concerned that, without clear guidance on the issue of "qualified" interpreter, the rule would be interpreted to mean "available, rather than qualified" interpreters. Some claimed that few public accommodations would understand the difference between a qualified interpreter and a person who simply knows a few signs or how to fingerspell.

In order to clarify what is meant by "qualified interpreter" the Department has added a definition of the term to the final rule. A qualified interpreter means an interpreter who is able to interpret effectively, accurately, and impartially both receptively and expressively, using any necessary specialized vocabulary. This definition focuses on the actual ability of the interpreter in a particular interpreting context to facilitate effective communication between the public accommodation and the individual with disabilities.

Public comment also revealed that public accommodations have at times asked persons who are deaf to provide family members or friends to interpret. In certain circumstances, notwithstanding that the family member or friend is able to interpret or is a certified interpreter, the family member or friend may not be qualified to render the necessary interpretation because of factors such as emotional or personal involvement or considerations of confidentiality that may adversely affect the ability to interpret "effectively, accurately, and impartially."

Readily achievable means easily accomplishable and able to be carried out without much difficulty or

"Readily achievable." The definition of "readily achievable" follows the statutory definition of that term in section 301(9) of the ADA. Readily achievable means easily accomplishable and able to be carried out without much

REGULATION

expense. In determining whether an action is readily achievable factors to be considered include--

(1) The nature and cost of the action needed under this part;

(2) The overall financial resources of the site or sites involved in the action; the number of persons employed at the site; the effect on expenses and resources; legitimate safety requirements that are necessary for safe operation, including crime prevention measures; or the impact otherwise of the action upon the operation of the site;

(3) The geographic separateness, and the administrative or fiscal relationship of the site or sites in question to any parent corporation or entity;

(4) If applicable, the overall financial resources of any parent corporation or entity; the overall size of the parent corporation or entity with respect to the number of its employees; the number, type, and location of its facilities; and

(5) If applicable, the type of operation or operations of any parent corporation or entity, including the composition, structure, and functions of the workforce of

ANALYSIS

difficulty or expense. The term is used as a limitation on the obligation to remove barriers under §§36.304(a), 36.305(a), 36.308(a), and 36.310(b). Further discussion of the meaning and application of the term "readily achievable" may be found in the preamble section for §36.304.

The definition lists factors to be considered in determining whether barrier removal is readily achievable in any particular circumstance. A significant number of commenters objected to §36.306 of the proposed rule, which listed identical factors to be considered for determining "readily achievable" and "undue burden" together in one section. They asserted that providing a consolidated section blurred the distinction between the level of effort required by a public accommodation under the two standards. The readily achievable standard is a "lower" standard than the "undue burden" standard in terms of the level of effort required, but the factors used in determining whether an action is readily achievable or would result in an undue burden are identical (see Education and Labor report at 109). Although the preamble to the proposed rule clearly delineated the relationship between the two standards, to eliminate any confusion the Department has deleted §36.306 of the proposed rule. That section, in any event, as other commenters noted, had merely repeated the lists of factors contained in the definitions of readily achievable and undue burden.

The list of factors included in the definition is derived from section 301(9) of the ADA. It reflects the congressional intention that a wide range of factors be considered in determining whether an action is readily achievable. It also takes into account that many local facilities are owned or operated by parent corporations or entities that conduct operations at many different sites. This section makes clear that, in some instances, resources beyond those of the local facility where the barrier must be removed may be relevant in determining whether an action is readily achievable. One must also evaluate the degree to which any parent entity has resources that may be allocated to the local facility.

The statutory list of factors in section 301(9) of the Act uses the term "covered entity" to refer to the larger entity of which a particular facility may be a part. "Covered entity" is not a defined term in the ADA and is not used consistently throughout the Act. The definition, therefore, substitutes the term "parent entity" in place of "covered entity" in paragraphs

REGULATION

the parent corporation or
entity.

ANALYSIS

(3), (4), and (5) when referring to the larger private entity
whose overall resources may be taken into account. This
usage is consistent with the House Judiciary Committee's use
of the term "parent company" to describe the larger entity of
which the local facility is a part (H.R. Rep. No. 485, 101st
Cong., 2d Sess., pt. 3, at 40-41, 54-55 (1990) [hereinafter
"Judiciary report"]).

A number of commenters asked for more specific guidance as to when and how the resources of a parent corporation or entity are to be taken into account in determining what
is readily achievable. The Department believes that this
complex issue is most appropriately resolved on a case-by-
case basis. As the comments reflect, there is a wide variety
of possible relationships between the site in question and any
parent corporation or other entity. It would be unwise to
posit legal ramifications under the ADA of even generic
relationships (e.g., banks involved in foreclosures or insurance companies operating as trustees or in other similar
fiduciary relationships), because any analysis will depend so
completely on the detailed fact situations and the exact nature
of the legal relationships involved. The final rule does,
however, reorder the factors to be considered. This shift and
the addition of the phrase "if applicable" make clear that the
line of inquiry concerning factors will start at the site involved in the action itself. This change emphasizes that the
overall resources, size, and operations of the parent corporation or entity should be considered to the extent appropriate
in light of "the geographic separateness, and the administrative or fiscal relationship of the site or sites in question to any
parent corporation or entity."

Although some commenters sought more specific numerical guidance on the definition of readily achievable, the
Department has declined to establish in the final rule any kind
of numerical formula for determining whether an action is
readily achievable. It would be difficult to devise a specific
ceiling on compliance costs that would take into account the
vast diversity of enterprises covered by the ADA's public
accommodations requirements and the economic situation
that any particular entity would find itself in at any moment.
The final rule, therefore, implements the flexible case-by-
case approach chosen by Congress.

A number of commenters requested that security considerations be explicitly recognized as a factor in determining

REGULATION

Religious entity means a religious organization or entity controlled by a religious organization, including a place of worship.

ANALYSIS

whether a barrier removal action is readily achievable. The Department believes that legitimate safety requirements, including crime prevention measures, may be taken into account so long as they are based on actual risks and are necessary for safe operation of the public accommodation. This point has been included in the definition.

Some commenters urged the Department not to consider acts of barrier removal in complete isolation from each other in determining whether they are readily achievable. The Department believes that it is appropriate to consider the cost of other barrier removal actions as one factor in determining whether a measure is readily achievable.

"Religious entity." The term "religious entity" is defined in accordance with section 307 of the ADA as a religious organization or entity controlled by a religious organization, including a place of worship. Section 36.102(e) of the rule states that the rule does not apply to any religious entity.

The ADA's exemption of religious organizations and religious entities controlled by religious organizations is very broad, encompassing a wide variety of situations. Religious organizations and entities controlled by religious organizations have no obligations under the ADA. Even when a religious organization carries out activities that would otherwise make it a public accommodation, the religious organization is exempt from ADA coverage. Thus, if a church itself operates a day care center, a nursing home, a private school, or a diocesan school system, the operations of the center, home, school, or schools would not be subject to the requirements of the ADA or this part. The religious entity would not lose its exemption merely because the services provided were open to the general public. The test is whether the church or other religious organization operates the public accommodation, not which individuals receive the public accommodation's services.

Religious entities that are controlled by religious organizations are also exempt from the ADA's requirements. Many religious organizations in the United States use lay boards and other secular or corporate mechanisms to operate schools and an array of social services. The use of a lay board or other mechanism does not itself remove the ADA's religious exemption. Thus, a parochial school, having religious doctrine in its curriculum and sponsored by a religious order, could be exempt either as a religious organization or as an entity con-

REGULATION

ANALYSIS

trolled by a religious organization, even if it has a lay board. The test remains a factual one -- whether the church or other religious organization controls the operations of the school or of the service or whether the school or service is itself a religious organization.

Although a religious organization or a religious entity that is controlled by a religious organization has no obligations under the rule, a public accommodation that is not itself a religious organization, but that operates a place of public accommodation in leased space on the property of a religious entity, which is not a place of worship, is subject to the rule's requirements if it is not under control of a religious organization. When a church rents meeting space, which is not a place of worship, to a local community group or to a private, independent day care center, the ADA applies to the activities of the local community group and day care center if a lease exists and consideration is paid.

Service animal means any guide dog, signal dog, or other animal individually trained to do work or perform tasks for the benefit of an individual with a disability, including, but not limited to, guiding individuals with impaired vision, alerting individuals with impaired hearing to intruders or sounds, providing minimal protection or rescue work, pulling a wheelchair, or fetching dropped items.

"Service animal." The term "service animal" encompasses any guide dog, signal dog, or other animal individually trained to provide assistance to an individual with a disability. The term is used in §36.302(c), which requires public accommodations generally to modify policies, practices, and procedures to accommodate the use of service animals in places of public accommodation.

Specified public transportation means transportation by bus, rail, or any other conveyance (other than by aircraft) that provides the general public with general or special service (including charter service) on a regular and continuing basis.

"Specified public transportation." The definition of "specified public transportation" is identical to the statutory definition in section 301(10) of the ADA. The term means transportation by bus, rail, or any other conveyance (other than by aircraft) that provides the general public with general or special service (including charter service) on a regular and continuing basis. It is used in category (7) of the definition of "place of public accommodation," which includes stations used for specified public transportation.

The effect of this definition, which excludes transporta-

REGULATION

ANALYSIS

tion by aircraft, is that it excludes privately operated airports from coverage as places of public accommodation. However, places of public accommodation located within airports would be covered by this part. Airports that are operated by public entities are covered by title II of the ADA and, if they are operated as part of a program receiving Federal financial assistance, by section 504 of the Rehabilitation Act. Privately operated airports are similarly covered by section 504 if they are operated as part of a program receiving Federal financial assistance. The operations of any portion of any airport that are under the control of an air carrier are covered by the Air Carrier Access Act. In addition, airports are covered as commercial facilities under this rule.

State means each of the several States, the District of Columbia, the Commonwealth of Puerto Rico, Guam, American Samoa, the Virgin Islands, the Trust Territory of the Pacific Islands, and the Commonwealth of the Northern Mariana Islands.

"State." The definition of "State" is identical to the statutory definition in section 3(3) of the ADA. The term is used in the definitions of "commerce" and "public entity" in §36.104.

Undue burden means significant difficulty or expense. In determining whether an action would result in an undue burden, factors to be considered include--

(1) The nature and cost of the action needed under this part;

(2) The overall financial resources of the site or sites involved in the action; the number of persons employed at the site; the effect on expenses and resources; legitimate safety requirements that are necessary for safe operation, including

"Undue burden." The definition of "undue burden" is analogous to the statutory definition of "undue hardship" in employment under section 101(10) of the ADA. The term undue burden means "significant difficulty or expense" and serves as a limitation on the obligation to provide auxiliary aids and services under §36.303 and §§36.309(b)(3) and (c)(3). Further discussion of the meaning and application of the term undue burden may be found in the preamble discussion of §36.303.

The definition lists factors considered in determining whether provision of an auxiliary aid or service in any particular circumstance would result in an undue burden. The factors to be considered in determining whether an action would result in an undue burden are identical to those to be considered in determining whether an action is readily achievable. However, "readily achievable" is a lower standard than "undue burden" in that it requires a lower level of effort on the part of the public accommodation (see Education and Labor report at 109).

REGULATION

crime prevention measures; or the impact otherwise of the action upon the operation of the site;

(3) The geographic separateness, and the administrative or fiscal relationship of the site or sites in question to any parent corporation or entity;

(4) If applicable, the overall financial resources of any parent corporation or entity; the overall size of the parent corporation or entity with respect to the number of its employees; the number, type, and location of its facilities; and

(5) If applicable, the type of operation or operations of any parent corporation or entity, including the composition, structure, and functions of the workforce of the parent corporation or entity.

ANALYSIS

Further analysis of the factors to be considered in determining undue burden may be found in the preamble discussion of the definition of the term "readily achievable."

REGULATION
Subpart B -- General Requirements

ANALYSIS
Subpart B -- General Requirements

Subpart B includes general prohibitions restricting a public accommodation from discriminating against people with disabilities by denying them the opportunity to benefit from goods or services, by giving them unequal goods or services, or by giving them different or separate goods or services. These general prohibitions are patterned after the basic, general prohibitions that exist in other civil rights laws that prohibit discrimination on the basis of race, sex, color, religion, or national origin.

§36.201 General.

(a) Prohibition of discrimination. No individual shall be discriminated against on the basis of disability in the full and equal enjoyment of the goods, services, facilities, privileges, advantages, or accommodations of any place of public accommodation by any private entity who owns, leases (or leases to), or operates a place of public accommodation.

(b) Landlord and tenant responsibilities. Both the landlord who owns the building that houses a place of public accommodation and the tenant who owns or operates the place of public accommodation are public accommodations subject to the requirements of this part. As between the parties, allocation of responsibility for complying with the obligations of this part may be determined by lease or other contract.

Section 36.201 General.

Section 36.201(a) contains the general rule that prohibits discrimination on the basis of disability in the full and equal enjoyment of goods, services, facilities, privileges, advantages, and accommodations of any place of public accommodation.

Full and equal enjoyment means the right to participate and to have an equal opportunity to obtain the same results as others to the extent possible with such accommodations as may be required by the Act and these regulations. It does not mean that an individual with a disability must achieve an identical result or level of achievement as persons without a disability. For example, an exercise class cannot exclude a person who uses a wheelchair because he or she cannot do all of the exercises and derive the same result from the class as persons without a disability.

Section 302(a) of the ADA states that the prohibition against discrimination applies to "any person who owns, leases (or leases to), or operates a place of public accommodation," and this language is reflected in §36.201(a). The coverage is quite extensive and would include sublessees, management companies, and any other entity that owns, leases, leases to, or operates a place of public accommodation, even if the operation is only for a short time.

The first sentence of paragraph (b) of §36.201 reiterates the general principle that both the landlord that owns the building that houses the place of public accommodation, as well as the tenant that owns or operates the place of public accommodation, are public accommodations subject to the requirements of this part. Although the statutory language could be interpreted as placing equal responsibility on all private entities, whether lessor, lessee, or operator of a public accommodation, the committee reports suggest that liability

ANALYSIS

may be allocated. Section 36.201(b) of that section of the proposed rule attempted to allocate liability in the regulation itself. Paragraph (b)(2) of that section made a specific allocation of liability for the obligation to take readily achievable measures to remove barriers, and paragraph (b)(3) made a specific allocation for the obligation to provide auxiliary aids.

Numerous commenters pointed out that these allocations would not apply in all situations. Some asserted that paragraph (b)(2) of the proposed rule only addressed the situation when a lease gave the tenant the right to make alterations with permission of the landlord, but failed to address other types of leases, e.g., those that are silent on the right to make alterations, or those in which the landlord is not permitted to enter a tenant's premises to make alterations. Several commenters noted that many leases contain other clauses more relevant to the ADA than the alterations clause. For example, many leases contain a "compliance clause," a clause which allocates responsibility to a particular party for compliance with all relevant Federal, State, and local laws. Many commenters pointed out various types of relationships that were left unaddressed by the regulation, e.g., sale and leaseback arrangements where the landlord is a financial institution with no control or responsibility for the building; franchises; subleases; and management companies which, at least in the hotel industry, often have control over operations but are unable to make modifications to the premises.

Some commenters raised specific questions as to how the barrier removal allocation would work as a practical matter. Paragraph (b)(2) of the proposed rule provided that the burden of making readily achievable modifications within the tenant's place of public accommodation would shift to the landlord when the modifications were not readily achievable for the tenant or when the landlord denied a tenant's request for permission to make such modifications. Commenters noted that the rule did not specify exactly when the burden would actually shift from tenant to landlord and whether the landlord would have to accept a tenant's word that a particular action is not readily achievable. Others questioned if the tenant should be obligated to use alternative methods of barrier removal before the burden shifts. In light of the fact that readily achievable removal of barriers can include such actions as moving of racks and displays, some commenters doubted the appropriateness of requiring a landlord to become involved in day-to-day operations of its tenants' businesses.

REGULATION

The Department received widely differing comments in response to the preamble question asking whether landlord and tenant obligations should vary depending on the length of time remaining on an existing lease. Many suggested that tenants should have no responsibilities in "shorter leases," which commenters defined as ranging anywhere from 90 days to three years. Other commenters pointed out that the time remaining on the lease should not be a factor in the rule's allocation of responsibilities, but is relevant in determining what is readily achievable for the tenant. The Department agrees with this latter approach and will interpret the rule in that manner.

In recognition of the somewhat limited applicability of the allocation scheme contained in the proposed rule, paragraphs (b)(2) and (b)(3) have been deleted from the final rule. The Department has substituted instead a statement that allocation of responsibility as between the parties for taking readily achievable measures to remove barriers and to provide auxiliary aids and services both in common areas and within places of public accommodation may be determined by the lease or other contractual relationships between the parties. The ADA was not intended to change existing landlord/tenant responsibilities as set forth in the lease. By deleting specific provisions from the rule, the Department gives full recognition to this principle. As between the landlord and tenant, the extent of responsibility for particular obligations may be, and in many cases probably will be, determined by contract.

The suggested allocation of responsibilities contained in the proposed rule may be used if appropriate in a particular situation. Thus, the landlord would generally be held responsible for making readily achievable changes and providing auxiliary aids and services in common areas and for modifying policies, practices, or procedures applicable to all tenants, and the tenant would generally be responsible for readily achievable changes, provision of auxiliary aids, and modification of policies within its own place of public accommodation.

Many commenters objected to the proposed rule's allocation of responsibility for providing auxiliary aids and services solely to the tenant, pointing out that this exclusive allocation may not be appropriate in the case of larger public accommodations that operate their businesses by renting space out to

ANALYSIS

smaller public accommodations. For example, large theaters often rent to smaller traveling companies and hospitals often rely on independent contractors to provide childbirth classes. Groups representing persons with disabilities objected to the proposed rule because, in their view, it permitted the large theater or hospital to evade ADA responsibilities by leasing to independent smaller entities. They suggested that these types of public accommodations are not really landlords because they are in the business of providing a service, rather than renting space, as in the case of a shopping center or office building landlord. These commenters believed that responsibility for providing auxiliary aids should shift to the landlord, if the landlord relies on a smaller public accommodation or independent contractor to provide services closely related to those of the larger public accommodation, and if the needed auxiliary aids prove to be an undue burden for the smaller public accommodation. The final rule no longer lists specific allocations to specific parties but, rather, leaves allocation of responsibilities to the lease negotiations. Parties are, therefore, free to allocate the responsibility for auxiliary aids.

Section 36.201(b)(4) of the proposed rule, which provided that alterations by a tenant on its own premises do not trigger a path of travel obligation on the landlord, has been moved to §36.403(d) of the final rule.

An entity that is not in and of itself a public accommodation, such as a trade association or performing artist, may become a public accommodation when it leases space for a conference or performance at a hotel, convention center, or stadium. For an entity to become a public accommodation when it is the lessee of space, however, the Department believes that consideration in some form must be given. Thus, a Boy Scout troop that accepts donated space does not become a public accommodation because the troop has not "leased" space, as required by the ADA.

As a public accommodation, the trade association or performing artist will be responsible for compliance with this part. Specific responsibilities should be allocated by contract, but, generally, the lessee should be responsible for providing auxiliary aids and services (which could include interpreters, braille programs, etc.) for the participants in its conference or performance as well as for assuring that displays are accessible to individuals with disabilities.

REGULATION

Some commenters suggested that the rule should allocate responsibilities for areas other than removal of barriers and auxiliary aids. The final rule leaves allocation of all areas to the lease negotiations. However, in general landlords should not be given responsibility for policies a tenant applies in operating its business, if such policies are solely those of the tenant. Thus, if a restaurant tenant discriminates by refusing to seat a patron, it would be the tenant, and not the landlord, who would be responsible, because the discriminatory policy is imposed solely by the tenant and not by the landlord. If, however, a tenant refuses to modify a "no pets" rule to allow service animals in its restaurant because the landlord mandates such a rule, then both the landlord and the tenant would be liable for violation of the ADA when a person with a service dog is refused entrance. The Department wishes to emphasize, however, that the parties are free to allocate responsibilities in any way they choose.

Private clubs are also exempt from the ADA. However, consistent with title II of the Civil Rights Act (42 U.S.C. 2000a(e),) a private club is considered a public accommodation to the extent that "the facilities of such establishment are made available to the customers or patrons" of a place of public accommodation. Thus, if a private club runs a day care center that is open exclusively to its own members, the club, like the church in the example above, would have no responsibility for compliance with the ADA. Nor would the day care center have any responsibilities because it is part of the private club exempt from the ADA.

On the other hand, if the private club rents to a day care center that is open to the public, then the private club would have the same obligations as any other public accommodation that functions as a landlord with respect to compliance with title III within the day care center. In such a situation, both the private club that "leases to" a public accommodation and the public accommodation lessee (the day care center) would be subject to the ADA. This same principle would apply if the private club were to rent to, for example, a bar association, which is not generally a public accommodation but which, as explained above, becomes a public accommodation when it leases space for a conference.

REGULATION

§36.202 Activities.

(a) Denial of participation. A public accommodation shall not subject an individual or class of individuals on the basis of a disability or disabilities of such individual or class, directly, or through contractual, licensing, or other arrangements, to a denial of the opportunity of the individual or class to participate in or benefit from the goods, services, facilities, privileges, advantages, or accommodations of a place of public accommodation.

(b) Participation in unequal benefit. A public accommodation shall not afford an individual or class of individuals, on the basis of a disability or disabilities of such individual or class, directly, or through contractual, licensing, or other arrangements, with the opportunity to participate in or benefit from a good, service, facility, privilege, advantage, or accommodation that is not equal to that afforded to other individuals.

(c) Separate benefit. A public accommodation shall not provide an individual or class of individuals, on the basis of a disability or disabilities of such individual or class, directly, or through contractual, licensing, or other arrangements with a good, service, facility,

ANALYSIS

Section 36.202 Activities.

Section 36.202 sets out the general forms of discrimination prohibited by title III of the ADA. These general prohibitions are further refined by the specific prohibitions in subpart C. Section 36.213 makes clear that the limitations on the ADA's requirements contained in subpart C, such as "necessity" (§36.301(a)) and "safety" (§36.301(b)), are applicable to the prohibitions in §36.202. Thus, it is unnecessary to add these limitations to §36.202 as has been requested by some commenters. In addition, the language of §36.202 very closely tracks the language of section 302(b)(1)(A) of the Act, and that statutory provision does not expressly contain these limitations.

Deny participation -- Section 36.202(a) provides that it is discriminatory to deny a person with a disability the right to participate in or benefit from the goods, services, facilities, privileges, advantages, or accommodations of a place of public accommodation.

A public accommodation may not exclude persons with disabilities on the basis of disability for reasons other than those specifically set forth in this part. For example, a public accommodation cannot refuse to serve a person with a disability because its insurance company conditions coverage or rates on the absence of persons with disabilities. This is a frequent basis of exclusion from a variety of community activities and is prohibited by this part.

Unequal benefit -- Section 36.202(b) prohibits services or accommodations that are not equal to those provided others. For example, persons with disabilities must not be limited to certain performances at a theater.

Separate benefit -- Section 36.202(c) permits different or separate benefits or services only when necessary to provide persons with disabilities opportunities as effective as those provided others. This paragraph permitting separate benefits "when necessary" should be read together with §36.203(a), which requires integration in "the most integrated setting appropriate to the needs of the individual." The preamble to that section provides further guidance on separate programs. Thus, this section would not prohibit the designation of parking spaces for persons with disabilities.

Each of the three paragraphs (a)-(c) prohibits discrimina-

REGULATION

privilege, advantage, or accommodation that is different or separate from that provided to other individuals, unless such action is necessary to provide the individual or class of individuals with a good, service, facility, privilege, advantage, or accommodation, or other opportunity that is as effective as that provided to others.

(d) Individual or class of individuals. For purposes of paragraphs (a) through (c) of this section, the term "individual or class of individuals" refers to the clients or customers of the public accommodation that enters into the contractual, licensing, or other arrangement.

ANALYSIS

tion against an individual or class of individuals "either directly or through contractual, licensing, or other arrangements." The intent of the contractual prohibitions of these paragraphs is to prohibit a public accommodation from doing indirectly, through a contractual relationship, what it may not do directly. Thus, the "individual or class of individuals" referenced in the three paragraphs is intended to refer to the clients and customers of the public accommodation that entered into a contractual arrangement. It is not intended to encompass the clients or customers of other entities. A public accommodation, therefore, is not liable under this provision for discrimination that may be practiced by those with whom it has a contractual relationship, when that discrimination is not directed against its own clients or customers. For example, if an amusement park contracts with a food service company to operate its restaurants at the park, the amusement park is not responsible for other operations of the food service company that do not involve clients or customers of the amusement park. Section 36.202(d) makes this clear by providing that the term "individual or class of individuals" refers to the clients or customers of the public accommodation that enters into the contractual, licensing, or other arrangement.

REGULATION

§36.203 Integrated settings.

(a) <u>General</u>. A public accommodation shall afford goods, services, facilities, privileges, advantages, and accommodations to an individual with a disability in the most integrated setting appropriate to the needs of the individual.

(b) <u>Opportunity to participate</u>. Notwithstanding the existence of separate or different programs or activities provided in accordance with this subpart, a public accommodation shall not deny an individual with a disability an opportunity to participate in such programs or activities that are not separate or different.

(c) <u>Accommodations and services</u>. (1) Nothing in this part shall be construed to require an individual with a disability to accept an accommodation, aid, service, opportunity, or benefit available under this part that such individual chooses not to accept.

(2) Nothing in the Act or this part authorizes the representative or guardian of an individual with a disability to decline food, water, medical treatment, or medical services for that individual.

ANALYSIS

Section 36.203 Integrated settings.

Section 36.203 addresses the integration of persons with disabilities. The ADA recognizes that the provision of goods and services in an integrated manner is a fundamental tenet of nondiscrimination on the basis of disability. Providing segregated accommodations and services relegates persons with disabilities to the status of second-class citizens. For example, it would be a violation of this provision to require persons with mental disabilities to eat in the back room of a restaurant or to refuse to allow a person with a disability the full use of a health spa because of stereotypes about the person's ability to participate. Section 36.203(a) states that a public accommodation shall afford goods, services, facilities, privileges, advantages, and accommodations to an individual with a disability in the most integrated setting appropriate to the needs of the individual. Section 36.203(b) specifies that, notwithstanding the existence of separate or different programs or activities provided in accordance with this section, an individual with a disability shall not be denied the opportunity to participate in such programs or activities that are not separate or different. Section 306.203(c), which is derived from section 501(d) of the Americans with Disabilities Act, states that nothing in this part shall be construed to require an individual with a disability to accept an accommodation, aid, service, opportunity, or benefit that he or she chooses not to accept.

Taken together, these provisions are intended to prohibit exclusion and segregation of individuals with disabilities and the denial of equal opportunities enjoyed by others, based on, among other things, presumptions, patronizing attitudes, fears, and stereotypes about individuals with disabilities. Consistent with these standards, public accommodations are required to make decisions based on facts applicable to individuals and not on the basis of presumptions as to what a class of individuals with disabilities can or cannot do.

Sections 36.203(b) and (c) make clear that individuals with disabilities cannot be denied the opportunity to participate in programs that are not separate or different. This is an important and overarching principle of the Americans with Disabilities Act. Separate, special, or different programs that are designed to provide a benefit to persons with disabilities cannot be used to restrict the participation of persons with disabilities in general, integrated activities.

REGULATION

For example, a person who is blind may wish to decline participating in a special museum tour that allows persons to touch sculptures in an exhibit and instead tour the exhibit at his or her own pace with the museum's recorded tour. It is not the intent of this section to require the person who is blind to avail himself or herself of the special tour. Modified participation for persons with disabilities must be a choice, not a requirement.

Further, it would not be a violation of this section for an establishment to offer recreational programs specially designed for children with mobility impairments in those limited circumstances. However, it would be a violation of this section if the entity then excluded these children from other recreational services made available to nondisabled children, or required children with disabilities to attend only designated programs.

Many commenters asked that the Department clarify a public accommodation's obligations within the integrated program when it offers a separate program, but an individual with a disability chooses not to participate in the separate program. It is impossible to make a blanket statement as to what level of auxiliary aids or modifications are required in the integrated program. Rather, each situation must be assessed individually. Assuming the integrated program would be appropriate for a particular individual, the extent to which that individual must be provided with modifications will depend not only on what the individual needs but also on the limitations set forth in subpart C. For example, it may constitute an undue burden for a particular public accommodation, which provides a full-time interpreter in its special guided tour for individuals with hearing impairments, to hire an additional interpreter for those individuals who choose to attend the integrated program. The Department cannot identify categorically the level of assistance or aid required in the integrated program.

The preamble to the proposed rule contained a statement that some interpreted as encouraging the continuation of separate schools, sheltered workshops, special recreational programs, and other similar programs. It is important to emphasize that §36.202(c) only calls for separate programs when such programs are "necessary" to provide as effective an opportunity to individuals with disabilities as to other individuals. Likewise, §36.203(a) only permits separate

REGULATION

programs when a more integrated setting would not be "appropriate." Separate programs are permitted, then, in only limited circumstances. The sentence at issue has been deleted from the preamble because it was too broadly stated and had been erroneously interpreted as Departmental encouragement of separate programs without qualification.

The proposed rule's reference in §36.203(b) to separate programs or activities provided in accordance with "this section" has been changed to "this subpart" in recognition of the fact that separate programs or activities may, in some limited circumstances, be permitted not only by §36.203(a) but also by §36.202(c).

In addition, some commenters suggested that the individual with the disability is the only one who can decide whether a setting is "appropriate" and what the "needs" are. Others suggested that only the public accommodation can make these determinations. The regulation does not give exclusive responsibility to either party. Rather, the determinations are to be made based on an objective view, presumably one which would take into account views of both parties.

Some commenters expressed concern that §36.203(c), which states that nothing in the rule requires an individual with a disability to accept special accommodations and services provided under the ADA, could be interpreted to allow guardians of infants or older people with disabilities to refuse medical treatment for their wards. Section 36.203(c) has been revised to make it clear that paragraph (c) is inapplicable to the concern of the commenters. A new paragraph (c)(2) has been added stating that nothing in the regulation authorizes the representative or guardian of an individual with a disability to decline food, water, medical treatment, or medical services for that individual. New paragraph (c) clarifies that neither the ADA nor the regulation alters current Federal law ensuring the rights of incompetent individuals with disabilities to receive food, water, and medical treatment. See, e.g., Child Abuse Amendments of 1984 (42 U.S.C. 5106a(b)(10), 5106g(10)); Rehabilitation Act of 1973, as amended (29 U.S.C 794); Developmentally Disabled Assistance and Bill of Rights Act (42 U.S.C. 6042).

Sections 36.203(c)(1) and (2) are based on section 501(d) of the ADA. Section 501(d) was designed to clarify that nothing in the ADA requires individuals with disabilities to

REGULATION

accept special accommodations and services for individuals with disabilities that may segregate them:

The Committee added this section [501(d)] to clarify that nothing in the ADA is intended to permit discriminatory treatment on the basis of disability, even when such treatment is rendered under the guise of providing an accommodation, service, aid or benefit to the individual with disability. For example, a blind individual may choose not to avail himself or herself of the right to go to the front of a line, even if a particular public accommodation has chosen to offer such a modification of a policy for blind individuals. Or, a blind individual may choose to decline to participate in a special museum tour that allows persons to touch sculptures in an exhibit and instead tour the exhibits at his or her own pace with the museum's recorded tour.

(Judiciary report at 71-72.) The Act is not to be construed to mean that an individual with disabilities must accept special accommodations and services for individuals with disabilities when that individual chooses to participate in the regular services already offered. Because medical treatment, including treatment for particular conditions, is not a special accommodation or service for individuals with disabilities under section 501(d), neither the Act nor this part provides affirmative authority to suspend such treatment. Section 501(d) is intended to clarify that the Act is not designed to foster discrimination through mandatory acceptance of special services when other alternatives are provided; this concern does not reach to the provision of medical treatment for the disabling condition itself.

Section 36.213 makes clear that the limitations contained in subpart C are to be read into subpart B. Thus, the integration requirement is subject to the various defenses contained in subpart C, such as safety, if eligibility criteria are at issue (§36.301(b)), or fundamental alteration and undue burden, if the concern is provision of auxiliary aids (§36.303(a)).

REGULATION

§36.204 Administrative methods.

A public accommodation shall not, directly or through contractual or other arrangements, utilize standards or criteria or methods of administration that have the effect of discrimina-ting on the basis of disability, or that perpetuate the discrimination of others who are subject to common administrative control.

ANALYSIS

Section 36.204 Administrative methods.

Section 36.204 specifies that an individual or entity shall not, directly, or through contractual or other arrangements, utilize standards or criteria or methods of administration that have the effect of discriminating on the basis of disability or that perpetuate the discrimination of others who are subject to common administrative control. The preamble discussion of §36.301 addresses eligibility criteria in detail.

Section 36.204 is derived from section 302(b)(1)(D) of the Americans with Disabilities Act, and it uses the same language used in the employment section of the ADA (section 102(b)(3)). Both sections incorporate a disparate impact standard to ensure the effectiveness of the legislative mandate to end discrimination. This standard is consistent with the interpretation of section 504 by the U.S. Supreme Court in Alexander v. Choate, 469 U.S. 287 (1985). The Court in Choate explained that members of Congress made numerous statements during passage of section 504 regarding eliminating architectural barriers, providing access to transportation, and eliminating discriminatory effects of job qualification procedures. The Court then noted: "These statements would ring hollow if the resulting legislation could not rectify the harms resulting from action that discriminated by effect as well as by design." Id at 297 (footnote omitted).

Of course, §36.204 is subject to the various limitations contained in subpart C including, for example, necessity (§36.301(a)), safety (§36.301(b)), fundamental alteration (§36.302(a)), readily achievable (§36.304(a)), and undue burden (§36.303(a)).

REGULATION

§36.205 Association.

A public accommodation shall not exclude or otherwise deny equal goods, services, facilities, privileges, advantages, accommodations, or other opportunities to an individual or entity because of the known disability of an individual with whom the individual or entity is known to have a relationship or association.

ANALYSIS

Section 36.205 Association.

Section 36.205 implements section 302(b)(1)(E) of the Act, which provides that a public accommodation shall not exclude or otherwise deny equal goods, services, facilities, privileges, advantages, accommodations, or other opportunities to an individual or entity because of the known disability of an individual with whom the individual or entity is known to have a relationship or association. This section is unchanged from the proposed rule.

The individuals covered under this section include any individuals who are discriminated against because of their known association with an individual with a disability. For example, it would be a violation of this part for a day care center to refuse admission to a child because his or her brother has HIV disease.

This protection is not limited to those who have a familial relationship with the individual who has a disability. If a place of public accommodation refuses admission to a person with cerebral palsy and his or her companions, the companions have an independent right of action under the ADA and this section.

During the legislative process, the term "entity" was added to section 302(b)(l)(E) to clarify that the scope of the provision is intended to encompass not only persons who have a known association with a person with a disability, but also entities that provide services to or are otherwise associated with such individuals. This provision was intended to ensure that entities such as health care providers, employees of social service agencies, and others who provide professional services to persons with disabilities are not subjected to discrimination because of their professional association with persons with disabilities. For example, it would be a violation of this section to terminate the lease of a entity operating an independent living center for persons with disabilities, or to seek to evict a health care provider because that individual or entity provides services to persons with mental impairments.

REGULATION

§36.206 Retaliation or coercion.

(a) No private or public entity shall discriminate against any individual because that individual has opposed any act or practice made unlawful by this part, or because that individual made a charge, testified, assisted, or participated in any manner in an investigation, proceeding, or hearing under the Act or this part.

(b) No private or public entity shall coerce, intimidate, threaten, or interfere with any individual in the exercise or enjoyment of, or on account of his or her having exercised or enjoyed, or on account of his or her having aided or encouraged any other individual in the exercise or enjoyment of, any right granted or protected by the Act or this part.

(c) Illustrations of conduct prohibited by this section include, but are not limited to:

(1) Coercing an individual to deny or limit the benefits, services, or advantages to which he or she is entitled under the Act or this part;

(2) Threatening, intimidating, or interfering with an individual with a disability who is seeking to obtain or use the goods, services,

ANALYSIS

Section 36.206 Retaliation or coercion.

Section 36.206 implements section 503 of the ADA, which prohibits retaliation against any individual who exercises his or her rights under the Act. This section is unchanged from the proposed rule. Paragraph (a) of §36.206 provides that no private entity or public entity shall discriminate against any individual because that individual has exercised his or her right to oppose any act or practice made unlawful by this part, or because that individual made a charge, testified, assisted, or participated in any manner in an investigation, proceeding, or hearing under the Act or this part.

Paragraph (b) provides that no private entity or public entity shall coerce, intimidate, threaten, or interfere with any individual in the exercise of his or her rights under this part or because that individual aided or encouraged any other individual in the exercise or enjoyment of any right granted or protected by the Act or this part.

Illustrations of practices prohibited by this section are contained in paragraph (c), which is modeled on a similar provision in the regulations issued by the Department of Housing and Urban Development to implement the Fair Housing Act (see 24 CFR 100.400(c)(l)). Prohibited actions may include:

1) Coercing an individual to deny or limit the benefits, services, or advantages to which he or she is entitled under the Act or this part;

2) Threatening, intimidating, or interfering with an individual who is seeking to obtain or use the goods, services, facilities, privileges, advantages, or accommodations of a public accommodation;

3) Intimidating or threatening any person because that person is assisting or encouraging an individual or group entitled to claim the rights granted or protected by the Act or this part to exercise those rights; or

4) Retaliating against any person because that person has participated in any investigation or action to enforce the Act or this part.

This section protects not only individuals who allege a

REGULATION

facilities, privileges, advantages, or accommodations of a public accommodation;

(3) Intimidating or threatening any person because that person is assisting or encouraging an individual or group entitled to claim the rights granted or protected by the Act or this part to exercise those rights; or

(4) Retaliating against any person because that person has participated in any investigation or action to enforce the Act or this part.

ANALYSIS

violation of the Act or this part, but also any individuals who support or assist them. This section applies to all investigations or proceedings initiated under the Act or this part without regard to the ultimate resolution of the underlying allegations. Because this section prohibits any act of retaliation or coercion in response to an individual's effort to exercise rights established by the Act and this part (or to support the efforts of another individual), the section applies not only to public accommodations that are otherwise subject to this part, but also to individuals other than public accommodations or to public entities. For example, it would be a violation of the Act and this part for a private individual, e.g., a restaurant customer, to harass or intimidate an individual with a disability in an effort to prevent that individual from patronizing the restaurant. It would, likewise, be a violation of the Act and this part for a public entity to take adverse action against an employee who appeared as a witness on behalf of an indvidual who sought to enforce the Act.

REGULATION

§36.207 Places of public accommodation located in private residences.

(a) When a place of public accommodation is located in a private residence, the portion of the residence used exclusively as a residence is not covered by this part, but that portion used exclusively in the operation of the place of public accommodation or that portion used both for the place of public accommodation and for residential purposes is covered by this part.

(b) The portion of the residence covered under paragraph (a) of this section extends to those elements used to enter the place of public accommodation, including the homeowner's front sidewalk, if any, the door or entryway, and hallways; and those portions of the residence, interior or exterior, available to or used by customers or clients, including restrooms.

ANALYSIS

Section 36.207 Places of public accommodation located in private residences.

A private home used exclusively as a residence is not covered by title III because it is neither a "commercial facility" nor a "place of public accommodation." In some situations, however, a private home is not used exclusively as a residence, but houses a place of public accommodation in all or part of a home (e.g., an accountant who meets with his or her clients at his or her residence). Section 36.207(a) provides that those portions of the private residence used in the operation of the place of public accommodation are covered by this part.

For instance, a home or a portion of a home may be used as a day care center during the day and a residence at night. If all parts of the house are used for the day care center, then the entire residence is a place of public accommodation because no part of the house is used exclusively as a residence. If an accountant uses one room in the house solely as his or her professional office, then a portion of the house is used exclusively as a place of public accommodation and a portion is used exclusively as a residence. Section 36.207 provides that when a portion of a residence is used exclusively as a residence, that portion is not covered by this part. Thus, the portions of the accountant's house, other than the professional office and areas and spaces leading to it, are not covered by this part. All of the requirements of this rule apply to the covered portions, including requirements to make reasonable modifications in policies, eliminate discriminatory eligibility criteria, take readily achievable measures to remove barriers or provide readily achievable alternatives (e.g., making house calls), provide auxiliary aids and services and undertake only accessible new construction and alterations.

Paragraph (b) was added in response to comments that sought clarification on the extent of coverage of the private residence used as the place of public accommodation. The final rule makes clear that the place of accommodation extends to all areas of the home used by clients and customers of the place of public accommodation. Thus, the ADA would apply to any door or entry way, hallways, a restroom, if used by customers and clients; and any other portion of the residence, interior or exterior, used by customers or clients of the public accommodation. This interpretation is simply an application of the general rule for all public accommodations,

REGULATION

which extends statutory requirements to all portions of the facility used by customers and clients, including, if applicable, restrooms, hallways, and approaches to the public accommodation. As with other public accommodations, barriers at the entrance and on the sidewalk leading up to the public accommodation, if the sidewalk is under the control of the public accommodation, must be removed if doing so is readily achievable.

The Department recognizes that many businesses that operate out of personal residences are quite small, often employing only the homeowner and having limited total revenues. In these circumstances the effect of ADA coverage would likely be quite minimal. For example, because the obligation to remove existing architectural barriers is limited to those that are easily accomplishable without much difficulty or expense (see §36.304), the range of required actions would be quite modest. It might not be readily achievable for such a place of public accommodation to remove any existing barriers. If it is not readily achievable to remove existing architectural barriers, a public accommodation located in a private residence may meet its obligations under the Act and this part by providing its goods or services to clients or customers with disabilities through the use of alternative measures, including delivery of goods or services in the home of the customer or client, to the extent that such alternative measures are readily achievable (see §36.305).

Some commenters asked for clarification as to how the new construction and alteration standards of subpart D will apply to residences. The new construction standards only apply to the extent that the residence or portion of the residence was designed or intended for use as a public accommodation. Thus, for example, if a portion of a home is designed or constructed for use exclusively as a lawyer's office or for use both as a lawyer's office and for residential purposes, then it must be designed in accordance with the new construction standards in the appendix. Likewise, if a homeowner is undertaking alterations to convert all or part of his residence to a place of public accommodation, that work must be done in compliance with the alterations standards in the appendix.

The preamble to the proposed rule addressed the applicable requirements when a commercial facility is located in a private residence. That situation is now addressed in §36.401(b) of subpart D.

REGULATION
§36.208 Direct threat.

(a) This part does not require a public accommodation to permit an individual to participate in or benefit from the goods, services, facilities, privileges, advantages and accommodations of that public accommodation when that individual poses a direct threat to the health or safety of others.

(b) Direct threat means a significant risk to the health or safety of others that cannot be eliminated by a modification of policies, practices, or procedures, or by the provision of auxiliary aids or services.

(c) In determining whether an individual poses a direct threat to the health or safety of others, a public accommodation must make an individualized assessment, based on reasonable judgment that relies on current medical knowledge or on the best available objective evidence, to ascertain: the nature, duration, and severity of the risk; the probability that the potential injury will actually occur; and whether reasonable modifications of policies, practices, or procedures will mitigate the risk.

ANALYSIS
Section 36.208 Direct threat.

Section 36.208(a) implements section 302(b)(3) of the Act by providing that this part does not require a public accommodation to permit an individual to participate in or benefit from the goods, services, facilities, privileges, advantages and accommodations of the public accommodation, if that individual poses a direct threat to the health or safety of others. This section is unchanged from the proposed rule.

The Department received a significant number of comments on this section. Commenters representing individuals with disabilities generally supported this provision, but suggested revisions to further limit its application. Commenters representing public accommodations generally endorsed modifications that would permit a public accommodation to exercise its own judgment in determining whether an individual poses a direct threat.

The inclusion of this provision is not intended to imply that persons with disabilities pose risks to others. It is intended to address concerns that may arise in this area. It establishes a strict standard that must be met before denying service to an individual with a disability or excluding that individual from participation.

Paragraph (b) of this section explains that a "direct threat" is a significant risk to the health or safety of others that cannot be eliminated by a modification of policies, practices, or procedures, or by the provision of auxiliary aids and services. This paragraph codifies the standard first applied by the Supreme Court in School Board of Nassau County v. Arline, 480 U.S. 273 (1987), in which the Court held that an individual with a contagious disease may be an "individual with handicaps" under section 504 of the Rehabilitation Act. In Arline, the Supreme Court recognized that there is a need to balance the interests of people with disabilities against legitimate concerns for public safety. Although persons with disabilities are generally entitled to the protection of this part, a person who poses a significant risk to others may be excluded if reasonable modifications to the public accommodation's policies, practices, or procedures will not eliminate that risk. The determination that a person poses a direct threat to the health or safety of others may not be based on generalizations or stereotypes about the effects of a particular disability; it must be based on an individual assessment that conforms to the requirements of paragraph (c) of this section.

REGULATION

Paragraph (c) establishes the test to use in determining whether an individual poses a direct threat to the health or safety of others. A public accommodation is required to make an individualized assessment, based on reasonable judgment that relies on current medical evidence or on the best available objective evidence, to determine: the nature, duration, and severity of the risk; the probability that the potential injury will actually occur; and whether reasonable modifications of policies, practices, or procedures will mitigate the risk. This is the test established by the Supreme Court in Arline. Such an inquiry is essential if the law is to achieve its goal of protecting disabled individuals from discrimination based on prejudice, stereotypes, or unfounded fear, while giving appropriate weight to legitimate concerns, such as the need to avoid exposing others to significant health and safety risks. Making this assessment will not usually require the services of a physician. Sources for medical knowledge include guidance from public health authorities, such as the U.S. Public Health Service, the Centers for Disease Control, and the National Institutes of Health, including the National Institute of Mental Health.

Many of the commenters sought clarification of the inquiry requirement. Some suggested that public accommodations should be prohibited from making any inquiries to determine if an individual with a disability would pose a direct threat to other persons. The Department believes that to preclude all such inquiries would be inappropriate. Under §36.301 of this part, a public accommodation is permitted to establish eligibility criteria necessary for the safe operation of the place of public accommodation. Implicit in that right is the right to ask if an individual meets the criteria. However, any eligibility or safety standard established by a public accommodation must be based on actual risk, not on speculation or stereotypes; it must be applied to all clients or customers of the place of public accommodation; and inquiries must be limited to matters necessary to the application of the standard.

Some commenters suggested that the test established in the Arline decision, which was developed in the context of an employment case, is too stringent to apply in a public accommodations context where interaction between the public accommodation and its client or customer is often very brief. One suggested alternative was to permit public accommodations to exercise "good faith" judgment in determining whether an individual poses a direct threat, particularly when a public accommodation is dealing with a client or customer engaged in disorderly or disruptive behavior.

The Department believes that the ADA clearly requires that any determination to exclude an individual from participation must be based on an objective standard. A public accommodation may establish neutral eligibility criteria as a condition of receiving its goods or services. As long as these criteria are necessary for the safe provision of the public accommodation's goods and services and applied neutrally to all clients or customers, regardless of whether they are individuals with disabilities, a person who is unable to meet the criteria may be excluded from participation without inquiry into the underlying reason for the inability to comply. In places of public accommodation such as restaurants, theaters, or hotels, where the contact between the public accommodation and its clients is transitory, the uniform application of an eligibility standard precluding violent or disruptive behavior by any client or customer should be sufficient to enable a public accommodation to conduct its business in an orderly manner.

Some other commenters asked for clarification of the application of this provision to persons, particularly children, who have short-term, contagious illnesses, such as fevers, influenza, or the common cold. It is common practice in schools and day care settings to exclude persons with such illnesses until the symptoms subside. The Department believes that these commenters misunderstand the scope of this rule. The ADA only prohibits discrimination against an individual with a disability. Under the ADA and this part, a "disability" is defined as a physical or mental impairment that substantially limits one or more major life activities. Common, short-term illnesses that predictably resolve themselves within a matter of days do not "substantially limit" a major life activity; therefore, it is not a violation of this part to exclude an individual from receiving the services of a public accommodation because of such transitory illness. However, this part does apply to persons who have long-term illnesses. Any determination with respect to a person who has a chronic or long-term illness must be made in compliance with the requirements of this section.

REGULATION
§36.209 Illegal use of drugs.

(a) <u>General</u>. (1) Except as provided in paragraph (b) of this section, this part does not prohibit discrimination against an individual based on that individual's current illegal use of drugs.

(2) A public accommodation shall not discriminate on the basis of illegal use of drugs against an individual who is not engaging in current illegal use of drugs and who--

(i) Has successfully completed a supervised drug rehabilitation program or has otherwise been rehabilitated successfully;

(ii) Is participating in a supervised rehabilitation program; or

(iii) Is erroneously regarded as engaging in such use.

(b) <u>Health and drug rehabilitation services</u>. (1) A public accommodation shall not deny health services, or services provided in connection with drug rehabilitation, to an individual on the basis of that individual's current illegal use of drugs, if the individual is otherwise entitled to such services.

(2) A drug rehabilitation or treatment program may

ANALYSIS
Section 36.209 Illegal use of drugs.

Section 36.209 effectuates section 510 of the ADA, which clarifies the Act's application to people who use drugs illegally. Paragraph (a) provides that this part does not prohibit discrimination based on an individual's current illegal use of drugs.

The Act and the regulation distinguish between illegal use of drugs and the legal use of substances, whether or not those substances are "controlled substances," as defined in the Controlled Substances Act (21 U.S.C. 812). Some controlled substances are prescription drugs that have legitimate medical uses. Section 36.209 does not affect use of controlled substances pursuant to a valid prescription, under supervision by a licensed health care professional, or other use that is authorized by the Controlled Substances Act or any other provision of Federal law. It does apply to illegal use of those substances, as well as to illegal use of controlled substances that are not prescription drugs. The key question is whether the individual's use of the substance is illegal, not whether the substance has recognized legal uses. Alcohol is not a controlled substance, so use of alcohol is not addressed by §36.209. Alcoholics are individuals with disabilities, subject to the protections of the statute.

A distinction is also made between the use of a substance and the status of being addicted to that substance. Addiction is a disability, and addicts are individuals with disabilities protected by the Act. The protection, however, does not extend to actions based on the illegal use of the substance. In other words, an addict cannot use the fact of his or her addiction as a defense to an action based on illegal use of drugs. This distinction is not artificial. Congress intended to deny protection to people who engage in the illegal use of drugs, whether or not they are addicted, but to provide protection to addicts so long as they are not currently using drugs.

A third distinction is the difficult one between current use and former use. The definition of "current illegal use of drugs" in §36.104, which is based on the report of the Conference Committee, H.R. Conf. Rep. No. 596, 101st Cong., 2d Sess. 64 (1990), is "illegal use of drugs that occurred recently enough to justify a reasonable belief that a person's drug use is current or that continuing use is a real and ongoing problem."

Paragraph (a)(2)(i) specifies that an individual who has

REGULATION

deny participation to individuals who engage in illegal use of drugs while they are in the program.

(c) Drug testing. (1) This part does not prohibit a public accommodation from adopting or administering reasonable policies or procedures, including but not limited to drug testing, designed to ensure that an individual who formerly engaged in the illegal use of drugs is not now engaging in current illegal use of drugs.

(2) Nothing in this paragraph (c) shall be construed to encourage, prohibit, restrict, or authorize the conducting of testing for the illegal use of drugs.

ANALYSIS

successfully completed a supervised drug rehabilitation program or has otherwise been rehabilitated successfully and who is not engaging in current illegal use of drugs is protected. Paragraph (a)(2)(ii) clarifies that an individual who is currently participating in a supervised rehabilitation program and is not engaging in current illegal use of drugs is protected. Paragraph (a)(2)(iii) provides that a person who is erroneously regarded as engaging in current illegal use of drugs, but who is not engaging in such use, is protected.

Paragraph (b) provides a limited exception to the exclusion of current illegal users of drugs from the protections of the Act. It prohibits denial of health services, or services provided in connection with drug rehabilitation, to an individual on the basis of current illegal use of drugs, if the individual is otherwise entitled to such services. As explained further in the discussion of §36.302, a health care facility that specializes in a particular type of treatment, such as care of burn victims, is not required to provide drug rehabilitation services, but it cannot refuse to treat an individual's burns on the grounds that the individual is illegally using drugs.

A commenter argued that health care providers should be permitted to use their medical judgment to postpone discretionary medical treatment of individuals under the influence of alcohol or drugs. The regulation permits a medical practitioner to take into account an individual's use of drugs in determining appropriate medical treatment. Section 36.209 provides that the prohibitions on discrimination in this part do not apply when the public accommodation acts on the basis of current illegal use of drugs. Although those prohibitions do apply under paragraph (b), the limitations established under this part also apply. Thus, under §36.208, a health care provider or other public accommodation covered under §36.209(b) may exclude an individual whose current illegal use of drugs poses a direct threat to the health or safety of others, and, under §36.301, a public accommodation may impose or apply eligibility criteria that are necessary for the provision of the services being offered, and may impose legitimate safety requirements that are necessary for safe operation. These same limitations also apply to individuals with disabilities who use alcohol or prescription drugs. The Department believes that these provisions address this commenter's concerns.

Other commenters pointed out that abstention from the use

REGULATION

of drugs is an essential condition for participation in some drug rehabilitation programs, and may be a necessary requirement in inpatient or residential settings. The Department believes that this comment is well-founded. Congress clearly did not intend to exclude from drug treatment programs the very individuals who need such programs because of their use of drugs. In such a situation, however, once an individual has been admitted to a program, abstention may be a necessary and appropriate condition to continued participation. The final rule therefore provides that a drug rehabilitation or treatment program may deny participation to individuals who use drugs while they are in the program.

Paragraph (c) expresses Congress' intention that the Act be neutral with respect to testing for illegal use of drugs. This paragraph implements the provision in section 510(b) of the Act that allows entities "to adopt or administer reasonable policies or procedures, including but not limited to drug testing," that ensure an individual who is participating in a supervised rehabilitation program, or who has completed such a program or otherwise been rehabilitated successfully, is no longer engaging in the illegal use of drugs. Paragraph (c) is not to be construed to encourage, prohibit, restrict, or authorize the conducting of testing for the illegal use of drugs.

Paragraph (c) of §36.209 clarifies that it is not a violation of this part to adopt or administer reasonable policies or procedures to ensure that an individual who formerly engaged in the illegal use of drugs is not currently engaging in illegal use of drugs. Any such policies or procedures must, of course, be reasonable, and must be designed to identify accurately the illegal use of drugs. This paragraph does not authorize inquiries, tests, or other procedures that would disclose use of substances that are not controlled substances or are taken under supervision by a licensed health care professional, or other uses authorized by the Controlled Substances Act or other provisions of Federal law, because such uses are not included in the definition of "illegal use of drugs."

One commenter argued that the rule should permit testing for lawful use of prescription drugs, but most favored the explanation that tests must be limited to unlawful use in order to avoid revealing the use of prescription medicine used to treat disabilities. Tests revealing legal use of prescription drugs might violate the prohibition in §36.301 of attempts to unnecessarily identify the existence of a disability.

REGULATION

§36.210 Smoking.

This part does not preclude the prohibition of, or the imposition of restrictions on, smoking in places of public accommodation.

ANALYSIS

Section 36.210 Smoking.

Section 36.210 restates the clarification in section 501(b) of the Act that the Act does not preclude the prohibition of, or imposition of restrictions on, smoking. Some commenters argued that §36.210 does not go far enough, and that the regulation should prohibit smoking in all places of public accommodation. The reference to smoking in section 501 merely clarifies that the Act does not require public accommodations to accommodate smokers by permitting them to smoke in places of public accommodations.

REGULATION

§36.211 Maintenance of accessible features.

(a) A public accommodation shall maintain in operable working condition those features of facilities and equipment that are required to be readily accessible to and usable by persons with disabilities by the Act or this part.

(b) This section does not prohibit isolated or temporary interruptions in service or access due to maintenance or repairs.

ANALYSIS

Section 36.211 Maintenance of accessible features.

Section 36.211 provides that a public accommodation shall maintain in operable working condition those features of facilities and equipment that are required to be readily accessible to and usable by persons with disabilities by the Act or this part. The Act requires that, to the maximum extent feasible, facilities must be accessible to, and usable by, individuals with disabilities. This section recognizes that it is not sufficient to provide features such as accessible routes, elevators, or ramps, if those features are not maintained in a manner that enables individuals with disabilities to use them. Inoperable elevators, locked accessible doors, or "accessible" routes that are obstructed by furniture, filing cabinets, or potted plants are neither "accessible to" nor "usable by" individuals with disabilities.

Some commenters objected that this section appeared to establish an absolute requirement and suggested that language from the preamble be included in the text of the regulation. It is, of course, impossible to guarantee that mechanical devices will never fail to operate. Paragraph (b) of the final regulation provides that this section does not prohibit isolated or temporary interruptions in service or access due to maintenance or repairs. This paragraph is intended to clarify that temporary obstructions or isolated instances of mechanical failure would not be considered violations of the Act or this part. However, allowing obstructions or "out of service" equipment to persist beyond a reasonable period of time would violate this part, as would repeated mechanical failures due to improper or inadequate maintenance. Failure of the public accommodation to ensure that accessible routes are properly maintained and free of obstructions, or failure to arrange prompt repair of inoperable elevators or other equipment intended to provide access, would also violate this part.

Other commenters requested that this section be expanded to include specific requirements for inspection and maintenance of equipment, for training staff in the proper operation of equipment, and for maintenance of specific items. The Department believes that this section properly establishes the general requirement for maintaining access and that further, more detailed requirements are not necessary.

REGULATION

§36.212 Insurance.

(a) This part shall not be construed to prohibit or restrict —

(1) An insurer, hospital or medical service company, health maintenance organization, or any agent, or entity that administers benefit plans, or similar organizations from underwriting risks, classifying risks, or administering such risks that are based on or not inconsistent with State law; or

(2) A person or organization covered by this part from establishing, sponsoring, observing or administering the terms of a bona fide benefit plan that are based on underwriting risks, classifying risks, or administering such risks that are based on or not inconsistent with State law; or

(3) A person or organization covered by this part from establishing, sponsoring, observing or administering the terms of a bona fide benefit plan that is not subject to State laws that regulate insurance.

(b) Paragraphs (a)(1), (2), and (3) of this section shall not be used as a subterfuge to evade the purposes of the Act or this part.

(c) A public accommodation shall not refuse to

ANALYSIS

Section 36.212 Insurance.

The Department received numerous comments on proposed §36.212. Most supported the proposed regulation but felt that it did not go far enough in protecting individuals with disabilities and persons associated with them from discrimination. Many commenters argued that language from the preamble to the proposed regulation should be included in the text of the final regulation. Other commenters argued that even that language was not strong enough, and that more stringent standards should be established. Only a few commenters argued that the Act does not apply to insurance underwriting practices or the terms of insurance contracts. These commenters cited language from the Senate committee report (S. Rep. No. 116, 101st Cong., 1st Sess., at 84-86 (1989) [hereinafter "Senate report"]), indicating that Congress did not intend to affect existing insurance practices.

The Department has decided to adopt the language of the proposed rule without change. Sections 36.212(a) and (b) restate section 501(c) of the Act, which provides that the Act shall not be construed to restrict certain insurance practices on the part of insurance companies and employers, as long as such practices are not used to evade the purposes of the Act. Section 36.212(c) is a specific application of §36.202(a), which prohibits denial of participation on the basis of disability. It provides that a public accommodation may not refuse to serve an individual with a disability because of limitations on coverage or rates in its insurance policies (see Judiciary report at 56).

Many commenters supported the requirements of §36.212(c) in the proposed rule because it addressed an important reason for denial of services by public accommodations. One commenter argued that services could be denied if the insurance coverage required exclusion of people whose disabilities were reasonably related to the risks involved in that particular place of public accommodation. Sections 36.208 and 36.301 establish criteria for denial of participation on the basis of legitimate safety concerns. This paragraph does not prohibit consideration of such concerns in insurance policies, but provides that any exclusion on the basis of disability must be based on the permissible criteria, rather than on the terms of the insurance contract.

Language in the committee reports indicates that Congress intended to reach insurance practices by prohibiting

REGULATION

serve an individual with a disability because its insurance company conditions coverage or rates on the absence of individuals with disabilities.

ANALYSIS

differential treatment of individuals with disabilities in insurance offered by public accommodations unless the differences are justified. "Under the ADA, a person with a disability cannot be denied insurance or be subject to different terms or conditions of insurance based on disability alone, if the disability does not pose increased risks" (Senate report at 84; Education and Labor report at 136). Section 501(c)(1) of the Act was intended to emphasize that "insurers may continue to sell to and underwrite individuals applying for life, health, or other insurance on an individually underwritten basis, or to service such insurance products, so long as the standards used are based on sound actuarial data and not on speculation" (Judiciary report at 70 (emphasis added); see also Senate report at 85; Education and Labor report at 137).

The committee reports indicate that underwriting and classification of risks must be "based on sound actuarial principles or be related to actual or reasonably anticipated experience" (see, e.g., Judiciary report at 71). Moreover, "while a plan which limits certain kinds of coverage based on classification of risk would be allowed . . ., the plan may not refuse to insure, or refuse to continue to insure, or limit the amount, extent, or kind of coverage available to an individual, or charge a different rate for the same coverage solely because of a physical or mental impairment, except where the refusal, limitation, or rate differential is based on sound actuarial principles or is related to actual or reasonably anticipated experience" (Senate report at 85; Education and Labor report at 136-37; Judiciary report at 71). The ADA, therefore, does not prohibit use of legitimate actuarial considerations to justify differential treatment of individuals with disabilities in insurance.

The committee reports provide some guidance on how nondiscrimination principles in the disability rights area relate to insurance practices. For example, a person who is blind may not be denied coverage based on blindness independent of actuarial risk classification. With respect to group health insurance coverage, an individual with a pre-existing condition may be denied coverage for that condition for the period specified in the policy, but cannot be denied coverage for illness or injuries unrelated to the pre-existing condition. Also, a public accommodation may offer insurance policies that limit coverage for certain procedures or treatments, but may not entirely deny coverage to a person with a disability.

ANALYSIS

The Department requested comment on the extent to which data that would establish statistically sound correlations are available. Numerous commenters cited pervasive problems in the availability and cost of insurance for individuals with disabilities and parents of children with disabilities. No commenters cited specific data, or sources of data, to support specific exclusionary practices. Several commenters reported that, even when statistics are available, they are often outdated and do not reflect current medical technology and treatment methods. Concern was expressed that adequate efforts are not made to distinguish those individuals who are high users of health care from individuals in the same diagnostic groups who may be low users of health care. One insurer reported that "hard data and actuarial statistics are not available to provide precise numerical justifications for every underwriting determination," but argued that decisions may be based on "logical principles generally accepted by actuarial science and fully consistent with state insurance laws." The commenter urged that the Department recognize the validity of information other than statistical data as a basis for insurance determinations.

The most frequent comment was a recommendation that the final regulation should require the insurance company to provide a copy of the actuarial data on which its actions are based when requested by the applicant. Such a requirement would be beyond anything contemplated by the Act or by Congress and has therefore not been included in the Department's final rule. Because the legislative history of the ADA clarifies that different treatment of individuals with disabilities in insurance may be justified by sound actuarial data, such actuarial data will be critical to any potential litigation on this issue. This information would presumably be obtainable in a court proceeding where the insurer's actuarial data was the basis for different treatment of persons with disabilities. In addition, under some State regulatory schemes, insurers may have to file such actuarial information with the State regulatory agency and this information may be obtainable at the State level.

A few commenters representing the insurance industry conceded that underwriting practices in life and health insurance are clearly covered, but argued that property and casualty insurance are not covered. The Department sees no reason for this distinction. Although life and health insurance are the areas where the regulation will have its greatest

REGULATION

application, the Act applies equally to unjustified discrimination in all types of insurance provided by public accommodations. A number of commenters, for example, reported difficulties in obtaining automobile insurance because of their disabilities, despite their having good driving records.

REGULATION

§36.213 Relationship of subpart B to subparts C and D of this part.

Subpart B of this part sets forth the general principles of nondiscrimination applicable to all entities subject to this part. Subparts C and D of this part provide guidance on the application of the statute to specific situations. The specific provisions, including the limitations on those provisions, control over the general provisions in circumstances where both specific and general provisions apply. **§§36.214-36.300: (Reserved)**

ANALYSIS

Section 36.213 Relationship of subpart B to subparts C and D.

This section explains that subpart B sets forth the general principles of nondiscrimination applicable to all entities subject to this regulation, while subparts C and D provide guidance on the application of this part to specific situations. The specific provisions in subparts C and D, including the limitations on those provisions, control over the general provisions in circumstances where both specific and general provisions apply. Resort to the general provisions of subpart B is only appropriate where there are no applicable specific rules of guidance in subparts C or D. This interaction between the specific requirements and the general requirements operates with regard to contractual obligations as well.

One illustration of this principle is its application to the obligation of a public accommodation to provide access to services by removal of architectural barriers or by alternatives to barrier removal. The general requirement, established in subpart B by §36.203, is that a public accommodation must provide its services to individuals with disabilities in the most integrated setting appropriate. This general requirement would appear to categorically prohibit "segregated" seating for persons in wheelchairs. Section 36.304, however, only requires removal of architectural barriers to the extent that removal is "readily achievable." If providing access to all areas of a restaurant, for example, would not be "readily achievable," a public accommodation may provide access to selected areas only. Also, §36.305 provides that, where barrier removal is not readily achievable, a public accommodation may use alternative, readily achievable methods of making services available, such as curbside service or home delivery. Thus, in this manner, the specific requirements of §§36.304 and 36.305 control over the general requirement of §36.203.

REGULATION
Subpart C -- Specific Requirements

ANALYSIS
Subpart C -- Specific Requirements

In general, subpart C implements the "specific prohibitions" that comprise section 302(b)(2) of the ADA. It also addresses the requirements of section 309 of the ADA regarding examinations and courses.

§36.301 Eligibility criteria.

(a) General. A public accommodation shall not impose or apply eligibility criteria that screen out or tend to screen out an individual with a disability or any class of individuals with disabilities from fully and equally enjoying any goods, services, facilities, privileges, advantages, or accommodations, unless such criteria can be shown to be necessary for the provision of the goods, services, facilities, privileges, advantages, or accommodations being offered.

(b) Safety. A public accommodation may impose legitimate safety requirements that are necessary for safe operation. Safety requirements must be based on actual risks and not on mere speculation, stereotypes, or generalizations about individuals with disabilities.

(c) Charges. A public accommodation may not impose a surcharge on a particular individual with a disability or any group of individuals with disabilities to cover the costs of mea-

Section 36.301 Eligibility criteria.

Section 36.301 of the rule prohibits the imposition or application of eligibility criteria that screen out or tend to screen out an individual with a disability or any class of individuals with disabilities from fully and equally enjoying any goods, services, facilities, privileges, advantages, and accommodations, unless such criteria can be shown to be necessary for the provision of the goods, services, facilities, privileges, advantages, or accommodations being offered. This prohibition is based on section 302(b)(2)(A)(i) of the ADA.

It would violate this section to establish exclusive or segregative eligibility criteria that would bar, for example, all persons who are deaf from playing on a golf course or all individuals with cerebral palsy from attending a movie theater, or limit the seating of individuals with Down's syndrome to only particular areas of a restaurant. The wishes, tastes, or preferences of other customers may not be asserted to justify criteria that would exclude or segregate individuals with disabilities.

Section 36.301 also prohibits attempts by a public accommodation to unnecessarily identify the existence of a disability; for example, it would be a violation of this section for a retail store to require an individual to state on a credit application whether the applicant has epilepsy, mental illness, or any other disability, or to inquire unnecessarily whether an individual has HIV disease.

Section 36.301 also prohibits policies that unnecessarily impose requirements or burdens on individuals with disabilities that are not placed on others. For example, public accommodations may not require that an individual with a disability be accompanied by an attendant. As provided by §36.306, however, a public accommodation is not required to provide services of a personal nature including assistance in toileting, eating, or dressing.

REGULATION

sures, such as the provision of auxiliary aids, barrier removal, alternatives to barrier removal, and reasonable modifications in policies, practices, or procedures, that are required to provide that individual or group with the nondiscriminatory treatment required by the Act or this part.

ANALYSIS

Paragraph (c) of §36.301 provides that public accommodations may not place a surcharge on a particular individual with a disability or any group of individuals with disabilities to cover the costs of measures, such as the provision of auxiliary aids and services, barrier removal, alternatives to barrier removal, and reasonable modifications in policies, practices, and procedures, that are required to provide that individual or group with the nondiscriminatory treatment required by the Act or this part.

A number of commenters inquired as to whether deposits required for the use of auxiliary aids, such as assistive listening devices, are prohibited surcharges. It is the Department's view that reasonable, completely refundable, deposits are not to be considered surcharges prohibited by this section. Requiring deposits is an important means of ensuring the availability of equipment necessary to ensure compliance with the ADA.

Other commenters sought clarification as to whether §36.301(c) prohibits professionals from charging for the additional time that it may take in certain cases to provide services to an individual with disabilities. The Department does not intend §36.301(c) to prohibit professionals who bill on the basis of time from charging individuals with disabilities on that basis. However, fees may not be charged for the provision of auxiliary aids and services, barrier removal, alternatives to barrier removal, reasonable modifications in policies, practices, and procedures, or any other measures necessary to ensure compliance with the ADA.

Other commenters inquired as to whether day care centers may charge for extra services provided to individuals with disabilities. As stated above, §36.302(c) is intended only to prohibit charges for measures necessary to achieve compliance with the ADA.

Another commenter asserted that charges may be assessed for home delivery provided as an alternative to barrier removal under §36.305, when home delivery is provided to all customers for a fee. Charges for home delivery are permissible if home delivery is not considered an alternative to barrier removal. If the public accommodation offers an alternative, such as curb, carry-out, or sidewalk service for which no surcharge is assessed, then it may charge for home delivery in accordance with its standard pricing for home delivery.

REGULATION

In addition, §36.301 prohibits the imposition of criteria that "tend to" screen out an individual with a disability. This concept, which is derived from current regulations under section 504 (see, e.g., 45 CFR 84.13), makes it discriminatory to impose policies or criteria that, while not creating a direct bar to individuals with disabilities, indirectly prevent or limit their ability to participate. For example, requiring presentation of a driver's license as the sole means of identification for purposes of paying by check would violate this section in situations where, for example, individuals with severe vision impairments or developmental disabilities or epilepsy are ineligible to receive a driver's license and the use of an alternative means of identification, such as another photo I.D. or credit card, is feasible.

A public accommodation may, however, impose neutral rules and criteria that screen out, or tend to screen out, individuals with disabilities, if the criteria are necessary for the safe operation of the public accommodation. Examples of safety qualifications that would be justifiable in appropriate circumstances would include height requirements for certain amusement park rides or a requirement that all participants in a recreational rafting expedition be able to meet a necessary level of swimming proficiency. Safety requirements must be based on actual risks and not on speculation, stereotypes, or generalizations about individuals with disabilities.

REGULATION

§36.302 Modifications in policies, practices, or procedures.

(a) General. A public accommodation shall make reasonable modifications in policies, practices, or procedures, when the modifications are necessary to afford goods, services, facilities, privileges, advantages, or accommodations to individuals with disabilities, unless the public accommodation can demonstrate that making the modifications would fundamentally alter the nature of the goods, services, facilities, privileges, advantages, or accommodations.

(b) Specialties. (1) General. A public accommodation may refer an individual with a disability to another public accommodation, if that individual is seeking, or requires, treatment or services outside of the referring public accommodation's area of specialization, and if, in the normal course of its operations, the referring public accommodation would make a similar referral for an individual without a disability who seeks or requires the same treatment or services.

(2) Illustration--medical specialties. A health care provider may refer an individual with a disability to another provider, if that individual is seeking, or

ANALYSIS

Section 36.302 Modifications in policies, practices, or procedures.

Section 36.302 of the rule prohibits the failure to make reasonable modifications in policies, practices, and procedures when such modifications may be necessary to afford any goods, services, facilities, privileges, advantages, or accommodations, unless the entity can demonstrate that making such modifications would fundamentally alter the nature of such goods, services, facilities, privileges, advantages, or accommodations. This prohibition is based on section 302(b)(2)(A)(ii) of the ADA.

For example, a parking facility would be required to modify a rule barring all vans or all vans with raised roofs, if an individual who uses a wheelchair-accessible van wishes to park in that facility, and if overhead structures are high enough to accommodate the height of the van. A department store may need to modify a policy of only permitting one person at a time in a dressing room, if an individual with mental retardation needs and requests assistance in dressing from a companion. Public accommodations may need to revise operational policies to ensure that services are available to individuals with disabilities. For instance, a hotel may need to adopt a policy of keeping an accessible room unoccupied until an individual with a disability arrives at the hotel, assuming the individual has properly reserved the room.

One example of application of this principle is specifically included in a new §36.302(d) on check-out aisles. That paragraph provides that a store with check-out aisles must ensure that an adequate number of accessible check-out aisles is kept open during store hours, or must otherwise modify its policies and practices, in order to ensure that an equivalent level of convenient service is provided to individuals with disabilities as is provided to others. For example, if only one check-out aisle is accessible, and it is generally used for express service, one way of providing equivalent service is to allow persons with mobility impairments to make all of their purchases at that aisle. This principle also applies with respect to other accessible elements and services. For example, a particular bank may be in compliance with the accessibility guidelines for new construction incorporated in Appendix A with respect to automated teller machines (ATM) at a new branch office by providing one accessible walk-up machine at that location, even though an adjacent walk-up ATM is not accessible and the drive-up ATM is not

REGULATION

requires, treatment or services outside of the referring provider's area of specialization, and if the referring provider would make a similar referral for an individual without a disability who seeks or requires the same treatment or services. A physician who specializes in treating only a particular condition cannot refuse to treat an individual with a disability for that condition, but is not required to treat the individual for a different condition.

(c) Service animals. (1) General. Generally, a public accommodation shall modify policies, practices, or procedures to permit the use of a service animal by an individual with a disability.

(2) Care or supervision of service animals. Nothing in this part requires a public accommodation to supervise or care for a service animal.

(d) Check-out aisles. A store with check-out aisles shall ensure that an adequate number of accessible check-out aisles is kept open during store hours, or shall otherwise modify its policies and practices, in order to ensure that an equivalent level of convenient service is provided to individuals with disabilities as is provided to others. If only one check-out aisle is accessible, and it

ANALYSIS

accessible. However, the bank would be in violation of this section if the accessible ATM was located in a lobby that was locked during evening hours while the drive-up ATM was available to customers without disabilities during those same hours. The bank would need to ensure that the accessible ATM was available to customers during the hours that any of the other ATM's was available.

A number of commenters inquired as to the relationship between this section and §36.307, "Accessible or special goods." Under §36.307, a public accommodation is not required to alter its inventory to include accessible or special goods that are designed for, or facilitate use by, individuals with disabilities. The rule enunciated in §36.307 is consistent with the "fundamental alteration" defense to the reasonable modifications requirement of §36.302. Therefore, §36.302 would not require the inventory of goods provided by a public accommodation to be altered to include goods with accessibility features. For example, §36.302 would not require a bookstore to stock brailled books or order brailled books, if it does not do so in the normal course of its business.

The rule does not require modifications to the legitimate areas of specialization of service providers. Section 36.302(b) provides that a public accommodation may refer an individual with a disability to another public accommodation, if that individual is seeking, or requires, treatment or services outside of the referring public accommodation's area of specialization, and if, in the normal course of its operations, the referring public accommodation would make a similar referral for an individual without a disability who seeks or requires the same treatment or services.

For example, it would not be discriminatory for a physician who specializes only in burn treatment to refer an individual who is deaf to another physician for treatment of an injury other than a burn injury. To require a physician to accept patients outside of his or her specialty would fundamentally alter the nature of the medical practice and, therefore, not be required by this section.

A clinic specializing exclusively in drug rehabilitation could similarly refuse to treat a person who is not a drug addict, but could not refuse to treat a person who is a drug addict simply because the patient tests positive for HIV. Conversely, a clinic that specializes in the treatment of indi-

REGULATION

is generally used for express service, one way of providing equivalent service is to allow persons with mobility impairments to make all their purchases at that aisle.

ANALYSIS

viduals with HIV could refuse to treat an individual that does not have HIV, but could not refuse to treat a person for HIV infection simply because that person is also a drug addict.

Some commenters requested clarification as to how this provision would apply to situations where manifestations of the disability in question, itself, would raise complications requiring the expertise of a different practitioner. It is not the Department's intention in §36.302(b) to prohibit a physician from referring an individual with a disability to another physician, if the disability itself creates specialized complications for the patient's health that the physician lacks the experience or knowledge to address (see Education and Labor report at 106).

Section 36.302(c)(1) requires that a public accommodation modify its policies, practices, or procedures to permit the use of a service animal by an individual with a disability in any area open to the general public. The term "service animal" is defined in §36.104 to include guide dogs, signal dogs, or any other animal individually trained to provide assistance to an individual with a disability.

A number of commenters pointed to the difficulty of making the distinction required by the proposed rule between areas open to the general public and those that are not. The ambiguity and uncertainty surrounding these provisions has led the Department to adopt a single standard for all public accommodations.

Section 36.302(c)(1) of the final rule now provides that "[g]enerally, a public accommodation shall modify policies, practices, and procedures to permit the use of a service animal by an individual with a disability." This formulation reflects the general intent of Congress that public accommodations take the necessary steps to accommodate service animals and to ensure that individuals with disabilities are not separated from their service animals. It is intended that the broadest feasible access be provided to service animals in all places of public accommodation, including movie theaters, restaurants, hotels, retail stores, hospitals, and nursing homes (see Education and Labor report at 106; Judiciary report at 59). The section also acknowledges, however, that, in rare circumstances, accommodation of service animals may not be required because a fundamental alteration would result in the nature of the goods, services, facilities, privileges, or accom-

REGULATION

ANALYSIS

modations offered or provided, or the safe operation of the public accommodation would be jeopardized.

As specified in §36.302(c)(2), the rule does not require a public accommodation to supervise or care for any service animal. If a service animal must be separated from an individual with a disability in order to avoid a fundamental alteration or a threat to safety, it is the responsibility of the individual with the disability to arrange for the care and supervision of the animal during the period of separation.

A museum would not be required by §36.302 to modify a policy barring the touching of delicate works of art in order to enhance the participation of individuals who are blind, if the touching threatened the integrity of the work. Damage to a museum piece would clearly be a fundamental alteration that is not required by this section.

REGULATION

§36.303 Auxiliary aids and services.

(a) <u>General</u>. A public accommodation shall take those steps that may be necessary to ensure that no individual with a disability is excluded, denied services, segregated or otherwise treated differently than other individuals because of the absence of auxiliary aids and services, unless the public accommodation can demonstrate that taking those steps would fundamentally alter the nature of the goods, services, facilities, privileges, advantages, or accommodations being offered or would result in an undue burden, i.e., significant difficulty or expense.

(b) <u>Examples</u>. The term "auxiliary aids and services" includes--

(1) Qualified interpreters, notetakers, computer-aided transcription services, written materials, telephone handset amplifiers, assistive listening devices, assistive listening systems, telephones compatible with hearing aids, closed caption decoders, open and closed captioning, telecommunications devices for deaf persons (TDD's), videotext displays, or other effective methods of making aurally delivered materials available to individuals with hearing impairments;

ANALYSIS

Section 36.303 Auxiliary aids and services.

Section 36.303 of the final rule requires a public accommodation to take such steps as may be necessary to ensure that no individual with a disability is excluded, denied services, segregated or otherwise treated differently than other individuals because of the absence of auxiliary aids and services, unless the public accommodation can demonstrate that taking such steps would fundamentally alter the nature of the goods, services, facilities, advantages, or accommodations being offered or would result in an undue burden. This requirement is based on section 302(b)(2)(A)(iii) of the ADA.

Implicit in this duty to provide auxiliary aids and services is the underlying obligation of a public accommodation to communicate effectively with its customers, clients, patients, or participants who have disabilities affecting hearing, vision, or speech. To give emphasis to this underlying obligation, §36.303(c) of the rule incorporates language derived from section 504 regulations for federally conducted programs (<u>see</u> <u>e.g.</u>, 28 CFR 39.160(a)) that requires that appropriate auxiliary aids and services be furnished to ensure that communication with persons with disabilities is as effective as communication with others.

Auxiliary aids and services include a wide range of services and devices for ensuring effective communication. Use of the most advanced technology is not required so long as effective communication is ensured. The Department's proposed §36.303(b) provided a list of examples of auxiliary aids and services that was taken from the definition of auxiliary aids and services in section 3(1) of the ADA and was supplemented by examples from regulations implementing section 504 in federally conducted programs (<u>see</u> <u>e.g.</u>, 28 CFR 39.103). A substantial number of commenters suggested that additional examples be added to this list. The Department has added several items to this list but wishes to clarify that the list is not an all-inclusive or exhaustive catalogue of possible or available auxiliary aids or services. It is not possible to provide an exhaustive list, and such an attempt would omit new devices that will become available with emerging technology.

The Department has added videotext displays, computer-aided transcription services, and open and closed captioning to the list of examples. Videotext displays have become an important means of accessing auditory communications

REGULATION

(2) Qualified readers, taped texts, audio recordings, Brailled materials, large print materials, or other effective methods of making visually delivered materials available to individuals with visual impairments;

(3) Acquisition or modification of equipment or devices; and

(4) Other similar services and actions.

(c) Effective communication. A public accommodation shall furnish appropriate auxiliary aids and services where necessary to ensure effective communication with individuals with disabilities.

(d) Telecommunication devices for the deaf (TDD's). (1) A public accommodation that offers a customer, client, patient, or participant the opportunity to make outgoing telephone calls on more than an incidental convenience basis shall make available, upon request, a TDD for the use of an individual who has impaired hearing or a communication disorder.

(2) This part does not require a public accommodation to use a TDD for receiving or making telephone calls incident to its operations.

ANALYSIS

through a public address system. Transcription services are used to relay aurally delivered material almost simultaneously in written form to persons who are deaf or hard of hearing. This technology is often used at conferences, conventions, and hearings. While the proposed rule expressly included television decoder equipment as an auxiliary aid or service, it did not mention captioning itself. The final rule rectifies this omission by mentioning both closed and open captioning.

In this section, the Department has changed the proposed rule's phrase, "orally delivered materials," to the phrase, "aurally delivered materials." This new phrase tracks the language in the definition of "auxiliary aids and services" in section 3 of the ADA and is meant to include nonverbal sounds and alarms and computer-generated speech.

Several persons and organizations requested that the Department replace the term "telecommunications devices for deaf persons" or "TDD's" with the term "text telephone." The Department has declined to do so. The Department is aware that the Architectural and Transportation Barriers Compliance Board has used the phrase "text telephone" in lieu of the statutory term "TDD" in its final accessibility guidelines. Title IV of the ADA, however, uses the term "Telecommunications Device for the Deaf," and the Department believes it would be inappropriate to abandon this statutory term at this time.

Paragraph (b)(2) lists examples of aids and services for making visually delivered materials accessible to persons with visual impairments. Many commenters proposed additional examples such as signage or mapping, audio description services, secondary auditory programs (SAP), telebraillers, and reading machines. While the Department declines to add these items to the list in the regulation, they may be considered appropriate auxiliary aids and services.

Paragraph (b)(3) refers to the acquisition or modification of equipment or devices. For example, tape players used for an audio-guided tour of a museum exhibit may require the addition of brailled adhesive labels to the buttons on a reasonable number of the tape players to facilitate their use by individuals who are blind. Similarly, permanent or portable assistive listening systems for persons with hearing impairments may be required at a hotel conference center.

REGULATION

(e) <u>Closed caption decoders</u>. Places of lodging that provide televisions in five or more guest rooms and hospitals that provide televisions for patient use shall provide, upon request, a means for decoding captions for use by an individual with impaired hearing.

(f) <u>Alternatives</u>. If provision of a particular auxiliary aid or service by a public accommodation would result in a fundamental alteration in the nature of the goods, services, facilities, privileges, advantages, or accommodations being offered or in an undue burden, i.e., significant difficulty or expense, the public accommodation shall provide an alternative auxiliary aid or service, if one exists, that would not result in such an alteration or such burden but would nevertheless ensure that, to the maximum extent possible, individuals with disabilities receive the goods, services, facilities, privileges, advantages, or accommodations offered by the public accommodation.

ANALYSIS

Several commenters suggested the addition of current technological innovations in microelectronics and computerized control systems (e.g., voice recognition systems, automatic dialing telephones, and infrared elevator and light control systems) to the list of auxiliary aids and services. The Department interprets auxiliary aids and services as those aids and services designed to provide effective communications, i.e., making aurally and visually delivered information available to persons with hearing, speech, and vision impairments. Methods of making services, programs, or activities accessible to, or usable by, individuals with mobility or manual dexterity impairments are addressed by other sections of this part, including the requirements for modifications in policies, practices, or procedures (§36.302), the elimination of existing architectural barriers (§36.304), and the provision of alternatives to barriers removal (§36.305).

Paragraph (b)(4) refers to other similar services and actions. Several commenters asked for clarification that "similar services and actions" include retrieving items from shelves, assistance in reaching a marginally accessible seat, pushing a barrier aside in order to provide an accessible route, or assistance in removing a sweater or coat. While retrieving an item from a shelf might be an "auxiliary aid or service" for a blind person who could not locate the item without assistance, it might be a readily achievable alternative to barrier removal for a person using a wheelchair who could not reach the shelf, or a reasonable modification to a self-service policy for an individual who lacked the ability to grasp the item. (Of course, a store would not be required to provide a personal shopper.) As explained above, auxiliary aids and services are those aids and services required to provide effective communications. Other forms of assistance are more appropriately addressed by other provisions of the final rule.

The auxiliary aid requirement is a flexible one. A public accommodation can choose among various alternatives as long as the result is effective communication. For example, a restaurant would not be required to provide menus in braille for patrons who are blind, if the waiters in the restaurant are made available to read the menu. Similarly, a clothing boutique would not be required to have brailled price tags if sales personnel provide price information orally upon request; and a bookstore would not be required to make available a sign language interpreter, because effective communication can be conducted by notepad.

REGULATION

A critical determination is what constitutes an effective auxiliary aid or service. The Department's proposed rule recommended that, in determining what auxiliary aid to use, the public accommodation consult with an individual before providing him or her with a particular auxiliary aid or service. This suggestion sparked a significant volume of public comment. Many persons with disabilities, particularly persons who are deaf or hard of hearing, recommended that the rule should require that public accommodations give "primary consideration" to the "expressed choice" of an individual with a disability. These commenters asserted that the proposed rule was inconsistent with congressional intent of the ADA, with the Department's proposed rule implementing title II of the ADA, and with longstanding interpretations of section 504 of the Rehabilitation Act.

Based upon a careful review of the ADA legislative history, the Department believes that Congress did not intend under title III to impose upon a public accommodation the requirement that it give primary consideration to the request of the individual with a disability. To the contrary, the legislative history demonstrates congressional intent to strongly encourage consulting with persons with disabilities. In its analysis of the ADA's auxiliary aids requirement for public accommodations, the House Education and Labor Committee stated that it "expects" that "public accommodation[s] will consult with the individual with a disability before providing a particular auxiliary aid or service" (Education and Labor report at 107). Some commenters also cited a different committee statement that used mandatory language as evidence of legislative intent to require primary consideration. However, this statement was made in the context of reasonable accommodations required by Title I with respect to employment (Education and Labor report at 67). Thus, the Department finds that strongly encouraging consultation with persons with disabilities, in lieu of mandating primary consideration of their expressed choice, is consistent with congressional intent.

The Department wishes to emphasize that public accommodations must take steps necessary to ensure that an individual with a disability will not be excluded, denied services, segregated or otherwise treated differently from other individuals because of the use of inappropriate or ineffective auxiliary aids. In those situations requiring an interpreter, the public accommodations must secure the services of a qualified interpreter, unless an undue burden would result.

REGULATION

ANALYSIS

In the analysis of §36.303(c) in the proposed rule, the Department gave as an example the situation where a note pad and written materials were insufficient to permit effective communication in a doctor's office when the matter to be decided was whether major surgery was necessary. Many commenters objected to this statement, asserting that it gave the impression that only decisions about major surgery would merit the provision of a sign language interpreter. The statement would, as the commenters also claimed, convey the impression to other public accommodations that written communications would meet the regulatory requirements in all but the most extreme situations. The Department, when using the example of major surgery, did not intent to limit the provision of interpreter services to the most extreme situations.

Other situations may also require the use of interpreters to ensure effective communication depending on the facts of the particular case. It is not difficult to imagine a wide range of communications involving areas such as health, legal matters, and finances that would be sufficiently lengthy or complex to require an interpreter for effective communication. In some situations, an effective alternative to use of a notepad or an interpreter may be the use of a computer terminal upon which the representative of the public accommodation and the customer or client can exchange typewritten messages.

Section 36.303(d) specifically addresses requirements for TDD's. Partly because of the availability of telecommunications relay services to be established under title IV of the ADA, §36.303(d)(2) provides that a public accommodation is not required to use a telecommunication device for the deaf (TDD) in receiving or making telephone calls incident to its operations. Several commenters were concerned that relay services would not be sufficient to provide effective access in a number of situations. Commenters argued that relay systems (1) do not provide effective access to the automated systems that require the caller to respond by pushing a button on a touch tone phone, (2) cannot operate fast enough to convey messages on answering machines, or to permit a TDD user to leave a recorded message, and (3) are not appropriate for calling crisis lines relating to such matters as rape, domestic violence, child abuse, and drugs where confidentiality is a concern. The Department believes that it is more appropriate for the Federal Communications Commission to address these issues in its rulemaking under title IV.

ADA Handbook

REGULATION

A public accommodation is, however, required to make a TDD available to an individual with impaired hearing or speech, if it customarily offers telephone service to its customers, clients, patients, or participants on more than an incidental convenience basis. Where entry to a place of public accommodation requires use of a security entrance telephone, a TDD or other effective means of communication must be provided for use by an individual with impaired hearing or speech.

In other words, individual retail stores, doctors' offices, restaurants, or similar establishments are not required by this section to have TDD's, because TDD users will be able to make inquiries, appointments, or reservations with such establishments through the relay system established under title IV of the ADA. The public accommodation will likewise be able to contact TDD users through the relay system. On the other hand, hotels, hospitals, and other similar establishments that offer nondisabled individuals the opportunity to make outgoing telephone calls on more than an incidental convenience basis must provide a TDD on request.

Section 36.303(e) requires places of lodging that provide televisions in five or more guest rooms and hospitals to provide, upon request, a means for decoding closed captions for use by an individual with impaired hearing. Hotels should also provide a TDD or similar device at the front desk in order to take calls from guests who use TDD's in their rooms. In this way guests with hearing impairments can avail themselves of such hotel services as making inquiries of the front desk and ordering room service. The term "hospital" is used in its general sense and should be interpreted broadly.

Movie theaters are not required by §36.303 to present open-captioned films. However, other public accommodations that impart verbal information through soundtracks on films, video tapes, or slide shows are required to make such information accessible to persons with hearing impairments. Captioning is one means to make the information accessible to individuals with disabilities.

The rule specifies that auxiliary aids and services include the acquisition or modification of equipment or devices. For example, tape players used for an audio-guided tour of a museum exhibit may require the addition of brailled adhesive labels to the buttons on a reasonable number of the tape players to facilitate their use by individuals who are blind.

REGULATION

Similarly, a hotel conference center may need to provide permanent or portable assistive listening systems for persons with hearing impairments.

As provided in §36.303(f), a public accommodation is not required to provide any particular aid or service that would result either in a fundamental alteration in the nature of the goods, services, facilities, privileges, advantages, or accommodations offered or in an undue burden. Both of these statutory limitations are derived from existing regulations and caselaw under section 504 and are to be applied on a case-by-case basis (see, e.g., 28 CFR 39.160(d) and Southeastern Community College v. Davis, 442 U.S. 397 (1979)). Congress intended that "undue burden" under §36.303 and "undue hardship," which is used in the employment provisions of title I of the ADA, should be determined on a case-by-case basis under the same standards and in light of the same factors (Judiciary report at 59). The rule, therefore, in accordance with the definition of undue hardship in section 101(10) of the ADA, defines undue burden as "significant difficulty or expense" (see §§36.104 and 36.303(a)) and requires that undue burden be determined in light of the factors listed in the definition in 36.104.

Consistent with regulations implementing section 504 in federally conducted programs (see, e.g., 28 CFR 39.160(d)), §36.303(f) provides that the fact that the provision of a particular auxiliary aid or service would result in an undue burden does not relieve a public accommodation from the duty to furnish an alternative auxiliary aid or service, if available, that would not result in such a burden.

Section §36.303(g) of the proposed rule has been deleted from this section and included in a new §36.306. That new section continues to make clear that the auxiliary aids requirement does not mandate the provision of individually prescribed devices, such as prescription eyeglasses or hearing aids.

The costs of compliance with the requirements of this section may not be financed by surcharges limited to particular individuals with disabilities or any group of individuals with disabilities (§36.301(c)).

REGULATION

§36.304 Removal of barriers.

(a) General. A public accommodation shall remove architectural barriers in existing facilities, including communication barriers that are structural in nature, where such removal is readily achievable, i.e., easily accomplishable and able to be carried out without much difficulty or expense.

(b) Examples. Examples of steps to remove barriers include, but are not limited to, the following actions--

(1) Installing ramps;

(2) Making curb cuts in sidewalks and entrances;

(3) Repositioning shelves;

(4) Rearranging tables, chairs, vending machines, display racks, and other furniture;

(5) Repositioning telephones;

(6) Adding raised markings on elevator control buttons;

(7) Installing flashing alarm lights;

(8) Widening doors;

(9) Installing offset

ANALYSIS

Section 36.304 Removal of barriers.

Section 36.304 requires the removal of architectural barriers and communication barriers that are structural in nature in existing facilities, where such removal is readily achievable, i.e., easily accomplishable and able to be carried out without much difficulty or expense. This requirement is based on section 302(b)(2)(A)(iv) of the ADA.

A number of commenters interpreted the phrase "communication barriers that are structural in nature" broadly to encompass the provision of communications devices such as TDD's, telephone handset amplifiers, assistive listening devices, and digital check-out displays. The statute, however, as read by the Department, limits the application of the phrase "communications barriers that are structural in nature" to those barriers that are an integral part of the physical structure of a facility. In addition to the communications barriers posed by permanent signage and alarm systems noted by Congress (see Education and Labor report at 110), the Department would also include among the communications barriers covered by §36.304 the failure to provide adequate sound buffers, and the presence of physical partitions that hamper the passage of sound waves between employees and customers. Given that §36.304's proper focus is on the removal of physical barriers, the Department believes that the obligation to provide communications equipment and devices such as TDD's, telephone handset amplifiers, assistive listening devices, and digital check-out displays is more appropriately determined by the requirements for auxiliary aids and services under §36.303 (see Education and Labor report at 107-108). The obligation to remove communications barriers that are structural in nature under §36.304, of course, is independent of any obligation to provide auxiliary aids and services under §36.303.

The statutory provision also requires the readily achievable removal of certain barriers in existing vehicles and rail passenger cars. This transportation requirement is not included in §36.304, but rather in §36.310(b) of the rule.

In striking a balance between guaranteeing access to individuals with disabilities and recognizing the legitimate cost concerns of businesses and other private entities, the ADA establishes different standards for existing facilities and new construction. In existing facilities, which are the subject of §36.304, where retrofitting may prove costly, a less rigorous degree of accessibility is required than in the case of new

REGULATION

hinges to widen doorways;

(10) Eliminating a turnstile or providing an alternative accessible path;

(11) Installing accessible door hardware;

(12) Installing grab bars in toilet stalls;

(13) Rearranging toilet partitions to increase maneuvering space;

(14) Insulating lavatory pipes under sinks to prevent burns;

(15) Installing a raised toilet seat;

(16) Installing a full-length bathroom mirror;

(17) Repositioning the paper towel dispenser in a bathroom;

(18) Creating designated accessible parking spaces;

(19) Installing an accessible paper cup dispenser at an existing inaccessible water fountain;

(20) Removing high pile, low density carpeting; or

(21) Installing vehicle hand controls.

(c) Priorities. A public

ANALYSIS

construction and alterations (see §§36.401-36.406) where accessibility can be more conveniently and economically incorporated in the initial stages of design and construction.

For example, a bank with existing automatic teller machines (ATM's) would have to remove barriers to the use of the ATM's, if it is readily achievable to do so. Whether or not it is necessary to take actions such as ramping a few steps or raising or lowering an ATM would be determined by whether the actions can be accomplished easily and without much difficulty or expense.

On the other hand, a newly constructed bank with ATM's would be required by §36.401 to have an ATM that is "readily accessible to and usable by" persons with disabilities in accordance with accessibility guidelines incorporated under §36.406.

The requirement to remove architectural barriers includes the removal of physical barriers of any kind. For example, §36.304 requires the removal, when readily achievable, of barriers caused by the location of temporary or movable structures, such as furniture, equipment, and display racks. In order to provide access to individuals who use wheelchairs, for example, restaurants may need to rearrange tables and chairs, and department stores may need to reconfigure display racks and shelves. As stated in §36.304(f), such actions are not readily achievable to the extent that they would result in a significant loss of selling or serving space. If the widening of all aisles in selling or serving areas is not readily achievable, then selected widening should be undertaken to maximize the amount of merchandise or the number of tables accessible to individuals who use wheelchairs. Access to goods and services provided in any remaining inaccessible areas must be made available through alternative methods to barrier removal, as required by §36.305.

Because the purpose of title III of the ADA is to ensure that public accommodations are accessible to their customers, clients, or patrons (as opposed to their employees, who are the focus of title I), the obligation to remove barriers under §36.304 does not extend to areas of a facility that are used exclusively as employee work areas.

Section 36.304(b) provides a wide-ranging list of the types of modest measures that may be taken to remove

REGULATION

accommodation is urged to take measures to comply with the barrier removal requirements of this section in accordance with the following order of priorities.

(1) First, a public accommodation should take measures to provide access to a place of public accommodation from public sidewalks, parking, or public transportation. These measures include, for example, installing an entrance ramp, widening entrances, and providing accessible parking spaces.

(2) Second, a public accommodation should take measures to provide access to those areas of a place of public accommodation where goods and services are made available to the public. These measures include, for example, adjusting the layout of display racks, rearranging tables, providing brailled and raised character signage, widening doors, providing visual alarms, and installing ramps.

(3) Third, a public accommodation should take measures to provide access to restroom facilities. These measures include, for example, removal of obstructing furniture or vending machines, widening of doors, installation of ramps, providing accessible signage,

ANALYSIS

barriers and that are likely to be readily achievable. The list includes examples of measures, such as adding raised letter markings on elevator control buttons and installing flashing alarm lights, that would be used to remove communications barriers that are structural in nature. It is not an exhaustive list, but merely an illustrative one. Moreover, the inclusion of a measure on this list does not mean that it is readily achievable in all cases. Whether or not any of these measures is readily achievable is to be determined on a case-by-case basis in light of the particular circumstances presented and the factors listed in the definition of readily achievable (§36.104).

A public accommodation generally would not be required to remove a barrier to physical access posed by a flight of steps, if removal would require extensive ramping or an elevator. Ramping a single step, however, will likely be readily achievable, and ramping several steps will in many circumstances also be readily achievable. The readily achievable standard does not require barrier removal that requires extensive restructuring or burdensome expense. Thus, where it is not readily achievable to do, the ADA would not require a restaurant to provide access to a restroom reachable only by a flight of stairs.

Like §36.405, this section permits deference to the national interest in preserving significant historic structures. Barrier removal would not be considered "readily achievable" if it would threaten or destroy the historic significance of a building or facility that is eligible for listing in the National Register of Historic Places under the National Historic Preservation Act (16 U.S.C. 470, et seq.), or is designated as historic under State or local law.

The readily achievable defense requires a less demanding level of exertion by a public accommodation than does the undue burden defense to the auxiliary aids requirements of §36.303. In that sense, it can be characterized as a "lower" standard than the undue burden standard. The readily achievable defense is also less demanding than the undue hardship defense in section 102(b)(5) of the ADA, which limits the obligation to make reasonable accommodation in employment. Barrier removal measures that are not easily accomplishable and are not able to be carried out without much difficulty or expense are not required under the readily achievable standard, even if they do not impose an undue burden or an undue hardship.

REGULATION

widening of toilet stalls, and installation of grab bars.

(4) Fourth, a public accommodation should take any other measures necessary to provide access to the goods, services, facilities, privileges, advantages, or accommodations of a place of public accommodation.

(d) Relationship to alterations requirements of subpart D of this part. (1) Except as provided in paragraph (d)(2) of this section, measures taken to comply with the barrier removal requirements of this section shall comply with the applicable requirements for alterations in §36.402 and §§36.404-36.406 of this part for the element being altered. The path of travel requirements of §36.403 shall not apply to measures taken solely to comply with the barrier removal requirements of this section.

(2) If, as a result of compliance with the alterations requirements specified in paragraph (d)(1) of this section, the measures required to remove a barrier would not be readily achievable, a public accommodation may take other readily achievable measures to remove the barrier that do not fully comply with the specified requirements. Such measures include, for

ANALYSIS

Section 36.304(f)(1) of the proposed rule, which stated that "barrier removal is not readily achievable if it would result in significant loss of profit or significant loss of efficiency of operation," has been deleted from the final rule. Many commenters objected to this provision because it impermissibly introduced the notion of profit into a statutory standard that did not include it. Concern was expressed that, in order for an action not to be considered readily achievable, a public accommodation would inappropriately have to show, for example, not only that the action could not be done without "much difficulty or expense", but that a significant loss of profit would result as well. In addition, some commenters asserted use of the word "significant," which is used in the definition of undue hardship under title I (the standard for interpreting the meaning of undue burden as a defense to title III's auxiliary aids requirements) (see §§36.104, 36.303(f)), blurs the fact that the readily achievable standard requires a lower level of effort on the part of a public accommodation than does the undue burden standard.

The obligation to engage in readily achievable barrier removal is a continuing one. Over time, barrier removal that initially was not readily achievable may later be required because of changed circumstances. Many commenters expressed support for the Department's position that the obligation to comply with §36.304 is continuing in nature. Some urged that the rule require public accommodations to assess their compliance on at least an annual basis in light of changes in resources and other factors that would be relevant to determining what barrier removal measures would be readily achievable.

Although the obligation to engage in readily achievable barrier removal is clearly a continuing duty, the Department has declined to establish any independent requirement for an annual assessment or self-evaluation. It is best left to the public accommodations subject to §36.304 to establish policies to assess compliance that are appropriate to the particular circumstances faced by the wide range of public accommodations covered by the ADA. However, even in the absence of an explicit regulatory requirement for periodic self-evaluations, the Department still urges public accommodations to establish procedures for an ongoing assessment of their compliance with the ADA's barrier removal requirements. The Department recommends that this process include appropriate consultation with individuals with disabili-

REGULATION

example, providing a ramp with a steeper slope or widening a doorway to a narrower width than that mandated by the alterations requirements. No measure shall be taken, however, that poses a significant risk to the health or safety of individuals with disabilities or others.

(e) Portable ramps. Portable ramps should be used to comply with this section only when installation of a permanent ramp is not readily achievable. In order to avoid any significant risk to the health or safety of individuals with disabilities or others in using portable ramps, due consideration shall be given to safety features such as nonslip surfaces, railings, anchoring, and strength of materials.

(f) Selling or serving space. The rearrangement of temporary or movable structures, such as furniture, equipment, and display racks is not readily achievable to the extent that it results in a significant loss of selling or serving space.

(g) Limitation on barrier removal obligations. (1) The requirements for barrier removal under §36.304 shall not be interpreted to exceed the standards for alterations in subpart D of this part.

ANALYSIS

ties or organizations representing them. A serious effort at self-assessment and consultation can diminish the threat of litigation and save resources by identifying the most efficient means of providing required access.

The Department has been asked for guidance on the best means for public accommodations to comply voluntarily with this section. Such information is more appropriately part of the Department's technical assistance effort and will be forthcoming over the next several months. The Department recommends, however, the development of an implementation plan designed to achieve compliance with the ADA's barrier removal requirements before they become effective on January 26, 1992. Such a plan, if appropriately designed and diligently executed, could serve as evidence of a good faith effort to comply with the requirements of §36.104. In developing an implementation plan for readily achievable barrier removal, a public accommodation should consult with local organizations representing persons with disabilities and solicit their suggestions for cost-effective means of making individual places of public accommodation accessible. Such organizations may also be helpful in allocating scarce resources and establishing priorities. Local associations of businesses may want to encourage this process and serve as the forum for discussions on the local level between disability rights organizations and local businesses.

Section 36.304(c) recommends priorities for public accommodations in removing barriers in existing facilities. Because the resources available for barrier removal may not be adequate to remove all existing barriers at any given time, §36.304(c) suggests priorities for determining which types of barriers should be mitigated or eliminated first. The purpose of these priorities is to facilitate long-term business planning and to maximize, in light of limited resources, the degree of effective access that will result from any given level of expenditure.

Although many commenters expressed support for the concept of establishing priorities, a significant number objected to their mandatory nature in the proposed rule. The Department shares the concern of these commenters that mandatory priorities would increase the likelihood of litigation and inappropriately reduce the discretion of public accommodations to determine the most effective mix of barrier removal measures to undertake in particular circumstances. Therefore, in the final rule the priorities are no longer mandatory.

REGULATION

(2) To the extent that relevant standards for alterations are not provided in subpart D of this part, then the requirements of §36.304 shall not be interpreted to exceed the standards for new construction in subpart D of this part.

(3) This section does not apply to rolling stock and other conveyances to the extent that §36.310 applies to rolling stock and other conveyances.

ANALYSIS

In response to comments that the priorities failed to address communications issues, the Department wishes to emphasize that the priorities encompass the removal of communications barriers that are structural in nature. It would be counter to the ADA's carefully wrought statutory scheme to include in this provision the wide range of communication devices that are required by the ADA's provisions on auxiliary aids and services. The final rule explicitly includes brailled and raised letter signage and visual alarms among the examples of steps to remove barriers provided in §36.304(c)(2).

Section 36.304(c)(1) places the highest priority on measures that will enable individuals with disabilities to physically enter a place of public accommodation. This priority on "getting through the door" recognizes that providing actual physical access to a facility from public sidewalks, public transportation, or parking is generally preferable to any alternative arrangements in terms of both business efficiency and the dignity of individuals with disabilities.

The next priority, which is established in §36.304(c)(2), is for measures that provide access to those areas of a place of public accommodation where goods and services are made available to the public. For example, in a hardware store, to the extent that it is readily achievable to do so, individuals with disabilities should be given access not only to assistance at the front desk, but also access, like that available to other customers, to the retail display areas of the store.

The Department agrees with those commenters who argued that access to the areas where goods and services are provided is generally more important than the provision of restrooms. Therefore, the final rule reverses priorities two and three of the proposed rule in order to give lower priority to accessible restrooms. Consequently, the third priority in the final rule (§36.304(c)(3)) is for measures to provide access to restroom facilities and the last priority is placed on any remaining measures required to remove barriers.

Section 36.304(d) requires that measures taken to remove barriers under §36.304 be subject to subpart D's requirements for alterations (except for the path of travel requirements in §36.403). It only permits deviations from the subpart D requirements when compliance with those requirements is not readily achievable. In such cases, §36.304(d) permits mea-

REGULATION

ANALYSIS

sures to be taken that do not fully comply with the subpart D requirements, so long as the measures do not pose a significant risk to the health or safety of individuals with disabilities or others.

This approach represents a change from the proposed rule which stated that "readily achievable" measures taken solely to remove barriers under §36.304 are exempt from the alterations requirements of subpart D. The intent of the proposed rule was to maximize the flexibility of public accommodations in undertaking barrier removal by allowing deviations from the technical standards of subpart D. It was thought that allowing slight deviations would provide access and release additional resources for expanding the amount of barrier removal that could be obtained under the readily achievable standard.

Many commenters, however, representing both businesses and individuals with disabilities, questioned this approach because of the likelihood that unsafe or ineffective measures would be taken in the absence of the subpart D standards for alterations as a reference point. Some advocated a rule requiring strict compliance with the subpart D standard.

The Department in the final rule has adopted the view of many commenters that (1) public accommodations should in the first instance be required to comply with the subpart D standards for alterations where it is readily achievable to do so and (2) safe, readily achievable measures must be taken when compliance with the subpart D standards is not readily achievable. Reference to the subpart D standards in this manner will promote certainty and good design at the same time that permitting slight deviations will expand the amount of barrier removal that may be achieved under §36.304.

Because of the inconvenience to individuals with disabilities and the safety problems involved in the use of portable ramps, §36.304(e) permits the use of a portable ramp to comply with §36.304(a) only when installation of a permanent ramp is not readily achievable. In order to promote safety, §36.304(e) requires that due consideration be given to the incorporation of features such as nonslip surfaces, railings, anchoring, and strength of materials in any portable ramp that is used.

Temporary facilities brought in for use at the site of a natural disaster are subject to the barrier removal requirements of §36.304.

REGULATION

A number of commenters requested clarification regarding how to determine when a public accommodation has discharged its obligation to remove barriers in existing facilities. For example, is a hotel required by §36.304 to remove barriers in all of its guest rooms? Or is some lesser percentage adequate? A new paragraph (g) has been added to §36.304 to address this issue. The Department believes that the degree of barrier removal required under §36.304 may be less, but certainly would not be required to exceed, the standards for alterations under the ADA Accessibility Guidelines incorporated by subpart D of this part (ADAAG). The ADA's requirements for readily achievable barrier removal in existing facilities are intended to be substantially less rigorous than those for new construction and alterations. It, therefore, would be obviously inappropriate to require actions under §36.304 that would exceed the ADAAG requirements. Hotels, then, in order to satisfy the requirements of §36.304, would not be required to remove barriers in a higher percentage of rooms than required by ADAAG. If relevant standards for alterations are not provided in ADAAG, then reference should be made to the standards for new construction.

REGULATION

§36.305 Alternatives to barrier removal.

(a) General. Where a public accommodation can demonstrate that barrier removal is not readily achievable, the public accommodation shall not fail to make its goods, services, facilities, privileges, advantages, or accommodations available through alternative methods, if those methods are readily achievable.

(b) Examples. Examples of alternatives to barrier removal include, but are not limited to, the following actions--

(1) Providing curb service or home delivery;

(2) Retrieving merchandise from inaccessible shelves or racks;

(3) Relocating activities to accessible locations;

(c) Multiscreen cinemas. If it is not readily achievable to remove barriers to provide access by persons with mobility impairments to all of the theaters of a multiscreen cinema, the cinema shall establish a film rotation schedule that provides reasonable access for individuals who use wheelchairs to all films. Reasonable notice shall be provided to the public as to the location and time of accessible showings.

ANALYSIS

Section 36.305 Alternatives to barrier removal.

Section 36.305 specifies that where a public accommodation can demonstrate that removal of a barrier is not readily achievable, the public accommodation must make its goods, services, facilities, privileges, advantages, or accommodations available through alternative methods, if such methods are readily achievable. This requirement is based on section 302(b)(2)(A)(v) of the ADA.

For example, if it is not readily achievable for a retail store to raise, lower, or remove shelves or to rearrange display racks to provide accessible aisles, the store must, if readily achievable, provide a clerk or take other alternative measures to retrieve inaccessible merchandise. Similarly, if it is not readily achievable to ramp a long flight of stairs leading to the front door of a restaurant or a pharmacy, the restaurant or the pharmacy must take alternative measures, if readily achievable, such as providing curb service or home delivery. If, within a restaurant, it is not readily achievable to remove physical barriers to a certain section of a restaurant, the restaurant must, where it is readily achievable to do so, offer the same menu in an accessible area of the restaurant.

Where alternative methods are used to provide access, a public accommodation may not charge an individual with a disability for the costs associated with the alternative method (see §36.301(c)). Further analysis of the issue of charging for alternative measures may be found in the preamble discussion of §36.301(c).

In some circumstances, because of security considerations, some alternative methods may not be readily achievable. The rule does not require a cashier to leave his or her post to retrieve items for individuals with disabilities, if there are no other employees on duty.

Section 36.305(c) of the proposed rule has been deleted and the requirements have been included in a new §36.306. That section makes clear that the alternative methods requirement does not mandate the provision of personal devices, such as wheelchairs, or services of a personal nature.

In the final rule, §36.305(c) provides specific requirements regarding alternatives to barrier removal in multiscreen cinemas. In some situations, it may not be readily achievable to remove enough barriers to provide access to all of the theaters

REGULATION

of a multiscreen cinema. If that is the case, §36.305(c) requires the cinema to establish a film rotation schedule that provides reasonable access for individuals who use wheelchairs to films being presented by the cinema. It further requires that reasonable notice be provided to the public as to the location and time of accessible showings. Methods for providing notice include appropriate use of the international accessibility symbol in a cinema's print advertising and the addition of accessibility information to a cinema's recorded telephone information line.

REGULATION

§36.306 Personal devices and services.

This part does not require a public accommodation to provide its customers, clients, or participants with personal devices, such as wheelchairs; individually prescribed devices, such as prescription eyeglasses or hearing aids; or services of a personal nature including assistance in eating, toileting, or dressing.

ANALYSIS

Section 36.306 Personal devices and services.

The final rule includes a new §36.306, entitled "Personal devices and services." Section 36.306 of the proposed rule, "Readily achievable and undue burden: Factors to be considered," was deleted for the reasons described in the preamble discussion of the definition of the term "readily achievable" in §36.104. In place of §§36.303(g) and 36.305(c) of the proposed rule, which addressed the issue of personal devices and services in the contexts of auxiliary aids and alternatives to barrier removal, §36.306 provides a general statement that the regulation does not require the provision of personal devices and services. This section states that a public accommodation is not required to provide its customers, clients, or participants with personal devices, such as wheelchairs; individually prescribed devices, such as prescription eyeglasses or hearing aids; or services of a personal nature including assistance in eating, toileting, or dressing.

This statement serves as a limitation on all the requirements of the regulation. The personal devices and services limitation was intended to have general application in the proposed rule in all contexts where it was relevant. The final rule, therefore, clarifies this point by including a general provision that will explicitly apply not just to auxiliary aids and services and alternatives to barrier removal, but across-the-board to include such relevant areas as modifications in policies, practices, and procedures (§36.302) and examinations and courses (§36.309), as well.

The Department wishes to clarify that measures taken as alternatives to barrier removal, such as retrieving items from shelves or providing curb service or home delivery, are not to be considered personal services. Similarly, minimal actions that may be required as modifications in policies, practices, or procedures under §36.302, such as a waiter's removing the cover from a customer's straw, a kitchen's cutting up food into smaller pieces, or a bank's filling out a deposit slip, are not services of a personal nature within the meaning of §36.306. (Of course, such modifications may be required under §36.302 only if they are "reasonable.") Similarly, this section does not preclude the short-term loan of personal receivers that are part of an assistive listening system.

Of course, if personal services are customarily provided to the customers or clients of a public accommodation, e.g., in a hospital or senior citizen center, then these personal services should also be provided to persons with disabilities using the public accommodation.

REGULATION

§36.307 Accessible or special goods.

(a) This part does not require a public accommodation to alter its inventory to include accessible or special goods that are designed for, or facilitate use by, individuals with disabilities.

(b) A public accommodation shall order accessible or special goods at the request of an individual with disabilities, if, in the normal course of its operation, it makes special orders on request for unstocked goods, and if the accessible or special goods can be obtained from a supplier with whom the public accommodation customarily does business.

(c) Examples of accessible or special goods include items such as brailled versions of books, books on audio cassettes, closed-captioned video tapes, special sizes or lines of clothing, and special foods to meet particular dietary needs.

ANALYSIS

Section 36.307 Accessible or special goods.

Section 36.307 establishes that the rule does not require a public accommodation to alter its inventory to include accessible or special goods with accessibility features that are designed for, or facilitate use by, individuals with disabilities. As specified in §36.307(c), accessible or special goods include such items as brailled versions of books, books on audio-cassettes, closed captioned video tapes, special sizes or lines of clothing, and special foods to meet particular dietary needs.

The purpose of the ADA's public accommodations requirements is to ensure accessibility to the goods offered by a public accommodation, not to alter the nature or mix of goods that the public accommodation has typically provided. In other words, a bookstore, for example, must make its facilities and sales operations accessible to individuals with disabilities, but is not required to stock brailled or large print books. Similarly, a video store must make its facilities and rental operations accessible, but is not required to stock closed-captioned video tapes. The Department has been made aware, however, that the most recent titles in video-tape rental establishments are, in fact, closed captioned.

Although a public accommodation is not required by §36.307(a) to modify its inventory, it is required by §36.307(b), at the request of an individual with disabilities, to order accessible or special goods that it does not customarily maintain in stock if, in the normal course of its operation, it makes special orders for unstocked goods, and if the accessible or special goods can be obtained from a supplier with whom the public accommodation customarily does business. For example, a clothing store would be required to order specially-sized clothing at the request of an individual with a disability, if it customarily makes special orders for clothing that it does not keep in stock, and if the clothing can be obtained from one of the store's customary suppliers.

One commenter asserted that the proposed rule could be interpreted to require a store to special order accessible or special goods of all types, even if only one type is specially ordered in the normal course of its business. The Department, however, intends for §36.307(b) to require special orders only of those particular types of goods for which a public accommodation normally makes special orders. For example, a book and recording store would not have to specially order brailled books if, in the normal course of its business, it only specially orders recordings and not books.

REGULATION

§36.308 Seating in assembly areas.

(a) Existing facilities.
(1) To the extent that it is readily achievable, a public accommodation in assembly areas shall--

(i) Provide a reasonable number of wheelchair seating spaces and seats with removable aisle-side arm rests; and

(ii) Locate the wheelchair seating spaces so that they--

(A) Are dispersed throughout the seating area;

(B) Provide lines of sight and choice of admission prices comparable to those for members of the general public;

(C) Adjoin an accessible route that also serves as a means of egress in case of emergency; and

(D) Permit individuals who use wheelchairs to sit with family members or other companions.

(2) If removal of seats is not readily achievable, a public accommodation shall provide, to the extent that it is readily achievable to do so, a portable chair or other means to permit a family member or other companion to sit with an individual who uses a wheelchair.

ANALYSIS

Section 36.308 Seating in assembly areas.

Section 36.308 establishes specific requirements for removing barriers to physical access in assembly areas, which include such facilities as theaters, concert halls, auditoriums, lecture halls, and conference rooms. This section does not address the provision of auxiliary aids or the removal of communications barriers that are structural in nature. These communications requirements are the focus of other provisions of the regulation (see §§36.303-36.304).

Individuals who use wheelchairs historically have been relegated to inferior seating in the back of assembly areas separate from accompanying family members and friends. The provisions of §36.308 are intended to promote integration and equality in seating.

In some instances it may not be readily achievable for auditoriums or theaters to remove seats to allow individuals with wheelchairs to sit next to accompanying family members or friends. In these situations, the final rule retains the requirement that the public accommodation provide portable chairs or other means to allow the accompanying individuals to sit with the persons in wheelchairs. Persons in wheelchairs should have the same opportunity to enjoy movies, plays, and similar events with their families and friends, just as other patrons do. The final rule specifies that portable chairs or other means to permit family members or companions to sit with individuals who use wheelchairs must be provided only when it is readily achievable to do so.

In order to facilitate seating of wheelchair users who wish to transfer to existing seating, paragraph (a)(1) of the final rule adds a requirement that, to the extent readily achievable, a reasonable number of seats with removable aisle-side armrests must be provided. Many persons in wheelchairs are able to transfer to existing seating with this relatively minor modification. This solution avoids the potential safety hazard created by the use of portable chairs and fosters integration. The final ADA Accessibility Guidelines incorporated by subpart D (ADAAG) also add a requirement regarding aisle seating that was not in the proposed guidelines. In situations when a person in a wheelchair transfers to existing seating, the public accommodation shall provide assistance in handling the wheelchair of the patron with the disability.

Likewise, consistent with ADAAG, the final rule adds in

REGULATION

(3) The requirements of paragraph (a) of this section shall not be interpreted to exceed the standards for alterations in subpart D of this part.

(b) <u>New construction and alterations</u>. The provision and location of wheelchair seating spaces in newly constructed or altered assembly areas shall be governed by the standards for new construction and alterations in subpart D of this part.

ANALYSIS

§36.308(a)(1)(ii)(B) a requirement that, to the extent readily achievable, wheelchair seating provide lines of sight and choice of admission prices comparable to those for members of the general public.

Finally, because Congress intended that the requirements for barrier removal in existing facilities be substantially less rigorous than those required for new construction and alterations, the final rule clarifies in §36.308(a)(3) that in no event can the requirements for existing facilities be interpreted to exceed the standards for alterations under ADAAG. For example, §4.33 of ADAAG only requires wheelchair spaces to be provided in more than one location when the seating capacity of the assembly area exceeds 300. Therefore, paragraph (a) of §36.308 may not be interpreted to require readily achievable dispersal of wheelchair seating in assembly areas with 300 or fewer seats. Similarly, §4.1.3(19) of ADAAG requires six accessible wheelchair locations in an assembly area with 301 to 500 seats. The reasonable number of wheelchair locations required by paragraph (a), therefore, may be less than six, but may not be interpreted to exceed six.

REGULATION

Proposed Section 36.309 Purchase of furniture and equipment.

Section 36.309 of the proposed rule would have required that newly purchased furniture or equipment made available for use at a place of public accommodation be accessible, to the extent such furniture or equipment is available, unless this requirement would fundamentally alter the goods, services, facilities, privileges, advantages, or accommodations offered, or would not be readily achievable. Proposed §36.309 has been omitted from the final rule because the Department has determined that its requirements are more properly addressed under other sections, and because there are currently no appropriate accessibility standards addressing many types of furniture and equipment.

Some types of equipment will be required to meet the accessibility requirements of subpart D. For example, ADAAG establishes technical and scoping requirements in new construction and alterations for automated teller machines and telephones. Purchase or modification of equipment is required in certain instances by the provisions in §§36.201 and 36.202. For example, an arcade may need to provide accessible video machines in order to ensure full and equal enjoyment of the facilities and to provide an opportunity to participate in the services and facilities it provides. The barrier removal requirements of §36.304 will apply as well to furniture and equipment (lowering shelves, rearranging furniture, adding braille labels to a vending machine).

REGULATION

§36.309 Examinations and courses.

(a) General. Any private entity that offers examinations or courses related to applications, licensing, certification, or credentialing for secondary or postsecondary education, professional, or trade purposes shall offer such examinations or courses in a place and manner accessible to persons with disabilities or offer alternative accessible arrangements for such individuals.

(b) Examinations. (1) Any private entity offering an examination covered by this section must assure that --

(i) The examination is selected and administered so as to best ensure that, when the examination is administered to an individual with a disability that impairs sensory, manual, or speaking skills, the examination results accurately reflect the individual's aptitude or achievement level or whatever other factor the examination purports to measure, rather than reflecting the individual's impaired sensory, manual, or speaking skills (except where those skills are the factors that the examination purports to measure);

(ii) An examination that

ANALYSIS

Section 36.309 Examinations and courses.

Section 36.309(a) sets forth the general rule that any private entity that offers examinations or courses related to applications, licensing, certification, or credentialing for secondary or postsecondary education, professional, or trade purposes shall offer such examinations or courses in a place and manner accessible to persons with disabilities or offer alternative accessible arrangements for such individuals.

Paragraph (a) restates section 309 of the Americans with Disabilities Act. Section 309 is intended to fill the gap that is created when licensing, certification, and other testing authorities are not covered by section 504 of the Rehabilitation Act or title II of the ADA. Any such authority that is covered by section 504, because of the receipt of Federal money, or by title II, because it is a function of a State or local government, must make all of its programs accessible to persons with disabilities, which includes physical access as well as modifications in the way the test is administered, e.g., extended time, written instructions, or assistance of a reader.

Many licensing, certification, and testing authorities are not covered by section 504, because no Federal money is received; nor are they covered by title II of the ADA because they are not State or local agencies. However, States often require the licenses provided by such authorities in order for an individual to practice a particular profession or trade. Thus, the provision was included in the ADA in order to assure that persons with disabilities are not foreclosed from educational, professional, or trade opportunities because an examination or course is conducted in an inaccessible site or without needed modifications.

As indicated in the "Application" section of this part (§36.102), §36.309 applies to any private entity that offers the specified types of examinations or courses. This is consistent with section 309 of the Americans with Disabilities Act, which states that the requirements apply to "any person" offering examinations or courses.

The Department received a large number of comments on this section, reflecting the importance of ensuring that the key gateways to education and employment are open to individuals with disabilities. The most frequent comments were objections to the fundamental alteration and undue burden provisions in §§36.309 (b)(3) and (c)(3) and to allowing

REGULATION

is designed for individuals with impaired sensory, manual, or speaking skills is offered at equally convenient locations, as often, and in as timely a manner as are other examinations; and

(iii) The examination is administered in facilities that are accessible to individuals with disabilities or alternative accessible arrangements are made.

(2) Required modifications to an examination may include changes in the length of time permitted for completion of the examination and adaptation of the manner in which the examination is given.

(3) A private entity offering an examination covered by this section shall provide appropriate auxiliary aids for persons with impaired sensory, manual, or speaking skills, unless that private entity can demonstrate that offering a particular auxiliary aid would fundamentally alter the measurement of the skills or knowledge the examination is intended to test or would result in an undue burden. Auxiliary aids and services required by this section may include taped examinations, interpreters or other effective methods of making orally delivered materials available to individuals with hearing

ANALYSIS

courses and examinations to be provided through alternative accessible arrangements, rather than in an integrated setting.

Although section 309 of the Act does not refer to a fundamental alteration or undue burden limitation, those limitations do appear in section 302(b)(2)(A)(iii) of the Act, which establishes the obligation of public accommodations to provide auxiliary aids and services. The Department, therefore, included it in the paragraphs of §36.309 requiring the provision of auxiliary aids. One commenter argued that similar limitations should apply to all of the requirements of §36.309, but the Department did not consider this extension appropriate.

Commenters who objected to permitting "alternative accessible arrangements" argued that such arrangements allow segregation and should not be permitted, unless they are the least restrictive available alternative, for example, for someone who cannot leave home. Some commenters made a distinction between courses, where interaction is an important part of the educational experience, and examinations, where it may be less important. Because the statute specifically authorizes alternative accessible arrangements as a method of meeting the requirements of section 309, the Department has not adopted this suggestion. The Department notes, however, that, while examinations of the type covered by §36.309 may not be covered elsewhere in the regulation, courses will generally be offered in a "place of education," which is included in the definition of "place of public accommodation" in §36.104, and, therefore, will be subject to the integrated setting requirement of §36.203.

Section 36.309(b) sets forth specific requirements for examinations. Examinations covered by this section would include a bar exam or the Scholastic Aptitude Test prepared by the Educational Testing Service. Paragraph (b)(l) is adopted from the Department of Education's section 504 regulation on admission tests to postsecondary educational programs (34 CFR 104.42(b)(3)). Paragraph (b)(1)(i) requires that a private entity offering an examination covered by the section must assure that the examination is selected and administered so as to best ensure that the examination accurately reflects an individual's aptitude or achievement level or other factor the examination purports to measure, rather than reflecting the individual's impaired sensory, manual, or speaking skills (except where those skills are the factors that the examination purports to measure).

REGULATION

impairments, brailled or large print examinations and answer sheets or qualified readers for individuals with visual impairments or learning disabilities, transcribers for individuals with manual impairments, and other similar services and actions.

(4) Alternative accessible arrangements may include, for example, provision of an examination at an individual's home with a proctor if accessible facilities or equipment are unavailable. Alternative arrangements must provide comparable conditions to those provided for nondisabled individuals.

(c) <u>Courses</u>. (1) Any private entity that offers a course covered by this section must make such modifications to that course as are necessary to ensure that the place and manner in which the course is given are accessible to individuals with disabilities.

(2) Required modifications may include changes in the length of time permitted for the completion of the course, substitution of specific requirements, or adaptation of the manner in which the course is conducted or course materials are distributed.

(3) A private entity that

ANALYSIS

Paragraph (b)(1)(ii) requires that any examination specially designed for individuals with disabilities be offered as often and in as timely a manner as other examinations. Some commenters noted that persons with disabilities may be required to travel long distances when the locations for examinations for individuals with disabilities are limited, for example, to only one city in a State instead of a variety of cities. The Department has therefore revised this paragraph to add a requirement that such examinations be offered at locations that are as convenient as the location of other examinations.

Commenters representing organizations that administer tests wanted to be able to require individuals with disabilities to provide advance notice and appropriate documentation, at the applicants' expense, of their disabilities and of any modifications or aids that would be required. The Department agrees that such requirements are permissible, provided that they are not unreasonable and that the deadline for such notice is no earlier than the deadline for others applying to take the examination. Requiring individuals with disabilities to file earlier applications would violate the requirement that examinations designed for individuals with disabilities be offered in as timely a manner as other examinations.

Examiners may require evidence that an applicant is entitled to modifications or aids as required by this section, but requests for documentation must be reasonable and must be limited to the need for the modification or aid requested. Appropriate documentation might include a letter from a physician or other professional, or evidence of a prior diagnosis or accommodation, such as eligibility for a special education program. The applicant may be required to bear the cost of providing such documentation, but the entity administering the examination cannot charge the applicant for the cost of any modifications or auxiliary aids, such as interpreters, provided for the examination.

Paragraph (b)(1)(iii) requires that examinations be administered in facilities that are accessible to individuals with disabilities or alternative accessible arrangements are made.

Paragraph (b)(2) gives examples of modifications to examinations that may be necessary in order to comply with this section. These may include providing more time for completion of the examination or a change in the manner of

REGULATION

offers a course covered by this section shall provide appropriate auxiliary aids and services for persons with impaired sensory, manual, or speaking skills, unless the private entity can demonstrate that offering a particular auxiliary aid or service would fundamentally alter the course or would result in an undue burden. Auxiliary aids and services required by this section may include taped texts, interpreters or other effective methods of making orally delivered materials available to individuals with hearing impairments, brailled or large print texts or qualified readers for individuals with visual impairments and learning disabilities, classroom equipment adapted for use by individuals with manual impairments, and other similar services and actions.

(4) Courses must be administered in facilities that are accessible to individuals with disabilities or alternative accessible arrangements must be made.

(5) Alternative accessible arrangements may include, for example, provision of the course through videotape, cassettes, or prepared notes. Alternative arrangements must provide comparable conditions to those provided for nondisabled individuals.

ANALYSIS

giving the examination, e.g., reading the examination to the individual.

Paragraph (b)(3) requires the provision of auxiliary aids and services, unless the private entity offering the examination can demonstrate that offering a particular auxiliary aid would fundamentally alter the examination or result in an undue burden. Examples of auxiliary aids include taped examinations, interpreters or other effective methods of making aurally delivered materials available to individuals with hearing impairments, readers for individuals with visual impairments or learning disabilities, and other similar services and actions. The suggestion that individuals with learning disabilities may need readers is included, although it does not appear in the Department of Education regulation, because, in fact, some individuals with learning disabilities have visual perception problems and would benefit from a reader.

Many commenters pointed out the importance of ensuring that modifications provide the individual with a disability an equal opportunity to demonstrate his or her knowledge or ability. For example, a reader who is unskilled or lacks knowledge of specific terminology used in the examination may be unable to convey the information in the questions or to follow the applicant's instructions effectively. Commenters pointed out that, for persons with visual impairments who read braille, braille provides the closest functional equivalent to a printed test. The Department has, therefore, added Brailled examinations to the examples of auxiliary aids and services that may be required. For similar reasons, the Department also added to the list of examples of auxiliary aids and services large print examinations and answer sheets; "qualified" readers; and transcribers to write answers.

A commenter suggested that the phrase "fundamentally alter the examination" in this paragraph of the proposed rule be revised to more accurately reflect the function affected. In the final rule the Department has substituted the phrase "fundamentally alter the measurement of the skills or knowledge the examination is intended to test."

Paragraph (b)(4) gives examples of alternative accessible arrangements. For instance, the private entity might be required to provide the examination at an individual's home with a proctor. Alternative arrangements must provide conditions for individuals with disabilities that are comparable to

REGULATION

the conditions under which other individuals take the examinations. In other words, an examination cannot be offered to an individual with a disability in a cold, poorly lit basement, if other individuals are given the examination in a warm, well lit classroom.

Some commenters who provide examinations for licensing or certification for particular occupations or professions urged that they be permitted to refuse to provide modifications or aids for persons seeking to take the examinations if those individuals, because of their disabilities, would be unable to perform the essential functions of the profession or occupation for which the examination is given, or unless the disability is reasonably determined in advance as not being an obstacle to certification. The Department has not changed its rule based on this comment. An examination is one stage of a licensing or certification process. An individual should not be barred from attempting to pass that stage of the process merely because he or she might be unable to meet other requirements of the process. If the examination is not the first stage of the qualification process, an applicant may be required to complete the earlier stages prior to being admitted to the examination. On the other hand, the applicant may not be denied admission to the examination on the basis of doubts about his or her abilities to meet requirements that the examination is not designed to test.

Paragraph (c) sets forth specific requirements for courses. Paragraph (c)(1) contains the general rule that any course covered by this section must be modified to ensure that the place and manner in which the course is given is accessible. Paragraph (c)(2) gives examples of possible modifications that might be required, including extending the time permitted for completion of the course, permitting oral rather than written delivery of an assignment by a person with a visual impairment, or adapting the manner in which the course is conducted (i.e., providing cassettes of class handouts to an individual with a visual impairment). In response to comments, the Department has added to the examples in paragraph (c)(2) specific reference to distribution of course materials. If course materials are published and available from other sources, the entity offering the course may give advance notice of what materials will be used so as to allow an individual to obtain them in braille or on tape, but materials provided by the course offerer must be made available in alternative formats for individuals with disabilities.

REGULATION

ANALYSIS

In language similar to that of paragraph (b), paragraph (c)(3) requires auxiliary aids and services, unless a fundamental alteration or undue burden would result, and paragraph (c)(4) requires that courses be administered in accessible facilities. Paragraph (c)(5) gives examples of alternative accessible arrangements. These may include provision of the course through videotape, cassettes, or prepared notes. Alternative arrangements must provide comparable conditions to those provided to others, including similar lighting, room temperature, and the like. An entity offering a variety of courses, to fulfill continuing education requirements for a profession, for example, may not limit the selection or choice of courses available to individuals with disabilities.

REGULATION

§36.310 Transportation provided by public accommodations.

(a) <u>General</u>. (1) A public accommodation that provides transportation services, but that is not primarily engaged in the business of transporting people, is subject to the general and specific provisions in subparts B, C, and D of this part for its transportation operations, except as provided in this section.

(2) <u>Examples</u>. Transportation services subject to this section include, but are not limited to, shuttle services operated between transportation terminals and places of public accommodation, customer shuttle bus services operated by private companies and shopping centers, student transportation systems, and transportation provided within recreational facilities such as stadiums, zoos, amusement parks, and ski resorts.

(b) <u>Barrier removal</u>. A public accommodation subject to this section shall remove transportation barriers in existing vehicles and rail passenger cars used for transporting individuals (not including barriers that can only be removed through the retrofitting of vehicles or rail passenger cars by the installation of a hydraulic or other lift) where such re-

ANALYSIS

Section 36.310 Transportation provided by public accommodations.

Section 36.310 contains specific provisions relating to public accommodations that provide transportation to their clients or customers. This section has been substantially revised in order to coordinate the requirements of this section with the requirements applicable to these transportation systems that will be contained in the regulations issued by the Secretary of Transportation pursuant to section 306 of the ADA, to be codified at 49 CFR part 37. The Department notes that, although the responsibility for issuing regulations applicable to transportation systems operated by public accommodations is divided between this Department and the Department of Transportation, enforcement authority is assigned only to the Department of Justice.

The Department received relatively few comments on this section of the proposed rule. Most of the comments addressed issues that are not specifically addressed in this part, such as the standards for accessible vehicles and the procedure for determining whether equivalent service is provided. Those standards will be contained in the regulation issued by the Department of Transportation. Other commenters raised questions about the types of transportation that will be subject to this section. In response to these inquiries, the Department has revised the list of examples contained in the regulation.

Paragraph (a)(1) states the general rule that covered public accommodations are subject to all of the specific provisions of subparts B, C, and D, except as provided in §36.310. Examples of operations covered by the requirements are listed in paragraph (a)(2). The stated examples include hotel and motel airport shuttle services, customer shuttle bus services operated by private companies and shopping centers, student transportation, and shuttle operations of recreational facilities such as stadiums, zoos, amusement parks, and ski resorts. This brief list is not exhaustive. The section applies to any fixed route or demand responsive transportation system operated by a public accommodation for the benefit of its clients or customers. The section does not apply to transportation services provided only to employees. Employee transportation will be subject to the regulations issued by the Equal Employment Opportunity Commission to implement title I of the Act. However, if employees and customers or clients are served by the same transportation system, the provisions of this section will apply.

REGULATION

moval is readily achievable.

(c) Requirements for vehicles and systems. A public accommodation subject to this section shall comply with the requirements pertaining to vehicles and transportation systems in the regulations issued by the Secretary of Transportation pursuant to section 306 of the Act.

§§36.311-36.400 [Reserved]

ANALYSIS

Paragraph (b) specifically provides that a public accommodation shall remove transportation barriers in existing vehicles to the extent that it is readily achievable to do so, but that the installation of hydraulic or other lifts is not required.

Paragraph (c) provides that public accommodations subject to this section shall comply with the requirements for transportation vehicles and systems contained in the regulations issued by the Secretary of Transportation.

REGULATION
Subpart D--New Construction and Alterations

ANALYSIS
Subpart D -- New Construction and Alterations.

Subpart D implements section 303 of the Act, which requires that newly constructed or altered places of public accommodation or commercial facilities be readily accessible to and usable by individuals with disabilities. This requirement contemplates a high degree of convenient access. It is intended to ensure that patrons and employees of places of public accommodation and employees of commercial facilities are able to get to, enter, and use the facility.

Potential patrons of places of public accommodation, such as retail establishments, should be able to get to a store, get into the store, and get to the areas where goods are being provided. Employees should have the same types of access, although those individuals require access to and around the employment area as well as to the area in which goods and services are provided.

The ADA is geared to the future -- its goal being that, over time, access will be the rule, rather than the exception. Thus, the Act only requires modest expenditures, of the type addressed in §36.304 of this part, to provide access to existing facilities not otherwise being altered, but requires all new construction and alterations to be accessible.

The Act does not require new construction or alterations; it simply requires that, when a public accommodation or other private entity undertakes the construction or alteration of a facility subject to the Act, the newly constructed or altered facility must be made accessible. This subpart establishes the requirements for new construction and alterations.

As explained under the discussion of the definition of "facility," §36.104, pending development of specific requirements, the Department will not apply this subpart to places of public accommodation located in mobile units, boats, or other conveyances.

REGULATION

§36.401 New construction.

(a) <u>General</u>. (1) Except as provided in paragraphs (b) and (c) of this section, discrimination for purposes of this part includes a failure to design and construct facilities for first occupancy after January 26, 1993, that are readily accessible to and usable by individuals with disabilities.

(2) For purposes of this section, a facility is designed and constructed for first occupancy after January 26, 1993, only--

(i) If the last application for a building permit or permit extension for the facility is certified to be complete, by a State, County, or local government after January 26, 1992 (or, in those jurisdictions where the government does not certify completion of applications, if the last application for a building permit or permit extension for the facility is received by the State, County, or local government after January 26, 1992); and

(ii) If the first certificate of occupancy for the facility is issued after January 26, 1993.

(b) <u>Commercial facilities located in private residences.</u>

ANALYSIS

Section 36.401 New construction.
General

Section 36.401 implements the new construction requirements of the ADA. Section 303(a)(l) of the Act provides that discrimination for purposes of section 302(a) of the Act includes a failure to design and construct facilities for first occupancy later than 30 months after the date of enactment (i.e., after January 26, 1993) that are readily accessible to and usable by individuals with disabilities.

Paragraph 36.40l(a)(l) restates the general requirement for accessible new construction. The proposed rule stated that "any public accommodation or other private entity responsible for design and construction" must ensure that facilities conform to this requirement. Various commenters suggested that the proposed language was not consistent with the statute because it substituted "private entity responsible for design and construction" for the statutory language; because it did not address liability on the part of architects, contractors, developers, tenants, owners, and other entities; and because it limited the liability of entities responsible for commercial facilities. In response, the Department has revised this paragraph to repeat the language of section 303(a) of the ADA. The Department will interpret this section in a manner consistent with the intent of the statute and with the nature of the responsibilities of the various entities for design, for construction, or for both.

Designed and constructed for first occupancy

According to paragraph (a)(2), a facility is subject to the new construction requirements only if a completed application for a building permit or permit extension is filed after January 26, 1992, and the facility is occupied after January 26, 1993.

The proposed rule set forth for comment two alternative ways by which to determine what facilities are subject to the Act and what standards apply. Paragraph (a)(2) of the final rule is a slight variation on Option One in the proposed rule. The reasons for the Department's choice of Option One are discussed later in this section.

Paragraph (a)(2) acknowledges that Congress did not contemplate having actual occupancy be the sole trigger for the accessibility requirements, because the statute prohibits a

REGULATION

(1) When a commercial facility is located in a private residence, the portion of the residence used exclusively as a residence is not covered by this subpart, but that portion used exclusively in the operation of the commercial facility or that portion used both for the commercial facility and for residential purposes is covered by the new construction and alterations requirements of this subpart.

(2) The portion of the residence covered under paragraph (b)(1) of this section extends to those elements used to enter the commercial facility, including the homeowner's front sidewalk, if any, the door or entryway, and hallways; and those portions of the residence, interior or exterior, available to or used by employees or visitors of the commercial facility, including restrooms.

(c) Exception for structural impracticability. (1) Full compliance with the requirements of this section is not required where an entity can demonstrate that it is structurally impracticable to meet the requirements. Full compliance will be considered structurally impracticable only in those rare circumstances when the unique characteristics of terrain prevent the incorpora-

ANALYSIS

failure to "design and construct for first occupancy," rather than requiring accessibility in facilities actually occupied after a particular date.

The commenters overwhelmingly agreed with the Department's proposal to use a date certain; many cited the reasons given in the preamble to the proposed rule. First, it is helpful for designers and builders to have a fixed date for accessible design, so that they can determine accessibility requirements early in the planning and design stage. It is difficult to determine accessibility requirements in anticipation of the actual date of first occupancy because of unpredictable and uncontrollable events (e.g., strikes affecting suppliers or labor, or natural disasters) that may delay occupancy. To redesign or reconstruct portions of a facility if it begins to appear that occupancy will be later than anticipated would be quite costly. A fixed date also assists those responsible for enforcing, or monitoring compliance with, the statute, and those protected by it.

The Department considered using as a trigger date for application of the accessibility standards the date on which a permit is granted. The Department chose instead the date on which a complete permit application is certified as received by the appropriate government entity. Almost all commenters agreed with this choice of a trigger date. This decision is based partly on information that several months or even years can pass between application for a permit and receipt of a permit. Design is virtually complete at the time an application is complete (i.e., certified to contain all the information required by the State, county, or local government). After an application is filed, delays may occur before the permit is granted due to numerous factors (not necessarily relating to accessibility): for example, hazardous waste discovered on the property, flood plain requirements, zoning disputes, or opposition to the project from various groups. These factors should not require redesign for accessibility if the application was completed before January 26, 1992. However, if the facility must be redesigned for other reasons, such as a change in density or environmental preservation, and the final permit is based on a new application, the rule would require accessibility if that application was certified complete after January 26, 1992.

The certification of receipt of a complete application for a building permit is an appropriate point in the process because

REGULATION

tion of accessibility features.

(2) If full compliance with this section would be structurally impracticable, compliance with this section is required to the extent that it is not structurally impracticable. In that case, any portion of the facility that can be made accessible shall be made accessible to the extent that it is not structurally impracticable.

(3) If providing accessibility in conformance with this section to individuals with certain disabilities (e.g., those who use wheelchairs) would be structurally impracticable, accessibility shall nonetheless be ensured to persons with other types of disabilities (e.g., those who use crutches or who have sight, hearing, or mental impairments) in accordance with this section.

(d) Elevator exemption. (1) For purposes of this paragraph (d) --

(i) Professional office of a health care provider means a location where a person or entity regulated by a State to provide professional services related to the physical or mental health of an individual makes such services available to the public. The facility housing the "professional office of a health care provider" only includes floor

ANALYSIS

certifications are issued in writing by governmental authorities. In addition, this approach presents a clear and objective standard.

However, a few commenters pointed out that in some jurisdictions it is not possible to receive a "certification" that an application is complete, and suggested that in those cases the fixed date should be the date on which an application for a permit is received by the government agency. The Department has included such a provision in §36.401(a)(2)(i).

The date of January 26, 1992, is relevant only with respect to the last application for a permit or permit extension for a facility. Thus, if an entity has applied for only a "foundation" permit, the date of that permit application has no effect, because the entity must also apply for and receive a permit at a later date for the actual superstructure. In this case, it is the date of the later application that would control, unless construction is not completed within the time allowed by the permit, in which case a third permit would be issued and the date of the application for that permit would be determinative for purposes of the rule.

Choice of Option One for defining "designed and constructed for first occupancy"

Under the option the Department has chosen for determining applicability of the new construction standards, a building would be considered to be "for first occupancy" after January 26, 1993, only (1) if the last application for a building permit or permit extension for the facility is certified to be complete (or, in some jurisdictions, received) by a State, county, or local government after January 26, 1992, and (2) if the first certificate of occupancy is issued after January 26, 1993. The Department also asked for comment on an Option Two, which would have imposed new construction requirements if a completed application for a building permit or permit extension was filed after the enactment of the ADA (July 26, 1990), and the facility was occupied after January 26, 1993.

The request for comment on this issue drew a large number of comments expressing a wide range of views. Most business groups and some disability rights groups favored Option One, and some business groups and most disability rights groups favored Option Two. Individuals and government entities were equally divided; several commenters proposed other options.

REGULATION

levels housing at least one health care provider, or any floor level designed or intended for use by at least one health care provider.

(ii) Shopping center or shopping mall means--

(A) A building housing five or more sales or rental establishments; or

(B) A series of buildings on a common site, either under common ownership or common control or developed either as one project or as a series of related projects, housing five or more sales or rental establishments. For purposes of this section, places of public accommodation of the types listed in paragraph (5) of the definition of "place of public accommodation" in section §36.104 are considered sales or rental establishments. The facility housing a "shopping center or shopping mall" only includes floor levels housing at least one sales or rental establishment, or any floor level designed or intended for use by at least one sales or rental establishment.

(2) This section does not require the installation of an elevator in a facility that is less than three stories or has less than 3000 square feet per story, except with respect to any facility that houses

ANALYSIS

Those favoring Option One pointed out that it is more reasonable in that it allows time for those subject to the new construction requirements to anticipate those requirements and to receive technical assistance pursuant to the Act. Numerous commenters said that time frames for designing and constructing some types of facilities (for example, health care facilities) can range from two to four years or more. They expressed concerns that Option Two, which would apply to some facilities already under design or construction as of the date the Act was signed, and to some on which construction began shortly after enactment, could result in costly redesign or reconstruction of those facilities. In the same vein, some Option One supporters found Option Two objectionable on due process grounds. In their view, Option Two would mean that in July 1991 (upon issuance of the final DOJ rule) the responsible entities would learn that ADA standards had been in effect since July 26, 1990, and this would amount to retroactive application of standards. Numerous commenters characterized Option Two as having no support in the statute and Option One as being more consistent with congressional intent.

Those who favored Option Two pointed out that it would include more facilities within the coverage of the new construction standards. They argued that because similar accessibility requirements are in effect under State laws, no hardship would be imposed by this option. Numerous commenters said that hardship would also be eliminated in light of their view that the ADA requires compliance with the Uniform Federal Accessibility Standards (UFAS) until issuance of DOJ standards. Those supporting Option Two claimed that it was more consistent with the statute and its legislative history.

The Department has chosen Option One rather than Option Two, primarily on the basis of the language of three relevant sections of the statute. First, section 303(a) requires compliance with accessibility standards set forth, or incorporated by reference in, regulations to be issued by the Department of Justice. Standing alone, this section cannot be read to require compliance with the Department's standards before those standards are issued (through this rulemaking). Second, according to section 310 of the statute, section 303 becomes effective on January 26, 1992. Thus, section 303 cannot impose requirements on the design of buildings before that date. Third, while section 306(d) of the Act requires compli-

REGULATION

one or more of the following:

(i) A shopping center or shopping mall, or a professional office of a health care provider.

(ii) A terminal, depot, or other station used for specified public transportation, or an airport passenger terminal. In such a facility, any area housing passenger services, including boarding and debarking, loading and unloading, baggage claim, dining facilities, and other common areas open to the public, must be on an accessible route from an accessible entrance.

(3) The elevator exemption set forth in this paragraph (d) does not obviate or limit in any way the obligation to comply with the other accessibility requirements established in paragraph (a) of this section. For example, in a facility that houses a shopping center or shopping mall, or a professional office of a health care provider, the floors that are above or below an accessible ground floor and that do not house sales or rental establishments or a professional office of a health care provider, must meet the requirements of this section but for the elevator.

ANALYSIS

ance with UFAS if final regulations have not been issued, that provision cannot reasonably be read to take effect until July 26, 1991, the date by which the Department of Justice must issue final regulations under title III.

Option Two was based on the premise that the interim standards in section 306(d) take effect as of the ADA's enactment (July 26, 1990), rather than on the date by which the Department of Justice regulations are due to be issued (July 26, 1991). The initial clause of section 306(d)(1) itself is silent on this question:

If final regulations have not been issued pursuant to this section, for new construction for which a . . . building permit is obtained prior to the issuance of final regulations . . . [interim standards apply].

The approach in Option Two relies partly on the language of section 310 of the Act, which provides that section 306, the interim standards provision, takes effect on the date of enactment. Under this interpretation the interim standards provision would prevail over the operative provision, section 303, which requires that new construction be accessible and which becomes effective January 26, 1992. This approach would also require construing the language of section 306(d)(1) to take effect before the Department's standards are due to be issued. The preferred reading of section 306 is that it would require that, if the Department's final standards had not been issued by July 26, 1991, UFAS would apply to certain buildings until such time as the Department's standards were issued.

General Substantive Requirements of the New Construction Provisions

The rule requires, as does the statute, that covered newly constructed facilities be readily accessible to and usable by individuals with disabilities. The phrase "readily accessible to and usable by individuals with disabilities" is a term that, in slightly varied formulations, has been used in the Architectural Barriers Act of 1968, the Fair Housing Act, the regulations implementing section 504 of the Rehabilitation Act of 1973, and current accessibility standards. It means, with respect to a facility or a portion of a facility, that it can be approached, entered, and used by individuals with disabilities (including mobility, sensory, and cognitive impairments) easily and conveniently. A facility that is constructed to meet the requirements of the rule's accessibility standards will be considered readily accessible and usable with respect to construction. To the extent that a particular type or element of a facility is not specifically addressed by the standards, the language of this section is the safest guide.

A private entity that renders an "accessible" building inaccessible in its operation, through policies or practices, may be in violation of section 302 of the Act. For example, a private entity can render an entrance to a facility inaccessible by keeping an accessible entrance open only during certain hours (whereas the facility is available to others for a greater length of time). A facility could similarly be rendered inaccessible if a person with disabilities is significantly limited in her or his choice of a range of accommodations.

Ensuring access to a newly constructed facility will include providing access to the facility from the street or parking lot, to the extent the responsible entity has control over the route from those locations. In some cases, the private entity will have no control over access at the point where streets, curbs, or sidewalks already exist, and in those instances the entity is encouraged to request modifications to a sidewalk, including installation of curb cuts, from a public entity responsible for them. However, as some commenters pointed out, there is no obligation for a private entity subject to title III of the ADA to seek or ensure compliance by a public entity with title II. Thus, although a locality may have an obligation under title II of the Act to install curb cuts at a particular location, that responsibility is separate from the private entity's title III obligation, and any involvement by a private entity in seeking cooperation from a public entity is purely voluntary in this context.

Work Areas

Proposed paragraph 36.401(b) addressed access to employment areas, rather than to the areas where goods or services are being provided. The preamble noted that the proposed paragraph provided guidance for new construction and alterations until more specific guidance was issued by the ATBCB and reflected in this Department's regulation. The entire paragraph has been deleted from this section in the final rule. The concepts of paragraphs (b) (1), (2), and (5) of the proposed rule are included, with modifications and expansion, in ADAAG. Paragraphs (3) and (4) of the proposed

REGULATION

rule, concerning fixtures and equipment, are not included in the rule or in ADAAG.

Some commenters asserted that questions relating to new construction and alterations of work areas should be addressed by the EEOC under title I, as employment concerns. However, the legislative history of the statute clearly indicates that the new construction and alterations requirements of title III were intended to ensure accessibility of new facilities to all individuals, including employees. The language of section 303 sweeps broadly in its application to all public accommodations and commercial facilities. EEOC's title I regulations will address accessibility requirements that come into play when "reasonable accommodation" to individual employees or applicants with disabilities is mandated under title I.

The issues dealt with in proposed §36.401(b)(1) and (2) are now addressed in ADAAG section 4.1.1(3). The Department's proposed paragraphs would have required that areas that will be used only by employees as work stations be constructed so that individuals with disabilities could approach, enter, and exit the areas. They would not have required that all individual work stations be constructed or equipped (for example, with shelves that are accessible or adaptable) to be accessible. This approach was based on the theory that, as long as an employee with disabilities could enter the building and get to and around the employment area, modifications in a particular work station could be instituted as a "reasonable accommodation" to that employee if the modifications were necessary and they did not constitute an undue hardship.

Almost all of the commenters agreed with the proposal to require access to a work area but not to require accessibility of each individual work station. This principle is included in ADAAG 4.1.1(3). Several of the comments related to the requirements of the proposed ADAAG and have been addressed in the accessibility standards.

Proposed paragraphs (b)(3) and (4) would have required that consideration be given to placing fixtures and equipment at accessible heights in the first instance, and to purchasing new equipment and fixtures that are adjustable. These paragraphs have not been included in the final rule because the rule in most instances does not establish accessibility standards for purchased equipment. (See discussion elsewhere in the preamble of proposed §36.309.) While the Department en-

ANALYSIS

courages entities to consider providing accessible or adjustable fixtures and equipment for employees, this rule does not require them to do so.

Paragraph (b)(5) of proposed §36.401 clarified that proposed paragraph (b) did not limit the requirement that employee areas other than individual work stations must be accessible. For example, areas that are employee "common use" areas and are not solely used as work stations (e.g., employee lounges, cafeterias, health units, exercise facilities) are treated no differently under this regulation than other parts of a building; they must be constructed or altered in compliance with the accessibility standards. This principle is not stated in §36.401 but is implicit in the requirements of this section and ADAAG.

Commercial Facilities in Private Residences

Section 36.401(b) of the final rule is a new provision relating to commercial facilities located in private residences. The proposed rule addressed these requirements in the preamble to §36.207, "Places of public accommodation located in private residences." The preamble stated that the approach for commercial facilities would be the same as that for places of public accommodation, i.e., those portions used exclusively as a commercial facility or used as both a commercial facility and for residential purposes would be covered. Because commercial facilities are only subject to new construction and alterations requirements, however, the covered portions would only be subject to subpart D. This approach is reflected in §36.401(b)(1).

The Department is aware that the statutory definition of "commercial facility" excludes private residences because they are "expressly exempted from coverage under the Fair Housing Act of 1968, as amended." However, the Department interprets that exemption as applying only to facilities that are exclusively residential. When a facility is used as both a residence and a commercial facility, the exemption does not apply.

Paragraph (b)(2) is similar to the new paragraph (b) under §36.207, "Places of public accommodation located in private residences." The paragraph clarifies that the covered portion includes not only the space used as a commercial facility, but also the elements used to enter the commercial facility, e.g.,

REGULATION

ANALYSIS

the homeowner's front sidewalk, if any; the doorway; the hallways; the restroom, if used by employees or visitors of the commercial facility; and any other portion of the residence, interior or exterior, used by employees or visitors of the commercial facility.

As in the case of public accommodations located in private residences, the new construction standards only apply to the extent that a portion of the residence is designed or intended for use as a commercial facility. Likewise, if a homeowner alters a portion of his home to convert it to a commercial facility, that work must be done in compliance with the alterations standards in the appendix A.

Structural Impracticability

Proposed §36.401(c) is included in the final rule with minor changes. It details a statutory exception to the new construction requirement: the requirement that new construction be accessible does not apply where an entity can demonstrate that it is structurally impracticable to meet the requirements of the regulation. This provision is also included in ADAAG, at section 4.1.1(5)(a).

Consistent with the legislative history of the ADA, this narrow exception will apply only in rare and unusual circumstances where unique characteristics of terrain make accessibility unusually difficult. Such limitations for topographical problems are analogous to an acknowledged limitation in the application of the accessibility requirements of the Fair Housing Amendments Act (FHAA) of 1988.

Almost all commenters supported this interpretation. Two commenters argued that the DOJ requirement is too limiting and would not exempt some buildings that should be exempted because of soil conditions, terrain, and other unusual site conditions. These commenters suggested consistency with HUD's Fair Housing Accessibility Guidelines (56 FR 9472 (1991)), which generally would allow exceptions from accessibility requirements, or allow compliance with less stringent requirements, on sites with slopes exceeding 10%.

The Department is aware of the provisions in HUD's guidelines, which were issued on March 6, 1991, after passage of the ADA and publication of the Department's proposed rule. The approach taken in these guidelines, which apply to

REGULATION

different types of construction and implement different statutory requirements for new construction, does not bind this Department in regulating under the ADA. The Department has included in the final rule the substance of the proposed provision, which is faithful to the intent of the statute, as expressed in the legislative history. (See Senate report at 70-71; Education and Labor report at 120.)

The limited structural impracticability exception means that it is acceptable to deviate from accessibility requirements only where unique characteristics of terrain prevent the incorporation of accessibility features and where providing accessibility would destroy the physical integrity of a facility. A situation in which a building must be built on stilts because of its location in marshlands or over water is an example of one of the few situations in which the exception for structural impracticability would apply.

This exception to accessibility requirements should not be applied to situations in which a facility is located in "hilly" terrain or on a plot of land upon which there are steep grades. In such circumstances, accessibility can be achieved without destroying the physical integrity of a structure, and is required in the construction of new facilities.

Some commenters asked for clarification concerning when and how to apply the ADA rules or the Fair Housing Accessibility Guidelines, especially when a facility may be subject to both because of mixed use. Guidance on this question is provided in the discussion of the definitions of place of public accommodation and commercial facility. With respect to the structural impracticability exception, a mixed-use facility could not take advantage of the Fair Housing exemption, to the extent that it is less stringent than the ADA exemption, except for those portions of the facility that are subject only to the Fair Housing Act.

As explained in the preamble to the proposed rule, in those rare circumstances in which it is structurally impracticable to achieve full compliance with accessibility requirements under the ADA, places of public accommodation and commercial facilities should still be designed and constructed to incorporate accessibility features to the extent that the features are structurally practicable. The accessibility requirements should not be viewed as an all-or-nothing proposition in such circumstances.

REGULATION

If it is structurally impracticable for a facility in its entirety to be readily accessible to and usable by people with disabilities, then those portions that can be made accessible should be made accessible. If a building cannot be constructed in compliance with the full range of accessibility requirements because of structural impracticability, then it should still incorporate those features that are structurally practicable. If it is structurally impracticable to make a particular facility accessible to persons who have particular types of disabilities, it is still appropriate to require it to be made accessible to persons with other types of disabilities. For example, a facility that is of necessity built on stilts and cannot be made accessible to persons who use wheelchairs because it is structurally impracticable to do so, must be made accessible for individuals with vision or hearing impairments or other kinds of disabilities.

Elevator Exemption

Section 36.401(d) implements the "elevator exemption" for new construction in section 303(b) of the ADA. The elevator exemption is an exception to the general requirement that new facilities be readily accessible to and usable by individuals with disabilities. Generally, an elevator is the most common way to provide individuals who use wheelchairs "ready access" to floor levels above or below the ground floor of a multi-story building. Congress, however, chose not to require elevators in new small buildings, that is, those with less than three stories or less that 3000 square feet per story. In buildings eligible for the exemption, therefore, "ready access" from the building entrance to a floor above or below the ground floor is not required, because the statute does not require that an elevator be installed in such buildings. The elevator exemption does not apply, however, to a facility housing a shopping center, a shopping mall, or the professional office of a health care provider, or other categories of facilities as determined by the Attorney General. For example, a new office building that will have only two stories, with no elevator planned, will not be required to have an elevator, even if each story has 20,000 square feet. In other words, having either less than 3000 square feet per story or less than three stories qualifies a facility for the exemption; it need not qualify for the exemption on both counts. Similarly, a facility that has five stories of 2800 square feet each qualifies for the exemption. If a facility has three or more stories at any point, it is not eligible for the elevator exemption unless all the stories are less than 3000 square feet.

REGULATION

The terms "shopping center or shopping mall" and "professional office of a health care provider" are defined in this section. They are substantively identical to the definitions included in the proposed rule in §36.104, "Definitions." They have been moved to this section because, as commenters pointed out, they are relevant only for the purposes of the elevator exemption, and inclusion in the general definitions section could give the incorrect impression that an office of a health care provider is not covered as a place of public accommodation under other sections of the rule, unless the office falls within the definition.

For purposes of §36.401, a "shopping center or shopping mall" is (1) a building housing five or more sales or rental establishments, or (2) a series of buildings on a common site, either under common ownership or common control or developed either as one project or as a series of related projects, housing five or more sales or rental establishments. The term "shopping center or shopping mall" only includes floor levels containing at least one sales or rental establishment, or any floor level that was designed or intended for use by at least one sales or rental establishment.

Any sales or rental establishment of the type that is included in paragraph (5) of the definition of "place of public accommodation" (for example, a bakery, grocery store, clothing store, or hardware store) is considered a sales or rental establishment for purposes of this definition; the other types of public accommodations (e.g., restaurants, laundromats, banks, travel services, health spas) are not.

In the preamble to the proposed rule, the Department sought comment on whether the definition of "shopping center or mall" should be expanded to include any of these other types of public accommodations. The Department also sought comment on whether a series of buildings should fall within the definition only if they are physically connected.

Most of those responding to the first question (overwhelmingly groups representing people with disabilities, or individual commenters) urged that the definition encompass more places of public accommodation, such as restaurants, motion picture houses, laundromats, dry cleaners, and banks. They pointed out that often it is not known what types of establishments will be tenants in a new facility. In addition, they noted that malls are advertised as entities, that their

REGULATION

ANALYSIS

appeal is in the "package" of services offered to the public, and that this package often includes the additional types of establishments mentioned.

Commenters representing business groups sought to exempt banks, travel services, grocery stores, drug stores, and freestanding retail stores from the elevator requirement. They based this request on the desire to continue the practice in some locations of incorporating mezzanines housing administrative offices, raised pharmacist areas, and raised areas in the front of supermarkets that house safes and are used by managers to oversee operations of check-out aisles and other functions. Many of these concerns are adequately addressed by ADAAG. Apart from those addressed by ADAAG, the Department sees no reason to treat a particular type of sales or rental establishment differently from any other. Although banks and travel services are not included as "sales or rental establishments," because they do not fall under paragraph (5) of the definition of place of public accommodation, grocery stores and drug stores are included.

The Department has declined to include places of public accommodation other than sales or rental establishments in the definition. The statutory definition of "public accommodation" (section 301(7)) lists 12 types of establishments that are considered public accommodations. Category (E) includes "a bakery, grocery store, clothing store, hardware store, shopping center, or other sales or rental establishment." This arrangement suggests that it is only these types of establishments that would make up a shopping center for purposes of the statute. To include all types of places of public accommodation, or those from 6 or 7 of the categories, as commenters suggest, would overly limit the elevator exemption; the universe of facilities covered by the definition of "shopping center" could well exceed the number of multitenant facilities not covered, which would render the exemption almost meaningless.

For similar reasons, the Department is retaining the requirement that a building or series of buildings must house five or more sales or rental establishments before it falls within the definition of "shopping center." Numerous commenters objected to the number and requested that the number be lowered from five to three or four. Lowering the number in this manner would include an inordinately large number of two-story multitenant buildings within the category of those required to have elevators.

REGULATION

ANALYSIS

The responses to the question concerning whether a series of buildings should be connected in order to be covered were varied. Generally, disability rights groups and some government agencies said a series of buildings should not have to be connected, and pointed to a trend in some areas to build shopping centers in a garden or village setting. The Department agrees that this design choice should not negate the elevator requirement for new construction. Some business groups answered the question in the affirmative, and some suggested a different definition of shopping center. For example, one commenter recommended the addition of a requirement that the five or more establishments be physically connected on the non-ground floors by a common pedestrian walkway or pathway, because otherwise a series of stand-alone facilities would have to comply with the elevator requirement, which would be unduly burdensome and perhaps infeasible. Another suggested use of what it characterized as the standard industry definition: "a group of retail stores and related business facilities, the whole planned, developed, operated and managed as a unit." While the rule's definition would reach a series of related projects that are under common control but were not developed as a single project, the Department considers such a facility to be a shopping center within the meaning of the statute. However, in light of the hardship that could confront a series of existing small stand-alone buildings if elevators were required in alterations, the Department has included a common access route in the definition of shopping center or shopping mall for purposes of §36.404.

Some commenters suggested that access to restrooms and other shared facilities open to the public should be required even if those facilities were not on a shopping floor. Such a provision with respect to toilet or bathing facilities is included in the elevator exception in final ADAAG 4.1.3(5).

For purposes of this subpart, the rule does not distinguish between a "shopping mall" (usually a building with a roofed-over common pedestrian area serving more than one tenant in which a majority of the tenants have a main entrance from the common pedestrian area) and a "shopping center" (e.g., a "shopping strip"). Any facility housing five or more of the types of sales or rental establishments described, regardless of the number of other types of places of public accommodation housed there (e.g., offices, movie theatres, restaurants), is a shopping center or shopping mall.

REGULATION

ANALYSIS

For example, a two-story facility built for mixed-use occupancy on both floors (e.g., by sales and rental establishments, a movie theater, restaurants, and general office space) is a shopping center or shopping mall if it houses five or more sales or rental establishments. If none of these establishments is located on the second floor, then only the ground floor, which contains the sales or rental establishments, would be a "shopping center or shopping mall," unless the second floor was designed or intended for use by at least one sales or rental establishment. In determining whether a floor was intended for such use, factors to be considered include the types of establishments that first occupied the floor, the nature of the developer's marketing strategy, i.e., what types of establishments were sought, and inclusion of any design features particular to rental and sales establishments.

A "professional office of a health care provider" is defined as a location where a person or entity regulated by a State to provide professional services related to the physical or mental health of an individual makes such services available to the public. In a two-story development that houses health care providers only on the ground floor, the "professional office of a health care provider" is limited to the ground floor unless the second floor was designed or intended for use by a health care provider. In determining if a floor was intended for such use, factors to be considered include whether the facility was constructed with special plumbing, electrical, or other features needed by health care providers, whether the developer marketed the facility as a medical office center, and whether any of the establishments that first occupied the floor was, in fact, a health care provider.

In addition to requiring that a building that is a shopping center, shopping mall, or the professional office of a health care provider have an elevator regardless of square footage or number of floors, the ADA (section 303(b)) provides that the Attorney General may determine that a particular category of facilities requires the installation of elevators based on the usage of the facilities. The Department, as it proposed to do, has added to the nonexempt categories terminals, depots, or other stations used for specified public transportation, and airport passenger terminals. Numerous commenters in all categories endorsed this proposal; none opposed it. It is not uncommon for an airport passenger terminal or train station, for example, to have only two floors, with gates on both floors. Because of the significance of transportation, because

REGULATION

ANALYSIS

a person with disabilities could be arriving or departing at any gate, and because inaccessible facilities could result in a total denial of transportation services, it is reasonable to require that newly constructed transit facilities be accessible, regardless of square footage or number of floors. One comment suggested an amendment that would treat terminals and stations similarly to shopping centers, by requiring an accessible route only to those areas used for passenger loading and unloading and for other passenger services. Paragraph (d)(2)(ii) has been modified accordingly.

Some commenters suggested that other types of facilities (e.g., educational facilities, libraries, museums, commercial facilities, and social service facilities) should be included in the category of nonexempt facilities. The Department has not found adequate justification for including any other types of facilities in the nonexempt category at this time.

Section 36.401(d)(2) establishes the operative requirements concerning the elevator exemption and its application to shopping centers and malls, professional offices of health care providers, transit stations, and airport passenger terminals. Under the rule's framework, it is necessary first to determine if a new facility (including one or more buildings) houses places of public accommodation or commercial facilities that are in the categories for which elevators are required. If so, and the facility is a shopping center or shopping mall, or a professional office of a health care provider, then any area housing such an office or a sales or rental establishment or the professional office of a health care provider is not entitled to the elevator exemption.

The following examples illustrate the application of these principles:

1. A shopping mall has an upper and a lower level. There are two "anchor stores" (in this case, major department stores at either end of the mall, both with exterior entrances and an entrance on each level from the common area). In addition, there are 30 stores (sales or rental establishments) on the upper level, all of which have entrances from a common central area. There are 30 stores on the lower level, all of which have entrances from a common central area. According to the rule, elevator access must be provided to each store and to each level of the anchor stores. This requirement could be satisfied with respect to the 60 stores through eleva-

REGULATION

tors connecting the two pedestrian levels, provided that an individual could travel from the elevator to any other point on that level (i.e., into any store through a common pedestrian area) on an accessible path.

2. A commercial (nonresidential) "townhouse" development is composed of 20 two-story attached buildings. The facility is developed as one project, with common ownership, and the space will be leased to retailers. Each building has one accessible entrance from a pedestrian walk to the first floor. From that point, one can enter a store on the first floor, or walk up a flight of stairs to a store on the second floor. All 40 stores must be accessible at ground floor level or by accessible vertical access from that level. This does not mean, however, that 20 elevators must be installed. Access could be provided to the second floor by an elevator from the pedestrian area on the lower level to an upper walkway connecting all the areas on the second floor.

3. In the same type of development, it is planned that retail stores will be housed exclusively on the ground floor, with only office space (not professional offices of health care providers) on the second. Elevator access need not be provided to the second floor because all the sales or rental establishments (the entities that make the facility a shopping center) are located on an accessible ground floor.

4. In the same type of development, the space is designed and marketed as medical or office suites, or as a medical office facility. Accessible vertical access must be provided to all areas, as described in example 2.

Some commenters suggested that building owners who knowingly lease or rent space to nonexempt places of public accommodation would violate §36.401. However, the Department does not consider leasing or renting inaccessible space in itself to constitute a violation of this part. Nor does a change in use of a facility, with no accompanying alterations (e.g., if a psychiatrist replaces an attorney as a tenant in a second-floor office, but no alterations are made to the office) trigger accessibility requirements.

Entities cannot evade the requirements of this section by constructing facilities in such a way that no story is intended to constitute a "ground floor." For example, if a private entity constructs a building whose main entrance leads only to

ANALYSIS

stairways or escalators that connect with upper or lower floors, the Department would consider at least one level of the facility a ground story.

The rule requires in §36.401(d)(3), consistent with the proposed rule, that, even if a building falls within the elevator exemption, the floor or floors other than the ground floor must nonetheless be accessible, except for elevator access, to individuals with disabilities, including people who use wheelchairs. This requirement applies to buildings that do not house sales or rental establishments or the professional offices of a health care provider as well as to those in which such establishments or offices are all located on the ground floor. In such a situation, little added cost is entailed in making the second floor accessible, because it is similar in structure and floor plan to the ground floor.

There are several reasons for this provision. First, some individuals who are mobility impaired may work on a building's second floor, which they can reach by stairs and the use of crutches; however, the same individuals, once they reach the second floor, may then use a wheelchair that is kept in the office. Secondly, because the first floor will be accessible, there will be little additional cost entailed in making the second floor, with the same structure and generally the same floor plan, accessible. In addition, the second floor must be accessible to those persons with disabilities who do not need elevators for level changes (for example, persons with sight or hearing impairments and those with certain mobility impairments). Finally, if an elevator is installed in the future for any reason, full access to the floor will be facilitated.

One commenter asserted that this provision goes beyond the Department's authority under the Act, and disagreed with the Department's claim that little additional cost would be entailed in compliance. However, the provision is taken directly from the legislative history (see Education and Labor report at 114).

One commenter said that where an elevator is not required, platform lifts should be required. Two commenters pointed out that the elevator exemption is really an exemption from the requirement for providing an accessible route to a second floor not served by an elevator. The Department agrees with the latter comment. Lifts to provide access between floors are not required in buildings that are not

REGULATION

required to have elevators. This point is specifically addressed in the appendix to ADAAG (§ 4.1.3(5)). ADAAG also addresses in detail the situations in which lifts are permitted or required.

REGULATION

§36.402 Alterations.

(a) <u>General</u>. (1) Any alteration to a place of public accommodation or a commercial facility, after January 26, 1992, shall be made so as to ensure that, to the maximum extent feasible, the altered portions of the facility are readily accessible to and usable by individuals with disabilities, including individuals who use wheelchairs.

(2) An alteration is deemed to be undertaken after January 26, 1992, if the physical alteration of the property begins after that date.

(b) <u>Alteration</u>. For the purposes of this part, an alteration is a change to a place of public accommodation or a commercial facility that affects or could affect the usability of the building or facility or any part thereof.

(1) Alterations include, but are not limited to, remodeling, renovation, rehabilitation, reconstruction, historic restoration, changes or rearrangement in structural parts or elements, and changes or rearrangement in the plan configuration of walls and full-height partitions. Normal maintenance, reroofing, painting or wallpapering, asbestos removal, or changes to

ANALYSIS

Section 36.402 Alterations.

Sections 36.402-36.405 implement section 303(a)(2) of the Act, which requires that alterations to existing facilities be made in a way that ensures that the altered portion is readily accessible to and usable by individuals with disabilities. This part does not require alterations; it simply provides that when alterations are undertaken, they must be made in a manner that provides access.

Section 36.402(a)(1) provides that any alteration to a place of public accommodation or a commercial facility, after January 26, 1992, shall be made so as to ensure that, to the maximum extent feasible, the altered portions of the facility are readily accessible to and usable by individuals with disabilities, including individuals who use wheelchairs.

The proposed rule provided that an alteration would be deemed to be undertaken after January 26, 1992, if the physical alteration of the property is in progress after that date. Commenters pointed out that this provision would, in some cases, produce an unjust result by requiring the redesign or retrofitting of projects initiated before this part established the ADA accessibility standards. The Department agrees that the proposed rule would, in some instances, unfairly penalize projects that were substantially completed before the effective date. Therefore, paragraph (a)(2) has been revised to specify that an alteration will be deemed to be undertaken after January 26, 1992, if the physical alteration of the property begins after that date. As a matter of interpretation, the Department will construe this provision to apply to alterations that require a permit from a State, County or local government, if physical alterations pursuant to the terms of the permit begin after January 26, 1992. The Department recognizes that this application of the effective date may require redesign of some facilities that were planned prior to the publication of this part, but no retrofitting will be required of facilities on which the physical alterations were initiated prior to the effective date of the Act. Of course, nothing in this section in any way alters the obligation of any facility to remove architectural barriers in existing facilities to the extent that such barrier removal is readily achievable.

Paragraph (b) provides that, for the purposes of this part, an "alteration" is a change to a place of public accommodation or a commercial facility that affects or could affect the usability of the building or facility or any part thereof. One

REGULATION

mechanical and electrical systems are not alterations unless they affect the usability of the building or facility.

(2) If existing elements, spaces, or common areas are altered, then each such altered element, space, or area shall comply with the applicable provisions of appendix A to this part.

(c) To the maximum extent feasible. The phrase "to the maximum extent feasible," as used in this section, applies to the occasional case where the nature of an existing facility makes it virtually impossible to comply fully with applicable accessibility standards through a planned alteration. In these circumstances, the alteration shall provide the maximum physical accessibility feasible. Any altered features of the facility that can be made accessible shall be made accessible. If providing accessibility in conformance with this section to individuals with certain disabilities (e.g., those who use wheelchairs) would not be feasible, the facility shall be made accessible to persons with other types of disabilities (e.g., those who use crutches, those who have impaired vision or hearing, or those who have other impairments).

ANALYSIS

commenter suggested that the concept of usability should apply only to those changes that affect access by persons with disabilities. The Department remains convinced that the Act requires the concept of "usability" to be read broadly to include any change that affects the usability of the facility, not simply changes that relate directly to access by individuals with disabilities.

The Department received a significant number of comments on the examples provided in paragraphs (b)(1) and (b)(2) of the proposed rule. Some commenters urged the Department to limit the application of this provision to major structural modifications, while others asserted that it should be expanded to include cosmetic changes such as painting and wallpapering. The Department believes that neither approach is consistent with the legislative history, which requires this Department's regulation to be consistent with the accessibility guidelines (ADAAG) developed by the Architectural and Transportation Barriers Compliance Board (ATBCB). Although the legislative history contemplates that, in some instances, the ADA accessibility standards will exceed the current MGRAD requirements, it also clearly indicates the view of the drafters that "minor changes such as painting or papering walls . . . do not affect usability" (Education and Labor report at 111, Judiciary report at 64), and, therefore, are not alterations. The proposed rule was based on the existing MGRAD definition of "alteration." The language of the final rule has been revised to be consistent with ADAAG, incorporated as Appendix A to this part.

Some commenters sought clarification of the intended scope of this section. The proposed rule contained illustrations of changes that affect usability and those that do not. The intent of the illustrations was to explain the scope of the alterations requirement; the effect was to obscure it. As a result of the illustrations, some commenters concluded that any alteration to a facility, even a minor alteration such as relocating an electrical outlet, would trigger an extensive obligation to provide access throughout an entire facility. That result was never contemplated.

Therefore, in this final rule paragraph (b)(1) has been revised to include the major provisions of paragraphs (b)(1) and (b)(2) of the proposed rule. The examples in the proposed rule have been deleted. Paragraph (b)(1) now provides that alterations include, but are not limited to, remodeling, renova-

REGULATION

ANALYSIS

tion, rehabilitation, reconstruction, historic restoration, changes or rearrangement in structural parts or elements, and changes or rearrangement in the plan configuration of walls and full-height partitions. Normal maintenance, reroofing, painting or wallpapering, asbestos removal, or changes to mechanical and electrical systems are not alterations unless they affect the usability of building or facility.

Paragraph (b)(2) of this final rule was added to clarify the scope of the alterations requirement. Paragraph (b)(2) provides that if existing elements, spaces, or common areas are altered, then each such altered element, space, or area shall comply with the applicable provisions of Appendix A (ADAAG). As provided in §36.403, if an altered space or area is an area of the facility that contains a primary function, then the requirements of that section apply.

Therefore, when an entity undertakes a minor alteration to a place of public accommodation or commercial facility, such as moving an electrical outlet, the new outlet must be installed in compliance with ADAAG. (Alteration of the elements listed in §36.403(c)(2) cannot trigger a path of travel obligation.) If the alteration is to an area, such as an employee lounge or locker room, that is not an area of the facility that contains a primary function, that area must comply with ADAAG. It is only when an alteration affects access to or usability of an area containing a primary function, as opposed to other areas or the elements listed in §36.403(c)(2), that the path of travel to the altered area must be made accessible.

The Department received relatively few comments on paragraph (c), which explains the statutory phrase "to the maximum extent feasible." Some commenters suggested that the regulation should specify that cost is a factor in determining whether it is feasible to make an altered area accessible. The legislative history of the ADA indicates that the concept of feasibility only reaches the question of whether it is possible to make the alteration accessible in compliance with this part. Costs are to be considered only when an alteration to an area containing a primary function triggers an additional requirement to make the path of travel to the altered area accessible.

Section 36.402(c) is, therefore, essentially unchanged from the proposed rule. At the recommendation of a

REGULATION

commenter, the Department has inserted the word "virtually" to modify "impossible" to conform to the language of the legislative history. It explains that the phrase "to the maximum extent feasible" as used in this section applies to the occasional case where the nature of an existing facility makes it virtually impossible to comply fully with applicable accessibility standards through a planned alteration. In the occasional cases in which full compliance is impossible, alterations shall provide the maximum physical accessibility feasible. Any features of the facility that are being altered shall be made accessible unless it is technically infeasible to do so. If providing accessibility in conformance with this section to individuals with certain disabilities (e.g., those who use wheelchairs) would not be feasible, the facility shall be made accessible to persons with other types of disabilities (e.g., those who use crutches or who have impaired vision or hearing, or those who have other types of impairments).

REGULATION

§36.403 Alterations: Path of travel.

(a) General. An alteration that affects or could affect the usability of or access to an area of a facility that contains a primary function shall be made so as to ensure that, to the maximum extent feasible, the path of travel to the altered area and the restrooms, telephones, and drinking fountains serving the altered area, are readily accessible to and usable by individuals with disabilities, including individuals who use wheelchairs, unless the cost and scope of such alterations is disproportionate to the cost of the overall alteration.

(b) Primary function. A "primary function" is a major activity for which the facility is intended. Areas that contain a primary function include, but are not limited to, the customer services lobby of a bank, the dining area of a cafeteria, the meeting rooms in a conference center, as well as offices and other work areas in which the activities of the public accommodation or other private entity using the facility are carried out. Mechanical rooms, boiler rooms, supply storage rooms, employee lounges or locker rooms, janitorial closets, entrances, corridors, and restrooms are not areas containing a primary function.

ANALYSIS

Section 36.403 Alterations: Path of travel.

Section 36.403 implements the statutory requirement that any alteration that affects or could affect the usability of or access to an area of a facility that contains a primary function shall be made so as to ensure that, to the maximum extent feasible, the path of travel to the altered area, and the restrooms, telephones, and drinking fountains serving the altered area, are readily accessible to and usable by individuals with disabilities, including individuals who use wheelchairs, unless the cost and scope of such alterations is disproportionate to the cost of the overall alteration. Paragraph (a) restates this statutory requirement.

Paragraph (b) defines a "primary function" as a major activity for which the facility is intended. This paragraph is unchanged from the proposed rule. Areas that contain a primary function include, but are not limited to, the customer services lobby of a bank, the dining area of a cafeteria, the meeting rooms in a conference center, as well as offices and all other work areas in which the activities of the public accommodation or other private entities using the facility are carried out. The concept of "areas containing a primary function" is analogous to the concept of "functional spaces" in §3.5 of the existing Uniform Federal Accessibility Standards, which defines "functional spaces" as "[t]he rooms and spaces in a building or facility that house the major activities for which the building or facility is intended."

Paragraph (b) provides that areas such as mechanical rooms, boiler rooms, supply storage rooms, employee lounges and locker rooms, janitorial closets, entrances, corridors, and restrooms are not areas containing a primary function. There may be exceptions to this general rule. For example, the availability of public restrooms at a place of public accommodation at a roadside rest stop may be a major factor affecting customers' decisions to patronize the public accommodation. In that case, a restroom would be considered to be an "area containing a primary function" of the facility.

Most of the commenters who addressed this issue supported the approach taken by the Department; but a few commenters suggested that areas not open to the general public or those used exclusively by employees should be excluded from the definition of primary function. The preamble to the proposed rule noted that the Department

REGULATION

(c) <u>Alterations to an area containing a primary function</u>. (1) Alterations that affect the usability of or access to an area containing a primary function include, but are not limited to --

(i) Remodeling merchandise display areas or employee work areas in a department store;

(ii) Replacing an inaccessible floor surface in the customer service or employee work areas of a bank;

(iii) Redesigning the assembly line area of a factory; or

(iv) Installing a computer center in an accounting firm.

(2) For the purposes of this section, alterations to windows, hardware, controls, electrical outlets, and signage shall not be deemed to be alterations that affect the usability of or access to an area containing a primary function.

(d) <u>Landlord/tenant</u>: If a tenant is making alterations as defined in §36.402 that would trigger the requirements of this section, those alterations by the tenant in areas that only the tenant occupies do not trigger a path of travel obligation upon the landlord with

ANALYSIS

considered an alternative approach to the definition of "primary function," under which a primary function of a commercial facility would be defined as a major activity for which the facility was intended, while a primary function of a place of public accommodation would be defined as an activity which involves providing significant goods, services, facilities, privileges, advantages, or accommodations. However, the Department concluded that, although portions of the legislative history of the ADA support this alternative, the better view is that the language now contained in §36.403(b) most accurately reflects congressional intent. No commenter made a persuasive argument that the Department's interpretation of the legislative history is incorrect.

When the ADA was introduced, the requirement to make alterations accessible was included in section 302 of the Act, which identifies the practices that constitute discrimination by a public accommodation. Because section 302 applies only to the operation of a place of public accommodation, the alterations requirement was intended only to provide access to clients and customers of a public accommodation. It was anticipated that access would be provided to employees with disabilities under the "reasonable accommodation" requirements of title I. However, during its consideration of the ADA, the House Judiciary Committee amended the bill to move the alterations provision from section 302 to section 303, which applies to commercial facilities as well as public accommodations. The Committee report accompanying the bill explains that:

New construction and alterations of both public accommodations and commercial facilities must be made readily accessible to and usable by individuals with disabilities . . . . Essentially, [this requirement] is designed to ensure that patrons <u>and employees</u> of public accommodations and commercial facilities are able to get to, enter and use the facility. . . . The rationale for making new construction accessible applies with equal force to alterations.

Judiciary report at 62-63 (emphasis added).

The ADA, as enacted, contains the language of section 303 as it was reported out of the Judiciary Committee. Therefore, the Department has concluded that the concept of "primary function" should be applied in the same manner to places of public accommodation and to commercial facilities, thereby

REGULATION

respect to areas of the facility under the landlord's authority, if those areas are not otherwise being altered.

(e) Path of travel. (1) A "path of travel" includes a continuous, unobstructed way of pedestrian passage by means of which the altered area may be approached, entered, and exited, and which connects the altered area with an exterior approach (including sidewalks, streets, and parking areas), an entrance to the facility, and other parts of the facility.

(2) An accessible path of travel may consist of walks and sidewalks, curb ramps and other interior or exterior pedestrian ramps; clear floor paths through lobbies, corridors, rooms, and other improved areas; parking access aisles; elevators and lifts; or a combination of these elements.

(3) For the purposes of this part, the term "path of travel" also includes the restrooms, telephones, and drinking fountains serving the altered area.

(f) Disproportionality. (1) Alterations made to provide an accessible path of travel to the altered area will be deemed disproportionate to the overall alteration when the cost exceeds 20% of the

ANALYSIS

including employee work areas in places of public accommodation within the scope of this section.

Paragraph (c) provides examples of alterations that affect the usability of or access to an area containing a primary function. The examples include: remodeling a merchandise display area or employee work areas in a department store; installing a new floor surface to replace an inaccessible surface in the customer service area or employee work areas of a bank; redesigning the assembly line area of a factory; and installing a computer center in an accounting firm. This list is illustrative, not exhaustive. Any change that affects the usability of or access to an area containing a primary function triggers the statutory obligation to make the path of travel to the altered area accessible.

When the proposed rule was drafted, the Department believed that the rule made it clear that the ADA would require alterations to the path of travel only when such alterations are not disproportionate to the alteration to the primary function area. However, the comments that the Department received indicated that many commenters believe that even minor alterations to individual elements would require additional alterations to the path of travel. To address the concern of these commenters, a new paragraph (c)(2) has been added to the final rule to provide that alterations to such elements as windows, hardware, controls (e.g. light switches or thermostats), electrical outlets, or signage will not be deemed to be alterations that affect the usability of or access to an area containing a primary function. Of course, each element that is altered must comply with ADAAG (Appendix A). The cost of alterations to individual elements would be included in the overall cost of an alteration for purposes of determining disproportionality and would be counted when determining the aggregate cost of a series of small alterations in accordance with §36.403(h) if the area is altered in a manner that affects access to or usability of an area containing a primary function.

Paragraph (d) concerns the respective obligations of landlords and tenants in the cases of alterations that trigger the path of travel requirement under §36.403. This paragraph was contained in the landlord/tenant section of the proposed rule, §36.201(b). If a tenant is making alterations upon its premises pursuant to terms of a lease that grant it the authority to do so (even if they constitute alterations that trigger the

REGULATION

cost of the alteration to the primary function area.

(2) Costs that may be counted as expenditures required to provide an accessible path of travel may include:

(i) Costs associated with providing an accessible entrance and an accessible route to the altered area, for example, the cost of widening doorways or installing ramps;

(ii) Costs associated with making restrooms accessible, such as installing grab bars, enlarging toilet stalls, insulating pipes, or installing accessible faucet controls;

(iii) Costs associated with providing accessible telephones, such as relocating the telephone to an accessible height, installing amplification devices, or installing a telecommunications device for deaf persons (TDD);

(iv) Costs associated with relocating an inaccessible drinking fountain.

(g) Duty to provide accessible features in the event of disproportionality. (1) When the cost of alterations necessary to make the path of travel to the altered area fully accessible is

ANALYSIS

path of travel requirement), and the landlord is not making alterations to other parts of the facility, then the alterations by the tenant on its own premises do not trigger a path of travel obligation upon the landlord in areas of the facility under the landlord's authority that are not otherwise being altered. The legislative history makes clear that the path of travel requirement applies only to the entity that is already making the alteration, and thus the Department has not changed the final rule despite numerous comments suggesting that the tenant be required to provide a path of travel.

Paragraph (e) defines a "path of travel" as a continuous, unobstructed way of pedestrian passage by means of which an altered area may be approached, entered, and exited; and which connects the altered area with an exterior approach (including sidewalks, streets, and parking areas), an entrance to the facility, and other parts of the facility. This concept of an accessible path of travel is analogous to the concepts of "accessible route" and "circulation path" contained in section 3.5 of the current UFAS. Some commenters suggested that this paragraph should address emergency egress. The Department disagrees. "Path of travel" as it is used in this section is a term of art under the ADA that relates only to the obligation of the public accommodation or commercial facility to provide additional accessible elements when an area containing a primary function is altered. The Department recognizes that emergency egress is an important issue, but believes that it is appropriately addressed in ADAAG (appendix A), not in this paragraph. Furthermore, ADAAG does not require changes to emergency egress areas in alterations.

Paragraph (e)(2) is drawn from section 3.5 of UFAS. It provides that an accessible path of travel may consist of walks and sidewalks, curb ramps and other interior or exterior pedestrian ramps; clear floor paths through lobbies, corridors, rooms, and other improved areas; parking access aisles; elevators and lifts; or a combination of such elements. Paragraph (e)(3) provides that, for the purposes of this part, the term "path of travel" also includes the restrooms, telephones, and drinking fountains serving an altered area.

Although the Act establishes an expectation that an accessible path of travel should generally be included when alterations are made to an area containing a primary function, Congress recognized that, in some circumstances, providing an accessible path of travel to an altered area may be sufficiently

REGULATION

disproportionate to the cost of the overall alteration, the path of travel shall be made accessible to the extent that it can be made accessible without incurring disproportionate costs.

(2) In choosing which accessible elements to provide, priority should be given to those elements that will provide the greatest access, in the following order:

(i) An accessible entrance;

(ii) An accessible route to the altered area;

(iii) At least one accessible restroom for each sex or a single unisex restroom;

(iv) Accessible telephones;

(v) Accessible drinking fountains; and

(vi) When possible, additional accessible elements such as parking, storage, and alarms.

(h) Series of smaller alterations. (1) The obligation to provide an accessible path of travel may not be evaded by performing a series of small alterations to the area served by a single path of travel if those alterations could have been

ANALYSIS

burdensome in comparison to the alteration being undertaken to the area containing a primary function as to render this requirement unreasonable. Therefore, Congress provided, in section 303(a)(2) of the Act, that alterations to the path of travel that are disproportionate in cost and scope to the overall alteration are not required.

The Act requires the Attorney General to determine at what point the cost of providing an accessible path of travel becomes disproportionate. The proposed rule provided three options for making this determination.

Two committees of Congress specifically addressed this issue: the House Committee on Education and Labor and the House Committee on the Judiciary. The reports issued by each committee suggested that accessibility alterations to a path of travel might be "disproportionate" if they exceed 30% of the alteration costs (Education and Labor report at 113; Judiciary report at 64). Because the Department believed that smaller percentage rates might be appropriate, the proposed rule sought comments on three options: 10%, 20%, or 30%.

The Department received a significant number of comments on this section. Commenters representing individuals with disabilities generally supported the use of 30% (or more); commenters representing covered entities supported a figure of 10% (or less). The Department believes that alterations made to provide an accessible path of travel to the altered area should be deemed disproportionate to the overall alteration when the cost exceeds 20% of the cost of the alteration to the primary function area. This approach appropriately reflects the intent of Congress to provide access for individuals with disabilities without causing economic hardship for the covered public accommodations and commercial facilities.

The Department has determined that the basis for this cost calculation shall be the cost of the alterations to the area containing the primary function. This approach will enable the public accommodation or other private entity that is making the alteration to calculate its obligation as a percentage of a clearly ascertainable base cost, rather than as a percentage of the "total" cost, an amount that will change as accessibility alterations to the path of travel are made.

Paragraph (f)(2) (paragraph (e)(2) in the proposed rule) is

REGULATION

performed as a single undertaking.

(2) (i) If an area containing a primary function has
been altered without providing an accessible path of
travel to that area, and
subsequent alterations of that
area, or a different
area on the same path of
travel, are undertaken within
three years of the original
alteration, the total cost of
alterations to the primary
function areas on that path of
travel during the preceding
three year period shall be
considered in determining
whether the cost of making
that path of travel accessible
is disproportionate.

(ii) Only alterations
undertaken after January 26,
1992, shall be considered in
determining if the cost of
providing an accessible path
of travel is disproportionate
to the overall cost of the
alterations.

ANALYSIS

unchanged. It provides examples of costs that may be counted
as expenditures required to provide an accessible path of
travel. They include:

-Costs associated with providing an accessible entrance and
an accessible route to the altered area, for example, the cost of
widening doorways or installing ramps;

- Costs associated with making restrooms accessible, such as
installing grab bars, enlarging toilet stalls, insulating pipes, or
installing accessible faucet controls;

- Costs associated with providing accessible telephones, such
as relocating telephones to an accessible height, installing
amplification devices, or installing telecommunications devices for deaf persons (TDD's);

- Costs associated with relocating an inaccessible drinking
fountain.

Paragraph (f)(1) of the proposed rule provided that when
the cost of alterations necessary to make the path of travel
serving an altered area fully accessible is disproportionate to
the cost of the overall alteration, the path of travel shall be
made accessible to the maximum extent feasible. In response
to the suggestion of a commenter, the Department has made an
editorial change in the final rule (paragraph (g)(1)) to clarify
that if the cost of providing a fully accessible path of travel is
disproportionate, the path of travel shall be made accessible
"to the extent that it can be made accessible without incurring
disproportionate costs."

Paragraph (g)(2) (paragraph (f)(2) in the NPRM) establishes that priority should be given to those elements that will
provide the greatest access, in the following order: an accessible entrance; an accessible route to the altered area; at least
one accessible restroom for each sex or a single unisex
restroom; accessible telephones; accessible drinking fountains;
and, whenever possible, additional accessible elements such as
parking, storage, and alarms. This paragraph is unchanged
from the proposed rule.

Paragraph (h) (paragraph (g) in the proposed rule) provides that the obligation to provide an accessible path of travel
may not be evaded by performing a series of small alterations
to the area served by a single path of travel if those alterations

REGULATION

ANALYSIS

could have been performed as a single undertaking. If an area containing a primary function has been altered without providing an accessible path of travel to serve that area, and subsequent alterations of that area, or a different area on the same path of travel, are undertaken within three years of the original alteration, the total cost of alterations to primary function areas on that path of travel during the preceding three year period shall be considered in determining whether the cost of making the path of travel serving that area accessible is disproportionate. Only alterations undertaken after January 26, 1992, shall be considered in determining if the cost of providing accessible features is disproportionate to the overall cost of the alterations.

REGULATION
§36.404 Alterations: Elevator exemption.

(a) This section does not require the installation of an elevator in an altered facility that is less than three stories or has less than 3,000 square feet per story, except with respect to any facility that houses a shopping center, a shopping mall, the professional office of a health care provider, a terminal, depot, or other station used for specified public transportation, or an airport passenger terminal.

(1) For the purposes of this section, "professional office of a health care provider" means a location where a person or entity regulated by a State to provide professional services related to the physical or mental health of an individual makes such services available to the public. The facility that houses a "professional office of a health care provider" only includes floor levels housing by at least one health care provider, or any floor level designed or intended for use by at least one health care provider.

(2) For the purposes of this section, shopping center or shopping mall means--

(i) A building housing five or more sales or rental establishments; or

ANALYSIS
Section 36.404 Alterations: Elevator Exemption.

Section 36.404 implements the elevator exemption in section 303(b) of the Act as it applies to altered facilities. The provisions of section 303(b) are discussed in the preamble to §36.401(d) above. The statute applies the same exemption to both new construction and alterations. The principal difference between the requirements of §36.401(d) and §36.404 is that, in altering an existing facility that is not eligible for the statutory exemption, the public accommodation or other private entity responsible for the alteration is not required to install an elevator if the installation of an elevator would be disproportionate in cost and scope to the cost of the overall alteration as provided in §36.403(f)(1). In addition, the standards referenced in §36.406 (ADAAG) provide that installation of an elevator in an altered facility is not required if it is "technically infeasible."

This section has been revised to define the terms "professional office of a health care provider" and "shopping center or shopping mall" for the purposes of this section. The definition of "professional office of a health care provider" is identical to the definition included in §36.401(d).

It has been brought to the attention of the Department that there is some misunderstanding about the scope of the elevator exemption as it applies to the professional office of a health care provider. A public accommodation, such as the professional office of a health care provider, is required to remove architectural barriers to its facility to the extent that such barrier removal is readily achievable (see §36.304), but it is not otherwise required by this part to undertake new construction or alterations. This part does not require that an existing two story building that houses the professional office of a health care provider be altered for the purpose of providing elevator access. If, however, alterations to the area housing the office of the health care provider are undertaken for other purposes, the installation of an elevator might be required, but only if the cost of the elevator is not disproportionate to the cost of the overall alteration. Neither the Act nor this part prohibits a health care provider from locating his or her professional office in an existing facility that does not have an elevator.

Because of the unique challenges presented in altering existing facilities, the Department has adopted a definition of "shopping center or shopping mall" for the purposes of this

REGULATION

(ii) A series of buildings on a common site, connected by a common pedestrian access route above or below the ground floor, that is either under common ownership or common control or developed either as one project or as a series of related projects, housing five or more sales or rental establishments. For purposes of this section, places of public accommodation of the types listed in paragraph (5) of the definition of "place of public accommodation" in §36.104 are considered sales or rental establishments. The facility housing a "shopping center or shopping mall" only includes floor levels housing at least one sales or rental establishment, or any floor level designed or intended for use by at least one sales or rental establishment.

(b) The exemption provided in paragraph (a) of this section does not obviate or limit in any way the obligation to comply with the other accessibility requirements established in this subpart. For example, alterations to floors above or below the accessible ground floor must be accessible regardless of whether the altered facility has an elevator.

ANALYSIS

section that is slightly different from the definition adopted under §36.401(d). For the purposes of this section, a "shopping center or shopping mall" is (1) a building housing five or more sales or rental establishments, or (2) a series of buildings on a common site, connected by a common pedestrian access route above or below the ground floor, either under common ownership or common control or developed either as one project or as a series of related projects, housing five or more sales or rental establishments. As is the case with new construction, the term "shopping center or shopping mall" only includes floor levels housing at least one sales or rental establishment, or any floor level that was designed or intended for use by at least one sales or rental establishment.

The Department believes that it is appropriate to use a different definition of "shopping center or shopping mall" for this section than for §36.401, in order to make it clear that a series of existing buildings on a common site that is altered for the use of sales or rental establishments does not become a "shopping center or shopping mall" required to install an elevator, unless there is a common means of pedestrian access above or below the ground floor. Without this exemption, separate, but adjacent, buildings that were initially designed and constructed independently of each other could be required to be retrofitted with elevators, if they were later renovated for a purpose not contemplated at the time of construction.

Like §36.401(d), §36.404 provides that the exemptions in this paragraph do not obviate or limit in any way the obligation to comply with the other accessibility requirements established in this subpart. For example, alterations to floors above or below the ground floor must be accessible regardless of whether the altered facility has an elevator. If a facility that is not required to install an elevator nonetheless has an elevator, that elevator shall meet, to the maximum extent feasible, the accessibility requirements of this section.

REGULATION

§36.405 Alterations: Historic preservation.

(a) Alterations to buildings or facilities that are eligible for listing in the National Register of Historic Places under the National Historic Preservation Act (16 U.S.C. 470 et seq.), or are designated as historic under State or local law, shall comply to the maximum extent feasible with section 4.1.7 of appendix A to this Part.

(b) If it is determined under the procedures set out in section 4.1.7 of appendix A that it is not feasible to provide physical access to an historic property that is a place of public accommodation in a manner that will not threaten or destroy the historic significance of the building or facility, alternative methods of access shall be provided pursuant to the requirements of subpart C of this part.

ANALYSIS

Section 36.405 Alterations: Historic preservation.

Section 36.405 gives effect to the intent of Congress, expressed in section 504(c) of the Act, that this part recognize the national interest in preserving significant historic structures. Commenters criticized the Department's use of descriptive terms in the proposed rule that are different from those used in the ADA to describe eligible historic properties. In addition, some commenters criticized the Department's decision to use the concept of "substantially impairing" the historic features of a property, which is a concept employed in regulations implementing section 504 of the Rehabilitation Act of 1973. Those commenters recommended that the Department adopt the criteria of "adverse effect" published by the Advisory Council on Historic Preservation under the National Historic Preservation Act (36 CFR 800.9) as the standard for determining whether an historic property may be altered.

The Department agrees with these comments to the extent that they suggest that the language of the rule should conform to the language employed by Congress in the ADA. Therefore, the language of this section has been revised to make it clear that this provision applies to buildings or facilities that are eligible for listing in the National Register of Historic Places under the National Historic Preservation Act (16 U.S.C. 470 et seq.) and to buildings or facilities that are designated as historic under State or local law. The Department believes, however, that the criteria of adverse effect employed under the National Historic Preservation Act are inappropriate for this rule because section 504(c) of the ADA specifies that special alterations provisions shall apply only when an alteration would "threaten or destroy the historic significance of qualified historic buildings and facilities."

The Department intends that the exception created by this section be applied only in those very rare situations in which it is not possible to provide access to an historic property using the special access provisions in ADAAG. Therefore, paragraph (a) of §36.405 has been revised to provide that alterations to historic properties shall comply, to the maximum extent feasible, with section 4.1.7 of ADAAG. Paragraph (b) of this section has been revised to provide that if it has been determined, under the procedures established in ADAAG, that it is not feasible to provide physical access to an historic property that is a place of public accommodation in a manner that will not threaten or destroy the historic significance of the property, alternative methods of access shall be provided pursuant to the requirements of Subpart C.

REGULATION

§36.406 Standards for new construction and alterations.

(a) New construction and alterations subject to this part shall comply with the standards for accessible design published as appendix A to this part (ADAAG).

(b) The chart in the appendix to this section provides guidance to the user in reading appendix A to this part (ADAAG) together with subparts A through D of this part, when determining requirements for a particular facility.

Appendix to section 36.406

This chart has no effect for purposes of compliance or enforcement. It does not necessarily provide complete or mandatory information.

§§36.407-36.500 [Reserved]

ANALYSIS

Section 36.406 Standards for New Construction and Alterations.

Section 36.406 implements the requirements of sections 306(b) and 306(c) of the Act, which require the Attorney General to promulgate standards for accessible design for buildings and facilities subject to the Act and this part that are consistent with the supplemental minimum guidelines and requirements for accessible design published by the Architectural and Transportation Barriers Compliance Board (ATBCB or Board) pursuant to section 504 of the Act. This section of the rule provides that new construction and alterations subject to this part shall comply with the standards for accessible design published as Appendix A to this part.

Appendix A contains the Americans with Disabilities Act Accessibility Guidelines for Buildings and Facilities (ADAAG), which is being published by the ATBCB as a final rule elsewhere in this issue of the Federal Register. As proposed in this Department's proposed rule, §36.406(a) adopts ADAAG as the accessibility standard applicable under this rule.

Paragraph (b) was not included in the proposed rule. It provides, in chart form, guidance for using ADAAG together with subparts A through D of this part when determining requirements for a particular facility. This chart is intended solely as guidance for the user; it has no effect for purposes of compliance or enforcement. It does not necessarily provide complete or mandatory information.

Proposed §36.406(b) is not included in the final rule. That provision, which would have taken effect only if the final rule had followed the proposed Option Two for §36.401(a), is unnecessary because the Department has chosen Option One, as explained in the preamble for that section.

Section 504(a) of the ADA requires the ATBCB to issue minimum guidelines to supplement the existing Minimum Guidelines and Requirements for Accessible Design (MGRAD) (36 CFR part 1190) for purposes of title III. According to section 504(b) of the Act, the guidelines are to establish additional requirements, consistent with the Act, "to ensure that buildings and facilities are accessible, in terms of architecture and design, ... and communication, to individuals with disabilities." Section 306(c) of the Act requires that the

REGULATION

accessibility standards included in the Department's regulations be consistent with the minimum guidelines, in this case ADAAG.

As explained in the ATBCB's preamble to ADAAG, the substance and form of the guidelines are drawn from several sources. They use as their model the 1984 Uniform Federal Accessibility Standards (UFAS) (41 CFR part 101, subpart 101-19.6, appendix), which are the standards implementing the Architectural Barriers Act. UFAS is based on the Board's 1982 MGRAD. ADAAG follows the numbering system and format of the private sector American National Standard Institute's ANSI A117.1 standards. (American National Specifications for Making Buildings and Facilities Accessible to and Usable by Physically Handicapped People (ANSI A117-1980) and American National Standard for Buildings and Facilities -- Providing Accessibility and Usability for Physically Handicapped People (ANSI A117.1-1986).) ADAAG supplements MGRAD. In developing ADAAG, the Board made every effort to be consistent with MGRAD and the current and proposed ANSI Standards, to the extent consistent with the ADA.

ADAAG consists of nine main sections and a separate appendix. Sections 1 through 3 contain general provisions and definitions. Section 4 contains scoping provisions and technical specifications applicable to all covered buildings and facilities. The scoping provisions are listed separately for new construction of sites and exterior facilities; new construction of buildings; additions; alterations; and alterations to historic properties. The technical specifications generally reprint the text and illustrations of the ANSI A117.1 standard, except where differences are noted by italics. Sections 5 through 9 of the guidelines are special application sections and contain additional requirements for restaurants and cafeterias, medical care facilities, business and mercantile facilities, libraries, and transient lodging. The appendix to the guidelines contains additional information to aid in understanding the technical specifications. The section numbers in the appendix correspond to the sections of the guidelines to which they relate. An asterisk after a section number indicates that additional information appears in the appendix.

ADAAG's provisions are further explained under Summary of ADAAG, below.

REGULATION

General Comments

One commenter urged the Department to move all or portions of subpart D, New Construction and Alterations, to the Appendix (ADAAG) or to duplicate portions of subpart D in the Appendix. The commenter correctly pointed out that subpart D is inherently linked to ADDAG, and that a self-contained set of rules would be helpful to users. The Department has attempted to simplify use of the two documents by deleting some paragraphs from subpart D (e.g., those relating to work areas), because they are included in ADAAG. However, the Department has retained in subpart D those sections that are taken directly from the statute or that give meaning to specific statutory concepts (e.g., structural impracticability, path of travel). While some of the subpart D provisions are duplicated in ADAAG, others are not. For example, issues relating to path of travel and disproportionality in alterations are not addressed in detail in ADAAG. (The structure and contents of the two documents are addressed below under Summary of ADAAG.) While the Department agrees that it would be useful to have one self-contained document, the different focuses of this rule and ADAAG do not permit this result at this time. However, the chart included in §36.406(b) should assist users in applying the provisions of subparts A through D, and ADAAG together.

Numerous business groups have urged the Department not to adopt the proposed ADAAG as the accessibility standards, because the requirements established are too high, reflect the "state of the art," and are inflexible, rigid, and impractical. Many of these objections have been lodged on the basis that ADAAG exceeds the statutory mandate to establish "minimum" guidelines. In the view of the Department, these commenters have misconstrued the meaning of the term "minimum guidelines." The statute clearly contemplates that the guidelines establish a level of access -- a minimum -- that the standards must meet or exceed. The guidelines are not to be "minimal" in the sense that they would provide for a low level of access. To the contrary, Congress emphasized that the ADA requires a "high degree of convenient access." Education and Labor report at 117-18. The legislative history explains that the guidelines may not "reduce, weaken, narrow or set less accessibility standards than those included in existing MGRAD" and should provide greater guidance in communication accessibility for individuals with hearing and vision impairments. Id. at 139. Nor did

REGULATION

Congress contemplate a set of guidelines less detailed than ADAAG; the statute requires that the ADA guidelines supplement the existing MGRAD. When it established the statutory scheme, Congress was aware of the content and purpose of the 1982 MGRAD; as ADAAG does with respect to ADA, MGRAD establishes a minimum level of access that the Architectural Barriers Act standards (i.e., UFAS) must meet or exceed, and includes a high level of detail.

Many of the same commenters urged the Department to incorporate as its accessibility standards the ANSI standard's technical provisions and to adopt the proposed scoping provisions under development by the Council of American Building Officials' Board for the Coordination of Model Codes (BCMC). They contended that the ANSI standard is familiar to and accepted by professionals, and that both documents are developed through consensus. They suggested that ADAAG will not stay current, because it does not follow an established cyclical review process, and that it is not likely to be adopted by nonfederal jurisdictions in State and local codes. They urged the Department and the Board to coordinate the ADAAG provisions and any substantive changes to them with the ANSI A117 committee in order to maintain a consistent and uniform set of accessibility standards that can be efficiently and effectively implemented at the State and local level through the existing building regulatory processes.

The Department shares the commenters' goal of coordination between the private sector and Federal standards, to the extent that coordination can lead to substantive requirements consistent with the ADA. A single accessibility standard, or consistent accessibility standards, that can be used for ADA purposes and that can be incorporated or referenced by State and local governments, would help to ensure that the ADA requirements are routinely implemented at the design stage. The Department plans to work toward this goal.

The Department, however, must comply with the requirements of the ADA, the Federal Advisory Committee Act (5 USC App. 1 et seq.) and the Administrative Procedure Act (5 USC 551 et seq.). Neither the Department nor the Board can adopt private requirements wholesale. Furthermore, neither the 1991 ANSI A117 Standard revision nor the BCMC process is complete. Although the ANSI and BCMC provisions are not final, the Board has carefully considered both the draft BCMC scoping provisions and draft ANSI technical standards

ANALYSIS

and included their language in ADAAG wherever consistent with the ADA.

Some commenters requested that, if the Department did not adopt ANSI by reference, the Department declare compliance with ANSI/BCMC to constitute equivalency with the ADA standards. The Department has not adopted this recommendation but has instead worked as a member of the ATBCB to ensure that its accessibility standards are practical and usable. In addition, as explained under subpart F, Certification of State Laws or Local Building Codes, the proper forum for further evaluation of this suggested approach would be in conjunction with the certification process.

Some commenters urged the Department to allow an additional comment period after the Board published its guidelines in final form, for purposes of affording the public a further opportunity to evaluate the appropriateness of including them as the Department's accessibility standards. Such an additional comment period is unnecessary and would unduly delay the issuance of final regulations. The Department put the public on notice, through the proposed rule, of its intention to adopt the proposed ADAAG, with any changes made by the Board, as the accessibility standards. As a member of the Board and of its ADA Task Force, the Department participated actively in the public hearings held on the proposed guidelines and in preparation of both the proposed and final versions of ADAAG. Many individuals and groups commented directly to the Department's docket, or at its public hearings, about ADAAG. The comments received on ADAAG, whether by the Board or by this Department, were thoroughly analyzed and considered by the Department in the context of whether the proposed ADAAG was consistent with the ADA and suitable for adoption as both guidelines and standards. The Department is convinced that ADAAG as adopted in its final form is appropriate for these purposes. The final guidelines, adopted here as standards, will ensure the high level of access contemplated by Congress, consistent with the ADA's balance between the interests of people with disabilities and the business community.

A few commenters, citing the Senate report (at 70) and the Education and Labor report (at 119), asked the Department to include in the regulations a provision stating that departures from particular technical and scoping requirements of the accessibility standards will be permitted so long as the

REGULATION

ANALYSIS

alternative methods used will provide substantially equivalent or greater access to and utilization of the facility. Such a provision is found in ADAAG 2.2 and by virtue of that fact is included in these regulations.

Comments on specific provisions of proposed ADAAG

During the course of accepting comments on its proposed rule, the Department received numerous comments on ADAAG. Those areas that elicited the heaviest response included assistive listening systems, automated teller machines, work areas, parking, areas of refuge, telephones (scoping for TDD's and volume controls) and visual alarms. Strenuous objections were raised by some business commenters to the proposed provisions of the guidelines concerning check-out aisles, counters, and scoping for hotels and nursing facilities. All these comments were considered in the same manner as other comments on the Department's proposed rule and, in the Department's view, have been addressed adequately in the final ADAAG.

Largely in response to comments, the Board made numerous changes from its proposal, including the following:

- Generally, at least 50% of public entrances to new buildings must be accessible, rather than all entrances, as would often have resulted from the proposed approach.

- Not all check-out aisles are required to be accessible.

- The final guidelines provide greater flexibility in providing access to sales counters, and no longer require a portion of every counter to be accessible.

- Scoping for TDD's or text telephones was increased. One TDD or text telephone, for speech and hearing impaired persons, must be provided at locations with 4, rather than 6, pay phones, and in hospitals and shopping malls. Use of portable (less expensive) TDD's is allowed.

- Dispersal of wheelchair seating areas in theaters will be required only where there are more than 300 seats, rather than in all cases. Seats with removable armrests (i.e., seats into which persons with mobility impairments can transfer) will also be required.

REGULATION

ANALYSIS

- Areas of refuge (areas with direct access to a stairway, and where people who cannot use stairs may await assistance during a emergency evacuation) will be required, as proposed, but the final provisions are based on the Uniform Building Code. Such areas are not required in alterations.

- Rather than requiring 5% of new hotel rooms to be accessible to people with mobility impairments, between 2 and 4% accessibility (depending on total number of rooms) is required. In addition, 1% of the rooms must have roll-in showers.

- The proposed rule reserved the provisions on alterations to homeless shelters. The final guidelines apply alterations requirements to homeless shelters, but the requirements are less stringent than those applied to other types of facilities.

- Parking spaces that can be used by people in vans (with lifts) will be required.

- As mandated by the ADA, the Board has established a procedure to be followed with respect to alterations to historic facilities.

Summary of ADAAG

This section of the preamble summarizes the structure of ADAAG, and highlights the more important portions.

- Sections 1 through 3

Sections 1 through 3 contain general requirements, including definitions.

- Section 4.1.1, Application

Section 4 contains scoping requirements. Section 4.1.1, Application, provides that all areas of newly designed or newly constructed buildings and facilities and altered portions of existing buildings and facilities required to be accessible by §4.1.6 must comply with the guidelines unless otherwise provided in §4.1.1 or a special application section. It addresses areas used only by employees as work areas, temporary structures, and general exceptions.

Section 4.1.1(3) preserves the basic principle of the

REGULATION

proposed rule: areas that may be used by employees with disabilities shall be designed and constructed so that an individual with a disability can approach, enter, and exit the area. The language has been clarified to provide that it applies to any area used only as a work area (not just to areas "that may be used by employees with disabilities"), and that the guidelines do not require that any area used as an individual work station be designed with maneuvering space or equipped to be accessible. The appendix to ADAAG explains that work areas must meet the guidelines' requirements for doors and accessible routes, and recommends, but does not require, that 5% of individual work stations be designed to permit a person using a wheelchair to maneuver within the space.

Further discussion of work areas is found in the preamble concerning proposed §36.401(b).

Section 4.1.1(5)(a) includes an exception for structural impracticability that corresponds to the one found in §36.401(c) and discussed in that portion of the preamble.

'Section 4.1.2, Accessible Sites and Exterior Facilities: New Construction

This section addresses exterior features, elements, or spaces such as parking, portable toilets, and exterior signage, in new construction. Interior elements and spaces are covered by §4.1.3.

The final rule retains the UFAS scoping for parking but also requires that at least one of every eight accessible parking spaces be designed with adequate adjacent space to deploy a lift used with a van. These spaces must have a sign indicating that they are van-accessible, but they are not to be reserved exclusively for van users.

'Section 4.1.3, Accessible Buildings: New Construction

This section establishes scoping requirements for new construction of buildings and facilities.

Sections 4.1.3(1) through (4) cover accessible routes, protruding objects, ground and floor surfaces, and stairs.

Section 4.1.3(5) generally requires elevators to serve each level in a newly constructed building, with four exceptions

REGULATION

included in the subsection. Exception 1 is the "elevator exception" established in §36.401(d), which must be read with this section. Exception 4 allows the use of platform lifts under certain conditions.

Section 4.1.3(6), Windows, is reserved. Section 4.1.3(7) applies to doors.

Under §4.1.3(8), at least 50% of all public entrances must be accessible. In addition, if a building is designed to provide access to enclosed parking, pedestrian tunnels, or elevated walkways, at least one entrance that serves each such function must be accessible. Each tenancy in a building must be served by an accessible entrance. Where local regulations (e.g., fire codes) require that a minimum number of exits be provided, an equivalent number of accessible entrances must be provided. (The latter provision does not require a greater number of entrances than otherwise planned.)

ADAAG §4.1.3(9), with accompanying technical requirements in §4.3, requires an area of rescue assistance (i.e., an area with direct access to an exit stairway and where people who are unable to use stairs may await assistance during an emergency evacuation) to be established on each floor of a multi-story building. This was one of the most controversial provisions in the guidelines. The final ADAAG is based on current Uniform Building Code requirements and retains the requirement that areas of refuge (renamed "areas of rescue assistance") be provided, but specifies that this requirement does not apply to buildings that have a supervised automatic sprinkler system. Areas of refuge are not required in alterations.

The next seven subsections deal with drinking fountains (§4.1.3(10)); toilet facilities (§4.1.3(11)); storage, shelving, and display units (§4.1.3(12)), controls and operating mechanisms (§4.1.3(13)), emergency warning systems (§4.1.3(14), detectable warnings (§4.1.3(15)), and building signage (§4.1.3(16)). Paragraph 11 requires that toilet facilities comply with §4.22, which requires one accessible toilet stall (60" x 60") in each newly constructed restroom. In response to public comments, the final rule requires that a second accessible stall (36" x 60") be provided in restrooms that have six or more stalls.

ADAAG §4.1.3(17) establishes requirements for accessi-

REGULATION

ANALYSIS

bility of pay phones to persons with mobility impairments, hearing impairments (requiring some phones with volume controls), and those who cannot use voice telephones.   It requires one interior "text telephone" to be provided at any facility that has a total of four or more public pay phones. (The term "text telephone" has been adopted to reflect current terminology and changes in technology.) In addition, text telephones will be required in specific locations, such as covered shopping malls, hospitals (in emergency rooms, waiting rooms, and recovery areas), and convention centers.

Paragraph 18 of §4.1.3 generally requires that at least five percent of fixed or built-in seating or tables be accessible.

Paragraph 19, covering assembly areas, specifies the number of wheelchair seating spaces and types and numbers of assistive listening systems required. It requires dispersal of wheelchair seating locations in facilities where there are more than 300 seats. The guidelines also require that at least one percent of all fixed seats be aisle seats without armrests (or with moveable armrests) on the aisle side to increase accessibility for persons with mobility impairments who prefer to transfer from their wheelchairs to fixed seating. In addition, the final ADAAG requires that fixed seating for a companion be located adjacent to each wheelchair location.

Paragraph 20 requires that where automated teller machines are provided, at least one must comply with §4.34, which, among other things, requires accessible controls, and instructions and other information that are accessible to persons with sight impairments.

Under paragraph 21, where dressing rooms are provided, five per cent or at least one must comply with §4.35.

'Section 4.1.5, Additions

Each addition to an existing building or facility is regarded as an alteration subject to §§36.402 through 36.406 of subpart D, including the date established in §36.402(a). But additions also have attributes of new construction, and to the extent that a space or element in the addition is newly constructed, each new space or element must comply with the applicable scoping provisions of §§4.1.1 to 4.1.3 for new construction, the applicable technical specifications of §§4.2 through 4.34, and any applicable special provisions in §§5 through 10. For

REGULATION

instance, if a restroom is provided in the addition, it must comply with the requirements for new construction. Construction of an addition does not, however, create an obligation to retrofit the entire existing building or facility to meet requirements for new construction. Rather, the addition is to be regarded as an alteration and to the extent that it affects or could affect the usability of or access to an area containing a primary function, the requirements in §4.1.6(2) are triggered with respect to providing an accessible path of travel to the altered area and making the restrooms, telephones, and drinking fountains serving the altered area accessible. For example, if a museum adds a new wing that does not have a separate entrance as part of the addition, an accessible path of travel would have to be provided through the existing building or facility unless it is disproportionate to the overall cost and scope of the addition as established in §36.403(f).

- Section 4.1.6, Alterations

An alteration is a change to a building or facility that affects or could affect the usability of or access to the building or facility or any part thereof. There are three general principles for alterations. First, if any existing element or space is altered, the altered element or space must meet new construction requirements (§4.1.6(1)(b)). Second, if alterations to the elements in a space when considered together amount to an alteration of the space, the entire space must meet new construction requirements (§4.1.6(1)(c)). Third, if the alteration affects or could affect the usability of or access to an area containing a primary function, the path of travel to the altered area and the restrooms, drinking fountains, and telephones serving the altered area must be made accessible unless it is disproportionate to the overall alterations in terms of cost and scope as determined under criteria established by the Attorney General (§4.1.6(2)).

Section 4.1.6 should be read with §§36.402 through 36.405. Requirements concerning alterations to an area serving a primary function are addressed with greater detail in the latter sections than in §4.1.6(2). Section 4.1.6(1)(j) deals with technical infeasibility. Section 4.1.6(3) contains special technical provisions for alterations to existing buildings and facilities.

REGULATION

ANALYSIS

- Section 4.1.7, Historic Preservation

This section contains scoping provisions and alternative requirements for alterations to qualified historic buildings and facilities. It clarifies the procedures under the National Historic Preservation Act and their application to alterations covered by the ADA. An individual seeking to alter a facility that is subject to the ADA guidelines and to State or local historic preservation statutes shall consult with the State Historic Preservation Officer to determine if the planned alteration would threaten or destroy the historic significance of the facility.

- Sections 4.2 Through 4.35

Sections 4.2 through 4.35 contain the technical specifications for elements and spaces required to be accessible by the scoping provisions (§§4.1 through 4.1.7) and special application sections (§§5 through 10). The technical specifications are the same as the 1980 version of ANSI A117.1 standard, except as noted in the text by italics.

- Sections 5 Through 9

These are special application sections and contain additional requirements for restaurants and cafeterias, medical care facilities, business and mercantile facilities, libraries, and transient lodging. For example, at least 5 percent, but not less than one, of the fixed tables in a restaurant must be accessible.

In §7, Business and Mercantile, paragraph 7.2 (Sales and Service Counters, Teller Windows, Information Counters) has been revised to provide greater flexibility in new construction than did the proposed rule. At least one of each type of sales or service counter where a cash register is located shall be made accessible. Accessible counters shall be dispersed throughout the facility. At counters such as bank teller windows or ticketing counters, alternative methods of compliance are permitted. A public accommodation may lower a portion of the counter, provide an auxiliary counter, or provide equivalent facilitation through such means as installing a folding shelf on the front of the counter at an accessible height to provide a work surface for a person using a wheelchair.

Section 7.3., Check-out Aisles, provides that, in new construction, a certain number of each design of check-out

ANALYSIS

aisle, as listed in a chart based on the total number of check-out aisles of each design, shall be accessible. The percentage of check-outs required to be accessible generally ranges from 20% to 40%. In a newly constructed or altered facility with less than 5,000 square feet of selling space, at least one of each type of check-out aisle must be accessible. In altered facilities with 5,000 or more square feet of selling space, at least one of each design of check-out aisle must be made accessible when altered, until the number of accessible aisles of each design equals the number that would be required for new construction.

- Section 9, Accessible Transient Lodging

Section 9 addresses two types of transient lodging: hotels, motels, inns, boarding houses, dormitories, resorts, and other similar places (§§9.1 through 9.4); and homeless shelters, halfway houses, transient group homes, and other social service establishments (§9.5). The interplay of the ADA and Fair Housing Act with respect to such facilities is addressed in the preamble discussion of the definition of "place of public accommodation" in §36.104.

The final rule establishes scoping requirements for accessibility of newly constructed hotels. Four percent of the first hundred rooms, and roughly two percent of rooms in excess of 100, must meet certain requirements for accessibility to persons with mobility or hearing impairments, and an additional identical percentage must be accessible to persons with hearing impairments. An additional 1% of the available rooms must be equipped with roll-in showers, raising the actual scoping for rooms accessible to persons with mobility impairments to 5% of the first hundred rooms and 3% thereafter. The final ADAAG also provides that when a hotel is being altered, one fully accessible room and one room equipped with visual alarms, notification devices, and amplified telephones shall be provided for each 25 rooms being altered until the number of accessible rooms equals that required under the new construction standard. Accessible rooms must be dispersed in a manner that will provide persons with disabilities with a choice of single or multiple-bed accommodations.

In new construction, homeless shelters and other social service entities must comply with ADAAG; at least one type of amenity in each common area must be accessible. In a

REGULATION

ANALYSIS

facility that is not required to have an elevator, it is not necessary to provide accessible amenities on the inaccessible floors if at least one of each type of amenity is provided in accessible common areas. The percentage of accessible sleeping accommodations required is the same as that required for other places of transient lodging. Requirements for facilities altered for use as a homeless shelter parallel the current MGRAD accessibility requirements for leased buildings. A shelter located in an altered facility must have at least one accessible entrance, accessible sleeping accommodations in a number equivalent to that established for new construction, at least one accessible toilet and bath, at least one accessible common area, and an accessible route connecting all accessible areas. All accessible areas in a homeless shelter in an altered facility may be located on one level.

Section 10, Transportation Facilities

Section 10 of ADAAG is reserved. On March 20, 1991, the ATBCB published a supplemental notice of proposed rulemaking (56 FR 11874) to establish special access requirements for transportation facilities. The Department anticipates that when the ATBCB issues final guidelines for transportation facilities, this part will be amended to include those provisions.

REGULATION

Subpart E - Enforcement.
§36.501 Private suits.

(a) <u>General</u>. Any person who is being subjected to discrimination on the basis of disability in violation of the Act or this part or who has reasonable grounds for believing that such person is about to be subjected to discrimination in violation of section 303 of the Act or subpart D of this part may institute a civil action for preventive relief, including an application for a permanent or temporary injunction, restraining order, or other order. Upon timely application, the court may, in its discretion, permit the Attorney General to intervene in the civil action if the Attorney General or his or her designee certifies that the case is of general public importance. Upon application by the complainant and in such circumstances as the court may deem just, the court may appoint an attorney for such complainant and may authorize the commencement of the civil action without the payment of fees, costs, or security. Nothing in this section shall require a person with a disability to engage in a futile gesture if the person has actual notice that a person or organization covered by title III of the Act or this part does not intend to comply with its provisions.

ANALYSIS

Subpart E -- Enforcement.

Because the Department of Justice does not have authority to establish procedures for judicial review and enforcement, subpart E generally restates the statutory procedures for enforcement.

Section 36.501 describes the procedures for private suits by individuals and the judicial remedies available. In addition to the language in section 308(a)(1) of the Act, §36.501(a) of this part includes the language from section 204(a) of the Civil Rights Act of 1964 (42 U.S.C. 2000a-3(a)) which is incorporated by reference in the ADA. A commenter noted that the proposed rule did not include the provision in section 204(a) allowing the court to appoint an attorney for the complainant and authorize the commencement of the civil action without the payment of fees, costs, or security. That provision has been included in the final rule.

Section 308(a)(1) of the ADA permits a private suit by an individual who has reasonable grounds for believing that he or she is "about to be" subjected to discrimination in violation of section 303 of the Act (subpart D of this part), which requires that new construction and alterations be readily accessible to and usable by individuals with disabilities. Authorizing suits to prevent construction of facilities with architectural barriers will avoid the necessity of costly retrofitting that might be required if suits were not permitted until after the facilities were completed. To avoid unnecessary suits, this section requires that the individual bringing the suit have "reasonable grounds" for believing that a violation is about to occur, but does not require the individual to engage in a futile gesture if he or she has notice that a person or organization covered by title III of the Act does not intend to comply with its provisions.

Section 36.501(b) restates the provisions of section 308(a)(2) of the Act, which states that injunctive relief for the failure to remove architectural barriers in existing facilities or the failure to make new construction and alterations accessible "shall include" an order to alter these facilities to make them readily accessible to and usable by persons with disabilities to the extent required by title III. The Report of the Energy and Commerce Committee notes that "an order to make a facility readily accessible to and usable by individuals with disabilities is mandatory" under this standard. H.R. Rep. No. 485, 101st Cong., 2d Sess., pt 4, at 64 (1990).

REGULATION

(b) <u>Injunctive relief</u>. In the case of violations of §36.304, §36.308, §36.310(b), §36.401, §36.402, §36.403, and §36.405 of this part, injunctive relief shall include an order to alter facilities to make such facilities readily accessible to and usable by individuals with disabilities to the extent required by the Act or this part. Where appropriate, injunctive relief shall also include requiring the provision of an auxiliary aid or service, modification of a policy, or provision of alternative methods, to the extent required by the Act or this part.

ANALYSIS

Also, injunctive relief shall include, where appropriate, requiring the provision of an auxiliary aid or service, modification of a policy, or provision of alternative methods, to the extent required by title III of the Act and this part.

REGULATION

§36.502 Investigations and compliance reviews.

(a) The Attorney General shall investigate alleged violations of the Act or this part.

(b) Any individual who believes that he or she or a specific class of persons has been subjected to discrimination prohibited by the Act or this part may request the Department to institute an investigation.

(c) Where the Attorney General has reason to believe that there may be a violation of this part, he or she may initiate a compliance review.

ANALYSIS

Section 36.502 is based on section 308(b)(1)(A)(i) of the Act, which provides that the Attorney General shall investigate alleged violations of title III and undertake periodic reviews of compliance of covered entities. Although the Act does not establish a comprehensive administrative enforcement mechanism for investigation and resolution of all complaints received, the legislative history notes that investigation of alleged violations and periodic compliance reviews are essential to effective enforcement of title III, and that the Attorney General is expected to engage in active enforcement and to allocate sufficient resources to carry out this responsibility. Judiciary Report at 67.

Many commenters argued for inclusion of more specific provisions for administrative resolution of disputes arising under the Act and this part in order to promote voluntary compliance and avoid the need for litigation. Administrative resolution is far more efficient and economical than litigation, particularly in the early stages of implementation of complex legislation when the specific requirements of the statute are not widely understood. The Department has added a new paragraph (c) to this section authorizing the Attorney General to initiate a compliance review where he or she has reason to believe there may be a violation of this rule.

REGULATION

§36.503 Suit by the Attorney General.

Following a compliance review or investigation under §36.502, or at any other time in his or her discretion, the Attorney General may commence a civil action in any appropriate United States district court if the Attorney General has reasonable cause to believe that --

(a) Any person or group of persons is engaged in a pattern or practice of discrimination in violation of the Act or this part; or

(b) Any person or group of persons has been discriminated against in violation of the Act or this part and the discrimination raises an issue of general public importance.

ANALYSIS

Section 36.503 describes the procedures for suits by the Attorney General set out in section 308(b)(1)(B) of the Act. If the Department has reasonable cause to believe that any person or group of persons is engaged in a pattern or practice of resistance to the full enjoyment of any of the rights granted by title III or that any person or group of persons has been denied any of the rights granted by title III and such denial raises an issue of general public importance, the Attorney General may commence a civil action in any appropriate United States district court. The proposed rule provided for suit by the Attorney General "or his or her designee." The reference to a "designee" has been omitted in the final rule because it is unnecessary. The Attorney General has delegated enforcement authority under the ADA to the Assistant Attorney General for Civil Rights. 55 Fed. Reg. 40653 (October 4, 1990) (to be codified at 28 CFR §0.50(l).)

REGULATION

§36.504 Relief.

(a) <u>Authority of court</u>. In a civil action under §36.503, the court —

(1) May grant any equitable relief that such court considers to be appropriate, including, to the extent required by the Act or this part —

(i) Granting temporary, preliminary, or permanent relief;

(ii) Providing an auxiliary aid or service, modification of policy, practice, or procedure, or alternative method; and

(iii) Making facilities readily accessible to and usable by individuals with disabilities;

(2) May award other relief as the court considers to be appropriate, including monetary damages to persons aggrieved when requested by the Attorney General; and

(3) May, to vindicate the public interest, assess a civil penalty against the entity in an amount —

(i) Not exceeding $50,000 for a first violation; and

(ii) Not exceeding $100,000 for any subsequent violation.

ANALYSIS

Section 36.504 describes the relief that may be granted in a suit by the Attorney General under section 308(b)(2) of the Act. In such an action, the court may grant any equitable relief it considers to be appropriate, including granting temporary, preliminary, or permanent relief, providing an auxiliary aid or service, modification of policy or alternative method, or making facilities readily accessible to and usable by individuals with disabilities, to the extent required by title III. In addition, a court may award such other relief as the court considers to be appropriate, including monetary damages to persons aggrieved, when requested by the Attorney General.

Furthermore, the court may vindicate the public interest by assessing a civil penalty against the covered entity in an amount not exceeding $50,000 for a first violation and not exceeding $100,000 for any subsequent violation. Section 36.504(b) of the rule adopts the standard of section 308(b)(3) of the Act. This section makes it clear that, in counting the number of previous determinations of violations for determining whether a "first" or "subsequent" violation has occurred, determinations in the same action that the entity has engaged in more than one discriminatory act are to be counted as a single violation. A "second violation" would not accrue to that entity until the Attorney General brought another suit against the entity and the entity was again held in violation. Again, all of the violations found in the second suit would be cumulatively considered as a "subsequent violation."

Section 36.504(c) clarifies that the terms "monetary damages" and "other relief" do not include punitive damages. They do include, however, all forms of compensatory damages, including out-of-pocket expenses and damages for pain and suffering.

Section 36.504(a)(3) is based on section 308(b)(2)(C) of the Act, which provides that, "to vindicate the public interest," a court may assess a civil penalty against the entity that has been found to be in violation of the Act in suits brought by the Attorney General. In addition, §36.504(d), which is taken from section 308(b)(5) of the Act, further provides that, in considering what amount of civil penalty, if any, is appropriate, the court shall give consideration to "any good faith effort or attempt to comply with this part." In evaluating such good faith, the court shall consider "among other factors

REGULATION

(b) Single violation. For purposes of paragraph (a)(3) of this section, in determining whether a first or subsequent violation has occurred, a determination in a single action, by judgment or settlement, that the covered entity has engaged in more than one discriminatory act shall be counted as a single violation.

(c) Punitive damages. For purposes of paragraph (a)(2) of this section, the terms "monetary damages" and "such other relief" do not include punitive damages.

(d) Judicial consideration. In a civil action under §36.503, the court, when considering what amount of civil penalty, if any, is appropriate, shall give consideration to any good faith effort or attempt to comply with this part by the entity. In evaluating good faith, the court shall consider, among other factors it deems relevant, whether the entity could have reasonably anticipated the need for an appropriate type of auxiliary aid needed to accommodate the unique needs of a particular individual with a disability.

ANALYSIS

it deems relevant, whether the entity could have reasonably anticipated the need for an appropriate type of auxiliary aid needed to accommodate the unique needs of a particular individual with a disability."

The "good faith" standard referred to in this section is not intended to imply a willful or intentional standard - that is, an entity cannot demonstrate good faith simply by showing that it did not willfully, intentionally, or recklessly disregard the law. At the same time, the absence of such a course of conduct would be a factor a court should weigh in determining the existence of good faith.

REGULATION

§36.505 Attorneys fees.

In any action or administrative proceeding commenced pursuant to the Act or this part, the court or agency, in its discretion, may allow the prevailing party, other than the United States, a reasonable attorney's fee, including litigation expenses, and costs, and the United States shall be liable for the foregoing the same as a private individual.

ANALYSIS

Section 36.505 states that courts are authorized to award attorneys fees, including litigation expenses and costs, as provided in section 505 of the Act. Litigation expenses include items such as expert witness fees, travel expenses, etc. The Judiciary Committee Report specifies that such items are included under the rubric of "attorneys fees" and not "costs" so that such expenses will be assessed against a plaintiff only under the standard set forth in Christiansburg Garment Co. v. Equal Employment Opportunity Commission, 434 U.S. 412 (1978). (Judiciary report at 73.)

REGULATION

§36.506 Alternative means of dispute resolution.

Where appropriate and to the extent authorized by law, the use of alternative means of dispute resolution, including settlement negotiations, conciliation, facilitation, mediation, factfinding, minitrials, and arbitration, is encouraged to resolve disputes arising under the Act and this part.

ANALYSIS

Section 36.506 restates section 513 of the Act, which encourages use of alternative means of dispute resolution.

REGULATION

§36.507 Effect of unavailability of technical assistance.

A public accommodation or other private entity shall not be excused from compliance with the requirements of this part because of any failure to receive technical assistance, including any failure in the development or dissemination of any technical assistance manual authorized by the Act.

ANALYSIS

Section 36.507 explains that, as provided in section 506(e) of the Act, a public accommodation or other private entity is not excused from compliance with the requirements of this part because of any failure to receive technical assistance.

REGULATION

§36.508 Effective date.

(a) General. Except as otherwise provided in this section and in this part, this part shall become effective on January 26, 1992.

(b) Civil actions. Except for any civil action brought for a violation of section 303 of the Act, no civil action shall be brought for any act or omission described in section 302 of the Act that occurs--

(1) Before July 26, 1992, against businesses with 25 or fewer employees and gross receipts of $1,000,000 or less.

(2) Before January 26, 1993, against businesses with 10 or fewer employees and gross receipts of $500,000 or less.

(c) Transportation services provided by public accommodations. Newly purchased or leased vehicles required to be accessible by §36.310 must be readily accessible to and usable by individuals with disabilities, including individuals who use wheelchairs, if the solicitation for the vehicle is made after August 25, 1990.

§§36.509-35.600 [Reserved]

ANALYSIS

Section 36.508 Effective Date.

In general, title III is effective 18 months after enactment of the Americans with Disabilities Act, i.e., January 26, 1992. However, there are several exceptions to this general rule contained throughout title III. Section 36.508 sets forth all of these exceptions in one place.

Paragraph (b) contains the rule on civil actions. It states that, except with respect to new construction and alterations, no civil action shall be brought for a violation of this part that occurs before July 26, 1992, against businesses with 25 or fewer employees and gross receipts of $1,000,000 or less; and before January 26, 1993, against businesses with 10 or fewer employees and gross receipts of $500,000 or less. In determining what constitutes gross receipts, it is appropriate to exclude amounts collected for sales taxes.

Paragraph (c) concerns transportation services provided by public accommodations not primarily engaged in the business of transporting people. The 18-month effective date applies to all of the transportation provisions except those requiring newly purchased or leased vehicles to be accessible. Vehicles subject to that requirement must be accessible to and usable by individuals with disabilities if the solicitation for the vehicle is made on or after August 26, 1990.

REGULATION

Subpart F--Certification of State Laws or Local Building Codes

ANALYSIS

Subpart F -- Certification of State Laws or Local Building Codes

Subpart F establishes procedures to implement section 308(b)(1)(A)(ii) of the Act, which provides that, on the application of a State or local government, the Attorney General may certify that a State law or local building code or similar ordinance meets or exceeds the minimum accessibility requirements of the Act. In enforcement proceedings, this certification will constitute rebuttable evidence that the law or code meets or exceeds the ADA's requirements.

Three significant changes, further explained below, were made from the proposed subpart, in response to comments. First, the State or local jurisdiction is required to hold a public hearing on its proposed request for certification and to submit to the Department, as part of the information and materials in support of a request for certification, a transcript of the hearing. Second, the time allowed for interested persons and organizations to comment on the request filed with the Department (§36.605(a)(1)) has been changed from 30 to 60 days. Finally, a new §36.608, Guidance concerning model codes, has been added.

§36.601 Definitions.

Assistant Attorney General means the Assistant Attorney General for Civil Rights or his or her designee.

Certification of equivalency means a final certification that a code meets or exceeds the minimum requirements of title III of the Act for accessibility and usability of facilities covered by that title.

Code means a State law or local building code or similar ordinance, or part thereof, that establishes accessibility requirements.

Model code means a nationally recognized docu-

Section 36.601 establishes the definitions to be used for purposes of this subpart. Two of the definitions have been modified, and a definition of "model code" has been added. First, in response to a comment, a reference to a code "or part thereof" has been added to the definition of "code." The purpose of this addition is to clarify that an entire code need not be submitted if only part of it is relevant to accessibility, or if the jurisdiction seeks certification of only some of the portions that concern accessibility. The Department does not intend to encourage "piecemeal" requests for certification by a single jurisdiction. In fact, the Department expects that in some cases, rather than certifying portions of a particular code and refusing to certify others, it may notify a submitting jurisdiction of deficiencies and encourage a reapplication that cures those deficiencies, so that the entire code can be certified eventually. Second, the definition of "submitting official" has been modified. The proposed rule defined the submitting official to be the State or local official who has principal responsibility for administration of a code. Commenters pointed out that in some cases more than one code within the same jurisdiction is relevant for purposes of certification. It was also suggested that the Department allow a State to submit a single application on behalf of the State,

REGULATION

ment developed by a private entity for use by State or local jurisdictions in developing codes as defined in this section. A model code is intended for incorporation by reference or adoption in whole or in part, with or without amendment, by State or local jurisdictions.

Preliminary determination of equivalency means a preliminary determination that a code appears to meet or exceed the minimum requirements of title III of the Act for accessibility and usability of facilities covered by that title.

Submitting official means the State or local official who --

(1) Has principal responsibility for administration of a code, or is authorized to submit a code on behalf of a jurisdiction; and

(2) Files a request for certification under this subpart.

ANALYSIS

as well as on behalf of any local jurisdictions required to follow the State accessibility requirements. Consistent with these comments, the Department has added to the definition language clarifying that the official can be one authorized to submit a code on behalf of a jurisdiction.

A definition of "model code" has been added in light of new §36.608.

Most commenters generally approved of the proposed certification process. Some approved of what they saw as the Department's attempt to bring State and local codes into alignment with the ADA. A State agency said that this section will be the backbone of the intergovernmental cooperation essential if the accessibility provisions of the ADA are to be effective.

Some comments disapproved of the proposed process as time consuming and laborious for the Department, although some of these comments pointed out that, if the Attorney General certified model codes on which State and local codes are based, many perceived problems would be alleviated. (This point is further addressed by new §36.608.)

Many of the comments received from business organizations, as well as those from some individuals and disability rights groups, addressed the relationship of the ADA requirements and their enforcement, to existing State and local codes and code enforcement systems. These commenters urged the Department to use existing code-making bodies for interpretations of the ADA, and to actively participate in the integration of the ADA into the text of the national model codes that are adopted by State and local enforcement agencies. These issues are discussed in preamble section 36.406 under General comments.

Many commenters urged the Department to evaluate or certify the entire code enforcement system (including any process for hearing appeals from builders of denials by the building code official of requests for variances, waivers, or modifications). Some urged that certification not be allowed in jurisdictions where waivers can be granted, unless there is a clearly identified decision-making process, with written rulings and notice to affected parties of any waiver or modification request. One commenter urged establishment of a dispute resolution mechanism, providing for interpretation

REGULATION

§36.602 General rule.

On the application of a State or local government, the Assistant Attorney General may certify that a code meets or exceeds the minimum requirements of the Act for the accessibility and usability of places of public accommodation and commercial facilities under this part by issuing a certification of equivalency. At any enforcement proceeding under title III of the Act, such certification shall be rebuttable evidence that such State law or local ordinance does meet or exceed the minimum requirements of title III.

ANALYSIS

(usually through a building official) and an administrative appeals mechanism (generally called Boards of Appeal, Boards of Construction Appeals, or Boards of Review), before certification could be granted.

The Department thoroughly considered these proposals but has declined to provide for certification of processes of enforcement or administration of State and local codes. The statute clearly authorizes the Department to certify the codes themselves for equivalency with the statute; it would be ill-advised for the Department at this point to inquire beyond the face of the code and written interpretations of it. It would be inappropriate to require those jurisdictions that grant waivers or modifications to establish certain procedures before they can apply for certification, or to insist that no deviations can be permitted. In fact, the Department expects that many jurisdictions will allow slight variations from a particular code, consistent with ADAAG itself. ADAAG includes in §2.2 a statement allowing departures from particular requirements where substantially equivalent or greater access and usability is provided. Several sections specifically allow for alternative methods providing equivalent facilitation and, in some cases, provide examples. (See, e.g., §4.31.9, Text Telephones; §7.2(2)(iii), Sales and Service Counters.) Section 4.1.6 includes less stringent requirements that are permitted in alterations, in certain circumstances.

However, in an attempt to ensure that it does not certify a code that in practice has been or will be applied in a manner that defeats its equivalency with the ADA, the Department will require that the submitting official include, with the application for certification, any relevant manuals, guides, or any other interpretive information issued that pertain to the code. (§36.603(c)(1).) The requirement that this information be provided is in addition to the NPRM's requirement that the official provide any pertinent formal opinions of the State Attorney General or the chief legal officer of the jurisdiction.

REGULATION

§36.603 Filing a request for certification.

(a) A submitting official may file a request for certification of a code under this subpart.

(b) Before filing a request for certification of a code, the submitting official shall ensure that --

(1) Adequate public notice of intention to file a request for certification, notice of a hearing, and notice of the location at which the request and materials can be inspected is published within the relevant jurisdiction;

(2) Copies of the proposed request and supporting materials are made available for public examination and copying at the office of the State or local agency charged with administration and enforcement of the code; and

(3) The local or State jurisdiction holds a public hearing on the record, in the State or locality, at which the public is invited to comment on the proposed request for certification.

(c) The submitting official shall include the following materials and information in support of the request:

(1) The text of the

ANALYSIS

The first step in the certification process is a request for certification, filed by a "submitting official" (§36.603). The Department will not accept requests for certification until after January 26, 1992, the effective date of this part. The Department received numerous comments from individuals and organizations representing a variety of interests, urging that the hearing required to be held by the Assistant Attorney General in Washington, D.C., after a preliminary determination of equivalency (§36.605(a)(2)), be held within the State or locality requesting certification, in order to facilitate greater participation by all interested parties. While the Department has not modified the requirement that it hold a hearing in Washington, it has added a new subparagraph 36.603(b)(3) requiring a hearing within the State or locality before a request for certification is filed. The hearing must be held after adequate notice to the public and must be on the record; a transcript must be provided with the request for certification. This procedure will insure input from the public at the State or local level and will also insure a Washington, D.C., hearing as mentioned in the legislative history.

The request for certification, along with supporting documents (§36.603(c)), must be filed in duplicate with the office of the Assistant Attorney General for Civil Rights. The Assistant Attorney General may request further information. The request and supporting materials will be available for public examination at the office of the Assistant Attorney General and at the office of the State or local agency charged with administration and enforcement of the code. The submitting official must publish public notice of the request for certification.

REGULATION

ANALYSIS

jurisdiction's code; any standard, regulation, code, or other relevant document incorporated by reference or otherwise referenced in the code; the law creating and empowering the agency; any relevant manuals, guides, or any other interpretive information issued that pertain to the code; and any formal opinions of the State Attorney General or the chief legal officer of the jurisdiction that pertain to the code;

(2) Any model code or statute on which the pertinent code is based, and an explanation of any differences between the model and the pertinent code;

(3) A transcript of the public hearing required by paragraph (b)(3) of this section; and

(4) Any additional information that the submitting official may wish to be considered.

(d) The submitting official shall file the original and one copy of the request and of supporting materials with the Assistant Attorney General. The submitting official shall clearly label the request as a "request for certification" of a code. A copy of the request and supporting materials will be available for public examination and copying at the

REGULATION

offices of the Assistant Attorney General in Washington, D.C. The submitting official shall ensure that copies of the request and supporting materials are available for public examination and copying at the office of the State or local agency charged with administration and enforcement of the code. The submitting official shall ensure that adequate public notice of the request for certification and of the location at which the request and materials can be inspected is published within the relevant jurisdiction.

(e) Upon receipt of a request for certification, the Assistant Attorney General may request further information that he or she considers relevant to the determinations required to be made under this subpart.

ANALYSIS

REGULATION

§36.604 Preliminary determination.

After consultation with the Architectural and Transportation Barriers Compliance Board, the Assistant Attorney General shall make a preliminary determination of equivalency or a preliminary determination to deny certification.

ANALYSIS

Next, under §36.604, the Assistant Attorney General's office will consult with the ATBCB and make a <u>preliminary</u> determination to either (1) find that the code is equivalent (make a "preliminary determination of equivalency") or (2) deny certification. The next step depends on which of these preliminary determinations is made.

REGULATION

§36.605 Procedure following preliminary determination of equivalency.

(a) If the Assistant Attorney General makes a preliminary determination of equivalency under §36.604, he or she shall inform the submitting official, in writing, of that preliminary determination. The Assistant Attorney General shall also -

(1) Publish a notice in the Federal Register that advises the public of the preliminary determination of equivalency with respect to the particular code, and invite interested persons and organizations, including individuals with disabilities, during a period of at least 60 days following publication of the notice, to file written comments relevant to whether a final certification of equivalency should be issued;

(2) After considering the information received in response to the notice described in paragraph (a) of this section, and after publishing a separate notice in the Federal Register, hold an informal hearing in Washington, D.C., at which interested persons, including individuals with disabilities, are provided an opportunity to express their views with respect to the preliminary determination of equivalency; and

ANALYSIS

If the preliminary determination is to find equivalency, the Assistant Attorney General, under §36.605, will inform the submitting official in writing of the preliminary determination and publish a notice in the Federal Register informing the public of the preliminary determination and inviting comment for 60 days. (This time period has been increased from 30 days in light of public comment pointing out the need for more time within which to evaluate the code.) After considering the information received in response to the comments, the Department will hold an informal hearing in Washington. This hearing will not be subject to the formal requirements of the Administrative Procedure Act. In fact, this requirement could be satisfied by a meeting with interested parties. After the hearing, the Assistant Attorney General's office will consult again with the ATBCB and make a final determination of equivalency or a final determination to deny the request for certification, with a notice of the determination published in the Federal Register.

REGULATION

(b) The Assistant Attorney General, after consultation with the Architectural and Transportation Barriers Compliance Board, and consideration of the materials and information submitted pursuant to this section and §36.603, shall issue either a certification of equivalency or a final determination to deny the request for certification. He or she shall publish notice of the certification of equivalency or denial of certification in the Federal Register.

ANALYSIS

REGULATION

§36.606 Procedure following preliminary denial of certification.

(a) If the Assistant Attorney General makes a preliminary determination to deny certification of a code under §36.604, he or she shall notify the submitting official of the determination. The notification may include specification of the manner in which the code could be amended in order to qualify for certification.

(b) The Assistant Attorney General shall allow the submitting official not less than 15 days to submit data, views, and arguments in opposition to the preliminary determination to deny certification. If the submitting official does not submit materials, the Assistant Attorney General shall not be required to take any further action. If the submitting official submits materials, the Assistant Attorney General shall evaluate those materials and any other relevant information. After evaluation of any newly submitted materials, the Assistant Attorney General shall make either a final denial of certification or a preliminary determination of equivalency.

ANALYSIS

If the preliminary determination is to deny certification, there will be no hearing (§36.606). The Department will notify the submitting official of the preliminary determination, and may specify how the code could be modified in order to receive a preliminary determination of equivalency. The Department will allow at least 15 days for the submitting official to submit relevant material in opposition to the preliminary denial. If none is received, no further action will be taken. If more information is received, the Department will consider it and make either a final decision to deny certification or a preliminary determination of equivalency. If at that stage the Assistant Attorney General makes a preliminary determination of equivalency, the hearing procedures set out in §36.605 will be followed.

REGULATION

§36.607 Effect of certification.

(a) (1) A certification shall be considered a certification of equivalency only with respect to those features or elements that are both covered by the certified code and addressed by the standards against which equivalency is measured.

(2) For example, if certain equipment is not covered by the code, the determination of equivalency cannot be used as evidence with respect to the question of whether equipment in a building built according to the code satisfies the Act's requirements with respect to such equipment. By the same token, certification would not be relevant to construction of a facility for children, if the regulations against which equivalency is measured do not address children's facilities.

(b) A certification of equivalency is effective only with respect to the particular edition of the code for which certification is granted. Any amendments or other changes to the code after the date of the certified edition are not considered part of the certification.

(c) A submitting official may reapply for certification of amendments or other changes to a code that has already received certification.

ANALYSIS

Section 36.607 addresses the effect of certification. First, certification will only be effective concerning those features or elements that are both (1) covered by the certified code and (2) addressed by the regulations against which they are being certified. For example, if children's facilities are not addressed by the Department's standards, and the building in question is a private elementary school, certification will not be effective for those features of the building to be used by children. And if the Department's regulations addressed equipment but the local code did not, a building's equipment would not be covered by the certification.

In addition, certification will be effective only for the particular edition of the code that is certified. Amendments will not automatically be considered certified, and a submitting official will need to reapply for certification of the changed or additional provisions.

Certification will not be effective in those situations where a State or local building code official allows a facility to be constructed or altered in a manner that does not follow the technical or scoping provisions of the certified code. Thus, if an official either waives an accessible element or feature or allows a change that does not provide equivalent facilitation, the fact that the Department has certified the code itself will not stand as evidence that the facility has been constructed or altered in accordance with the minimum accessibility requirements of the ADA. The Department's certification of a code is effective only with respect to the standards in the code; it is not to be interpreted to apply to a State or local government's application of the code. The fact that the Department has certified a code with provisions concerning waivers, variances, or equivalent facilitation shall not be interpreted as an endorsement of actions taken pursuant to those provisions.

REGULATION

36.608 Guidance concerning model codes.

Upon application by an authorized representative of a private entity responsible for developing a model code, the Assistant Attorney General may review the relevant model code and issue guidance concerning whether and in what respects the model code is consistent with the minimum requirements of the Act for the accessibility and usability of places of public accommodation and commercial facilities under this part.

§§36.609-36.999 [Reserved]

ANALYSIS

The final rule includes a new §36.608 concerning model codes. It was drafted in response to concerns raised by numerous commenters, many of which have been discussed under General comments (§36.406). It is intended to assist in alleviating the difficulties posed by attempting to certify possibly tens of thousands of codes. It is included in recognition of the fact that many codes are based on, or incorporate, model or consensus standards developed by nationally recognized organizations (e.g., the American National Standards Institute (ANSI); Building Officials and Code Administrators (BOCA) International; Council of American Building Officials (CABO) and its Board for the Coordination of Model Codes (BCMC); Southern Building Code Congress International (SBCCI)). While the Department will not certify or "precertify" model codes, as urged by some commenters, it does wish to encourage the continued viability of the consensus and model code process consistent with the purposes of the ADA.

The new section therefore allows an authorized representative of a private entity responsible for developing a model code to apply to the Assistant Attorney General for review of the code. The review process will be informal and will not be subject to the procedures of §§36.602 through 36.607. The result of the review will take the form of guidance from the Assistant Attorney General as to whether and in what respects the model code is consistent with the ADA's requirements. The guidance will not be binding on any entity or on the Department; it will assist in evaluations of individual State or local codes and may serve as a basis for establishing priorities for consideration of individual codes. The Department anticipates that this approach will foster further cooperation among various government levels, the private entities developing standards, and individuals with disabilities.

RESOURCE LIST

Resource List

This Resource List contains separate sections for government and non-governmental organizations.

I. Easy Reference Guide for Government Agencies

The following is intended as an Easy Reference Guide to assist the reader in identifying the relevant government agency for several areas of interest:

For questions pertaining to:	Consult these government agencies:
employment	Equal Employment Opportunity Commission (R,TA,E) President's Committee on Employment of People with Disabilities (TA) Small Business Administration (TA) National Institute on Disability and Rehabilitation Research (TA)
public accommodations	Department of Justice (R,TA,E)
public services	Department of Justice (R,TA,E)
rehabilitation and independent living services	Department of Education (P)
tax law provisions	Department of Treasury (TA)
accessibility	Architectural and Transportation Barriers Compliance Board (G,TA)
work incentive	Social Security Administration (P)

Key
R: issued regulations
TA: provides technical assistance on how to comply
E: has enforcement authority
P: administers programs relevant to successful implementation of the Act
G: issues guidelines

II. Government Agencies

Civil Rights Division
Office on the Americans with Disabilities Act
U.S. Department of Justice
P.O. Box 66118
Washington, D.C. 20035-6118
(202) 514-0301 (voice)
(202) 514-0383 (TDD)

Regulations, technical assistance, and enforcement for titles II (public services) and III (public accommodations).

Equal Employment Opportunity Commission
1801 L Street NW
Washington, D.C. 20507
800-669-EEOC (voice)
800-800-3302 (TDD)

Regulations, technical assistance, and enforcement for title I (employment).

Department of Transportation
400 Seventh Street SW
Room 10424
Washington, D.C. 20590
(202) 366-9305
(202) 755-7687 (TDD)

Regulations, technical assistance, and enforcement for title II and III transportation provisions.

Architectural and Transportation Barriers Compliance Board
1111 18th Street NW
Suite 501
Washington, D.C. 20036
800-USA-ABLE
800-USA-ABLE (TDD)

Americans with Disabilities Act Accessibility Guidelines (ADAAG) required under title III (public accommodations) and technical assistance on architectural, transportation, and communications accessibility issues.

Federal Communications Commission
1919 M Street NW
Washington, D.C. 20554
(202) 632-7260 (voice)
(202) 632-6999 (TDD)

Regulations, technical assistance and enforcement for title IV (communications).

The following agencies implement programs relating to, or are responsible for provisions pertaining to, the implementation of titles I, II, and III of the ADA.

Internal Revenue Service
Office of the Chief Counsel
P.O. Box 7604
Ben Franklin Station
Washington, D.C. 20044
(202) 566-3292 (voice only)

The Internal Revenue Service provides technical assistance on various tax code provisions designed to encourage businesses to hire people with disabilities. See Appendix G for an explanation of these provisions.

_____

National Council on Disability
800 Independence Avenue SW
Suite 814
Washington, D.C. 20591
(202) 267-3846 (voice)
(202) 267-3232 (TDD)

Charged by statute with responsibility for developing recommendations for federal disability policy and overseeing the research priorities for the National Institute on Disability and Rehabilitation Research.

_____

Small Business Administration
Office of Advocacy
Office of Economic Research
409 Third Street SW
Fifth Floor
Washington, D.C. 20416
(202) 205-6530 (voice only)

_____

President's Committee on Employment of People with Disabilities
1331 F Street NW
Third Floor
Washington, D.C. 20004
(202) 376-6200 (voice)
(202) 376-6205 (TDD)

Provides technical assistance on employment provisions of ADA directly and through its Governors' Committees on Employment of People with Disabilities.

_____

Rehabilitation Services Administration
U.S. Department of Education
Mary E. Switzer Building
Room 3028
330 C Street SW
Washington, D.C. 20202-2531
(202) 732-1282 (voice and TDD)

Administers the principal Federal service programs designed to rehabilitate, employ, and promote the independent living of people with disabilities. See the description of Rehabilitation Act of 1973 programs contained in Appendix item L, Related Federal Disability Laws, for further information about these programs.

National Institute on Disability and Rehabilitation Research
U.S. Department of Education
400 Maryland Avenue SW
Washington, D.C. 20202-2572
(202) 732-1134 (voice)
(202) 732-5079 (TDD)

Administers the principal Federal disability research programs, the Technology Related Assistance for Individuals with Disabilities Act, and ADA technical assistance centers. See the description of Rehabilitation Act of 1973 programs contained in Appendix item L, Related Federal Disability Laws, for further information about these programs.

Public Health Service
U.S. Department of Health and Human Services
Centers for Disease Control
Mail Stop C09
1600 Clifton Road NE
Atlanta, Georgia 30333
(404) 639-2237 (voice only)

The ADA in certain circumstances permits the reassignment of individuals with certain contagious diseases specified by the Public Health Service from food handling jobs to another job if the risk posed by the individual may not be eliminated by a reasonable accommodation. The Public Health service issued its proposed list of such diseases in May 1991, with publication of the final list expected in the autumn of 1991.

Administration on Developmental Disabilities
U.S. Department of Health and Human Services
Program Operations Division
200 Independence Avenue SW
Room 329D
Washington, D.C. 20201
(202) 245-2897 (voice)
(202) 245-2890 (TDD)

ADD administers the Developmental Disabilities Act, designed to promote community integration and maximum independence for people with developmental disabilities. ADD administers the Protection and Advocacy Program for Developmentally Disabled individuals. See the description of Developmental Disabilities Assistance and Bill of Rights Act programs contained in Appendix item L, Related Federal Disability Laws, for further information on the Protection and Advocacy system.

Social Security Administration
Office of Disability
Room 545
Altimeyer Building
6401 Security Boulevard
Baltimore, Maryland 21235
(301) 965-3424 (voice only)

SSA administers programs that provide incentives for individuals receiving Social Security Disability Insurance (SSDI) or SSI (Supplemental Security Income) to obtain gainful employment.

Office of Federal Contract Compliance Programs
U.S. Department of Labor
200 Constitution Ave. NW
Washington, D.C. 20210
(202) 523-9501 (voice only)

Enforcement agency for section 503 of the Rehabilitation Act, which, unlike the ADA, includes an affirmative action requirement affecting certain Federal contractors.

National Library Services for the Blind and Physically Handicapped
1291 Taylor Street NW
Washington, D.C. 20542
(202) 707-5100 (voice)
(202) 707-0744 (TDD)

A free national library program that lends braille and cassette tapes versions of up to 59,000 unique books and magazines that are typically found in public libraries to individuals with visual disabilities. Over 20 million books and magazines were circulated to a readership of 695,350 in 1990.

III. Non-Government Organizations

What follows is a partial listing of organizations offering assistance in implementing the employment, public services, and public accommodations provisions of the ADA.

Virtually all of the organizations listed below provide information and referral services on ADA matters. Many publish newsletters and/or journals and hold meetings at least annually at which ADA implementation issues have been, and are likely to continue to be, a popular subject for panels, speakers, and workshops to address. Some of these organizations also hold periodic seminars on the ADA that are occasionally open to non-members as well as members. Specific information on these activities, as well as membership information, may be obtained from the organizations.

Many of these organizations are in the process of developing additional ADA-related services and products following the publication by the Equal Employment Opportunity Commission and the Department of Justice of final regulations for titles I, II, and III of the ADA on July 26, 1991. An effort was made to obtain the most current information available from these organizations concerning their ADA-related activities as of the September, 1991, publication deadline for this handbook. Wherever possible, mention of planned activities that may be of interest to the reader has been made in the annotations.

Inclusion in the list below does not constitute an endorsement by the Equal Employment Opportunity Commission or the Department of Justice of these organizations or of any legal interpretations of the Americans with Disabilities Act offered by them.

1. Disability

This section is subdivided into cross-disability and disability-specific listings. Cross-disability organizations provide services to individuals with different types of disabilities. For more information you may contact either the Equal Employment Opportunity Commission or the Department of Justice (see Government listings above).

a. Cross-Disability

Disability Rights Education and Defense Fund
2212 Sixth Street
Berkeley, California 94710
(510) 644-2555 (voice)
(510) 644-2629 (TDD)
(800) 466-4232 (voice and TDD: operational beginning December 1, 1991)

Specializes in training and technical assistance for people with disabilities and their representatives, State and local government units, businesses and trade associations; also public policy advocacy and litigation.

Independent Living Research Utilization
2323 South Shephard Street
Suite 1000
Houston, Texas 77019
(713) 520-0232 (voice)
(713) 520-5136 (TDD)

Provides information and technical assistance pertaining to independent living and disability rights; will provide information on how to contact the community-based independent living center closest to the inquirer.

National Council on Independent Living
Troy Atrium
Fourth Street and Broadway
Troy, N.Y. 12180
(518) 274-1979 (voice)
(518) 274-0701 (TDD)

Umbrella organization representing community based independent living centers. Will provide referral information on services offered by centers, and will locate the center closest to the inquirer. See also Independent Living Research Utilization entry.

National Organization on Disability
910 16th Street NW
Suite 600
Washington, D.C. 20006
(202) 293-5960 (voice)
(202) 293-5968 (TDD)

Issued fact sheet on the ADA to its 3,000 Communities in Action, consisting primarily of mayors' offices on disability policy, who are pledged to bring about changes promoting the full integration of people with disabilities into their communities; offers a 10 minute video narrated by Charles Kuralt, "Community Partners at Work," available only to its affiliated Communities in Action for community showings; offers to any local organization camera-ready copies of public service announcements promoting changes consistent with the goals of the ADA.

World Institute on Disability
510 16th Street
Suite 100
Oakland, California 94612
(415) 763-4100 (voice and TDD)

Cross-disability research, training and policy development center; involved in assisting businesses interested in marketing products and ideas to the 43 million individuals with disabilities in the United States.

b. Disability-Specific

Alexander Graham Bell Association for the Deaf, Inc.
3417 Volta Place NW
Washington, D.C. 20007
(202) 337-5220 (voice and TDD)

Information and referral; planned ADA brochure for fall 1991.

American Amputee Foundation
P.O. Box 250218
Hillcrest Station
Little Rock, Arkansas 72225
(501) 666-2523 (voice only)

Self-help information and referral network offering technical assistance, information on assistive devices, videos, some financial assistance, and publications, including a comprehensive national resource directory.

American Civil Liberties Union AIDS Project
132 West 43rd Street
New York, New York 10036
(212) 944-9800 (voice only)

Distributes brochure on how the ADA applies to people with AIDS.

American Council of the Blind
1115 15th Street NW
Suite 720
Washington, D.C. 20005
(202) 467-5081 (voice only)
(800) 424-8666 (Monday through Friday 3-5:30 EST only)

Advocacy, educational, and information sharing activities; provides access to several Special Interest affiliates, such as American Blind Lawyers Association, Guide Dog Users, Inc., and Council of Citizens with Low Vision, Intl.

American Foundation for the Blind
15 West 16th Street
New York, New York 10011
(212) 620-2000 (voice)
(212) 620-2158 (TDD)

Offers information on assistive technology; has a listing of jobs held by individuals who are blind indicating how adaptations were made in various employment situations; sells products, some unique and some designed by AFB; provides evaluations of assistive technology.

American Printing House for the Blind
1839 Frankfort Avenue
Louisville, Kentucky 40206-0085
(502) 895-2405 (voice only)

One of several braille publishers in the United States; also distributes materials in large print and audio recordings; distributes instructional aids, education computer software, and textbooks for children.

American Speech-Language-Hearing Association
10801 Rockville Pike
Rockville, Maryland 20852
(301) 897-5700 (voice and TDD)
(800) 638-8255 (consumer hotline number; voice and TDD)

Distributes technical information pieces; developing an ADA brochure; seminars available to non-members as well as members; consumer hotline number.

Association of Persons in Supported Employment
5001 W. Broad Street
Suite 34
Richmond, Virginia 23230
(804) 282-3655 (voice only)

Assists businesses interested in developing supported employment programs in obtaining necessary support services; current projects include a train the trainer Social Security Administration work incentive program; members include rehabilitation service personnel, consumers of supported employment services and their families.

The Association for Severely Handicapped Individuals
7010 Roosevelt Way, NE
Seattle, Washington 98115
(206) 523-8446 (voice)
(206) 524-6198 (TDD)

Epilepsy Foundation of America
4351 Garden City Drive
Landover, Maryland 20785
(301) 459-3700 (voice only)

Developing manual scheduled for publication in fall 1991 on the ADA as it applies to people with epilepsy.

Helen Keller Center for Deaf-Blind Youth and Adults
111 Middle Neck Road
Sands Point, New York 11050
(516) 944-8900 (voice and TDD)

The only rehabilitation facility in the United States devoted solely to the needs of individuals who are deaf-blind. Offers training for service providers; information and referral from its central and nine regional offices.

Learning Disabilities Association of America
4156 Library Road
Pittsburgh, Pennsylvania 15234
(412) 341-1515 (voice only)

Organization composed primarily of parents and professionals with 500 State and local chapters.

Legal Action Center
236 Massachusetts Avenue NE
Suite 510
Washington, D.C. 20002
(202) 544-5478 (voice only)

Provides information and technical assistance on the ADA as it affects individuals with current or past drug abuse or alcohol-related problems, and individuals with AIDS or who test positive for the HIV virus.

National Alliance for the Mentally Ill
2101 Wilson Blvd.
Suite 302
Arlington, Virginia 22201
(703) 524-7600 (voice only)

Represents primarily families; planning an ADA fact sheet/pamphlet; 1,046 State and local affiliates.

National Association for the Physically Handicapped
4230 Emerick Street
Saginaw, Michigan 48602
(517) 799-3060 (voice only)

National Association for Retarded Citizens
1522 K St. NW
Suite 516
Washington, D.C. 20005
(202) 785-3388 (voice)
(202) 785-3411 (TDD)

1300 State and local chapters representing 140,000 individuals with mental retardation and their families; offers technical assistance and fact sheet on the ADA.

National Association of the Deaf
814 Thayer Avenue
Silver Spring, Maryland 20910-4500
(301) 587-1788 (voice)
(301) 587-1789 (TDD)

Members include consumers, parents, and teachers; has 22,000 members and chapters in all 50 States; provides basic information and referral on deafness and accommodations for people who are deaf.

National Easter Seals Society
1350 New York Ave NW
Washington, D.C. 20005
(202) 347-3066 (voice)
(202) 347-7385 (TDD)

Some of Easter Seals' 175 affiliates are training businesses on the requirements for titles I (employment) and III (public accommodations) of ADA. Videotape "Nobody is Burning Wheelchairs"; provides technical assistance on public accommodations provisions.

National Federation of the Blind
1800 Johnson Street
Baltimore, Maryland 21230
(301) 659-9314 (voice only)

Some legal referrals and advocacy; publications on employment issues; computer bulletin board; technical assistance; sells aids and devices; large exhibit at annual conferences on available adaptive equipment.

National Head Injury Foundation
1140 Connecticut Avenue NW
Suite 812
Washington, D.C. 20036
(202) 296-6443 (voice only)
(800) 444-6443 (families, consumers; voice only)

Chapters or contacts in every State; referral information on medical and vocational rehabilitation and employment options.

National Information Center on Deafness
Gallaudet University
800 Florida Avenue NE
Washington, D.C. 20002
(202) 651-5051 (voice)
(202) 651-5052 (TDD)

Publications on workplace accommodations for people who are deaf; has list of manufacturers and up-to-date information on topics related to deafness and hearing loss; developing updated ADA materials on the employment of individuals who are deaf; will provide information on how to obtain the services of a qualified interpreter.

National Mental Health Consumers' Association
311 South Juniper Street
Room 902
Philadelphia, Pennsylvania 19107
(215) 735-2465 (voice only)
(215) 735-1273 (TDD)
(800) 688-4226 (voice only)

A clearinghouse providing technical assistance to assist in the development and successful operation of consumer operated self-help programs for people with mental illnesses; distributes information on the ADA to individuals and organizations.

National Organization for Rare Disorders
Fairwood Professional Building
P.O. Box 8923
New Fairfield, Connecticut 06812-1783
(800) 999-6673 (voice only)
(203) 746-6518 (voice only)

Umbrella group for associations representing individuals with rare disorders, defined as those with an incidence of less than 200,000 in the population. There are about 5,000 such known disorders affecting an estimated 20 million Americans. Serves as a clearinghouse offering information and resources on support groups, research on the disorders, and how to seek or keep employment, among other issues.

National Spinal Cord Injury Association
600 West Cummings Park
Suite 2000
Woburn, Massachusetts 01801
(617) 935-2722 (voice only)

Serves consumers, families, and professionals; provides information and referral on rehabilitation and employment options.

Paralyzed Veterans of America
801 18th Street NW
Washington, D.C. 20006
(202) 872-1300 (voice only)

Guidebook on access to hotels and motels used by American Institute of Architects (to be revised in accordance with ADA); disseminates information about tax benefits for businesses accommodating consumers and employees with disabilities; promotes access to outdoors and wilderness areas.

Rochester Institute of Technology
National Center on Employment for the Deaf
Lyndon Baines Johnson Building
P.O. Box 9887
Rochester, New York 14623-0887
(716) 475-6219 (voice)
(716) 475-6205 (TDD)

Serves as a job placement office for deaf individuals, primarily graduates of the National Technical Institute for the Deaf; posts job listings from employers from all over the country; provides information on companies interested in hiring individuals with deafness or hearing loss; assists in updating of resumes; referral information.

Self-Help for Hard of Hearing People
7800 Wisconsin Avenue NW
Bethesda, Maryland 20814
(301) 657-2248 (voice)
(301) 657-2249 (TDD)

Serves consumers and professionals; provides technical assistance to hospitals on meeting the needs of individuals with hearing impairments; videotape and information packet on employing people with hearing loss.

Telecommunications for the Deaf, Inc.
8719 Colesville Road
Suite 300
Silver Spring, Maryland 20910
(301) 589-3786 (voice)
(301) 589-3006 (TDD)

Publishes and sells a nationwide Telecommunications Device for the Deaf (TDD) directory; information on visually-based accommodations for deaf and hearing impaired people, such as alarms, decoders, and TDD's. Sells decoders and a videotape on how to use TDD's.

United Cerebral Palsy
1522 K Street NW
Suite 1112
Washington, D.C. 20005
(202) 842-1266 (voice only)

Conducts, as part of a joint venture called the National Center for Access Unlimited, various training and technical assistance activities for businesses; published monograph on accessible design; plans to publish additional monograph on personnel practices and a consumer-oriented rights manual by the spring of 1992.

2. Disability-Business-Rehabilitation

The Dole Foundation for Employment of People with Disabilities
1819 H Street NW
Suite 850
Washington, D.C. 20006
(202) 457-0318 (voice and TDD)

A public foundation that funds employment-related projects including technical assistance and training projects; part of a partnership of corporations and philanthropic organizations committed to funding training, technical assistance, and educational projects promoting the integration of people with disabilities into society.

Goodwill Industries of America
9200 Wisconsin Avenue
Bethesda, Maryland 20814
(301) 530-6500 (voice only)

Represents 179 vocational rehabilitation facilities of many types; brochure on ADA; conducts seminars and publications for members.

Industry-Labor Council of National Center for Disability Services
201 I.U. Willets Road
Albertson, New York 11507
(516) 747-6323 (voice)
(516) 747-5355 (TDD)

Membership organization serving 152 mostly Fortune 500 corporations and labor unions; conducts training seminars for members and non-members on multiple aspects of employing people with disabilities; information hotline service; assists in recruiting efforts by businesses; audiovisual library.

Inter-National Association of Business, Industry and Rehabilitation
P.O. Box 15242
Washington, D.C. 20003
(202) 543-6353 (voice only)

Represents businesses, labor unions and job placement service organizations sponsoring federally funded Projects with Industry programs. These organizations are public-private partnerships that competitively employ people with disabilities. (See the description of Rehabilitation Act of 1973 programs contained in Appendix item L, Related Federal Disability Laws, for additional information about this program.) Also represents similar programs which are not federally funded. Provides technical assistance, referral information.

Mainstream, Inc.
Suite 1010
1030 15th Street NW
Washington, D.C. 20005
(202) 898-1400 (voice and TDD)

Customized training, mostly for businesses, associations and service providers on multiple aspects of employing people with disabilities. Produces kit of ADA-related materials; placement programs in Dallas and Washington, D.C.

National Association of Rehabilitation Facilities
1910 Association Drive
Suite 200
Reston, Virginia 22091-1502
(703) 648-9300 (voice only)

Training for members, which include providers of rehabilitation services; developing revised manual for primarily employers and question and answer materials on ADA. NARF has a toll free number that individuals can call to obtain referral information on the availability of public and private medical and vocational rehabilitation options. That number is (800) 368-3513. Information about model rehabilitation programs for service providers is also available at that number.

National Association of Rehabilitation Facilities in the Private Sector
P.O. Box 697
Brookline, Massachusetts 02146
(617) 566-4432 (voice only)

Serves approximately 3,000 individual and corporate members, which include private sector rehabilitation professionals and facilities in diverse fields. Will send, for a nominal fee, a printout of members in inquirer's locale. Offers for $35 its directory of members, organized geographically and by specialty area.

National Rehabilitation Association
633 South Washington Street
Alexandria, Virginia 22314
(703) 836-0850 (voice)
(703) 836-0852 (TDD)

Specializes in visiting hotels and providing information on how to make them accessible; 62 chapters with 17,000 members including people with disabilities, families, service providers, and businesses.

Rehabilitation Services Administration
U.S. Department of Education
Mary E. Switzer Building
Room 3028
330 C Street SW
Washington, D.C. 20202
(202) 732-1282 (voice)
(202) 732-1330 (TDD)

Each State has one or more agencies that provide rehabilitation services to individuals with disabilities. RSA will provide information on how to contact the agency in your State and provide additional information on other federally funded community-based employment and independent living related services and programs, including the Independent Living program, Projects with Industry, and supported employment programs.

3. Business

U.S. Chamber of Commerce
Labor and Human Resources Department
1615 H St. NW
Washington, D.C. 20062
(202) 463-5502 (voice only)

Published booklet *What Businesses Must Know About the Americans with Disabilities Act.*

National Association of Wholesale Distributors
1725 K St. NW
Suite 700
Washington, D.C. 20006
(202) 872-0885 (voice only)

Federation of 114 national associations. Planning to publish information book on ADA as it applies to wholesale distributors by the end of 1991.

National Restaurant Association
1200 17th Street NW
Washington, D.C. 20036
(202) 331-5988 (general information) (voice only)
(202) 331-5985 (physical accessibility questions) (voice only)
(202) 331-5910 (other legal questions) (voice only)

Has an employment brochure; legal department takes technical assistance calls; 800 technical assistance number for members.

National Retail Federation
701 Pennsylvania Avenue
Suite 710
Washington, D.C. 20004

Umbrella group representing 20 national associations representing over 1 million establishments employing 16 million people. Conducts training seminars; planning an ADA compliance manual.

Society for Human Resources Management
606 North Washington Street
Alexandria, Virginia 22314
(703) 548-3440 (ask for Technical and Information Services unit) (voice only)

Serves human resources professionals, including EEO professionals.
Planning publication of overview of employment provisions in November, 1991.

4. Advocacy/Legal

Listing the following organizations does not constitute an endorsement by the Department of Justice or the Equal Employment Opportunity Commission of the legal interpretations of the Americans with Disabilities Act held by these groups. The Department of Justice and the Equal Employment Opportunity Commission believe that an accurate understanding of the ADA can prevent the filing of unnecessary and unfounded charges and strongly support efforts to resolve disputes arising under the ADA wherever possible through means other than the filing of charges or lawsuits.

a. Cross Disability

American Bar Association
Commission on Mental and Physical Disability Law
1800 M Street NW
Washington, D.C. 20036
(202) 331-2240 (voice)
(312) 988-5168 (TDD)

Clearinghouse answering legal inquiries on ADA for a fee; has on file *Mental and Physical Disability Law Reporter* for past fifteen years, which includes coverage of title V Rehabilitation Act cases; library available by appointment only; offers, through its ADA Project, training on legal and compliance issues for businesses, disability organizations, State and local government agencies, and law firms.

Disability Rights Education and Defense Fund
2212 Sixth Street
Berkeley, California 94710
(510) 644-2555 (voice)
(510) 644-2629 (TDD)
(800) 466-4232 (voice and TDD: operational beginning December 1, 1991)

Employment Law Center
1663 Mission Street
Suite 400
San Francisco, California 94103
(415) 864-8848 (voice only)

Engages in policy work and litigates selected employment law reform cases under State and federal disability law.

National Disability Action Center
1101 15th Street NW
Suite 1215
Washington, D.C. 20005
(202) 775-9231 (voice and TDD)

Public Interest Law Center of Philadelphia
125 South Ninth Street
Seventh Floor, Suite 700
Philadelphia, Pennsylvania 19107
(215) 627-7100 (voice only)

Western Law Center for the Handicapped
1441 West Olympic Boulevard
Los Angeles 90015
(213) 736-1031 (voice only)

b. Disability-Specific

American Civil Liberties Union AIDS Project
132 West 43rd Street
New York, New York 10036
(212) 944-9800 (voice only)

Legal Action Center
153 Waverly Place
New York, New York 10014
(212) 243-1313 (voice only)

Technical assistance and litigation for individuals with current or past drug abuse or alcohol problems, and individuals with AIDS or who test positive for the HIV virus.

National Association of Protection and Advocacy Systems
900 Second Street NE
Suite 211
Washington, D.C. 20002
(202) 408-9514 (voice)
(202) 408-9521 (TDD)

Represents federally funded Protection and Advocacy agencies. See the description of Developmental Disabilities Assistance and Bill of Rights Act programs contained in Appendix item L, Related Federal Disability Laws, for a description of this program.

National Center on Law and the Deaf
800 Florida Avenue NE
Room 326 Ely Center
Washington, D.C. 20002
(202) 651-5373 (voice and TDD)

National Mental Health Law Project
1101 15th Street NW
Suite 1212
Washington, D.C. 20005
(202) 467-5730 (voice)
(202) 467-4232 (TDD)

---

5. Information Databases on Disability

ABLEDATA
Newington Children's Hospital
181 East Cedar Street
Newington, Connecticut 06111
(800) 344-5405 (voice and TDD)
(203) 667-5405 (voice and TDD)

A national database providing information on 16,000 products for people with disabilities produced by 2,000 companies. Information/products focus on such areas as attendant/personal care, mobility, communications, and recreation. Printouts of up to 8 pages of product information are free of charge, with sliding scale for more extensive listings; open from 8-5 Eastern Standard Time, from Monday through Friday.

Mental Health Policy Resource Center
1730 Rhode Island Avenue NW
Suite 308
Washington, D.C. 20036
(202) 775-8826 (voice only)

Runs on-line database, available by subscription, containing documents on the ADA as it pertains to people with mental disabilities; publishing manuscript reviewing section 503 Rehabillitation Act case law ruling on reasonable accommodations for people with mental disabilities in autumn 1991; non-circulating library with ADA-related materials open to public by appointment .

National Rehabilitation Information Center (NARIC)
8455 Colesville Road
Suite 935
Silver Spring, Maryland 20910
(301) 588-9284 (voice and TDD)
(800) 346-2742 (voice and TDD)

A library and information center on disability and rehabilitation. Collects and disseminates the results of federally funded research projects. Collection includes commercially published books, journal articles, and audiovisual materials. Currently has more than 30,000 documents. NARIC has information specialists who will perform searches for the caller. Phone either of the numbers listed above between 8 A.M. and 6 P.M. EST Monday through Friday and ask to speak with an information specialist.

National Information Center for Children and Youth with Handicaps (NICHCY)
P.O. Box 1492
Washington, D.C. 20013
(703) 893-6061 (local, voice/TDD)
(800) 999-5599 (toll free, voice/TDD)

Information and referral service for people with disabilities, their families and professionals. Disseminates publications and information on self-help advocacy, ADA, and broad array of disability matters. Has particular expertise in matters of concern to children with disabilities and their parents.

6. Technology

ABLEDATA
Newington Children's Hospital
181 East Cedar Street
Newington, Connecticut 06111
(800) 344-5405 (voice and TDD)
(203) 667-5405 (voice and TDD)

See listing under category 5, Information Databases on Disability.

Apple Computer
Worldwide Disability Solutions Group
20525 Mariani Avenue
Cupertino, California 95014
(408) 974-7910 (voice only)

Program and resource referral source with extensive database on accommodations for people with disabilities produced by Apple and other companies; publishes consumer booklet, videotapes.

IBM National Support Center for Persons with Disabilities
P.O. Box 2150
Atlanta, Georgia 30301
(800) 426-2133 (voice and TDD)

Clearinghouse with extensive database on adaptive technology produced by IBM and other companies; publishes "resource guides", organized by disability (vision, mobility, hearing, speech); offers training program for people with disabilities in computer skills; offers discounts on computer systems.

Job Accommodation Network
West Virginia University
809 Allen Hall
P.O. Box 6123
Morgantown, West Virginia 26506-6123
(800) 526-7234 (U.S. other than West Virginia; voice or TDD)
(800) 526-4698 (West Virginia; voice and TDD)
(800) 526-2262 (Canada; voice and TDD)

Free service for those seeking information on how to accommodate particular functional limitations; has database with information on over 16,000 specific reasonable accommodations. An information specialist will assist the caller in obtaining relevant information. JAN provides information on accommodations that are not technology-based as well.

Rehabilitation Engineering Society of America
1101 Connecticut Avenue NW
Suite 700
Washington, D.C. 20036
(202) 857-1199 (voice only)

Clearinghouse of information on rehabilitation technology; provides technical assistance to States; membership includes rehabilitation technology specialists, manufacturers, and rehabilitation professionals; publishes *Assistive Technology Sourcebook*.

7. Accessibility and Job Accommodations

American National Standards Institute
11 West 42nd Street
13th Floor
New York, New York 10036
(212) 642-4900 (voice only)

Provides information concerning architectural standards to make buildings accessible to people with disabilities.

American Institute of Architects
Public Affairs Department
1735 New York Avenue NW
Washington, D.C. 20006
(202) 626-7461 (voice only)

Offers bibliographies on periodicals and books on barrier-free design and an information packet on how the ADA applies to architectural design.

Job Accommodation Network
West Virginia University
809 Allen Hall
P.O. Box 6123
Morgantown, West Virginia 26506-6123
(800) 526-7234 (U.S. other than West Virginia; voice or TDD)
(800) 526-4698 (West Virginia; voice or TDD)
(800) 526-2262 (Canada; voice or TDD)

See listing under category 6, Technology.

National Captioning Institute
5203 Leesburg Pike
Suite 1500
Falls Church, Virginia 22041
(703) 998-2400 (voice and TDD)

Develops, and is one of several distributors of, closed-captioning decoders; research on closed captioning and new technologies; distributes some decoders to needy individuals.

Registry of Interpreters for the Deaf
8719 Colesville Road
Suite 310
Silver Spring, Maryland 20910-3919
(301) 608-0050 (voice and TDD)

Will refer inquirer to interpreter service agencies in inquirer's locale; publishes annually updated directory of interpreters certified under RID's National Testing System. There are other certifications systems in use. For information on how to obtain the services of a qualified interpreter, contact the National Information Center on Deafness at (202) 651-5051 (voice) or (202) 651-5052 (TDD).

8. Alternative Dispute Resolution Information and Services

American Arbitration Association
140 West 51st Street
New York, New York 10020
(212) 484-4060 (voice only)

Provides information on mediation, arbitration, and other means of dispute resolution other than litigation. Will provide a list of "neutrals" (mediators or arbitrators with subject matter expertise) and refer the interested parties to one of its 35 local offices for scheduling of hearing and processing of the case.

Standing Committee on Dispute Resolution
American Bar Association
1800 M Street NW
Washington, DC 20036
(202) 331-2258 (voice only)

Publishes *Dispute Resolution Programs*, a directory listing "neutrals" (mediators or arbitrators with subject matter expertise) and self-identfied dispute resolution programs, every two years.

Appendix A

Public Law 101-336
The Americans with
Disabilities Act of 1990

PUBLIC LAW 101-336   JULY 26, 1990   104 STAT. 327

One Hundred First Congress of the United States of America
At the Second Session
Begun and held at the City of Washington on Tuesday, the twenty-third day of January, one thousand nine hundred and ninety.

An Act: To establish a clear and comprehensive prohibition of discrimination on the basis of disability.

Be it enacted by the Senate and House of Representatives of the United States of America in Congress assembled,

SECTION 1. SHORT TITLE; TABLE OF CONTENTS.   *42 USC 12101 note.*

(a) Short Title. This Act may be cited as the "Americans with Disabilities Act of 1990."

(b) Table of Contents. The table of contents is as follows:

ADA Handbook

TITLE V MISCELLANEOUS PROVISIONS

SEC. 2. FINDINGS AND PURPOSES.   *42USC 12101.*

(a) Findings. The Congress finds that

(1) some 43,000,000 Americans have one or more physical or mental disabilities, and this number is increasing as the population as a whole is growing older;

(2) historically, society has tended to isolate and segregate individuals with disabilities, and, despite some improvements, such forms of discrimination against individuals with disabilities continue to be a serious and pervasive social problem;

(3) discrimination against individuals with disabilities persists in such critical areas as employment, housing, public accommodations, education, transportation, communication, recreation, institutionalization, health services, voting, and access to public services;

(4) unlike individuals who have experienced discrimination on the basis of race, color, sex, national origin, religion, or age, individuals who have experienced discrimination on the basis of disability have often had no legal recourse to redress such discrimination;

(5) individuals with disabilities continually encounter various forms of discrimination, including outright intentional exclusion, the discriminatory effects of architectural, transportation, and communication barriers, overprotective rules and policies, failure to make modifications to existing facilities and practices, exclusionary qualification standards and criteria, segregation, and relegation to lesser services, programs, activities, benefits, jobs, or other opportunities;

(6) census data, national polls, and other studies have documented that people with disabilities, as a group, occupy an inferior status in our society, and are severely disadvantaged socially, vocationally, economically, and educationally;

(7) individuals with disabilities are a discrete and insular minority who have been faced with restrictions and limitations, subjected to a history of purposeful unequal treatment, and relegated to a position of political powerlessness in our society, based on characteristics that are beyond the control of such individuals and resulting from stereotypic assumptions not truly indicative of the individual ability of such individuals to participate in, and contribute to, society;

(8) the Nation's proper goals regarding individuals with disabilities are to assure equality of opportunity, full participation, independent living, and economic self-sufficiency for such individuals; and

(9) the continuing existence of unfair and unnecessary discrimination and prejudice denies people with disabilities the opportunity to compete on an equal basis and to pursue those opportunities for which our free society is justifiably famous, and costs the United States billions of dollars in unnecessary expenses resulting from dependency and nonproductivity.

(b) Purpose. It is the purpose of this Act

(1) to provide a clear and comprehensive national mandate for the elimination of discrimination against individuals with disabilities;

(2) to provide clear, strong, consistent, enforceable standards addressing discrimination against individuals with disabilities;

(3) to ensure that the Federal Government plays a central role in enforcing the standards established in this Act on behalf of individuals with disabilities; and

(4) to invoke the sweep of congressional authority, including the power to enforce the fourteenth amendment and to regulate commerce, in order to address the major areas of discrimination faced day-to-day by people with disabilities.

SEC. 3. DEFINITIONS.   *42 USC 12102*

As used in this Act:

(1) Auxiliary aids and services. The term "auxiliary aids and services" includes

(A) qualified interpreters or other effective methods of making aurally delivered materials available to individuals with hearing impairments;

(B) qualified readers, taped texts, or other effective methods of making visually delivered materials available to individuals with visual impairments;

(C) acquisition or modification of equipment or devices; and

(D) other similar services and actions.

(2) Disability. The term "disability" means, with respect to an individual

(A) a physical or mental impairment that substantially limits one or more of the major life activities of such individual;

(B) a record of such an impairment; or

(C) being regarded as having such an impairment.

(3) State. The term "State" means each of the several States, the District of Columbia, the Commonwealth of Puerto Rico, Guam, American Samoa, the Virgin Islands, the Trust Territory of the Pacific Islands, and the Commonwealth of the Northern Mariana Islands.

TITLE I EMPLOYMENT

SEC. 101. DEFINITIONS.   *42 USC 12111*

As used in this title:

(1) Commission. The term "Commission" means the Equal Employment Opportunity Commission established by section 705 of the Civil Rights Act of 1964 (42 U.S.C. 2000e-4).

(2) Covered entity. The term "covered entity" means an employer, employment agency,

labor organization, or joint labor-management committee.

(3) Direct threat. The term "direct threat" means a significant risk to the health or safety of others that cannot be eliminated by reasonable accommodation.

(4) Employee. The term "employee" means an individual employed by an employer.

(5) Employer.

(A) In general. The term "employer" means a person engaged in an industry affecting commerce who has 15 or more employees for each working day in each of 20 or more calendar weeks in the current or preceding calendar year, and any agent of such person, except that, for two years following the effective date of this title, an employer means a person engaged in an industry affecting commerce who has 25 or more employees for each working day in each of 20 or more calendar weeks in the current or preceding year, and any agent of such person.

(B) Exceptions. The term "employer" does not include

(i) the United States, a corporation wholly owned by the government of the United States, or an Indian tribe; or

(ii) a bona fide private membership club (other than a labor organization) that is exempt from taxation under section 501(c) of the Internal Revenue Code of 1986.

(6) Illegal use of drugs.

(A) In general. The term "illegal use of drugs" means the use of drugs, the possession or distribution of which is unlawful under the Controlled Substances Act (21 U.S.C. 812). Such term does not include the use of a drug taken under supervision by a licensed health care professional, or other uses authorized by the Controlled Substances Act or other provisions of Federal law.

(B) Drugs. The term "drug" means a controlled substance, as defined in schedules I through V of section 202 of the Controlled Substances Act.

(7) Person, etc. The terms "person", "labor organization", "employment agency", "commerce", and "industry affecting commerce", shall have the same meaning given such terms in section 701 of the Civil Rights Act of 1964 (42 U.S.C. 2000e).

(8) Qualified individual with a disability. The term "qualified individual with a disability" means an individual with a disability who, with or without reasonable accommodation, can perform the essential functions of the employment position that such individual holds or desires. For the purposes of this title, consideration shall be given to the employer's judgment as to what functions of a job are essential, and if an employer has prepared a written description before advertising or interviewing applicants for the job, this description shall be considered evidence of the essential functions of the job.

(9) Reasonable accommodation. The term "reasonable accommodation" may include

(A) making existing facilities used by employees readily accessible to and usable by individuals with disabilities; and

(B) job restructuring, part-time or modified work schedules, reassignment to a vacant position, acquisition or modification of equipment or devices, appropriate adjustment or modifications of examinations, training materials or policies, the provision of qualified readers or interpreters, and other similar accommodations for individuals with disabilities.

(10) Undue hardship.

(A) In general. The term "undue hardship" means an action requiring significant difficulty or expense, when considered in light of the factors set forth in subparagraph (B).

(B) Factors to be considered. In determining whether an accommodation would impose an undue hardship on a covered entity, factors to be considered include

(i) the nature and cost of the accommodation needed under this Act;

(ii) the overall financial resources of the facility or facilities involved in the provision of the reasonable accommodation; the number of persons employed at such facility; the effect on expenses and resources, or the impact otherwise of such accommodation upon the operation of the facility;

(iii) the overall financial resources of the covered entity; the overall size of the business of a covered entity with respect to the number of its employees; the number, type, and location of its facilities; and

(iv) the type of operation or operations of the covered entity, including the composition, structure, and functions of the workforce of such entity; the geographic separateness, administrative, or fiscal relationship of the facility or facilities in question to the covered entity.

SEC. 102. DISCRIMINATION.   *42 USC 12112.*

(a) General Rule. No covered entity shall discriminate against a qualified individual with a disability because of the disability of such individual in regard to job application procedures, the hiring, advancement, or discharge of employees, employee compensation, job training, and other terms, conditions, and privileges of employment.

(b) Construction. As used in subsection (a), the term "discriminate" includes

(1) limiting, segregating, or classifying a job applicant or employee in a way that adversely affects the opportunities or status of such applicant or employee because of the disability of such applicant or employee;

(2) participating in a contractual or other arrangement or relationship that has the effect of subjecting a covered entity's qualified applicant or employee with a disability to the discrimination prohibited by this title (such relationship includes a relationship with an employment or referral agency, labor union, an organization providing fringe benefits to an employee of the covered entity, or an organization providing training and apprenticeship programs);

(3) utilizing standards, criteria, or methods of administration

(A) that have the effect of discrimination on the basis of disability;
or

(B) that perpetuate the discrimination of others who are subject to common administrative control;

(4) excluding or otherwise denying equal jobs or benefits to a qualified individual because of the known disability of an individual with whom the qualified individual is known to have a relationship or association;

(5) (A) not making reasonable accommodations to the known physical or mental limitations of an otherwise qualified individual with a disability who is an applicant or employee, unless such covered entity can demonstrate that the accommodation would impose an undue hardship on the operation of the business of such covered entity; or

(B) denying employment opportunities to a job applicant or employee who is an otherwise qualified individual with a disability, if such denial is based on the need of such covered entity to make reasonable accommodation to the physical or mental impairments of the employee or applicant;

(6) using qualification standards, employment tests or other selection criteria that screen out

or tend to screen out an individual with a disability or a class of individuals with disabilities unless the standard, test or other selection criteria, as used by the covered entity, is shown to be job-related for the position in question and is consistent with business necessity; and

(7) failing to select and administer tests concerning employment in the most effective manner to ensure that, when such test is administered to a job applicant or employee who has a disability that impairs sensory, manual, or speaking skills, such test results accurately reflect the skills, aptitude, or whatever other factor of such applicant or employee that such test purports to measure, rather than reflecting the impaired sensory, manual, or speaking skills of such employee or applicant (except where such skills are the factors that the test purports to measure).

(c) Medical Examinations and Inquiries.

(1) In general. The prohibition against discrimination as referred to in subsection (a) shall include medical examinations and inquiries.

(2) Preemployment.

(A) Prohibited examination or inquiry. Except as provided in paragraph (3), a covered entity shall not conduct a medical examination or make inquiries of a job applicant as to whether such applicant is an individual with a disability or as to the nature or severity of such disability.

(B) Acceptable inquiry. A covered entity may make preemployment inquiries into the ability of an applicant to perform job-related functions.

(3) Employment entrance examination. A covered entity may require a medical examination after an offer of employment has been made to a job applicant and prior to the commencement of the employment duties of such applicant, and may condition an offer of employment on the results of such examination, if

(A) all entering employees are subjected to such an examination regardless of disability;

(B) information obtained regarding the medical condition or history of the applicant is collected and maintained on separate forms and in separate medical files and is treated as a confidential medical record, except that

(i) supervisors and managers may be informed regarding necessary restrictions on the work or duties of the employee and necessary accommodations;

(ii) first aid and safety personnel may be informed, when appropriate, if the disability might require emergency treatment; and

(iii) government officials investigating compliance with this Act shall be provided relevant information on request; and

(C) the results of such examination are used only in accordance with this title.

(4) Examination and inquiry.

(A) Prohibited examinations and inquiries. A covered entity shall not require a medical examination and shall not make inquiries of an employee as to whether such employee is an individual with a disability or as to the nature or severity of the disability, unless such examination or inquiry is shown to be job-related and consistent with business necessity.

(B) Acceptable examinations and inquiries. A covered entity may conduct voluntary medical examinations, including voluntary medical histories, which are part of an employee health program available to employees at that work site. A covered entity may make inquiries into the ability of an employee to perform job-related functions.

(C) Requirement. Information obtained under subparagraph (B) regarding the medical condition or history of any employee are subject to the requirements of subparagraphs (B) and (C) of paragraph (3).

SEC. 103. DEFENSES.   *42 USC 12113.*

(a) In General. It may be a defense to a charge of discrimination under this Act that an alleged application of qualification standards, tests, or selection criteria that screen out or tend to screen out or otherwise deny a job or benefit to an individual with a disability has been shown to be job-related and consistent with business necessity, and such performance cannot be accomplished by reasonable accommodation, as required under this title.

(b) Qualification Standards. The term "qualification standards" may include a requirement that an individual shall not pose a direct threat to the health or safety of other individuals in the workplace.

(c) Religious Entities.

(1) In general. This title shall not prohibit a religious corporation, association, educational institution, or society from giving preference in employment to individuals of a particular religion to perform work connected with the carrying on by such corporation, association, educational institution, or society of its activities.

(2) Religious tenets requirement. Under this title, a religious organization may require that all applicants and employees conform to the religious tenets of such organization.

(d) List of Infectious and Communicable Diseases.

(1) In general. The Secretary of Health and Human Services, not later than 6 months after the date of enactment of this Act, shall

(A) review all infectious and communicable diseases which may be transmitted through handling the food supply;

(B) publish a list of infectious and communicable diseases which are transmitted through handling the food supply;

(C) publish the methods by which such diseases are transmitted; and

(D) widely disseminate such information regarding the list of diseases and their modes of transmissability to the general public.

Such list shall be updated annually.

(2) Applications. In any case in which an individual has an infectious or communicable disease that is transmitted to others through the handling of food, that is included on the list developed by the Secretary of Health and Human Services under paragraph (1), and which cannot be eliminated by reasonable accommodation, a covered entity may refuse to assign or continue to assign such individual to a job involving food handling.

(3) Construction. Nothing in this Act shall be construed to preempt, modify, or amend any State, county, or local law, ordinance, or regulation applicable to food handling which is designed to protect the public health from individuals who pose a significant risk to the health or safety of others, which cannot be eliminated by reasonable accommodation, pursuant to the list of infectious or communicable diseases and the modes of transmissability published by the Secretary of Health and Human Services.

SEC. 104. ILLEGAL USE OF DRUGS AND ALCOHOL.   *42 USC 12114.*

(a) Qualified Individual With a Disability. For purposes of this title, the term "qualified individual with a disability" shall not include any employee or applicant who is currently engaging in the illegal use of drugs, when the covered entity acts on the basis of such use.

(b) Rules of Construction. Nothing in subsection (a) shall be construed to exclude as a qualified individual with a disability an individual who

(1) has successfully completed a supervised drug rehabilitation program and is no longer engaging in the illegal use of drugs, or has otherwise been rehabilitated successfully and is no longer engaging in such use;

(2) is participating in a supervised rehabilitation program and is no longer engaging in such use; or

(3) is erroneously regarded as engaging in such use, but is not engaging in such use; except that it shall not be a violation of this Act for a covered entity to adopt or administer reasonable policies or procedures, including but not limited to drug testing, designed to ensure that an individual described in paragraph (1) or (2) is no longer engaging in the illegal use of drugs.

(c) Authority of Covered Entity. A covered entity

(1) may prohibit the illegal use of drugs and the use of alcohol at the workplace by all employees;

(2) may require that employees shall not be under the influence of alcohol or be engaging in the illegal use of drugs at the workplace;

(3) may require that employees behave in conformance with the requirements established under the Drug-Free Workplace Act of 1988 (41 U.S.C. 701 et seq.);

(4) may hold an employee who engages in the illegal use of drugs or who is an alcoholic to the same qualification standards for employment or job performance and behavior that such entity holds other employees, even if any unsatisfactory performance or behavior is related to the drug use or alcoholism of such employee; and

(5) may, with respect to Federal regulations regarding alcohol and the illegal use of drugs, require that

(A) employees comply with the standards established in such regulations of the Department of Defense, if the employees of the covered entity are employed in an industry subject to such regulations, including complying with regulations (if any) that apply to employment in sensitive positions in such an industry, in the case of employees of the covered entity who are employed in such positions (as defined in the regulations of the Department of Defense);

(B) employees comply with the standards established in such regulations of the Nuclear Regulatory Commission, if the employees of the covered entity are employed in an industry subject to such regulations, including complying with regulations (if any) that apply to employment in sensitive positions in such an industry, in the case of employees of the covered entity who are employed in such positions (as defined in the regulations of the Nuclear Regulatory Commission); and

(C) employees comply with the standards established in such regulations of the Department of Transportation, if the employees of the covered entity are employed in a transportation industry subject to such regulations, including complying with such regulations (if any) that apply to employment in sensitive positions in such an industry, in the case of employees of the covered entity who are employed in such positions (as defined in the regulations of the Department of Transportation).

(d) Drug Testing.

(1) In general. For purposes of this title, a test to determine the illegal use of drugs shall not be considered a medical examination.

(2) Construction. Nothing in this title shall be construed to encourage, prohibit, or authorize the conducting of drug testing for the illegal use of drugs by job applicants or employees or making employment decisions based on such test results.

(e) Transportation Employees. Nothing in this title shall be construed to encourage, prohibit, restrict, or authorize the otherwise lawful exercise by entities subject to the jurisdiction of the Department of Transportation of authority to

(1) test employees of such entities in, and applicants for, positions involving safety-sensitive duties for the illegal use of drugs and for on-duty impairment by alcohol; and

(2) remove such persons who test positive for illegal use of drugs and on-duty impairment by alcohol pursuant to paragraph (1) from safety-sensitive duties in implementing subsection (c).

SEC. 105. POSTING NOTICES.   *42 USC 12115.*

Every employer, employment agency, labor organization, or joint labor-management committee covered under this title shall post notices in an accessible format to applicants, employees, and members describing the applicable provisions of this Act, in the manner prescribed by section 711 of the Civil Rights Act of 1964 (42 U.S.C. 2000e-10).

SEC. 106. REGULATIONS.   *42 USC 12116.*

Not later than 1 year after the date of enactment of this Act, the Commission shall issue regulations in an accessible format to carry out this title in accordance with subchapter II of chapter 5 of title 5, United States Code.

SEC. 107. ENFORCEMENT.   *42 USC 12117.*

Regulations.

(a) Powers, Remedies, and Procedures. The powers, remedies, and procedures set forth in sections 705, 706, 707, 709, and 710 of the Civil Rights Act of 1964 (42 U.S.C. 2000e-4, 2000e-5, 2000e-6, 2000e-8, and 2000e-9) shall be the powers, remedies, and procedures this title provides to the Commission, to the Attorney General, or to any person alleging discrimination on the basis of disability in violation of any provision of this Act, or regulations promulgated under section 106, concerning employment.

(b) Coordination. The agencies with enforcement authority for actions which allege employment discrimination under this title and under the Rehabilitation Act of 1973 shall develop procedures to ensure that administrative complaints filed under this title and under the Rehabilitation Act of 1973 are dealt with in a manner that avoids duplication of effort and prevents imposition of inconsistent or conflicting standards for the same requirements under this title and the Rehabilitation Act of 1973. The Commission, the Attorney General, and the Office of Federal Contract Compliance Programs shall establish such coordinating mechanisms (similar to provisions contained in the joint regulations promulgated by the Commission and the Attorney General at part 42 of title 28 and part 1691 of title 29, Code of Federal Regulations, and the Memorandum of Understanding between the Commission and the Office of Federal Contract Compliance Programs dated January 16, 1981 (46 Fed. Reg. 7435, January 23, 1981)) in regulations implementing this title and Rehabilitation Act of 1973 not later than 18 months after the date of enactment of this Act.

SEC. 108. EFFECTIVE DATE.　　　　　　　　　　　　　*42 USC 12111 note.*

This title shall become effective 24 months after the date of enactment.

TITLE II PUBLIC SERVICES　　　　　　　　　　　　　　*42 USC 12131.*

Subtitle A Prohibition Against Discrimination and Other Generally Applicable Provisions

SEC. 201. DEFINITION.　　　　*42 USC 12115.*

As used in this title:
　　(1) Public entity. The term "public entity" means
　　(A) any State or local government;
　　(B) any department, agency, special purpose district, or other instrumentality of a State or States or local government; and
　　(C) the National Railroad Passenger Corporation, and any commuter authority (as defined in section 103(8) of the Rail Passenger Service Act).
　　(2) Qualified individual with a disability. The term "qualified individual with a disability" means an individual with a disability who, with or without reasonable modifications to rules, policies, or practices, the removal of architectural, communication, or transportation barriers, or the provision of auxiliary aids and services, meets the essential eligibility requirements for the receipt of services or the participation in programs or activities provided by a public entity.

SEC. 202. DISCRIMINATION.　　　　　　　　　　　　　*42 USC 12132.*

Subject to the provisions of this title, no qualified individual with a disability shall, by reason of such disability, be excluded from participation in or be denied the benefits of the services, programs, or activities of a public entity, or be subjected to discrimination by any such entity.

SEC. 203. ENFORCEMENT.　　　　　　　　　　　　　　*42 USC 12132.*

The remedies, procedures, and rights set forth in section 505 of the Rehabilitation Act of 1973 (29 U.S.C. 794a) shall be the remedies, procedures, and rights this title provides to any person alleging discrimination on the basis of disability in violation of section 202.

SEC. 204. REGULATIONS.　　　　　　　　　　　　　　*42 USC 12134.*

(a) In General. Not later than 1 year after the date of enactment of this Act, the Attorney General shall promulgate regulations in an accessible format that implement this subtitle. Such regulations shall not include any matter within the scope of the authority of the Secretary of Transportation under section 223, 229, or 244.
(b) Relationship to Other Regulations. Except for "program accessibility, existing facilities", and "communications", regulations under subsection (a) shall be consistent with this Act and with the coordination regulations under part 41 of title 28, Code of Federal Regulations (as promulgated by the Department of Health, Education, and Welfare on January 13, 1978), applicable to

recipients of Federal financial assistance under section 504 of the Rehabilitation Act of 1973 (29 U.S.C. 794). With respect to "program accessibility, existing facilities", and "communications", such regulations shall be consistent with regulations and analysis as in part 39 of title 28 of the Code of Federal Regulations, applicable to federally conducted activities under such section 504.

(c) Standards. Regulations under subsection (a) shall include standards applicable to facilities and vehicles covered by this subtitle, other than facilities, stations, rail passenger cars, and vehicles covered by subtitle B. Such standards shall be consistent with the minimum guidelines and requirements issued by the Architectural and Transportation Barriers Compliance Board in accordance with section 504(a) of this Act.

SEC. 205. EFFECTIVE DATE.   *42 USC 12131 note.*

(a) General Rule. Except as provided in subsection (b), this subtitle shall become effective 18 months after the date of enactment of this Act.

(b) Exception. Section 204 shall become effective on the date of enactment of this Act.

Subtitle B Actions Applicable to Public Transportation Provided by Public Entities Considered Discriminatory

PART I PUBLIC TRANSPORTATION OTHER THAN BY AIRCRAFT OR CERTAIN RAIL OPERATIONS

SEC. 221. DEFINITIONS.   *42 USC 12141.*

As used in this part:

(1) Demand responsive system. The term "demand responsive system" means any system of providing designated public transportation which is not a fixed route system.

(2) Designated public transportation. The term "designated public transportation" means transportation (other than public school transportation) by bus, rail, or any other conveyance (other than transportation by aircraft or intercity or commuter rail transportation (as defined in section 241)) that provides the general public with general or special service (including charter service) on a regular and continuing basis.

(3) Fixed route system. The term "fixed route system" means a system of providing designated public transportation on which a vehicle is operated along a prescribed route according to a fixed schedule.

(4) Operates. The term "operates", as used with respect to a fixed route system or demand responsive system, includes operation of such system by a person under a contractual or other arrangement or relationship with a public entity.

(5) Public school transportation. The term "public school transportation" means transportation by schoolbus vehicles of schoolchildren, personnel, and equipment to and from a public elementary or secondary school and school-related activities.

(6) Secretary. The term "Secretary" means the Secretary of Transportation.

SEC. 222. PUBLIC ENTITIES OPERATING FIXED ROUTE SYSTEMS.   *42 USC 12142.*

(a) Purchase and Lease of New Vehicles. It shall be considered discrimination for purposes of section 202 of this Act and section 504 of the Rehabilitation Act of 1973 (29 U.S.C. 794) for a public entity which operates a fixed route system to purchase or lease a new bus, a new rapid rail vehicle, a new light rail vehicle, or any other new vehicle to be used on such system, if the solicitation for such purchase or lease is made after the 30th day following the effective date of this subsection and if such bus, rail vehicle, or other vehicle is not readily accessible to and usable by individuals with disabilities, including individuals who use wheelchairs.

(b) Purchase and Lease of Used Vehicles. Subject to subsection (c)(1), it shall be considered discrimination for purposes of section 202 of this Act and section 504 of the Rehabilitation Act of 1973 (29 U.S.C. 794) for a public entity which operates a fixed route system to purchase or lease, after the 30th day following the effective date of this subsection, a used vehicle for use on such system unless such entity makes demonstrated good faith efforts to purchase or lease a used vehicle for use on such system that is readily accessible to and usable by individuals with disabilities, including individuals who use wheelchairs.

(c) Remanufactured Vehicles.

(1) General rule. Except as provided in paragraph (2), it shall be considered discrimination for purposes of section 202 of this Act and section 504 of the Rehabilitation Act of 1973 (29 U.S.C. 794) for a public entity which operates a fixed route system

(A) to remanufacture a vehicle for use on such system so as to extend its usable life for 5 years or more, which remanufacture begins (or for which the solicitation is made) after the 30th day following the effective date of this subsection; or

(B) to purchase or lease for use on such system a remanufactured vehicle which has been remanufactured so as to extend its usable life for 5 years or more, which purchase or lease occurs after such 30th day and during the period in which the usable life is extended;

unless, after remanufacture, the vehicle is, to the maximum extent feasible, readily accessible to and usable by individuals with disabilities, including individuals who use wheelchairs.

(2) Exception for historic vehicles.

(A) General rule. If a public entity operates a fixed route system any segment of which is included on the National Register of Historic Places and if making a vehicle of historic character to be used solely on such segment readily accessible to and usable by individuals with disabilities would significantly alter the historic character of such vehicle, the public entity only has to make (or to purchase or lease a remanufactured vehicle with) those modifications which are necessary to meet the requirements of paragraph (1) and which do not significantly alter the historic character of such vehicle.

(B) Vehicles of historic character defined by regulations. For purposes of this paragraph and section 228(b), a vehicle of historic character shall be defined by the regulations issued by the Secretary to carry out this subsection.

SEC. 223. PARATRANSIT AS A COMPLEMENT TO FIXED ROUTE SERVICE. *42 USC 12143.*

(a) General Rule. It shall be considered discrimination for purposes of section 202 of this Act and section 504 of the Rehabilitation Act of 1973 (29 U.S.C. 794) for a public entity which operates a fixed route system (other than a system which provides solely commuter bus service) to fail to provide with respect to the operations of its fixed route system, in accordance with this section, paratransit and other special transportation services to individuals with disabilities, including individuals who use wheelchairs, that are sufficient to provide to such individuals a level of service (1) which is comparable to the level of designated public transportation services provided to individuals without disabilities using such system; or (2) in the case of response time, which is comparable, to the extent practicable, to the level of designated public transportation services provided to individuals without disabilities using such system.

(b) Issuance of Regulations. Not later than 1 year after the effective date of this subsection, the Secretary shall issue final regulations to carry out this section.

(c) Required Contents of Regulations.

(1) Eligible recipients of service. The regulations issued under this section shall require each public entity which operates a fixed route system to provide the paratransit and other special transportation services required under this section

(A)(i) to any individual with a disability who is unable, as a result of a physical or mental impairment (including a vision impairment) and without the assistance of another individual (except an operator of a wheelchair lift or other boarding assistance device), to board, ride, or disembark from any vehicle on the system which is readily accessible to and usable by individuals with disabilities;

(ii) to any individual with a disability who needs the assistance of a wheelchair lift or other boarding assistance device (and is able with such assistance) to board, ride, and disembark from any vehicle which is readily accessible to and usable by individuals with disabilities if the individual wants to travel on a route on the system during the hours of operation of the system at a time (or within a reasonable period of such time) when such a vehicle is not being used to provide designated public transportation on the route; and

(iii) to any individual with a disability who has a specific impairment-related condition which prevents such individual from traveling to a boarding location or from a disembarking location on such system;

(B) to one other individual accompanying the individual with the disability; and

(C) to other individuals, in addition to the one individual described in subparagraph (B), accompanying the individual with a disability provided that space for these additional individuals is available on the paratransit vehicle carrying the individual with a disability and that the transportation of such additional individuals will not result in a denial of service to individuals with disabilities.

For purposes of clauses (i) and (ii) of subparagraph (A), boarding or disembarking from a vehicle does not include travel to the boarding location or from the disembarking location.

(2) Service area. The regulations issued under this section shall require the provision of paratransit and special transportation services required under this section in the service area of each public entity which operates a fixed route system, other than any portion of the service area in which the public entity solely provides commuter bus service.

(3) Service criteria. Subject to paragraphs (1) and (2), the regulations issued under this section shall establish minimum service criteria for determining the level of services to be required under this section.

(4) Undue financial burden limitation. The regulations issued under this section shall provide that, if the public entity is able to demonstrate to the satisfaction of the Secretary that the provi-

sion of paratransit and other special transportation services otherwise required under this section would impose an undue financial burden on the public entity, the public entity, notwithstanding any other provision of this section (other than paragraph (5)), shall only be required to provide such services to the extent that providing such services would not impose such a burden.

(5) Additional services. The regulations issued under this section shall establish circumstances under which the Secretary may require a public entity to provide, notwithstanding paragraph (4), paratransit and other special transportation services under this section beyond the level of paratransit and other special transportation services which would otherwise be required under paragraph (4).

(6) Public participation. The regulations issued under this section shall require that each public entity which operates a fixed route system hold a public hearing, provide an opportunity for public comment, and consult with individuals with disabilities in preparing its plan under paragraph (7).

(7) Plans. The regulations issued under this section shall require that each public entity which operates a fixed route system

(A) within 18 months after the effective date of this subsection, submit to the Secretary, and commence implementation of, a plan for providing paratransit and other special transportation services which meets the requirements of this section; and

(B) on an annual basis thereafter, submit to the Secretary, and commence implementation of, a plan for providing such services.

(8) Provision of services by others. The regulations issued under this section shall

(A) require that a public entity submitting a plan to the Secretary under this section identify in the plan any person or other public entity which is providing a paratransit or other special transportation service for individuals with disabilities in the service area to which the plan applies; and

(B) provide that the public entity submitting the plan does not have to provide under the plan such service for individuals with disabilities.

(9) Other provisions. The regulations issued under this section shall include such other provisions and requirements as the Secretary determines are necessary to carry out the objectives of this section.

(d) Review of Plan.

(1) General rule. The Secretary shall review a plan submitted under this section for the purpose of determining whether or not such plan meets the requirements of this section, including the regulations issued under this section.

(2) Disapproval. If the Secretary determines that a plan reviewed under this subsection fails to meet the requirements of this section, the Secretary shall disapprove the plan and notify the public entity which submitted the plan of such disapproval and the reasons therefor.

(3) Modification of disapproved plan. Not later than 90 days after the date of disapproval of a plan under this subsection, the public entity which submitted the plan shall modify the plan to meet the requirements of this section and shall submit to the Secretary, and commence implementation of, such modified plan.

(e) Discrimination Defined. As used in subsection (a), the term "discrimination" includes

(1) a failure of a public entity to which the regulations issued under this section apply to submit, or commence implementation of, a plan in accordance with subsections (c)(6) and (c)(7);

(2) a failure of such entity to submit, or commence implementation of, a modified plan in

accordance with subsection (d)(3);

(3) submission to the Secretary of a modified plan under subsection (d)(3) which does not meet the requirements of this section; or

(4) a failure of such entity to provide paratransit or other special transportation services in accordance with the plan or modified plan the public entity submitted to the Secretary under this section.

(f) Statutory Construction. Nothing in this section shall be construed as preventing a public entity

(1) from providing paratransit or other special transportation services at a level which is greater than the level of such services which are required by this section,

(2) from providing paratransit or other special transportation services in addition to those paratransit and special transportation services required by this section, or

(3) from providing such services to individuals in addition to those individuals to whom such services are required to be provided by this section.

SEC. 224. PUBLIC ENTITY OPERATING A DEMAND RESPONSIVE SYSTEM. *42 USC 12144.*

If a public entity operates a demand responsive system, it shall be considered discrimination, for purposes of section 202 of this Act and section 504 of the Rehabilitation Act of 1973 (29 U.S.C. 794), for such entity to purchase or lease a new vehicle for use on such system, for which a solicitation is made after the 30th day following the effective date of this section, that is not readily accessible to and usable by individuals with disabilities, including individuals who use wheelchairs, unless such system, when viewed in its entirety, provides a level of service to such individuals equivalent to the level of service such system provides to individuals without disabilities.

SEC. 225. TEMPORARY RELIEF WHERE LIFTS ARE UNAVAILABLE. *42 USC 12145.*

(a) Granting. With respect to the purchase of new buses, a public entity may apply for, and the Secretary may temporarily relieve such public entity from the obligation under section 222(a) or 224 to purchase new buses that are readily accessible to and usable by individuals with disabilities if such public entity demonstrates to the satisfaction of the Secretary

(1) that the initial solicitation for new buses made by the public entity specified that all new buses were to be lift-equipped and were to be otherwise accessible to and usable by individuals with disabilities;

(2) the unavailability from any qualified manufacturer of hydraulic, electromechanical, or other lifts for such new buses;

(3) that the public entity seeking temporary relief has made good faith efforts to locate a qualified manufacturer to supply the lifts to the manufacturer of such buses in sufficient time to comply with such solicitation; and

(4) that any further delay in purchasing new buses necessary to obtain such lifts would significantly impair transportation services in the community served by the public entity.

(b) Duration and Notice to Congress. Any relief granted under subsection (a) shall be limited in duration by a specified date, and the appropriate committees of Congress shall be notified of any such relief granted.

(c) Fraudulent Application. If, at any time, the Secretary has reasonable cause to believe that any relief granted under subsection (a) was fraudulently applied for, the Secretary shall

(1) cancel such relief if such relief is still in effect; and

(2) take such other action as the Secretary considers appropriate.

SEC. 226. NEW FACILITIES.

42 USC 12146.

For purposes of section 202 of this Act and section 504 of the Rehabilitation Act of 1973 (29 U.S.C. 794), it shall be considered discrimination for a public entity to construct a new facility to be used in the provision of designated public transportation services unless such facility is readily accessible to and usable by individuals with disabilities, including individuals who use wheelchairs.

SEC. 227. ALTERATIONS OF EXISTING FACILITIES.

42 USC 12147.

(a) General Rule. With respect to alterations of an existing facility or part thereof used in the provision of designated public transportation services that affect or could affect the usability of the facility or part thereof, it shall be considered discrimination, for purposes of section 202 of this Act and section 504 of the Rehabilitation Act of 1973 (29 U.S.C. 794), for a public entity to fail to make such alterations (or to ensure that the alterations are made) in such a manner that, to the maximum extent feasible, the altered portions of the facility are readily accessible to and usable by individuals with disabilities, including individuals who use wheelchairs, upon the completion of such alterations. Where the public entity is undertaking an alteration that affects or could affect usability of or access to an area of the facility containing a primary function, the entity shall also make the alterations in such a manner that, to the maximum extent feasible, the path of travel to the altered area and the bathrooms, telephones, and drinking fountains serving the altered area, are readily accessible to and usable by individuals with disabilities, including individuals who use wheelchairs, upon completion of such alterations, where such alterations to the path of travel or the bathrooms, telephones, and drinking fountains serving the altered area are not disproportionate to the overall alterations in terms of cost and scope (as determined under criteria established by the Attorney General).

(b) Special Rule for Stations.

(1) General rule. For purposes of section 202 of this Act and section 504 of the Rehabilitation Act of 1973 (29 U.S.C. 794), it shall be considered discrimination for a public entity that provides designated public transportation to fail, in accordance with the provisions of this subsection, to make key stations (as determined under criteria established by the Secretary by regulation) in rapid rail and light rail systems readily accessible to and usable by individuals with disabilities, including individuals who use wheelchairs.

(2) Rapid rail and light rail key stations.

(A) Accessibility. Except as otherwise provided in this paragraph, all key stations (as determined under criteria established by the Secretary by regulation) in rapid rail and light rail systems shall be made readily accessible to and usable by individuals with disabilities, including individuals who use wheelchairs, as soon as practicable but in no event later than the last day of the 3-year period beginning on the effective date of this paragraph.

(B) Extension for extraordinarily expensive structural changes. The Secretary may extend the 3-year period under subparagraph (A) up to a 30-year period for key stations in a rapid rail or light rail system which stations need extraordinarily expensive structural changes to, or replacement of, existing facilities; except that by the last day of the 20th year following the date of the enactment of this Act at least 2/3 of such key stations must be readily accessible to and usable by individuals with disabilities.

(3) Plans and milestones. The Secretary shall require the appropriate public entity to develop and submit to the Secretary a plan for compliance with this subsection

(A) that reflects consultation with individuals with disabilities affected by such plan and the results of a public hearing and public comments on such plan, and

(B) that establishes milestones for achievement of the requirements of this subsection.

SEC.228. PUBLIC TRANSPORTATION PROGRAMS AND ACTIVITIES IN EXISTING FACILITIES AND ONE CAR PER TRAIN RULE.   *42 USC 12148.*

(a) Public Transportation Programs and Activities in Existing Facilities.

(1) In general. With respect to existing facilities used in the provision of designated public transportation services, it shall be considered discrimination, for purposes of section 202 of this Act and section 504 of the Rehabilitation Act of 1973 (29 U.S.C. 794), for a public entity to fail to operate a designated public transportation program or activity conducted in such facilities so that, when viewed in the entirety, the program or activity is readily accessible to and usable by individuals with disabilities.

(2) Exception. Paragraph (1) shall not require a public entity to make structural changes to existing facilities in order to make such facilities accessible to individuals who use wheelchairs, unless and to the extent required by section 227(a) (relating to alterations) or section 227(b) (relating to key stations).

(3) Utilization. Paragraph (1) shall not require a public entity to which paragraph (2) applies, to provide to individuals who use wheelchairs services made available to the general public at such facilities when such individuals could not utilize or benefit from such services provided at such facilities.

(b) One Car Per Train Rule.

(1) General rule. Subject to paragraph (2), with respect to 2 or more vehicles operated as a train by a light or rapid rail system, for purposes of section 202 of this Act and section 504 of the Rehabilitation Act of 1973 (29 U.S.C. 794), it shall be considered discrimination for a public entity to fail to have at least 1 vehicle per train that is accessible to individuals with disabilities, including individuals who use wheelchairs, as soon as practicable but in no event later than the last day of the 5-year period beginning on the effective date of this section.

(2) Historic trains. In order to comply with paragraph (1) with respect to the remanufacture of a vehicle of historic character which is to be used on a segment of a light or rapid rail system which is included on the National Register of Historic Places, if making such vehicle readily accessible to and usable by individuals with disabilities would significantly alter the historic character of such vehicle, the public entity which operates such system only has to make (or to purchase or lease a remanufactured vehicle with) those modifications which are necessary to meet the requirements of section 222(c)(1) and which do not significantly alter the historic character of such vehicle.

SEC. 229. REGULATIONS.   *42 USC 12149.*

(a) In General. Not later than 1 year after the date of enactment of this Act, the Secretary of Transportation shall issue regulations, in an accessible format, necessary for carrying out this part (other than section 223).

(b) Standards. The regulations issued under this section and section 223 shall include standards applicable to facilities and vehicles covered by this subtitle. The standards shall be consistent with the minimum guidelines and requirements issued by the Architectural and Transportation Barriers Compliance Board in accordance with section 504 of this Act.

SEC. 230. INTERIM ACCESSIBILITY REQUIREMENTS.   *42 USC 12150.*

If final regulations have not been issued pursuant to section 229, for new construction or alterations for which a valid and appropriate State or local building permit is obtained prior to the issuance of final regulations under such section, and for which the construction or alteration authorized by such permit begins within one year of the receipt of such permit and is completed under the terms of such permit, compliance with the Uniform Federal Accessibility Standards in effect at the time the building permit is issued shall suffice to satisfy the requirement that facilities be readily accessible to and usable by persons with disabilities as required under sections 226 and 227, except that, if such final regulations have not been issued one year after the Architectural and Transportation Barriers Compliance Board has issued the supplemental minimum guidelines required under section 504(a) of this Act, compliance with such supplemental minimum guidelines shall be necessary to satisfy the requirement that facilities be readily accessible to and usable by persons with disabilities prior to issuance of the final regulations.

SEC. 231. EFFECTIVE DATE.   *42 USC 12141 note.*

(a) General Rule. Except as provided in subsection (b), this part shall become effective 18 months after the date of enactment of this Act.

(b) Exception. Sections 222, 223 (other than subsection (a)), 224, 225, 227(b), 228(b), and 229 shall become effective on the date of enactment of this Act.

PART II PUBLIC TRANSPORTATION BY INTERCITY AND COMMUTER RAIL

SEC. 241. DEFINITIONS.   *42 USC 12161.*

As used in this part:

(1) Commuter authority. The term "commuter authority" has the meaning given such term in section 103(8) of the Rail Passenger Service Act (45 U.S.C. 502(8)).

(2) Commuter rail transportation. The term "commuter rail transportation" has the meaning given the term "commuter service" in section 103(9) of the Rail Passenger Service Act (45 U.S.C. 502(9)).

(3) Intercity rail transportation. The term "intercity rail transportation" means transportation provided by the National Railroad Passenger Corporation.

(4) Rail passenger car. The term "rail passenger car" means, with respect to intercity rail

transportation, single-level and bi-level coach cars, single-level and bi-level dining cars, single-level and bi-level sleeping cars, single-level and bi-level lounge cars, and food service cars.

(5) Responsible person. The term "responsible person" means

(A) in the case of a station more than 50 percent of which is owned by a public entity, such public entity;

(B) in the case of a station more than 50 percent of which is owned by a private party, the persons providing intercity or commuter rail transportation to such station, as allocated on an equitable basis by regulation by the Secretary of Transportation; and

(C) in a case where no party owns more than 50 percent of a station, the persons providing intercity or commuter rail transportation to such station and the owners of the station, other than private party owners, as allocated on an equitable basis by regulation by the Secretary of Transportation.

(6) Station. The term "station" means the portion of a property located appurtenant to a right-of-way on which intercity or commuter rail transportation is operated, where such portion is used by the general public and is related to the provision of such transportation, including passenger platforms, designated waiting areas, ticketing areas, restrooms, and, where a public entity providing rail transportation owns the property, concession areas, to the extent that such public entity exercises control over the selection, design, construction, or alteration of the property, but such term does not include flag stops.

SEC. 242.INTERCITY AND COMMUTER RAIL ACTIONS CONSIDERED DISCRIMINATORY.

42 USC 12162.

(a) Intercity Rail Transportation.

(1) One car per train rule. It shall be considered discrimination for purposes of section 202 of this Act and section 504 of the Rehabilitation Act of 1973 (29 U.S.C. 794) for a person who provides intercity rail transportation to fail to have at least one passenger car per train that is readily accessible to and usable by individuals with disabilities, including individuals who use wheelchairs, in accordance with regulations issued under section 244, as soon as practicable, but in no event later than 5 years after the date of enactment of this Act.

(2) New intercity cars.

(A) General rule. Except as otherwise provided in this subsection with respect to individuals who use wheelchairs, it shall be considered discrimination for purposes of section 202 of this Act and section 504 of the Rehabilitation Act of 1973 (29 U.S.C. 794) for a person to purchase or lease any new rail passenger cars for use in intercity rail transportation, and for which a solicitation is made later than 30 days after the effective date of this section, unless all such rail cars are readily accessible to and usable by individuals with disabilities, including individuals who use wheelchairs, as prescribed by the Secretary of Transportation in regulations issued under section 244.

(B) Special rule for single-level passenger coaches for individuals who use wheelchairs. Single-level passenger coaches shall be required to

(i) be able to be entered by an individual who uses a wheelchair;

(ii) have space to park and secure a wheelchair;

(iii) have a seat to which a passenger in a wheelchair can transfer, and a space to fold and store such passenger's wheelchair; and

(iv) have a restroom usable by an individual who uses a wheelchair, only to the extent provided in paragraph (3).

(C) Special rule for single-level dining cars for individuals who use wheelchairs. Single-level dining cars shall not be required to

(i) be able to be entered from the station platform by an individual who uses a wheelchair; or

(ii) have a restroom usable by an individual who uses a wheelchair if no restroom is provided in such car for any passenger.

(D) Special rule for bi-level dining cars for individuals who use wheelchairs. Bi-level dining cars shall not be required to

(i) be able to be entered by an individual who uses a wheelchair;

(ii) have space to park and secure a wheelchair;

(iii) have a seat to which a passenger in a wheelchair can transfer, or a space to fold and store such passenger's wheelchair; or

(iv) have a restroom usable by an individual who uses a wheelchair.

(3) Accessibility of single-level coaches.

(A) General rule. It shall be considered discrimination for purposes of section 202 of this Act and section 504 of the Rehabilitation Act of 1973 (29 U.S.C. 794) for a person who provides intercity rail transportation to fail to have on each train which includes one or more single-level rail passenger coaches

(i) a number of spaces

(I) to park and secure wheelchairs (to accommodate individuals who wish to remain in their wheelchairs) equal to not less than one-half of the number of single-level rail passenger coaches in such train; and

(II) to fold and store wheelchairs (to accommodate individuals who wish to transfer to coach seats) equal to not less than one-half of the number of single-level rail passenger coaches in such train,

as soon as practicable, but in no event later than 5 years after the date of enactment of this Act; and

(ii) a number of spaces

(I) to park and secure wheelchairs (to accommodate individuals who wish to remain in their wheelchairs) equal to not less than the total number of single-level rail passenger coaches in such train; and

(II) to fold and store wheelchairs (to accommodate individuals who wish to transfer to coach seats) equal to not less than the total number of single-level rail passenger coaches in such train,

as soon as practicable, but in no event later than 10 years after the date of enactment of this Act.

(B) Location. Spaces required by subparagraph (A) shall be located in single-level rail passenger coaches or food service cars.

(C) Limitation. Of the number of spaces required on a train by subparagraph (A), not more than two spaces to park and secure wheelchairs nor more than two spaces to fold and store wheelchairs shall be located in any one coach or food service car.

(D) Other accessibility features. Single-level rail passenger coaches and food service cars on which the spaces required by subparagraph (A) are located shall have a restroom usable by an individual who uses a wheelchair and shall be able to be entered from the station platform by an individual who uses a wheelchair.

(4) Food service.

(A) Single-level dining cars. On any train in which a single-level dining car is used to provide food service

(i) if such single-level dining car was purchased after the date of enactment of this Act, table service in such car shall be provided to a passenger who uses a wheelchair if

(I) the car adjacent to the end of the dining car through which a wheelchair may enter is itself accessible to a wheelchair;

(II) such passenger can exit to the platform from the car such passenger occupies, move down the platform, and enter the adjacent accessible car described in subclause (I) without the necessity of the train being moved within the station; and

(III) space to park and secure a wheelchair is available in the dining car at the time such passenger wishes to eat (if such passenger wishes to remain in a wheelchair), or space to store and fold a wheelchair is available in the dining car at the time such passenger wishes to eat (if such passenger wishes to transfer to a dining car seat); and

(ii) appropriate auxiliary aids and services, including a hard surface on which to eat, shall be provided to ensure that other equivalent food service is available to individuals with disabilities, including individuals who use wheelchairs, and to passengers traveling with such individuals.

Unless not practicable, a person providing intercity rail transportation shall place an accessible car adjacent to the end of a dining car described in clause (i) through which an individual who uses a wheelchair may enter.

(B) Bi-level dining cars. On any train in which a bi-level dining car is used to provide food service

(i) if such train includes a bi-level lounge car purchased after the date of enactment of this Act, table service in such lounge car shall be provided to individuals who use wheelchairs and to other passengers; and

(ii) appropriate auxiliary aids and services, including a hard surface on which to eat, shall be provided to ensure that other equivalent food service is available to individuals with disabilities, including individuals who use wheelchairs, and to passengers traveling with such individuals.

(b) Commuter Rail Transportation.

(1) One car per train rule. It shall be considered discrimination for purposes of section 202 of this Act and section 504 of the Rehabilitation Act of 1973 (29 U.S.C. 794) for a person who provides commuter rail transportation to fail to have at least one passenger car per train that is readily accessible to and usable by individuals with disabilities, including individuals who use wheelchairs, in accordance with regulations issued under section 244, as soon as practicable, but in no event later than 5 years after the date of enactment of this Act.

(2) New commuter rail cars.

(A) General rule. It shall be considered discrimination for purposes of section 202 of this Act and section 504 of the Rehabilitation Act of 1973 (29 U.S.C. 794) for a person to purchase or lease any new rail passenger cars for use in commuter rail transportation, and for which a solicitation is made later than 30 days after the effective date of this section, unless all such rail cars are readily accessible to and usable by individuals with disabilities, including individuals who use wheelchairs, as prescribed by the Secretary of Transportation in regulations issued under section 244.

(B) Accessibility. For purposes of section 202 of this Act and section 504 of the Rehabilitation Act of 1973 (29 U.S.C. 794), a requirement that a rail passenger car used in commuter rail transportation be accessible to or readily accessible to and usable by individuals with disabilities, including individuals who use wheelchairs, shall not be construed to require

(i) a restroom usable by an individual who uses a wheelchair if no restroom is provided in such car for any passenger;

(ii) space to fold and store a wheelchair; or

(iii) a seat to which a passenger who uses a wheelchair can transfer.

(c) Used Rail Cars. It shall be considered discrimination for purposes of section 202 of this Act and section 504 of the Rehabilitation Act of 1973 (29 U.S.C. 794) for a person to purchase or lease a used rail passenger car for use in intercity or commuter rail transportation, unless such person makes demonstrated good faith efforts to purchase or lease a used rail car that is readily accessible to and usable by individuals with disabilities, including individuals who use wheelchairs, as prescribed by the Secretary of Transportation in regulations issued under section 244.

(d) Remanufactured Rail Cars.

(1) Remanufacturing. It shall be considered discrimination for purposes of section 202 of this Act and section 504 of the Rehabilitation Act of 1973 (29 U.S.C. 794) for a person to remanufacture a rail passenger car for use in intercity or commuter rail transportation so as to extend its usable life for 10 years or more, unless the rail car, to the maximum extent feasible, is made readily accessible to and usable by individuals with disabilities, including individuals who use wheelchairs, as prescribed by the Secretary of Transportation in regulations issued under section 244.

(2) Purchase or lease. It shall be considered discrimination for purposes of section 202 of this Act and section 504 of the Rehabilitation Act of 1973 (29 U.S.C. 794) for a person to purchase or lease a remanufactured rail passenger car for use in intercity or commuter rail transportation unless such car was remanufactured in accordance with paragraph (1).

(e) Stations.

(1) New stations. It shall be considered discrimination for purposes of section 202 of this Act and section 504 of the Rehabilitation Act of 1973 (29 U.S.C. 794) for a person to build a new station for use in intercity or commuter rail transportation that is not readily accessible to and usable by individuals with disabilities, including individuals who use wheelchairs, as prescribed by the Secretary of Transportation in regulations issued under section 244.

(2) Existing stations.

(A) Failure to make readily accessible.

(i) General rule. It shall be considered discrimination for purposes of section 202 of this Act and section 504 of the Rehabilitation Act of 1973 (29 U.S.C. 794) for a responsible person to fail to make existing stations in the intercity rail transportation system, and existing key stations in commuter rail transportation systems, readily accessible to and usable by individuals with disabilities, including individuals who use wheelchairs, as prescribed by the Secretary of Transportation in regulations issued under section 244.

(ii) Period for compliance.

(I) Intercity rail. All stations in the intercity rail transportation system shall be made readily accessible to and usable by individuals with disabilities, including individuals who use wheelchairs, as soon as practicable, but in no event later than 20 years after the date of enactment of this Act.

(II) Commuter rail. Key stations in commuter rail transportation systems shall be made readily accessible to and usable by individuals with disabilities, including individuals who use wheelchairs, as soon as practicable but in no event later than 3 years after the date of enactment of this Act, except that the time limit may be extended by the Secretary of Transportation up to 20 years after the date of enactment of this Act in a case where the raising of the entire passenger platform is the only means available of attaining accessibility or where other extraordinarily expensive structural changes are necessary to attain accessibility.

(iii) Designation of key stations. Each commuter authority shall designate the key stations in its commuter rail transportation system, in consultation with individuals with disabilities and organizations representing such individuals, taking into consideration such factors as high ridership and whether such station serves as a transfer or feeder station. Before the final designation of key stations under this clause, a commuter authority shall hold a public hearing.

(iv) Plans and milestones. The Secretary of Transportation shall require the appropriate person to develop a plan for carrying out this subparagraph that reflects consultation with individuals with disabilities affected by such plan and that establishes milestones for achievement of the requirements of this subparagraph.

(B) Requirement when making alterations.

(i) General rule. It shall be considered discrimination, for purposes of section 202 of this Act and section 504 of the Rehabilitation Act of 1973 (29 U.S.C. 794), with respect to alterations of an existing station or part thereof in the intercity or commuter rail transportation systems that affect or could affect the usability of the station or part thereof, for the responsible person, owner, or person in control of the station to fail to make the alterations in such a manner that, to the maximum extent feasible, the altered portions of the station are readily accessible to and usable by individuals with disabilities, including individuals who use wheelchairs, upon completion of such alterations.

(ii) Alterations to a primary function area. It shall be considered discrimination, for purposes of section 202 of this Act and section 504 of the Rehabilitation Act of 1973 (29 U.S.C. 794), with respect to alterations that affect or could affect the usability of or access to an area of the station containing a primary function, for the responsible person, owner, or person in control of the station to fail to make the alterations in such a manner that, to the maximum extent feasible, the path of travel to the altered area, and the bathrooms, telephones, and drinking fountains serving the altered area, are readily accessible to and usable by individuals with disabilities, including individuals who use wheelchairs, upon completion of such alterations, where such alterations to the path of travel or the bathrooms, telephones, and drinking fountains serving the altered area are not disproportionate to the overall alterations in terms of cost and scope (as determined under criteria established by the Attorney General).

(C) Required cooperation. It shall be considered discrimination for purposes of section 202 of this Act and section 504 of the Rehabilitation Act of 1973 (29 U.S.C. 794) for an owner, or person in control, of a station governed by subparagraph (A) or (B) to fail to provide reasonable cooperation to a responsible person with respect to such station in that responsible person's efforts to comply with such subparagraph. An owner, or person in control, of a station shall be liable to a responsible person for any failure to provide reasonable cooperation as required by this subparagraph. Failure to receive reasonable cooperation required by this subparagraph shall not be a defense to a claim of discrimination under this Act.

SEC. 243. CONFORMANCE OF ACCESSIBILITY STANDARDS.   *42 USC 12163.*

Accessibility standards included in regulations issued under this part shall be consistent with the minimum guidelines issued by the Architectural and Transportation Barriers Compliance Board under section 504(a) of this Act.

SEC. 244. REGULATIONS.   *42 USC 12164.*

Not later than 1 year after the date of enactment of this Act, the Secretary of Transportation shall issue regulations, in an accessible format, necessary for carrying out this part.

SEC. 245. INTERIM ACCESSIBILITY REQUIREMENTS.   *42 USC 12165.*

(a) Stations. If final regulations have not been issued pursuant to section 244, for new construction or alterations for which a valid and appropriate State or local building permit is obtained prior to the issuance of final regulations under such section, and for which the construction or alteration authorized by such permit begins within one year of the receipt of such permit and is completed under the terms of such permit, compliance with the Uniform Federal Accessibility Standards in effect at the time the building permit is issued shall suffice to satisfy the requirement that stations be readily accessible to and usable by persons with disabilities as required under section 242(e), except that, if such final regulations have not been issued one year after the Architectural and Transportation Barriers Compliance Board has issued the supplemental minimum guidelines required under section 504(a) of this Act, compliance with such supplemental minimum guidelines shall be necessary to satisfy the requirement that stations be readily accessible to and usable by persons with disabilities prior to issuance of the final regulations.
(b) Rail Passenger Cars. If final regulations have not been issued pursuant to section 244, a person shall be considered to have complied with the requirements of section 242 (a) through (d) that a rail passenger car be readily accessible to and usable by individuals with disabilities, if the design for such car complies with the laws and regulations (including the Minimum Guidelines and Requirements for Accessible Design and such supplemental minimum guidelines as are issued under section 504(a) of this Act) governing accessibility of such cars, to the extent that such laws and regulations are not inconsistent with this part and are in effect at the time such design is substantially completed.

SEC. 246. EFFECTIVE DATE.   *42 USC 12161 note.*

(a) General Rule. Except as provided in subsection (b), this part shall become effective 18 months after the date of enactment of this Act.
(b) Exception. Sections 242 and 244 shall become effective on the date of enactment of this Act.

TITLE III PUBLIC ACCOMMODATIONS AND SERVICES OPERATED BY PRIVATE ENTITIES

SEC. 301. DEFINITIONS.   *42 USC 12181.*

As used in this title:

(1) Commerce. The term "commerce" means travel, trade, traffic, commerce, transportation, or communication

(A) among the several States;

(B) between any foreign country or any territory or possession and any State; or

(C) between points in the same State but through another State or foreign country.

(2) Commercial facilities. The term "commercial facilities" means facilities

(A) that are intended for nonresidential use; and

(B) whose operations will affect commerce. Such term shall not include railroad locomotives, railroad freight cars, railroad cabooses, railroad cars described in section 242 or covered under this title, railroad rights-of-way, or facilities that are covered or expressly exempted from coverage under the Fair Housing Act of 1968 (42 U.S.C. 3601 et seq.).

(3) Demand responsive system. The term "demand responsive system" means any system of providing transportation of individuals by a vehicle, other than a system which is a fixed route system.

(4) Fixed route system. The term "fixed route system" means a system of providing transportation of individuals (other than by aircraft) on which a vehicle is operated along a prescribed route according to a fixed schedule.

(5) Over-the-road bus. The term "over-the-road bus" means a bus characterized by an elevated passenger deck located over a baggage compartment.

(6) Private entity. The term "private entity" means any entity other than a public entity (as defined in section 201(1)).

(7) Public accommodation. The following private entities are considered public accommodations for purposes of this title, if the operations of such entities affect commerce

(A) an inn, hotel, motel, or other place of lodging, except for an establishment located within a building that contains not more than five rooms for rent or hire and that is actually occupied by the proprietor of such establishment as the residence of such proprietor;

(B) a restaurant, bar, or other establishment serving food or drink;

(C) a motion picture house, theater, concert hall, stadium, or other place of exhibition or entertainment;

(D) an auditorium, convention center, lecture hall, or other place of public gathering;

(E) a bakery, grocery store, clothing store, hardware store, shopping center, or other sales or rental establishment;

(F) a laundromat, dry-cleaner, bank, barber shop, beauty shop, travel service, shoe repair service, funeral parlor, gas station, office of an accountant or lawyer, pharmacy, insurance office, professional office of a health care provider, hospital, or other service establishment;

(G) a terminal, depot, or other station used for specified public transportation;

(H) a museum, library, gallery, or other place of public display or collection;

(I) a park, zoo, amusement park, or other place of recreation;

(J) a nursery, elementary, secondary, undergraduate, or postgraduate private school, or other place of education;

(K) a day care center, senior citizen center, homeless shelter, food bank, adoption agency, or other social service center establishment; and

(L) a gymnasium, health spa, bowling alley, golf course, or other place of exercise or recreation.

(8) Rail and railroad. The terms "rail" and "railroad" have the meaning given the term "railroad" in section 202(e) of the Federal Railroad Safety Act of 1970 (45 U.S.C. 431(e)).

(9) Readily achievable. The term "readily achievable" means easily accomplishable and able to be carried out without much difficulty or expense. In determining whether an action is readily achievable, factors to be considered include

(A) the nature and cost of the action needed under this Act;

(B) the overall financial resources of the facility or facilities involved in the action; the number of persons employed at such facility; the effect on expenses and resources, or the impact otherwise of such action upon the operation of the facility;

(C) the overall financial resources of the covered entity; the overall size of the business of a covered entity with respect to the number of its employees; the number, type, and location of its facilities; and

(D) the type of operation or operations of the covered entity, including the composition, structure, and functions of the workforce of such entity; the geographic separateness, administrative or fiscal relationship of the facility or facilities in question to the covered entity.

(10) Specified public transportation. The term "specified public transportation" means transportation by bus, rail, or any other conveyance (other than by aircraft) that provides the general public with general or special service (including charter service) on a regular and continuing basis.

(11) Vehicle. The term "vehicle" does not include a rail passenger car, railroad locomotive, railroad freight car, railroad caboose, or a railroad car described in section 242 or covered under this title.

SEC. 302. PROHIBITION OF DISCRIMINATION BY PUBLIC ACCOMMODATIONS.

42 USC 12182.

(a) General Rule. No individual shall be discriminated against on the basis of disability in the full and equal enjoyment of the goods, services, facilities, privileges, advantages, or accommodations of any place of public accommodation by any person who owns, leases (or leases to), or operates a place of public accommodation.

(b) Construction.

(1) General prohibition.

(A) Activities.

(i) Denial of participation. It shall be discriminatory to subject an individual or class of individuals on the basis of a disability or disabilities of such individual or class, directly, or through contractual, licensing, or other arrangements, to a denial of the opportunity of the individual or class to participate in or benefit from the goods, services, facilities, privileges, advantages, or accommodations of an entity.

(ii) Participation in unequal benefit. It shall be discriminatory to afford an individual or class of individuals, on the basis of a disability or disabilities of such individual or class, directly, or through contractual, licensing, or other arrangements with the opportunity to participate in or benefit from a good, service, facility, privilege, advantage, or accommodation that is not equal to that afforded to other individuals.

(iii) Separate benefit. It shall be discriminatory to provide an individual or class of individuals, on the basis of a disability or disabilities of such individual or class, directly, or through contractual, licensing, or other arrangements with a good, service, facility, privilege, advantage, or accommodation that is different or separate from that provided to other individuals, unless such action is necessary to provide the individual or class of individuals with a good, service, facility, privilege, advantage, or accommodation, or other opportunity that is as effective as that provided to others.

(iv) Individual or class of individuals. For purposes of clauses (i) through (iii) of this subparagraph, the term "individual or class of individuals" refers to the clients or customers of the covered public accommodation that enters into the contractual, licensing or other arrangement.

(B) Integrated settings. Goods, services, facilities, privileges, advantages, and accommodations shall be afforded to an individual with a disability in the most integrated setting appropriate to the needs of the individual.

(C) Opportunity to participate. Notwithstanding the existence of separate or different programs or activities provided in accordance with this section, an individual with a disability shall not be denied the opportunity to participate in such programs or activities that are not separate or different.

(D) Administrative methods. An individual or entity shall not, directly or through contractual or other arrangements, utilize standards or criteria or methods of administration

(i) that have the effect of discriminating on the basis of disability;
or

(ii) that perpetuate the discrimination of others who are subject to common administrative control.

(E) Association. It shall be discriminatory to exclude or otherwise deny equal goods, services, facilities, privileges, advantages, accommodations, or other opportunities to an individual or entity because of the known disability of an individual with whom the individual or entity is known to have a relationship or association.

(2) Specific prohibitions.

(A) Discrimination. For purposes of subsection (a), discrimination includes

(i) the imposition or application of eligibility criteria that screen out or tend to screen out an individual with a disability or any class of individuals with disabilities from fully and equally enjoying any goods, services, facilities, privileges, advantages, or accommodations, unless such criteria can be shown to be necessary for the provision of the goods, services, facilities, privileges, advantages, or accommodations being offered;

(ii) a failure to make reasonable modifications in policies, practices, or procedures, when such modifications are necessary to afford such goods, services, facilities, privileges, advantages, or accommodations to individuals with disabilities, unless the entity can demonstrate that making such modifications would fundamentally alter the nature of such goods, services, facilities, privileges, advantages, or accommodations;

(iii) a failure to take such steps as may be necessary to ensure that no individual with a disability is excluded, denied services, segregated or otherwise treated differently than other individuals because of the absence of auxiliary aids and services, unless the entity can demonstrate that taking such steps would fundamentally alter the nature of the good, service, facility, privilege, advantage, or accommodation being offered or would result in an undue burden;

(iv) a failure to remove architectural barriers, and communication barriers that are structural in nature, in existing facilities, and transportation barriers in existing vehicles and rail passenger cars used by an establishment for transporting individuals (not including barriers that can only be removed through the retrofitting of vehicles or rail passenger cars by the installation of a hydraulic or other lift), where such removal is readily achievable; and

(v) where an entity can demonstrate that the removal of a barrier under clause (iv) is not readily achievable, a failure to make such goods, services, facilities, privileges, advantages, or accommodations available through alternative methods if such methods are readily achievable.

(B) Fixed route system.

(i) Accessibility. It shall be considered discrimination for a private entity which operates a fixed route system and which is not subject to section 304 to purchase or lease a vehicle with a seating capacity in excess of 16 passengers (including the driver) for use on such system, for which a solicitation is made after the 30th day following the effective date of this subparagraph, that is not readily accessible to and usable by individuals with disabilities, including individuals who use wheelchairs.

(ii) Equivalent service. If a private entity which operates a fixed route system and which is not subject to section 304 purchases or leases a vehicle with a seating capacity of 16 passengers or less (including the driver) for use on such system after the effective date of this subparagraph that is not readily accessible to or usable by individuals with disabilities, it shall be considered discrimination for such entity to fail to operate such system so that, when viewed in its entirety, such system ensures a level of service to individuals with disabilities, including individuals who use wheelchairs, equivalent to the level of service provided to individuals without disabilities.

(C) Demand responsive system. For purposes of subsection (a), discrimination includes

(i) a failure of a private entity which operates a demand responsive system and which is not subject to section 304 to operate such system so that, when viewed in its entirety, such system ensures a level of service to individuals with disabilities, including individuals who use wheelchairs, equivalent to the level of service provided to individuals without disabilities; and

(ii) the purchase or lease by such entity for use on such system of a vehicle with a seating capacity in excess of 16 passengers (including the driver), for which solicitations are made after the 30th day following the effective date of this subparagraph, that is not readily accessible to and usable by individuals with disabilities (including individuals who use wheelchairs) unless such entity can demonstrate that such system, when viewed in its entirety, provides a level of service to individuals with disabilities equivalent to that provided to individuals without disabilities.

(D) Over-the- road buses.

(i) Limitation on applicability. Subparagraphs (B) and (C) do not apply to over-the-road buses.

(ii) Accessibility requirements. For purposes of subsection (a), discrimination includes (I) the purchase or lease of an over-the-road bus which does not comply with the regulations issued under section 306(a)(2) by a private entity which provides transportation of individuals and which is not primarily engaged in the business of transporting people, and (II) any other failure of such entity to comply with such regulations.

(3) Specific Construction. Nothing in this title shall require an entity to permit an individual to participate in or benefit from the goods, services, facilities, privileges, advantages and accommodations of such entity where such individual poses a direct threat to the health or safety of others.

The term "direct threat" means a significant risk to the health or safety of others that cannot be eliminated by a modification of policies, practices, or procedures or by the provision of auxiliary aids or services.

SEC. 303. NEW CONSTRUCTION AND ALTERATIONS IN PUBLIC ACCOMMODATIONS AND COMMERCIAL FACILITIES.   *42 USC 12183.*

(a) Application of Term. Except as provided in subsection (b), as applied to public accommodations and commercial facilities, discrimination for purposes of section 302(a) includes

(1) a failure to design and construct facilities for first occupancy later than 30 months after the date of enactment of this Act that are readily accessible to and usable by individuals with disabilities, except where an entity can demonstrate that it is structurally impracticable to meet the requirements of such subsection in accordance with standards set forth or incorporated by reference in regulations issued under this title; and

(2) with respect to a facility or part thereof that is altered by, on behalf of, or for the use of an establishment in a manner that affects or could affect the usability of the facility or part thereof, a failure to make alterations in such a manner that, to the maximum extent feasible, the altered portions of the facility are readily accessible to and usable by individuals with disabilities, including individuals who use wheelchairs. Where the entity is undertaking an alteration that affects or could affect usability of or access to an area of the facility containing a primary function, the entity shall also make the alterations in such a manner that, to the maximum extent feasible, the path of travel to the altered area and the bathrooms, telephones, and drinking fountains serving the altered area, are readily accessible to and usable by individuals with disabilities where such alterations to the path of travel or the bathrooms, telephones, and drinking fountains serving the altered area are not disproportionate to the overall alterations in terms of cost and scope (as determined under criteria established by the Attorney General).

(b) Elevator. Subsection (a) shall not be construed to require the installation of an elevator for facilities that are less than three stories or have less than 3,000 square feet per story unless the building is a shopping center, a shopping mall, or the professional office of a health care provider or unless the Attorney General determines that a particular category of such facilities requires the installation of elevators based on the usage of such facilities.

SEC. 304. PROHIBITION OF DISCRIMINATION IN SPECIFIED PUBLIC TRANSPORTATION SERVICES PROVIDED BY PRIVATE ENTITIES.   *42 USC 12184.*

(a) General Rule. No individual shall be discriminated against on the basis of disability in the full and equal enjoyment of specified public transportation services provided by a private entity that is primarily engaged in the business of transporting people and whose operations affect commerce.

(b) Construction. For purposes of subsection (a), discrimination includes

(1) the imposition or application by a entity described in subsection (a) of eligibility criteria that screen out or tend to screen out an individual with a disability or any class of individuals with disabilities from fully enjoying the specified public transportation services provided by the entity, unless such criteria can be shown to be necessary for the provision of the services being offered;

(2) the failure of such entity to

(A) make reasonable modifications consistent with those required under section 302(b)(2)(A)(ii);

(B) provide auxiliary aids and services consistent with the requirements of section 302(b)(2)(A)(iii); and

(C) remove barriers consistent with the requirements of section 302(b)(2)(A) and with the requirements of section 303(a)(2);

(3) the purchase or lease by such entity of a new vehicle (other than an automobile, a van with a seating capacity of less than 8 passengers, including the driver, or an over-the-road bus) which is to be used to provide specified public transportation and for which a solicitation is made after the 30th day following the effective date of this section, that is not readily accessible to and usable by individuals with disabilities, including individuals who use wheelchairs; except that the new vehicle need not be readily accessible to and usable by such individuals if the new vehicle is to be used solely in a demand responsive system and if the entity can demonstrate that such system, when viewed in its entirety, provides a level of service to such individuals equivalent to the level of service provided to the general public;

(4)(A) the purchase or lease by such entity of an over-the-road bus which does not comply with the regulations issued under section 306(a)(2); and

(B) any other failure of such entity to comply with such regulations; and

(5) the purchase or lease by such entity of a new van with a seating capacity of less than 8 passengers, including the driver, which is to be used to provide specified public transportation and for which a solicitation is made after the 30th day following the effective date of this section that is not readily accessible to or usable by individuals with disabilities, including individuals who use wheelchairs; except that the new van need not be readily accessible to and usable by such individuals if the entity can demonstrate that the system for which the van is being purchased or leased, when viewed in its entirety, provides a level of service to such individuals equivalent to the level of service provided to the general public;

(6) the purchase or lease by such entity of a new rail passenger car that is to be used to provide specified public transportation, and for which a solicitation is made later than 30 days after the effective date of this paragraph, that is not readily accessible to and usable by individuals with disabilities, including individuals who use wheelchairs; and

(7) the remanufacture by such entity of a rail passenger car that is to be used to provide specified public transportation so as to extend its usable life for 10 years or more, or the purchase or lease by such entity of such a rail car, unless the rail car, to the maximum extent feasible, is made readily accessible to and usable by individuals with disabilities, including individuals who use wheelchairs.

(c) Historical or Antiquated Cars.

(1) Exception. To the extent that compliance with subsection (b)(2)(C) or (b)(7) would significantly alter the historic or antiquated character of a historical or antiquated rail passenger car, or a rail station served exclusively by such cars, or would result in violation of any rule,

regulation, standard, or order issued by the Secretary of Transportation under the Federal Railroad Safety Act of 1970, such compliance shall not be required.

(2) Definition. As used in this subsection, the term "historical or antiquated rail passenger car" means a rail passenger car

(A) which is not less than 30 years old at the time of its use for transporting individuals;

(B) the manufacturer of which is no longer in the business of manufacturing rail passenger cars; and

(C) which (i) has a consequential association with events or persons significant to the past; or

(ii) embodies, or is being restored to embody, the distinctive characteristics of a type of rail passenger car used in the past, or to represent a time period which has passed.

SEC. 305. STUDY.   *42 USC 12185.*

a) Purposes. The Office of Technology Assessment shall undertake a study to determine

(1) the access needs of individuals with disabilities to over-the-road buses and over-the-road bus service; and

(2) the most cost-effective methods for providing access to over-the-road buses and over-the-road bus service to individuals with disabilities, particularly individuals who use wheelchairs, through all forms of boarding options.

(b) Contents. The study shall include, at a minimum, an analysis of the following:

(1) The anticipated demand by individuals with disabilities for accessible over-the-road buses and over-the-road bus service.

(2) The degree to which such buses and service, including any service required under sections 304(b)(4) and 306(a)(2), are readily accessible to and usable by individuals with disabilities.

(3) The effectiveness of various methods of providing accessibility to such buses and service to individuals with disabilities.

(4) The cost of providing accessible over-the-road buses and bus service to individuals with disabilities, including consideration of recent technological and cost saving developments in equipment and devices.

(5) Possible design changes in over-the-road buses that could enhance accessibility, including the installation of accessible restrooms which do not result in a loss of seating capacity.

(6) The impact of accessibility requirements on the continuation of over-the-road bus service, with particular consideration of the impact of such requirements on such service to rural communities.

(c) Advisory Committee. In conducting the study required by subsection (a), the Office of Technology Assessment shall establish an advisory committee, which shall consist of

(1) members selected from among private operators and manufacturers of over-the-road buses;

(2) members selected from among individuals with disabilities, particularly individuals who use wheelchairs, who are potential riders of such buses; and

(3) members selected for their technical expertise on issues included in the study, including manufacturers of boarding assistance equipment and devices.

The number of members selected under each of paragraphs (1) and (2) shall be equal, and the total number of members selected under paragraphs (1) and (2) shall exceed the number of members selected under paragraph (3).

(d) Deadline. The study required by subsection (a), along with recommendations by the Office of Technology Assessment, including any policy options for legislative action, shall be submitted to the President and Congress within 36 months after the date of the enactment of this Act. If *President* the President determines that compliance with the regulations issued pursuant to section *of U.S.* 306(a)(2)(B) on or before the applicable deadlines specified in section 306(a)(2)(B) will result in a significant reduction in intercity over-the-road bus service, the President shall extend each such deadline by 1 year.

(e) Review. In developing the study required by subsection (a), the Office of Technology Assessment shall provide a preliminary draft of such study to the Architectural and Transportation Barriers Compliance Board established under section 502 of the Rehabilitation Act of 1973 (29 U.S.C. 792). The Board shall have an opportunity to comment on such draft study, and any such comments by the Board made in writing within 120 days after the Board's receipt of the draft study shall be incorporated as part of the final study required to be submitted under subsection (d).

SEC. 306. REGULATIONS.   *42 USC 12186.*

(a) Transportation Provisions.

(1) General rule. Not later than 1 year after the date of the enactment of this Act, the Secretary of Transportation shall issue regulations in an accessible format to carry out sections 302(b)(2) (B) and (C) and to carry out section 304 (other than subsection (b)(4)).

(2) Special rules for providing access to over-the-road buses.

(A) Interim requirements.

(i) Issuance. Not later than 1 year after the date of the enactment of this Act, the Secretary of Transportation shall issue regulations in an accessible format to carry out sections 304(b)(4) and 302(b)(2)(D)(ii) that require each private entity which uses an over-the-road bus to provide transportation of individuals to provide accessibility to such bus; except that such regulations shall not require any structural changes in over-the-road buses in order to provide access to individuals who use wheelchairs during the effective period of such regulations and shall not require the purchase of boarding assistance devices to provide access to such individuals.

(ii) Effective period. The regulations issued pursuant to this subparagraph shall be effective until the effective date of the regulations issued under subparagraph (B).

(B) Final requirement.

(i) Review of study and interim requirements. The Secretary shall review the study submitted under section 305 and the regulations issued pursuant to subparagraph (A).

(ii) Issuance. Not later than 1 year after the date of the submission of the study under section 305, the Secretary shall issue in an accessible format new regulations to carry out sections 304(b)(4) and 302(b)(2)(D)(ii) that require, taking into account the purposes of the study under section 305 and any recommendations resulting from such study, each private entity which uses an over-the-road bus to provide transportation to individuals to provide accessibility to such bus to individuals with disabilities, including individuals who use wheelchairs.

(iii) Effective period. Subject to section 305(d), the regulations issued pursuant to this subparagraph shall take effect

> (I) with respect to small providers of transportation (as defined by the Secretary), 7 years after the date of the enactment of this Act; and

> (II) with respect to other providers of transportation, 6 years after such date of enactment.

> (C) Limitation on requiring installation of accessible restrooms. The regulations issued pursuant to this paragraph shall not require the installation of accessible restrooms in over-the-road buses if such installation would result in a loss of seating capacity.

(3) Standards. The regulations issued pursuant to this subsection shall include standards applicable to facilities and vehicles covered by sections 302(b)(2) and 304.

(b) Other Provisions. Not later than 1 year after the date of the enactment of this Act, the Attorney General shall issue regulations in an accessible format to carry out the provisions of this title not referred to in subsection (a) that include standards applicable to facilities and vehicles covered under section 302.

(c) Consistency With ATBCB Guidelines. Standards included in regulations issued under subsections (a) and (b) shall be consistent with the minimum guidelines and requirements issued by the Architectural and Transportation Barriers Compliance Board in accordance with section 504 of this Act.

(d) Interim Accessibility Standards.

(1) Facilities. If final regulations have not been issued pursuant to this section, for new construction or alterations for which a valid and appropriate State or local building permit is obtained prior to the issuance of final regulations under this section, and for which the construction or alteration authorized by such permit begins within one year of the receipt of such permit and is completed under the terms of such permit, compliance with the Uniform Federal Accessibility Standards in effect at the time the building permit is issued shall suffice to satisfy the requirement that facilities be readily accessible to and usable by persons with disabilities as required under section 303, except that, if such final regulations have not been issued one year after the Architectural and Transportation Barriers Compliance Board has issued the supplemental minimum guidelines required under section 504(a) of this Act, compliance with such supplemental minimum guidelines shall be necessary to satisfy the requirement that facilities be readily accessible to and usable by persons with disabilities prior to issuance of the final regulations.

(2) Vehicles and rail passenger cars. If final regulations have not been issued pursuant to this section, a private entity shall be considered to have complied with the requirements of this title, if any, that a vehicle or rail passenger car be readily accessible to and usable by individuals with disabilities, if the design for such vehicle or car complies with the laws and regulations (including the Minimum Guidelines and Requirements for Accessible Design and such supplemental minimum guidelines as are issued under section 504(a) of this Act) governing accessibility of such vehicles or cars, to the extent that such laws and regulations are not inconsistent with this title and are in effect at the time such design is substantially completed.

SEC. 307. EXEMPTIONS FOR PRIVATE CLUBS AND RELIGIOUS ORGANIZATIONS.

42 USC 12187.

The provisions of this title shall not apply to private clubs or establishments exempted from coverage under title II of the Civil Rights Act of 1964 (42 U.S.C. 2000-a(e)) or to religious organizations or entities controlled by religious organizations, including places of worship.

SEC. 308. ENFORCEMENT.   *42 USC 12188.*

(a) In General.

   (1) Availability of remedies and procedures. The remedies and procedures set forth in section 204(a) of the Civil Rights Act of 1964 (42 U.S.C. 2000a-3(a)) are the remedies and procedures this title provides to any person who is being subjected to discrimination on the basis of disability in violation of this title or who has reasonable grounds for believing that such person is about to be subjected to discrimination in violation of section 303. Nothing in this section shall require a person with a disability to engage in a futile gesture if such person has actual notice that a person or organization covered by this title does not intend to comply with its provisions.

   (2) Injunctive relief. In the case of violations of sections 302(b)(2)(A)(iv) and section 303(a), injunctive relief shall include an order to alter facilities to make such facilities readily accessible to and usable by individuals with disabilities to the extent required by this title. Where appropriate, injunctive relief shall also include requiring the provision of an auxiliary aid or service, modification of a policy, or provision of alternative methods, to the extent required by this title.

(b) Enforcement by the Attorney General.

   (1) Denial of rights.

      (A) Duty to investigate.

      (i) In general. The Attorney General shall investigate alleged violations of this title, and shall undertake periodic reviews of compliance of covered entities under this title.

      (ii) Attorney General Certification. On the application of a State or local government, the Attorney General may, in consultation with the Architectural and Transportation Barriers Compliance Board, and after prior notice and a public hearing at which persons, including individuals with disabilities, are provided an opportunity to testify against such certification, certify that a State law or local building code or similar ordinance that establishes accessibility requirements meets or exceeds the minimum requirements of this Act for the accessibility and usability of covered facilities under this title. At any enforcement proceeding under this section, such certification by the Attorney General shall be rebuttable evidence that such State law or local ordinance does meet or exceed the minimum requirements of this Act.

      (B) Potential violation. If the Attorney General has reasonable cause to believe that

      (i) any person or group of persons is engaged in a pattern or practice of discrimination under this title; or

      (ii) any person or group of persons has been discriminated against under this title and such discrimination raises an issue of general public importance,
the Attorney General may commence a civil action in any appropriate United States district court.

   (2) Authority of court. In a civil action under paragraph (1)(B), the court

      (A) may grant any equitable relief that such court considers to be appropriate, including, to the extent required by this title

      (i) granting temporary, preliminary, or permanent relief;

      (ii) providing an auxiliary aid or service, modification of policy, practice, or procedure, or alternative method; and

      (iii) making facilities readily accessible to and usable by individuals with disabilities;

(B) may award such other relief as the court considers to be appropriate, including monetary damages to persons aggrieved when requested by the Attorney General; and

(C) may, to vindicate the public interest, assess a civil penalty against the entity in an amount

(i) not exceeding $50,000 for a first violation; and

(ii) not exceeding $100,000 for any subsequent violation.

(3) Single violation. For purposes of paragraph (2)(C), in determining whether a first or subsequent violation has occurred, a determination in a single action, by judgment or settlement, that the covered entity has engaged in more than one discriminatory act shall be counted as a single violation.

(4) Punitive damages. For purposes of subsection (b)(2)(B), the term "monetary damages" and "such other relief" does not include punitive damages.

(5) Judicial consideration. In a civil action under paragraph (1)(B), the court, when considering what amount of civil penalty, if any, is appropriate, shall give consideration to any good faith effort or attempt to comply with this Act by the entity. In evaluating good faith, the court shall consider, among other factors it deems relevant, whether the entity could have reasonably anticipated the need for an appropriate type of auxiliary aid needed to accommodate the unique needs of a particular individual with a disability.

SEC. 309. EXAMINATIONS AND COURSES.   *42 USC 12189.*

Any person that offers examinations or courses related to applications, licensing, certification, or credentialing for secondary or postsecondary education, professional, or trade purposes shall offer such examinations or courses in a place and manner accessible to persons with disabilities or offer alternative accessible arrangements for such individuals.

SEC. 310. EFFECTIVE DATE.   *42 USC 12181 note.*

(a) General Rule. Except as provided in subsections (b) and (c), this title shall become effective 18 months after the date of the enactment of this Act.

(b) Civil Actions. Except for any civil action brought for a violation of section 303, no civil action shall be brought for any act or omission described in section 302 which occurs

(1) during the first 6 months after the effective date, against businesses that employ 25 or fewer employees and have gross receipts of $1,000,000 or less; and

(2) during the first year after the effective date, against businesses that employ 10 or fewer employees and have gross receipts of $500,000 or less.

(c) Exception. Sections 302(a) for purposes of section 302(b)(2) (B) and (C) only, 304(a) for purposes of section 304(b)(3) only, 304(b)(3), 305, and 306 shall take effect on the date of the enactment of this Act.

TITLE IV TELECOMMUNICATIONS

SEC. 401. TELECOMMUNICATIONS RELAY SERVICES FOR HEARING-IMPAIRED AND SPEECH-IMPAIRED INDIVIDUALS.

(a) Telecommunications. Title II of the Communications Act of 1934 (47 U.S.C. 201 et seq.) is amended by adding at the end thereof the following new section:
"SEC. 225. TELECOMMUNICATIONS SERVICES FOR HEARING-IMPAIRED AND SPEECH-IMPAIRED INDIVIDUALS.   *State and local Governments. 47 USC 225.*

"(a) Definitions. As used in this section
     "(1) Common carrier or carrier. The term `common carrier' or `carrier' includes any common carrier engaged in interstate communication by wire or radio as defined in section 3(h) and any common carrier engaged in intrastate communication by wire or radio, notwithstanding sections 2(b) and 221(b).
     "(2) TDD. The term `TDD' means a Telecommunications Device for the Deaf, which is a machine that employs graphic communication in the transmission of coded signals through a wire or radio communication system.
     "(3) Telecommunications relay services. The term `telecommunications relay services' means telephone transmission services that provide the ability for an individual who has a hearing impairment or speech impairment to engage in communication by wire or radio with a hearing individual in a manner that is functionally equivalent to the ability of an individual who does not have a hearing impairment or speech impairment to communicate using voice communication services by wire or radio. Such term includes services that enable two-way communication between an individual who uses a TDD or other nonvoice terminal device and an individual who does not use such a device.
"(b) Availability of Telecommunications Relay Services.
     "(1) In general. In order to carry out the purposes established under section 1, to make available to all individuals in the United States a rapid, efficient nationwide communication service, and to increase the utility of the telephone system of the Nation, the Commission shall ensure that interstate and intrastate telecommunications relay services are available, to the extent possible and in the most efficient manner, to hearing-impaired and speech-impaired individuals in the United States.
     "(2) Use of General Authority and Remedies. For the purposes of administering and enforcing the provisions of this section and the regulations prescribed thereunder, the Commission shall have the same authority, power, and functions with respect to common carriers engaged in intrastate communication as the Commission has in administering and enforcing the provisions of this title with respect to any common carrier engaged in interstate communication. Any violation of this section by any common carrier engaged in intrastate communication shall be subject to the same remedies, penalties, and procedures as are applicable to a violation of this Act by a common carrier engaged in interstate communication.
"(c) Provision of Services. Each common carrier providing telephone voice transmission services shall, not later than 3 years after the date of enactment of this section, provide in compliance with the regulations prescribed under this section, throughout the area in which it

offers service, telecommunications relay services, individually, through designees, through a competitively selected vendor, or in concert with other carriers. A common carrier shall be considered to be in compliance with such regulations

"(1) with respect to intrastate telecommunications relay services in any State that does not have a certified program under subsection (f) and with respect to interstate telecommunications relay services, if such common carrier (or other entity through which the carrier is providing such relay services) is in compliance with the Commission's regulations under subsection (d); or

"(2) with respect to intrastate telecommunications relay services in any State that has a certified program under subsection (f) for such State, if such common carrier (or other entity through which the carrier is providing such relay services) is in compliance with the program certified under subsection (f) for such State.

"(d) Regulations.

"(1) In general. The Commission shall, not later than 1 year after the date of enactment of this section, prescribe regulations to implement this section, including regulations that

"(A) establish functional requirements, guidelines, and operations procedures for telecommunications relay services;

"(B) establish minimum standards that shall be met in carrying out subsection (c);

"(C) require that telecommunications relay services operate every day for 24 hours per day;

"(D) require that users of telecommunications relay services pay rates no greater than the rates paid for functionally equivalent voice communication services with respect to such factors as the duration of the call, the time of day, and the distance from point of origination to point of termination;

"(E) prohibit relay operators from failing to fulfill the obligations of common carriers by refusing calls or limiting the length of calls that use telecommunications relay services;

"(F) prohibit relay operators from disclosing the content of any relayed conversation and from keeping records of the content of any such conversation beyond the duration of the call; and

"(G) prohibit relay operators from intentionally altering a relayed conversation.

"(2) Technology. The Commission shall ensure that regulations prescribed to implement this section encourage, consistent with section 7(a) of this Act, the use of existing technology and do not discourage or impair the development of improved technology.

"(3) Jurisdictional separation of costs.

"(A) In general. Consistent with the provisions of section 410 of this Act, the Commission shall prescribe regulations governing the jurisdictional separation of costs for the services provided pursuant to this section.

"(B) Recovering costs. Such regulations shall generally provide that costs caused by interstate telecommunications relay services shall be recovered from all subscribers for every interstate service and costs caused by intrastate telecommunications relay services shall be recovered from the intrastate jurisdiction. In a State that has a certified program under subsection (f), a State commission shall permit a common carrier to recover the costs incurred in providing intrastate telecommunications relay services by a method consistent with the requirements of this section.

"(e) Enforcement.

"(1) In general. Subject to subsections (f) and (g), the Commission shall enforce this section.

"(2) Complaint. The Commission shall resolve, by final order, a complaint alleging a violation of this section within 180 days after the date such complaint is filed.

"(f) Certification.

"(1) State documentation. Any State desiring to establish a State program under this section shall submit documentation to the Commission that describes the program of such State for implementing intrastate telecommunications relay services and the procedures and remedies available for enforcing any requirements imposed by the State program.

"(2) Requirements for certification. After review of such documentation, the Commission shall certify the State program if the Commission determines that

"(A) the program makes available to hearing-impaired and speech-impaired individuals, either directly, through designees, through a competitively selected vendor, or through regulation of intrastate common carriers, intrastate telecommunications relay services in such State in a manner that meets or exceeds the requirements of regulations prescribed by the Commission under subsection (d); and

"(B) the program makes available adequate procedures and remedies for enforcing the requirements of the State program.

"(3) Method of funding. Except as provided in subsection (d), the Commission shall not refuse to certify a State program based solely on the method such State will implement for funding intrastate telecommunication relay services.

"(4) Suspension or revocation of certification. The Commission may suspend or revoke such certification if, after notice and opportunity for hearing, the Commission determines that such certification is no longer warranted. In a State whose program has been suspended or revoked, the Commission shall take such steps as may be necessary, consistent with this section, to ensure continuity of telecommunications relay services.

"(g) Complaint.

"(1) Referral of complaint. If a complaint to the Commission alleges a violation of this section with respect to intrastate telecommunications relay services within a State and certification of the program of such State under subsection (f) is in effect, the Commission shall refer such complaint to such State.

"(2) Jurisdiction of commission. After referring a complaint to a State under paragraph (1), the Commission shall exercise jurisdiction over such complaint only if

"(A) final action under such State program has not been taken on such complaint by such State

"(i) within 180 days after the complaint is filed with such State; or

"(ii) within a shorter period as prescribed by the regulations of such State; or

"(B) the Commission determines that such State program is no longer qualified for certification under subsection (f).".

(b) Conforming Amendments. The Communications Act of 1934 (47 U.S.C. 151 et seq.) is amended

(1) in section 2(b) (47 U.S.C. 152(b)), by striking "section 224" and inserting "sections 224 and 225"; and

(2) in section 221(b) (47 U.S.C. 221(b)), by striking "section 301" and inserting "sections 225 and 301".

SEC. 402. CLOSED-CAPTIONING OF PUBLIC SERVICE ANNOUNCEMENTS.

Section 711 of the Communications Act of 1934 is amended to read as follows:

"SEC. 711. CLOSED-CAPTIONING OF PUBLIC SERVICE ANNOUNCEMENTS.

47 USC 611.

"Any television public service announcement that is produced or funded in whole or in part by any agency or instrumentality of Federal Government shall include closed captioning of the verbal content of such announcement. A television broadcast station licensee

"(1) shall not be required to supply closed captioning for any such announcement that fails to include it; and

"(2) shall not be liable for broadcasting any such announcement without transmitting a closed caption unless the licensee intentionally fails to transmit the closed caption that was included with the announcement.".

TITLE V MISCELLANEOUS PROVISIONS

SEC. 501. CONSTRUCTION.   *42 USC 12201.*

(a) In General. Except as otherwise provided in this Act, nothing in this Act shall be construed to apply a lesser standard than the standards applied under title V of the Rehabilitation Act of 1973 (29 U.S.C. 790 et seq.) or the regulations issued by Federal agencies pursuant to such title.

(b) Relationship to Other Laws. Nothing in this Act shall be construed to invalidate or limit the remedies, rights, and procedures of any Federal law or law of any State or political subdivision of any State or jurisdiction that provides greater or equal protection for the rights of individuals with disabilities than are afforded by this Act. Nothing in this Act shall be construed to preclude the prohibition of, or the imposition of restrictions on, smoking in places of employment covered by title I, in transportation covered by title II or III, or in places of public accommodation covered by title III.

(c) Insurance. Titles I through IV of this Act shall not be construed to prohibit or restrict

(1) an insurer, hospital or medical service company, health maintenance organization, or any agent, or entity that administers benefit plans, or similar organizations from underwriting risks, classifying risks, or administering such risks that are based on or not inconsistent with State law; or

(2) a person or organization covered by this Act from establishing, sponsoring, observing or administering the terms of a bona fide benefit plan that are based on underwriting risks, classifying risks, or administering such risks that are based on or not inconsistent with State law; or

(3) a person or organization covered by this Act from establishing, sponsoring, observing or administering the terms of a bona fide benefit plan that is not subject to State laws that regulate insurance.

Paragraphs (1), (2), and (3) shall not be used as a subterfuge to evade the purposes of title I and III.

(d) Accommodations and Services. Nothing in this Act shall be construed to require an individual with a disability to accept an accommodation, aid, service, opportunity, or benefit which such individual chooses not to accept.

SEC. 502. STATE IMMUNITY.

42 USC 12202.

A State shall not be immune under the eleventh amendment to the Constitution of the United States from an action in Federal or State court of competent jurisdiction for a violation of this Act. In any action against a State for a violation of the requirements of this Act, remedies (including remedies both at law and in equity) are available for such a violation to the same extent as such remedies are available for such a violation in an action against any public or private entity other than a State.

SEC. 503. PROHIBITION AGAINST RETALIATION AND COERCION.   *42 USC 12203.*

(a) Retaliation. No person shall discriminate against any individual because such individual has opposed any act or practice made unlawful by this Act or because such individual made a charge, testified, assisted, or participated in any manner in an investigation, proceeding, or hearing under this Act.

(b) Interference, Coercion, or Intimidation. It shall be unlawful to coerce, intimidate, threaten, or interfere with any individual in the exercise or enjoyment of, or on account of his or her having exercised or enjoyed, or on account of his or her having aided or encouraged any other individual in the exercise or enjoyment of, any right granted or protected by this Act.

(c) Remedies and Procedures. The remedies and procedures available under sections 107, 203, and 308 of this Act shall be available to aggrieved persons for violations of subsections (a) and (b), with respect to title I, title II and title III, respectively.

SEC. 504. REGULATIONS BY THE ARCHITECTURAL AND TRANSPORTATION BARRIERS COMPLIANCE BOARD.   *42 USC 12204.*

(a) Issuance of Guidelines. Not later than 9 months after the date of enactment of this Act, the Architectural and Transportation Barriers Compliance Board shall issue minimum guidelines that shall supplement the existing Minimum Guidelines and Requirements for Accessible Design for purposes of titles II and III of this Act.

(b) Contents of Guidelines. The supplemental guidelines issued under subsection (a) shall establish additional requirements, consistent with this Act, to ensure that buildings, facilities, rail passenger cars, and vehicles are accessible, in terms of architecture and design, transportation, and communication, to individuals with disabilities.

(c) Qualified Historic Properties.

(1) In general. The supplemental guidelines issued under subsection (a) shall include procedures and requirements for alterations that will threaten or destroy the historic significance of qualified historic buildings and facilities as defined in 4.1.7(1)(a) of the Uniform Federal Accessibility Standards.

(2) Sites eligible for listing in national register. With respect to alterations of buildings or facilities that are eligible for listing in the National Register of Historic Places under the National Historic Preservation Act (16 U.S.C. 470 et seq.), the guidelines described in paragraph (1) shall, at a minimum, maintain the procedures and requirements established in 4.1.7 (1) and (2) of the Uniform Federal Accessibility Standards.

(3) Other sites. With respect to alterations of buildings or facilities designated as historic under State or local law, the guidelines described in paragraph (1) shall establish procedures equivalent to those established by 4.1.7(1) (b) and (c) of the Uniform Federal Accessibility Standards, and shall require, at a minimum, compliance with the requirements established in 4.1.7(2) of such standards.

SEC. 505. ATTORNEY'S FEES.
42 USC 12205.

In any action or administrative proceeding commenced pursuant to this Act, the court or agency, in its discretion, may allow the prevailing party, other than the United States, a reasonable attorney's fee, including litigation expenses, and costs, and the United States shall be liable for the foregoing the same as a private individual.

SEC. 506. TECHNICAL ASSISTANCE.
42 USC 12206.

(a) Plan for Assistance.

(1) In general. Not later than 180 days after the date of enactment of this Act, the Attorney General, in consultation with the Chair of the Equal Employment Opportunity Commission, the Secretary of Transportation, the Chair of the Architectural and Transportation Barriers Compliance Board, and the Chairman of the Federal Communications Commission, shall develop a plan to assist entities covered under this Act, and other Federal agencies, in understanding the responsibility of such entities and agencies under this Act.

(2) Publication of plan. The Attorney General shall publish the plan referred to in paragraph (1) for public comment in accordance with subchapter II of chapter 5 of title 5, United States Code (commonly known as the Administrative Procedure Act).

(b) Agency and Public Assistance. The Attorney General may obtain the assistance of other Federal agencies in carrying out subsection (a), including the National Council on Disability, the President's Committee on Employment of People with Disabilities, the Small Business Administration, and the Department of Commerce.

(c) Implementation.

(1) Rendering assistance. Each Federal agency that has responsibility under paragraph (2) for implementing this Act may render technical assistance to individuals and institutions that have rights or duties under the respective title or titles for which such agency has responsibility.

(2) Implementation of titles.

(A) Title I. The Equal Employment Opportunity Commission and the Attorney General shall implement the plan for assistance developed under subsection (a), for title I.

(B) Title II.

(i) Subtitle a. The Attorney General shall implement such plan for assistance for subtitle A of title II.

(ii) Subtitle b. The Secretary of Transportation shall implement such plan for assistance for subtitle B of title II.

(C) Title III. The Attorney General, in coordination with the Secretary of Transportation and the Chair of the Architectural Transportation Barriers Compliance Board, shall implement such plan for assistance for title III, except for section 304, the plan for assistance for which shall be implemented by the Secretary of Transportation.

(D) Title IV. The Chairman of the Federal Communications Commission, in coordination with the Attorney General, shall implement such plan for assistance for title IV.

(3) Technical assistance manuals. Each Federal agency that has responsibility under paragraph (2) for implementing this Act shall, as part of its implementation responsibilities, ensure the availability and provision of appropriate technical assistance manuals to individuals or entities with rights or duties under this Act no later than six months after applicable final regulations are published under titles I, II, III, and IV.

(d) Grants and Contracts.

(1) In general. Each Federal agency that has responsibility under subsection (c)(2) for implementing this Act may make grants or award contracts to effectuate the purposes of this section, subject to the availability of appropriations. Such grants and contracts may be awarded to individuals, institutions not organized for profit and no part of the net earnings of which inures to the benefit of any private shareholder or individual (including educational institutions), and associations representing individuals who have rights or duties under this Act. Contracts may be awarded to entities organized for profit, but such entities may not be the recipients or grants described in this paragraph.

(2) Dissemination of information. Such grants and contracts, among other uses, may be designed to ensure wide dissemination of information about the rights and duties established by this Act and to provide information and technical assistance about techniques for effective compliance with this Act.

(e) Failure to Receive Assistance. An employer, public accommodation, or other entity covered under this Act shall not be excused from compliance with the requirements of this Act because of any failure to receive technical assistance under this section, including any failure in the development or dissemination of any technical assistance manual authorized by this section.

SEC. 507. FEDERAL WILDERNESS AREAS. *42 USC 12207.*

(a) Study. The National Council on Disability shall conduct a study and report on the effect that wilderness designations and wilderness land management practices have on the ability of individuals with disabilities to use and enjoy the National Wilderness Preservation System as established under the Wilderness Act (16 U.S.C. 1131 et seq.).

(b) Submission of Report. Not later than 1 year after the enactment of this Act, the National Council on Disability shall submit the report required under subsection (a) to Congress.

(c) Specific Wilderness Access.

(1) In general. Congress reaffirms that nothing in the Wilderness Act is to be construed as prohibiting the use of a wheelchair in a wilderness area by an individual whose disability requires use of a wheelchair, and consistent with the Wilderness Act no agency is required to provide any form of special treatment or accommodation, or to construct any facilities or modify any conditions of lands within a wilderness area in order to facilitate such use.

(2) Definition. For purposes of paragraph (1), the term "wheelchair" means a device designed solely for use by a mobility-impaired person for locomotion, that is suitable for use in an indoor pedestrian area.

SEC. 508. TRANSVESTITES. *42 USC 12208.*

For the purposes of this Act, the term "disabled" or "disability" shall not apply to an individual solely because that individual is a transvestite.

SEC. 509. COVERAGE OF CONGRESS AND THE AGENCIES OF THE LEGISLATIVE BRANCH. *42 USC 12209.*

(a) Coverage of the Senate.

(1) Commitment to Rule XLII. The Senate reaffirms its commitment to Rule XLII of the Standing Rules of the Senate which provides as follows:

"No member, officer, or employee of the Senate shall, with respect to employment by the Senate or any office thereof

"(a) fail or refuse to hire an individual;

"(b) discharge an individual; or

"(c) otherwise discriminate against an individual with respect to promotion, compensation, or terms, conditions, or privileges of employment

on the basis of such individual's race, color, religion, sex, national origin, age, or state of physical handicap.".

(2) Application to Senate employment. The rights and protections provided pursuant to this Act, the Civil Rights Act of 1990 (S. 2104, 101st Congress), the Civil Rights Act of 1964, the Age Discrimination in Employment Act of 1967, and the Rehabilitation Act of 1973 shall apply with respect to employment by the United States Senate.

(3) Investigation and adjudication of claims. All claims raised by any individual with respect to Senate employment, pursuant to the Acts referred to in paragraph (2), shall be investigated and adjudicated by the Select Committee on Ethics, pursuant to S. Res. 338, 88th Congress, as amended, or such other entity as the Senate may designate.

(4) Rights of employees. The Committee on Rules and Administration shall ensure that Senate employees are informed of their rights under the Acts referred to in paragraph (2).

(5) Applicable Remedies. When assigning remedies to individuals found to have a valid claim under the Acts referred to in paragraph (2), the Select Committee on Ethics, or such other entity as the Senate may designate, should to the extent practicable apply the same remedies applicable to all other employees covered by the Acts referred to in paragraph (2). Such remedies shall apply exclusively.

(6) Matters Other Than Employment.

(A) In General. The rights and protections under this Act shall, subject to subparagraph (B), apply with respect to the conduct of the Senate regarding matters other than employment.

(B) Remedies. The Architect of the Capitol shall establish remedies and procedures to be utilized with respect to the rights and protections provided pursuant to subparagraph (A). Such remedies and procedures shall apply exclusively, after approval in accordance with subparagraph (C).

(C) Proposed remedies and procedures. For purposes of subparagraph (B), the Architect of the Capitol shall submit proposed remedies and procedures to the Senate Committee on Rules and Administration. The remedies and procedures shall be effective upon the approval of the Committee on Rules and Administration.

(7) Exercise of rulemaking power. Notwithstanding any other provision of law, enforcement and adjudication of the rights and protections referred to in paragraph (2) and (6)(A) shall be within the exclusive jurisdiction of the United States Senate. The provisions of paragraph (1), (3), (4), (5), (6)(B), and (6)(C) are enacted by the Senate as an exercise of the rulemaking power of the Senate, with full recognition of the right of the Senate to change its rules, in the same manner, and to the same extent, as in the case of any other rule of the Senate.

(b) Coverage of the House of Representatives.

(1) In general. Notwithstanding any other provision of this Act or of law, the purposes of this Act shall, subject to paragraphs (2) and (3), apply in their entirety to the House of Representatives.

(2) Employment in the house.

(A) Application. The rights and protections under this Act shall, subject to subparagraph (B), apply with respect to any employee in an employment position in the House of Representatives and any employing authority of the House of Representatives.

(B) Administration.

(i) In general. In the administration of this paragraph, the remedies and procedures made applicable pursuant to the resolution described in clause (ii) shall apply exclusively.

(ii) Resolution. The resolution referred to in clause (i) is House Resolution 15 of the One Hundred First Congress, as agreed to January 3, 1989, or any other provision that continues in effect the provisions of, or is a successor to, the Fair Employment Practices Resolution (House Resolution 558 of the One Hundredth Congress, as agreed to October 4, 1988).

(C) Exercise of rulemaking power. The provisions of subparagraph (B) are enacted by the House of Representatives as an exercise of the rulemaking power of the House of Representatives, with full recognition of the right of the House to change its rules, in the same manner, and to the same extent as in the case of any other rule of the House.

(3) Matters other than employment.

(A) In general. The rights and protections under this Act shall, subject to subparagraph (B), apply with respect to the conduct of the House of Representatives regarding matters other than employment.

(B) Remedies. The Architect of the Capitol shall establish remedies and procedures to be utilized with respect to the rights and protections provided pursuant to subparagraph (A). Such remedies and procedures shall apply exclusively, after approval in accordance with subparagraph (C).

(C) Approval. For purposes of subparagraph (B), the Architect of the Capitol shall submit proposed remedies and procedures to the Speaker of the House of Representatives. The remedies and procedures shall be effective upon the approval of the Speaker, after consultation with the House Office Building Commission.

(c) Instrumentalities of Congress.

(1) In general. The rights and protections under this Act shall, subject to paragraph (2), apply with respect to the conduct of each instrumentality of the Congress.

(2) Establishment of remedies and procedures by instrumentalities. The chief official of each instrumentality of the Congress shall establish remedies and procedures to be utilized with respect to the rights and protections provided pursuant to paragraph (1). Such remedies and procedures shall apply exclusively.

(3) Report to congress. The chief official of each instrumentality of the Congress shall, after

establishing remedies and procedures for purposes of paragraph (2), submit to the Congress a report describing the remedies and procedures.

(4) Definition of instrumentalities. For purposes of this section, instrumentalities of the Congress include the following: the Architect of the Capitol, the Congressional Budget Office, the General Accounting Office, the Government Printing Office, the Library of Congress, the Office of Technology Assessment, and the United States Botanic Garden.

(5) Construction. Nothing in this section shall alter the enforcement procedures for individuals with disabilities provided in the General Accounting Office Personnel Act of 1980 and regulations promulgated pursuant to that Act.

SEC. 510. ILLEGAL USE OF DRUGS.   *42 USC 12210.*

(a) In General. For purposes of this Act, the term "individual with a disability" does not include an individual who is currently engaging in the illegal use of drugs, when the covered entity acts on the basis of such use.

(b) Rules of Construction. Nothing in subsection (a) shall be construed to exclude as an individual with a disability an individual who

(1) has successfully completed a supervised drug rehabilitation program and is no longer engaging in the illegal use of drugs, or has otherwise been rehabilitated successfully and is no longer engaging in such use;

(2) is participating in a supervised rehabilitation program and is no longer engaging in such use; or

(3) is erroneously regarded as engaging in such use, but is not engaging in such use; except that it shall not be a violation of this Act for a covered entity to adopt or administer reasonable policies or procedures, including but not limited to drug testing, designed to ensure that an individual described in paragraph (1) or (2) is no longer engaging in the illegal use of drugs; however, nothing in this section shall be construed to encourage, prohibit, restrict, or authorize the conducting of testing for the illegal use of drugs.

(c) Health and Other Services. Notwithstanding subsection (a) and section 511(b)(3), an individual shall not be denied health services, or services provided in connection with drug rehabilitation, on the basis of the current illegal use of drugs if the individual is otherwise entitled to such services.

(d) Definition of Illegal use of drugs.

(1) In general. The term "illegal use of drugs" means the use of drugs, the possession or distribution of which is unlawful under the Controlled Substances Act (21 U.S.C. 812). Such term does not include the use of a drug taken under supervision by a licensed health care professional, or other uses authorized by the Controlled Substances Act or other provisions of Federal law.

(2) Drugs. The term "drug" means a controlled substance, as defined in schedules I through V of section 202 of the Controlled Substances Act.

SEC. 511. DEFINITIONS.   *42 USC 12211.*

(a) Homosexuality and Bisexuality. For purposes of the definition of "disability" in section 3(2), homosexuality and bisexuality are not impairments and as such are not disabilities under this Act.

(b) Certain Conditions. Under this Act, the term "disability" shall not include

(1) transvestism, transsexualism, pedophilia, exhibitionism, voyeurism, gender identity disorders not resulting from physical impairments, or other sexual behavior disorders;

(2) compulsive gambling, kleptomania, or pyromania; or

(3) psychoactive substance use disorders resulting from current illegal use of drugs.

SEC. 512. AMENDMENTS TO THE REHABILITATION ACT.   *42 USC 12115.*

(a) Definition of Handicapped Individual. Section 7(8) of the Rehabilitation Act of 1973 (29 U.S.C. 706(8)) is amended by redesignating subparagraph (C) as subparagraph (D), and by inserting after subparagraph (B) the following subparagraph:

"(C)(i) For purposes of title V, the term `individual with handicaps' does not include an individual who is currently engaging in the illegal use of drugs, when a covered entity acts on the basis of such use.

"(ii) Nothing in clause (i) shall be construed to exclude as an individual with handicaps an individual who

"(I) has successfully completed a supervised drug rehabilitation program and is no longer engaging in the illegal use of drugs, or has otherwise been rehabilitated successfully and is no longer engaging in such use;

"(II) is participating in a supervised rehabilitation program and is no longer engaging in such use; or

"(III) is erroneously regarded as engaging in such use, but is not engaging in such use; except that it shall not be a violation of this Act for a covered entity to adopt or administer reasonable policies or procedures, including but not limited to drug testing, designed to ensure that an individual described in subclause (I) or (II) is no longer engaging in the illegal use of drugs.

"(iii) Notwithstanding clause (i), for purposes of programs and activities providing health services and services provided under titles I, II and III, an individual shall not be excluded from the benefits of such programs or activities on the basis of his or her current illegal use of drugs if he or she is otherwise entitled to such services.

"(iv) For purposes of programs and activities providing educational services, local educational agencies may take disciplinary action pertaining to the use or possession of illegal drugs or alcohol against any handicapped student who currently is engaging in the illegal use of drugs or in the use of alcohol to the same extent that such disciplinary action is taken against nonhandicapped students. Furthermore, the due process procedures at 34 CFR 104.36 shall not apply to such disciplinary actions.

"(v) For purposes of sections 503 and 504 as such sections relate to employment, the term 'individual with handicaps' does not include any individual who is an alcoholic whose current use of alcohol prevents such individual from performing the duties of the job in question or whose employment, by reason of such current alcohol abuse, would constitute a direct threat to property or the safety of others.".

(b) Definition of Illegal Drugs. Section 7 of the Rehabilitation Act of 1973 (29 U.S.C. 706) is amended by adding at the end the following new paragraph:

"(22)(A) The term `drug' means a controlled substance, as defined in schedules I through V of section 202 of the Controlled Substances Act (21 U.S.C. 812).

"(B) The term 'illegal use of drugs' means the use of drugs, the possession or distribution of which is unlawful under the Controlled Substances Act. Such term does not include the use of a drug taken under supervision by a licensed health care professional, or other uses authorized by the Controlled Substances Act or other provisions of Federal law."

(c) Conforming Amendments. Section 7(8)(B) of the Rehabilitation Act of 1973 (29 U.S.C. 706(8)(B)) is amended

(1) in the first sentence, by striking "Subject to the second sentence of this subparagraph," and inserting "Subject to subparagraphs (C) and (D),"; and

(2) by striking the second sentence.

SEC. 513. ALTERNATIVE MEANS OF DISPUTE RESOLUTION.   *42 USC 12212.*

Where appropriate and to the extent authorized by law, the use of alternative means of dispute resolution, including settlement negotiations, conciliation, facilitation, mediation, factfinding, minitrials, and arbitration, is encouraged to resolve disputes arising under this Act.

SEC. 514. SEVERABILITY.   *42 USC 12213.*

Should any provision in this Act be found to be unconstitutional by a court of law, such provision shall be severed from the remainder of the Act, and such action shall not affect the enforceability of the remaining provisions of the Act.

Approved July 26, 1990.

LEGISLATIVE HISTORY-S. 933 (H.R. 2273):
HOUSE REPORTS: No. 101-485, Pt. 1 (Comm. on Public Works and Transportation), Pt. 2 (Comm. on Education and Labor), Pt. 3 (Comm. on the Judiciary), and Pt. 4 (Comm. on Energy and Commerce) all accompanying H.R. 2272; and No. 101-558 and No. 101-569 both from (Comm. of Conference).
SENATE REPORTS: No. 101-116 (Comm. on Labor and Human Resources).
CONGRESSIONAL RECORD:
　Vol. 135 (1989): Sept. 7, considered and passed by Senate.
　Vol. 136 (1990): May 17, 22, H.R. 2273 considered and passed House; S. 933 passed in lieu.
　　July 11, Senate recommitted conference report.
　　July 12, House agreed to conference report.
　　July 13, Senate agreed to conference report.
WEEKLY COMPILATION OF PRESIDENTIAL DOCUMENTS, Vol. 26 (1990): July 26, Presidential remarks and statement.

APPENDIX B

ADA ACCESSIBILITY GUIDELINES

1. PURPOSE.

This document sets guidelines for accessibility to places of public accommodation and commercial facilities by individuals with disabilities. These guidelines are to be applied during the design, construction, and alteration of such buildings and facilities to the extent required by regulations issued by Federal agencies, including the Department of Justice, under the Americans with Disabilities Act of 1990.

The technical specifications 4.2 through 4.35, of these guidelines are the same as those of the American National Standard Institute's document A117.1-1980, except as noted in this text by italics. However, sections 4.1.1 through 4.1.7 and sections 5 through 10 are different from ANSI A117.1 in their entirety and are printed in standard type.

The illustrations and text of ANSI A117.1 are reproduced with permission from the American National Standards Institute. Copies of the standard may be purchased from the American National Standards Institute at 1430 Broadway, New York, New York 10018.

2. GENERAL.

2.1 Provisions for Adults. *The specifications in these guidelines are based upon adult dimensions and anthropometrics.*

2.2* Equivalent Facilitation. *Departures from particular technical and scoping requirements of this guideline by the use of other designs and technologies are permitted where the alternative designs and technologies used will provide substantially equivalent or greater access to and usability of the facility.*

3. MISCELLANEOUS INSTRUCTIONS AND DEFINITIONS.

3.1 Graphic Conventions. Graphic conventions are shown in Table 1. Dimensions that are not marked minimum or maximum are absolute, unless otherwise indicated in the text or captions.

Table 1
Graphic Conventions

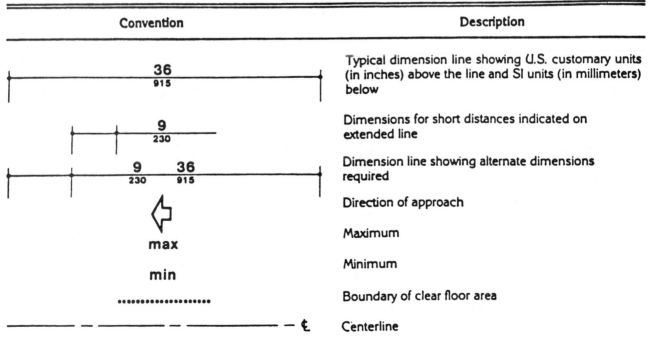

Convention	Description
36 / 915	Typical dimension line showing U.S. customary units (in inches) above the line and SI units (in millimeters) below
9 / 230	Dimensions for short distances indicated on extended line
9 36 / 230 915	Dimension line showing alternate dimensions required
	Direction of approach
max	Maximum
min	Minimum
....	Boundary of clear floor area
— — — — — — ₵	Centerline

3.2 Dimensional Tolerances. All dimensions are subject to conventional building industry tolerances for field conditions.

3.3 Notes. The text of *these guidelines* does not contain notes or footnotes. Additional information, explanations, and advisory materials are located in the Appendix. Paragraphs marked with an asterisk have related, non-mandatory material in the Appendix. In the Appendix, the corresponding paragraph numbers are preceded by an A.

3.4 General Terminology.

comply with. Meet one or more specifications of *these guidelines*.

if, if ... then. Denotes a specification that applies only when the conditions described are present.

may. Denotes an option or alternative.

shall. Denotes a mandatory specification or requirement.

should. Denotes an advisory specification or recommendation.

3.5 Definitions.

Access Aisle. An accessible pedestrian space between elements, such as parking spaces, seating, and desks, that provides clearances appropriate for use of the elements.

Accessible. Describes a site, building, facility, or portion thereof that complies with *these guidelines*.

Accessible Element. An *element* specified by *these guidelines* (for example, telephone, controls, and the like).

Accessible Route. A continuous unobstructed path connecting all accessible elements and spaces of a building or facility. Interior accessible routes may include corridors, floors, ramps, elevators, lifts, and clear floor space at fixtures. Exterior accessible routes may include parking access aisles, curb ramps, *crosswalks at vehicular ways*, walks, ramps, and lifts.

Accessible Space. *Space that complies with these guidelines.*

Adaptability. The ability of certain building spaces and elements, such as kitchen counters, sinks, and grab bars, to be added or altered so as to accommodate the needs of *individuals with or without disabilities* or to accommodate the needs of persons with different types or degrees of disability.

Addition. *An expansion, extension, or increase in the gross floor area of a building or facility.*

Administrative Authority. A governmental agency that adopts or enforces regulations and *guidelines* for the design, construction, or *alteration* of buildings and facilities.

Alteration. *An alteration is a change to a building or facility made by, on behalf of, or for the use of a public accommodation or commercial facility, that affects or could affect the usability of the building or facility or part thereof. Alterations include, but are not limited to, remodeling, renovation, rehabilitation, reconstruction, historic restoration, changes or rearrangement of the structural parts or elements, and changes or rearrangement in the plan configuration of walls and full-height partitions. Normal maintenance, reroofing, painting or wallpapering, or changes to mechanical and electrical systems are not alterations unless they affect the usability of the building or facility.*

Area of Rescue Assistance. *An area, which has direct access to an exit, where people who are unable to use stairs may remain temporarily in safety to await further instructions or assistance during emergency evacuation.*

Assembly Area. A room or space accommodating a *group of* individuals for recreational, educational, political, social, or amusement purposes, or for the consumption of food and drink.

Automatic Door. A door equipped with a power-operated mechanism and controls that open and close the door automatically upon receipt of a momentary actuating signal. The switch that begins the automatic cycle may be a photoelectric device, floor mat, or manual switch (see power-assisted door).

Building. Any structure used and intended for supporting or sheltering any use or occupancy.

Circulation Path. An exterior or interior way of passage from one place to another for pedestrians, including, but not limited to, walks, hallways, courtyards, stairways, and stair landings.

Clear. Unobstructed.

Clear Floor Space. The minimum unobstructed floor or ground space required to accommodate a single, stationary wheelchair and occupant.

Closed Circuit Telephone. A telephone with dedicated line(s) such as a house phone, courtesy phone or phone that must be used to gain entrance to a facility.

Common Use. Refers to those interior and exterior rooms, spaces, or elements that are made available for the use of a restricted group of people (for example, occupants of a homeless shelter, the occupants of an office building, or the guests of such occupants).

Cross Slope. The slope that is perpendicular to the direction of travel (see running slope).

Curb Ramp. A short ramp cutting through a curb or built up to it.

Detectable Warning. A standardized surface feature built in or applied to walking surfaces or other elements to warn visually impaired people of hazards on a circulation path.

Dwelling Unit. A single unit which provides a kitchen or food preparation area, in addition to rooms and spaces for living, bathing, sleeping, and the like. Dwelling units include a single family home or a townhouse used as a transient group home; an apartment building used as a shelter; guestrooms in a hotel that provide sleeping accommodations and food preparation areas; and other similar facilities used on a transient basis. For purposes of these guidelines, use of the term "Dwelling Unit" does not imply the unit is used as a residence.

Egress, Means of. A continuous and unobstructed way of exit travel from any point in a building or facility to a public way. A means of egress comprises vertical and horizontal travel and may include intervening room spaces, doorways, hallways, corridors, passageways, balconies, ramps, stairs, enclosures, lobbies, horizontal exits, courts and yards. An accessible means of egress is one that complies with these guidelines and does not include stairs, steps, or escalators. Areas of rescue assistance or evacuation elevators may be included as part of accessible means of egress.

Element. An architectural or mechanical component of a building, facility, space, or site, e.g., telephone, curb ramp, door, drinking fountain, seating, or water closet.

Entrance. Any access point to a building or portion of a building or facility used for the purpose of entering. An entrance includes the approach walk, the vertical access leading to the entrance platform, the entrance platform itself, vestibules if provided, the entry door(s) or gate(s), and the hardware of the entry door(s) or gate(s).

Facility. All or any portion of buildings, structures, site improvements, complexes, equipment, roads, walks, passageways, parking lots, or other real or personal property located on a site.

Ground Floor. Any occupiable floor less than one story above or below grade with direct access to grade. A building or facility always has at least one ground floor and may have more than one ground floor as where a split level entrance has been provided or where a building is built into a hillside.

Mezzanine or Mezzanine Floor. That portion of a story which is an intermediate floor level placed within the story and having occupiable space above and below its floor.

Marked Crossing. A crosswalk or other identified path intended for pedestrian use in crossing a vehicular way.

Multifamily Dwelling. Any building containing more than two dwelling units.

Occupiable. A room or enclosed space designed for human occupancy in which individuals congregate for amusement, educational or similar purposes, or in which occupants are engaged at labor, and which is equipped with means of egress, light, and ventilation.

Operable Part. A part of a piece of equipment or appliance used to insert or withdraw objects, or to activate, deactivate, or adjust the equipment or appliance (for example, coin slot, pushbutton, handle).

Path of Travel. (Reserved).

Power-assisted Door. A door used *for human passage* with a mechanism that helps to open the door, or relieves the opening resistance of a door, upon the activation of a switch or a continued force applied to the door itself.

Public Use. Describes interior or exterior rooms or spaces that are made available to the general public. Public use may be provided at a building or facility that is privately or publicly owned.

Ramp. A walking surface which has a running slope greater than 1:20.

Running Slope. The slope that is parallel to the direction of travel (see cross slope).

Service Entrance. An entrance intended primarily for delivery of goods or services.

Signage. *Displayed* verbal, symbolic, *tactile,* and pictorial information.

Site. A parcel of land bounded by a property line or a designated portion of a public right-of-way.

Site Improvement. Landscaping, paving for pedestrian and vehicular ways, outdoor lighting, recreational facilities, and the like, added to a site.

Sleeping Accommodations. Rooms in which people sleep; for example, dormitory and hotel or motel guest rooms or suites.

Space. A definable area, e.g., room, toilet room, hall, assembly area, entrance, storage room, alcove, courtyard, or lobby.

Story. That portion of a building included between the upper surface of a floor and upper surface of the floor or roof next above. If such portion of a building does not include occupiable space, it is not considered a story for purposes of these guidelines. There may be more than one floor level within a story as in the case of a mezzanine or mezzanines.

Structural Frame. The structural frame shall be considered to be the columns and the girders, beams, trusses and spandrels having direct connections to the columns and all other members which are essential to the stability of the building as a whole.

Tactile. Describes an object that can be perceived using the sense of touch.

Text Telephone. Machinery or equipment that employs interactive graphic (i.e., typed) communications through the transmission of coded signals across the standard telephone network. Text telephones can include, for example, devices known as TDD's (telecommunication display devices or telecommunication devices for deaf persons) or computers.

Transient Lodging. A building, facility, or portion thereof, excluding inpatient medical care facilities, that contains one or more dwelling units or sleeping accommodations. Transient lodging may include, but is not limited to, resorts, group homes, hotels, motels, and dormitories.

Vehicular Way. A route intended for vehicular traffic, such as a street, driveway, or parking lot.

Walk. An exterior pathway with a prepared surface intended for pedestrian use, including general pedestrian areas such as plazas and courts.

NOTE: Sections 4.1.1 through 4.1.7 are different from ANSI A117.1 in their entirety and are printed in standard type (ANSI A117.1 does not include scoping provisions).

4. ACCESSIBLE ELEMENTS AND SPACES: SCOPE AND TECHNICAL REQUIREMENTS.

4.1 Minimum Requirements

4.1.1* Application.

(1) General. All areas of newly designed or newly constructed buildings and facilities required to be accessible by 4.1.2 and 4.1.3 and altered portions of existing buildings and facilities required to be accessible by 4.1.6 shall comply with these guidelines, 4.1 through 4.35, unless otherwise provided in this section or as modified in a special application section.

(2) Application Based on Building Use. Special application sections 5 through 10 provide additional requirements for restaurants and cafeterias, medical care facilities, business and mercantile, libraries, accessible transient lodging, and transportation facilities. When a building or facility contains more than one use covered by a special application section, each portion shall comply with the requirements for that use.

(3)* Areas Used Only by Employees as Work Areas. Areas that are used only as work areas shall be designed and constructed so that individuals with disabilities can approach, enter, and exit the areas. These guidelines do not require that any areas used only as work areas be constructed to permit maneuvering within the work area or be constructed or equipped (i.e., with racks or shelves) to be accessible.

(4) Temporary Structures. These guidelines cover temporary buildings or facilities as well as permanent facilities. Temporary buildings and facilities are not of permanent construction but are extensively used or are essential for public use for a period of time. Examples of temporary buildings or facilities covered by these guidelines include, but are not limited to: reviewing stands, temporary classrooms, bleacher areas, exhibit areas, temporary banking facilities, temporary health screening services, or temporary safe pedestrian passageways around a construction site. Structures,

sites and equipment directly associated with the actual processes of construction, such as scaffolding, bridging, materials hoists, or construction trailers are not included.

(5) General Exceptions.

(a) In new construction, a person or entity is not required to meet fully the requirements of these guidelines where that person or entity can demonstrate that it is structurally impracticable to do so. Full compliance will be considered structurally impracticable only in those rare circumstances when the unique characteristics of terrain prevent the incorporation of accessibility features. If full compliance with the requirements of these guidelines is structurally impracticable, a person or entity shall comply with the requirements to the extent it is not structurally impracticable. Any portion of the building or facility which can be made accessible shall comply to the extent that it is not structurally impracticable.

(b) Accessibility is not required to (i) observation galleries used primarily for security purposes; or (ii) in non-occupiable spaces accessed only by ladders, catwalks, crawl spaces, very narrow passageways, or freight (non-passenger) elevators, and frequented only by service personnel for repair purposes; such spaces include, but are not limited to, elevator pits, elevator penthouses, piping or equipment catwalks.

4.1.2 Accessible Sites and Exterior Facilities: New Construction. An accessible site shall meet the following minimum requirements:

(1) At least one accessible route complying with 4.3 shall be provided within the boundary of the site from public transportation stops, accessible parking spaces, passenger loading zones if provided, and public streets or sidewalks, to an accessible building entrance.

(2) At least one accessible route complying with 4.3 shall connect accessible buildings, accessible facilities, accessible elements, and accessible spaces that are on the same site.

(3) All objects that protrude from surfaces or posts into circulation paths shall comply with 4.4.

(4) Ground surfaces along accessible routes and in accessible spaces shall comply with 4.5.

(5) (a) If parking spaces are provided for self-parking by employees or visitors, or both, then accessible spaces complying with 4.6 shall be provided in each such parking area in conformance with the table below. Spaces required by the table need not be provided in the particular lot. They may be provided in a different location if equivalent or greater accessibility, in terms of distance from an accessible entrance, cost and convenience is ensured.

Total Parking in Lot	Required Minimum Number of Accessible Spaces
1 to 25	1
26 to 50	2
51 to 75	3
76 to 100	4
101 to 150	5
151 to 200	6
201 to 300	7
301 to 400	8
401 to 500	9
501 to 1000	2 percent of total
1001 and over	20 plus 1 for each 100 over 1000

Except as provided in (b), access aisles adjacent to accessible spaces shall be 60 in (1525 mm) wide minimum.

(b) One in every eight accessible spaces, but not less than one, shall be served by an access aisle 96 in (2440 mm) wide minimum and shall be designated "van accessible" as required by 4.6.4. The vertical clearance at such spaces shall comply with 4.6.5. All such spaces may be grouped on one level of a parking structure.

EXCEPTION: Provision of all required parking spaces in conformance with "Universal Parking Design" (see appendix A4.6.3) is permitted.

(c) If passenger loading zones are provided, then at least one passenger loading zone shall comply with 4.6.6.

(d) At facilities providing medical care and other services for persons with mobility impairments, parking spaces complying with 4.6 shall be provided in accordance with 4.1.2(5)(a) except as follows:

(i) Outpatient units and facilities: 10 percent of the total number of parking spaces provided serving each such outpatient unit or facility;

(ii) Units and facilities that specialize in treatment or services for persons with mobility impairments: 20 percent of the total number of parking spaces provided serving each such unit or facility.

(e)*Valet parking: Valet parking facilities shall provide a passenger loading zone complying with 4.6.6 located on an accessible route to the entrance of the facility. Paragraphs 5(a), 5(b), and 5(d) of this section do not apply to valet parking facilities.

(6) If toilet facilities are provided on a site, then each such public or common use toilet facility shall comply with 4.22. If bathing facilities are provided on a site, then each such public or common use bathing facility shall comply with 4.23.

For single user portable toilet or bathing units clustered at a single location, at least 5% but no less than one toilet unit or bathing unit complying with 4.22 or 4.23 shall be installed at each cluster whenever typical inaccessible units are provided. Accessible units shall be identified by the International Symbol of Accessibility.

EXCEPTION: Portable toilet units at construction sites used exclusively by construction personnel are not required to comply with 4.1.2(6).

(7) Building Signage. Signs which designate permanent rooms and spaces shall comply with 4.30.1, 4.30.4, 4.30.5 and 4.30.6. Other signs which provide direction to, or information about, functional spaces of the building shall comply with 4.30.1, 4.30.2, 4.30.3, and 4.30.5. Elements and spaces of accessible facilities which shall be identified by the International Symbol of Accessibility and which shall comply with 4.30.7 are:

(a) Parking spaces designated as reserved for individuals with disabilities;

(b) Accessible passenger loading zones;

(c) Accessible entrances when not all are accessible (inaccessible entrances shall have directional signage to indicate the route to the nearest accessible entrance);

(d) Accessible toilet and bathing facilities when not all are accessible.

4.1.3 Accessible Buildings: New Construction.
Accessible buildings and facilities shall meet the following minimum requirements:

(1) At least one accessible route complying with 4.3 shall connect accessible building or facility entrances with all accessible spaces and elements within the building or facility.

(2) All objects that overhang or protrude into circulation paths shall comply with 4.4.

(3) Ground and floor surfaces along accessible routes and in accessible rooms and spaces shall comply with 4.5.

(4) Interior and exterior stairs connecting levels that are not connected by an elevator, ramp, or other accessible means of vertical access shall comply with 4.9.

(5)* One passenger elevator complying with 4.10 shall serve each level, including mezzanines, in all multi-story buildings and facilities unless exempted below. If more than one elevator is provided, each full passenger elevator shall comply with 4.10.

EXCEPTION 1: Elevators are not required in facilities that are less than three stories or that have less than 3000 square feet per story unless the building is a shopping center, a shopping mall, or the professional office of a health care provider, or another type of facility as determined by the Attorney General. The elevator exemption set forth in this paragraph does not obviate or limit in any way the obligation to comply with the other accessibility requirements established in section 4.1.3. For example, floors above or below the accessible ground floor must meet the requirements of this section except for elevator service. If toilet or bathing facilities are provided on a level not served by an elevator, then toilet or bathing facilities must be provided on the accessible ground floor. In new construction if a building or facility is eligible for this exemption but a full passenger elevator is nonetheless planned, that elevator shall meet the requirements of 4.10 and shall serve each level in the building. A full passenger elevator that provides service from a garage to only one level of a building or facility is not required to serve other levels.

EXCEPTION 2: Elevator pits, elevator penthouses, mechanical rooms, piping or equipment catwalks are exempted from this requirement.

EXCEPTION 3: Accessible ramps complying with 4.8 may be used in lieu of an elevator.

EXCEPTION 4: Platform lifts (wheelchair lifts) complying with 4.11 of this guideline and applicable state or local codes may be used in lieu of an elevator only under the following conditions:

(a) To provide an accessible route to a performing area in an assembly occupancy.

(b) To comply with the wheelchair viewing position line-of-sight and dispersion requirements of 4.33.3.

(c) To provide access to incidental occupiable spaces and rooms which are not open to the general public and which house no more than five persons, including but not limited to equipment control rooms and projection booths.

(d) To provide access where existing site constraints or other constraints make use of a ramp or an elevator infeasible.

(6) Windows: (Reserved).

(7) Doors:

(a) At each accessible entrance to a building or facility, at least one door shall comply with 4.13.

(b) Within a building or facility, at least one door at each accessible space shall comply with 4.13.

(c) Each door that is an element of an accessible route shall comply with 4.13.

(d) Each door required by 4.3.10, Egress, shall comply with 4.13.

(8) In new construction, at a minimum, the requirements in (a) and (b) below shall be satisfied independently:

(a)(i) At least 50% of all public entrances (excluding those in (b) below) must be accessible. At least one must be a ground floor entrance. Public entrances are any entrances that are not loading or service entrances.

(ii) Accessible entrances must be provided in a number at least equivalent to the number of exits required by the applicable building/fire codes. (This paragraph does not require an increase in the total number of entrances planned for a facility.)

(iii) An accessible entrance must be provided to each tenancy in a facility (for example, individual stores in a strip shopping center).

One entrance may be considered as meeting more than one of the requirements in (a). Where feasible, accessible entrances shall be the entrances used by the majority of people visiting or working in the building.

(b)(i) In addition, if direct access is provided for pedestrians from an enclosed parking garage to the building, at least one direct entrance from the garage to the building must be accessible.

(ii) If access is provided for pedestrians from a pedestrian tunnel or elevated walkway, one entrance to the building from each tunnel or walkway must be accessible.

One entrance may be considered as meeting more than one of the requirements in (b).

Because entrances also serve as emergency exits whose proximity to all parts of buildings and facilities is essential, it is preferable that all entrances be accessible.

(c) If the only entrance to a building, or tenancy in a facility, is a service entrance, that entrance shall be accessible.

(d) Entrances which are not accessible shall have directional signage complying with 4.30.1,

4.30.2, 4.30.3, and 4.30.5, which indicates the location of the nearest accessible entrance.

(9)* In buildings or facilities, or portions of buildings or facilities, required to be accessible, accessible means of egress shall be provided in the same number as required for exits by local building/life safety regulations. Where a required exit from an occupiable level above or below a level of accessible exit discharge is not accessible, an area of rescue assistance shall be provided on each such level (in a number equal to that of inaccessible required exits). Areas of rescue assistance shall comply with 4.3.11. A horizontal exit, meeting the requirements of local building/life safety regulations, shall satisfy the requirement for an area of rescue assistance.

EXCEPTION: Areas of rescue assistance are not required in buildings or facilities having a supervised automatic sprinkler system.

(10)* Drinking Fountains:

(a) Where only one drinking fountain is provided on a floor there shall be a drinking fountain which is accessible to individuals who use wheelchairs in accordance with 4.15 and one accessible to those who have difficulty bending or stooping. (This can be accommodated by the use of a "hi-lo" fountain; by providing one fountain accessible to those who use wheelchairs and one fountain at a standard height convenient for those who have difficulty bending; by providing a fountain accessible under 4.15 and a water cooler; or by such other means as would achieve the required accessibility for each group on each floor.)

(b) Where more than one drinking fountain or water cooler is provided on a floor, at least 50% of those provided shall comply with 4.15 and shall be on an accessible route.

(11) Toilet Facilities: If toilet rooms are provided, then each public and common use toilet room shall comply with 4.22. Other toilet rooms provided for the use of occupants of specific spaces (i.e., a private toilet room for the occupant of a private office) shall be adaptable. If bathing rooms are provided, then each public and common use bathroom shall comply with 4.23. Accessible toilet rooms and bathing facilities shall be on an accessible route.

(12) Storage, Shelving and Display Units:

(a) If fixed or built-in storage facilities such as cabinets, shelves, closets, and drawers are provided in accessible spaces, at least one of each type provided shall contain storage space complying with 4.25. Additional storage may be provided outside of the dimensions required by 4.25.

(b) Shelves or display units allowing self-service by customers in mercantile occupancies shall be located on an accessible route complying with 4.3. Requirements for accessible reach range do not apply.

(13) Controls and operating mechanisms in accessible spaces, along accessible routes, or as parts of accessible elements (for example, light switches and dispenser controls) shall comply with 4.27.

(14) If emergency warning systems are provided, then they shall include both audible alarms and visual alarms complying with 4.28. Sleeping accommodations required to comply with 9.3 shall have an alarm system complying with 4.28. Emergency warning systems in medical care facilities may be modified to suit standard health care alarm design practice.

(15) Detectable warnings shall be provided at locations as specified in 4.29.

(16) Building Signage:

(a) Signs which designate permanent rooms and spaces shall comply with 4.30.1, 4.30.4, 4.30.5 and 4.30.6.

(b) Other signs which provide direction to or information about functional spaces of the building shall comply with 4.30.1, 4.30.2, 4.30.3, and 4.30.5.

EXCEPTION: Building directories, menus, and all other signs which are temporary are not required to comply.

(17) Public Telephones:

(a) If public pay telephones, public closed circuit telephones, or other public telephones are provided, then they shall comply with 4.31.2 through 4.31.8 to the extent required by the following table:

Number of each type of telephone provided on each floor	Number of telephones required to comply with 4.31.2 through 4.31.8[1]
1 or more single unit	1 per floor
1 bank[2]	1 per floor
2 or more banks[2]	1 per bank. Accessible unit may be installed as a single unit in proximity (either visible or with signage) to the bank. At least one public telephone per floor shall meet the requirements for a forward reach telephone[3].

[1] Additional public telephones may be installed at any height. Unless otherwise specified, accessible telephones may be either forward or side reach telephones.

[2] A bank consists of two or more adjacent public telephones, often installed as a unit.

[3] EXCEPTION: For exterior installations only, if dial tone first service is available, then a side reach telephone may be installed instead of the required forward reach telephone (i.e., one telephone in proximity to each bank shall comply with 4.31).

(b)* All telephones required to be accessible and complying with 4.31.2 through 4.31.8 shall be equipped with a volume control. In addition, 25 percent, but never less than one, of all other public telephones provided shall be equipped with a volume control and shall be dispersed among all types of public telephones, including closed circuit telephones, throughout the building or facility. Signage complying with applicable provisions of 4.30.7 shall be provided.

(c) The following shall be provided in accordance with 4.31.9:

(i) If a total number of four or more public pay telephones (including both interior and exterior phones) is provided at a site, and at least one is in an interior location, then at least one interior public text telephone shall be provided.

(ii) If an interior public pay telephone is provided in a stadium or arena, in a convention center, in a hotel with a convention center, or in a covered mall, at least one interior public text telephone shall be provided in the facility.

(iii) if a public pay telephone is located in or adjacent to a hospital emergency room, hospital recovery room, or hospital waiting room, one public text telephone shall be provided at each such location.

(d) Where a bank of telephones in the interior of a building consists of three or more public pay telephones, at least one public pay telephone in each such bank shall be equipped with a shelf and outlet in compliance with 4.31.9(2).

(18) If fixed or built-in seating or tables (including, but not limited to, study carrels and student laboratory stations), are provided in accessible public or common use areas, at least five percent (5%), but not less than one, of the fixed or built-in seating areas or tables shall comply with 4.32. An accessible route shall lead to and through such fixed or built-in seating areas, or tables.

(19)* Assembly areas:

(a) In places of assembly with fixed seating accessible wheelchair locations shall comply with 4.33.2, 4.33.3, and 4.33.4 and shall be provided consistent with the following table:

Capacity of Seating in Assembly Areas	Number of Required Wheelchair Locations
4 to 25	1
26 to 50	2
51 to 300	4
301 to 500	6
over 500	6, plus 1 additional space for each total seating capacity increase of 100

In addition, one percent, but not less than one, of all fixed seats shall be aisle seats with no armrests on the aisle side, or removable or folding armrests on the aisle side. Each such seat shall be identified by a sign or marker. Signage notifying patrons of the availability of such seats shall be posted at the ticket office. Aisle seats are not required to comply with 4.33.4.

(b) This paragraph applies to assembly areas where audible communications are integral to the use of the space (e.g., concert and lecture halls, playhouses and movie theaters, meeting rooms, etc.). Such assembly areas, if (1) they accommodate at least 50 persons, or if they have audio-amplification systems, and (2) they have fixed seating, shall have a permanently installed assistive listening system complying with 4.33. For other assembly areas, a permanently installed assistive listening system, or an adequate number of electrical outlets or other supplementary wiring necessary to support a portable assistive listening system shall be provided. The minimum number of receivers to be provided shall be equal to 4 percent of the total number of seats, but in no case less than two. Signage complying with applicable provisions of 4.30 shall be installed to notify patrons of the availability of a listening system.

(20) Where automated teller machines (ATMs) are provided, each ATM shall comply with the requirements of 4.34 except where two or more are provided at a location, then only one must comply.

EXCEPTION: Drive-up-only automated teller machines are not required to comply with 4.27.2, 4.27.3 and 4.34.3.

(21) Where dressing and fitting rooms are provided for use by the general public, patients, customers or employees, 5 percent, but never less than one, of dressing rooms for each type of use in each cluster of dressing rooms shall be accessible and shall comply with 4.35.

Examples of types of dressing rooms are those serving different genders or distinct and different functions as in different treatment or examination facilities.

4.1.4 (Reserved).

4.1.5 Accessible Buildings: Additions.
Each addition to an existing building or facility shall be regarded as an alteration. Each space or element added to the existing building or facility shall comply with the applicable provisions of 4.1.1 to 4.1.3, Minimum Requirements (for New Construction) and the applicable technical specifications of 4.2 through 4.35 and sections 5 through 10. Each addition that

affects or could affect the usability of an area containing a primary function shall comply with 4.1.6(2).

4.1.6 Accessible Buildings: Alterations.

(1) General. Alterations to existing buildings and facilities shall comply with the following:

(a) No alteration shall be undertaken which decreases or has the effect of decreasing accessibility or usability of a building or facility below the requirements for new construction at the time of alteration.

(b) If existing elements, spaces, or common areas are altered, then each such altered element, space, feature, or area shall comply with the applicable provisions of 4.1.1 to 4.1.3 Minimum Requirements (for New Construction). If the applicable provision for new construction requires that an element, space, or common area be on an accessible route, the altered element, space, or common area is not required to be on an accessible route except as provided in 4.1.6(2) (Alterations to an Area Containing a Primary Function.)

(c) If alterations of single elements, when considered together, amount to an alteration of a room or space in a building or facility, the entire space shall be made accessible.

(d) No alteration of an existing element, space, or area of a building or facility shall impose a requirement for greater accessibility than that which would be required for new construction. For example, if the elevators and stairs in a building are being altered and the elevators are, in turn, being made accessible, then no accessibility modifications are required to the stairs connecting levels connected by the elevator. If stair modifications to correct unsafe conditions are required by other codes, the modifications shall be done in compliance with these guidelines unless technically infeasible.

(e) At least one interior public text telephone complying with 4.31.9 shall be provided if:

(i) alterations to existing buildings or facilities with less than four exterior or interior public pay telephones would increase the total number to four or more telephones with at least one in an interior location; or

(ii) alterations to one or more exterior or interior public pay telephones occur in an existing building or facility with four or more public telephones with at least one in an interior location.

(f) If an escalator or stair is planned or installed where none existed previously and major structural modifications are necessary for such installation, then a means of accessible vertical access shall be provided that complies with the applicable provisions of 4.7, 4.8, 4.10, or 4.11.

(g) In alterations, the requirements of 4.1.3(9), 4.3.10 and 4.3.11 do not apply.

(h)*Entrances: If a planned alteration entails alterations to an entrance, and the building has an accessible entrance, the entrance being altered is not required to comply with 4.1.3(8), except to the extent required by 4.1.6(2). If a particular entrance is not made accessible, appropriate accessible signage indicating the location of the nearest accessible entrance(s) shall be installed at or near the inaccessible entrance, such that a person with disabilities will not be required to retrace the approach route from the inaccessible entrance.

(i) If the alteration work is limited solely to the electrical, mechanical, or plumbing system, or to hazardous material abatement, or automatic sprinkler retrofitting, and does not involve the alteration of any elements or spaces required to be accessible under these guidelines, then 4.1.6(2) does not apply.

(j) EXCEPTION: In alteration work, if compliance with 4.1.6 is technically infeasible, the alteration shall provide accessibility to the maximum extent feasible. Any elements or features of the building or facility that are being altered and can be made accessible shall be made accessible within the scope of the alteration.

Technically Infeasible. Means, with respect to an alteration of a building or a facility, that it has little likelihood of being accomplished because existing structural conditions would require removing or altering a load-bearing member which is an essential part of the structural frame; or because other existing physical or site constraints prohibit modification or addition of elements, spaces, or features which are in full and strict compliance with the minimum requirements for new construction and which are necessary to provide accessibility.

(k) EXCEPTION:

(i) These guidelines do not require the installation of an elevator in an altered facility that is less than three stories or has less than 3,000 square feet per story unless the building is a shopping center, a shopping mall, the professional office of a health care provider, or another type of facility as determined by the Attorney General.

(ii) The exemption provided in paragraph (i) does not obviate or limit in any way the obligation to comply with the other accessibility requirements established in these guidelines. For example, alterations to floors above or below the ground floor must be accessible regardless of whether the altered facility has an elevator. If a facility subject to the elevator exemption set forth in paragraph (i) nonetheless has a full passenger elevator, that elevator shall meet, to the maximum extent feasible, the accessibility requirements of these guidelines.

(2) Alterations to an Area Containing a Primary Function: In addition to the requirements of 4.1.6(1), an alteration that affects or could affect the usability of or access to an area containing a primary function shall be made so as to ensure that, to the maximum extent feasible, the path of travel to the altered area and the restrooms, telephones, and drinking fountains serving the altered area, are readily accessible to and usable by individuals with disabilities, unless such alterations are disproportionate to the overall alterations in terms of cost and scope (as determined under criteria established by the Attorney General).

(3) Special Technical Provisions for Alterations to Existing Buildings and Facilities:

(a) Ramps: Curb ramps and interior or exterior ramps to be constructed on sites or in existing buildings or facilities where space limitations prohibit the use of a 1:12 slope or less may have slopes and rises as follows:

(i) A slope between 1:10 and 1:12 is allowed for a maximum rise of 6 inches.

(ii) A slope between 1:8 and 1:10 is allowed for a maximum rise of 3 inches. A slope steeper than 1:8 is not allowed.

(b) Stairs: Full extension of handrails at stairs shall not be required in alterations where such extensions would be hazardous or impossible due to plan configuration.

(c) Elevators:

(i) If safety door edges are provided in existing automatic elevators, automatic door reopening devices may be omitted (see 4.10.6).

(ii) Where existing shaft configuration or technical infeasibility prohibits strict compliance with 4.10.9, the minimum car plan dimensions may be reduced by the minimum amount necessary, but in no case shall the inside car area be smaller than 48 in by 48 in.

(iii) Equivalent facilitation may be provided with an elevator car of different dimensions when usability can be demonstrated and when all other elements required to be accessible comply with the applicable provisions of 4.10. For example, an elevator of 47 in by 69 in (1195 mm by 1755 mm) with a door opening on the narrow dimension, could accommodate the standard wheelchair clearances shown in Figure 4.

(d) Doors:

(i) Where it is technically infeasible to comply with clear opening width requirements of 4.13.5, a projection of 5/8 in maximum will be permitted for the latch side stop.

(ii) If existing thresholds are 3/4 in high or less, and have (or are modified to have) a beveled edge on each side, they may remain.

(e) Toilet Rooms:

(i) Where it is technically infeasible to comply with 4.22 or 4.23, the installation of at least one unisex toilet/bathroom per floor, located in the same area as existing toilet facilities, will be permitted in lieu of modifying existing toilet facilities to be accessible. Each unisex toilet room shall contain one water closet complying with 4.16 and one lavatory complying with 4.19, and the door shall have a privacy latch.

(ii) Where it is technically infeasible to install a required standard stall (Fig. 30(a)), or where other codes prohibit reduction of the fixture count (i.e., removal of a water closet in order to create a double-wide stall), either alternate stall (Fig.30(b)) may be provided in lieu of the standard stall.

(iii) When existing toilet or bathing facilities are being altered and are not made accessible, signage complying with 4.30.1, 4.30.2, 4.30.3, 4.30.5, and 4.30.7 shall be provided indicating the location of the nearest accessible toilet or bathing facility within the facility.

(f) Assembly Areas:

(i) Where it is technically infeasible to disperse accessible seating throughout an altered assembly area, accessible seating areas may be clustered. Each accessible seating area shall have provisions for companion seating and shall be located on an accessible route that also serves as a means of emergency egress.

(ii) Where it is technically infeasible to alter all performing areas to be on an accessible route, at least one of each type of performing area shall be made accessible.

(g) Platform Lifts (Wheelchair Lifts): In alterations, platform lifts (wheelchair lifts) complying with 4.11 and applicable state or local codes may be used as part of an accessible route. The use of lifts is not limited to the four conditions in exception 4 of 4.1.3(5).

(h) Dressing Rooms: In alterations where technical infeasibility can be demonstrated, one dressing room for each sex on each level shall be made accessible. Where only unisex dressing rooms are provided, accessible unisex dressing rooms may be used to fulfill this requirement.

4.1.7 Accessible Buildings: Historic Preservation.

(1) Applicability:

(a) General Rule. Alterations to a qualified historic building or facility shall comply with 4.1.6 Accessible Buildings: Alterations, the applicable technical specifications of 4.2

through 4.35 and the applicable special application sections 5 through 10 unless it is determined in accordance with the procedures in 4.1.7(2) that compliance with the requirements for accessible routes (exterior and interior), ramps, entrances, or toilets would threaten or destroy the historic significance of the building or facility in which case the alternative requirements in 4.1.7(3) may be used for the feature.

EXCEPTION: (Reserved).

(b) Definition. A qualified historic building or facility is a building or facility that is:

(i) Listed in or eligible for listing in the National Register of Historic Places; or

(ii) Designated as historic under an appropriate State or local law.

(2) Procedures:

(a) Alterations to Qualified Historic Buildings and Facilities Subject to Section 106 of the National Historic Preservation Act:

(i) Section 106 Process. Section 106 of the National Historic Preservation Act (16 U.S.C. 470 f) requires that a Federal agency with jurisdiction over a Federal, federally assisted, or federally licensed undertaking consider the effects of the agency's undertaking on buildings and facilities listed in or eligible for listing in the National Register of Historic Places and give the Advisory Council on Historic Preservation a reasonable opportunity to comment on the undertaking prior to approval of the undertaking.

(ii) ADA Application. Where alterations are undertaken to a qualified historic building or facility that is subject to section 106 of the National Historic Preservation Act, the Federal agency with jurisdiction over the undertaking shall follow the section 106 process. If the State Historic Preservation Officer or Advisory Council on Historic Preservation agrees that compliance with the requirements for accessible routes (exterior and interior), ramps, entrances, or toilets would threaten or destroy the historic significance of the building or facility, the alternative requirements in 4.1.7(3) may be used for the feature.

(b) Alterations to Qualified Historic Buildings and Facilities Not Subject to Section 106 of the National Historic Preservation Act. Where alterations are undertaken to a qualified historic building or facility that is not subject to section 106 of the National Historic Preservation Act, if the entity undertaking the alterations believes that compliance with the requirements for accessible routes (exterior and interior), ramps, entrances, or toilets would threaten or destroy the historic significance of the building or facility and that the alternative requirements in 4.1.7(3) should be used for the feature, the entity should consult with the State Historic Preservation Officer. If the State Historic Preservation Officer agrees that compliance with the accessibility requirements for accessible routes (exterior and interior), ramps, entrances or toilets would threaten or destroy the historical significance of the building or facility, the alternative requirements in 4.1.7(3) may be used.

(c) Consultation With Interested Persons. Interested persons should be invited to participate in the consultation process, including State or local accessibility officials, individuals with disabilities, and organizations representing individuals with disabilities.

(d) Certified Local Government Historic Preservation Programs. Where the State Historic Preservation Officer has delegated the consultation responsibility for purposes of this section to a local government historic preservation program that has been certified in accordance with section 101(c) of the National Historic Preservation Act of 1966 (16 U.S.C. 470a (c)) and implementing regulations (36 CFR 61.5), the responsibility may be carried out by the appropriate local government body or official.

(3) Historic Preservation: Minimum Requirements:

(a) At least one accessible route complying with 4.3 from a site access point to an accessible entrance shall be provided.

EXCEPTION: A ramp with a slope no greater than 1:6 for a run not to exceed 2 ft (610 mm) may be used as part of an accessible route to an entrance.

(b) At least one accessible entrance complying with 4.14 which is used by the public shall be provided.

EXCEPTION: If it is determined that no entrance used by the public can comply with 4.14, then access at any entrance not used by the general public but open (unlocked) with directional signage at the primary entrance may be used. The accessible entrance shall also have a notification system. Where security is a problem, remote monitoring may be used.

(c) If toilets are provided, then at least one toilet facility complying with 4.22 and 4.1.6 shall be provided along an accessible route that complies with 4.3. Such toilet facility may be unisex in design.

(d) Accessible routes from an accessible entrance to all publicly used spaces on at least the level of the accessible entrance shall be provided. Access shall be provided to all levels of a building or facility in compliance with 4.1 whenever practical.

(e) Displays and written information, documents, etc., should be located where they can be seen by a seated person. Exhibits and signage displayed horizontally (e.g., open books), should be no higher than 44 in (1120 mm) above the floor surface.

NOTE: The technical provisions of sections 4.2 through 4.35 are the same as those of the American National Standard Institute's document A117.1-1980, except as noted in the text.

4.2 Space Allowance and Reach Ranges.

4.2.1* Wheelchair Passage Width. The minimum clear width for single wheelchair passage shall be 32 in (815 mm) at a point and 36 in (915 mm) continuously (see Fig. 1 and 24(e)).

4.2.2 Width for Wheelchair Passing. The minimum width for two wheelchairs to pass is 60 in (1525 mm) (see Fig. 2).

4.2.3* Wheelchair Turning Space. The space required for a wheelchair to make a 180-degree turn is a clear space of 60 in (1525 mm) diameter (see Fig. 3(a)) or a T-shaped space (see Fig. 3(b)).

4.2.4* Clear Floor or Ground Space for Wheelchairs.

4.2.4.1 Size and Approach. The minimum clear floor or ground space required to accommodate a single, stationary wheelchair and occupant is 30 in by 48 in (760 mm by 1220 mm) (see Fig. 4(a)). The minimum clear floor or ground space for wheelchairs may be positioned for forward or parallel approach to an object (see Fig. 4(b) and (c)). Clear floor or ground space for wheelchairs may be part of the knee space required under some objects.

4.2.4.2 Relationship of Maneuvering Clearance to Wheelchair Spaces. One full unobstructed side of the clear floor or ground space for a wheelchair shall adjoin or overlap an accessible route or adjoin another wheelchair clear floor space. If a clear floor space is located in an alcove or otherwise confined on all or part of three sides, additional maneuvering clearances shall be provided as shown in Fig. 4(d) and (e).

4.2.4.3 Surfaces for Wheelchair Spaces. Clear floor or ground spaces for wheelchairs shall comply with 4.5.

4.2.5* Forward Reach. If the clear floor space only allows forward approach to an object, the maximum high forward reach allowed shall be 48 in (1220 mm) (see Fig. 5(a)). *The minimum low forward reach is 15 in (380 mm).* If the high forward reach is over an obstruction, reach and clearances shall be as shown in Fig. 5(b).

4.2.6* Side Reach. If the clear floor space allows parallel approach by a person in a wheelchair, the maximum high side reach allowed shall be 54 in (1370 mm) and the low side reach shall be no less than 9 in (230 mm) above the floor (Fig. 6(a) and (b)). If the side reach is over an obstruction, the reach and clearances shall be as shown in Fig 6(c).

4.3 Accessible Route.

4.3.1* General. All walks, halls, corridors, aisles, *skywalks, tunnels,* and other spaces

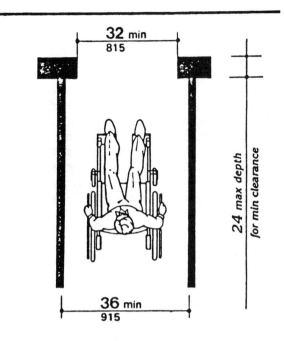

Fig. 1
Minimum Clear Width
for Single Wheelchair

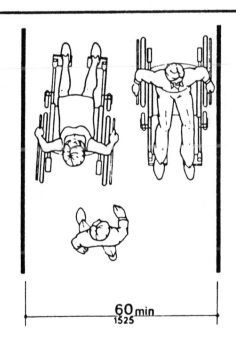

Fig. 2
Minimum Clear Width
for Two Wheelchairs

that are part of an accessible route shall comply with 4.3.

4.3.2 Location.

(1) At least one accessible route *within the boundary of the site* shall be provided from public transportation stops, accessible parking, and accessible passenger loading zones, and public streets or sidewalks to the accessible building entrance they serve. *The accessible route shall, to the maximum extent feasible, coincide with the route for the general public.*

(2) At least one accessible route shall connect accessible buildings, facilities, elements, and spaces that are on the same site.

(3) At least one accessible route shall connect accessible building or facility entrances with all accessible spaces and elements and with all accessible dwelling units within the building or facility.

(4) An accessible route shall connect at least one accessible entrance of each accessible dwelling unit with those exterior and interior spaces and facilities that serve the accessible dwelling unit.

4.3.3 Width. The minimum clear width of an accessible route shall be 36 in (915 mm) except at doors (see 4.13.5 and 4.13.6). If a person in a wheelchair must make a turn around an obstruction, the minimum clear width of the accessible route shall be as shown in Fig. 7(a) and (b).

4.3.4 Passing Space. If an accessible route has less than 60 in (1525 mm) clear width, then passing spaces at least 60 in by 60 in (1525 mm by 1525 mm) shall be located at reasonable intervals not to exceed 200 ft (61 m). A T-intersection of two corridors or walks is an acceptable passing place.

4.3.5 Head Room. Accessible routes shall comply with 4.4.2.

4.3.6 Surface Textures. The surface of an accessible route shall comply with 4.5.

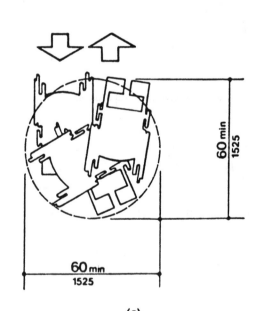

(a)
60-in (1525-mm)-Diameter Space

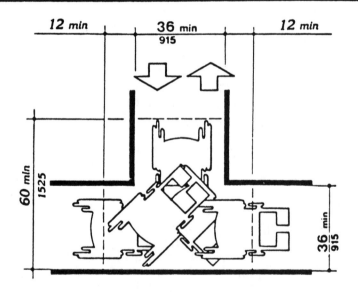

(b)
T-Shaped Space for 180° Turns

Fig. 3
Wheelchair Turning Space

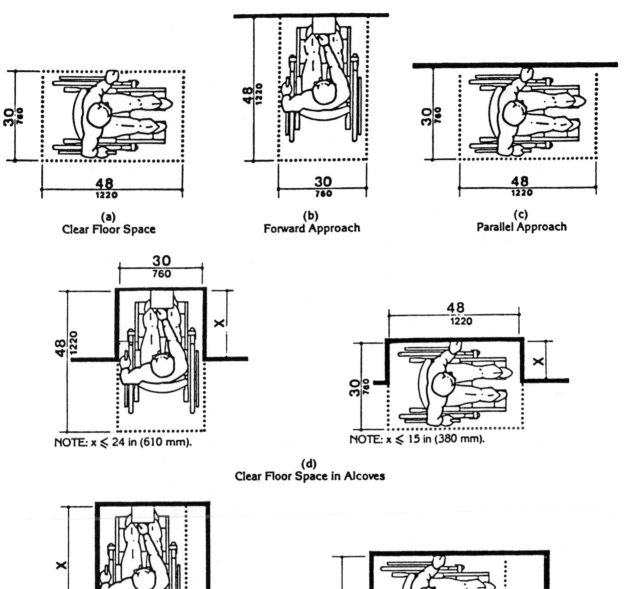

(a)
Clear Floor Space

(b)
Forward Approach

(c)
Parallel Approach

NOTE: x ≤ 24 in (610 mm).

NOTE: x ≤ 15 in (380 mm).

(d)
Clear Floor Space in Alcoves

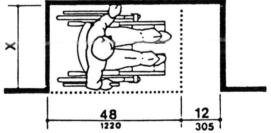

NOTE: If x > 24 in (610 mm), then an additional maneuvering clearance of 6 in (150 mm) shall be provided as shown.

NOTE: If x > 15 in (380 mm), then an additional maneuvering clearance of 12 in (305 mm) shall be provided as shown.

(e)
Additional Maneuvering Clearances for Alcoves

Fig. 4
Minimum Clear Floor Space for Wheelchairs

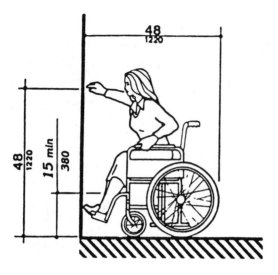
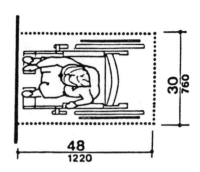

(a)
High Forward Reach Limit

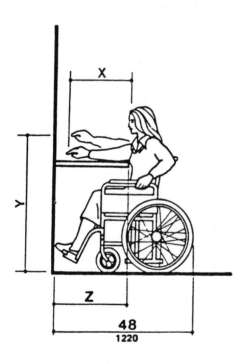
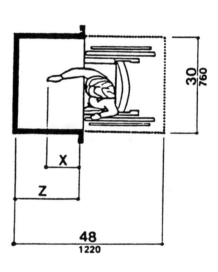

NOTE: x shall be ≤ 25 in (635 mm); z shall be ≥ x. When x < 20 in (510 mm), then y shall be 48 in (1220 mm) maximum. When x is 20 to 25 in (510 to 635 mm), then y shall be 44 in (1120 mm) maximum.

(b)
Maximum Forward Reach over an Obstruction

Fig. 5
Forward Reach

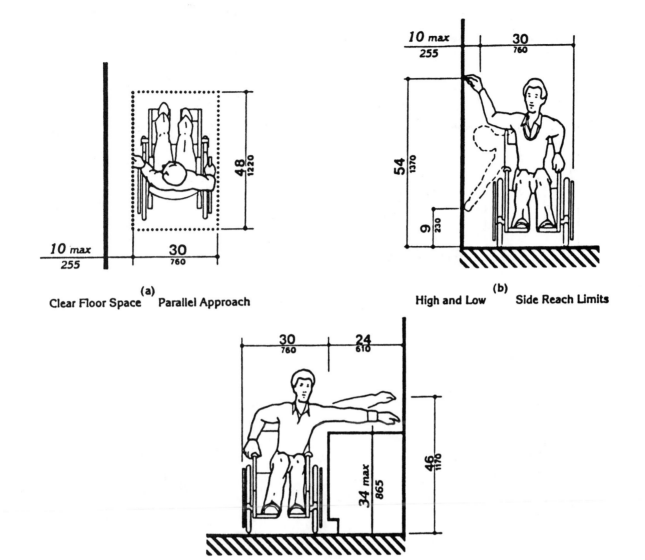

(a)
Clear Floor Space   Parallel Approach

(b)
High and Low   Side Reach Limits

(c)
Maximum Side Reach over Obstruction

Fig. 6
Side Reach

4.3.7 Slope. An accessible route with a running slope greater than 1:20 is a ramp and shall comply with 4.8. Nowhere shall the cross slope of an accessible route exceed 1:50.

4.3.8 Changes in Levels. Changes in levels along an accessible route shall comply with 4.5.2. If an accessible route has changes in level greater than 1/2 in (13 mm), then a curb

ramp, ramp, elevator, or platform lift *(as permitted in 4.1.3 and 4.1.6)* shall be provided that complies with 4.7, 4.8, 4.10, or 4.11, respectively. An accessible route does not include stairs, steps, or escalators. See definition of "egress, means of" in 3.5.

4.3.9 Doors. Doors along an accessible route shall comply with 4.13.

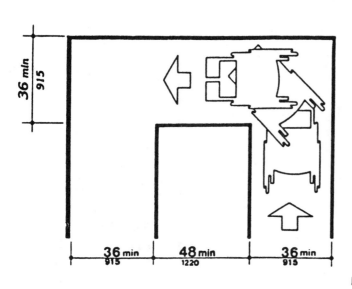

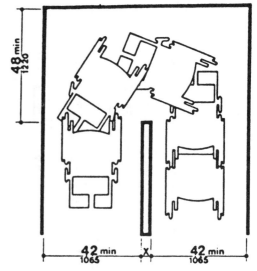

NOTE: Dimensions shown apply when x < 48 in (1220 mm).

(a)
90° Turn

(b)
Turns around an Obstruction

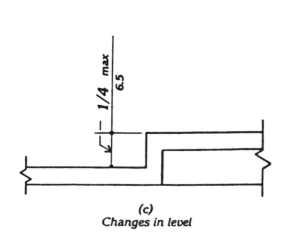

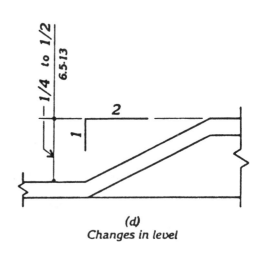

(c)
Changes in level

(d)
Changes in level

Fig. 7
Accessible Route

4.3.10* Egress. Accessible routes serving any accessible space or element shall also serve as a means of egress for emergencies or connect to an accessible area of *rescue assistance.*

4.3.11 *Areas of Rescue Assistance.*

4.3.11.1 *Location and Construction.* *An area of rescue assistance shall be one of the following:*

(1) A portion of a stairway landing within a smokeproof enclosure (complying with local requirements).

(2) A portion of an exterior exit balcony located immediately adjacent to an exit stairway when the balcony complies with local requirements for exterior exit balconies. Openings to the interior of the building located within 20 feet (6 m) of the

area of rescue assistance shall be protected with fire assemblies having a three-fourths hour fire protection rating.

(3) A portion of a one-hour fire-resistive corridor (complying with local requirements for fire-resistive construction and for openings) located immediately adjacent to an exit enclosure.

(4) A vestibule located immediately adjacent to an exit enclosure and constructed to the same fire-resistive standards as required for corridors and openings.

(5) A portion of a stairway landing within an exit enclosure which is vented to the exterior and is separated from the interior of the building with not less than one-hour fire-resistive doors.

(6) When approved by the appropriate local authority, an area or a room which is separated from other portions of the building by a smoke barrier. Smoke barriers shall have a fire-resistive rating of not less than one hour and shall completely enclose the area or room. Doors in the smoke barrier shall be tight-fitting smoke- and draft-control assemblies having a fire-protection rating of not less than 20 minutes and shall be self-closing or automatic closing. The area or room shall be provided with an exit directly to an exit enclosure. Where the room or area exits into an exit enclosure which is required to be of more than one-hour fire-resistive construction, the room or area shall have the same fire-resistive construction, including the same opening protection, as required for the adjacent exit enclosure.

(7) An elevator lobby when elevator shafts and adjacent lobbies are pressurized as required for smokeproof enclosures by local regulations and when complying with requirements herein for size, communication, and signage. Such pressurization system shall be activated by smoke detectors on each floor located in a manner approved by the appropriate local authority. Pressurization equipment and its duct work within the building shall be separated from other portions of the building by a minimum two-hour fire-resistive construction.

4.3.11.2 Size. Each area of rescue assistance shall provide at least two accessible areas each being not less than 30 inches by 48 inches (760 mm by 1220 mm). The area of rescue

assistance shall not encroach on any required exit width. The total number of such 30-inch by 48-inch (760 mm by 1220 mm) areas per story shall be not less than one for every 200 persons of calculated occupant load served by the area of rescue assistance.

EXCEPTION: The appropriate local authority may reduce the minimum number of 30-inch by 48-inch (760 mm by 1220 mm) areas to one for each area of rescue assistance on floors where the occupant load is less than 200.

4.3.11.3* Stairway Width. Each stairway adjacent to an area of rescue assistance shall have a minimum clear width of 48 inches between handrails.

4.3.11.4* Two-way Communication. A method of two-way communication, with both visible and audible signals, shall be provided between each area of rescue assistance and the primary entry. The fire department or appropriate local authority may approve a location other than the primary entry.

4.3.11.5 Identification. Each area of rescue assistance shall be identified by a sign which states "AREA OF RESCUE ASSISTANCE" and displays the international symbol of accessibility. The sign shall be illuminated when exit sign illumination is required. Signage shall also be installed at all inaccessible exits and where otherwise necessary to clearly indicate the direction to areas of rescue assistance. In each area of rescue assistance, instructions on the use of the area under emergency conditions shall be posted adjoining the two-way communication system.

4.4 Protruding Objects.

4.4.1* General. Objects projecting from walls (for example, telephones) with their leading edges between 27 in and 80 in (685 mm and 2030 mm) above the finished floor shall protrude no more than 4 in (100 mm) into walks, halls, corridors, passageways, or aisles (see Fig. 8(a)). Objects mounted with their leading edges at or below 27 in (685 mm) above the finished floor may protrude any amount (see Fig. 8(a) and (b)). Free-standing objects mounted on posts or pylons may overhang 12 in (305 mm) maximum from 27 in to 80 in (685 mm to 2030 mm) above the ground or

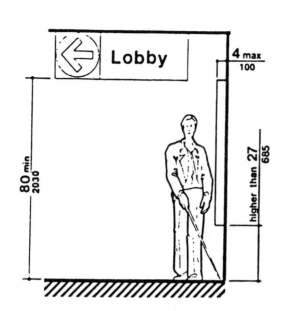
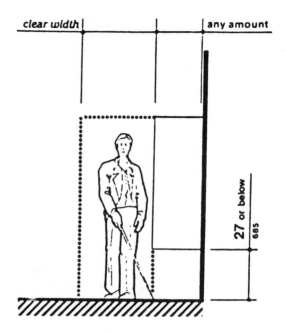

Fig. 8 (a)
Walking Parallel to a Wall

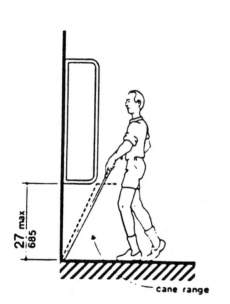

Fig. 8 (b)
Walking Perpendicular to a Wall

Fig. 8
Protruding Objects

finished floor (see Fig. 8(c) and (d)). Protruding objects shall not reduce the clear width of an accessible route or maneuvering space (see Fig. 8(e)).

4.4.2 Head Room. Walks, halls, corridors, passageways, aisles, or other circulation spaces shall have 80 in (2030 mm) minimum clear head room (see Fig. 8(a)). *If vertical clearance of an area adjoining an accessible route is reduced to less than 80 in (nominal dimension), a barrier to warn blind or visually-impaired persons shall be provided (see Fig. 8(c-1)).*

4.5 Ground and Floor Surfaces.

4.5.1* General. Ground and floor surfaces along accessible routes and in accessible rooms and spaces including floors, walks, ramps, stairs, and curb ramps, shall be stable, firm, slip-resistant, and shall comply with 4.5.

4.5.2 Changes in Level. Changes in level up to 1/4 in (6 mm) may be vertical and without edge treatment *(see Fig. 7(c)).* Changes in level between 1/4 in and 1/2 in (6 mm and 13 mm)

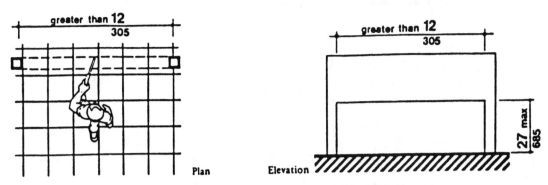

Fig. 8 (c) Free-Standing Overhanging Objects

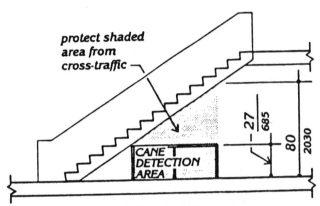

Fig. 8 (c-1) Overhead Hazards

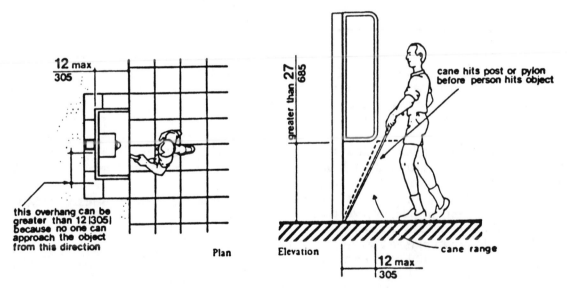

Fig. 8 (d)
Objects Mounted on Posts or Pylons

Fig. 8
Protruding Objects *(Continued)*

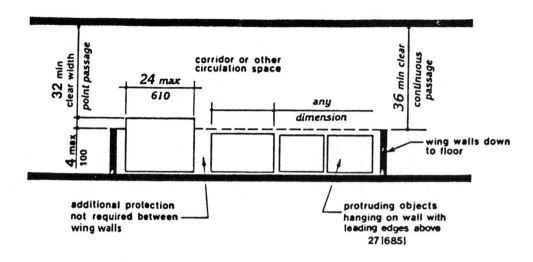

Fig. 8 (e)
Example of Protection around Wall-Mounted Objects and Measurements of Clear Widths

Fig. 8
Protruding Objects *(Continued)*

---

shall be beveled with a slope no greater than 1:2 *(see Fig. 7(d))*. Changes in level greater than 1/2 in (13 mm) shall be accomplished by means of a ramp that complies with 4.7 or 4.8.

4.5.3* Carpet. If carpet or carpet tile is used on a ground or floor surface, then it shall be securely attached; have a firm cushion, pad, or backing, or no cushion or pad; and have a level loop, textured loop, level cut pile, or level cut/ uncut pile texture. The maximum pile *thickness* shall be 1/2 in (13 mm) (see Fig. 8(f)). Exposed edges of carpet shall be fastened to floor surfaces and have trim along the entire length of the exposed edge. Carpet edge trim shall comply with 4.5.2.

4.5.4 Gratings. If gratings are located in walking surfaces, then they shall have spaces no greater than 1/2 in (13 mm) wide in one direction *(see Fig. 8(g))*. If gratings have elongated openings, then they shall be placed so that the long dimension is perpendicular to the dominant direction of travel *(see Fig. 8(h))*.

4.6 Parking and Passenger Loading Zones.

4.6.1 Minimum Number. *Parking spaces required to be accessible by 4.1 shall comply with 4.6.2 through 4.6.5. Passenger loading zones required to be accessible by 4.1 shall comply with 4.6.5 and 4.6.6.*

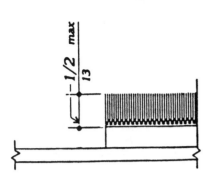

Fig. 8 (f)
Carpet Pile Thickness

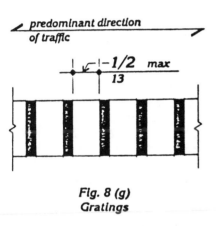

Fig. 8 (g)
Gratings

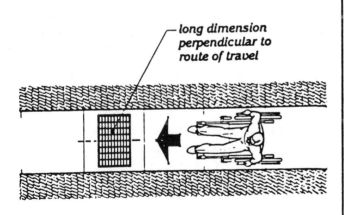

Fig. 8 (h)
Grating Orientation

4.6.2 Location. *Accessible parking spaces serving* a particular building shall be located on the shortest accessible route of travel *from adjacent parking* to an accessible entrance. *In parking facilities* that do not serve a particular building, *accessible parking* shall be located on the shortest accessible route *of travel* to an accessible pedestrian entrance of the parking facility. *In buildings with multiple accessible entrances with adjacent parking, accessible parking spaces shall be dispersed and located closest to the accessible entrances.*

4.6.3* Parking Spaces. *Accessible* parking spaces shall be at least 96 in (2440 mm) wide. Parking access aisles shall be part of an accessible route to the building or facility entrance and shall comply with 4.3. Two accessible parking spaces may share a common access aisle (see Fig. 9). Parked vehicle overhangs shall not reduce the clear width of an accessible route. *Parking spaces and access aisles shall be level with surface slopes not exceeding 1:50 (2%) in all directions.*

4.6.4* Signage. Accessible parking spaces shall be designated as reserved by a sign showing the symbol of accessibility (see 4.30.7). *Spaces complying with 4.1.2(5)(b) shall have an additional sign "Van-Accessible" mounted below the symbol of accessibility.* Such signs shall be located so they cannot be obscured by a vehicle parked in the space.

4.6.5* Vertical Clearance. *Provide minimum vertical clearance of 114 in (2895 mm) at accessible passenger loading zones and along at least one vehicle access route to such areas from site entrance(s) and exit(s). At parking spaces complying with 4.1.2(5)(b), provide minimum vertical clearance of 98 in (2490 mm) at the parking space and along at least one vehicle access route to such spaces from site entrance(s) and exit(s).*

4.6.6 Passenger Loading Zones. Passenger loading zones shall provide an access aisle at least 60 in (1525 mm) wide and 20 ft (240 in) (6100 mm) long adjacent and parallel to the vehicle pull-up space (see Fig. 10). If there are curbs between the access aisle and the vehicle pull-up space, then a curb ramp complying with 4.7 shall be provided. *Vehicle standing spaces and access aisles shall be level with*

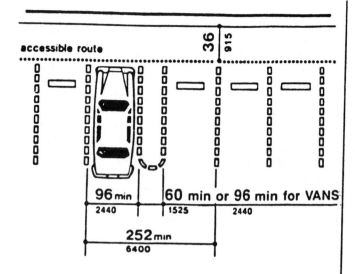

accessible route

36 / 915

96 min / 2440

60 min or 96 min for VANS / 1525

2440

252 min / 6400

Fig. 9
Dimensions of Parking Spaces

surface slopes not exceeding 1:50 (2%) in all directions.

4.7 Curb Ramps.

4.7.1 Location. Curb ramps complying with 4.7 shall be provided wherever an accessible route crosses a curb.

4.7.2 Slope. Slopes of curb ramps shall comply with 4.8.2. The slope shall be measured as shown in Fig. 11. *Transitions from ramps to walks, gutters, or streets shall be flush and free of abrupt changes. Maximum slopes of adjoining gutters, road surface immediately adjacent to the curb ramp, or accessible route shall not exceed 1:20.*

4.7.3 Width. The minimum width of a curb ramp shall be 36 in (915 mm), exclusive of flared sides.

4.7.4 Surface. Surfaces of curb ramps shall comply with 4.5.

4.7.5 Sides of Curb Ramps. If a curb ramp is located where pedestrians must walk across the ramp, *or where it is not protected by hand-rails or guardrails*, it shall have flared sides; the maximum slope of the flare shall be 1:10 (see Fig. 12(a)). Curb ramps with returned curbs

may be used where pedestrians would not normally walk across the ramp (see Fig. 12(b)).

4.7.6 Built-up Curb Ramps. Built-up curb ramps shall be located so that they do not project into vehicular traffic lanes (see Fig. 13).

4.7.7 *Detectable Warnings.* A curb ramp shall have a *detectable* warning complying with 4.29.2. *The detectable warning shall extend the full width and depth of the curb ramp.*

4.7.8 Obstructions. Curb ramps shall be located or protected to prevent their obstruction by parked vehicles.

4.7.9 Location at Marked Crossings. Curb ramps at marked crossings shall be wholly contained within the markings, excluding any flared sides (see Fig. 15).

4.7.10 Diagonal Curb Ramps. If diagonal (or corner type) curb ramps have returned curbs or other well-defined edges, such edges shall be parallel to the direction of pedestrian flow. The bottom of diagonal curb ramps shall have 48 in (1220 mm) minimum clear space as shown in Fig. 15(c) and (d). If diagonal curb ramps are provided at marked crossings, the 48 in (1220 mm) clear space shall be within the markings (see Fig. 15(c) and (d)). If diagonal curb ramps have flared sides, they shall also have at least a 24 in (610 mm) long segment of straight curb located on each side of the curb ramp and within the marked crossing (see Fig. 15(c)).

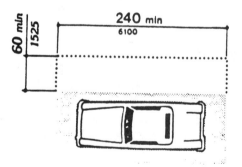

60 min / 1525

240 min / 6100

Fig. 10
Access Aisle at Passenger Loading Zones

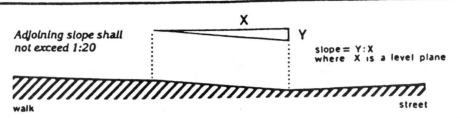

Fig. 11
Measurement of Curb Ramp Slopes

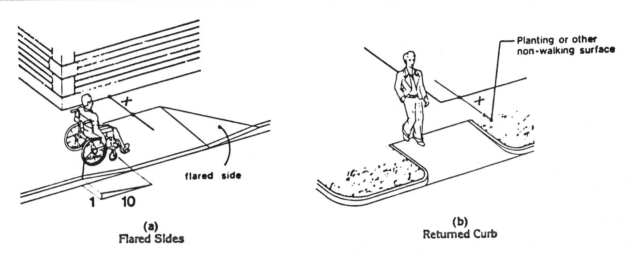

(a)
Flared Sides

(b)
Returned Curb

If X is less than 48 in,
then the slope of the flared side
shall not exceed 1:12.

Fig. 12
Sides of Curb Ramps

4.7.11 Islands. Any raised islands in crossings shall be cut through level with the street or have curb ramps at both sides and a level area at least 48 in (1220 mm) long between the curb ramps in the part of the island intersected by the crossings (see Fig. 15(a) and (b)).

4.8 Ramps.

4.8.1* General. Any part of an accessible route with a slope greater than 1:20 shall be considered a ramp and shall comply with 4.8.

4.8.2* Slope and Rise. The least possible slope shall be used for any ramp. The maximum slope of a ramp in new construction shall be 1:12. The maximum rise for any run shall be 30 in (760 mm) (see Fig. 16). Curb ramps

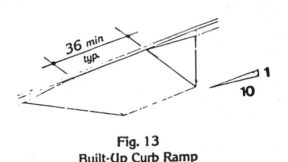

Fig. 13
Built-Up Curb Ramp

and ramps to be constructed on existing sites or in existing buildings or facilities may have slopes and rises as *allowed in 4.1.6(3)(a)* if space limitations prohibit the use of a 1:12 slope or less.

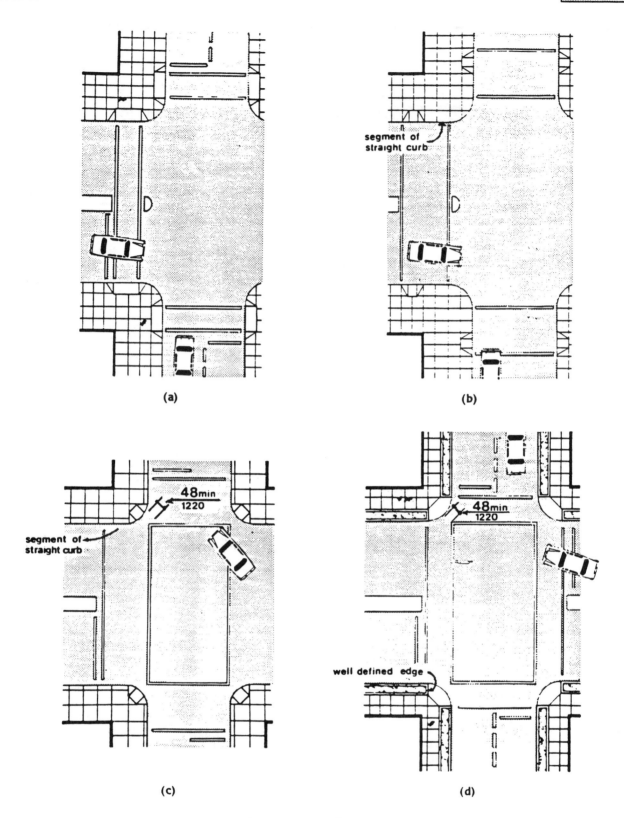

(a)   **(b)**

(c)   **(d)**

Fig. 15
Curb Ramps at Marked Crossings

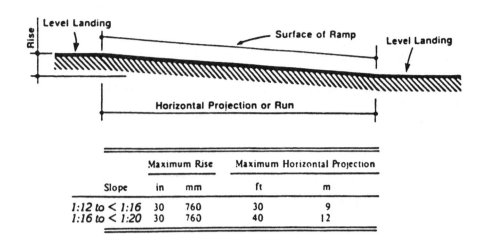

	Maximum Rise		Maximum Horizontal Projection	
Slope	in	mm	ft	m
1:12 to < 1:16	30	760	30	9
1:16 to < 1:20	30	760	40	12

Fig. 16
Components of a Single Ramp Run and Sample Ramp Dimensions

4.8.3 Clear Width. The minimum clear width of a ramp shall be 36 in (915 mm).

4.8.4* Landings. Ramps shall have level landings at bottom and top of *each ramp and each ramp run.* Landings shall have the following features:

(1) The landing shall be at least as wide as the ramp run leading to it.

(2) The landing length shall be a minimum of 60 in (1525 mm) clear.

(3) If ramps change direction at landings, the minimum landing size shall be 60 in by 60 in (1525 mm by 1525 mm).

(4) If a doorway is located at a landing, then the area in front of the doorway shall comply with 4.13.6.

4.8.5* Handrails. If a ramp run has a rise greater than 6 in (150 mm) or a horizontal projection greater than 72 in (1830 mm), then it shall have handrails on both sides. Handrails are not required on curb ramps *or adjacent to seating in assembly areas.* Handrails shall comply with 4.26 and shall have the following features:

(1) Handrails shall be provided along both sides of ramp segments. The inside handrail on switchback or dogleg ramps shall always be continuous.

(2) If handrails are not continuous, they shall extend at least 12 in (305 mm) beyond the top and bottom of the ramp segment and shall be parallel with the floor or ground surface (see Fig. 17).

(3) The clear space between the handrail and the wall shall be 1 - 1/2 in (38 mm).

(4) Gripping surfaces shall be continuous.

(5) *Top of handrail gripping surfaces shall be mounted between 34 in and 38 in (865 mm and 965 mm) above ramp surfaces.*

(6) *Ends of handrails shall be either rounded or returned smoothly to floor, wall, or post.*

(7) *Handrails shall not rotate within their fittings.*

4.8.6 Cross Slope and Surfaces. The cross slope of ramp surfaces shall be no greater than 1:50. Ramp surfaces shall comply with 4.5.

4.8.7 Edge Protection. Ramps and landings with drop-offs shall have curbs, walls, railings, or projecting surfaces that prevent people from slipping off the ramp. Curbs shall be a minimum of 2 in (50 mm) high (see Fig. 17).

4.8.8 Outdoor Conditions. Outdoor ramps and their approaches shall be designed so that water will not accumulate on walking surfaces.

4.9 Stairs.

4.9.1* Minimum Number. *Stairs required to be accessible by 4.1 shall comply with 4.9.*

4.9.2 Treads and Risers. On any given flight of stairs, all steps shall have uniform riser heights and uniform tread widths. Stair treads shall be no less than 11 in (280 mm) wide, measured from riser to riser (see Fig. 18(a)). *Open risers are not permitted.*

4.9.3 Nosings. The undersides of nosings shall not be abrupt. The radius of curvature at the leading edge of the tread shall be no greater than 1/2 in (13 mm). Risers shall be sloped or the underside of the nosing shall have an angle not less than 60 degrees from the horizontal. Nosings shall project no more than 1-1/2 in (38 mm) (see Fig. 18).

4.9.4 Handrails. Stairways shall have handrails at both sides of all stairs. Handrails shall comply with 4.26 and shall have the following features:

(1) Handrails shall be continuous along both sides of stairs. The inside handrail on switchback or dogleg stairs shall always be continuous (see Fig. 19(a) and (b)).

(2) If handrails are not continuous, they shall extend at least 12 in (305 mm) beyond the top riser and at least 12 in (305 mm) plus the width of one tread beyond the bottom riser. At the top, the extension shall be parallel with the floor or ground surface. At the bottom, the handrail shall continue to slope for a distance of the width of one tread from the bottom riser; the remainder of the extension shall be horizontal (see Fig. 19(c) and (d)). Handrail extensions shall comply with 4.4.

(3) The clear space between handrails and wall shall be 1-1/2 in (38 mm).

(4) Gripping surfaces shall be uninterrupted by newel posts, other construction elements, or obstructions.

(5) *Top of handrail gripping surface shall be mounted between 34 in and 38 in (865 mm and 965 mm) above stair nosings.*

(6) *Ends of handrails shall be either rounded or returned smoothly to floor, wall or post.*

(7) *Handrails shall not rotate within their fittings.*

4.9.5 Detectable Warnings at Stairs. *(Reserved).*

4.9.6 Outdoor Conditions. Outdoor stairs and their approaches shall be designed so that water will not accumulate on walking surfaces.

4.10 Elevators.

4.10.1 General. *Accessible* elevators shall be on an accessible route and shall comply with 4.10 and with the *ASME A17.1-1990,* Safety Code for Elevators and Escalators. *Freight elevators shall not be considered as meeting the requirements of this section unless the only elevators provided are used as combination passenger and freight elevators for the public and employees.*

4.10.2 Automatic Operation. Elevator operation shall be automatic. Each car shall be equipped with a self-leveling feature that will automatically bring the car to floor landings within a tolerance of 1/2 in (13 mm) under rated loading to zero loading conditions. This self-leveling feature shall be automatic and independent of the operating device and shall correct the overtravel or undertravel.

4.10.3 Hall Call Buttons. Call buttons in elevator lobbies and halls shall be centered at 42 in (1065 mm) above the floor. Such call buttons shall have visual signals to indicate when each call is registered and when each call is answered. Call buttons shall be a minimum of 3/4 in (19 mm) in the smallest dimension. The button designating the up direction shall be on top. (See Fig. 20.) *Buttons shall be raised or flush. Objects mounted beneath hall call buttons shall not project into the elevator lobby more than 4 in (100 mm).*

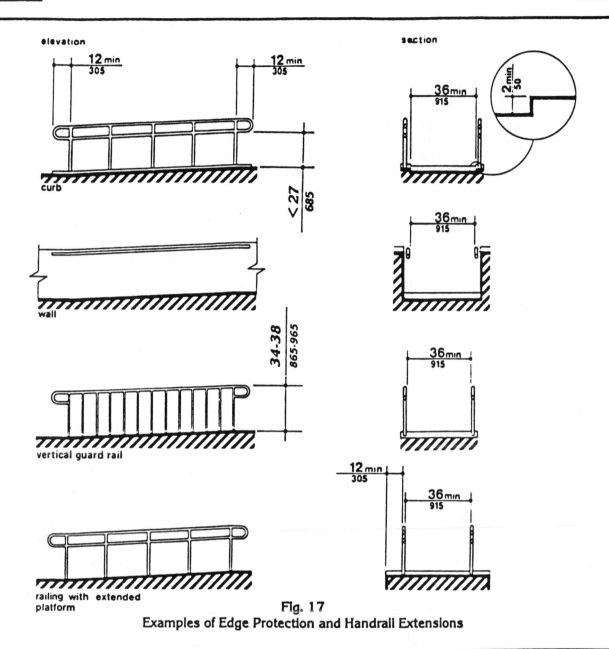

Fig. 17
Examples of Edge Protection and Handrail Extensions

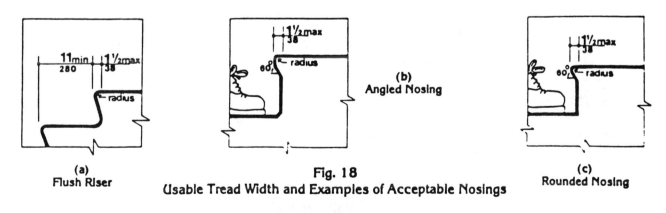

(a)
Flush Riser

(b)
Angled Nosing

(c)
Rounded Nosing

Fig. 18
Usable Tread Width and Examples of Acceptable Nosings

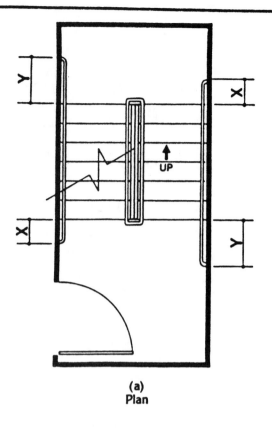

(a)
Plan

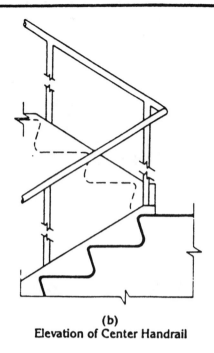

(b)
Elevation of Center Handrail

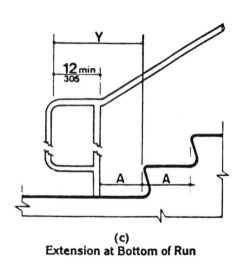

(c)
Extension at Bottom of Run

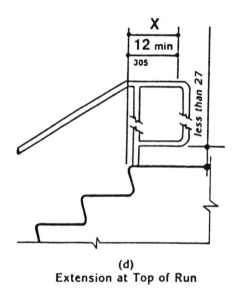

(d)
Extension at Top of Run

NOTE:

*X is the 12 in minimum handrail extension required
at each top riser.*

*Y is the minimum handrail extension of 12 in plus the
width of one tread that is required at each bottom riser.*

Fig. 19
Stair Handrails

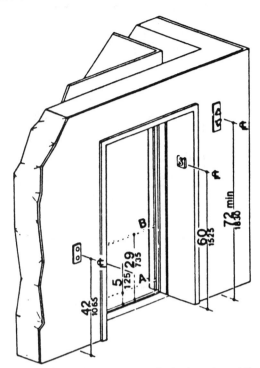

NOTE: The automatic door reopening device is activated if an object passes through either line A or line B. Line A and line B represent the vertical locations of the door reopening device not requiring contact.

Fig. 20
Hoistway and Elevator Entrances

4.10.4 Hall Lanterns. A visible and audible signal shall be provided at each hoistway entrance to indicate which car is answering a call. Audible signals shall sound once for the up direction and twice for the down direction or shall have verbal annunciators that say "up" or "down." Visible signals shall have the following features:

(1) Hall lantern fixtures shall be mounted so that their centerline is at least 72 in (1830 mm) above the lobby floor. (See Fig. 20.)

(2) Visual elements shall be at least 2-1/2 in (64 mm) in the smallest dimension.

(3) Signals shall be visible from the vicinity of the hall call button (see Fig. 20). In-car lanterns located in cars, visible from the vicinity of hall call buttons, and conforming to the above requirements, shall be acceptable.

4.10.5 Raised and Braille Characters on Hoistway Entrances. All elevator hoistway entrances shall have *raised and Braille* floor designations provided on both jambs. The centerline of the characters shall be 60 in (1525 mm) *above finish* floor. Such characters shall be 2 in (50 mm) high and shall comply with 4.30.4. Permanently applied plates are acceptable if they are permanently fixed to the jambs. (See Fig. 20).

4.10.6* Door Protective and Reopening Device. Elevator doors shall open and close automatically. They shall be provided with a reopening device that will stop and reopen a car door and hoistway door automatically if the door becomes obstructed by an object or person. The device shall be capable of completing these operations without requiring contact for an obstruction passing through the opening at heights of 5 in and 29 in (125 mm and 735 mm) above finish floor (see Fig. 20). Door reopening devices shall remain effective for at least 20 seconds. After such an interval, doors may close in accordance with the requirements of *ASME A17.1-1990.*

4.10.7* Door and Signal Timing for Hall Calls. The minimum acceptable time from notification that a car is answering a call until the doors of that car start to close shall be calculated from the following equation:

$$T = D/(1.5 \text{ ft/s) or } T = D/(445 \text{ mm/s})$$

where T total time in seconds and D distance (in feet or millimeters) from a point in the lobby or corridor 60 in (1525 mm) directly in front of the farthest call button controlling that car to the centerline of its hoistway door (see Fig. 21). For cars with in-car lanterns, T begins when the lantern is visible from the vicinity of hall call buttons and an audible signal is sounded. *The minimum acceptable notification time shall be 5 seconds.*

4.10.8 Door Delay for Car Calls. The minimum time for elevator doors to remain fully open in response to a car call shall be 3 seconds.

4.10.9 Floor Plan of Elevator Cars. The floor area of elevator cars shall provide space for wheelchair users to enter the car, maneuver

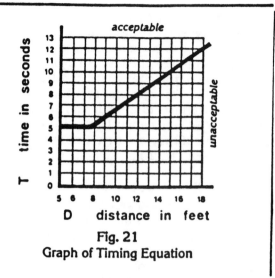

Fig. 21
Graph of Timing Equation

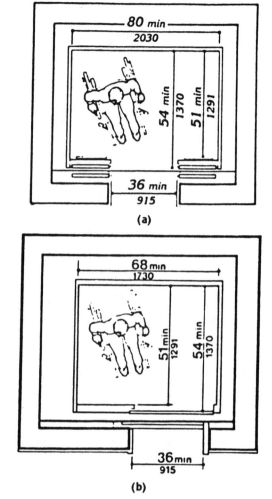

(a)

(b)

Fig. 22
Minimum Dimensions of Elevator Cars

within reach of controls, and exit from the car. Acceptable door opening and inside dimensions shall be as shown in Fig. 22. The clearance between the car platform sill and the edge of any hoistway landing shall be no greater than 1-1/4 in (32 mm).

4.10.10 Floor Surfaces. Floor surfaces shall comply with 4.5.

4.10.11 Illumination Levels. The level of illumination at the car controls, platform, and car threshold and landing sill shall be at least 5 footcandles (53.8 lux).

4.10.12* Car Controls. Elevator control panels shall have the following features:

(1) Buttons. All control buttons shall be at least 3/4 in (19 mm) in their smallest dimension. They *shall* be *raised* or flush.

(2) Tactile, *Braille,* and Visual Control Indicators. All control buttons shall be designated by *Braille and by raised* standard alphabet characters for letters, arabic characters for numerals, or standard symbols as shown in Fig. 23(a), and as required in *ASME A17.1-1990. Raised and Braille* characters and symbols shall comply with 4.30. The call button for the main entry floor shall be designated by a *raised* star at the left of the floor designation (see Fig. 23(a)). All raised designations for control buttons shall be placed immediately to the left of the button to which they apply. Applied plates,

permanently attached, are an acceptable means to provide raised control designations. Floor buttons shall be provided with visual indicators to show when each call is registered. The visual indicators shall be extinguished when each call is answered.

(3) Height. All floor buttons shall be no higher than 54 in (1370 mm) above the *finish* floor *for side approach and* 48 in (1220 mm) *for front approach.* Emergency controls, including the emergency alarm and emergency stop, shall be grouped at the bottom of the panel and shall have their centerlines no less than 35 in (890 mm) above the finish floor (see Fig. 23(a) and (b)).

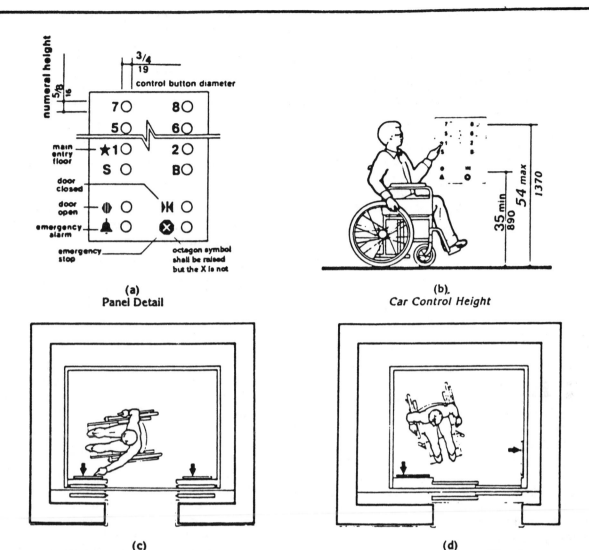

(a)
Panel Detail

(b).
Car Control Height

(c)
Alternate Locations of Panel
with Center Opening Door

(d)
Alternate Locations of Panel
with Side Opening Door

Fig. 23
Car Controls

(4) Location. Controls shall be located on a front wall if cars have center opening doors, and at the side wall or at the front wall next to the door if cars have side opening doors (see Fig. 23(c) and (d)).

4.10.13* Car Position Indicators. In elevator cars, a visual car position indicator shall be provided above the car control panel or over the door to show the position of the elevator in the hoistway. As the car passes or stops at a floor served by the elevators, the :orresponding numerals shall illuminate,

and an audible signal shall sound. Numerals shall be a minimum of 1/2 in (13 mm) high. The audible signal shall be no less than 20 decibels with a frequency no higher than 1500 Hz. An automatic verbal announcement of the floor number at which a car stops or which a car passes may be substituted for the audible signal.

4.10.14* Emergency Communications. If provided, emergency two-way communication systems between the elevator and a point outside the hoistway shall comply with *ASME*

A17.1-1990. The highest operable part of a two-way communication system shall be a maximum of *48 in (1220 mm)* from the floor of the car. It shall be identified by a raised symbol and lettering complying with 4.30 and located adjacent to the device. If the system uses a handset then the length of the cord from the panel to the handset shall be at least 29 in (735 mm). *If the system is located in a closed compartment the compartment door hardware shall conform to 4.27, Controls and Operating Mechanisms. The emergency intercommunication system shall not require voice communication.*

4.11 Platform Lifts (Wheelchair Lifts).

4.11.1 Location. *Platform lifts (wheelchair lifts) permitted by 4.1 shall comply with the requirements of 4.11.*

4.11.2* Other Requirements. If platform lifts *(wheelchair lifts)* are used, they shall comply with 4.2.4, 4.5, 4.27, and *ASME A17.1 Safety Code for Elevators and Escalators, Section XX,* 1990.

4.11.3 Entrance. *If platform lifts are used then they shall facilitate unassisted entry, operation, and exit from the lift in compliance with 4.11.2.*

4.12 Windows.

4.12.1* General. *(Reserved).*

4.12.2* Window Hardware. *(Reserved).*

4.13 Doors.

4.13.1 General. *Doors required to be accessible by 4.1 shall comply with the requirements of 4.13.*

4.13.2 Revolving Doors and Turnstiles. Revolving doors or turnstiles shall not be the only means of passage at an accessible entrance or along an accessible route. *An accessible gate or door shall be provided adjacent to the turnstile or revolving door and shall be so designed as to facilitate the same use pattern.*

4.13.3 Gates. Gates, including ticket gates, shall meet all applicable specifications of 4.13.

4.13.4 Double-Leaf Doorways. If doorways have two *independently operated* door leaves, then at least one leaf shall meet the specifications in 4.13.5 and 4.13.6. That leaf shall be an active leaf.

4.13.5 Clear Width. Doorways shall have a minimum clear opening of 32 in (815 mm) with the door open 90 degrees, measured between the face of the door and the *opposite* stop (see Fig. 24(a), (b), (c), and (d)). Openings more than 24 in (610 mm) in depth shall comply with 4.2.1 and 4.3.3 (see Fig. 24(e)).

EXCEPTION: Doors not requiring full user passage, such as shallow closets, may have the clear opening reduced to 20 in (510 mm) minimum.

4.13.6 Maneuvering Clearances at Doors. Minimum maneuvering clearances at doors that are not automatic or power-assisted shall be as shown in Fig. 25. The floor or ground area within the required clearances shall be level and clear.

EXCEPTION: Entry doors to acute care hospital bedrooms for in-patients shall be exempted from the requirement for space at the latch side of the door (see dimension "x" in Fig. 25) if the door is at least 44 in (1120 mm) wide.

4.13.7 Two Doors in Series. The minimum space between two hinged or pivoted doors in series shall be 48 in (1220 mm) plus the width of any door swinging into the space. Doors in series shall swing either in the same direction or away from the space between the doors (see Fig. 26).

4.13.8* Thresholds at Doorways. Thresholds at doorways shall not exceed 3/4 in (19 mm) in height for exterior sliding doors or 1/2 in (13 mm) for other types of doors. Raised thresholds and floor level changes at accessible doorways shall be beveled with a slope no greater than 1:2 (see 4.5.2).

4.13.9* Door Hardware. Handles, pulls, latches, locks, and other operating devices on accessible doors shall have a shape that is easy

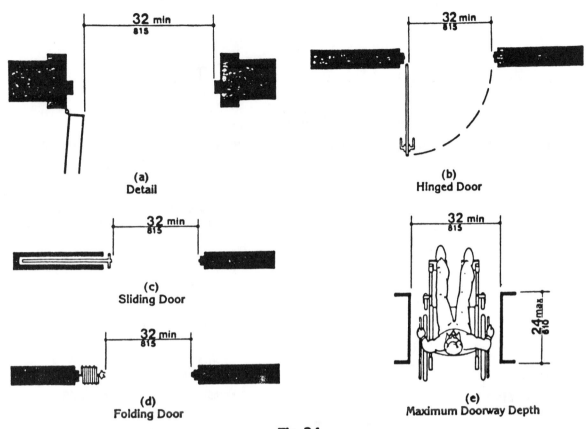

Fig. 24
Clear Doorway Width and Depth

to grasp with one hand and does not require tight grasping, tight pinching, or twisting of the wrist to operate. Lever-operated mechanisms, push-type mechanisms, and U-shaped handles are acceptable designs. When sliding doors are fully open, operating hardware shall be exposed and usable from both sides. *Hardware required for accessible door passage shall be mounted no higher than 48 in (1220 mm) above finished floor.*

4.13.10° Door Closers. If a door has a closer, then the sweep period of the closer shall be adjusted so that from an open position of 70 degrees, the door will take at least 3 seconds to move to a point 3 in (75 mm) from the latch, measured to the leading edge of the door.

4.13.11° Door Opening Force. The maximum force for pushing or pulling open a door shall be as follows:

(1) Fire doors shall have the minimum opening force allowable by the appropriate administrative authority.

(2) Other doors.

(a) exterior hinged doors: *(Reserved)*.

(b) interior hinged doors: 5 lbf (22.2N)

(c) sliding or folding doors: 5 lbf (22.2N)

These forces do not apply to the force required to retract latch bolts or disengage other devices that may hold the door in a closed position.

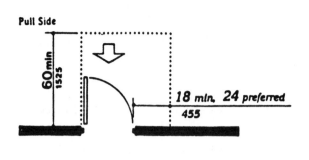

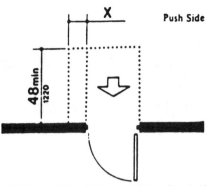

NOTE: x = 12 in (305 mm) if door has both a closer and latch.

(a)
Front Approaches — Swinging Doors

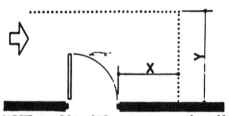

NOTE: x = 36 in (915 mm) minimum if y = 60 in (1525 mm); x = 42 in (1065 mm) minimum if y = 54 in (1370 mm).

NOTE: y = 48 in (1220 mm) minimum if door has both a latch and closer.

(b)
Hinge Side Approaches — Swinging Doors

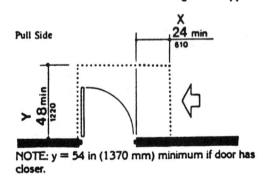

NOTE: y = 54 in (1370 mm) minimum if door has closer.

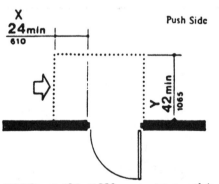

NOTE: y = 48 in (1220 mm) minimum if door has closer.

(c)
Latch Side Approaches — Swinging Doors

NOTE: All doors in alcoves shall comply with the clearances for front approaches.

Fig. 25
Maneuvering Clearances at Doors

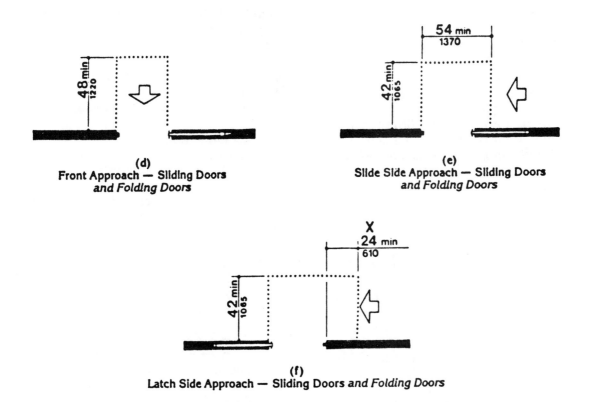

(d)
Front Approach — Sliding Doors
and Folding Doors

(e)
Slide Side Approach — Sliding Doors
and Folding Doors

(f)
Latch Side Approach — Sliding Doors *and Folding Doors*

NOTE: All doors in alcoves shall comply with the clearances for front approaches.

Fig. 25
Maneuvering Clearances at Doors *(Continued)*

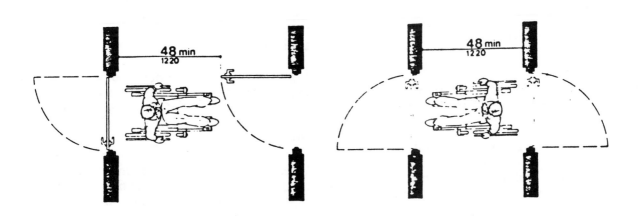

Fig. 26
Two Hinged Doors in Series

4.13.12* Automatic Doors and Power-Assisted Doors. If an automatic door is used, then it shall comply with *ANSI/BHMA A156.10-1985.* Slowly opening, low-powered, automatic doors shall *comply with ANSI A156.19-1984.* Such doors shall not open to back check faster than 3 seconds and shall require no more than 15 lbf (66.6N) to stop door movement. If a power-assisted door is used, its door-opening force shall comply with 4.13.11 and its closing shall conform to the requirements in *ANSI A156.19-1984.*

4.14 Entrances.

4.14.1 Minimum Number. *Entrances required to be accessible by 4.1* shall be part of an accessible route complying with 4.3. Such entrances shall be connected by an accessible route to public transportation stops, to accessible parking and passenger loading zones, and to public streets or sidewalks if available (see 4.3.2(1)). They shall also be connected by an accessible route to all accessible spaces or elements within the building or facility.

4.14.2 Service Entrances. A service entrance shall not be the sole accessible entrance unless it is the only entrance to a building or facility (for example, in a factory or garage).

4.15 Drinking Fountains and Water Coolers.

4.15.1 Minimum Number. *Drinking fountains or water coolers required to be accessible by 4.1* shall comply with 4.15.

4.15.2* Spout Height. Spouts shall be no higher than 36 in (915 mm), measured from the floor or ground surfaces to the spout outlet (see Fig. 27(a)).

4.15.3 Spout Location. The spouts of drinking fountains and water coolers shall be at the front of the unit and shall direct the water flow in a trajectory that is parallel or nearly parallel to the front of the unit. The spout shall provide a flow of water at least 4 in (100 mm) high so as to allow the insertion of a cup or glass under the flow of water. *On an accessible drinking fountain with a round or oval bowl, the spout must be positioned so the flow of water is within 3 in (75 mm) of the front edge of the fountain.*

4.15.4 Controls. Controls shall comply with 4.27.4. *Unit controls shall be front mounted or side mounted near the front edge.*

4.15.5 Clearances.

(1) Wall- and post-mounted cantilevered units shall have a clear knee space between the bottom of the apron and the floor or ground at least 27 in (685 mm) high, 30 in (760 mm) wide, and 17 in to 19 in (430 mm to 485 mm) deep (see Fig. 27(a) and (b)). Such units shall also have a minimum clear floor space 30 in by 48 in (760 mm by 1220 mm) to allow a person in a wheelchair to approach the unit facing forward.

(2) Free-standing or built-in units not having a clear space under them shall have a clear floor space at least 30 in by 48 in (760 mm by 1220 mm) that allows a person in a wheelchair to make a parallel approach to the unit (see Fig. 27(c) and (d)). This clear floor space shall comply with 4.2.4.

4.16 Water Closets.

4.16.1 General. Accessible water closets shall comply with 4.16.

4.16.2 Clear Floor Space. Clear floor space for water closets not in stalls shall comply with Fig. 28. Clear floor space may be arranged to allow either a left-handed or right-handed approach.

4.16.3* Height. The height of water closets shall be 17 in to 19 in (430 mm to 485 mm), measured to the top of the toilet seat (see Fig. 29(b)). *Seats shall not be sprung to return to a lifted position.*

4.16.4* Grab Bars. Grab bars for water closets not located in stalls shall comply with 4.26 and Fig. 29. *The grab bar behind the water closet shall be 36 in (915 mm) minimum.*

4.16.5* Flush Controls. Flush controls shall be hand operated *or automatic* and shall comply with 4.27.4. Controls for flush valves shall be mounted on the wide side of toilet areas no more than 44 in (1120 mm) above the floor.

4.16.6 Dispensers. Toilet paper dispensers shall be installed within reach, as shown in Fig. 29(b). *Dispensers that control delivery, or that do not permit continuous paper flow, shall not be used.*

4.17 Toilet Stalls.

4.17.1 Location. Accessible toilet stalls shall be on an accessible route and shall meet the requirements of 4.17.

4.17.2 Water Closets. Water closets in accessible stalls shall comply with 4.16.

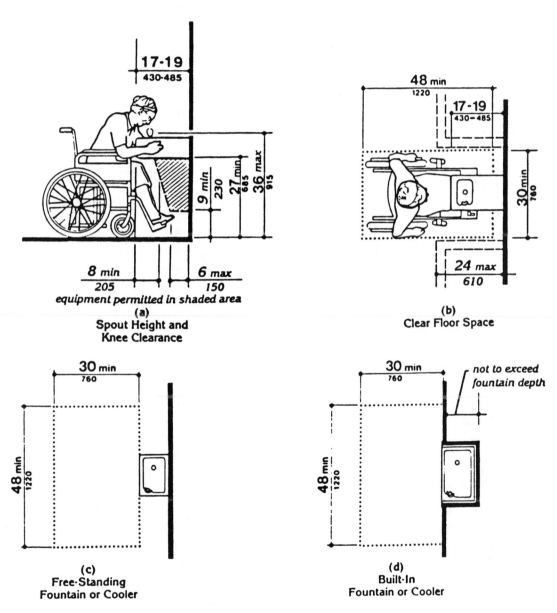

(a)
Spout Height and
Knee Clearance

(b)
Clear Floor Space

(c)
Free-Standing
Fountain or Cooler

(d)
Built-In
Fountain or Cooler

Fig. 27
Drinking Fountains and Water Coolers

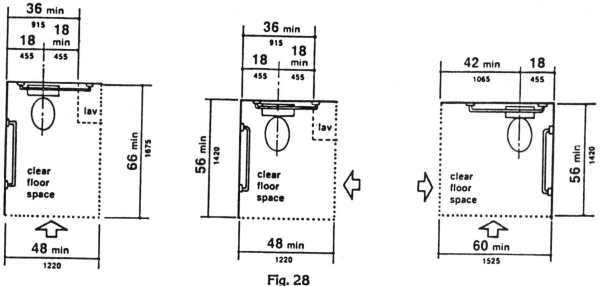

Fig. 28
Clear Floor Space at Water Closets

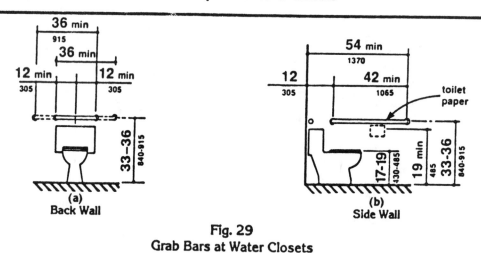

Fig. 29
Grab Bars at Water Closets

4.17.3* Size and Arrangement. The size and arrangement of the standard toilet stall shall comply with Fig. 30(a), *Standard Stall.* Standard toilet stalls with a minimum depth of 56 in (1420 mm) (see Fig. 30(a)) shall have wall-mounted water closets. If the depth of a standard toilet stall is increased at least 3 in (75 mm), then a floor-mounted water closet may be used. Arrangements shown for standard toilet stalls may be reversed to allow either a left- or right-hand approach. Additional stalls shall be provided in conformance with 4.22.4.

EXCEPTION: In instances of alteration work where provision of a standard stall (Fig. 30(a))

is technically infeasible or where plumbing code requirements prevent combining existing stalls to provide space, either alternate stall (Fig. 30(b)) may be provided in lieu of the standard stall.

4.17.4 Toe Clearances. In standard stalls, the front partition and at least one side partition shall provide a toe clearance of at least 9 in (230 mm) above the floor. If the depth of the stall is greater than 60 in (1525 mm), then the toe clearance is not required.

4.17.5* Doors. Toilet stall doors, *including door hardware,* shall comply with 4.13. *If toilet stall approach is from the latch side of the stall door, clearance between the door side of the*

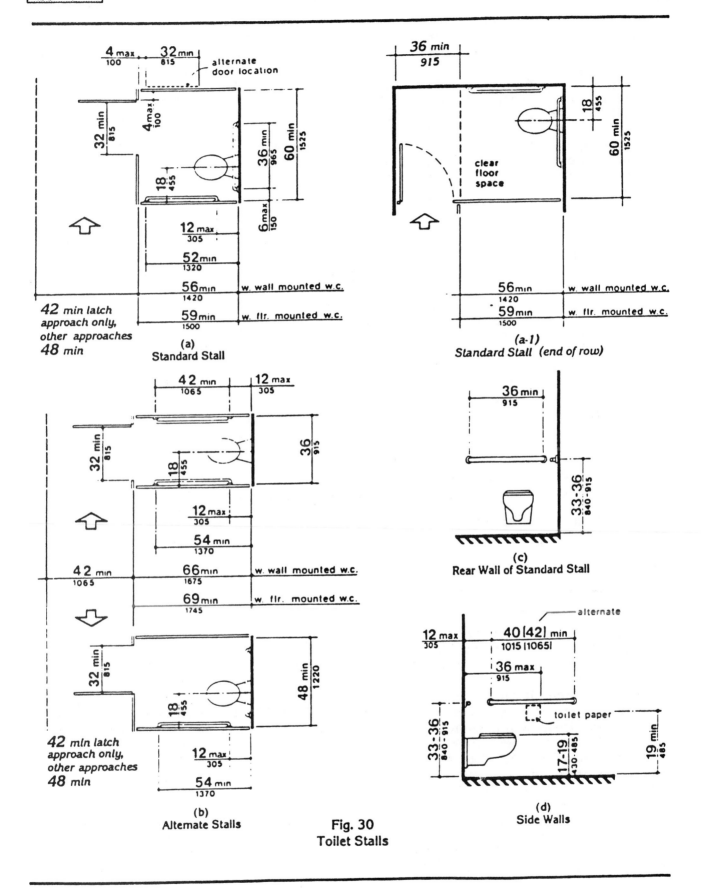

42 min latch approach only, other approaches 48 min

(a)
Standard Stall

(a-1)
Standard Stall (end of row)

(c)
Rear Wall of Standard Stall

42 min latch approach only, other approaches 48 min

(b)
Alternate Stalls

(d)
Side Walls

Fig. 30
Toilet Stalls

stall and any obstruction may be reduced to a minimum of 42 in (1065 mm) (Fig. 30).

4.17.6 Grab Bars. Grab bars complying with the length and positioning shown in Fig. 30(a), (b), (c), and (d) shall be provided. Grab bars may be mounted with any desired method as long as they have a gripping surface at the locations shown and do not obstruct the required clear floor area. Grab bars shall comply with 4.26.

4.18 Urinals.

4.18.1 General. Accessible urinals shall comply with 4.18.

4.18.2 Height. Urinals shall be stall-type or wall-hung with an elongated rim at a maximum of 17 in (430 mm) above the finish floor.

4.18.3 Clear Floor Space. A clear floor space 30 in by 48 in (760 mm by 1220 mm) shall be provided in front of urinals to allow forward approach. This clear space shall adjoin or overlap an accessible route and shall comply with 4.2.4. *Urinal shields that do not extend beyond the front edge of the urinal rim may be provided with 29 in (735 mm) clearance between them.*

4.18.4 Flush Controls. Flush controls shall be hand operated or automatic, and shall comply with 4.27.4, and shall be mounted no more than 44 in (1120 mm) above the finish floor.

4.19 Lavatories and Mirrors.

4.19.1 General. The requirements of 4.19 shall apply to lavatory fixtures, vanities, and built-in lavatories.

4.19.2 Height and Clearances. Lavatories shall be mounted with *the rim or counter surface no higher than 34 in (865 mm) above the finish floor.* Provide a clearance of at least 29 in (735 mm) above the finish floor to the bottom of the apron. Knee and toe clearance shall comply with Fig. 31.

4.19.3 Clear Floor Space. A clear floor space 30 in by 48 in (760 mm by 1220 mm) complying with 4.2.4 shall be provided in front of a lavatory to allow forward approach. Such

clear floor space shall adjoin or overlap an accessible route and shall extend a maximum of 19 in (485 mm) underneath the lavatory (see Fig. 32).

4.19.4 Exposed Pipes and Surfaces. Hot water and drain pipes under lavatories shall be insulated or otherwise *configured to protect against contact.* There shall be no sharp or abrasive surfaces under lavatories.

4.19.5 Faucets. Faucets shall comply with 4.27.4. Lever-operated, push-type, and electronically controlled mechanisms are examples of acceptable designs. *If self-closing valves are*

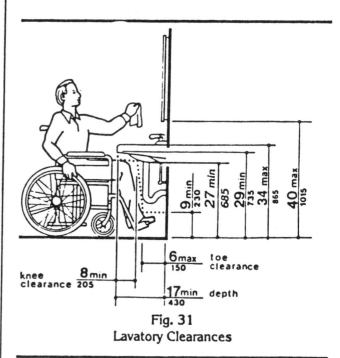

Fig. 31
Lavatory Clearances

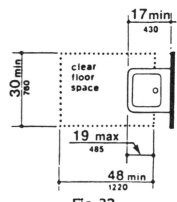

Fig. 32
Clear Floor Space at Lavatories

used the faucet *shall remain* open for at least 10 seconds.

4.19.6* Mirrors. Mirrors shall be mounted with the bottom edge *of the reflecting surface* no higher than 40 in (1015 mm) *above the finish* floor (see Fig. 31).

4.20 Bathtubs.

4.20.1 General. Accessible bathtubs shall comply with 4.20.

4.20.2 Floor Space. Clear floor space in front of bathtubs shall be as shown in Fig. 33.

4.20.3 Seat. An in-tub seat or a seat at the head end of the tub shall be provided as shown in Fig. 33 and 34. The structural strength of seats and their attachments shall comply with 4.26.3. Seats shall be mounted securely and shall not slip during use.

4.20.4 Grab Bars. Grab bars complying with 4.26 shall be provided as shown in Fig. 33 and 34.

4.20.5 Controls. Faucets and other controls complying with 4.27.4 shall be located as shown in Fig. 34.

4.20.6 Shower Unit. A shower spray unit with a hose at least 60 in (1525 mm) long that can be used *both* as a fixed shower head *and* as a hand-held shower shall be provided.

4.20.7 Bathtub Enclosures. If provided, enclosures for bathtubs shall not obstruct controls or transfer from wheelchairs onto bathtub seats or into tubs. Enclosures on bathtubs shall not have tracks mounted on their rims.

4.21 Shower Stalls.

4.21.1* General. Accessible shower stalls shall comply with 4.21.

4.21.2 Size and Clearances. Except as specified in 9.1.2, shower stall size and clear floor space shall comply with Fig. 35(a) or (b). The shower stall in Fig. 35(a) shall be 36 in by 36 in (915 mm by 915 mm). Shower stalls required by 9.1.2 shall comply with Fig. 57(a)

or (b). The shower stall in Fig. 35(b) will fit into the space required for a bathtub.

4.21.3 Seat. A seat shall be provided in shower stalls 36 in by 36 in (915 mm by 915 mm) and shall be as shown in Fig. 36. The seat shall be mounted 17 in to 19 in (430 mm to 485 mm) from the bathroom floor and shall extend the full depth of the stall. In a 36 in by 36 in (915 mm by 915 mm) shower stall, the seat shall be on the wall opposite the controls. *Where a fixed seat is provided in a 30 in by 60 in minimum (760 mm by 1525 mm) shower stall, it shall be a folding type and shall be mounted on the wall adjacent to the controls as shown in Fig. 57.* The structural strength of seats and their attachments shall comply with 4.26.3.

4.21.4 Grab Bars. Grab bars complying with 4.26 shall be provided as shown in Fig. 37.

4.21.5 Controls. Faucets and other controls complying with 4.27.4 shall be located as shown in Fig. 37. In shower stalls 36 in by 36 in (915 mm by 915 mm), all controls, faucets, and the shower unit shall be mounted on the side wall opposite the seat.

4.21.6 Shower Unit. A shower spray unit with a hose at least 60 in (1525 mm) long that can be used *both* as a fixed shower head *and* as a hand-held shower shall be provided.

EXCEPTION: In unmonitored facilities where vandalism is a consideration, a fixed shower head mounted at 48 in (1220 mm) above the shower floor may be used in lieu of a hand-held shower head.

4.21.7 Curbs. If provided, curbs in shower stalls 36 in by 36 in (915 mm by 915 mm) shall be no higher than *1/2 in (13 mm).* Shower stalls that are 30 in by 60 in (760 mm by 1525 mm) minimum shall not have curbs.

4.21.8 Shower Enclosures. If provided, enclosures for shower stalls shall not obstruct controls or obstruct transfer from wheelchairs onto shower seats.

4.22 Toilet Rooms.

4.22.1 Minimum Number. *Toilet facilities required to be accessible by 4.1 shall comply*

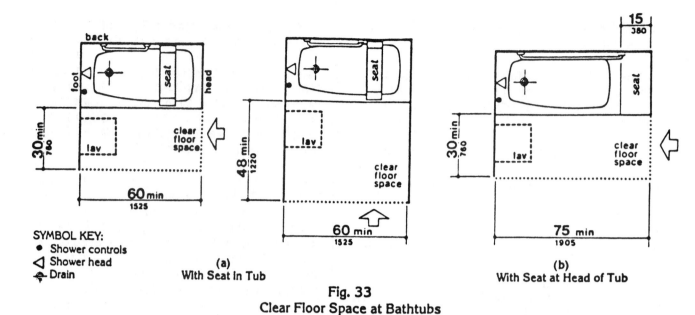

SYMBOL KEY:
- ● Shower controls
- ◁ Shower head
- ⊕ Drain

(a)
With Seat in Tub

(b)
With Seat at Head of Tub

Fig. 33
Clear Floor Space at Bathtubs

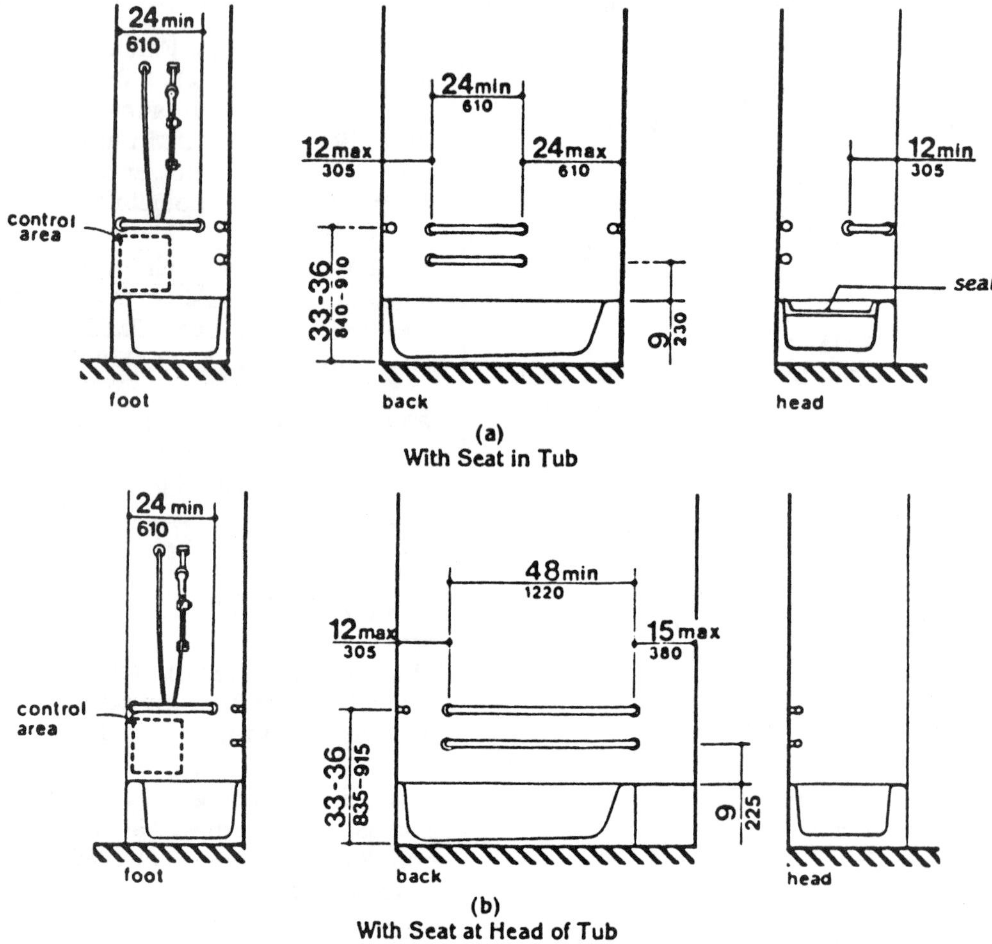

(a)
With Seat in Tub

(b)
With Seat at Head of Tub

Fig. 34
Grab Bars at Bathtubs

with 4.22. Accessible toilet rooms shall be on an accessible route.

4.22.2 Doors. All doors to accessible toilet rooms shall comply with 4.13. Doors shall not swing into the clear floor space required for any fixture.

4.22.3* Clear Floor Space. The accessible fixtures and controls required in 4.22.4, 4.22.5, 4.22.6, and 4.22.7 shall be on an accessible route. An unobstructed turning space complying with 4.2.3 shall be provided within an accessible toilet room. The clear floor space at fixtures and controls, the accessible route, and the turning space may overlap.

4.22.4 Water Closets. If toilet stalls are provided, then at least one shall be a standard toilet stall complying with 4.17; *where 6 or more stalls are provided, in addition to the stall complying with 4.17.3, at least one stall 36 in (915 mm) wide with an outward swinging, self-closing door and parallel grab bars complying with Fig. 30(d) and 4.26 shall be provided. Water closets in such stalls shall comply with 4.16.* If water closets are not in stalls, then at least one shall comply with 4.16.

4.22.5 Urinals. If urinals are provided, *then* at least one shall comply with 4.18.

4.22.6 Lavatories and Mirrors. If lavatories and mirrors are provided, *then* at least one of each shall comply with 4.19.

4.22.7 Controls and Dispensers. If controls, dispensers, receptacles, or other

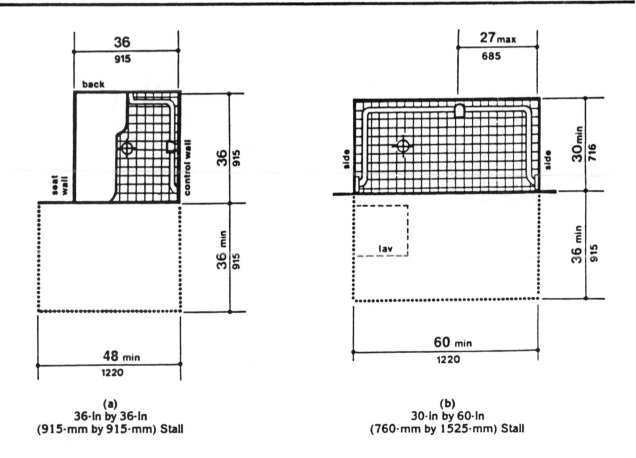

(a)
36-in by 36-in
(915-mm by 915-mm) Stall

(b)
30-in by 60-in
(760-mm by 1525-mm) Stall

Fig. 35
Shower Size and Clearances

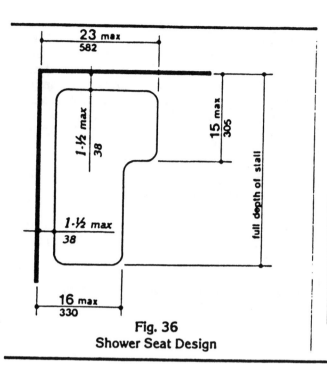

**Fig. 36
Shower Seat Design**

equipment are provided, *then* at least one of each shall be on an accessible route and shall comply with 4.27.

4.23 Bathrooms, Bathing Facilities, and Shower Rooms.

4.23.1 Minimum Number. Bathrooms, bathing facilities, or shower rooms *required to be accessible by 4.1* shall comply with 4.23 and shall be on an accessible route.

4.23.2 Doors. Doors to accessible bathrooms shall comply with 4.13. Doors shall not swing into the floor space required for any fixture.

4.23.3* Clear Floor Space. The accessible fixtures and controls required in 4.23.4, 4.23.5, 4.23.6, 4.23.7, 4.23.8, and 4.23.9 shall be on an accessible route. An unobstructed turning

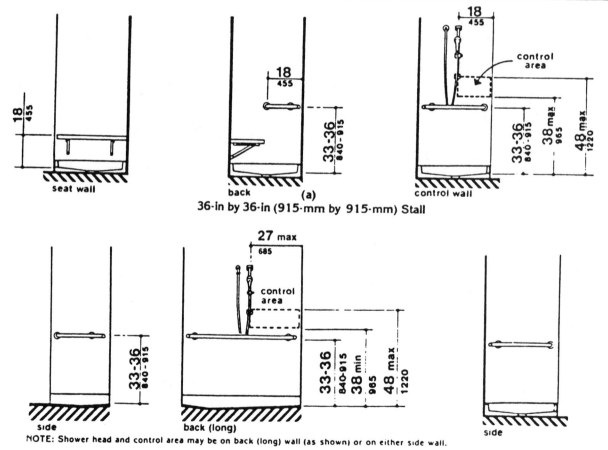

NOTE: Shower head and control area may be on back (long) wall (as shown) or on either side wall.

(b)
30-in by 60-in (760-mm by 1525-mm) Stall

**Fig. 37
Grab Bars at Shower Stalls**

space complying with 4.2.3 shall be provided within an accessible bathroom. The clear floor spaces at fixtures and controls, the accessible route, and the turning space may overlap.

4.23.4 Water Closets. If toilet stalls are provided, then at least one shall be a standard toilet stall complying with 4.17; *where 6 or more stalls are provided, in addition to the stall complying with 4.17.3, at least one stall 36 in (915 mm) wide with an outward swinging, self-closing door and parallel grab bars complying with Fig. 30(d) and 4.26 shall be provided. Water closets in such stalls shall comply with 4.16.* If water closets are not in stalls, then at least one shall comply with 4.16.

4.23.5 Urinals. If urinals are provided, then at least one shall comply with 4.18.

4.23.6 Lavatories and Mirrors. If lavatories and mirrors are provided, then at least one of each shall comply with 4.19.

4.23.7 Controls and Dispensers. If controls, dispensers, receptacles, or other equipment *are* provided, *then* at least one of each shall be on an accessible route and shall comply with 4.27.

4.23.8 Bathing and Shower Facilities. If tubs or showers are provided, then at least one accessible tub that complies with 4.20 or at least one accessible shower that complies with 4.21 shall be provided.

4.23.9* Medicine Cabinets. If medicine cabinets are provided, at least one shall be located with a usable shelf no higher than 44 in (1120 mm) above the floor space. The floor space shall comply with 4.2.4.

4.24 Sinks.

4.24.1 General. Sinks *required to be accessible by 4.1* shall comply with 4.24.

4.24.2 Height. Sinks shall be mounted with the counter or rim no higher than 34 in (865 mm) *above the finish* floor.

4.24.3 Knee Clearance. Knee clearance that is at least 27 in (685 mm) high, 30 in (760 mm) wide, and 19 in (485 mm) deep shall be pro-

vided underneath sinks.

4.24.4 Depth. Each sink shall be a maximum of 6-1/2 in (165 mm) deep.

4.24.5 Clear Floor Space. A clear floor space at least 30 in by 48 in (760 mm by 1220 mm) complying with 4.2.4 shall be provided in front of a sink to allow forward approach. The clear floor space shall be on an accessible route and shall extend a maximum of 19 in (485 mm) underneath the sink (see Fig. 32).

4.24.6 Exposed Pipes and Surfaces. Hot water and drain pipes exposed under sinks shall be insulated or otherwise *configured so as to protect against contact.* There shall be no sharp or abrasive surfaces under sinks.

4.24.7 Faucets. Faucets shall comply with 4.27.4. Lever-operated, push-type, touch-type, or electronically controlled mechanisms are acceptable designs.

4.25 Storage.

4.25.1 General. *Fixed* storage facilities such as cabinets, shelves, closets, and drawers *required to be accessible by 4.1* shall comply with 4.25.

4.25.2 Clear Floor Space. A clear floor space at least 30 in by 48 in (760 mm by 1220 mm) complying with 4.2.4 that allows either a forward or parallel approach by a person using a wheelchair shall be provided at accessible storage facilities.

4.25.3 Height. Accessible storage spaces shall be within at least one of the reach ranges specified in 4.2.5 and 4.2.6 *(see Fig. 5 and Fig. 6).* Clothes rods or shelves shall be a maximum of 54 in (1370 mm) *above the finish floor for a side approach. Where the distance from the wheelchair to the clothes rod or shelf exceeds 10 in (255 mm) (as in closets without accessible doors) the height and depth to the rod or shelf shall comply with Fig. 38(a) and Fig. 38(b).*

4.25.4 Hardware. Hardware for accessible storage facilities shall comply with 4.27.4. Touch latches and U-shaped pulls are acceptable.

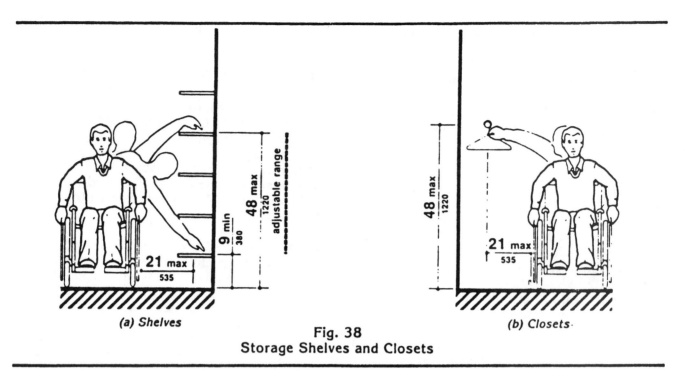

(a) Shelves

Fig. 38
Storage Shelves and Closets

(b) Closets

4.26 Handrails, Grab Bars, and Tub and Shower Seats.

4.26.1* General. All handrails, grab bars, and tub and shower seats *required to be accessible by 4.1, 4.8, 4.9, 4.16, 4.17, 4.20 or 4.21* shall comply with 4.26.

4.26.2* Size and Spacing of Grab Bars and Handrails. The diameter or width of the gripping surfaces of a handrail or grab bar shall be 1-1/4 in to 1-1/2 in (32 mm to 38 mm), or the shape shall provide an equivalent gripping surface. If handrails or grab bars are mounted adjacent to a wall, the space between the wall and the grab bar shall be 1-1/2 in (38 mm) (see Fig. 39(a), (b), (c), and (e)). Handrails may be located in a recess if the recess is a maximum of 3 in (75 mm) deep and extends at least 18 in (455 mm) above the top of the rail (see Fig. 39(d)).

4.26.3 Structural Strength. The structural strength of grab bars, tub and shower seats, fasteners, and mounting devices shall meet the following specification:

(1) Bending stress in a grab bar or seat induced by the maximum bending moment from the application of 250 lbf (1112N) shall be less than the allowable stress for the material of the grab bar or seat.

(2) Shear stress induced in a grab bar or seat by the application of 250 lbf (1112N) shall be less than the allowable shear stress for the material of the grab bar or seat. If the connection between the grab bar or seat and its mounting bracket or other support is considered to be fully restrained, then direct and torsional shear stresses shall be totaled for the combined shear stress, which shall not exceed the allowable shear stress.

(3) Shear force induced in a fastener or mounting device from the application of 250 lbf (1112N) shall be less than the allowable lateral load of either the fastener or mounting device or the supporting structure, whichever is the smaller allowable load.

(4) Tensile force induced in a fastener by a direct tension force of 250 lbf (1112N) plus the maximum moment from the application of 250 lbf (1112N) shall be less than the allowable withdrawal load between the fastener and the supporting structure.

(5) Grab bars shall not rotate within their fittings.

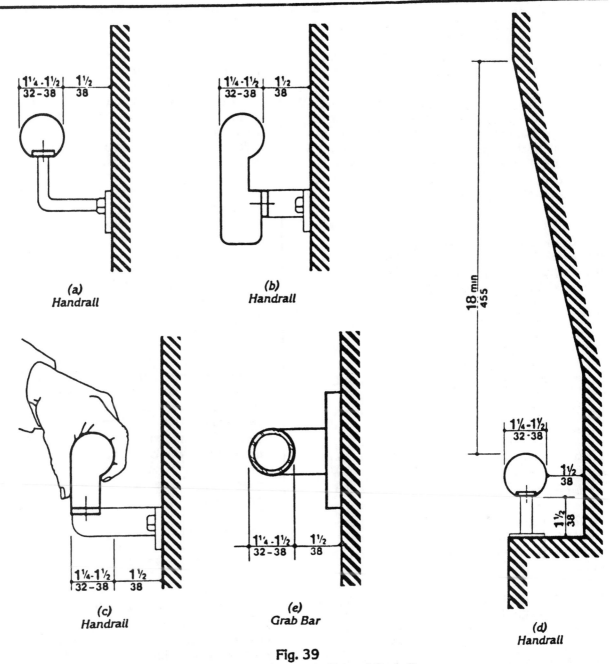

Fig. 39
Size and Spacing of Handrails and Grab Bars

4.26.4 Eliminating Hazards. A handrail or grab bar and any wall or other surface adjacent to it shall be free of any sharp or abrasive elements. Edges shall have a minimum radius of 1/8 in (3.2 mm).

4.27 Controls and Operating Mechanisms.

4.27.1 General. Controls and operating mechanisms *required to be accessible by 4.1* shall comply with 4.27.

4.27.2 Clear Floor Space. Clear floor space complying with 4.2.4 that allows a forward or a parallel approach by a person using a wheelchair shall be provided at controls, dispensers, receptacles, and other operable equipment.

4.27.3* Height. The highest operable part of controls, dispensers, receptacles, and other operable equipment shall be placed within at least one of the reach ranges specified in 4.2.5 and 4.2.6. Electrical and communications system receptacles on walls shall be mounted no less than 15 in (380 mm) above the floor.

EXCEPTION: These requirements do not apply where the use of special equipment dictates otherwise or where electrical and communications systems receptacles are not normally intended for use by building occupants.

4.27.4 Operation. Controls and operating mechanisms shall be operable with one hand and shall not require tight grasping, pinching, or twisting of the wrist. The force required to activate controls shall be no greater than 5 lbf (22.2 N).

4.28 Alarms.

4.28.1 General. Alarm systems required to be accessible by 4.1 shall comply with 4.28. At a minimum, visual signal appliances shall be provided in buildings and facilities in each of the following areas: restrooms and any other general usage areas (e.g., meeting rooms), hallways, lobbies, and any other area for common use.

4.28.2* Audible Alarms. If provided, audible emergency alarms shall produce a sound that exceeds the prevailing equivalent sound level in the room or space by at least 15 dbA or exceeds any maximum sound level with a duration of 60 seconds by 5 dbA, whichever is louder. Sound levels for alarm signals shall not exceed 120 dbA.

4.28.3* Visual Alarms. Visual alarm signal appliances shall be integrated into the building or facility alarm system. If single station audible alarms are provided then single station visual alarm signals shall be provided. Visual alarm signals shall have the following minimum photometric and location features:

(1) The lamp shall be a xenon strobe type or equivalent.

(2) The color shall be clear or nominal white (i.e., unfiltered or clear filtered white light).

(3) The maximum pulse duration shall be two-tenths of one second (0.2 sec) with a maximum duty cycle of 40 percent. The pulse duration is defined as the time interval between initial and final points of 10 percent of maximum signal.

(4) The intensity shall be a minimum of 75 candela.

(5) The flash rate shall be a minimum of 1 Hz and a maximum of 3 Hz.

(6) The appliance shall be placed 80 in (2030 mm) above the highest floor level within the space or 6 in (152 mm) below the ceiling, whichever is lower.

(7) In general, no place in any room or space required to have a visual signal appliance shall be more than 50 ft (15 m) from the signal (in the horizontal plane). In large rooms and spaces exceeding 100 ft (30 m) across, without obstructions 6 ft (2 m) above the finish floor, such as auditoriums, devices may be placed around the perimeter, spaced a maximum 100 ft (30 m) apart, in lieu of suspending appliances from the ceiling.

(8) No place in common corridors or hallways in which visual alarm signalling appliances are required shall be more than 50 ft (15 m) from the signal.

4.28.4* Auxiliary Alarms. Units and sleeping accommodations shall have a visual alarm connected to the building emergency alarm system or shall have a standard 110-volt electrical receptacle into which such an alarm can be connected and a means by which a signal from the building emergency alarm system can trigger such an auxiliary alarm. When visual alarms are in place the signal shall be visible in all areas of the unit or room. Instructions for use of the auxiliary alarm or receptacle shall be provided.

4.29 Detectable Warnings.

4.29.1 General. Detectable warnings required by 4.1 and 4.7 shall comply with 4.29.

4.29.2* Detectable Warnings on Walking Surfaces. Detectable warnings shall consist of raised truncated domes with a diameter of nominal 0.9 in (23 mm), a height of nominal 0.2 in (5 mm) and a center-to-center spacing of nominal 2.35 in (60 mm) and shall contrast visually with adjoining surfaces, either light-on-dark, or dark-on-light.

The material used to provide contrast shall be an integral part of the walking surface. Detectable warnings used on interior surfaces shall differ from adjoining walking surfaces in resiliency or sound-on-cane contact.

4.29.3 Detectable Warnings on Doors To Hazardous Areas. (Reserved).

4.29.4 Detectable Warnings at Stairs. (Reserved).

4.29.5 Detectable Warnings at Hazardous Vehicular Areas. If a walk crosses or adjoins a vehicular way, and the walking surfaces are not separated by curbs, railings, or other elements between the pedestrian areas and vehicular areas, the boundary between the areas shall be defined by a continuous detectable warning which is 36 in (915 mm) wide, complying with 4.29.2.

4.29.6 Detectable Warnings at Reflecting Pools. The edges of reflecting pools shall be protected by railings, walls, curbs, or detectable warnings complying with 4.29.2.

4.29.7 Standardization. (Reserved).

4.30 Signage.

4.30.1* General. Signage required to be accessible by 4.1 shall comply with the applicable provisions of 4.30.

4.30.2* Character Proportion. Letters and numbers on signs shall have a width-to-height ratio between 3:5 and 1:1 and a stroke-width-to-height ratio between 1:5 and 1:10.

4.30.3 Character Height. Characters and numbers on signs shall be sized according to the viewing distance from which they are to be read. The minimum height is measured using an upper case X. Lower case characters are permitted.

Height Above Finished Floor	Minimum Character Height
Suspended or Projected Overhead in compliance with 4.4.2	3 in (75 mm) minimum

4.30.4* Raised and Brailled Characters and Pictorial Symbol Signs (Pictograms). Letters and numerals shall be raised 1/32 in, upper case, sans serif or simple serif type and shall be accompanied with Grade 2 Braille. Raised characters shall be at least 5/8 in (16 mm) high, but no higher than 2 in (50 mm). Pictograms shall be accompanied by the equivalent verbal description placed directly below the pictogram. The border dimension of the pictogram shall be 6 in (152 mm) minimum in height.

4.30.5* Finish and Contrast. The characters and background of signs shall be eggshell, matte, or other non-glare finish. Characters and symbols shall contrast with their background — either light characters on a dark background or dark characters on a light background.

4.30.6 Mounting Location and Height. Where permanent identification is provided for rooms and spaces, signs shall be installed on the wall adjacent to the latch side of the door. Where there is no wall space to the latch side of the door, including at double leaf doors, signs shall be placed on the nearest adjacent wall. Mounting height shall be 60 in (1525 mm) above the finish floor to the centerline of the sign. Mounting location for such signage shall be so that a person may approach within 3 in (76 mm) of signage without encountering protruding objects or standing within the swing of a door.

4.30.7* Symbols of Accessibility.

(1) Facilities and elements required to be identified as accessible by 4.1 shall use the international symbol of accessibility. The

(a)
Proportions
International Symbol of Accessibility

(b)
Display Conditions
International Symbol of Accessibility

(c)
International TDD Symbol

(d)
International Symbol of Access for Hearing Loss

Fig. 43
International Symbols

symbol shall be displayed as shown in Fig. 43(a) and (b).

(2) *Volume Control Telephones. Telephones required to have a volume control by 4.1.3(17)(b) shall be identified by a sign containing a depiction of a telephone handset with radiating sound waves.*

(3) *Text Telephones. Text telephones required by 4.1.3 (17)(c) shall be identified by the international TDD symbol (Fig 43(c)). In addition, if a facility has a public text telephone, directional signage indicating the location of the nearest text telephone shall be placed adjacent to all banks of telephones which do not contain a text telephone. Such directional signage shall include the international TDD symbol. If a facility has no banks of telephones, the directional signage shall be provided at the entrance (e.g., in a building directory).*

(4) *Assistive Listening Systems. In assembly areas where permanently installed assistive listening systems are required by 4.1.3(19)(b) the availability of such systems shall be identified with signage that includes the international symbol of access for hearing loss (Fig 43(d)).*

4.30.8* Illumination Levels. *(Reserved).*

4.31 Telephones.

4.31.1 General. Public telephones *required to be accessible by 4.1* shall comply with 4.31.

4.31.2 Clear Floor or Ground Space. A clear floor or ground space at least 30 in by 48 in (760 mm by 1220 mm) that allows either a forward or parallel approach by a person using a wheelchair shall be provided at telephones (see Fig. 44). The clear floor or ground space shall comply with 4.2.4. Bases, enclosures, and fixed seats shall not impede approaches to telephones by people who use wheelchairs.

4.31.3* Mounting Height. The highest operable part of the telephone shall be within the reach ranges specified in 4.2.5 or 4.2.6.

4.31.4 *Protruding Objects.* *Telephones shall comply with 4.4.*

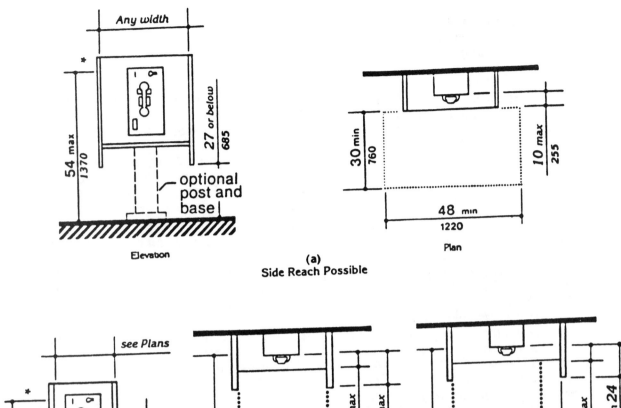

(a)
Side Reach Possible

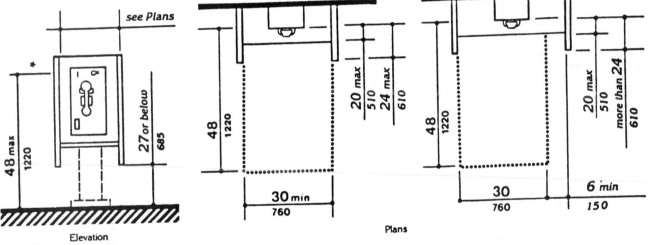

(b)
Forward Reach Required

*Height to highest operable
parts which are essential to
basic operation of telephone.

Fig. 44
Mounting Heights and Clearances for Telephones

4.31.5 Hearing Aid Compatible and Volume Control Telephones Required by 4.1.

(1) Telephones shall be hearing aid compatible.

(2) Volume controls. *capable of a minimum of 12 dBA and a maximum of 18 dBA above* normal, *shall be provided in accordance with 4.1.3. If an automatic reset is provided then 18 dBA may be exceeded.*

4.31.6 Controls. Telephones shall have pushbutton controls where service for such equipment is available.

4.31.7 Telephone Books. Telephone books, if provided, shall be located *in a position that complies with the reach ranges specified in 4.2.5 and 4.2.6.*

4.31.8 Cord Length. The cord from the telephone to the handset shall be at least 29 in (735 mm) long.

4.31.9* Text Telephones Required by 4.1.

(1) Text telephones used with a pay telephone shall be permanently affixed within, or adjacent to, the telephone enclosure. If an acoustic coupler is used, the telephone cord shall be sufficiently long to allow connection of the text telephone and the telephone receiver.

(2) Pay telephones designed to accommodate a portable text telephone shall be equipped with a shelf and an electrical outlet within or adjacent to the telephone enclosure. The telephone handset shall be capable of being placed flush on the surface of the shelf. The shelf shall be capable of accommodating a text telephone and shall have 6 in (152 mm) minimum vertical clearance in the area where the text telephone is to be placed.

(3) Equivalent facilitation may be provided. For example, a portable text telephone may be made available in a hotel at the registration desk if it is available on a 24-hour basis for use with nearby public pay telephones. In this instance, at least one pay telephone shall comply with paragraph 2 of this section. In addition, if an acoustic coupler is used, the telephone handset cord shall be sufficiently long so as to allow connection of the text telephone and the telephone receiver. Directional signage shall be provided and shall comply with 4.30.7.

4.32 *Fixed or Built-in* Seating and Tables.

4.32.1 Minimum Number. Fixed or built-in seating or tables *required to be accessible by 4.1* shall comply with 4.32.

4.32.2 Seating. If seating spaces for people in wheelchairs are provided at *fixed* tables or counters, clear floor space complying with 4.2.4 shall be provided. Such clear floor space

shall not overlap knee space by more than 19 in (485 mm) (see Fig. 45).

4.32.3 Knee Clearances. If seating for people in wheelchairs is provided at tables *or* counters, knee spaces at least 27 in (685 mm) high, 30 in (760 mm) wide, and 19 in (485 mm) deep shall be provided (see Fig. 45).

4.32.4* Height of Tables or Counters. The tops of *accessible* tables and *counters* shall be from 28 in to 34 in (710 mm to 865 mm) *above the finish* floor or ground.

4.33 Assembly Areas.

4.33.1 Minimum Number. Assembly *and associated* areas *required to be accessible by 4.1* shall comply with 4.33.

4.33.2* Size of Wheelchair Locations. Each wheelchair location shall provide minimum clear ground or floor spaces as shown in Fig. 46.

4.33.3* Placement of Wheelchair Locations. Wheelchair areas shall be an integral part of any fixed seating plan and shall be *provided so as to provide people with physical disabilities a choice of admission prices and lines of sight comparable to those for members of the general public. They shall* adjoin an accessible route that also serves as a means of egress in case of emergency. At least one *companion fixed seat shall be provided next to each wheelchair seating area. When the seating capacity exceeds 300, wheelchair spaces shall be provided in more than one location. Readily removable seats may be installed in wheelchair spaces when the spaces are not required to accommodate wheelchair users.*

EXCEPTION: Accessible viewing positions may be clustered for bleachers, balconies, and other areas having sight lines that require slopes of greater than 5 percent. Equivalent accessible viewing positions may be located on levels having accessible egress.

4.33.4 Surfaces. The ground or floor at wheelchair locations shall be level and shall comply with 4.5.

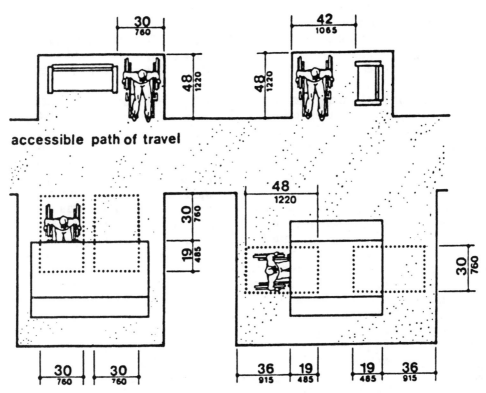

accessible path of travel

Fig. 45
Minimum Clearances for Seating and Tables

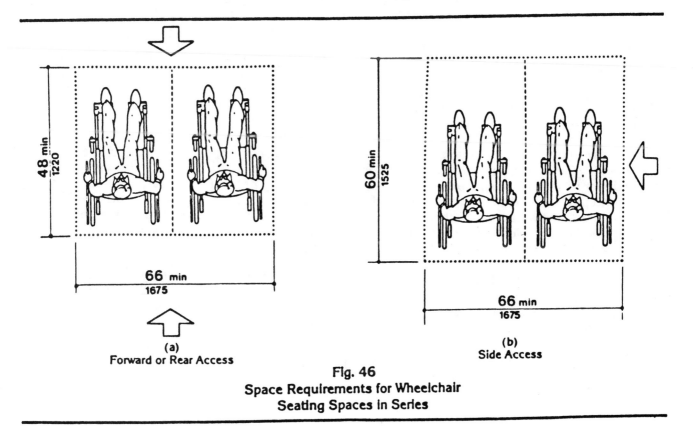

(a)
Forward or Rear Access

(b)
Side Access

Fig. 46
Space Requirements for Wheelchair
Seating Spaces in Series

4.33.5 Access to Performing Areas.
An accessible route shall connect wheelchair seating locations with performing areas, including stages, arena floors, dressing rooms, locker rooms, and other spaces used by performers.

4.33.6* Placement of Listening Systems.
If the listening system provided serves individual fixed seats, then such seats shall be located within a 50 ft (15 m) viewing distance of the stage or playing area and shall have a complete view of the stage or playing area.

4.33.7* Types of Listening Systems.
Assistive listening systems (ALS) are intended to augment standard public address and audio systems by providing signals which can be received directly by persons with special receivers or their own hearing aids and which eliminate or filter background noise. The type of assistive listening system appropriate for a particular application depends on the characteristics of the setting, the nature of the program, and the intended audience. Magnetic induction loops, infra-red and radio frequency systems are types of listening systems which are appropriate for various applications.

4.34 Automated Teller Machines.

4.34.1 General.
Each machine required to be accessible by 4.1.3 shall be on an accessible route and shall comply with 4.34.

4.34.2 Controls.
Controls for user activation shall comply with the requirements of 4.27.

4.34.3 Clearances and Reach Range.
Free standing or built-in units not having a clear space under them shall comply with 4.27.2 and 4.27.3 and provide for a parallel approach and both a forward and side reach to the unit allowing a person in a wheelchair to access the controls and dispensers.

4.34.4 Equipment for Persons with Vision Impairments.
Instructions and all information for use shall be made accessible to and independently usable by persons with vision impairments.

4.35 Dressing and Fitting Rooms.

4.35.1 General.
Dressing and fitting rooms required to be accessible by 4.1 shall comply with 4.35 and shall be on an accessible route.

4.35.2 Clear Floor Space.
A clear floor space allowing a person using a wheelchair to make a 180-degree turn shall be provided in every accessible dressing room entered through a swinging or sliding door. No door shall swing into any part of the turning space. Turning space shall not be required in a private dressing room entered through a curtained opening at least 32 in (815 mm) wide if clear floor space complying with section 4.2 renders the dressing room usable by a person using a wheelchair.

4.35.3 Doors.
All doors to accessible dressing rooms shall be in compliance with section 4.13.

4.35.4 Bench.
Every accessible dressing room shall have a 24 in by 48 in (610 mm by 1220 mm) bench fixed to the wall along the longer dimension. The bench shall be mounted 17 in to 19 in (430 mm to 485 mm) above the finish floor. Clear floor space shall be provided alongside the bench to allow a person using a wheelchair to make a parallel transfer onto the bench. The structural strength of the bench and attachments shall comply with 4.26.3. Where installed in conjunction with showers, swimming pools, or other wet locations, water shall not accumulate upon the surface of the bench and the bench shall have a slip-resistant surface.

4.35.5 Mirror.
Where mirrors are provided in dressing rooms of the same use, then in an accessible dressing room, a full-length mirror, measuring at least 18 in wide by 54 in high (460 mm by 1370 mm), shall be mounted in a position affording a view to a person on the bench as well as to a person in a standing position.

NOTE: Sections 4.1.1 through 4.1.7 and sections 5 through 10 are different from ANSI A117.1 in their entirety and are printed in standard type.

5. RESTAURANTS AND CAFETERIAS.

5.1* General. Except as specified or modified in this section, restaurants and cafeterias shall comply with the requirements of 4.1 to 4.35. Where fixed tables (or dining counters where food is consumed but there is no service) are provided, at least 5 percent, but not less than one, of the fixed tables (or a portion of the dining counter) shall be accessible and shall comply with 4.32 as required in 4.1.3(18). In establishments where separate areas are designated for smoking and non-smoking patrons, the required number of accessible fixed tables (or counters) shall be proportionally distributed between the smoking and non-smoking areas. In new construction, and where practicable in alterations, accessible fixed tables (or counters) shall be distributed throughout the space or facility.

5.2 Counters and Bars. Where food or drink is served at counters exceeding 34 in (865 mm) in height for consumption by customers seated on stools or standing at the counter, a portion of the main counter which is 60 in (1525 mm) in length minimum shall be provided in compliance with 4.32 or service shall be available at accessible tables within the same area.

5.3 Access Aisles. All accessible fixed tables shall be accessible by means of an access aisle at least 36 in (915 mm) clear between parallel edges of tables or between a wall and the table edges.

5.4 Dining Areas. In new construction, all dining areas, including raised or sunken dining areas, loggias, and outdoor seating areas, shall be accessible. In non-elevator buildings, an accessible means of vertical access to the mezzanine is not required under the following conditions: 1) the area of mezzanine seating measures no more than 33 percent of the area of the total accessible seating area; 2) the same services and decor are provided in an accessible space usable by the general public; and, 3) the accessible areas are not restricted to use by people with disabilities. In alterations, accessibility to raised or sunken dining areas, or to all parts of outdoor seating areas is not required provided that the same services and decor are provided in an accessible space usable by the general public and are not restricted to use by people with disabilities.

5.5 Food Service Lines. Food service lines shall have a minimum clear width of 36 in (915 mm), with a preferred clear width of 42 in (1065 mm) to allow passage around a person using a wheelchair. Tray slides shall be mounted no higher than 34 in (865 mm) above the floor (see Fig. 53). If self-service shelves

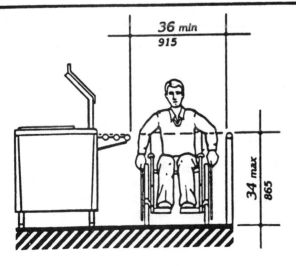

Fig. 53
Food Service Lines

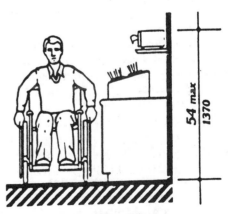

Fig. 54
Tableware Areas

are provided, at least 50 percent of each type must be within reach ranges specified in 4.2.5 and 4.2.6.

5.6 Tableware and Condiment Areas.
Self-service shelves and dispensing devices for tableware, dishware, condiments, food and beverages shall be installed to comply with 4.2 (see Fig. 54).

5.7 Raised Platforms. In banquet rooms or spaces where a head table or speaker's lectern is located on a raised platform, the platform shall be accessible in compliance with 4.8 or 4.11. Open edges of a raised platform shall be protected by placement of tables or by a curb.

5.8 Vending Machines and Other Equipment. Spaces for vending machines and other equipment shall comply with 4.2 and shall be located on an accessible route.

5.9 Quiet Areas. (Reserved).

6. MEDICAL CARE FACILITIES.

6.1 General. Medical care facilities included in this section are those in which people receive physical or medical treatment or care and where persons may need assistance in responding to an emergency and where the period of stay may exceed twenty-four hours. In addition to the requirements of 4.1 through 4.35, medical care facilities and buildings shall comply with 6.

(1) Hospitals - general purpose hospitals, psychiatric facilities, detoxification facilities — At least 10 percent of patient bedrooms and toilets, and all public use and common use areas are required to be designed and constructed to be accessible.

(2) Hospitals and rehabilitation facilities that specialize in treating conditions that affect mobility, or units within either that specialize in treating conditions that affect mobility — All patient bedrooms and toilets, and all public use and common use areas are required to be designed and constructed to be accessible.

(3) Long term care facilities, nursing homes — At least 50 percent of patient bedrooms and toilets, and all public use and common use areas are required to be designed and constructed to be accessible.

(4) Alterations to patient bedrooms.

(a) When patient bedrooms are being added or altered as part of a planned renovation of an entire wing, a department, or other discrete area of an existing medical facility, a percentage of the patient bedrooms that are being added or altered shall comply with 6.3. The percentage of accessible rooms provided shall be consistent with the percentage of rooms required to be accessible by the applicable requirements of 6.1(1), 6.1(2), or 6.1(3), until the number of accessible patient bedrooms in the facility equals the overall number that would be required if the facility were newly constructed. (For example, if 20 patient bedrooms are being altered in the obstetrics department of a hospital, 2 of the altered rooms must be made accessible. If, within the same hospital, 20 patient bedrooms are being altered in a unit that specializes in treating mobility impairments, all of the altered rooms must be made accessible.) Where toilet/bath rooms are part of patient bedrooms which are added or altered and required to be accessible, each such patient toilet/bathroom shall comply with 6.4.

(b) When patient bedrooms are being added or altered individually, and not as part of an alteration of the entire area, the altered patient bedrooms shall comply with 6.3, unless either: a) the number of accessible rooms provided in the department or area containing the altered patient bedroom equals the number of accessible patient bedrooms that would be required if the percentage requirements of 6.1(1), 6.1(2), or 6.1(3) were applied to that department or area; or b) the number of accessible patient bedrooms in the facility equals the overall number that would be required if the facility were newly constructed. Where toilet/bathrooms are part of patient bedrooms which are added or altered and required to be accessible, each such toilet/bathroom shall comply with 6.4.

6.2 Entrances.

At least one accessible entrance that complies with 4.14 shall be protected from the weather by canopy or roof overhang. Such entrances shall incorporate a passenger loading zone that complies with 4.6.6.

6.3 Patient Bedrooms.

Provide accessible patient bedrooms in compliance with 4.1 through 4.35. Accessible patient bedrooms shall comply with the following:

(1) Each bedroom shall have a door that complies with 4.13.

EXCEPTION: Entry doors to acute care hospital bedrooms for in-patients shall be exempted from the requirement in 4.13.6 for maneuvering space at the latch side of the door if the door is at least 44 in (1120 mm) wide.

(2) Each bedroom shall have adequate space to provide a maneuvering space that complies with 4.2.3. In rooms with 2 beds, it is preferable that this space be located between beds.

(3) Each bedroom shall have adequate space to provide a minimum clear floor space of 36 in (915 mm) along each side of the bed and to provide an accessible route complying with 4.3.3 to each side of each bed.

6.4 Patient Toilet Rooms.

Where toilet/bath rooms are provided as a part of a patient bedroom, each patient bedroom that is required to be accessible shall have an accessible toilet/bath room that complies with 4.22 or 4.23 and shall be on an accessible route.

7. BUSINESS AND MERCANTILE.

7.1 General.

In addition to the requirements of 4.1 to 4.35, the design of all areas used for business transactions with the public shall comply with 7.

7.2 Sales and Service Counters, Teller Windows, Information Counters.

(1) In department stores and miscellaneous retail stores where counters have cash registers and are provided for sales or distribution of goods or services to the public, at least one of each type shall have a portion of the counter which is at least 36 in (915 mm) in length with a maximum height of 36 in (915 mm) above the finish floor. It shall be on an accessible route complying with 4.3. The accessible counters must be dispersed throughout the building or facility. In alterations where it is technically infeasible to provide an accessible counter, an auxiliary counter meeting these requirements may be provided.

(2) At ticketing counters, teller stations in a bank, registration counters in hotels and motels, box office ticket counters, and other counters that may not have a cash register but at which goods or services are sold or distributed, either:

(i) a portion of the main counter which is a minimum of 36 in (915 mm) in length shall be provided with a maximum height of 36 in (915 mm); or

(ii) an auxiliary counter with a maximum height of 36 in (915 mm) in close proximity to the main counter shall be provided; or

(iii) equivalent facilitation shall be provided (e.g., at a hotel registration counter, equivalent facilitation might consist of: (1) provision of a folding shelf attached to the main counter on which an individual with disabilities can write, and (2) use of the space on the side of the counter or at the concierge desk, for handing materials back and forth).

All accessible sales and service counters shall be on an accessible route complying with 4.3.

(3)* Assistive Listening Devices. (Reserved)

7.3* Check-out Aisles.

(1) In new construction, accessible check-out aisles shall be provided in conformance with the table below:

Total Check-out Aisles of Each Design	Minimum Number of Accessible Check-out Aisles (of each design)
1 – 4	1
5 – 8	2
8 – 15	3
over 15	3, plus 20% of additional aisles

EXCEPTION: In new construction, where the selling space is under 5000 square feet, only one check-out aisle is required to be accessible.

EXCEPTION: In alterations, at least one check-out aisle shall be accessible in facilities under 5000 square feet of selling space. In facilities of 5000 or more square feet of selling space, at least one of each design of check-out aisle shall be made accessible when altered until the number of accessible check-out aisles of each design equals the number required in new construction.

Examples of check-out aisles of different "design" include those which are specifically designed to serve different functions. Different "design" includes but is not limited to the following features - length of belt or no belt; or permanent signage designating the aisle as an express lane.

(2) Clear aisle width for accessible check-out aisles shall comply with 4.2.1 and maximum adjoining counter height shall not exceed 38 in (965 mm) above the finish floor. The top of the lip shall not exceed 40 in (1015 mm) above the finish floor.

(3) Signage identifying accessible check-out aisles shall comply with 4.30.7 and shall be mounted above the check-out aisle in the same location where the check-out number or type of check-out is displayed.

7.4 Security Bollards.
Any device used to prevent the removal of shopping carts from store premises shall not prevent access or egress to people in wheelchairs. An alternate entry that is equally convenient to that provided for the ambulatory population is acceptable.

8. | LIBRARIES.

8.1 General.
In addition to the requirements of 4.1 to 4.35, the design of all public areas of a library shall comply with 8, including reading and study areas, stacks, reference rooms, reserve areas, and special facilities or collections.

8.2 Reading and Study Areas.
At least 5 percent or a minimum of one of each element of fixed seating, tables, or study carrels shall comply with 4.2 and 4.32. Clearances between fixed accessible tables and between study carrels shall comply with 4.3.

8.3 Check-Out Areas.
At least one lane at each check-out area shall comply with 7.2(1). Any traffic control or book security gates or turnstiles shall comply with 4.13.

8.4 Card Catalogs and Magazine Displays.
Minimum clear aisle space at card catalogs and magazine displays shall comply with Fig. 55. Maximum reach height shall comply with 4.2, with a height of 48 in (1220 mm) preferred irrespective of approach allowed.

8.5 Stacks.
Minimum clear aisle width between stacks shall comply with 4.3, with a minimum clear aisle width of 42 in (1065 mm) preferred where possible. Shelf height in stack areas is unrestricted (see Fig. 56).

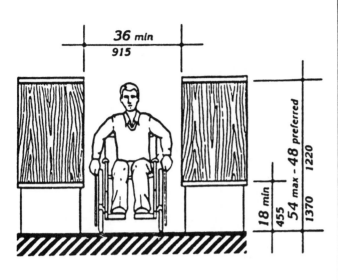

Fig. 55
Card Catalog

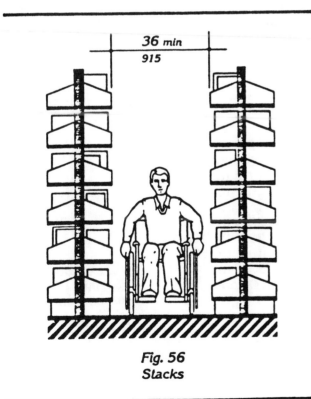

Fig. 56
Stacks

9. ACCESSIBLE TRANSIENT LODGING.

(1) Except as specified in the special technical provisions of this section, accessible transient lodging shall comply with the applicable requirements of 4.1 through 4.35. Transient lodging includes facilities or portions thereof used for sleeping accommodations, when not classed as a medical care facility.

9.1 Hotels, Motels, Inns, Boarding Houses, Dormitories, Resorts and Other Similar Places of Transient Lodging.

9.1.1 General. All public use and common use areas are required to be designed and constructed to comply with section 4 (Accessible Elements and Spaces: Scope and Technical Requirements).

EXCEPTION: Sections 9.1 through 9.4 do not apply to an establishment located within a building that contains not more than five rooms for rent or hire and that is actually occupied by the proprietor of such establishment as the residence of such proprietor.

9.1.2 Accessible Units, Sleeping Rooms, and Suites. Accessible sleeping rooms or suites that comply with the requirements of 9.2 (Requirements for Accessible Units, Sleeping Rooms, and Suites) shall be provided in conformance with the table below. In addition, in hotels, of 50 or more sleeping rooms or suites, additional accessible sleeping rooms or suites that include a roll-in shower shall also be provided in conformance with the table below. Such accommodations shall comply with the requirements of 9.2, 4.21, and Figure 57(a) or (b).

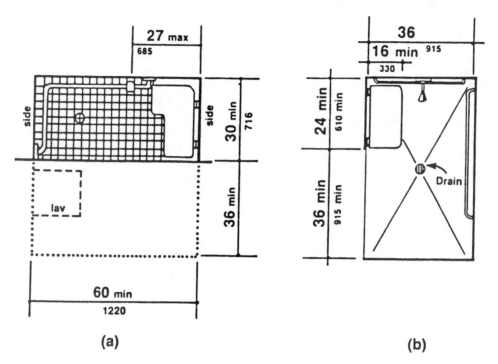

Fig. 57
Roll-in Shower with Folding Seat

Number of Rooms	Accessible Rooms	Rooms with Roll-in Showers
1 to 25	1	
26 to 50	2	
51 to 75	3	1
76 to 100	4	1
101 to 150	5	2
151 to 200	6	2
201 to 300	7	3
301 to 400	8	4
401 to 500	9	4 plus one for each additional 100 over 400
501 to 1000	2% of total	
1001 and over	20 plus 1 for each 100 over 1000	

9.1.3 Sleeping Accommodations for Persons with Hearing Impairments.
In addition to those accessible sleeping rooms and suites required by 9.1.2, sleeping rooms and suites that comply with 9.3 (Visual Alarms, Notification Devices, and Telephones) shall be provided in conformance with the following table:

Number of Elements	Accessible Elements
1 to 25	1
26 to 50	2
51 to 75	3
76 to 100	4
101 to 150	5
151 to 200	6
201 to 300	7
301 to 400	8
401 to 500	9
501 to 1000	2% of total
1001 and over	20 plus 1 for each 100 over 1000

9.1.4 Classes of Sleeping Accommodations.

(1) In order to provide persons with disabilities a range of options equivalent to those available to other persons served by the facility, sleeping rooms and suites required to be accessible by 9.1.2 shall be dispersed among the various classes of sleeping accommodations available to patrons of the place of transient lodging. Factors to be considered include room size, cost, amenities provided, and the number of beds provided.

(2) Equivalent Facilitation. For purposes of this section, it shall be deemed equivalent facilitation if the operator of a facility elects to limit construction of accessible rooms to those intended for multiple occupancy, provided that such rooms are made available at the cost of a single-occupancy room to an individual with disabilities who requests a single-occupancy room.

9.1.5. Alterations to Accessible Units, Sleeping Rooms, and Suites.
When sleeping rooms are being altered in an existing facility, or portion thereof, subject to the requirements of this section, at least one sleeping room or suite that complies with the requirements of 9.2 (Requirements for Accessible Units, Sleeping Rooms, and Suites) shall be provided for each 25 sleeping rooms, or fraction thereof, of rooms being altered until the number of such rooms provided equals the number required to be accessible with 9.1.2. In addition, at least one sleeping room or suite that complies with the requirements of 9.3 (Visual Alarms, Notification Devices, and Telephones) shall be provided for each 25 sleeping rooms, or fraction thereof, of rooms being altered until the number of such rooms equals the number required to be accessible by 9.1.3.

9.2 Requirements for Accessible Units, Sleeping Rooms and Suites.

9.2.1 General. Units, sleeping rooms, and suites required to be accessible by 9.1 shall comply with 9.2.

9.2.2 Minimum Requirements. An accessible unit, sleeping room or suite shall be on an accessible route complying with 4.3 and have the following accessible elements and spaces.

(1) Accessible sleeping rooms shall have a 36 in (915 mm) clear width maneuvering space located along both sides of a bed, except that where two beds are provided, this requirement can be met by providing a 36 in (915 mm) wide maneuvering space located between the two beds.

(2) An accessible route complying with 4.3 shall connect all accessible spaces and elements, including telephones, within the unit, sleeping room, or suite. This is not intended to require an elevator in multi-story units as long as the spaces identified in 9.2.2(6) and (7) are on accessible levels and the accessible sleeping area is suitable for dual occupancy.

(3) Doors and doorways designed to allow passage into and within all sleeping rooms, suites or other covered units shall comply with 4.13.

(4) If fixed or built-in storage facilities such as cabinets, shelves, closets, and drawers are provided in accessible spaces, at least one of each type provided shall contain storage space complying with 4.25. Additional storage may be provided outside of the dimensions required by 4.25.

(5) All controls in accessible units, sleeping rooms, and suites shall comply with 4.27.

(6) Where provided as part of an accessible unit, sleeping room, or suite, the following spaces shall be accessible and shall be on an accessible route:

(a) the living area.

(b) the dining area.

(c) at least one sleeping area.

(d) patios, terraces, or balconies.

EXCEPTION: The requirements of 4.13.8 and 4.3.8 do not apply where it is necessary to utilize a higher door threshold or a change in level to protect the integrity of the unit from wind/water damage. Where this exception results in patios, terraces or balconies that are not at an accessible level, equivalent facilitation shall be provided. (E.g., equivalent facilitation at a hotel patio or balcony might consist of providing raised decking or a ramp to provide accessibility.)

(e) at least one full bathroom (i.e., one with a water closet, a lavatory, and a bathtub or shower).

(f) if only half baths are provided, at least one half bath.

(g) carports, garages or parking spaces.

(7) Kitchens, Kitchenettes, or Wet Bars. When provided as accessory to a sleeping room or suite, kitchens, kitchenettes, wet bars, or similar amenities shall be accessible. Clear floor space for a front or parallel approach to cabinets, counters, sinks, and appliances shall be provided to comply with 4.2.4. Countertops and sinks shall be mounted at a maximum height of 34 in (865 mm) above the floor. At least fifty percent of shelf space in cabinets or refrigerator/freezers shall be within the reach ranges of 4.2.5 or 4.2.6 and space shall be designed to allow for the operation of cabinet and/or appliance doors so that all cabinets and appliances are accessible and usable. Controls and operating mechanisms shall comply with 4.27.

(8) Sleeping room accommodations for persons with hearing impairments required by 9.1 and complying with 9.3 shall be provided in the accessible sleeping room or suite.

9.3 Visual Alarms, Notification Devices and Telephones.

9.3.1 General. In sleeping rooms required to comply with this section, auxiliary visual alarms shall be provided and shall comply with 4.28.4. Visual notification devices shall also be provided in units, sleeping rooms and suites to alert room occupants of incoming telephone calls and a door knock or bell. Notification devices shall **not** be connected to auxiliary visual alarm signal appliances. Permanently installed telephones shall have volume controls complying with 4.31.5; an accessible electrical outlet within 4 ft (1220 mm) of a telephone connection shall be provided to facilitate the use of a text telephone.

9.3.2 Equivalent Facilitation. For purposes of this section, equivalent facilitation shall include the installation of electrical outlets (including outlets connected to a facility's central alarm system) and telephone wiring in sleeping rooms and suites to enable persons with hearing impairments to utilize portable visual alarms and communication devices provided by the operator of the facility.

9.4 Other Sleeping Rooms and Suites. Doors and doorways designed to allow passage into and within all sleeping units or other covered units shall comply with 4.13.5.

9.5 Transient Lodging in Homeless Shelters, Halfway Houses, Transient Group Homes, and Other Social Service Establishments.

9.5.1 New Construction. In new construction all public use and common use areas are required to be designed and constructed to comply with section 4. At least one of each type of amenity (such as washers, dryers and similar equipment installed for the use of occupants) in each common area shall be accessible and shall be located on an accessible route to any accessible unit or sleeping accommodation.

EXCEPTION: Where elevators are not provided as allowed in 4.1.3(5), accessible amenities are not required on inaccessible floors as long as one of each type is provided in common areas on accessible floors.

9.5.2 Alterations.

(1) Social service establishments which are not homeless shelters:

(a) The provisions of 9.5.3 and 9.1.5 shall apply to sleeping rooms and beds.

(b) Alteration of other areas shall be consistent with the new construction provisions of 9.5.1.

(2) Homeless shelters. If the following elements are altered, the following requirements apply:

(a) at least one public entrance shall allow a person with mobility impairments to approach, enter and exit including a minimum clear door width of 32 in (815 mm).

(b) sleeping space for homeless persons as provided in the scoping provisions of 9.1.2 shall include doors to the sleeping area with a minimum clear width of 32 in (815 mm) and maneuvering space around the beds for persons with mobility impairments complying with 9.2.2(1).

(c) at least one toilet room for each gender or one unisex toilet room shall have a minimum clear door width of 32 in (815 mm), minimum turning space complying with 4.2.3, one water closet complying with 4.16, one lavatory complying with 4.19 and the door shall have a privacy latch; and, if provided, at least one tub or shower shall comply with 4.20 or 4.21, respectively.

(d) at least one common area which a person with mobility impairments can approach, enter and exit including a minimum clear door width of 32 in (815 mm).

(e) at least one route connecting elements (a), (b), (c) and (d) which a person with mobility impairments can use including minimum clear width of 36 in (915 mm), passing space complying with 4.3.4, turning space complying with 4.2.3 and changes in levels complying with 4.3.8.

(f) homeless shelters can comply with the provisions of (a)-(e) by providing the above elements on one accessible floor.

9.5.3. Accessible Sleeping Accommodations in New Construction.
Accessible sleeping rooms shall be provided in conformance with the table in 9.1.2 and shall comply with 9.2 Accessible Units, Sleeping Rooms and Suites (where the items are provided). Additional sleeping rooms that comply with 9.3 Sleeping Accommodations for Persons with Hearing Impairments shall be provided in conformance with the table provided in 9.1.3.

In facilities with multi-bed rooms or spaces, a percentage of the beds equal to the table provided in 9.1.2 shall comply with 9.2.2(1).

10. TRANSPORTATION FACILITIES. (Reserved).

APPENDIX

This appendix contains *materials of an advisory nature* and provides additional information that should help the reader to understand the minimum requirements of the *guidelines* or to design buildings or facilities for greater accessibility. The paragraph numbers correspond to the sections or paragraphs of the *guideline* to which the material relates and are therefore not consecutive (for example, A4.2.1 contains additional information relevant to 4.2.1). Sections *of the guidelines* for which additional material appears in this appendix have been indicated by an asterisk. *Nothing in this appendix shall in any way obviate any obligation to comply with the requirements of the guidelines itself.*

A2.2 Equivalent Facilitation. *Specific examples of equivalent facilitation are found in the following sections:*

4.1.6(3)(c)	Elevators in Alterations
4.31.9	Text Telephones
7.2	Sales and Service Counters, Teller Windows, Information Counters
9.1.4	Classes of Sleeping Accommodations
9.2.2(6)(d)	Requirements for Accessible Units, Sleeping Rooms, and Suites

A4.1.1 Application.

A4.1.1(3) Areas Used Only by Employees as Work Areas. *Where there are a series of individual work stations of the same type (e.g., laboratories, service counters, ticket booths), 5%, but not less than one, of each type of work station should be constructed so that an individual with disabilities can maneuver within the work stations. Rooms housing individual offices in a typical office building must meet the requirements of the guidelines concerning doors, accessible routes, etc. but do not need to allow for maneuvering space around individual desks. Modifications required to permit maneuvering within the work area may be accomplished as a reasonable accommodation to individual employees with disabilities under Title I of the ADA. Consideration should also be given to placing shelves in employee work areas at a* convenient height for accessibility or installing commercially available shelving that is adjustable so that reasonable accommodations can be made in the future.

If work stations are made accessible they should comply with the applicable provisions of 4.2 through 4.35.

A4.1.2 Accessible Sites and Exterior Facilities: New Construction.

A4.1.2(5)(e) Valet Parking. *Valet parking is not always usable by individuals with disabilities. For instance, an individual may use a type of vehicle controls that render the regular controls inoperable or the driver's seat in a van may be removed. In these situations, another person cannot park the vehicle. It is recommended that some self-parking spaces be provided at valet parking facilities for individuals whose vehicles cannot be parked by another person and that such spaces be located on an accessible route to the entrance of the facility.*

A4.1.3 Accessible Buildings: New Construction.

A4.1.3(5) *Only full passenger elevators are covered by the accessibility provisions of 4.10. Materials and equipment hoists, freight elevators not intended for passenger use, dumbwaiters, and construction elevators are not covered by these guidelines. If a building is exempt from the elevator requirement, it is not necessary to provide a platform lift or other means of vertical access in lieu of an elevator.*

Under Exception 4, platform lifts are allowed where existing conditions make it impractical to install a ramp or elevator. Such conditions generally occur where it is essential to provide access to small raised or lowered areas where space may not be available for a ramp. Examples include, but are not limited to, raised pharmacy platforms, commercial offices raised above a sales floor, or radio and news booths.

A4.1.3(9) *Supervised automatic sprinkler systems have built in signals for monitoring features of the system such as the opening and closing of water control valves, the power supplies for needed pumps, water tank levels, and for indicating conditions that will impair the satisfactory operation of the sprinkler system.*

Because of these monitoring features, supervised automatic sprinkler systems have a high level of satisfactory performance and response to fire conditions.

A4.1.3(10) *If an odd number of drinking fountains is provided on a floor, the requirement in 4.1.3(10)(b) may be met by rounding down the odd number to an even number and calculating 50% of the even number. When more than one drinking fountain on a floor is required to comply with 4.15, those fountains should be dispersed to allow wheelchair users convenient access. For example, in a large facility such as a convention center that has water fountains at several locations on a floor, the accessible water fountains should be located so that wheelchair users do not have to travel a greater distance than other people to use a drinking fountain.*

A4.1.3(17)(b) *In addition to the requirements of section 4.1.3(17)(b), the installation of additional volume controls is encouraged. Volume controls may be installed on any telephone.*

A4.1.3(19)(a) *Readily removable or folding seating units may be installed in lieu of providing an open space for wheelchair users. Folding seating units are usually two fixed seats that can be easily folded into a fixed center bar to allow for one or two open spaces for wheelchair users when necessary. These units are more easily adapted than removable seats which generally require the seat to be removed in advance by the facility management.*

Either a sign or a marker placed on seating with removable or folding arm rests is required by this section. Consideration should be given for ensuring identification of such seats in a darkened theater. For example, a marker which contrasts (light on dark or dark on light) and which also reflects light could be placed on the side of such seating so as to be visible in a lighted auditorium and also to reflect light from a flashlight.

A4.1.6 Accessible Buildings: Alterations.

A4.1.6(1)(h) *When an entrance is being altered, it is preferable that those entrances being altered be made accessible to the extent feasible.*

A4.2 Space Allowances and Reach Ranges.

A4.2.1 Wheelchair Passage Width.

(1) Space Requirements for Wheelchairs. Many persons who use wheelchairs need a 30 in (760 mm) clear opening width for doorways, gates, and the like, when the latter are entered head-on. If the *person* is unfamiliar with a building, if competing traffic is heavy, if sudden or frequent movements are needed, or if the wheelchair must be turned at an opening, then greater clear widths are needed. For most situations, the addition of an inch of leeway on either side is sufficient. Thus, a minimum clear width of 32 in (815 mm) will provide adequate clearance. However, when an opening or a restriction in a passageway is more than 24 in (610 mm) long, it is essentially a passageway and must be at least 36 in (915 mm) wide.

(2) Space Requirements for Use of Walking Aids. Although people who use walking aids can maneuver through clear width openings of 32 in (815 mm), they need 36 in (915 mm) wide passageways and walks for comfortable gaits. Crutch tips, often extending down at a wide angle, are a hazard in narrow passageways where they might not be seen by other pedestrians. Thus, the 36 in (915 mm) width provides a safety allowance both for the person *with a disability* and for others.

(3) Space Requirements for Passing. Ablebodied *persons* in winter clothing, walking

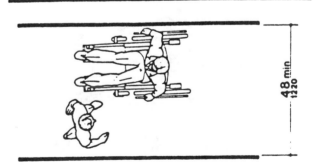

Fig. A1
Minimum Passage Width for One Wheelchair and One Ambulatory Person

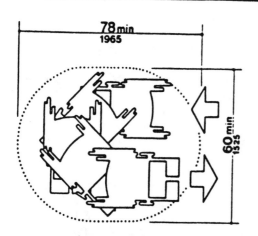

Fig. A2
Space Needed for Smooth U-Turn in a Wheelchair

straight ahead with arms swinging, need 32 in (815 mm) of width, which includes 2 in (50 mm) on either side for sway, and another 1 in (25 mm) tolerance on either side for clearing nearby objects or other pedestrians. Almost all wheelchair users and those who use walking aids can also manage within this 32 in (815 mm) width for short distances. Thus, two streams of traffic can pass in 64 in (1625 mm) in a comfortable flow. Sixty inches (1525 mm) provides a minimum width for a somewhat more restricted flow. If the clear width is less than 60 in (1525 mm), two wheelchair users will not be able to pass but will have to seek a wider place for passing. Forty-eight inches (1220 mm) is the minimum width needed for an ambulatory person to pass a nonambulatory or semi-ambulatory person. Within this 48 in (1220 mm) width, the ambulatory person will have to twist to pass a wheelchair user, a person with a *service animal*, or a

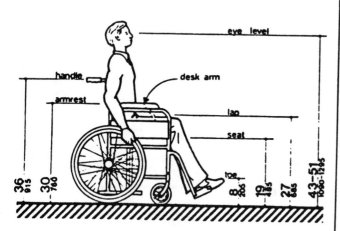

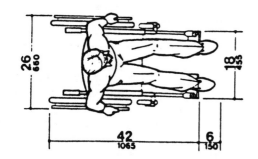

NOTE: Footrests may extend further for tall people

Fig. A3
Dimensions of Adult-Sized Wheelchairs

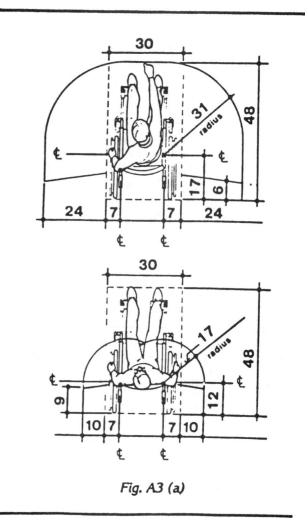

Fig. A3 (a)

semi-ambulatory person. There will be little leeway for swaying or missteps (see Fig. A1).

A4.2.3 Wheelchair Turning Space.
These guidelines specify a minimum space of 60 in (1525 mm) diameter or a 60 in by 60 in (1525 mm by 1525 mm) T-shaped space for a pivoting 180-degree turn of a wheelchair. This space is usually satisfactory for turning around, but many people will not be able to turn without repeated tries and bumping into surrounding objects. The space shown in Fig. A2 will allow most wheelchair users to complete U-turns without difficulty.

A4.2.4 Clear Floor or Ground Space for Wheelchairs.
The wheelchair and user shown in Fig. A3 represent typical dimensions for a large adult male. The space requirements in this *guideline* are based upon maneuvering clearances that will accommodate most wheelchairs. Fig. A3 provides a uniform reference for design not covered by this *guideline*.

A4.2.5 & A4.2.6 Reach.
Reach ranges for persons seated in wheelchairs may be further clarified by Fig. A3(a). These drawings approximate in the plan view the information shown in Fig. 4, 5, and 6.

A4.3 Accessible Route.

A4.3.1 General.

(1) Travel Distances. Many people with mobility impairments can move at only very slow speeds; for many, traveling 200 ft (61 m) could take about 2 minutes. This assumes a rate of about 1.5 ft/s (455 mm/s) on level ground. It also assumes that the traveler would move continuously. However, on trips over 100 ft (30 m), disabled people are apt to rest frequently, which substantially increases their trip times. Resting periods of 2 minutes for every 100 ft (30 m) can be used to estimate travel times for people with severely limited stamina. In inclement weather, slow progress and resting can greatly increase a disabled person's exposure to the elements.

(2) Sites. Level, indirect routes or those with running slopes lower than 1:20 can sometimes provide more convenience than direct routes with maximum allowable slopes or with ramps.

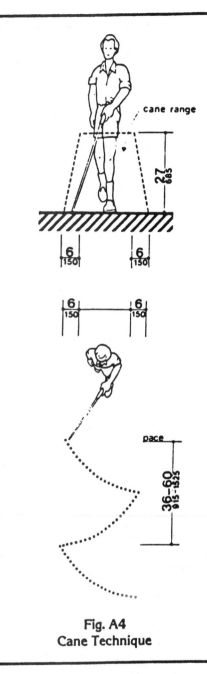

Fig. A4
Cane Technique

A4.3.10 Egress. Because people with disabilities may visit, be employed or be a resident in any building, emergency management plans with specific provisions to ensure their safe evacuation also play an essential role in fire safety and life safety.

A4.3.11.3 Stairway Width. *A 48 inch (1220 mm) wide exit stairway is needed to allow assisted evacuation (e.g., carrying a person in a wheelchair) without encroaching on the exit path for ambulatory persons.*

A4.3.11.4 Two-way Communication. *It is essential that emergency communication not be dependent on voice communications alone because the safety of people with hearing or speech impairments could be jeopardized. The visible signal requirement could be satisfied with something as simple as a button in the area of rescue assistance that lights, indicating that help is on the way, when the message is answered at the point of entry.*

A4.4 Protruding Objects.

A4.4.1 General. *Service animals* are trained to recognize and avoid hazards. However, most people with severe impairments of vision use the long cane as an aid to mobility. The two principal cane techniques are the touch technique, where the cane arcs from side to side and touches points outside both shoulders; and the diagonal technique, where the cane is held in a stationary position diagonally across the body with the cane tip touching or just above the ground at a point outside one shoulder and the handle or grip extending to a point outside the other shoulder. The touch technique is used primarily in uncontrolled areas, while the diagonal technique is used primarily in certain limited, controlled, and familiar environments. Cane users are often trained to use both techniques.

Potential hazardous objects are noticed only if they fall within the detection range of canes (see Fig. A4). Visually impaired people walking toward an object can detect an overhang if its lowest surface is not higher than 27 in (685 mm). When walking alongside *protruding* objects, they cannot detect overhangs. Since proper cane and *service animal* techniques keep people away from the edge of a path or from walls, a slight overhang of no more than 4 in (100 mm) is not hazardous.

A4.5 Ground and Floor Surfaces.

A4.5.1 General. *People who have difficulty walking or maintaining balance or who use crutches, canes, or walkers, and those with restricted gaits are particularly sensitive to slipping and tripping hazards. For such people, a stable and regular surface is necessary for safe walking, particularly on stairs. Wheelchairs can be propelled most easily on surfaces that are hard, stable, and regular. Soft loose*

surfaces such as shag carpet, loose sand or gravel, wet clay, and irregular surfaces such as cobblestones can significantly impede wheelchair movement.

Slip resistance is based on the frictional force necessary to keep a shoe heel or crutch tip from slipping on a walking surface under conditions likely to be found on the surface. *While the* <u>dynamic</u> *coefficient of friction during walking varies in a complex and non-uniform way, the* <u>static</u> *coefficient of friction, which can be measured in several ways, provides a close approximation of the slip resistance of a surface. Contrary to popular belief, some slippage is* <u>necessary</u> *to walking, especially for persons with restricted gaits; a truly "non-slip" surface could not be negotiated.*

The Occupational Safety and Health Administration recommends that walking surfaces have a static coefficient of friction of 0.5. A research project sponsored by the Architectural and Transportation Barriers Compliance Board (Access Board) conducted tests with persons with disabilities and concluded that a higher coefficient of friction was needed by such persons. A static coefficient of friction of 0.6 is recommended for accessible routes and 0.8 for ramps.

It is recognized that the coefficient of friction varies considerably due to the presence of contaminants, water, floor finishes, and other factors not under the control of the designer or builder and not subject to design and construction guidelines and that compliance would be difficult to measure on the building site. Nevertheless, many common building materials suitable for flooring are now labeled with information on the static coefficient of friction. While it may not be possible to compare one product directly with another, or to guarantee a constant measure, builders and designers are encouraged to specify materials with appropriate values. As more products include information on slip resistance, improved uniformity in measurement and specification is likely. The Access Board's advisory guidelines on Slip Resistant Surfaces provides additional information on this subject.

Cross slopes on walks and ground or floor surfaces can cause considerable difficulty in propelling a wheelchair in a straight line.

A4.5.3 Carpet. Much more needs to be done in developing both quantitative and qualitative criteria for carpeting (*i.e., problems associated with texture and weave need to be studied*). However, certain functional characteristics are well established. When both carpet and padding are used, it is desirable to have minimum movement (preferably none) between the floor and the pad and the pad and the carpet which would allow the carpet to hump or warp. In heavily trafficked areas, a thick, soft (plush) pad or cushion, particularly in combination with long carpet pile, makes it difficult for individuals in wheelchairs and those with other ambulatory disabilities to get about. Firm carpeting can be achieved through proper selection and combination of pad and carpet, sometimes with the elimination of the pad or cushion, and with proper installation. *Carpeting designed with a weave that causes a zig-zag effect when wheeled across is strongly discouraged.*

A4.6 Parking and Passenger Loading Zones.

A4.6.3 Parking Spaces. *The increasing use of vans with side-mounted lifts or ramps by persons with disabilities has necessitated some revisions in specifications for parking spaces and adjacent access aisles. The typical accessible parking space is 96 in (2440 mm) wide with an adjacent 60 in (1525 mm) access aisle. However, this aisle does not permit lifts or ramps to be deployed and still leave room for a person using a wheelchair or other mobility aid to exit the lift platform or ramp. In tests conducted with actual lift/van/wheelchair combinations, (under a Board-sponsored Accessible Parking and Loading Zones Project) researchers found that a space and aisle totaling almost 204 in (5180 mm) wide was needed to deploy a lift and exit conveniently. The "van accessible" parking space required by these guidelines provides a 96 in (2440 mm) wide space with a 96 in (2440 mm) adjacent access aisle which is just wide enough to maneuver and exit from a side mounted lift. If a 96 in (2440 mm) access aisle is placed between two spaces, two "van accessible" spaces are created. Alternatively, if the wide access aisle is provided at the end of a row (an area often unused), it may be possible to provide the wide access aisle without additional space (see Fig. A5(a)).*

A sign is needed to alert van users to the presence of the wider aisle, but the space is not intended to be restricted only to vans.

"Universal" Parking Space Design. An alternative to the provision of a percentage of spaces with a wide aisle, and the associated need to include additional signage, is the use of what has been called the "universal" parking space design. Under this design, all accessible spaces are 132 in (3350 mm) wide with a 60 in (1525 mm) access aisle (see Fig. A5(b)). One

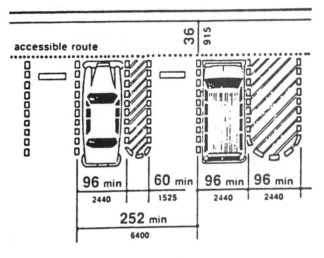

(a)
Van Accessible Space at End Row

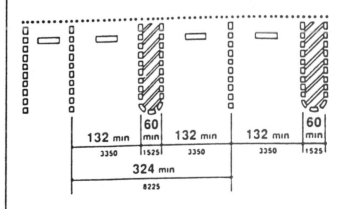

(b)
Universal Parking Space Design

Fig. A5
Parking Space Alternatives

advantage to this design is that no additional signage is needed because all spaces can accommodate a van with a side-mounted lift or ramp. Also, there is no competition between cars and vans for spaces since all spaces can accommodate either. Furthermore, the wider space permits vehicles to park to one side or the other within the 132 in (3350 mm) space to allow persons to exit and enter the vehicle on either the driver or passenger side, although, in some cases, this would require exiting or entering without a marked access aisle.

An essential consideration for any design is having the access aisle level with the parking space. Since a person with a disability, using a lift or ramp, must maneuver within the access aisle, the aisle cannot include a ramp or sloped area. The access aisle must be connected to an accessible route to the appropriate accessible entrance of a building or facility. The parking access aisle must either blend with the accessible route or have a curb ramp complying with 4.7. Such a curb ramp opening must be located within the access aisle boundaries, not within the parking space boundaries. Unfortunately, many facilities are designed with a ramp that is blocked when any vehicle parks in the accessible space. Also, the required dimensions of the access aisle cannot be restricted by planters, curbs or wheel stops.

A4.6.4 Signage. Signs designating parking places for disabled people can be seen from a driver's seat if the signs are mounted high enough above the ground and located at the front of a parking space.

A4.6.5 *Vertical Clearance.* High-top vans, which disabled people or transportation services often use, require higher clearances in parking garages than automobiles.

A4.8 Ramps.

A4.8.1 General. Ramps are essential for wheelchair users if elevators or lifts are not available to connect different levels. However, some people who use walking aids have difficulty with ramps and prefer stairs.

A4.8.2 Slope and Rise. *Ramp slopes between 1:16 and 1:20 are preferred.* The ability to manage an incline is related to both its slope and its length. Wheelchair users with

disabilities affecting *their* arms or with low stamina have serious difficulty using inclines. Most ambulatory people and most people who use wheelchairs can manage a slope of 1:16. Many people cannot manage a slope of 1:12 for 30 ft (9 m).

A4.8.4 *Landings.* *Level landings are essential toward maintaining an aggregate slope that complies with these guidelines. A ramp landing that is not level causes individuals using wheelchairs to tip backward or bottom out when the ramp is approached.*

A4.8.5 Handrails. The requirements for stair and ramp handrails in this *guideline* are for adults. When children are principal users in a building or facility, a second set of handrails at an appropriate height can assist them and aid in preventing accidents.

A4.9 Stairs.

A4.9.1 *Minimum Number.* *Only interior and exterior stairs connecting levels that are not connected by an elevator, ramp, or other accessible means of vertical access have to comply with 4.9.*

A4.10 Elevators.

A4.10.6 Door Protective and Reopening Device. The required door reopening device would hold the door open for 20 seconds if the doorway remains obstructed. After 20 seconds, the door may begin to close. However, if designed in accordance with *ASME A17.1-1990*, the door closing movement could still be stopped if a person or object exerts sufficient force at any point on the door edge.

A4.10.7 Door and Signal Timing for Hall Calls. This paragraph allows variation in the location of call buttons, advance time for warning signals, and the door-holding period used to meet the time requirement.

A4.10.12 Car Controls. Industry-wide standardization of elevator control panel design would make all elevators significantly more convenient for use by people with severe visual impairments. In many cases, it will be possible to locate the highest control on elevator panels within 48 in (1220 mm) from the floor.

A4.10.13 Car Position Indicators. A special button may be provided that would activate the audible signal within the given elevator only for the desired trip, rather than maintaining the audible signal in constant operation.

A4.10.14 Emergency Communications. A device that requires no handset is easier to use by people who have difficulty reaching. *Also, small handles on handset compartment doors are not usable by people who have difficulty grasping.*

Ideally, emergency two-way communication systems should provide both voice and visual display intercommunication so that persons with hearing impairments and persons with vision impairments can receive information regarding the status of a rescue. A voice intercommunication system cannot be the only means of communication because it is not accessible to people with speech and hearing impairments. While a voice intercommunication system is not required, at a minimum, the system should provide both an audio and visual indication that a rescue is on the way.

A4.11 Platform Lifts (Wheelchair Lifts).

A4.11.2 Other Requirements. *Inclined stairway chairlifts, and inclined and vertical platform lifts (wheelchair lifts) are available* for short-distance, vertical transportation of people with disabilities. Care should be taken in selecting lifts *as some lifts are not equally suitable for use by both wheelchair users and semi-ambulatory individuals.*

A4.12 Windows.

A4.12.1 General. *Windows intended to be operated by occupants in accessible spaces should comply with 4.12.*

A4.12.2 Window Hardware. *Windows requiring pushing, pulling, or lifting to open (for example, double-hung, sliding, or casement and awning units without cranks) should require no more than 5 lbf (22.2 N) to open or close. Locks, cranks, and other window hardware should comply with 4.27.*

A4.13 Doors.

A4.13.8 Thresholds at Doorways. Thresholds and surface height changes in doorways are particularly inconvenient for wheelchair users who also have low stamina or restrictions in arm movement because complex maneuvering is required to get over the level change while operating the door.

A4.13.9 Door Hardware. Some disabled persons must push against a door with their chair or walker to open it. Applied kickplates on doors with closers can reduce required maintenance by withstanding abuse from wheelchairs and canes. To be effective, they should cover the door width, less approximately 2 in (51 mm), up to a height of 16 in (405 mm) from its bottom edge and be centered across the *width of the door.*

A4.13.10 Door Closers. Closers with delayed action features give a person more time to maneuver through doorways. They are particularly useful on frequently used interior doors such as entrances to toilet rooms.

A4.13.11 Door Opening Force. Although most people with disabilities can exert at least 5 lbf (22.2N), both pushing and pulling from a stationary position, a few people with severe disabilities cannot exert 3 lbf (13.13N). Although some people cannot manage the allowable forces in this guideline and many others have difficulty, door closers must have certain minimum closing forces to close doors satisfactorily. Forces for pushing or pulling doors open are measured with a push-pull scale under the following conditions:

(1) Hinged doors: Force applied perpendicular to the door at the door opener or 30 in (760 mm) from the hinged side, whichever is farther from the hinge.

(2) Sliding or folding doors: Force applied parallel to the door at the door pull or latch.

(3) Application of force: Apply force gradually so that the applied force does not exceed the resistance of the door. In high-rise buildings, air-pressure differentials may require a modification of this specification in order to meet the functional intent.

A4.13.12 Automatic Doors and Power-Assisted Doors. Sliding automatic doors do not need guard rails and are more convenient for wheelchair users and visually impaired people to use. If slowly opening automatic doors can be reactivated before their closing cycle is completed, they will be more convenient in busy doorways.

A4.15 Drinking Fountains and Water Coolers.

A4.15.2 Spout Height. *Two drinking fountains, mounted side by side or on a single post, are usable by people with disabilities and people who find it difficult to bend over.*

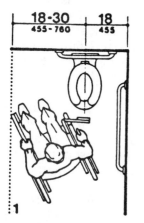

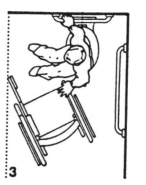

18-30 / 455-760   18 / 455

1 Takes transfer position, swings footrest out of the way, sets brakes.

2 Removes armrest, transfers.

3 Moves wheelchair out of the way, changes position (some people fold chair or pivot it 90° to the toilet).

4 Positions on toilet, releases brake.

(a)
Diagonal Approach

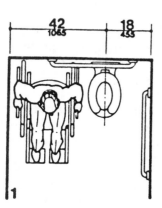
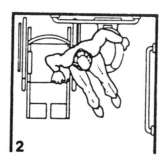
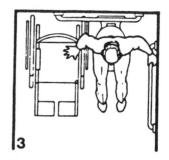

42 / 1065   18 / 455

1 Takes transfer position, removes armrest, sets brakes.

2 Transfers.

3 Positions on toilet.

(b)
Side Approach

Fig. A6
Wheelchair Transfers

A4.16 Water Closets.

A4.16.3 Height. Height preferences for toilet seats vary considerably among disabled people. Higher seat heights may be an advantage to some ambulatory disabled people, but are often a disadvantage for wheelchair users and others. Toilet seats 18 in (455 mm) high seem to be a reasonable compromise. Thick seats and filler rings are available to adapt standard fixtures to these requirements.

A4.16.4 Grab Bars. Fig. A6(a) and (b) show the diagonal and side approaches most commonly used to transfer from a wheelchair to a water closet. Some wheelchair users can transfer from the front of the toilet while others use a 90-degree approach. Most people who use the two additional approaches can also use either the diagonal approach or the side approach.

A4.16.5 Flush Controls. Flush valves and related plumbing can be located behind walls or to the side of the toilet, or a toilet seat lid can be provided if plumbing fittings are directly behind the toilet seat. Such designs reduce the chance of injury and imbalance caused by leaning back against the fittings. Flush controls for tank-type toilets have a standardized mounting location on the left side of the tank (facing the tank). Tanks can be obtained by special order with controls mounted on the right side. If administrative authorities require flush controls for flush valves to be located in a position that conflicts with the location of the rear grab bar, then that bar may be split or shifted toward the wide side of the toilet area.

A4.17 Toilet Stalls.

A4.17.3 Size and Arrangement. This section requires use of the 60 in (1525 mm) standard stall (Figure 30(a)) and permits the 36 in (915 mm) or 48 in (1220 mm) wide alternate stall (Figure 30(b)) only in alterations where provision of the standard stall is technically infeasible or where local plumbing codes prohibit reduction in the number of fixtures. A standard stall provides a clear space on one side of the water closet to enable persons who use wheelchairs to perform a side or diagonal transfer from the wheelchair to the water closet. However, some persons with disabilities who use mobility aids such as walkers, canes or crutches

are better able to use the two parallel grab bars in the 36 in (915 mm) wide alternate stall to achieve a standing position.

In large toilet rooms, where six or more toilet stalls are provided, it is therefore required that a 36 in (915 mm) wide stall with parallel grab bars be provided in addition to the standard stall required in new construction. The 36 in (915 mm) width is necessary to achieve proper use of the grab bars; wider stalls would position the grab bars too far apart to be easily used and narrower stalls would position the grab bars too close to the water closet. Since the stall is primarily intended for use by persons using canes, crutches and walkers, rather than wheelchairs, the length of the stall could be conventional. The door, however, must swing outward to ensure a usable space for people who use crutches or walkers.

A4.17.5 Doors. To make it easier for wheelchair users to close toilet stall doors, doors can be provided with closers, spring hinges, or a pull bar mounted on the inside surface of the door near the hinge side.

A4.19 Lavatories and Mirrors.

A4.19.6 Mirrors. If mirrors are to be used by both ambulatory people and wheelchair users, then they must be at least 74 in (1880 mm) high at their topmost edge. A single full length mirror can accommodate all people, including children.

A4.21 Shower Stalls.

A4.21.1 General. Shower stalls that are 36 in by 36 in (915 mm by 915 mm) wide provide additional safety to people who have difficulty maintaining balance because all grab bars and walls are within easy reach. Seated people use the walls of 36 in by 36 in (915 mm by 915 mm) showers for back support. Shower stalls that are 60 in (1525 mm) wide and have no curb may increase usability of a bathroom by wheelchair users because the shower area provides additional maneuvering space.

A4.22 Toilet Rooms.

A4.22.3 Clear Floor Space. In many small facilities, single-user restrooms may be the only facilities provided for all building users. In addition, the guidelines allow the use of "unisex" or "family" accessible toilet rooms in alterations when technical infeasibility can be demonstrated. Experience has shown that the provision of accessible "unisex" or single-user restrooms is a reasonable way to provide access for wheelchair users and any attendants, especially when attendants are of the opposite sex. Since these facilities have proven so useful, it is often considered advantageous to install a "unisex" toilet room in new facilities in addition to making the multi-stall restrooms accessible, especially in shopping malls, large auditoriums, and convention centers.

Figure 28 (section 4.16) provides minimum clear floor space dimensions for toilets in accessible "unisex" toilet rooms. The dotted lines designate the minimum clear floor space, depending on the direction of approach, required for wheelchair users to transfer onto the water closet. The dimensions of 48 in (1220 mm) and 60 in (1525 mm), respectively, correspond to the space required for the two common transfer approaches utilized by wheelchair users (see Fig. A6). It is important to keep in mind that the placement of the lavatory to the immediate side of the water closet will preclude the side approach transfer illustrated in Figure A6(b).

To accommodate the side transfer, the space adjacent to the water closet must remain clear of obstruction for 42 in (1065 mm) from the centerline of the toilet (Figure 28) and the lavatory must not be located within this clear space. A turning circle or T-turn, the clear floor space at the lavatory, and maneuvering space at the door must be considered when determining the possible wall locations. A privacy latch or other accessible means of ensuring privacy during use should be provided at the door.

RECOMMENDATIONS:

1. In new construction, accessible single-user restrooms may be desirable in some situations because they can accommodate a wide variety of building users. However, they cannot be used in lieu of making the multi-stall toilet rooms accessible as required.

2. Where strict compliance to the guidelines for accessible toilet facilities is technically infeasible in the alteration of existing facilities, accessible "unisex" toilets are a reasonable alternative.

3. In designing accessible single-user restrooms, the provisions of adequate space to allow a side transfer will provide accommodation to the largest number of wheelchair users.

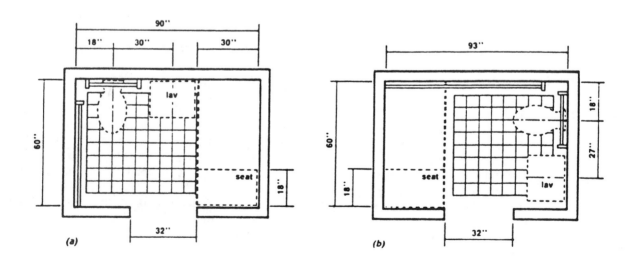

Fig. A7

A4.23 Bathrooms, Bathing Facilities, and Shower Rooms.

A4.23.3 Clear Floor Space. *Figure A7 shows two possible configurations of a toilet room with a roll-in shower. The specific shower shown is designed to fit exactly within the dimensions of a standard bathtub. Since the shower does not have a lip, the floor space can be used for required maneuvering space. This would permit a toilet room to be smaller than would be permitted with a bathtub and still provide enough floor space to be considered accessible. This design can provide accessibility in facilities where space is at a premium (i.e., hotels and medical care facilities). The alternate roll-in shower (Fig. 57b) also provides sufficient room for the "T-turn" and does not require plumbing to be on more than one wall.*

A4.23.9 Medicine Cabinets. Other alternatives for storing medical and personal care items are very useful to disabled people. Shelves, drawers, and floor-mounted cabinets can be provided within the reach ranges of disabled people.

A4.26 Handrails, Grab Bars, and Tub and Shower Seats.

A4.26.1 General. Many disabled people rely heavily upon grab bars and handrails to maintain balance and prevent serious falls. Many people brace their forearms between supports and walls to give them more leverage and stability in maintaining balance or for lifting. The grab bar clearance of 1-1/2 in (38 mm) required in this guideline is a safety clearance to prevent injuries resulting from arms slipping through the openings. It also provides adequate gripping room.

A4.26.2 Size and Spacing of Grab Bars and Handrails. This specification allows for alternate shapes of handrails as long as they allow an opposing grip similar to that provided by a circular section of 1-1/4 in to 1-1/2 in (32 mm to 38 mm).

A4.27 Controls and Operating Mechanisms.

A4.27.3 Height. *Fig. A8 further illustrates*

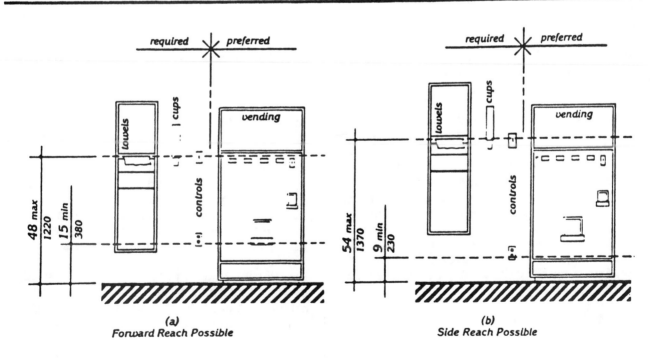

Fig. A8
Control Reach Limitations

mandatory and advisory control mounting height provisions for typical equipment.

Electrical receptacles installed to serve individual appliances and not intended for regular or frequent use by building occupants are not required to be mounted within the specified reach ranges. Examples would be receptacles installed specifically for wall-mounted clocks, refrigerators, and microwave ovens.

A4.28 Alarms.

A4.28.2 Audible Alarms. Audible emergency signals must have an intensity and frequency that can attract the attention of individuals who have partial hearing loss. People over 60 years of age generally have difficulty perceiving frequencies higher than 10,000 Hz. *An alarm signal which has a periodic element to its signal, such as single stroke bells (clang-pause-clang-pause), hi-low (up-down-up-down) and fast whoop (on-off-on-off) are best. Avoid continuous or reverberating tones. Select a signal which has a sound characterized by three or four clear tones without a great deal of "noise" in between.*

A4.28.3 Visual Alarms. The specifications in this section do not preclude the use of zoned or coded alarm systems.

A4.28.4 Auxiliary Alarms. Locating visual emergency alarms in rooms where persons who are deaf may work or reside alone can ensure that they will always be warned when an emergency alarm is activated. To be effective, such devices must be located and oriented so that they will spread signals and reflections throughout a space or raise the overall light level sharply. *However, visual alarms alone are not necessarily the best means to alert sleepers. A study conducted by Underwriters Laboratory (UL) concluded that a flashing light more than seven times brighter was required (110 candela v. 15 candela, at the same distance) to awaken sleepers as was needed to alert awake subjects in a normal daytime illuminated room.*

For hotel and other rooms where people are likely to be asleep, a signal-activated vibrator placed between mattress and box spring or under a pillow was found by UL to be much more effective in alerting sleepers. Many readily available devices are sound-activated so that they could respond to an alarm clock, clock

radio, wake-up telephone call or room smoke detector. Activation by a building alarm system can either be accomplished by a separate circuit activating an auditory alarm which would, in turn, trigger the vibrator or by a signal transmitted through the ordinary 110-volt outlet. Transmission of signals through the power line is relatively simple and is the basis of common, inexpensive remote light control systems sold in many department and electronic stores for home use. So-called "wireless" intercoms operate on the same principal.

A4.29 Detectable Warnings.

A4.29.2 Detectable Warnings on Walking Surfaces. *The material used to provide contrast should contrast by at least 70%. Contrast in percent is determined by:*

$$Contrast = [(B_1 - B_2)/B_1] \times 100$$

*where B_1 = light reflectance value (LRV) of the lighter area
and B_2 = light reflectance value (LRV) of the darker area.*

Note that in any application both white and black are never absolute; thus, B_1 never equals 100 and B_2 is always greater than 0.

A4.30 Signage.

A4.30.1 General. In building complexes where finding locations independently on a routine basis may be a necessity (for example, college campuses), tactile maps or prerecorded instructions can be very helpful to visually impaired people. Several maps and auditory instructions have been developed and tested for specific applications. The type of map or instructions used must be based on the information to be communicated, which depends highly on the type of buildings or users.

Landmarks that can easily be distinguished by visually impaired individuals are useful as orientation cues. Such cues include changes in illumination level, bright colors, unique patterns, wall murals, location of special equipment or other architectural features.

Many people with disabilities have limitations in movement of their heads and reduced peripheral vision. Thus, signage positioned perpendicular to the path of travel is easiest for them to notice. People can generally distinguish signage within an angle of 30 degrees to either side of the centerlines of their faces without moving their heads.

A4.30.2 Character Proportion. The legibility of printed characters is a function of the viewing distance, character height, the ratio of the stroke width to the height of the character, the contrast of color between character and background, and print font. The size of characters must be based upon the intended viewing distance. A severely nearsighted person may have to be much closer to recognize a character of a given size than a person with normal visual acuity.

A4.30.4 Raised and Brailled Characters and Pictorial Symbol Signs (Pictograms). *The standard dimensions for literary Braille are as follows:*

Dot diameter	*.059 in.*
Inter-dot spacing	*.090 in.*
Horizontal separation between cells	*.241 in.*
Vertical separation between cells	*.395 in.*

Raised borders around *signs containing* raised characters may make them confusing to read unless the border is set far away from the characters. *Accessible signage with descriptive materials about public buildings, monuments, and objects of cultural interest may not provide sufficiently detailed and meaningful information. Interpretive guides, audio tape devices, or other methods may be more effective in presenting such information.*

A4.30.5 Finish and Contrast. *An eggshell finish (11 to 19 degree gloss on 60 degree glossimeter) is recommended. Research indicates that signs are more legible for persons with low vision when characters contrast with their background by at least 70 percent. Contrast in percent shall be determined by:*

$$Contrast = [(B_1 - B_2)/B_1] \times 100$$

where B_1 = light reflectance value (LRV) of the lighter area
and B_2 = light reflectance value (LRV) of the darker area.

Note that in any application both white and black are never absolute; thus, B_1 never equals 100 and B_2 is always greater than 0.

The greatest readability is usually achieved through the use of light-colored characters or symbols on a dark background.

A4.30.7 Symbols of Accessibility for Different Types of Listening Systems. *Paragraph 4 of this section requires signage indicating the availability of an assistive listening system. An appropriate message should be displayed with the international symbol of access for hearing loss since this symbol conveys general accessibility for people with hearing loss. Some suggestions are:*

> *INFRARED*
> *ASSISTIVE LISTENING SYSTEM*
> *AVAILABLE*
> *——PLEASE ASK——*

> *AUDIO LOOP IN USE*
> *TURN T-SWITCH FOR*
> *BETTER HEARING*
> *——OR ASK FOR HELP——*

> *FM*
> *ASSISTIVE LISTENING*
> *SYSTEM AVAILABLE*
> *——PLEASE ASK——*

The symbol may be used to notify persons of the availability of other auxiliary aids and services such as: real time captioning, captioned note taking, sign language interpreters, and oral interpreters.

A4.30.8 Illumination Levels. *Illumination levels on the sign surface shall be in the 100 to 300 lux range (10 to 30 footcandles) and shall be uniform over the sign surface. Signs shall be located such that the illumination level on the surface of the sign is not significantly exceeded by the ambient light or visible bright lighting source behind or in front of the sign.*

A4.31 Telephones.

A4.31.3 Mounting Height. In localities where the dial-tone first system is in operation, calls can be placed at a coin telephone through the operator without inserting coins. The operator button is located at a height of 46 in (1170 mm) if the coin slot of the telephone is at 54 in (1370 mm). A generally available public telephone with a coin slot mounted lower on the equipment would allow universal installation of telephones at a height of 48 in (1220 mm) or less to all operable parts.

A4.31.9 Text Telephones. *A public text telephone may be an integrated text telephone pay phone unit or a conventional portable text telephone that is permanently affixed within, or adjacent to, the telephone enclosure. In order to be usable with a pay phone, a text telephone which is not a single integrated text telephone pay phone unit will require a shelf large enough (10 in (255mm) wide by 10 in (255 mm) deep with a 6 in (150 mm) vertical clearance minimum) to accommodate the device, an electrical outlet, and a power cord. Movable or portable text telephones may be used to provide equivalent facilitation. A text telephone should be readily available so that a person using it may access the text telephone easily and conveniently. As currently designed pocket-type text telephones for personal use do not accommodate a wide range of users. Such devices would not be considered substantially equivalent to conventional text telephones. However, in the future as technology develops this could change.*

A4.32 *Fixed or Built-in* Seating and Tables.

A4.32.4 Height of *Tables or Counters.* Different types of work require different *table or counter* heights for comfort and optimal performance. Light detailed work such as writing requires a *table or counter* close to elbow height for a standing person. Heavy manual work such as rolling dough requires *a counter or table* height about 10 in (255 mm) below elbow height for a standing person. This principle of *high/low table or counter heights* also applies for seated persons; however, the limiting condition for seated manual work is clearance under the *table or counter.*

Table A1 shows convenient *counter heights* for seated persons. The great variety of heights for comfort and optimal performance indicates a need for alternatives or a compromise in height if people who stand and people who sit will be using the same counter area.

Table A1
Convenient Heights of Tables and Counters for Seated People[1]

Conditions of Use	Short Women in mm		Tall Men in mm	
Seated in a wheelchair:				
Manual work–				
Desk or removeable armrests	26	660	30	760
Fixed, full-size armrests[2]	32[3]	815	32[3]	815
Light detailed work:				
Desk or removable armrests	29	735	34	865
Fixed, full-size armrests[2]	32[3]	815	34	865
Seated in a 16-in. (405-mm)				
High chair:				
Manual work	26	660	27	685
Light detailed work	28	710	31	785

[1] All dimensions are based on a work-surface thickness of 1 1/2 in (38 mm) and a clearance of 1 1/2 in (38 mm) between legs and the underside of a work surface.

[2] This type of wheelchair arm does not interfere with the positioning of a wheelchair under a work surface.

[3] This dimension is limited by the height of the armrests: a lower height would be preferable. Some people in this group prefer lower work surfaces, which require positioning the wheelchair back from the edge of the counter.

A4.33 Assembly Areas.

A4.33.2 Size of Wheelchair Locations. Spaces large enough for two wheelchairs allow people who are coming to a performance together to sit together.

A4.33.3 Placement of Wheelchair Locations. The location of wheelchair areas can be planned so that a variety of positions within the seating area are provided. This will allow choice in viewing and price categories.

Building/life safety codes set minimum distances between rows of fixed seats with consideration of the number of seats in a row, the exit aisle width and arrangement, and the location of exit doors. "Continental" seating, with a greater number of seats per row and a *commensurate increase in row spacing and exit doors, facilitates emergency egress for all people and increases ease of access to mid-row seats especially for people who walk with difficulty. Consideration of this positive attribute of "continental" seating should be included along with all other factors in the design of fixed seating areas.*

Table A2. Summary of Assistive Listening Devices

System	Advantages	Disadvantages	Typical Applications
Induction Loop Transmitter: Transducer wired to induction loop around listening area. Receiver: Self-contained induction receiver or personal hearing aid with telecoil.	Cost-Effective Low Maintenance Easy to use Unobtrusive May be possible to integrate into existing public address system. Some hearing aids can function as receivers.	Signal spills over to adjacent rooms. Susceptible to electrical interference. Limited portability Inconsistent signal strength. Head position affects signal strength. Lack of standards for induction coil performance.	Meeting areas Theaters Churches and Temples Conference rooms Classrooms TV viewing
FM Transmitter: Flashlight-sized worn by speaker. Receiver: With personal hearing aid via DAI or induction neck-loop and telecoil; or self-contained with earphone(s).	Highly portable Different channels allow use by different groups within the same room. High user mobility Variable for large range of hearing losses.	High cost of receivers Equipment fragile Equipment obtrusive High maintenance Expensive to maintain Custom fitting to individual user may be required.	Classrooms Tour groups Meeting areas Outdoor events One-on-one
Infrared Transmitter: Emitter in line-of-sight with receiver. Receiver: Self-contained. Or with personal hearing aid via DAI or induction neckloop and telecoil.	Easy to use Insures privacy or confidentiality Moderate cost Can often be integrated into existing public address system.	Line-of-sight required between emitter and receiver. Ineffective outdoors Limited portability Requires installation	Theaters Churches and Temples Auditoriums Meetings requiring confidentiality TV viewing

Source: Rehab Brief, National Institute on Disability and Rehabilitation Research, Washington, DC, Vol. XII, No. 10, (1990).

A4.33.6 Placement of Listening Systems. A distance of 50 ft (15 m) allows a person to distinguish performers' facial expressions.

A4.33.7 Types of Listening Systems. *An assistive listening system appropriate for an assembly area for a group of persons or where the specific individuals are not known in advance, such as a playhouse, lecture hall or movie theater, may be different from the system appropriate for a particular individual provided as an auxiliary aid or as part of a reasonable accommodation. The appropriate device for an individual is the type that individual can use, whereas the appropriate system for an assembly area will necessarily be geared toward the "average" or aggregate needs of various individuals.* A listening system that can be used from any seat in a seating area is the most flexible way to meet this specification. Earphone jacks with variable volume controls can benefit only people who have slight hearing loss and do not help people who use hearing aids. At the present time, *magnetic induction* loops are the most feasible type of listening system for people who use hearing aids *equipped with "T-coils,"* but people without hearing aids or those with hearing aids not equipped with inductive pick-ups cannot use them *without special receivers.* Radio frequency systems can be extremely effective and inexpensive. People without hearing aids can use them, but people with hearing aids need a special receiver to use them as they are presently designed. If hearing aids had a jack to allow a by-pass of microphones, then radio frequency systems would be suitable for people with and without hearing aids. Some listening systems may be subject to interference from other equipment and feedback from hearing aids of people who are using the systems. Such interference can be controlled by careful engineering design that anticipates feedback sources in the surrounding area.

Table A2, reprinted from a National Institute of Disability and Rehabilitation Research "Rehab Brief," shows some of the advantages and disadvantages of different types of assistive listening systems. In addition, the Architectural and Transportation Barriers Compliance Board (Access Board) has published a pamphlet on Assistive Listening Systems which lists demonstration centers across the country where technical assistance can be obtained in selecting and installing appropriate systems. The state of New York has also adopted a detailed technical specification which may be useful.

A5.0 Restaurants and Cafeterias.

A5.1 General. *Dining counters (where there is no service) are typically found in small carry-out restaurants, bakeries, or coffee shops and may only be a narrow eating surface attached to a wall. This section requires that where such a dining counter is provided, a portion of the counter shall be at the required accessible height.*

A7.0 Business and Mercantile.

A7.2(3) Assistive Listening Devices. *At all sales and service counters, teller windows, box offices, and information kiosks where a physical barrier separates service personnel and customers, it is recommended that at least one permanently installed assistive listening device complying with 4.33 be provided at each location or series. Where assistive listening devices are installed, signage should be provided identifying those stations which are so equipped.*

A7.3 Check-out Aisles. *Section 7.2 refers to counters without aisles; section 7.3 concerns check-out aisles. A counter without an aisle (7.2) can be approached from more than one direction such as in a convenience store. In order to use a check-out aisle (7.3), customers must enter a defined area (an aisle) at a particular point, pay for goods, and exit at a particular point.*

APPENDIX C

UNIFORM FEDERAL ACCESSIBILITY STANDARDS

UNIFORM FEDERAL ACCESSIBILITY STANDARDS

INTRODUCTION

GENERAL SERVICES ADMINISTRATION

DEPARTMENT OF DEFENSE

DEPARTMENT OF HOUSING AND URBAN DEVELOPMENT

U.S. POSTAL SERVICE

This document presents uniform standards for the design, construction, and alteration of buildings so that physically handicapped persons will have ready access to and use of them in accordance with the Architectural Barriers Act, 42 U.S.C. 4151-4157. The document embodies an agreement to minimize the differences between the standards previously used by four agencies (the General Services Administration, the departments of Housing and Urban Development and Defense, and the United States Postal Service) that are authorized to issue standards under the Architectural Barriers Act, and between those standards and the access standards recommended for facilities that are not federally funded or constructed.

The four standard-setting agencies establish and enforce standards for design, construction, and alteration of particular types of buildings and facilities. The General Services Administration (GSA) prescribes standards for all buildings subject to the Architectural Barriers Act that are not covered by standards issued by the other three standard-setting agencies; the Department of Defense (DoD) prescribes standards for DoD installations; the Department of Housing and Urban Development (HUD) prescribes standards for residential structures covered by the Architectural Barriers Act except those funded or constructed by DoD; and the U.S. Postal Service (USPS) prescribes standards for postal facilities. Each of the four agencies issues standards in accordance with its statutory authority.

To ensure compliance with the standards, Congress established the Architectural and Transportation Barriers Compliance Board (ATBCB) in Section 502 of the Rehabilitation Act of 1973 (the Rehabilitation Act), 29 U.S.C. 792. The ATBCB is composed of members representing eleven Federal agencies (the four standard-setting agencies; the departments of Education, Health and Human Services, Interior, Justice, Labor, and Transportation; and the Veterans Administration) and eleven members appointed by the President from the general public. A 1978 amendment to Section 502 of the Rehabilitation Act added to the ATBCB's functions the responsibility to issue minimum guidelines (Guidelines) and requirements for the standards established by the four standard-setting agencies. The final rule that established the Guidelines now in effect was published in the *Federal Register* on August 4, 1982 (47 FR 33862) and is codified at 36 CFR part 1190.

The four standard-setting agencies determined that the uniform standards adopted by them would, as much as possible, not only comply with the Guidelines adopted by the ATBCB but also be consistent with the standards published by the American National Standards Institute (ANSI) for general use. ANSI is a nongovernmental national organization that publishes a wide variety of recommended standards. ANSI's standards for barrier-free design are developed by a committee made up of 52 organizations representing associations of handicapped people, rehabilitation professionals, design professionals, builders, and manufacturers. The standards, which are called ANSI A117.1, "Specifications for Making Buildings and Facilities Accessible to, and Usable by, Physically Handicapped People," are developed using the consensus process. The original ANSI A117.1, adopted in 1961, formed the technical basis for the first accessibility standards adopted by the federal government and most state governments. The current edition, ANSI A117.1-1980, is based on research funded by HUD. It has generally been accepted by the private sector and has been recommended for use in model state and local building codes by the Council of American Building Officials.

In keeping with the objective of uniformity between federal requirements and those commonly applied by state and local governments, the Uniform Federal Accessibility Standards (UFAS) follows ANSI A117.1-1980 in format. Both the UFAS scope provisions, which establish the minimum number of elements and spaces required to comply with standards, and the UFAS technical requirements meet or exceed the comparable provisions of the Guidelines.

The UFAS was published in the *Federal Register* on August 7, 1984 (49 FR 31528). Each of the standard-setting agencies has taken action in accordance with its own procedures, including internally prescribed rulemaking and the Administrative Procedure Act where applicable, to incorporate the UFAS in its own standards, regulations, or other directives. GSA adopted the UFAS in 41 CFR 101-19.6, effective August 7, 1984. HUD adopted the UFAS in 24 CFR part 40, effective October 4, 1984. USPS adopted the UFAS in Handbook RE-4, "Standards for Facility Accessibility by the Physically Handicapped," effective November 15, 1984. DoD adopted the UFAS by revising Chapter 18 of DoD 4270.1-M, "Construction Criteria," by memorandum dated May 8, 1985.

For further information contact:

Kathleen Fields, General Services Administration, 18th and F Streets, N.W., Room 3044, Washington, D.C. 20405, (202) 566-0038.

Judith Gilliom, Department of Defense, Office of the Deputy Assistant Secretary of Defense (Equal Opportunity), Room 3E317, The Pentagon, Washington, D.C. 20301, (202) 697-8661.

Margaret Milner, Department of Housing and Urban Development, 451 7th Street, S.W., Room 9220, Washington, D.C. 20410, (202) 755-6454.

Melinda Hulsey, Real Estate and Buildings Department, U.S. Postal Service, 475 L'Enfant Plaza West, S.W., Washington, D.C. 20260-6424, (202) 268-3139.

For TDD communication, call Margaret Milner, (202) 426-6030. These are not toll-free numbers.

1. PURPOSE.

This document sets standards for facility accessibility by physically handicapped persons for Federal and federally-funded facilities. These standards are to be applied during the design, construction, and altera-tion of buildings and facilities to the extent required by the Architectural Barriers Act of 1968, as amended.

The technical provisions of these standards are the same as those of the American National Standard Institute's document A117.1-1980, except as noted in this text and on figures by italics.

2. GENERAL.

2.1 Authority. *These standards were jointly developed by the General Services Administration, the Department of Housing and Urban Development, the Department of Defense, and the United States Postal Service, under the authority of sections 2, 3, 4, and 4a, respectively, of the Architectural Barriers Act of 1968, as amended, Pub. L. No. 90-480, 42 U.S.C. 4151-4157.*

2.2 Provisions For Adults. The specifications in *these standards* are based upon adult dimensions and anthropometrics.

3. MISCELLANEOUS INSTRUCTIONS AND DEFINITIONS.

3.1 Graphic Conventions. Graphic conventions are shown in Table 1. Dimensions that are not marked "minimum" or "maximum" are absolute, unless other-wise indicated in the text or captions.

3.2 Dimensional Tolerances. All dimensions are subject to conventional building industry tolerances for field conditions.

3.3 Notes. The text of *these standards* does not contain notes or footnotes. Additional information, explanations, and advisory materials are located in the Appendix. Paragraphs marked with an asterisk have related, nonmandatory material in the Appendix. In the Appendix, the corresponding paragraph numbers are preceded by an A.

3.4 General Terminology.

comply with. Meet one or more specifications of this standard.

if, if...then. Denotes a specification that applies only when the conditions described are present.

may. Denotes an option or alternative.

Table 1
Graphic Conventions

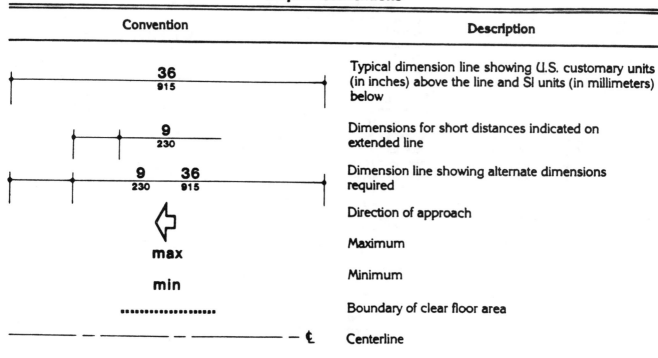

Convention	Description
36 / 915	Typical dimension line showing U.S. customary units (in inches) above the line and SI units (in millimeters) below
9 / 230	Dimensions for short distances indicated on extended line
9 / 230 36 / 915	Dimension line showing alternate dimensions required
	Direction of approach
max	Maximum
min	Minimum
....	Boundary of clear floor area
℄	Centerline

shall. Denotes a mandatory specification or requirement.

should. Denotes an advisory specification or recommendation.

3.5 Definitions. The following terms shall, for the purpose of *these standards*, have the meaning indicated in this section.

Access Aisle. An accessible pedestrian space between elements, such as parking spaces, seating, and desks, that provides clearances appropriate for use of the elements.

Accessible. Describes a site, building, facility, or portion thereof that complies with *these standards* and that can be approached, entered, and used by physically disabled people.

Accessible Element. An *element* specified by *these standards* (for example, telephone, controls, and the like).

Accessible Route. A continuous unobstructed path connecting all accessible elements and spaces in a building or facility. Interior accessible routes may include corridors, floors, ramps, elevators, lifts, and clear floor space at fixtures. Exterior accessible routes may include parking access aisles, curb ramps, walks, ramps, and lifts.

Accessible Space. *Space that complies with these standards.*

Adaptability. The ability of certain building *spaces and* elements, such as kitchen counters, sinks, and grab bars, to be *added or* altered so as to accommodate the needs of either disabled or nondisabled *persons*, or to accommodate the needs of persons with different types or degrees of disability.

Addition. An expansion, extension, or increase in the gross floor area of a building or facility.

Administrative Authority. A governmental agency that adopts or enforces regulations and standards for the design, construction, or alteration of buildings and facilities.

Alteration. As applied to a building or structure, means a change or rearrangement in the structural parts or elements, or in the means of egress or in moving from one location or position to another. It does not include normal maintenance, repair, reroofing, interior decoration, or changes to mechanical and electrical systems.

Assembly Area. A room or space accommodating fifty or more individuals for religious, recreational, educational, political, social, or amusement purposes, or for the consumption of food and drink, including all connected rooms or spaces with a common means of egress and ingress. Such areas as conference rooms would have to be accessible in accordance with other parts of this standard but would not have to meet all of the criteria associated with assembly areas.

Automatic Door. A door equipped with a power-operated mechanism and controls that open and close the door automatically upon receipt of a momentary actuating signal. The switch that begins the automatic cycle may be a photoelectric device, floor mat, or manual switch mounted on or near the door itself (see power-assisted door).

Circulation Path. An exterior or interior way of passage from one place to another for pedestrians, including, but not limited to, walks, hallways, courtyards, stairways, and stair landings.

Clear. Unobstructed.

Common Use. Refers to those interior and exterior rooms, spaces, or elements that are made available for the use of a restricted group of people (for example, residents of an apartment building, the occupants of an office building, or the guests of such residents or occupants).

Cross Slope. The slope that is perpendicular to the direction of travel (see running slope).

Curb Ramp. A short ramp cutting through a curb or built up to it.

Dwelling Unit. A single unit of residence which provides a kitchen or food preparation area, in addition to rooms and spaces for living, bathing, sleeping, and the like. A single family home is a dwelling unit, and dwelling units are to be found in such housing types as townhouses and apartment buildings.

Egress, Means of. An accessible route of exit that meets all applicable code specifications of the regulatory building agency having jurisdiction over the building or facility.

Element. An architectural or mechanical component of a building, facility, space, or site, e.g., telephone, curb ramp, door, drinking fountain, seating, water closet.

Entrance. Any access point to a building or portion of building or facility used for the purpose of entering. An entrance includes the approach walk, the vertical access leading to the entrance platform, the entrance platform itself, vestibules if provided, the entry door(s) or gate(s), and the hardware of the entry door(s) or gate(s). The principal entrance of a building or facility is the main door through which most people enter.

Essential Features. Those elements and spaces that make a building or facility usable by, or serve the needs of, its occupants or users. Essential features include but are not limited to entrances, toilet rooms, and accessible routes. Essential features do not include those spaces that house the major activities for which the building or facility is intended, such as classrooms and offices.

Extraordinary Repair. The replacement or renewal of any element of an existing building or facility for purposes other than normal maintenance.

Facility. All or any portion of a building, structure, or area, including the site on which such building, structure or area is located, wherein specific services are provided or activities performed.

Full and Fair Cash Value. Full and fair cash value is calculated for the estimated date on which work will commence on a project and means:

(1) The assessed valuation of a building or facility as recorded in the assessor's office of the municipality and as equalized at one hundred percent (100%) valuation, or
(2) The replacement cost, or
(3) The fair market value.

Functional Spaces. The rooms and spaces in a building or facility that house the major activities for which the building or facility is intended.

Housing. A building, facility, or portion thereof, excluding inpatient health care facilities, that contains one or more dwelling units or sleeping accommodations. Housing may include, but is not limited to, one and two-family dwellings, apartments, group homes, hotels, motels, dormitories, and mobile homes.

Marked Crossing. A crosswalk or other identified path intended for pedestrian use in crossing a vehicular way.

Multifamily Dwelling. Any building containing more than two dwelling units.

Operable Part. A part of a piece of equipment or appliance used to insert or withdraw objects, or to activate, deactivate, or adjust the equipment or appliance (for example, coin slot, pushbutton, handle).

Physically Handicapped. An individual who has a physical impairment, including impaired sensory, manual, or speaking abilities, which results in a functional limitation in access to and use of a building or facility.

Power-assisted Door. A door used for human passage with a mechanism that helps to open the door, or relieve the opening resistance of a door, upon the activation of a switch or a continued force applied to the door itself. If the switch or door is released, such doors immediately begin to close or close completely within 3 to 30 seconds (see automatic door).

Public Use. Describes interior or exterior rooms or spaces that are made available to the general public. Public use may be provided at a building or facility that is privately or publicly owned.

Ramp. A walking surface in an accessible space that has a running slope greater than 1:20.

Running Slope. The slope that is parallel to the direction of travel (see cross slope).

Service Entrance. An entrance intended primarily for delivery of services.

Signage. Verbal, symbolic, tactile, and pictorial information.

Site. A parcel of land bounded by a property line or a designated portion of a public right-of-way.

Site Improvement. Landscaping, paving for pedestrian and vehicular ways, outdoor lighting, recreational facilities, and the like, added to a site.

Sleeping Accommodations. Rooms in which people sleep, for example, dormitory and hotel or motel guest rooms.

Space. A definable area, e.g., toilet room, hall, assembly area, entrance, storage room, alcove, courtyard, or lobby.

Structural Impracticability. Changes having little likelihood of being accomplished without removing or altering a load-bearing structural member and/or incurring an increased cost of 50 percent or more of the value of the element of the building or facility involved.

Tactile. Describes an object that can be perceived using the sense of touch.

Tactile Warning. A standardized surface texture applied to or built into walking surfaces or other elements to warn visually impaired people of hazards in the path of travel.

Temporary. Applies to facilities that are not of permanent construction but are extensively used or essential for public use for a given (short) period of time, for example, temporary classrooms or classroom buildings at schools and colleges, or facilities around a major construction site to make passage accessible, usable, and safe for everybody. Structures directly associated with the actual processes of major construction, such as porto potties, scaffolding, bridging, trailers, and the like, are not included. Temporary as applied to elements means installed for less than 6 months and not required for safety reasons.

Vehicular Way. A route intended for vehicular traffic, such as a street, driveway, or parking lot.

Walk. An exterior pathway with a prepared surface intended for pedestrian use, including general pedestrian areas such as plazas and courts.

4. ACCESSIBLE ELEMENTS AND SPACES: SCOPE AND TECHNICAL REQUIREMENTS.

4.1 Minimum Requirements.

4.1.1 Accessible Sites and Exterior Facilities: New Construction. An accessible site shall meet the following minimum requirements:

(1) At least one accessible route complying with 4.3 shall be provided within the boundary of the site from public transportation stops, accessible parking

spaces, passenger loading zones if provided, and public streets or sidewalks to an accessible building entrance.

(2) At least one accessible route complying with 4.3 shall connect accessible buildings, facilities, elements, and spaces that are on the same site.

(3) All objects that protrude from surfaces or posts into circulation paths shall comply with 4.4.

(4) Ground surfaces along accessible routes and in accessible spaces shall comply with 4.5.

(5) (a) *If parking spaces are provided for employees or visitors, or both, then accessible spaces, complying with 4.6, shall be provided in each such parking area in conformance with the following table:*

Total Parking in Lot	Required Minimum Number of Accessible Spaces
1 to 25	1
26 to 50	2
51 to 75	3
76 to 100	4
101 to 150	5
151 to 200	6
201 to 300	7
301 to 400	8
401 to 500	9
501 to 1000	*
1001 and over	**

* 2 percent of total.
** 20 plus 1 for each 100 over 1000.

EXCEPTION: *The total number of accessible parking spaces may be distributed among parking lots, if greater accessibility is achieved.*

EXCEPTION: *This does not apply to parking provided for official government vehicles owned or leased by the government and used exclusively for government purposes.*

(b) *If passenger loading zones are provided, then at least one passenger loading zone shall comply with 4.6.5.*

(c) *Parking spaces for side lift vans are accessible parking spaces and may be used to meet the requirements of this paragraph.*

(d) *Parking spaces at accessible housing complying with 4.6 shall be provided in accordance with the following:*

(i) *Where parking is provided for all residents, one accessible parking space shall be provided for each accessible dwelling unit; and*

(ii) *Where parking is provided for only a portion of the residents, an accessible parking space shall be provided on request of the occupant of an accessible dwelling unit;*

(iii) *Where parking is provided for visitors, 2 percent of the spaces, or at least one, shall be accessible.*

(e) *Parking spaces at health care facilities complying with 4.6 shall be provided in accordance with the following:*

(i) *General health care facilities, employee and visitor parking: Comply with Table 4.1.1(5)(a);*

(ii) *Outpatient facilities: 10 percent of the total number of parking spaces provided;*

(iii) *Spinal cord injury facilities, employee and visitor parking: 20 percent of total parking spaces provided.*

(6) *If toilet facilities are provided on a site, then each such public or common use toilet facility shall comply with 4.22. If bathing facilities are provided on a site, then each such public or common use bathing facility shall comply with 4.23.*

EXCEPTION: *These provisions are not mandatory for single user portable toilet or bathing units clustered at a single location; however, at least one toilet unit complying with 4.22 or one bathing unit complying with 4.23 should be installed at each location whenever standard units are provided.*

(7) *All signs shall comply with 4.30. Elements and spaces of accessible facilities which shall be identified by the International Symbol of Accessibility are:*

(a) *Parking spaces designated as reserved for physically handicapped people;*
(b) *passenger loading zones;*
(c) *accessible entrances;*
(d) *accessible toilet and bathing facilities.*

4.1.2 Accessible Buildings: *New Construction.*
Accessible buildings and facilities shall meet the following minimum requirements:

(1) At least one accessible route complying with 4.3 shall connect accessible building or facility entrances with all accessible spaces and elements within the building or facility.

(2) All objects that overhang circulation paths shall comply with 4.4.

(3) Ground and floor surfaces along accessible routes and in accessible rooms and spaces shall comply with 4.5.

(4) Stairs connecting levels that are not connected by an elevator shall comply with 4.9.

(5) One passenger elevator complying with 4.10 shall serve each level in all multi-story buildings and facilities. If more than one elevator is provided, each elevator shall comply with 4.10.

EXCEPTION: Elevator pits, elevator penthouses, mechanical rooms, piping or equipment catwalks are excepted from this requirement.

EXCEPTION: Accessible ramps complying with 4.8 or, if no other alternative is feasible, accessible platform lifts complying with 4.11 may be used in lieu of an elevator.

(6) Windows. (Reserved).

(7) Doors:

(a) At each accessible entrance to a building or facility, at least one door shall comply with 4.13.

(b) Within a building or facility, at least one door at each accessible space shall comply with 4.13.

(c) Each door that is an element of an accessible route shall comply with 4.13.

(d) Each door required by 4.3.10, Egress, shall comply with 4.13.

EXCEPTION: In multiple-story buildings and facilities where at-grade egress from each floor is impossible, either of the following is permitted: the provision within each story of approved fire and smoke partitions that create horizontal exits, or, the provision within each floor of areas of refuge approved by agencies having authority for safety.

(8) At least one principal entrance at each grade floor level to a building or facility shall comply with 4.14, Entrances. When a building or facility has entrances which normally serve any of the following functions: transportation facilities, passenger loading zones, accessible parking facilities, taxi stands, public streets and sidewalks, or accessible interior vertical access, then at least one of the entrances serving each such function shall comply with 4.14, Entrances. Because entrances also serve as emergency exits, whose proximity to all parts of buildings and facilities is essential, it is preferable that all or most exits be accessible.

(9) If drinking fountains or water coolers are provided, approximately 50 percent of those provided on each floor shall comply with 4.15 and shall be on an accessible route. If only one drinking fountain or water cooler is provided on any floor, it shall comply with 4.15.

(10) If toilet facilities are provided, then each public and common use toilet room shall comply with 4.22. Other toilet rooms shall be adaptable. If bathing facilities are provided, then each public and common use bathroom shall comply with 4.23. Accessible toilet rooms and bathing facilities shall be on an accessible route.

(11) If storage facilities such as cabinets, shelves, closets, and drawers are provided in accessible spaces, at least one of each type provided shall contain storage space complying with 4.25. Additional storage may be provided outside of the dimensions shown in Fig. 38.

(12) Controls and operating mechanisms in accessible spaces, along accessible routes, or as parts of accessible elements (for example, light switches and dispenser controls) shall comply with 4.27.

(13) If emergency warning systems are provided, then they shall include both audible alarms complying with 4.28.2 and visual alarms complying with 4.28.3. In facilities with sleeping accommodations, the sleeping accommodations shall have an alarm system complying with 4.28.4. Emergency warning systems in health care facilities may be modified to suit standard health care alarm design practice.

(14) Tactile warnings shall be provided at hazardous conditions as specified in 4.29.3.

(15) If signs are provided, they shall comply with 4.30. In addition, permanent signage that identifies rooms and spaces shall also comply with 4.30.4 and 4.30.6.

EXCEPTION: The provisions of 4.30.4 are not mandatory for temporary information on room and space signage, such as current occupant's name, provided the permanent room or space identification complies with 4.30.4.

(16) Public telephones:

(a) If public telephones are provided, then accessible public telephones shall comply with 4.31, Telephones, and the following table:

Number of public telephones provided on each floor:	Number of telephones required to be accessible:*
1 or more single unit installations	1 per floor
1 bank**	1 per floor
2 or more banks**	1 per bank. Accessible unit may be installed as a single unit in proximity (either visible or with signage) to the bank. At least one public telephone per floor shall meet the requirements for a forward reach telephone.***

*Additional public telephones may be installed at any height. Unless otherwise specified, accessible telephones may be either forward or side reach telephones.

**A bank consists of two or more adjacent public telephones, often installed as a unit.

***EXCEPTION:* For exterior installations only, if dial tone first service is not available, then a side reach telephone may be installed instead of the required forward reach telephone (i.e., one telephone in proximity to each bank shall comply with 4.31).

(b) At least one of the public telephones complying with 4.31, Telephones, shall be equipped with a volume control. The installation of additional volume controls is encouraged, and these may be installed on any public telephone provided.

(17) If fixed or built-in seating, tables, or work surfaces are provided in accessible spaces, at least 5 percent, but always at least one, of seating spaces, tables, or work surfaces shall comply with 4.32.

(18) Assembly areas:

(a) If places of assembly are provided, they shall comply with the following table:

Capacity of Seating & Assembly Areas	Number of Required Wheelchair Locations
50 to 75	3
76 to 100	4
101 to 150	5
151 to 200	6
201 to 300	7
301 to 400	8
401 to 500	9
501 to 1,000	*
over 1,000	**

* 2 percent of total.
** 20 plus 1 for each 100 over 1,000.

(b) Assembly areas with audio-amplification systems shall have a listening system complying with 4.33 to assist a reasonable number of people, but no fewer than two, with severe hearing loss. For assembly areas without amplification systems and for spaces used primarily as meeting and conference rooms, a permanently installed or portable listening system shall be provided. If portable systems are used for conference or meeting rooms, the system may serve more than one room.

4.1.3 Accessible Housing. Accessible housing shall comply with the requirements of 4.1 and 4.34 except as noted below:

(1) *Elevators:* Where provided, elevators shall comply with 4.10. Elevators or other accessible means of vertical movement are not required in residential facilities when:

(a) No accessible dwelling units are located above or below the accessible grade level; and

(b) At least one of each type of common area and amenity provided for use of residents and visitors is available at the accessible grade level.

(2) *Entrances:* Entrances complying with 4.14 shall be provided as necessary to achieve access to and egress from buildings and facilities.

EXCEPTION: In projects consisting of one-to-four family dwellings where accessible entrances would be extraordinarily costly due to site conditions or local code restrictions, accessible entrances are required only to those buildings containing accessible dwelling units.

(3) *Common Areas:* At least one of each type of common area and amenity in each project shall be accessible and shall be located on an accessible route to any accessible dwelling unit.

4.1.4 Occupancy Classifications. Buildings and facilities shall comply with these standards to the extent noted in this section for various occupancy classifications, unless otherwise modified by a special application section. Occupancy classifications, and the facilities covered under each category include, but are not necessarily limited to, the listing which follows:

(1) *General Exceptions.* Accessibility is not required to elevator pits, elevator penthouses, mechanical rooms, piping or equipment catwalks, lookout galleries, electrical and telephone closets, and general utility rooms.

(2) *Military Exclusions.* The following facilities need not be designed to be accessible, but accessibility is recommended since the intended use of the facility may change with time.

(a) Unaccompanied personnel housing, closed messes, vehicle and aircraft maintenance facilities, where all work is performed by able-bodied military personnel, and, in general, all facilities which are intended for use or occupancy by able-bodied military personnel only.

(b) Those portions of Reserve and National Guard facilities which are designed and constructed primarily for use by able-bodied military personnel. This exclusion does not apply to those portions of a building or facility which may be open to the public or which may be used by the public during the conduct of normal business or which may be used by physically handicapped persons employed or seeking employment at such building or facility. These portions of the building or facility shall be accessible.

(c) Where the number of accessible spaces required is determined by the design capacity of a facility (such as parking or assembly areas), the number of able-bodied military persons used in determining the design capacity need not be counted when computing the number of accessible spaces required.

(3) *Military Housing.* In the case of military housing, which is primarily available for able-bodied military personnel and their dependents, at least 5

percent of the total but at least one unit (on an installation-by-installation basis) of all housing constructed will be designed and built to be either accessible or readily and easily modifiable to be accessible, but in any event, modification of individual units (including the making of adaptations), will be accomplished on a high priority basis when a requirement is identified. Common areas such as walks, streets, parking and play areas, and common entrances to multi-unit facilities shall be designed and built to be accessible.

(4) Assembly. Assembly occupancy includes, among others, the use of a building or structure, or a portion thereof, for the gathering together of persons for purposes such as civic, social or religious functions, recreation, food or drink consumption, or awaiting transportation. A room or space used for assembly purposes by less than fifty (50) persons and accessory to another occupancy shall be included as a part of that major occupancy. For purposes of these standards, assembly occupancies shall include the following:

Facilities	Application
Amusement arcades	All areas for which the intended use will require public access or which may result in employment of physically handicapped persons.
Amusement park structures	
Arenas	
Armories	
Art galleries	
Auditoriums	
Banquet halls	
Bleachers	
Bowling alleys	
Carnivals	
Churches	
Clubs	
Community halls	
Courtrooms (public areas)	
Dance halls	
Drive-in theaters	
Exhibition halls	
Fairs	
Funeral parlors	
Grandstands	
Gymnasiums	
Motion picture theaters	
Indoor & outdoor swimming pools	
Indoor & outdoor tennis courts	
Lecture halls	
Libraries*	
Museums	
Night clubs	
Passenger stations	
Pool & billiard halls	
Restaurants**	
Skating rinks	

Facilities	Application
Stadiums	All areas for which the intended use will require public access or which may result in employment of physically handicapped persons.
Taverns & bars	
Television studios admitting audiences	
Theaters	

*See Part 8 for special applications.
**See Part 5 for special applications.

(5) Business. Business occupancy includes, among others, the use of a building or structure, or a portion thereof, for office, professional or service type transactions, including storage of records and accounts.

Facilities	Application
Animal hospitals, kennels, pounds	All areas for which the intended use will require public access or which may result in employment of physically handicapped persons.
Automobile and other motor vehicle showrooms	
Banks	
Barber shops	
Beauty shops	
Car wash	
Civic administration	
Clinic, outpatient	
Dry cleaning	
Educational above 12th grade	
Electronic data processing	
Fire stations	
Florists & nurseries	
Laboratories: testing & research	
Laundries	
Motor vehicle service stations	
Police stations	
Post offices*	
Print shops	
Professional services: attorney, dentist, physician, engineer, etc.	
Radio & T.V. stations	
Telephone exchanges	

*See Part 9 for special applications.

(6) Educational. Educational occupancy includes, among others, the use of a building or structure, or portion thereof, by six or more persons at any time for educational purposes through the 12th grade.

Schools for business or vocational training shall conform to the requirements of the trade, vocation or business taught.

Facilities	Application
Academies Kindergarten Nursery schools Schools	All areas shall comply.

(7) Factory Industrial. Factory industrial occupancy includes, among others, the use of a building or structure, or portion thereof, for assembling, disassembling, fabricating, finishing, manufacturing, packaging, processing or other operations that are not classified as a Hazardous Occupancy.

Facilities	Application

Aircraft
Appliances
Athletic equipment
Automobile and other
  motor vehicle
Bakeries
Beverages
Bicycles
Boats, building
Brick and masonry
Broom or brush
Business machines
Canvas or similar
Cameras and photo
  equipment
Carpets & rugs, including
  cleaning
Ceramic products
Clothing
Construction &
  agricultural machinery
Disinfectants
Dry cleaning & dyeing
Electronics
Engines, including
  rebuilding
Film, photographic
Food processing
Foundries
Furniture
Glass products
Gypsum
Hemp products
Ice
Jute products
Laundries
Leather products
Machinery
Metal
Motion pictures &
  television film
Musical instruments
Optical goods
Paper products
Plastic products
	All areas for which the intended use will require public access or which may result in employment of physically handicapped persons.

Facilities	Application

Printing or publishing
Recreational vehicles
Refuse incineration
Shoes
Soaps & detergents
Steel products:
  fabrication, assembly
Textiles
Tobacco
Trailers
Upholstering
Wood, distribution
Millwork
Woodworking, cabinet
Postal mail:
  processing facilities*
	All areas for which the intended use will require public access or which may result in employment of physically handicapped persons.

*See Part 9 for special applications.

(8) Hazardous. Hazardous occupancy includes, among others, the use of a building or structure, or a portion thereof, that involves the manufacturing, processing, generation or storage of corrosive, highly toxic, highly combustible, flammable or explosive materials that constitute a high fire or explosive hazard, including loose combustible fibers, dust and unstable materials.

Facilities	Application
Combustible dust Combustible fibers Combustible liquid Corrosive liquids Explosive material Flammable gas Flammable liquid Liquified petroleum gas Nitromethane Oxidizing materials Organic peroxide	All areas for which the intended use will require public access or which may result in employment of physically handicapped persons.

(9) Institutional. Institutional occupancy includes, among others, the use of a building or structure, or any portion thereof, in which people have physical or medical treatment or care, or in which the liberty of the occupants is restricted. Institutional occupancies shall include the following subgroups:

(a) Institutional occupancies for the care of children, including:

Facilities	Application
Child care facilities	All public use, common use, or areas which may result in employment of physically handicapped persons.

(b) Institutional occupancies used for medical or other treatment or care of persons, some of whom are suffering from physical or mental illness, disease or infirmity, including:

Facilities	Application
Long Term Care Facilities: (including Skilled Nursing Facilities, Intermediate Care Facilities, Bed & Care, and Nursing Homes).	At least 50 percent of patient toilets and bedrooms; all public use, common use or areas which may result in employment of physically handicapped persons.
Outpatient Facilities:	All patient toilets and bedrooms, all public use, common use, or areas which may result in employment of physically handicapped persons.

Hospital*:

Facilities	Application
General Purpose Hospital:	At least 10 percent of patient toilets and bedrooms, all public use, common use, or areas which may result in employment of physically handicapped persons.
Special Purpose Hospital: (Hospitals that treat conditions that affect mobility).	All patient toilets and bedrooms, all public use, common use, or areas which may result in employment of physically handicapped persons.

* See Part 6 for special applications.

(c) Institutional occupancies where the occupants are under some degree of restraint or restriction for security reasons including:

Facilities	Application
Jails Prisons Reformatories Other detention or correctional facilities	5 percent of residential units available, or at least one unit, whichever is greater; all common use, visitor use, or areas which may result in employment of physically handicapped persons.

(10) Mercantile*. Mercantile occupancy includes, among others, all buildings and structures or parts thereof, for the display and sale of merchandise, and involving stocks of goods, wares or merchandise incidental to such purposes and accessible to the public.

Facilities	Application
Department stores Drug stores Markets Retail stores Shopping centers Sales rooms	All areas for which the intended use will require public access or which may result in employment of physically handicapped persons.

* See Part 7 for special applications.

(11) Residential. Residential occupancy includes, among others, the use of a building or structure, or portion thereof, for sleeping accommodations when not classed as an institutional occupancy. Residential occupancies shall comply with the requirements of 4.1 and 4.34 except as follows:

(a) Residential occupancies where the occupants are primarily transient in nature (less than 30 days) including:

Facilities	Application
Hotels Motels Boarding houses	5 percent of the total units, or at least one, whichever is greater, and all public use, common use, and areas which may result in employment of physically handicapped persons.

(b) Residential occupancies in multiple dwellings where the occupants are primarily permanent in nature, including:

Facilities	Application
Multifamily housing (Apartment houses):	
Federally assisted	5 percent of the total, or at least one unit, whichever is greater, in projects of 15 or more dwelling units, or as determined by the appropriate Federal agency following a local needs assessment conducted by local government bodies or states under applicable regulations.
Federally owned	5 percent of the total, or at least one unit, whichever is greater.
Dormitories	5 percent of the total, or at least one unit, whichever is greater.

(c) Residential occupancies in one (1) and two (2) family dwellings where the occupancies are primarily permanent in nature and not classified as preceding residential categories or as institutional.

Facilities	Application
One and two family dwelling:	
Federally assisted, rental	5 percent of the total, or at least one unit, whichever is greater, in projects of 15 or more dwelling units, or as determined by the appropriate Federal agency following a local needs assessment conducted by local government bodies or states under applicable regulations.
Federally assisted, homeownership	To be determined by home buyer.
Federally owned	5 percent of the total, or at least one unit, whichever is greater.

(12) Storage. Storage occupancy includes, among others, the use of a building or structure, or portion thereof, for storage that is not classified as a Hazardous Occupancy.

Facilities	Application
Metal desks	All areas for which the intended use will require public access or which may result in employment of physically handicapped persons shall comply.
Electrical coils	
Electrical motors	
Dry cell batteries	
Metal parts	
Empty cans	
Stoves	
Washers & Dryers	
Metal cabinets	
Glass bottles with noncombustible liquid	
Mirrors	
Foods in non-combustible containers	
Frozen foods	
Meats	
Fresh fruits and vegetables	
Dairy products	
Beer or wine up to 12 percent alcohol	
Distribution transformers	

Facilities	Application
Cement in bags	All areas for which the intended use will require public access or which may result in employment of physically handicapped persons shall comply.
Electrical insulators	
Gypsum board	
Inert pigments	
Dry insecticides	

(13) Utility and Miscellaneous. Utility and miscellaneous occupancies include, among others, accessory buildings and structures, such as:

Facilities	Application
Fences over 6 ft. high	All areas for which the intended use will require public access or which may result in employment of physically handicapped persons shall comply.
Tanks	
Cooling towers	
Retaining walls	
Buildings of less than 1,000 sq. ft. such as: Private garages Carports Sheds Agricultural buildings	

4.1.5 Accessible Buildings: Additions.
Each addition to an existing building shall comply with 4.1.1 to 4.1.4 of 4.1, Minimum Requirements, except as follows:

(1) **Entrances.** If a new addition to a building or facility does not have an entrance, then at least one entrance in the existing building or facility shall comply with 4.1.4, Entrances.

(2) **Accessible route.** If the only accessible entrance to the addition is located in the existing building or facility, then at least one accessible route shall comply with 4.3, Accessible Route, and shall provide access through the existing building or facility to all rooms, elements, and spaces in the new addition.

(3) **Toilet and bathing facilities.** If there are no toilet rooms and bathing facilities in the addition and these facilities are provided in the existing building, then at least one toilet and bathing facility in the existing building shall comply with 4.22, Toilet Rooms, or 4.23, Bathrooms, Bathing Facilities, and Shower Rooms.

(4) **Elements, spaces, and common areas.** If elements, spaces, or common areas are located in the existing building and they are not provided in the addition, then consideration should be given to making those elements, spaces, and common areas accessible in the existing building.

EXCEPTIONS: Mechanical rooms, storage areas, and other such minor additions which normally are not frequented by the public or employees of the facility are excepted from 4.1.5.

(5) Housing: (Reserved).

4.1.6 Accessible Buildings: Alterations.

(1) General. Alterations to existing buildings or facilities shall comply with the following:

(a) If existing elements, spaces, essential features, or common areas are altered, then each such altered element, space, feature, or area shall comply with the applicable provisions of 4.1.1 to 4.1.4 of 4.1, Minimum Requirements.

(b) If power-driven vertical access equipment (e.g., escalator) is planned or installed where none existed previously, or if new stairs (other than stairs installed to meet emergency exit requirements) requiring major structural changes are planned or installed where none existed previously, then a means of accessible vertical access shall be provided that complies with 4.7, Curb Ramps; 4.8, Ramps; 4.10, Elevators; or 4.11, Platform Lifts; except to the extent where it is structurally impracticable in transit facilities.

(c) If alterations of single elements, when considered together, amount to an alteration of a space of a building or facility, the entire space shall be made accessible.

(d) No alteration of an existing element, space, or area of a building shall impose a requirement for greater accessibility than that which would be required for new construction. For example, if the elevators and stairs in a building are being altered and the elevators are, in turn, being made accessible, then no accessibility modifications are required to the stairs connecting levels connected by the elevator.

(e) If the alteration work is limited solely to the electrical, mechanical, or plumbing system and does not involve the alteration of any elements and spaces required to be accessible under these standards, then 4.1.6(3) does not apply.

(f) No new accessibility alterations will be required of existing elements or spaces previously constructed or altered in compliance with earlier standards issued pursuant to the Architectural Barriers Act of 1968, as amended.

(g) Mechanical rooms and other spaces which normally are not frequented by the public or employees of the building or facility or which by nature of their use are not required by the Architectural Barriers Act to be accessible are excepted from the requirements of 4.1.6.

(2) Where a building or facility is vacated and it is totally altered, then it shall be altered to comply with 4.1.1 to 4.1.5 of 4.1, Minimum Requirements, except to the extent where it is structurally impracticable.

(3) Where substantial alteration occurs to a building or facility, then each element or space that is altered or added shall comply with the applicable provisions of 4.1.1 to 4.1.4 of 4.1, Minimum Requirements, except to the extent where it is structurally impracticable. The altered building or facility shall contain:

(a) At least one accessible route complying with 4.3, Accessible Route, and 4.1.6(a);

(b) At least one accessible entrance complying with 4.14, Entrances. If additional entrances are altered then they shall comply with 4.1.6(a); and

(c) The following toilet facilities, whichever is greater:

(i) At least one toilet facility for each sex in the altered building complying with 4.22, Toilet Rooms, and 4.23, Bathrooms, Bathing Facilities, and Shower Rooms.

(ii) At least one toilet facility for each sex on each substantially altered floor, where such facilities are provided, complying with 4.22, Toilet Rooms; and 4.23, Bathrooms, Bathing Facilities, and Shower Rooms.

(d) In making the determination as to what constitutes "substantial alteration," the agency issuing standards for the facility shall consider the total cost of all alterations (including but not limited to electrical, mechanical, plumbing, and structural changes) for a building or facility within any twelve (12) month period. For guidance in implementing this provision, an alteration to any building or facility is to be considered substantial if the total cost for this twelve month period amounts to 50 percent or more of the full and fair cash value of the building as defined in 3.5.

EXCEPTION: If the cost of the elements and spaces required by 4.1.6(3)(a), (b), or (c) exceeds 15 percent of the total cost of all other alterations, then a schedule may be established by the standard-setting and/or funding agency to provide the required improvements within a 5-year period.

EXCEPTION: Consideration shall be given to providing accessible elements and spaces in each altered building or facility complying with:

(i)   4.6, Parking and Passenger Loading Zones,
(ii)   4.15, Drinking Fountains and Water Coolers,
(iii)   4.25, Storage,
(iv)   4.28, Alarms,
(v)   4.31, Telephones,
(vi)   4.32, Seating, Tables, and Work Surfaces,
(vii)   4.33, Assembly Areas.

(4) Special technical provisions for alterations to existing buildings or facilities:

(a) *Ramps. Curb ramps and ramps to be con-structed on existing sites or in existing buildings or facilities may have slopes and rises as shown in Table 2 if space limitations prohibit the use of a 1:12 slope or less.*

Table 2
Allowable Ramp Dimensions for Construction in Existing Sites, Buildings, and Facilities

Slope*	Maximum Rise		Maximum Run	
	in	mm	ft	m
Steeper than 1:10 but no steeper than 1:8	3	75	2	0.6
Steeper than 1:12 but no steeper than 1:10	6	150	5	1.5

*A slope steeper than 1:8 not allowed.

(b) *Stairs. Full extension of stair handrails shall not be required in alterations where such extensions would be hazardous or impossible due to plan configuration.*

(c) *Elevators.*

(i) *If a safety door edge is provided in existing automatic elevators, then the automatic door reopen-ing devices may be omitted (see 4.10.6).*

(ii) *Where existing shaft or structural elements prohibit strict compliance with 4.10.9, then the minimum floor area dimensions may be reduced by the minimum amount necessary, but in no case shall they be less than 48 in by 48 in (1220 mm by 1220 mm).*

(d) *Doors.*

(i) *Where existing elements prohibit strict com-pliance with the clearance requirements of 4.13.5, a projection of 5/8 in (16 mm) maximum will be per-mitted for the latch side door stop.*

(ii) *If existing thresholds measure 3/4 in (19 mm) high or less, and are beveled or modified to provide a beveled edge on each side, then they may be retained.*

(e) *Toilet rooms. Where alterations to existing facilities make strict compliance with 4.22 and 4.23 structurally impracticable, the addition of one "unisex" toilet per floor containing one water closet complying with 4.16 and one lavatory complying*

with 4.19, located adjacent to existing toilet facilities, will be acceptable in lieu of making existing toilet facilities for each sex accessible.

EXCEPTION: In instances of alteration work where provision of a standard stall (Fig. 30(a)) is structurally impracticable or where plumbing code requirements prevent combining existing stalls to provide space, an alternate stall (Fig. 30(b)) may be provided in lieu of the standard stall.

(f) *Assembly areas.*

(i) *In alterations where it is structurally impractic-able to disperse seating throughout the assembly area, seating may be located in collected areas as structurally feasible. Seating shall adjoin an access-ible route that also serves as a means of emergency egress.*

(ii) *In alterations where it is structurally imprac-ticable to alter all performing areas to be on an accessible route, then at least one of each type shall be made accessible.*

(5) *Housing. (Reserved).*

4.1.7 Accessible Buildings: Historic Preservation.

(1) *Applicability.*

(a) *As a general rule, the accessibility provisions of part 4 shall be applied to "qualified" historic buildings and facilities. "Qualified" buildings or facilities are those buildings and facilities that are eligible for listing in the National Register of Historic Places, or such properties designated as historic under a statute of the appropriate state or local government body. Comments of the Advisory Council on Historic Preservation shall be obtained when required by Section 106 of the National Historic Preservation Act of 1966, as amended, 16 U.S.C. 470 and 36 CFR Part 800, before any alteration to a qualified historic building.*

(b) *The Advisory Council shall determine, on a case-by-case basis, whether provisions required by part 4 for accessible routes (exterior and interior), ramps, entrances, toilets, parking, and displays and signage, would threaten or destroy the historic significance of the building or facility.*

(c) *If the Advisory Council determines that any of the accessibility requirements for features listed in 4.1.7(1) would threaten or destroy the historic significance of a building or facility, then the special application provisions of 4.1.7(2) for that fea-ture may be utilized. The special application pro-visions listed under 4.1.7(2) may only be utilized following a written determination by the Advisory Council that application of a requirement contained in part 4 would threaten or destroy the historic integrity of a qualified building or facility.*

(2) Historic Preservation: Minimum Requirements.

(a) *At least one accessible route complying with 4.3 from a site access point to an accessible entrance shall be provided.*

EXCEPTION: *A ramp with a slope no greater than 1:6 for a run not to exceed 2 ft (610 mm) may be used as part of an accessible route at an entrance.*

(b) *At least one accessible entrance which is used by the public complying with 4.14 shall be provided.*

EXCEPTION: *If it is determined that no entrance used by the public can comply with 4.14, then access at any entrance not used by the general public but open (unlocked) with directional signs at the primary entrance may be used.*

(c) *If toilets are provided, then at least one toilet facility complying with 4.22 and 4.1.6 shall be provided along an accessible route that complies with 4.3. Such toilet facility may be "unisex" in design.*

(d) *Accessible routes from an accessible entrance to all publicly used spaces on at least the level of the accessible entrance shall be provided. Access should be provided to all levels of a building or facility in compliance with 4.1 whenever practical.*

(e) *Displays and written information, documents, etc., should be located where they can be seen by a seated person. Exhibits and signage displayed horizontally, e.g., books, should be no higher than 44 in (1120 mm) above the floor surface.*

4.2 Space Allowance and Reach Ranges

4.2.1* Wheelchair Passage Width. The minimum clear width for single wheelchair passage shall be 32 in (815 mm) at a point and 36 in (915 mm) continuously (see Fig. 1 and 24(e)).

4.2.2 Width for Wheelchair Passing. The minimum width for two wheelchairs to pass is 60 in (1525 mm) (see Fig. 2).

4.2.3* Wheelchair Turning Space. The space required for a wheelchair to make a 180-degree turn is a clear space of 60 in (1525 mm) diameter (see Fig. 3(a)) or a T-shaped space (see Fig. 3(b)).

4.2.4* Clear Floor or Ground Space for Wheelchairs.

4.2.4.1 Size and Approach. The minimum clear floor or ground space required to accommodate a single, stationary wheelchair occupant is 30 in by 48 in (760 mm by 1220 mm) (see Fig. 4(a)). The minimum clear floor or ground space for wheelchairs may be positioned for forward or parallel approach to an object

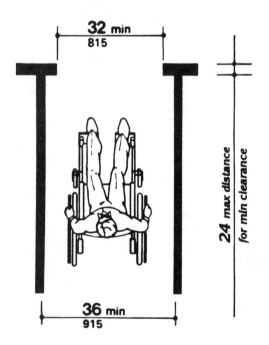

**Fig. 1
Minimum Clear Width
for Single Wheelchair**

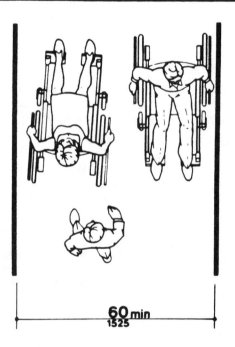

**Fig. 2
Minimum Clear Width
for Two Wheelchairs**

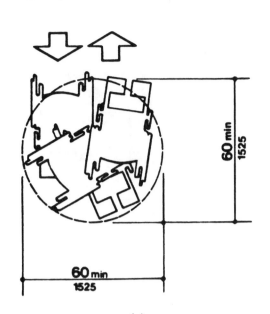

(a)
60-in (1525-mm)-Diameter Space

(b)
T-Shaped Space for 180° Turns

Fig. 3
Wheelchair Turning Space

(see Fig. 4(b) and (c)). Clear floor or ground space for wheelchairs may be part of the knee space required under some objects.

4.2.4.2 Relationship of Maneuvering Clearance to Wheelchair Spaces. One full unobstructed side of the clear floor or ground space for a wheelchair shall adjoin or overlap an accessible route or adjoin another wheelchair clear floor space. If a clear floor space is located in an alcove or otherwise confined on all or part of three sides, additional maneuvering clearances shall be provided as shown in Fig. 4(d) and (e).

4.2.4.3 Surfaces for Wheelchair Spaces. Clear floor or ground spaces for wheelchairs shall comply with 4.5.

4.2.5 Forward Reach. If the clear floor space only allows forward approach to an object, the maximum high forward reach allowed shall be 48 in (1220 mm) (see Fig. 5(a)). *The minimum low forward reach is 15 in (380 mm).* If the high forward reach is over an obstruction, reach and clearances shall be as shown in Fig. 5(b).

4.2.6* Side Reach. If the clear floor space allows parallel approach by a person in a wheelchair, the maximum high side reach allowed shall be 54 in (1370 mm) and the low side reach shall be no less than 9 in (230 mm) above the floor (Fig. 6(a) and (b)).

If the side reach is over an obstruction, the reach and clearances shall be as shown in Fig. 6(c).

4.3 Accessible Route.

4.3.1* General. All walks, halls, corridors, aisles, and other spaces that are part of an accessible route shall comply with 4.3.

4.3.2 Location.

(1) At least one accessible route *within the boundary of the site* shall be provided from public transportation stops, accessible parking, and accessible passenger loading zones, and public streets or sidewalks to the accessible building entrance they serve.

(2) At least one accessible route shall connect accessible buildings, facilities, elements, and spaces that are on the same site.

(3) At least one accessible route shall connect accessible building or facility entrances with all accessible spaces and elements and with all accessible dwelling units within the building or facility.

(4) An accessible route shall connect at least one accessible entrance of each accessible dwelling unit with those exterior and interior spaces and facilities that serve the accessible dwelling unit.

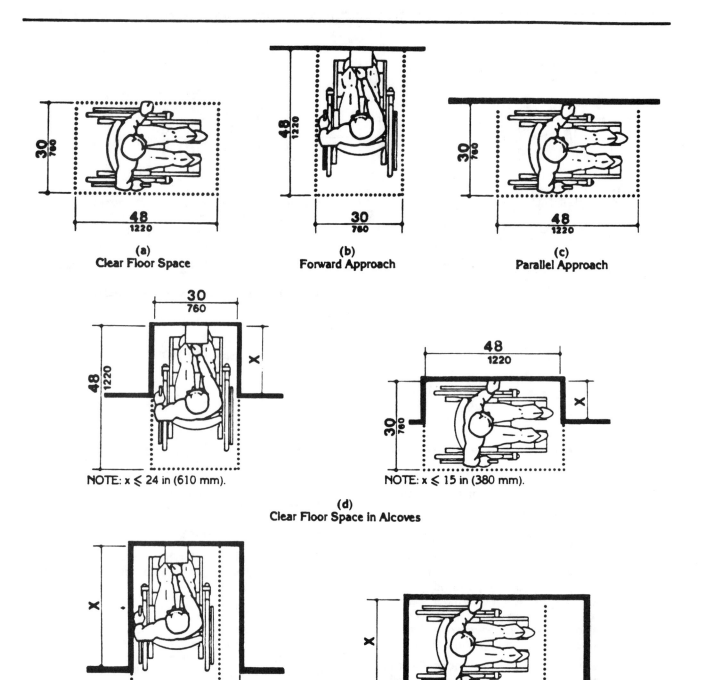

(a)
Clear Floor Space

(b)
Forward Approach

(c)
Parallel Approach

NOTE: x ≤ 24 in (610 mm).

NOTE: x ≤ 15 in (380 mm).

(d)
Clear Floor Space in Alcoves

NOTE: If x > 24 in (610 mm), then an additional maneuvering clearance of 6 in (150 mm) shall be provided as shown.

NOTE: If x > 15 in (380 mm), then an additional maneuvering clearance of 12 in (305 mm) shall be provided as shown.

(e)
Additional Maneuvering Clearances for Alcoves

Fig. 4
Minimum Clear Floor Space for Wheelchairs

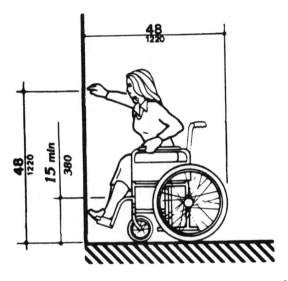

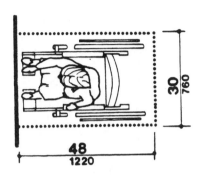

(a)
High Forward Reach Limit

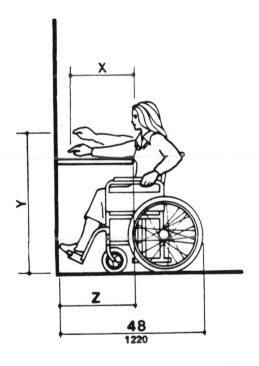

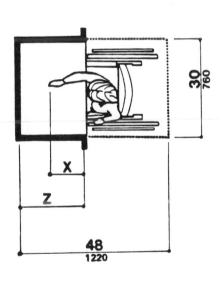

NOTE: x shall be ≤ 25 in (635 mm); z shall be ≥ x. When x < 20 in (510 mm), then y shall be 48 in (1220 mm) maximum. When x is 20 to 25 in (510 to 635 mm), then y shall be 44 in (1120 mm) maximum.

(b)
Maximum Forward Reach over an Obstruction

Fig. 5
Forward Reach

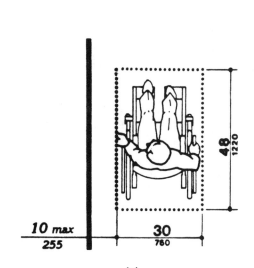

(a)
Clear Floor Space   Parallel Approach

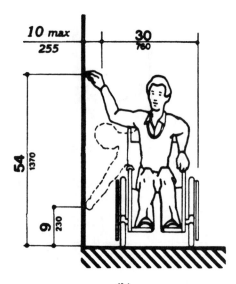

(b)
High and Low   Side Reach Limits

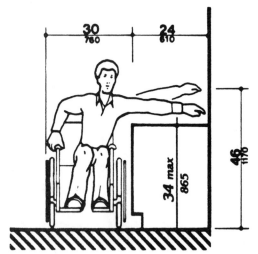

(c)
Maximum Side Reach over Obstruction

Fig. 6
Side Reach

4.3.3 Width. The minimum clear width of an accessible route shall be 36 in (915 mm) except at doors (see 4.13.5). If a person in a wheelchair must make a turn around an obstruction, the minimum clear width of the accessible route shall be as shown in Fig. 7.

4.3.4 Passing Space. If an accessible route has less than 60 in (1525 mm) clear width, then passing spaces at least 60 in by 60 in (1525 mm by 1525 mm) shall be located at reasonable intervals not to exceed 200 ft (61 m). A T-intersection of two corridors or walks is an acceptable passing place.

4.3.5 Head Room. Accessible routes shall comply with 4.4.2.

4.3.6 Surface Textures. The surface of an accessible route shall comply with 4.5.

4.3.7 Slope. An accessible route with a running slope greater than 1:20 is a ramp and shall comply with 4.8. Nowhere shall the cross slope of an accessible route exceed 1:50.

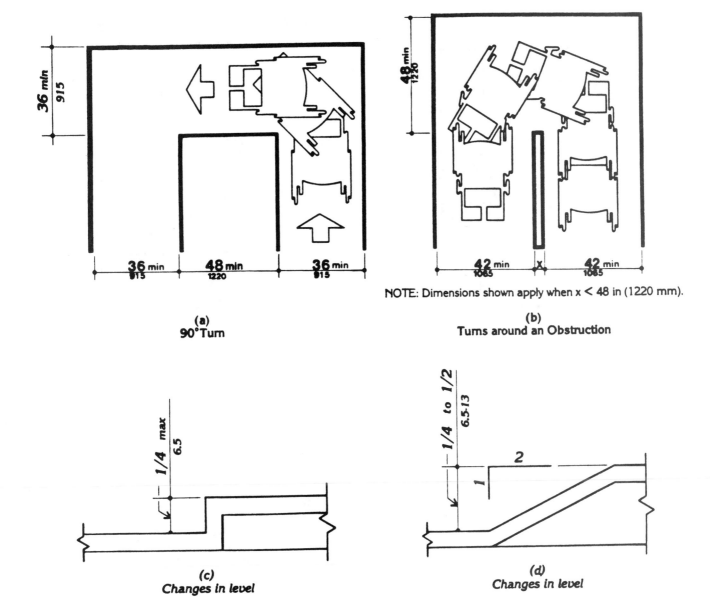

(a)
90° Turn

(b)
Turns around an Obstruction

NOTE: Dimensions shown apply when x < 48 in (1220 mm).

(c)
Changes in level

(d)
Changes in level

Fig. 7
Width of Accessible Route

4.3.8 Changes in Levels. Changes in levels along an accessible route shall comply with 4.5.2. If an accessible route has changes in level greater than 1/2 in (13 mm), then a curb ramp, ramp, elevator, or platform lift shall be provided that complies with 4.7, 4.8, 4.10, or 4.11, respectively. Stairs shall not be part of an accessible route.

4.3.9 Doors. Doors along an accessible route shall comply with 4.13.

4.3.10* Egress. Accessible routes serving any accessible space or element shall also serve as a means of egress for emergencies or connect to an accessible place of refuge. Such accessible routes and places of refuge shall comply with the requirements of the administrative authority having jurisdiction. *Where fire code provisions require more than one means of egress from any space or room, then more than one accessible means of egress shall also be provided for handicapped people. Arrange egress so as to be readily accessible from all accessible rooms and spaces.*

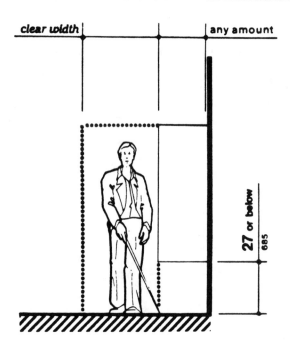

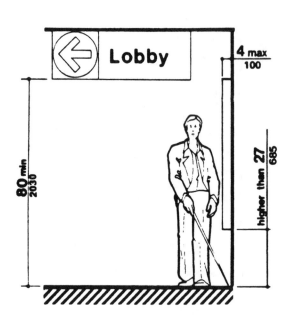

(a)
Walking Parallel to a Wall

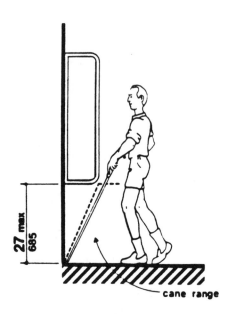

(b)
Walking Perpendicular to a Wall

Fig. 8
Protruding Objects

4.4 Protruding Objects.

4.4.1* General. Objects projecting from walls (for example, telephones) with their leading edges between 27 in and 80 in (685 mm and 2030 mm) above the finished floor shall protrude no more than 4 in (100 mm) into walks, halls, corridors, passageways, or aisles (see Fig. 8(a)). Objects mounted with their leading edges at or below 27 in (685 mm) above the finished floor may protrude any amount (see Fig. 8(a) and (b)). Free-standing objects mounted on posts or pylons may overhang 12 in (305 mm) maximum from 27 in to 80 in (685 mm to 2030 mm) above the ground or finished floor (see Fig. 8(c) and (d)). Protruding objects shall not reduce the clear width of an accessible route or maneuvering space (see Fig. 8(e)).

4.4.2 Head Room. Walks, halls, corridors, passageways, aisles, or other circulation spaces shall have 80 in (2030 mm) minimum clear head room (see Fig. 8(a)). *If vertical clearance of an area adjoining an accessible route is reduced to less than 80 in (nominal dimension), a barrier to warn blind or visually-impaired persons shall be provided (see Fig. 8(c)).*

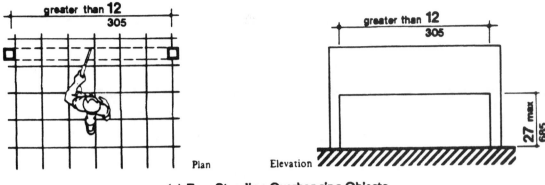

(c) Free-Standing Overhanging Objects

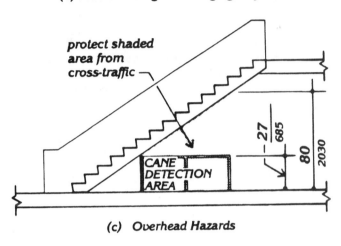

(c) Overhead Hazards

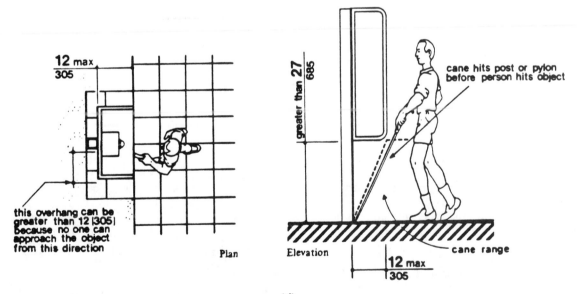

(d)
Objects Mounted on Posts or Pylons

Fig. 8
Protruding Objects *(Continued)*

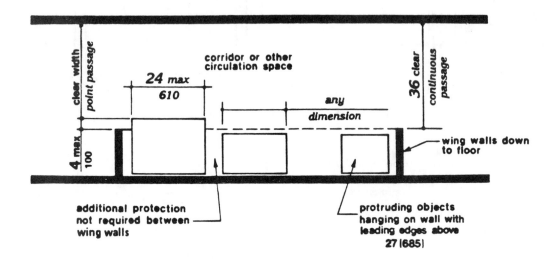

(e)
Example of Protection around Wall-Mounted Objects and Measurements of Clear Widths

Fig. 8
Protruding Objects *(Continued)*

4.5 Ground and Floor Surfaces.

4.5.1* General. Ground and floor surfaces along accessible routes and in accessible rooms and spaces, including floors, walks, ramps, stairs, and curb ramps, shall be stable, firm, *slip-resistant*, and shall comply with 4.5.

4.5.2 Changes in Level. Changes in level up to 1/4 in (6 mm) may be vertical and without edge treatment *(see Fig. 7(c))*. Changes in level between 1/4 in and 1/2 in (6 mm and 13 mm) shall be beveled with a slope no greater than 1:2 *(see Fig. 7(d))*. Changes in level greater than 1/2 in (13 mm) shall be accomplished by means of a ramp that complies with 4.7 or 4.8.

4.5.3* Carpet. If carpet or carpet tile is used on a ground or floor surface, then it shall be securely attached; have a firm cushion, pad, or backing or no cushion or pad; and have a level loop, textured loop, level cut pile, or level cut/uncut pile texture. The maximum pile height shall be 1/2 in (13 mm). Exposed edges of carpet shall be fastened to floor surfaces and have trim along the entire length of the exposed edge. Carpet edge trim shall comply with 4.5.2. *If carpet tile is used on an accessible ground or floor surface, it shall have a maximum combined thickness of pile, cushion, and backing height of 1/2 in (13 mm) (see Fig. 8(f)).*

4.5.4 Gratings. If gratings are located in walking surfaces, then they shall have spaces no greater than 1/2 in (13 mm) wide in one direction *(see Fig. 8(g))*. If gratings have elongated openings, then they shall be placed so that the long dimension is perpendicular to the dominant direction of travel *(see Fig. 8(h))*.

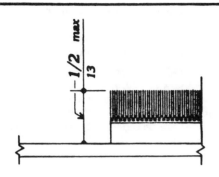

Fig. 8(f)
Carpet Tile Thickness

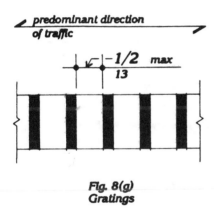

Fig. 8(g)
Gratings

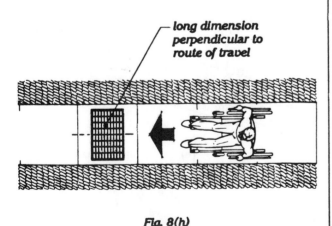

Fig. 8(h)
Grating Orientation

4.6 Parking and Passenger Loading Zones.

4.6.1 Minimum Number. *Parking spaces required to be accessible by 4.1 shall comply with 4.6.2 through 4.6.4. Passenger loading zones required to be accessible by 4.1 shall comply with 4.6.5 and 4.6.6.*

4.6.2 Location. Parking spaces for disabled people and accessible passenger loading zones that serve a particular building shall be *the spaces or zones located closest to the nearest accessible entrance on an accessible route.* In separate parking structures or lots that do not serve a particular building, parking spaces for disabled people shall be located on the shortest possible circulation route to an accessible pedestrian entrance of the parking facility.

4.6.3* Parking Spaces. Parking spaces for disabled people shall be at least 96 in (2440 mm) wide and shall have an adjacent access aisle 60 in (1525 mm) wide minimum (see Fig. 9). Parking access aisles shall be part of an accessible route to the building or facility entrance and shall comply with 4.3. Two accessible parking spaces may share a common access aisle. Parked vehicle overhangs shall not reduce the clear width of an accessible circulation route. *Parking spaces and access aisles shall be level with surface slopes not exceeding 1:50 in all directions.*

EXCEPTION: If accessible parking spaces for vans designed for handicapped persons are provided, each should have an adjacent access aisle at least 96 in (2440 mm) wide complying with 4.5, Ground and Floor Surfaces.

4.6.4* Signage. Accessible parking spaces shall be designated as reserved for the disabled by a sign showing the symbol of accessibility (see 4.30.5). Such signs shall not be obscured by a vehicle parked in the space.

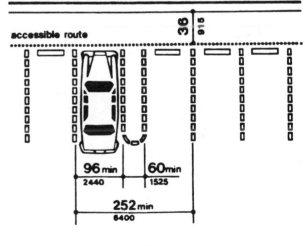

Fig. 9
Dimensions of Parking Spaces

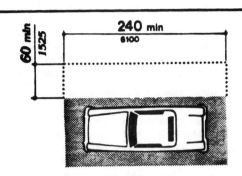

Fig. 10
Access Aisle at Passenger Loading Zones

4.6.5 Passenger Loading Zones. Passenger loading zones shall provide an access aisle at least 60 in (1525 mm) wide and 20 ft (6 m) long adjacent and parallel to the vehicle pull-up space (see Fig. 10). If there are curbs between the access aisle and the vehicle pull-up space, then a curb ramp complying with 4.7 shall be provided. *Vehicle standing spaces and access aisles shall be level with surface slopes not exceeding 1:50 in all directions.*

4.6.6 Vertical Clearance. *Provide minimum vertical clearances of 114 in at accessible passenger loading zones and along vehicle access routes to such areas from site entrances. If accessible van parking spaces are provided, then the minimum vertical clearance should be 114 in.*

4.7 Curb Ramps.

4.7.1 Location. Curb ramps complying with 4.7 shall be provided wherever an accessible route crosses a curb.

4.7.2 Slope. Slopes of curb ramps shall comply with 4.8.2. The slope shall be measured as shown in Fig. 11. *Transitions from ramps to walks, gutters, or streets shall be flush and free of abrupt changes. Maximum slopes of adjoining gutters, road surface immediately adjacent to the curb ramp, or accessible route shall not exceed 1:20.*

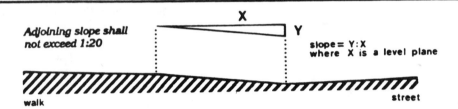

Fig. 11
Measurement of Curb Ramp Slopes

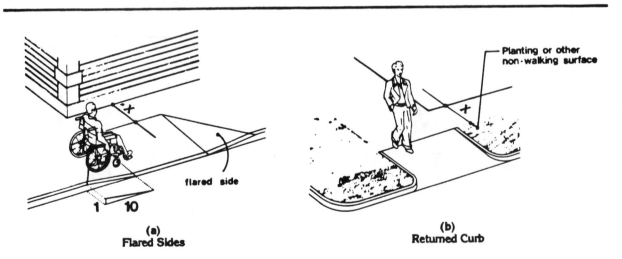

(a)
Flared Sides

(b)
Returned Curb

If X is less than 48 in, then the slope of the flared side shall not exceed 1:12.

Fig. 12
Sides of Curb Ramps

4.7.3 Width. The minimum width of a curb ramp shall be 36 in (915 mm), exclusive of flared sides.

4.7.4 Surface. Surfaces of curb ramps shall comply with 4.5.

4.7.5 Sides of Curb Ramps. If a curb ramp is located where pedestrians must walk across the ramp, *or where it is not protected by handrails or guardrails,* then it shall have flared sides; the maximum slope of the flare shall be 1:10 (see Fig. 12(a)). Curb ramps with returned curbs may be used where pedestrians would not normally walk across the ramp (see Fig. 12(b)).

4.7.6 Built-up Curb Ramps. Built-up curb ramps shall be located so that they do not project into vehicular traffic lanes (see Fig. 13).

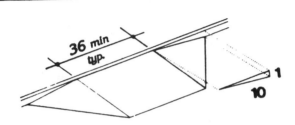

Fig. 13
Built-Up Curb Ramp

4.7.7 Warning Textures. *(Removed and reserved).*

4.7.8 Obstructions. Curb ramps shall be located or protected to prevent their obstruction by parked vehicles.

4.7.9 Location at Marked Crossings. Curb ramps at marked crossings shall be wholly contained within the markings, excluding any flared sides (see Fig. 15).

4.7.10 Diagonal Curb Ramps. If diagonal (or corner type) curb ramps have returned curbs or other well-defined edges, such edges shall be parallel to the direction of pedestrian flow. The bottom of diagonal curb ramps shall have 48 in (1220 mm) minimum clear space as shown in Fig. 15(c) and (d). If diagonal curb ramps are provided at marked crossings, the 48 in (1220 mm) clear space shall be within the markings (see Fig. 15(c) and (d)). If diagonal curb ramps have flared sides, they shall also have at least a 24 in (610 mm) long segment of straight curb located on each side of the curb ramp and within the marked crossing (see Fig. 15(c)).

4.7.11 Islands. Any raised islands in crossings shall be cut through level with the street or have curb ramps at both sides and a level area at least 48 in (1220 mm) long in the part of the island intersected by the crossings (see Fig. 15(a) and (b)).

4.7.12 Uncurbed Intersections. *(Removed and reserved).*

4.8 Ramps.

4.8.1* General. Any part of an accessible route with a slope greater than 1:20 shall be considered a ramp and shall comply with 4.8.

4.8.2* Slope and Rise. The least possible slope shall be used for any ramp. The maximum slope of a ramp in new construction shall be 1:12. The maximum rise for any run shall be 30 in (760 mm) (see Fig. 16). Curb ramps and ramps to be constructed on existing sites or in existing buildings or facilities may have slopes and rises as shown in Table 2 if space limitations prohibit the use of a 1:12 slope or less *(see 4.1.6).*

4.8.3 Clear Width. The minimum clear width of a ramp shall be 36 in (915 mm).

4.8.4 Landings. Ramps shall have level landings at the bottom and top of each run. Landings shall have the following features:

(1) The landing shall be at least as wide as the ramp run leading to it.

(2) The landing length shall be a minimum of 60 in (1525 mm) clear.

(3) If ramps change direction at landings, the minimum landing size shall be 60 in by 60 in (1525 mm by 1525 mm).

(4) If a doorway is located at a landing, then the area in front of the doorway shall comply with 4.13.6.

4.8.5* Handrails. If a ramp run has a rise greater than 6 in (250 mm) or a horizontal projection greater than 72 in (1830 mm), then it shall have handrails on both sides. Handrails are not required on curb ramps. Handrails shall comply with 4.26 and shall have the following features:

(1) Handrails shall be provided along both sides of ramp segments. The inside handrail on switchback or dogleg ramps shall always be continuous.

(2) If handrails are not continuous, they shall extend at least 12 in (305 mm) beyond the top and bottom of the ramp segment and shall be parallel with the floor or ground surface.

(3) The clear space between the handrail and the wall shall be 1-1/2 in (38 mm).

(4) Gripping surfaces shall be continuous.

(5) *Top of handrail gripping surfaces shall be mounted between 30 in and 34 in (760 mm and 865 mm) above ramp surfaces.*

(6) *Ends of handrails shall be either rounded or returned smoothly to floor, wall, or post.*

(7) *Handrails shall not rotate within their fittings.*

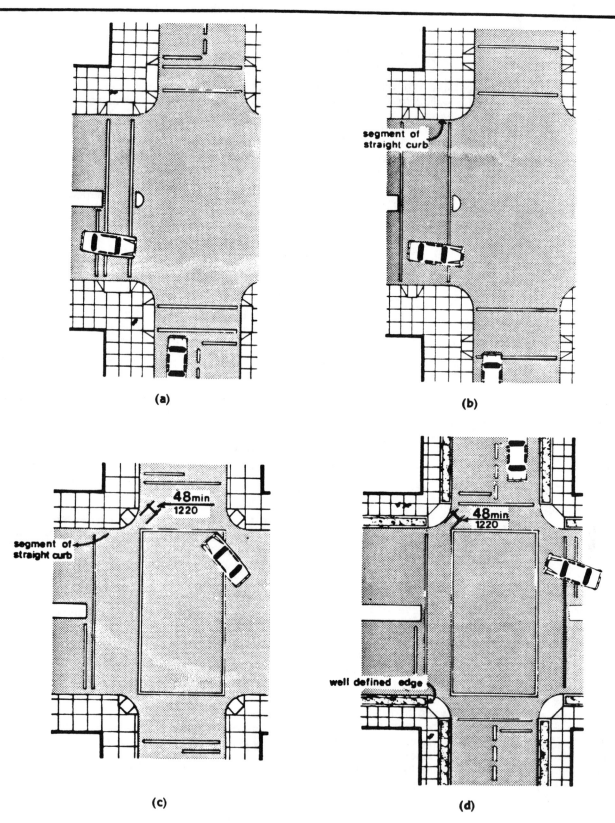

(a)

(b)

(c)

(d)

Fig. 15
Curb Ramps at Marked Crossings

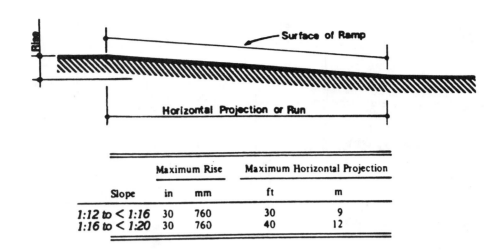

Fig. 16
Components of a Single Ramp Run and Sample Ramp Dimensions

Slope	Maximum Rise		Maximum Horizontal Projection	
	in	mm	ft	m
1:12 to < 1:16	30	760	30	9
1:16 to < 1:20	30	760	40	12

4.8.6 Cross Slope and Surfaces. The cross slope of ramp surfaces shall be no greater than 1:50. Ramp surfaces shall comply with 4.5.

4.8.7 Edge Protection. Ramps and landings with drop-offs shall have curbs, walls, railings, or projecting surfaces that prevent people from slipping off the ramp. Curbs shall be a minimum of 2 in (50 mm) high (see Fig. 17).

4.8.8 Outdoor Conditions. Outdoor ramps and their approaches shall be designed so that water will not accumulate on walking surfaces.

4.9 Stairs.

4.9.1 Minimum Number. Stairs *required to be accessible by 4.1 shall comply with 4.9.*

4.9.2 Treads and Risers. On any given flight of stairs, all steps shall have uniform riser heights and uniform tread widths. Stair treads shall be no less than 11 in (280 mm) wide, measured from riser to riser (see Fig. 18(a)). *Open risers are not permitted on accessible routes.*

4.9.3 Nosings. The undersides of nosings shall not be abrupt. The radius of curvature at the leading edge of the tread shall be no greater than 1/2 in (13 mm). Risers shall be sloped or the underside of the nosing shall have an angle not less than 60 degrees from the horizontal. Nosings shall project no more than 1-1/2 in (38 mm) (see Fig. 18).

4.9.4 Handrails. Stairways shall have handrails at both sides of all stairs. Handrails shall comply with 4.26 and shall have the following features:

(1) Handrails shall be continuous along both sides of stairs. The inside handrail on switchback or dogleg stairs shall always be continuous (see Fig. 19(a) and (b)).

(2) If handrails are not continuous, they shall extend at least 12 in (305 mm) beyond the top riser and at least 12 in (305 mm) plus the width of one tread beyond the bottom riser. At the top, the extension shall be parallel with the floor or ground surface. At the bottom, the handrail shall continue to slope for a distance of the width of one tread from the bottom riser; the remainder of the extension shall be horizontal (see Fig. 19(c) and (d)). Handrail extensions shall comply with 4.4.

(3) The clear space between handrails and wall shall be 1-1/2 in (38 mm).

(4) Gripping surfaces shall be uninterrupted by newel posts, other construction elements, or obstructions.

(5) *Top of handrail gripping surface shall be mounted between 30 in and 34 in (760 mm and 865 mm) above stair nosings.*

(6) *Ends of handrails shall be either rounded or returned smoothly to floor, wall, or post.*

(7) *Handrails shall not rotate within their fittings.*

4.9.5 Tactile Warnings at Stairs. *(Removed and reserved).*

4.9.6 Outdoor Conditions. Outdoor stairs and their approaches shall be designed so that water will not accumulate on walking surfaces.

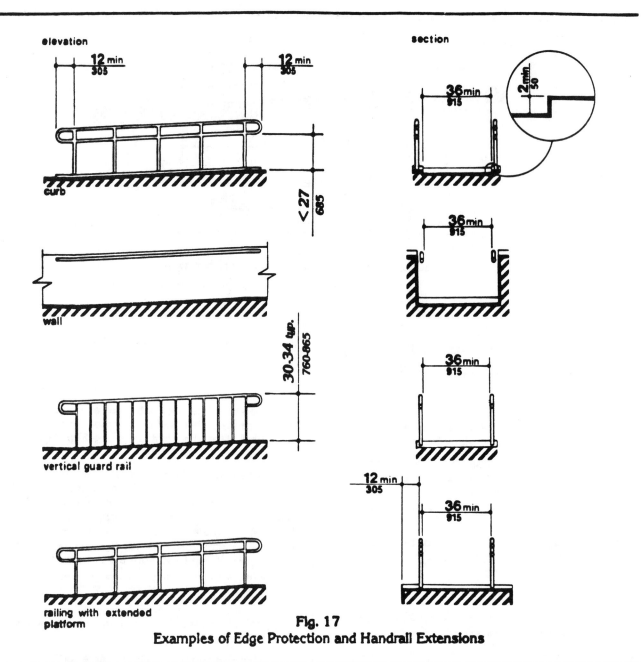

Fig. 17
Examples of Edge Protection and Handrail Extensions

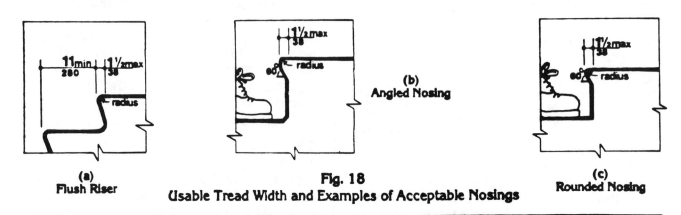

(a)
Flush Riser

(b)
Angled Nosing

(c)
Rounded Nosing

Fig. 18
Usable Tread Width and Examples of Acceptable Nosings

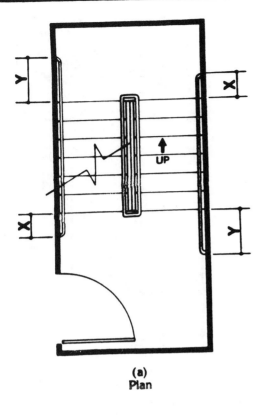

(a)
Plan

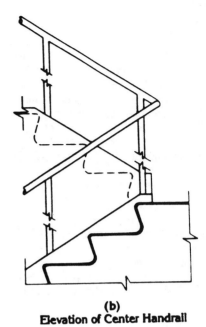

(b)
Elevation of Center Handrail

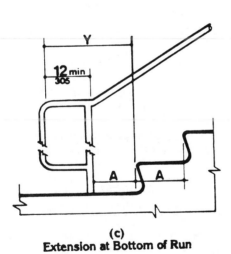

(c)
Extension at Bottom of Run

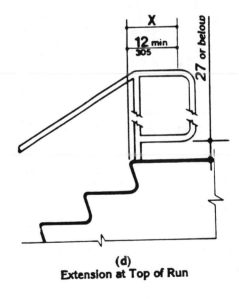

(d)
Extension at Top of Run

NOTE:

X is the 12 in minimum handrail extension required at each top riser.

Y is the minimum handrail extension of 12 in plus the width of one tread that is required at each bottom riser.

Fig. 19
Stair Handrails

4.10 Elevators.

4.10.1 General. *Accessible* elevators shall be on an accessible route and shall comply with 4.10 and with the American National Standard Safety Code for Elevators, Dumbwaiters, Escalators, and Moving Walks, ANSI A17.1-1978 and A17.1a-1979. This standard does not preclude the use of residential or fully enclosed wheelchair lifts when appropriate and approved by administrative authorities. *Freight elevators shall not be considered as meeting the requirements of this section, unless the only elevators provided are used as combination passenger and freight elevators for the public and employees.*

4.10.2 Automatic Operation. Elevator operation shall be automatic. Each car shall be equipped with a self-leveling feature that will automatically bring the car to floor landings within a tolerance of 1/2 in (13 mm) under rated loading to zero loading conditions. This self-leveling feature shall be automatic and independent of the operating device and shall correct the over-travel or undertravel.

4.10.3 Hall Call Buttons. Call buttons in elevator lobbies and halls shall be centered at 42 in (1065 mm) above the floor. Such call buttons shall have visual signals to indicate when each call is registered and when each call is answered. Call buttons shall be a minimum of 3/4 in (19 mm) in the smallest dimension. The button designating the up direction shall be on top (see Fig. 20). *Buttons shall be raised or flush. Objects mounted beneath hall call buttons shall not project into the elevator lobby more than 4 in (100 mm).*

4.10.4 Hall Lanterns. A visible and audible signal shall be provided at each hoistway entrance to indicate which car is answering a call. Audible signals shall sound once for the up direction and twice for the down direction or shall have verbal annunciators that say "up" or "down." Visible signals shall have the following features:

(1) Hall lantern fixtures shall be mounted so that their centerline is at least 72 in (1830 mm) above the lobby floor.

(2) Visual elements shall be at least 2-1/2 in (64 mm) in the smallest dimension.

(3) Signals shall be visible from the vicinity of the hall call button. In-car lanterns located in cars, visible from the vicinity of hall call buttons, and conforming to the above requirements, shall be acceptable (see Fig. 20).

4.10.5 *Raised* Characters on Hoistway Entrances. All elevator hoistway entrances shall have *raised* floor designations provided on both jambs. The centerline of the characters shall be 60 in (1525 mm) from the floor. Such characters shall be 2 in (50 mm) high and shall comply with 4.30. Permanently applied plates are acceptable if they are permanently fixed to the jambs. (See Fig. 20).

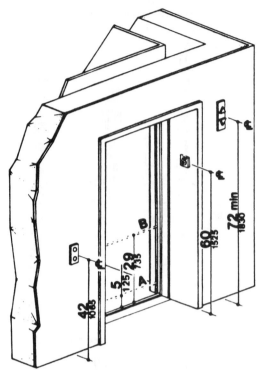

NOTE: The automatic door reopening device is activated if an object passes through either line A or line B. Line A and line B represent the vertical locations of the door reopening device not requiring contact.

**Fig. 20
Hoistway and Elevator Entrances**

4.10.6* Door Protective and Reopening Device. Elevator doors shall open and close automatically. They shall be provided with a reopening device that will stop and reopen a car door and hoistway door automatically if the door becomes obstructed by an object or person. The device shall be capable of completing these operations without requiring contact for an obstruction passing through the opening at heights of 5 in and 29 in (125 mm and 735 mm) from the floor (see Fig. 20). Door reopening devices shall remain effective for at least 20 seconds. After such an interval, doors may close in accordance with the requirements of ANSI A17.1-1978 and A17.1a-1979.

4.10.7* Door and Signal Timing for Hall Calls. The minimum acceptable time from notification that a car is answering a call until the doors of that car start to close shall be calculated from the following equation:

$$T = \frac{D}{1.5 \text{ ft/s}} \qquad \text{or } T = \frac{D}{445 \text{ mm/s}}$$

where T = total time in seconds and D = distance (in feet or millimeters) from a point in the lobby or corridor 60 in (1525 mm) directly in front of the farthest call button controlling that car to the centerline of its hoistway door (see Fig. 21). For cars with in-car lanterns, T begins when the lantern is visible from the vicinity of hall call buttons and an audible signal is sounded. *The minimum acceptable notification time shall be 5 seconds.*

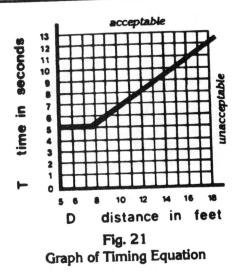

Fig. 21
Graph of Timing Equation

4.10.8 Door Delay for Car Calls. The minimum time for elevator doors to remain fully open in response to a car call shall be 3 seconds.

4.10.9 Floor Plan of Elevator Cars. The floor area of elevator cars shall provide space for wheelchair users to enter the car, maneuver within reach of controls, and exit from the car. Acceptable door opening and inside dimensions shall be as shown in Fig. 22. The clearance between the car platform sill and the edge of any hoistway landing shall be no greater than 1-1/4 in (32 mm).

4.10.10 Floor Surfaces. Floor surfaces shall comply with 4.5.

4.10.11 Illumination Levels. The level of illumination at the car controls, platform, and car threshold and landing sill shall be at least 5 footcandles (53.8 lux).

4.10.12* Car Controls. Elevator control panels shall have the following features:

(1) Buttons. All control buttons shall be at least 3/4 in (19 mm) in their smallest dimension. They may be *raised* or flush.

(2) Tactile and Visual Control Indicators. All control buttons shall be designated by *raised* standard alphabet characters for letters, arabic characters for numerals, or standard symbols as shown in Fig. 23(a), and as required in ANSI A17.1-1978 and A17.1a-1979. Raised characters and symbols shall comply with 4.30. The call button for the main entry floor shall be

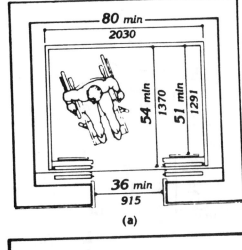

(a)

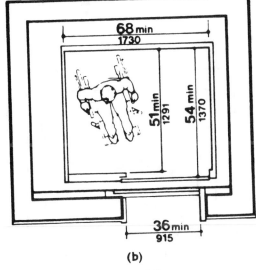

(b)

Fig. 22
Minimum Dimensions of Elevator Cars

designated by a *raised* star at the left of the floor designation (see Fig. 23(a)). All *raised* designations for control buttons shall be placed immediately to the left of the button to which they apply. Applied plates, permanently attached, are an acceptable means to provide *raised* control designations. Floor buttons shall be provided with visual indicators to show when each call is registered. The visual indicators shall be extinguished when each call is answered.

(3) Height. All floor buttons shall be no higher than 48 in (1220 mm), *unless there is a substantial increase in cost, in which case the maximum mounting height may be increased to 54 in (1370 mm),* above the floor. Emergency controls, including the emergency alarm and emergency stop, shall be grouped at the bottom of the panel and shall have their centerlines no less than 35 in (890 mm) above the floor (see Fig. 23(a) and (b)).

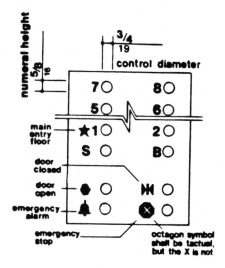

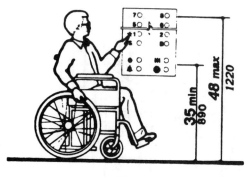

(a)
Panel Detail

(b)
Control Height

(c)
Alternate Locations of Panel with Center Opening Door

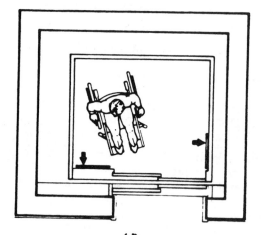

(d)
Alternate Locations of Panel with Side Opening Door

Fig. 23
Car Controls

(4) Location. Controls shall be located on a front wall if cars have center opening doors, and at the side wall or at the front wall next to the door if cars have side opening doors (see Fig. 23(c) and (d)).

4.10.13* Car Position Indicators. In elevator cars, a visual car position indicator shall be provided above the car control panel or over the door to show the position of the elevator in the hoistway. As the car passes or stops at a floor served by the elevators, the corresponding numerals shall illuminate, and an audible signal shall sound. Numerals shall be a minimum of 1/2 in (13 mm) high. The audible signal shall be no less than 20 decibels with a frequency no higher than

1500 Hz. An automatic verbal announcement of the floor number at which a car stops or which a car passes may be substituted for the audible signal.

4.10.14* Emergency Communications. If provided, emergency two-way communication systems between the elevator and a point outside the hoistway shall comply with ANSI A17.1-1978 and A17.1a-1979. The highest operable part of a two-way communication system shall be a maximum of 48 in (1220 mm) from the floor of the car. It shall be identified by a raised or recessed symbol and lettering complying with 4.30 and located adjacent to the device. If the system uses a handset, then the length of the cord from the panel to the handset shall be at least 29 in (735 mm). *If the system is located in a closed compartment, the compartment door hardware shall conform to 4.27, Controls and Operating Mechanisms. The emergency intercommunication system shall not require voice communication.*

4.11* Platform Lifts.

4.11.1 Location. *Platform lifts permitted by 4.1 shall comply with the requirements of 4.11.*

4.11.2 Other Requirements. If platform lifts are used, they shall comply with 4.2.4, 4.5, 4.27, and the applicable safety regulations of administrative authorities having jurisdiction.

4.11.3 *Entrance.* *If platform lifts are used, then they should facilitate unassisted entry and exit from the lift in compliance with 4.11.2.*

4.12 Windows. (Reserved).

4.13 Doors.

4.13.1 General. *Doors required to be accessible by 4.1 shall comply with the requirements of 4.13.*

4.13.2 Revolving Doors and Turnstiles. Revolving doors or turnstiles shall not be the only means of passage at an accessible entrance or along an accessible route. *An accessible gate or door shall be provided adjacent to the turnstile or revolving door and shall be so designed as to facilitate the same use pattern.*

4.13.3 Gates. Gates, including ticket gates, shall meet all applicable specifications of 4.13.

4.13.4 Double-Leaf Doorways. If doorways have two *independently* operated door leaves, then at least one leaf shall meet the specifications in 4.13.5 and 4.13.6. That leaf shall be an active leaf.

4.13.5 Clear Width. Doorways shall have a minimum clear opening of 32 in (815 mm) with the door open 90 degrees, measured between the face of the door and the stop (see Fig. 24(a), (b), (c), and (d)). Openings more than 24 in (610 mm) in depth shall comply with 4.2.1 and 4.3.3 (see Fig. 24(e)).

EXCEPTION: Doors not requiring full user passage, such as shallow closets, may have the clear opening reduced to 20 in (510 mm) minimum.

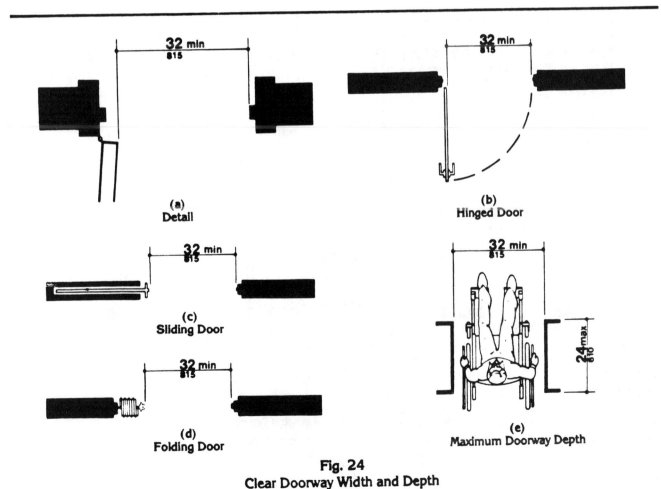

(a)
Detail

(b)
Hinged Door

(c)
Sliding Door

(d)
Folding Door

(e)
Maximum Doorway Depth

Fig. 24
Clear Doorway Width and Depth

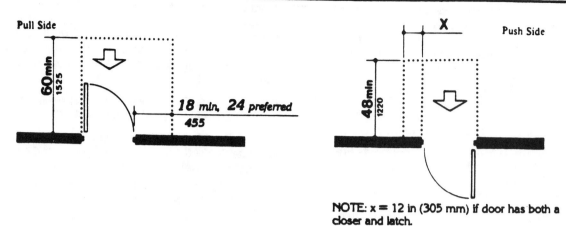

NOTE: x = 12 in (305 mm) if door has both a
closer and latch.

(a)
Front Approaches — Swinging Doors

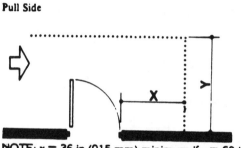

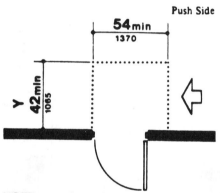

NOTE: x = 36 in (915 mm) minimum if y = 60 in
(1525 mm); x = 42 in (1065 mm) minimum if y =
54 in (1370 mm).

NOTE: y = 48 in (1220 mm) minimum if door has
both a latch and closer.

(b)
Hinge Side Approaches — Swinging Doors

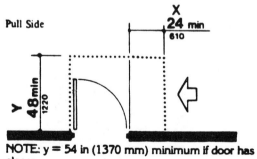

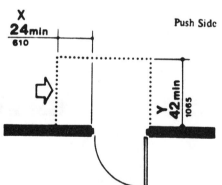

NOTE: y = 54 in (1370 mm) minimum if door has
closer.

NOTE: y = 48 in (1220 mm) minimum if door has
closer.

(c)
Latch Side Approaches — Swinging Doors

NOTE: All doors in alcoves shall comply with the clearances for front approaches.

Fig. 25
Maneuvering Clearances at Doors

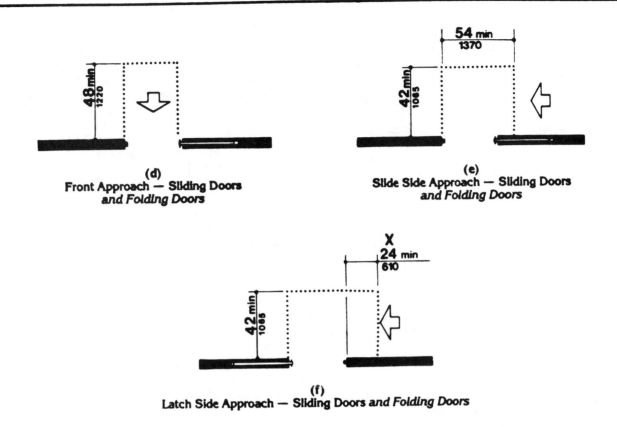

(d)
Front Approach — Sliding Doors
and Folding Doors

(e)
Slide Side Approach — Sliding Doors
and Folding Doors

(f)
Latch Side Approach — Sliding Doors *and Folding Doors*

NOTE: All doors in alcoves shall comply with the clearances for front approaches.

Fig. 25
Maneuvering Clearances at Doors *(Continued)*

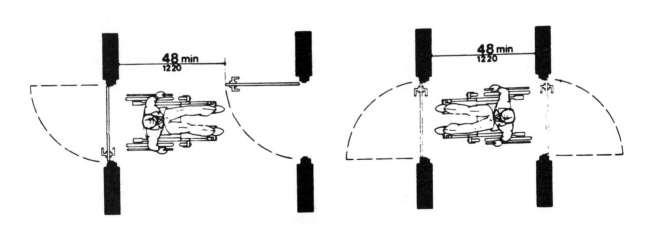

Fig. 26
Two Hinged Doors in Series

4.13.6 Maneuvering Clearances at Doors.

Minimum maneuvering clearances at doors that are not automatic or power-assisted shall be as shown in Fig. 25. The floor or ground area within the required clearances shall be level and clear. Entry doors to acute care hospital bedrooms for in-patients shall be exempted from the requirement for space at the latch side of the door (see dimension "x" in Fig. 25) if the door is at least 44 in (1120 mm) wide.

4.13.7 Two Doors in Series.

The minimum space between two hinged or pivoted doors in series shall be 48 in (1220 mm) plus the width of any door swinging into the space. Doors in series shall swing either in the same direction or away from the space between the doors (see Fig. 26).

4.13.8* Thresholds at Doorways.

Thresholds at doorways shall not exceed 3/4 in (19 mm) in height for exterior sliding doors or 1/2 in (13 mm) for other types of doors. Raised thresholds and floor level changes at accessible doorways shall be beveled with a slope no greater than 1:2 (see 4.5.2).

4.13.9* Door Hardware.

Handles, pulls, latches, locks, and other operating devices on accessible doors shall have a shape that is easy to grasp with one hand and does not require tight grasping, tight pinching, or twisting of the wrist to operate. Lever-operated mechanisms, push-type mechanisms, and U-shaped handles are acceptable designs. When sliding doors are fully open, operating hardware shall be exposed and usable from both sides. In dwelling units, only doors at accessible entrances to the unit itself shall comply with the requirements of this paragraph. Doors to hazardous areas shall have hardware complying with 4.29.3. *Mount no hardware required for accessible door passage higher than 48 in (1220 mm) above finished floor.*

4.13.10* Door Closers.

If a door has a closer, then the sweep period of the closer shall be adjusted so that from an open position of 70 degrees, the door will take at least 3 seconds to move to a point 3 in (75 mm) from the latch, measured to the leading edge of the door.

4.13.11* Door Opening Force.

The maximum force for pushing or pulling open a door shall be as follows:

(1) Fire doors shall have the minimum opening force allowable by the appropriate administrative authority.

(2) Other doors.

(a) exterior hinged doors: *(Reserved)*.

(b) interior hinged doors: 5 lbf (22.2N)

(c) sliding or folding doors: 5 lbf (22.2N)

These forces do not apply to the force required to retract latch bolts or disengage other devices that may hold the door in a closed position.

4.13.12* Automatic Doors and Power-Assisted Doors.

If an automatic door is used, then it shall comply with American National Standard for Power-Operated Doors, ANSI A156.10-1979. Slowly opening, low-powered, automatic doors shall be considered a type of custom design installation as described in paragraph 1.1.1 of ANSI A156.10-1979. Such doors shall not open to back check faster than 3 seconds and shall require no more than 15 lbf (66.6N) to stop door movement. If a power-assisted door is used, its door-opening force shall comply with 4.13.11 and its closing shall conform to the requirements in section 10 of ANSI A156.10-1979.

4.14 Entrances.

4.14.1 Minimum Number.

Entrances required to be accessible by 4.1 shall be part of an accessible route and shall comply with 4.3. Such entrances shall be connected by an accessible route to public transportation stops, to accessible parking and passenger loading zones, and to public streets or sidewalks if available (see 4.3.2(1)). They shall also be connected by an accessible route to all accessible spaces or elements within the building or facility.

4.14.2 Service Entrances.

A service entrance shall not be the sole accessible entrance unless it is the only entrance to a building or facility (for example, in a factory or garage).

4.15 Drinking Fountains and Water Coolers.

4.15.1 Minimum Number.

Drinking fountains or water coolers required to be accessible by 4.1 shall comply with 4.15.

4.15.2* Spout Height.

Spouts shall be no higher than 36 in (915 mm), measured from the floor or ground surfaces to the spout outlet (see Fig. 27(a)).

4.15.3 Spout Location.

The spouts of drinking fountains and water coolers shall be at the front of the unit and shall direct the water flow in a trajectory that is parallel or nearly parallel to the front of the unit. The spout shall provide a flow of water at least 4 in (100 mm) high so as to allow the insertion of a cup or glass under the flow of water.

4.15.4 Controls.

Controls shall comply with 4.27.4. *Unit controls shall be front mounted or side mounted near the front edge.*

4.15.5 Clearances.

(1) Wall- and post-mounted cantilevered units shall have a clear knee space between the bottom of the apron and the floor or ground at least 27 in (685 mm) high, 30 in (760 mm) wide, and 17 in to 19 in (430 mm to 485 mm) deep (see Fig. 27(a) and (b)). Such units shall also have a minimum clear floor space 30 in by 48 in (760 mm by 1220 mm) to allow a person in a wheelchair to approach the unit facing forward.

(2) Free-standing or built-in units not having a clear space under them shall have a clear floor space at least 30 in by 48 in (760 mm by 1220 mm) that allows a person in a wheelchair to make a parallel approach to the unit (see Fig. 27(c) and (d)). This clear floor space shall comply with 4.2.4.

4.16 Water Closets.

4.16.1 General. Accessible water closets shall comply with 4.16. For water closets in *accessible* dwelling units, see 4.34.5.2.

4.16.2 Clear Floor Space. Clear floor space for water closets not in stalls shall comply with Fig. 28. Clear floor space may be arranged to allow either a left-handed or right-handed approach.

4.16.3* Height. The height of water closets shall be 17 in to 19 in (430 mm to 485 mm), measured to the top of the toilet seat (see Fig. 29(b)). *Seats shall not be sprung to return to a lifted position.*

4.16.4* Grab Bars. Grab bars for water closets not located in stalls shall comply with Fig. 29 and 4.26.

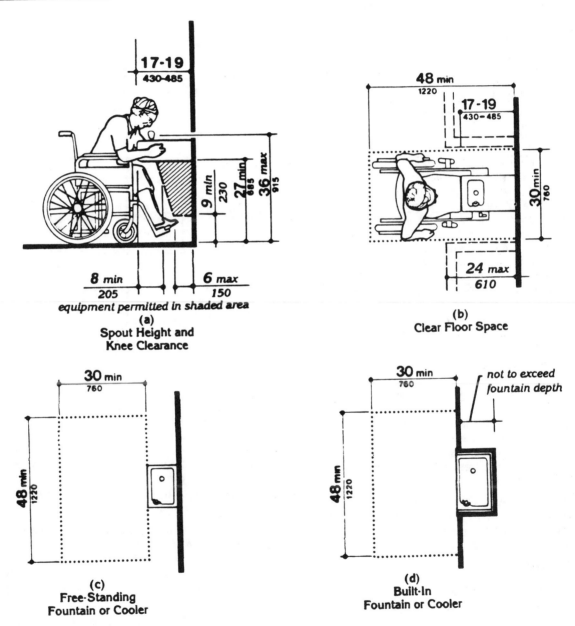

(a)
Spout Height and Knee Clearance

(b)
Clear Floor Space

(c)
Free-Standing Fountain or Cooler

(d)
Built-In Fountain or Cooler

Fig. 27
Drinking Fountains and Water Coolers

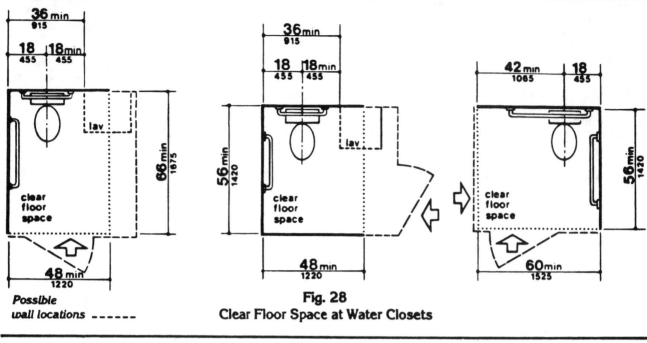

Possible wall locations ------

Fig. 28
Clear Floor Space at Water Closets

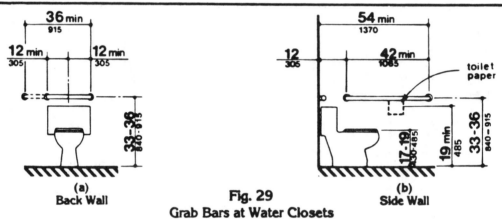

(a)
Back Wall

Fig. 29
Grab Bars at Water Closets

(b)
Side Wall

4.16.5* Flush Controls. Flush controls shall be hand operated *or automatic* and shall comply with 4.27.4. Controls for flush valves shall be mounted on the wide side of toilet areas no more than 44 in (1120 mm) above the floor.

4.16.6 Dispensers. Toilet paper dispensers shall be installed within reach, as shown in Fig. 29(b). *Dispensers that control delivery, or that do not permit continuous paper flow, shall not be used.*

4.17 Toilet Stalls.

4.17.1 Location. Accessible toilet stalls shall be on an accessible route and shall meet the requirements of 4.17.

4.17.2 Water Closets. Water closets in *accessible* stalls shall comply with 4.16.

4.17.3 Size and Arrangement. The size and

arrangement of toilet stalls shall comply with Fig. 30(a). Toilet stalls with a minimum depth of 56 in (1420 mm) (see Fig. 30(a)) shall have wall-mounted water closets. If the depth of toilet stalls is increased at least 3 in (75 mm), then a floor-mounted water closet may be used. Arrangements shown for stalls may be reversed to allow either a left- or right-hand approach.

EXCEPTION: In instances of alteration work where provision of a standard stall (Fig. 30(a)) is structurally impracticable or where plumbing code requirements prevent combining existing stalls to provide space, an alternate stall (Fig. 30(b)) may be provided in lieu of the standard stall.

4.17.4 Toe Clearances. In standard stalls, the front partition and at least one side partition shall provide a toe clearance of at least 9 in (230 mm) above the floor. If the depth of the stall is greater than 60 in (1525 mm), then the toe clearance is not required.

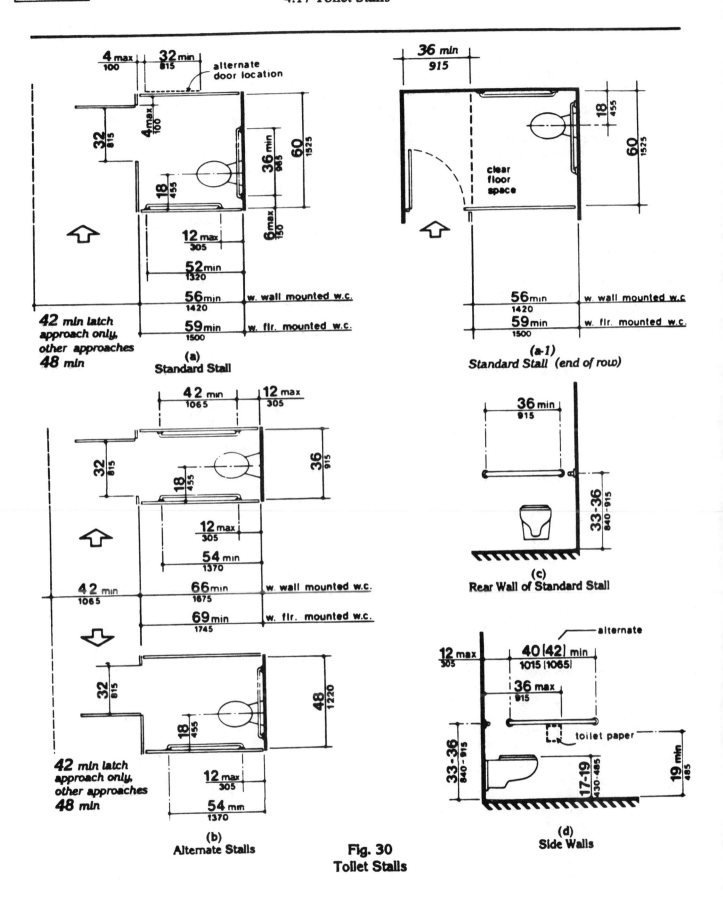

(a)
Standard Stall

42 min latch approach only, other approaches 48 min

(a-1)
Standard Stall (end of row)

(b)
Alternate Stalls

42 min latch approach only, other approaches 48 min

(c)
Rear Wall of Standard Stall

(d)
Side Walls

Fig. 30
Toilet Stalls

4.17.5* Doors. Toilet stall doors shall comply with 4.13. *If toilet stall approach is from the latch side of the stall door, clearance between the door side of the stall and any obstruction may be reduced to a minimum of 42 in (1065 mm).*

4.17.6 Grab Bars. Grab bars complying with the length and positioning shown in Fig. 30(a), (b), (c), and (d) shall be provided. Grab bars may be mounted with any desired method as long as they have a gripping surface at the locations shown and do not obstruct the required clear floor area. Grab bars shall comply with 4.26.

4.18 Urinals.

4.18.1 General. Accessible urinals shall comply with 4.18.

4.18.2 Height. Urinals shall be stall-type or wall-hung with an elongated rim at a maximum of 17 in (430 mm) above the floor.

4.18.3 Clear Floor Space. A clear floor space 30 in by 48 in (760 mm by 1220 mm) shall be provided in front of urinals to allow forward approach. This clear space shall adjoin or overlap an accessible route and shall comply with 4.2.4. *Urinal shields that do not extend beyond the front edge of the urinal rim may be provided with 29 in (735 mm) clearance between them.*

4.18.4 Flush Controls. Flush controls shall be hand operated or automatic, and shall comply with 4.27.4, and shall be mounted no more than 44 in (1120 mm) above the floor.

4.19 Lavatories and Mirrors.

4.19.1 General. The requirements of 4.19 shall apply to lavatory fixtures, vanities, and built-in lavatories.

4.19.2 Height and Clearances. Lavatories shall be mounted with *the rim or counter surface no higher than 34 in (865 mm) above the finished floor.* Provide a clearance of at least 29 in (735 mm) from the floor to the bottom of the apron. Knee and toe clearance shall comply with Fig. 31.

4.19.3 Clear Floor Space. A clear floor space 30 in by 48 in (760 mm by 1220 mm) complying with 4.2.4 shall be provided in front of a lavatory to allow forward approach. Such clear floor space shall adjoin or overlap an accessible route and shall extend a maximum of 19 in (485 mm) underneath the lavatory (see Fig. 32).

4.19.4 Exposed Pipes and Surfaces. Hot water and drain pipes under lavatories shall be insulated or otherwise covered. There shall be no sharp or abrasive surfaces under lavatories.

4.19.5 Faucets. Faucets shall comply with 4.27.4. Lever-operated, push-type, and electronically controlled mechanisms are examples of acceptable designs. Self-closing valves are allowed if the faucet remains open for at least 10 seconds.

4.19.6* Mirrors. Mirrors shall be mounted with the bottom edge *of the reflecting surface* no higher than 40 in (1015 mm) from the floor (see Fig. 31).

4.20 Bathtubs.

4.20.1 General. Accessible bathtubs shall comply with 4.20. For bathtubs in *accessible* dwelling units, see 4.34.5.4.

4.20.2 Floor Space. Clear floor space in front of bathtubs shall be as shown in Fig. 33.

4.20.3 Seat. An in-tub seat or a seat at the head end of the tub shall be provided as shown in Fig. 33 and 34. The structural strength of seats and their attachments shall comply with 4.26.3. Seats shall be mounted securely and shall not slip during use.

4.20.4 Grab Bars. Grab bars complying with 4.26 shall be provided as shown in Fig. 33 and 34.

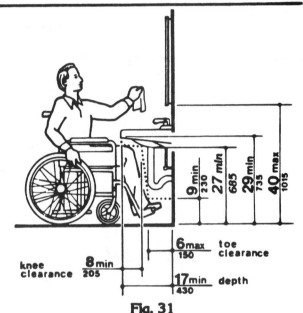

Fig. 31
Lavatory Clearances

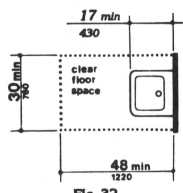

Fig. 32
Clear Floor Space at Lavatories

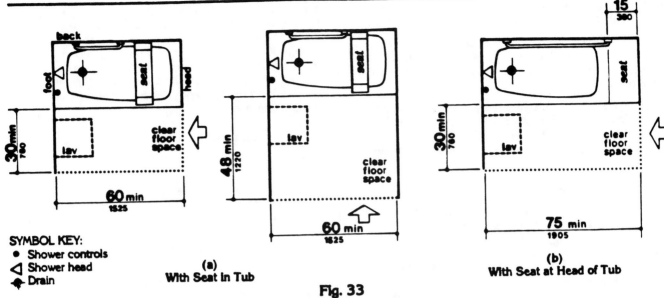

SYMBOL KEY:
- ● Shower controls
- ◁ Shower head
- ✦ Drain

(a)
With Seat in Tub

(b)
With Seat at Head of Tub

Fig. 33
Clear Floor Space at Bathtubs

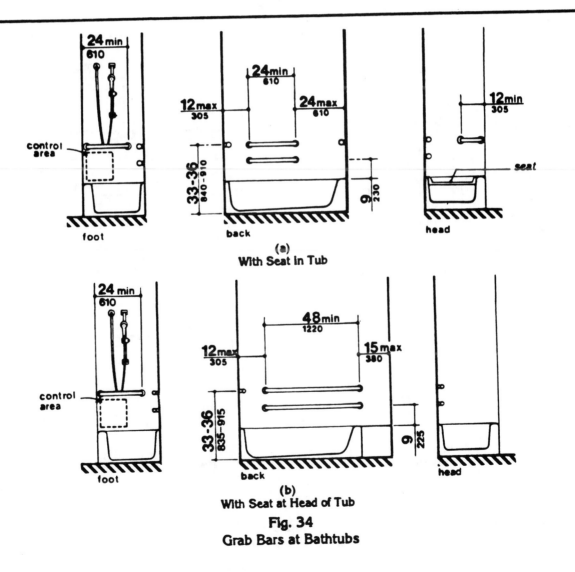

(a)
With Seat in Tub

(b)
With Seat at Head of Tub

Fig. 34
Grab Bars at Bathtubs

4.20.5 Controls. Faucets and other controls complying with 4.27.4 shall be located as shown in Fig. 34.

4.20.6 Shower Unit. A shower spray unit with a hose at least 60 in (1525 mm) long that can be used as a fixed shower head or as a hand-held shower shall be provided.

4.20.7 Bathtub Enclosures. If provided, enclosures for bathtubs shall not obstruct controls or transfer from wheelchairs onto bathtub seats or into tubs. Enclosures on bathtubs shall not have tracks mounted on their rims.

4.21 Shower Stalls.

4.21.1* General. Accessible shower stalls shall comply with 4.21. For shower stalls in *accessible* dwelling units, see 4.34.5.5.

4.21.2 Size and Clearances. Shower stall size and clear floor space shall comply with Fig. 35(a) or (b). The shower stall in Fig. 35(a) shall be 36 in by 36 in (915 mm by 915 mm). The shower stall in Fig. 35(b) will fit into the space required for a bathtub.

4.21.3 Seat. A seat shall be provided in shower stalls 36 in by 36 in (915 mm by 915 mm) and shall be as shown in Fig. 36. The seat shall be mounted 17 in to 19 in (430 mm to 485 mm) from the bathroom floor and shall extend the full depth of the stall. The seat shall be on the wall opposite the controls. The structural strength of seats and their attachments shall comply with 4.26.3.

4.21.4 Grab Bars. Grab bars complying with 4.26 shall be provided as shown in Fig. 37.

4.21.5 Controls. Faucets and other controls complying with 4.27.4 shall be located as shown in Fig. 37. In shower stalls 36 in by 36 in (915 mm by 915 mm), all controls, faucets, and the shower unit shall be mounted on the side wall opposite the seat.

4.21.6 Shower Unit. A shower spray unit with a hose at least 60 in (1525 mm) long that can be used as a fixed shower head or as a hand-held shower shall be provided.

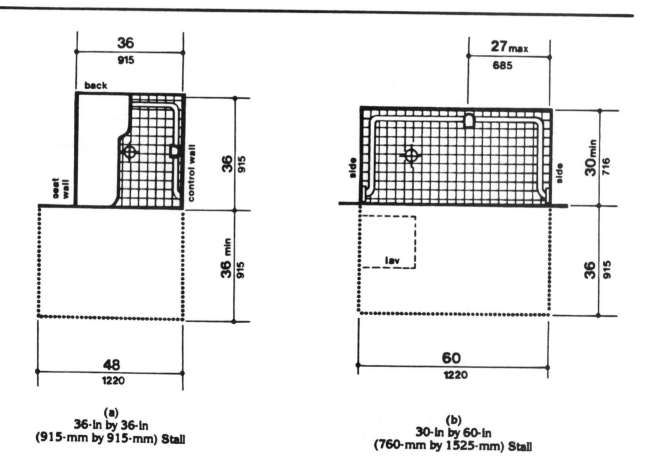

(a)
36-in by 36-in
(915-mm by 915-mm) Stall

(b)
30-in by 60-in
(760-mm by 1525-mm) Stall

Fig. 35
Shower Size and Clearances

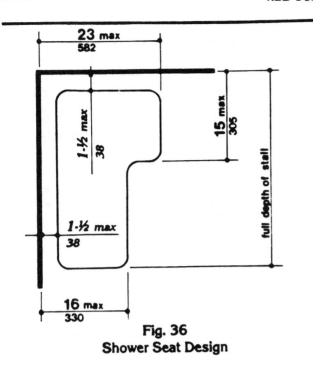

Fig. 36
Shower Seat Design

EXCEPTION: In unmonitored facilities where vandalism is a consideration, a fixed shower head mounted at 48 in (1220 mm) above the shower floor may be used in lieu of a hand-held shower head.

4.21.7 Curbs. If provided, curbs in shower stalls 36 in by 36 in (915 mm by 915 mm) shall be no higher than 1/2 in (13 mm). Shower stalls that are 30 in by 60 in (760 mm by 1525 mm) shall not have curbs.

4.21.8 Shower Enclosures. If provided, enclosures for shower stalls shall not obstruct controls or obstruct transfer from wheelchairs onto shower seats.

4.22 Toilet Rooms.

4.22.1 Minimum Number. *Toilet facilities required to be accessible by 4.1* shall comply with 4.22. Accessible toilet rooms shall be on an accessible route.

4.22.2 Doors. All doors to accessible toilet rooms shall comply with 4.13. Doors shall not swing into the clear floor space required for any fixture.

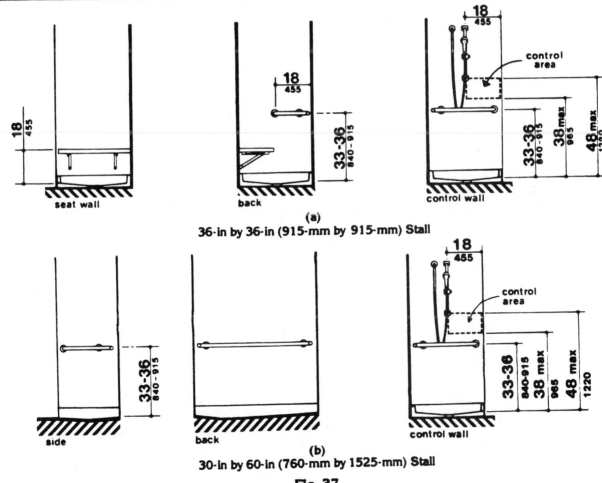

(a)
36-in by 36-in (915-mm by 915-mm) Stall

(b)
30-in by 60-in (760-mm by 1525-mm) Stall

Fig. 37
Grab Bars at Shower Stalls

4.22.3 Clear Floor Space. The accessible fixtures and controls required in 4.22.4, 4.22.5, 4.22.6, and 4.22.7 shall be on an accessible route. An unobstructed turning space complying with 4.2.3 shall be provided within an accessible toilet room. The clear floor space at fixtures and controls, the accessible route, and the turning space may overlap.

EXCEPTION: In toilet rooms with only one water closet and one lavatory, a clear floor space of 30 in by 60 in (815 mm by 1525 mm) may be used in lieu of the unobstructed turning space.

4.22.4 Water Closets. If toilet stalls are provided, then at least one shall comply with 4.17; its water closet shall comply with 4.16. If water closets are not in stalls, then at least one shall comply with 4.16.

4.22.5 Urinals. If urinals are provided, *then* at least one shall comply with 4.18.

4.22.6 Lavatories and Mirrors. If lavatories and mirrors are provided, *then* at least one of each shall comply with 4.19.

4.22.7 Controls and Dispensers. If controls, dispensers, receptacles, or other equipment is provided, *then* at least one of each shall be on an accessible route and shall comply with 4.27.

4.23 Bathrooms, Bathing Facilities, and Shower Rooms.

4.23.1 Minimum Number. Bathrooms, bathing facilities, or shower rooms *required to be accessible by 4.1* shall comply with 4.23 and shall be on an accessible route. For adaptable bathrooms in accessible dwelling units, see 4.34.5.

4.23.2 Doors. Doors to accessible bathrooms shall comply with 4.13. Doors shall not swing into the floor space required for any fixture.

4.23.3 Clear Floor Space. The accessible fixtures and controls required in 4.23.4, 4.23.5, 4.23.6, 4.23.7, 4.23.8, and 4.23.9 shall be on an accessible route. An unobstructed turning space complying with 4.2.3 shall be provided within an accessible bathroom. The clear floor spaces at fixtures and controls, the accessible route, and the turning space may overlap.

EXCEPTION: In bathrooms with only one water closet, one lavatory, and one bathtub or shower, a clear floor space of 30 in by 60 in (760 mm by 1525 mm) may be used in lieu of the unobstructed turning space.

4.23.4 Water Closets. If toilet stalls are provided, then at least one shall comply with 4.17; its water closet shall comply with 4.16. If water closets are not in stalls, then at least one shall comply with 4.16.

4.23.5 Urinals. If urinals are provided, then at least one shall comply with 4.18.

4.23.6 Lavatories and Mirrors. If lavatories and mirrors are provided, then at least one of each shall comply with 4.19.

4.23.7 Controls and Dispensers. If controls, dispensers, receptacles, or other equipment is provided, *then* at least one of each shall be on an accessible route and shall comply with 4.27.

4.23.8 Bathing and Shower Facilities. If tubs or showers are provided, then at least one accessible tub that complies with 4.20 or at least one accessible shower that complies with 4.21 shall be provided.

4.23.9* Medicine Cabinets. If medicine cabinets are provided, at least one shall be located with a usable shelf no higher than 44 in (1120 mm) above the floor space. The floor space shall comply with 4.2.4.

4.24 Sinks.

4.24.1 General. *Sinks required to be accessible by 4.1* shall comply with 4.24. Sinks in kitchens of accessible dwelling units shall comply with 4.34.6.5.

4.24.2 Height. Sinks shall be mounted with the counter or rim no higher than 34 in (865 mm) from the floor.

4.24.3 Knee Clearance. Knee clearance that is *at least* 27 in (685 mm) high, 30 in (760 mm) wide, and 19 in (485 mm) deep shall be provided underneath sinks.

4.24.4 Depth. Each sink shall be a maximum of 6-1/2 in (165 mm) deep.

4.24.5 Clear Floor Space. A clear floor space at least 30 in by 48 in (760 mm by 1220 mm) complying with 4.2.4 shall be provided in front of a sink to allow forward approach. The clear floor space shall be on an accessible route and shall extend a maximum of 19 in (485 mm) underneath the sink (see Fig. 32).

4.24.6 Exposed Pipes and Surfaces. Hot water and drain pipes exposed under sinks shall be insulated or otherwise covered. There shall be no sharp or abrasive surfaces under sinks.

4.24.7 Faucets. Faucets shall comply with 4.27.4. Lever-operated, push-type, touch-type, or electronically controlled mechanisms are acceptable designs.

4.25 Storage.

4.25.1 General. *Fixed* storage facilities such as cabinets, shelves, closets, and drawers *required to be accessible by 4.1* shall comply with 4.25.

4.25.2 Clear Floor Space. A clear floor space at least 30 in by 48 in (760 mm by 1220 mm) complying with 4.2.4 that allows either a forward or parallel approach by a person using a wheelchair shall be provided at accessible storage facilities.

4.25.3 Height. Accessible storage spaces shall be within at least one of the reach ranges specified in 4.2.5 and 4.2.6. Clothes rods shall be a maximum of 54 in (1370 mm) from the floor (see Fig. 38).

4.25.4 Hardware. Hardware for accessible storage facilities shall comply with 4.27.4. Touch latches and U-shaped pulls are acceptable.

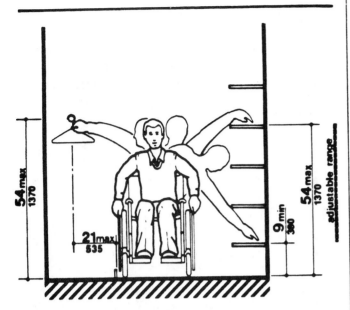

Fig. 38
Storage Shelves and Closets

4.26 Handrails, Grab Bars, and Tub and Shower Seats.

4.26.1* General. All handrails, grab bars, and tub and shower seats *required to be accessible by 4.1, 4.8, or 4.9* shall comply with 4.26.

4.26.2* Size and Spacing of Grab Bars and Handrails. The diameter or width of the gripping surfaces of a handrail or grab bar shall be 1·1/4 in to 1·1/2 in (32 mm to 38 mm), or the shape shall provide an equivalent gripping surface. If handrails or grab bars are mounted adjacent to a wall, the space between the wall and the grab bar shall be 1·1/2 in (38 mm) (see Fig. 39(a), (b), and (c)). Handrails may be located in a recess if the recess is a maximum of 3 in (75 mm) deep and extends at least 18 in (455 mm) above the top of the rail (see Fig. 39(d)).

4.26.3 Structural Strength. The structural strength of grab bars, tub and shower seats, fasteners, and mounting devices shall meet the following specification:

(1) Bending stress in a grab bar or seat induced by the maximum bending moment from the application of 250 lbf (1112N) shall be less than the allowable stress for the material of the grab bar or seat.

(2) Shear stress induced in a grab bar or seat by the application of 250 lbf (1112N) shall be less than the allowable shear stress for the material of the grab bar or seat. If the connection between the grab bar or seat and its mounting bracket or other support is considered to be fully restrained, then direct and torsional shear stresses shall be totaled for the combined shear stress, which shall not exceed the allowable shear stress.

(3) Shear force induced in a fastener or mounting device from the application of 250 lbf (1112N) shall be less than the allowable lateral load of either the fastener or mounting device or the supporting structure, whichever is the smaller allowable load.

(4) Tensile force induced in a fastener by a direct tension force of 250 lbf (1112N) plus the maximum moment from the application of 250 lbf (1112N) shall be less than the allowable withdrawal and the supporting structure.

(5) Grab bars shall not rotate within their fittings.

4.26.4 Eliminating Hazards. A handrail or grab bar and any wall or other surface adjacent to it shall be free of any sharp or abrasive elements. Edges shall have a minimum radius of 1/8 in (3.2 mm).

4.27 Controls and Operating Mechanisms.

4.27.1 General. Controls and operating mechanisms *required to be accessible by 4.1* shall comply with 4.27.

4.27.2 Clear Floor Space. Clear floor space complying with 4.2.4 that allows a forward or a parallel approach by a person using a wheelchair shall be provided at controls, dispensers, receptacles, and other operable equipment.

4.27.3* Height. The highest operable part of all controls, dispensers, receptacles, and other operable equipment shall be placed within at least one of the reach ranges specified in 4.2.5 and 4.2.6. Except where the use of special equipment dictates otherwise, electrical and communications system receptacles on walls shall be mounted no less than 15 in (380 mm) above the floor.

4.27.4 Operation. Controls and operating mechanisms shall be operable with one hand and shall not require tight grasping, pinching, or twisting of the wrist. The force required to activate controls shall be no greater than 5 lbf (22.2 N).

4.28 Alarms.

4.28.1 General. *Alarm systems required to be accessible by 4.1 shall comply with 4.28.*

4.28.2* Audible Alarms. If provided, audible emergency alarms shall produce a sound that exceeds the prevailing equivalent sound level in the room or space by at least 15 decibels or exceeds any maximum sound level with a duration of 30 seconds by 5 decibels, whichever is louder. Sound levels for alarm signals shall not exceed 120 decibels.

4.28.3* Visual Alarms. If provided, electrically powered internally illuminated emergency exit signs shall flash as a visual emergency alarm in conjunction with audible emergency alarms. The flashing frequency of visual alarm devices shall be less than 5 Hz. If such alarms use electricity from the building as a power source, then they shall be installed on the same system as the audible emergency alarms.

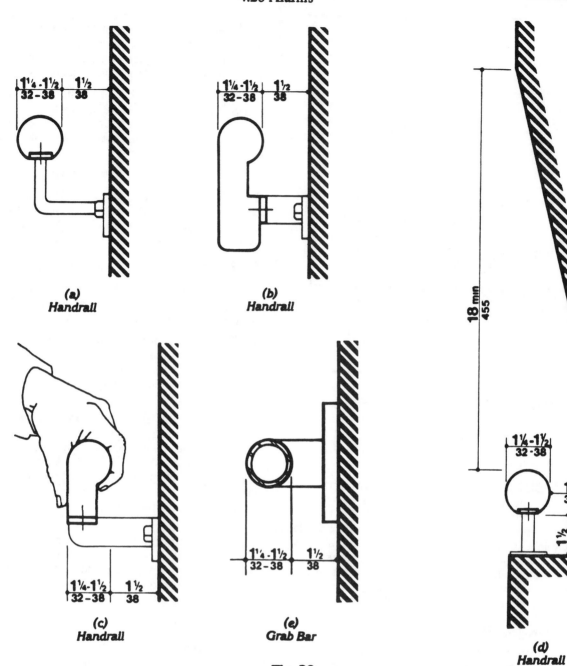

(a)
Handrail

(b)
Handrail

(c)
Handrail

(e)
Grab Bar

(d)
Handrail

18 min
455

Fig. 39
Size and Spacing of Handrails and Grab Bars

EXCEPTIONS:

(1) Visual alarm devices that are mounted adjacent to emergency exit signs may be used in lieu of flashing exit signs.

(2) Specialized systems utilizing advanced technology may be substituted for the visual systems specified above if equivalent protection is afforded handicapped users of the building or facility.

4.28.4* Auxiliary Alarms. Accessible sleeping accommodations shall have a visual alarm connected to the building emergency alarm system or shall have a standard 110-volt electrical receptacle into which such an alarm could be connected. Instructions for use of the auxiliary alarm or connection shall be provided.

4.29 Tactile Warnings.

4.29.1 General. Tactile warnings *required to be accessible by 4.1* shall comply with 4.29.

4.29.2* Tactile Warnings on Walking Surfaces. *(Reserved).*

4.29.3* Tactile Warnings on Doors to Hazardous Areas. Doors that lead to areas that might prove dangerous to a blind person (for example, doors to loading platforms, boiler rooms, stages, and the like) shall be made identifiable to the touch by a textured surface on the door handle, knob, pull, or other operating hardware. This textured surface may be made by knurling or roughing or by a material applied to the contact surface. Such textured surfaces shall not be provided for emergency exit doors or any doors other than those to hazardous areas.

4.29.4 Tactile Warnings at Stairs. *(Reserved)*.

4.29.5* Tactile Warnings at Hazardous Vehicular Areas. *(Reserved)*.

4.29.6* Tactile Warnings at Reflecting Pools. *(Reserved)*.

4.29.7* Standardization. Textured surfaces for tactile *door* warnings shall be standard within a building, facility, site, or complex of buildings.

4.30 Signage.

4.30.1* General. *Signage required to be accessible by 4.1 shall comply with 4.30.*

4.30.2* Character Proportion. Letters and numbers on signs shall have a width-to-height ratio between 3:5 and 1:1 and a stroke width-to-height ratio between 1:5 and 1:10.

4.30.3* Color Contrast. Characters and symbols shall contrast with their background — either light characters on a dark background or dark characters on a light background.

4.30.4* Raised or Indented Characters or Symbols. Letters and numbers on signs shall be raised or incised 1/32 in (0.8 mm) minimum and shall be sans serif characters. Raised characters or symbols shall be at least 5/8 in (16 mm) high, but no higher than 2 in (50 mm). Indented characters or symbols shall have a stroke width of at least 1/4 in (6 mm). Symbols or pictographs on signs shall be raised or indented 1/32 in (0.8 mm) minimum.

4.30.5 Symbols of Accessiblity. Accessible facilities *required to be* identified *by 4.1, shall use* the international symbol of accessibility. The symbol shall be displayed as shown in Fig. 43.

4.30.6 *Mounting Location and Height. Interior signage shall be located alongside the door on the latch side and shall be mounted at a height of between 54 in and 66 in (1370 mm and 1675 mm) above the finished floor.*

4.31 Telephones.

4.31.1 General. *Public telephones required to be accessible by 4.1 shall comply with 4.31.*

4.31.2 Clear Floor or Ground Space. A clear floor or ground space at least 30 in by 48 in (760 mm by 1220 mm) that allows either a forward or parallel

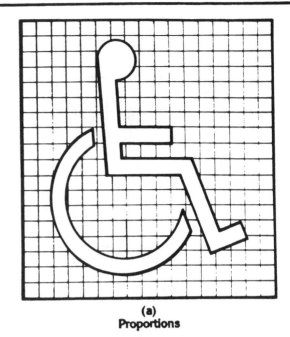

(a)
Proportions

(b)
Display Conditions

Fig. 43
International Symbol of Accessibility

approach by a person using a wheelchair shall be provided at telephones (see Fig. 44). The clear floor or ground space shall comply with 4.2.4. Bases, enclosures, and fixed seats shall not impede approaches to telephones by people who use wheelchairs.

4.31.3* Mounting Height. The highest operable part of the telephone shall be within the reach ranges specified in 4.2.5 or 4.2.6.

4.31.4 *Protruding Objects. Telephones shall comply with 4.4.*

4.31.5* Equipment for Hearing Impaired People. Telephones shall be equipped with a receiver that generates a magnetic field in the area of the receiver cap. *Volume controls shall be provided in accordance with 4.1.2.*

4.31.6 Controls. Telephones shall have pushbutton controls where service for such equipment is available.

4.31.7 Telephone Books. Telephone books, if provided, shall be located *in a position that complies with the reach ranges specified in 4.2.5 and 4.2.6.*

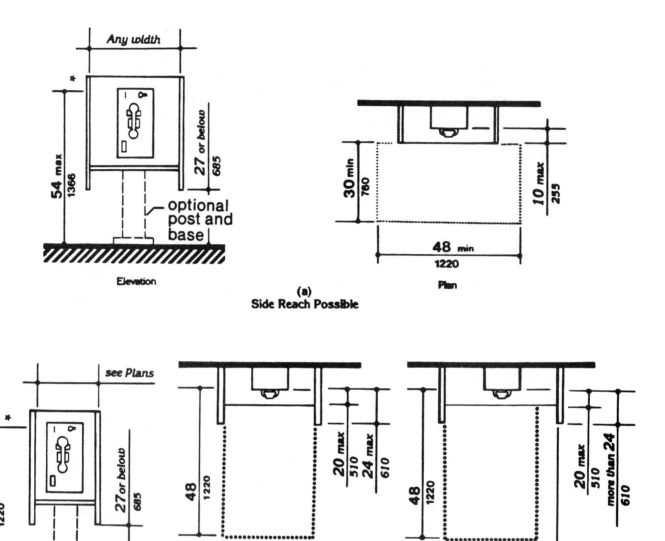

Fig. 44
Mounting Heights and Clearances for Telephones

Height to highest operable parts which are essential to basic operation of telephone.

4.31.8 Cord Length. The cord from the telephone to the handset shall be at least 29 in (735 mm) long.

4.32 Seating, Tables, and Work Surfaces.

4.32.1 Minimum Number. Fixed or built-in seating, tables, or work surfaces *required to be accessible by 4.1 shall comply with 4.32.*

4.32.2 Seating. If seating spaces for people in wheelchairs are provided at tables, counters, or work surfaces, clear floor space complying with 4.2.4 shall be provided. Such clear floor space shall not overlap knee space by more than 19 in (485 mm) (see Fig. 45).

4.32.3 Knee Clearances. If seating for people in wheelchairs is provided at tables, counters, and work surfaces, knee spaces at least 27 in (685 mm) high, 30 in (760 mm) wide, and 19 in (485 mm) deep shall be provided (see Fig. 45).

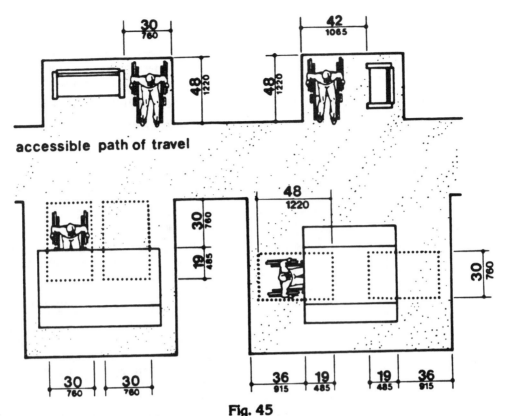

Fig. 45
Minimum Clearances for Seating and Tables

4.32.4* Height of Work Surfaces. The tops of tables and work surfaces shall be from 28 in to 34 in (710 mm to 865 mm) from the floor or ground.

4.33 Assembly Areas.

4.33.1 Minimum Number. Assembly and associated areas required to be accessible by 4.1 shall comply with 4.33.

4.33.2* Size of Wheelchair Locations. Each wheelchair location shall provide minimum clear ground or floor spaces as shown in Fig. 46.

4.33.3* Placement of Wheelchair Locations. Wheelchair areas shall be an integral part of any fixed seating plan and shall be dispersed throughout the seating area. They shall adjoin an accessible route that also serves as a means of egress in case of emergency and shall be located to provide lines of sight comparable to those for all viewing areas.

EXCEPTION: Accessible viewing positions may be clustered for bleachers, balconies, and other areas having sight lines that require slopes of greater than 5 percent. Equivalent accessible viewing positions may be located on levels having accessible egress.

4.33.4 Surfaces. The ground or floor at wheelchair locations shall be level and shall comply with 4.5.

4.33.5 Access to Performing Areas. An accessible route shall connect wheelchair seating locations with performing areas, including stages, arena floors, dressing rooms, locker rooms, and other spaces used by performers.

4.33.6* Placement of Listening Systems. If the listening system provided serves individual fixed seats, then such seats shall be located within a 50 ft (15 m) viewing distance of the stage or playing area and shall have a complete view of the stage or playing area.

4.33.7* Types of Listening Systems. Audio loops and radio frequency systems are two acceptable types of listening systems.

4.34 Dwelling Units.

4.34.1 General. The requirements of 4.34 apply to dwelling units *required to be accessible by 4.1.*

4.34.2* Minimum Requirements. An accessible dwelling unit shall be on an accessible route. An accessible dwelling unit shall have the following accessible elements and spaces as a minimum:

(1) Common spaces and facilities serving individual accessible dwelling units (for example, entry walks, trash disposal facilities, and mail boxes) shall comply with 4.2 through 4.33.

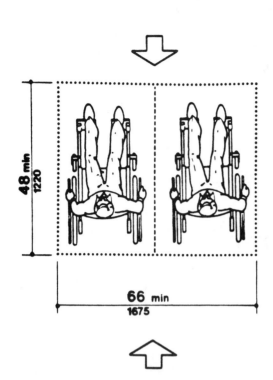

(a)
Forward or Rear Access

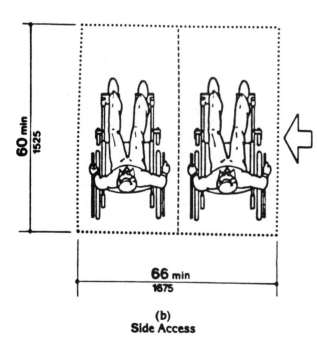

(b)
Side Access

Fig. 46
Space Requirements for Wheelchair
Seating Spaces in Series

(2) Accessible spaces shall have maneuvering space complying with 4.2.2 and 4.2.3 and surfaces complying with 4.5.

(3) At least one accessible route complying with 4.3 shall connect the accessible entrances with all accessible spaces and elements within the dwelling units.

(4) *See 4.1.1(5)(d) — Parking.*

(5) *Removed and reserved.*

(6) Doors to and in accessible spaces that are intended for passage shall comply with 4.13, *except that the provisions of 4.13.9 apply only to the doors at accessible entrances to the unit itself.*

(7) At least one accessible entrance to the dwelling unit shall comply with 4.14.

(8) Storage in accessible spaces in dwelling units, including cabinets, shelves, closets, and drawers, shall comply with 4.25.

(9) All controls in accessible spaces shall comply with 4.27. Those portions of heating, ventilating, and airconditioning equipment requiring regular, periodic maintenance and adjustment by the resident of a dwelling shall be accessible to people in wheelchairs. If air distribution registers must be placed in or close to ceilings for proper air circulation, this specification shall not apply to the registers.

(10) Emergency alarms *as required by 4.1 and* complying with 4.28.4 shall be provided in the dwelling unit.

(11) *Removed and reserved.*

(12) At least one full bathroom shall comply with 4.34.5. A full bathroom shall include a water closet, a lavatory, and a bathtub or a shower.

(13) The kitchen shall comply with 4.34.6.

(14) If laundry facilities are provided, they shall comply with 4.34.7.

(15) The following spaces shall be accessible and shall be on an accessible route:

(a) The living area.

(b) The dining area.

(c) The sleeping area, or the bedroom in one bedroom dwelling units, or at least two bedrooms or sleeping spaces in dwelling units with two or more bedrooms.

(d) Patios, terraces, balconies, carports, and garages, if provided with the dwelling unit.

4.34.3 Adaptability. The specifications for 4.34.5 and 4.34.6 *include* the concept of adaptability. *Accessible dwelling units may be designed for either permanent accessibility or adaptability.*

4.34.4 Consumer Information. To ensure that the existence of adaptable features will be known to the owner or occupant of a dwelling, the following consumer information shall be provided in each *adaptable* dwelling unit available for *occupancy:*

(1) Notification of the alternate heights available for the kitchen counter and sink, and the existence of removable cabinets and bases, if provided, under counters, sinks, and lavatories.

(2) Notification of the provisions for the installation of grab bars at toilets, bathtubs, and showers.

(3) Notification that the dwelling unit is equipped to have a visual emergency alarm installed.

(4) Identification of the location where information and instructions are available for changing the height of counters, removing cabinets and bases, installing a visual emergency alarm system, and installing grab bars.

(5) Notification that the dwelling unit has been designed in accordance with this *Uniform Federal Accessibility Standards.*

In addition, the *parties who will be responsible for making adaptations* shall be provided with the following information:

(1) Instructions for adjusting or replacing kitchen counter and sink heights and for removing cabinets.

(2) A scale drawing showing methods and locations for the installation of grab bars.

(3) A scale drawing showing the location of adjustable or replaceable counter areas and removable cabinets.

(4) Identification of the location of any equipment and parts required for adjusting or replacing counter tops, cabinets, and sinks.

(5) Instructions for installing a visual emergency alarm system, if the dwelling unit is equipped for such an installation.

4.34.5* Bathrooms. *Accessible* or adaptable bathrooms shall be on an accessible route and shall comply with the requirements of 4.34.5.

4.34.5.1 Doors. Doors shall not swing into the clear floor space required for any fixture.

4.34.5.2 Water Closets.

(1) Clear floor space at the water closet shall be as shown in Fig. 47(a). The water closet may be located with the clear area at either the right or left side of the toilet.

(2) The height of the water closet shall be at least 15 in (380 mm), *and no more than 19 in (485 mm),* measured to the top of the toilet seat.

(3) Structural reinforcement or other provisions that will allow installation of grab bars shall be provided in the locations shown in Fig. 47(b). If provided, grab bars shall be installed as shown in Fig. 29 and shall comply with 4.26.

(4) The toilet paper dispenser shall be installed within reach as shown in Fig. 47(b).

4.34.5.3 Lavatory, Mirrors, and Medicine Cabinets.

(1) The lavatory and mirrors shall comply with 4.22.6.

(2) If a cabinet is provided under the lavatory in adaptable bathrooms, then it shall be removable to provide the clearances specified in 4.22.6.

(3) If a medicine cabinet is provided above the lavatory, then the bottom of the medicine cabinet shall be located with a usable shelf no higher than 44 in (1120 mm) above the floor.

4.34.5.4 Bathtubs. If a bathtub is provided, then it shall have the following features:

(1) Floor space. Clear floor space at bathtubs shall be as shown in Fig. 33.

(2) Seat. An in-tub seat or a seat at the head end of the tub shall be provided as shown in Fig. 33 and 34. The structural strength of seats and their attachments shall comply with 4.26.3. Seats shall be mounted securely and shall not slip during use.

(3) Grab bars. Structural reinforcement or other provisions that will allow installation of grab bars shall be provided in the locations shown in Fig. 48. If provided, grab bars shall be installed as shown in Fig. 34 and shall comply with 4.26.

(4) Controls. Faucets and other controls shall be located as shown in Fig. 34 and shall comply with 4.27.4.

(5) Shower unit. A shower spray unit with a hose at least 60 in (1525 mm) long that can be used as a fixed shower head or as a hand-held shower shall be provided.

4.34.5.5 Showers. If a shower is provided, it shall have the following features:

(1) Size and clearances. Shower stall size and clear floor space shall comply with either Fig. 35(a) or (b). The shower stall in Fig. 35(a) shall be 36 in by 36 in (915 mm by 915 mm). The shower stall in Fig. 35(b) will fit into the same space as a standard 60 in (1525 mm) long bathtub.

(2) Seat. A seat shall be provided in the shower stall in Fig. 35(a) as shown in Fig. 36. The seat shall be 17 in to 19 in (430 mm to 485 mm) high measured from the bathroom floor and shall extend the full depth of the stall. The seat shall be on the wall opposite the controls. The structural strength of seats and their attachments shall comply with 4.26.3. Seats shall be mounted securely and shall not slip during use.

(3) Grab bars. Structural reinforcement or other provisions that will allow installation of grab bars shall be provided in the locations shown in Fig. 49. If provided, grab bars shall be installed as shown in Fig. 37 and shall comply with 4.26.

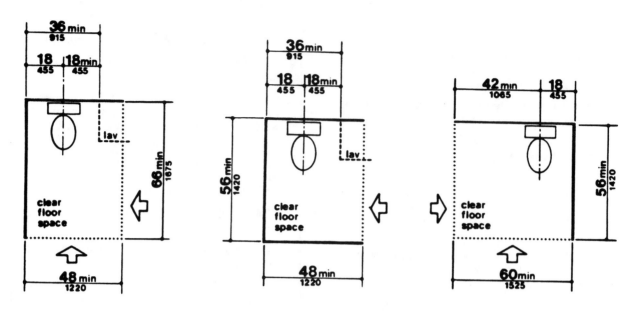

(a)
Clear Floor Space for Adaptable Bathrooms

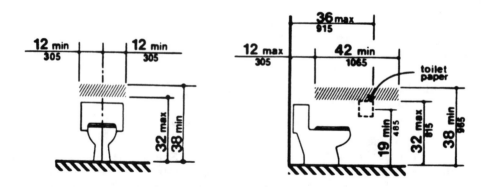

NOTE: The hatched areas are reinforced to receive grab bars.

(b)
Reinforced Areas for Installation of Grab Bars

Fig. 47
Water Closets in Adaptable Bathrooms

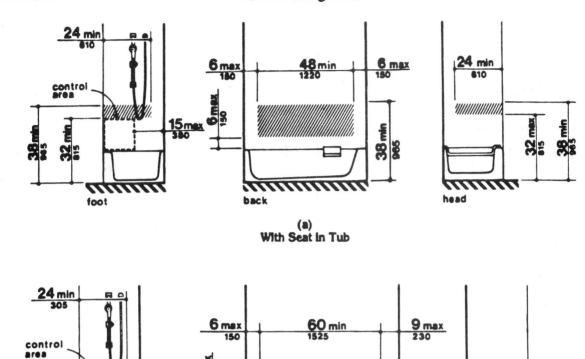

(a)
With Seat in Tub

(b)
With Seat at Head of Tub

NOTE: The hatched areas are reinforced to receive grab bars.

Fig. 48
Location of Grab Bars and Controls of Adaptable Bathtubs

(4) Controls. Faucets and other controls shall be located as shown in Fig. 37 and shall comply with 4.27.4. In the shower stall in Fig. 35(a), all controls, faucets, and the shower unit shall be mounted on the side wall opposite the seat.

(5) Shower unit. A shower spray unit with a hose at least 60 in (1525 mm) long that can be used as a fixed shower head at various heights or as a hand-held shower shall be provided.

4.34.5.6 Bathtub and Shower Enclosures.
Enclosures for bathtubs or shower stalls shall not obstruct controls or transfer from wheelchairs onto shower or bathtub seats. Enclosures on bathtubs shall not have tracks mounted on their rims.

4.34.5.7 Clear Floor Space. Clear floor space at fixtures may overlap.

4.34.6 Kitchens. *Accessible or adaptable* kitchens and their components shall be on an accessible route and shall comply with the requirements of 4.34.6.

4.34.6.1* Clearance. Clearances between all opposing base cabinets, counter tops, appliances, or walls shall be 40 in (1015 mm) minimum, except in U-shaped kitchens, where such clearance shall be 60 in (1525 mm) minimum.

4.34.6.2 Clear Floor Space. A clear floor space at least 30 in by 48 in (760 mm by 1220 mm) complying with 4.2.4 that allows either a forward or a parallel approach by a person in a wheelchair shall be provided at all appliances in the kitchen, including the range or cooktop, oven, refrigerator/freezer, dishwasher, and trash compactor. Laundry equipment located in the kitchen shall comply with 4.34.7.

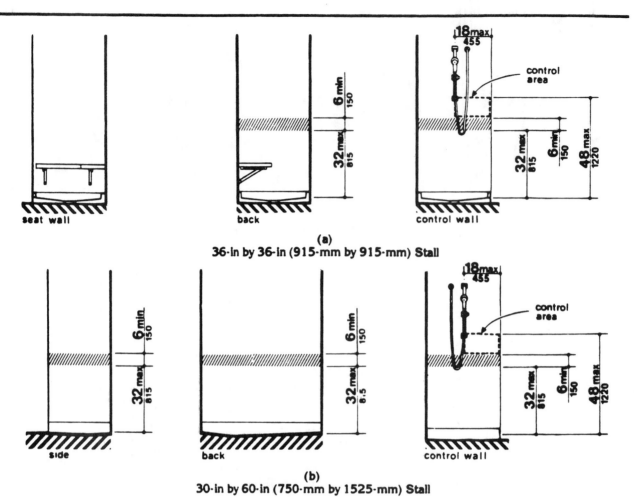

(a)
36-in by 36-in (915-mm by 915-mm) Stall

(b)
30-in by 60-in (750-mm by 1525-mm) Stall

NOTE: The hatched areas are reinforced to receive grab bars.

Fig. 49
Location of Grab Bars and Controls of Adaptable Showers

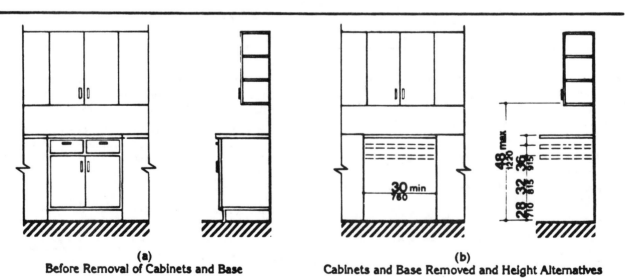

(a)
Before Removal of Cabinets and Base

(b)
Cabinets and Base Removed and Height Alternatives

Fig. 50
Counter Work Surface

4.34.6.3 Controls. All controls in kitchens shall comply with 4.27.

4.34.6.4 Work Surfaces. At least one 30 in (760 mm) section of counter shall provide a work surface that complies with the following requirements (see Fig. 50):

(1) The counter shall be *mounted at a maximum height of 34 in (865 mm) above the floor, measured from the floor to the top of the counter surface, or shall be* adjustable or replaceable as a unit to provide alternative heights of 28 in, 32 in, and 36 in (710 mm, 815 mm, and 915 mm), measured from the top of the counter surface.

(2) Base cabinets, if provided, shall be removable under the full 30 in (760 mm) minimum frontage of the counter. The finished floor shall extend under the counter to the wall.

(3) Counter thickness and supporting structure shall be 2 in (50 mm) maximum over the required clear area.

(4) A clear floor space 30 in by 48 in (760 mm by 1220 mm) shall allow a forward approach to the counter. Nineteen inches (485 mm) maximum of the clear floor space may extend underneath the counter. The knee space shall have a minimum clear width of 30 in (760 mm) and a minimum clear depth of 19 in (485 mm).

(5) There shall be no sharp or abrasive surfaces under such counters.

4.34.6.5* Sink. The sink and surrounding counter shall comply with the following requirements (see Fig. 51):

(1) The sink and surrounding counter shall be *mounted at a maximum height of 34 in (865 mm) above the floor, measured from the floor to the top of the counter surface, or shall* be adjustable or replaceable as a unit to provide alternative heights of 28 in, 32 in, and 36 in (710 mm, 815 mm, and 915 mm), measured from the floor to the top of the counter surface or sink rim. The total width of sink and counter area shall be 30 in (760 mm).

(2) Rough-in plumbing shall be located to accept connections of supply and drain pipes for sinks mounted at the height of 28 in (710 mm).

(3) The depth of a sink bowl shall be no greater than 6-1/2 in (165 mm). Only one bowl of double-or triple-bowl sinks needs to meet this requirement.

(4) Faucets shall comply with 4.27.4. Lever-operated or push-type mechanisms are two acceptable designs.

(5) Base cabinets, if provided, shall be removable under the full 30 in (760 mm) minimum frontage of the sink and surrounding counter. The finished flooring shall extend under the counter to the wall.

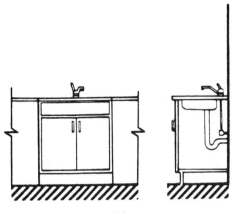

(a)
Before Removal of Cabinets and Base

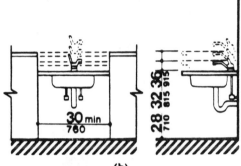

(b)
**Cabinets and Base Removed
and Height Alternatives**

**Fig. 51
Kitchen Sink**

(6) Counter thickness and supporting structure shall be 2 in (50 mm) maximum over the required clear space.

(7) A clear floor space 30 in by 48 in (760 mm by 1220 mm) shall allow forward approach to the sink. Nineteen inches (485 mm) maximum of the clear floor space may extend underneath the sink. The knee space shall have a clear width of 30 in (760 mm) and a clear depth of 19 in (485 mm).

(8) There shall be no sharp or abrasive surfaces under sinks. Hot water and drain pipes under sinks shall be insulated or otherwise covered.

4.34.6.6* Ranges and Cooktops. Ranges and cooktops shall comply with 4.34.6.2 and 4.34.6.3. If ovens or cooktops have knee spaces underneath, then they shall be insulated or otherwise protected on the exposed contact surfaces to prevent burns, abrasions, or electrical shock. The clear floor space may overlap the knee space, if provided, by 19 in (485 mm) maximum. The location of controls for ranges and cook-tops shall not require reaching across burners.

4.34.6.7* Ovens. Ovens shall comply with 4.34.6.2 and 4.34.6.3. Ovens shall be of the self-cleaning type or be located adjacent to an adjustable height counter with knee space below (see Fig. 52). For side-opening ovens, the door latch side shall be next to the open counter space, and there shall be a pull-out shelf under the oven extending the full width of the oven and pulling out not less than 10 in (255 mm) when fully extended. Ovens shall have controls on front panels; they may be located on either side of the door.

4.34.6.8* Refrigerator/Freezers. Refrigerator/ freezers shall comply with 4.34.6.3. *Provision shall be made for refrigerators which are:*

(1) Of the vertical side-by-side refrigerator/freezer type; or

(2) Of the over-and-under type and meet the following requirements:

(a) Have at least 50 percent of the freezer space below 54 in (1370 mm) above the floor.

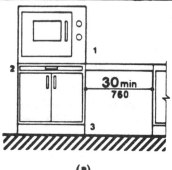

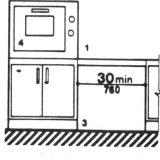

(a)
Side-Hinged Door

(b)
Bottom-Hinged Door

SYMBOL KEY:
1. Countertop or wall-mounted oven.
2. Pull-out board preferred with side-opening door.
3. Clear open space.
4. Bottom-hinged door.

Fig. 52
Ovens without Self-Cleaning Feature

(b) Have 100 percent of the refrigerator space and controls below 54 in (1370 mm).

Freezers with less than 100 percent of the storage volume within the limits specified in 4.2.5 or 4.2.6 shall be the self-defrosting type.

4.34.6.9 Dishwashers. Dishwashers shall comply with 4.34.6.2 and 4.34.6.3. Dishwashers shall have all rack space accessible from the front of the machine for loading and unloading dishes.

4.34.6.10* Kitchen Storage. Cabinets, drawers, and shelf areas shall comply with 4.25 and shall have the following features:

(1) Maximum height shall be 48 in (1220 mm) for at least one shelf of all cabinets and storage shelves mounted above work counters (see Fig. 50).

(2) Door pulls or handles for wall cabinets shall be mounted as close to the bottom of cabinet doors as possible. Door pulls or handles for base cabinets shall be mounted as close to the top of cabinet doors as possible.

4.34.7 Laundry Facilities. If laundry equipment is provided within individual accessible dwelling units, or if separate laundry facilities serve one or more accessible dwelling units, then they shall meet the requirements of 4.34.7.1 through 4.34.7.3.

4.34.7.1 Location. Laundry facilities and laundry equipment shall be on an accessible route.

4.34.7.2 Washing Machines and Clothes Dryers. Washing machines and clothes dryers in common use laundry rooms shall be front loading.

4.34.7.3 Controls. Laundry equipment shall comply with 4.27.

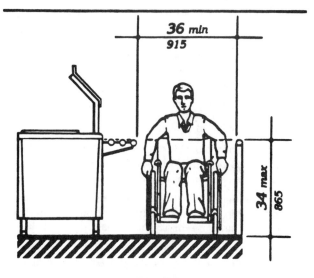

Fig. 53
Food Service Lines

5. RESTAURANTS AND CAFETERIAS.

5.1 General. In addition to the requirements of 4.1 to 4.33, the design of at least 5 percent of all fixed seating or tables in a restaurant or cafeteria shall comply with 4.32. Access aisles between tables shall comply with 4.3. Where practical, accessible tables should be distributed throughout the space or facility. In restaurants or cafeterias where there are mezzanine levels, loggias, or raised platforms, accessibility to all such spaces is not required providing that the same services and decorative character are provided in spaces located on accessible routes.

5.2 Food Service Lines. Food service lines shall have a minimum clear width of 36 in (915 mm), with a preferred clear width of 42 in (1065 mm) where passage of stopped wheelchairs by pedestrians is desired. Tray slides shall be mounted no higher than 34 in (865 mm) above the floor. If self-service shelves are provided, a reasonable portion must be within the ranges shown in Fig. 53.

5.3 Tableware Areas. Install tableware, dishware, condiment, food and beverage display shelves, and dispensing devices in compliance with 4.2 (see Fig. 54).

5.4 Vending Machines. Install vending machines in compliance with 4.27.

6. HEALTH CARE.

6.1 General. In addition to the requirements of 4.1 to 4.33, Health Care buildings and facilities shall comply with 6.

6.2 Entrances. At least one accessible entrance that complies with 4.14 shall be protected from the weather by canopy or roof overhang. Such entrances shall incorporate a passenger loading zone that complies with 4.6.5 (see 4.13.6).

6.3 Patient Bedrooms. Provide accessible patient bedrooms in compliance with 4. Accessible patient bedrooms shall comply with the following:

(1) Each bedroom shall have a turning space that complies with 4.2.3, and preferably that is located near the entrance.

(2) Each one-bed room shall have a minimum clear floor space of 36 in (915 mm) along each side of the bed, and 42 in (1065 mm) between the foot of the bed and the wall.

(3) Each two-bed room shall have a minimum clear floor space of 42 in (1065 mm), preferably 48 in (1220 mm), between the foot of the bed and the wall; 36 in (915 mm) between the side of the bed and the wall; and 48 in (1220 mm) between beds.

(4) Each four-bed room shall have a minimum clear floor space of 48 in (1220 mm) from the foot of the bed to the foot of the opposing bed; 36 in (915 mm) between the side of the bed and the wall; and 48 in (1220 mm) between beds.

(5) Each bedroom shall have a door that complies with 4.13.

6.4 Patient Toilet Rooms. Provide each patient bedroom that is required to be accessible with an accessible toilet room that complies with 4.22 or 4.23.

7. MERCANTILE.

7.1 General. In addition to the requirements of 4.1 to 4.33, the design of all areas used for business transactions with the public shall comply with 7.

7.2 Service Counters. Where service counters exceeding 36 in (915 mm) in height are provided for standing sales or distribution of goods to the public, an auxiliary counter or a portion of the main counter shall be provided with a maximum height of between 28 in to 34 in (710 mm to 865 mm) above the floor in compliance with 4.32.4.

7.3 Check-Out Aisles. At least one accessible check-out aisle shall be provided in buildings or facilities with check-out aisles. Clear aisle width shall comply with 4.2.1 and maximum adjoining counter height shall not exceed 36 in (915 mm) above the floor.

7.4 Security Bollards. Any device used to prevent the removal of shopping carts from store premises shall not prevent access or egress to those in wheelchairs. An alternate entry that is equally convenient to that provided for the ambulatory population is acceptable.

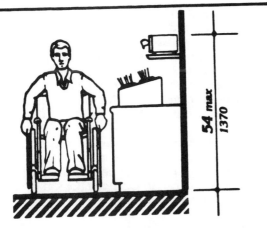

Fig. 54
Tableware Areas

54 max
1370

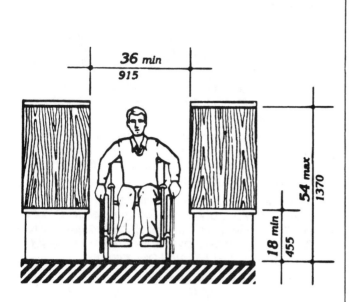

Fig. 55
Card Catalog

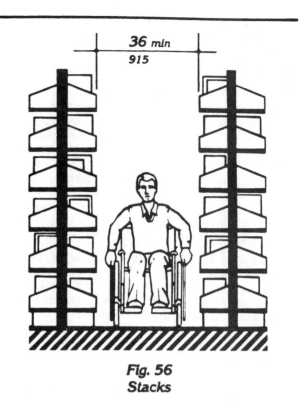

Fig. 56
Stacks

8. | LIBRARIES.

8.1 General. *In addition to the requirements of 4.1 to 4.33, the design of all public areas of a library shall comply with 8, including reading and study areas, stacks, reference rooms, reserve areas, and special facilities or collections. As provided, elements such as public toilet rooms, telephones, and parking shall be accessible.*

8.2 Reading and Study Areas. *At least 5 percent or a minimum of one of each element of fixed seating, tables, or study carrels shall comply with 4.2 and 4.32. Clearances between fixed accessible tables and study carrels shall comply with 4.3.*

8.3 Check-Out Areas. *At least one lane at each check-out area shall comply with 4.32. Any traffic control or book security gates or turnstiles shall comply with 4.13.*

8.4 Card Catalogs. *Minimum clear aisle space at card catalogs, magazine displays, or reference stacks shall comply with Fig. 55. Maximum reach height shall comply with 4.2, with a height of 48 in (1370 mm) preferred, irrespective of reach allowed.*

8.5 Stacks. *Minimum clear aisle width between stacks shall comply with 4.3, with a minimum clear aisle width of 42 in (1065 mm) preferred where possible. Shelf height in stack areas is unrestricted (see Fig. 56).*

9. | POSTAL FACILITIES.

9.1 General. *In addition to the requirements of 4.1 to 4.33, the design of U.S. postal facilities shall comply with the requirements of 9. In addition, employee toilet rooms, water fountains, lunchrooms, lounges, attendance-recording equipment, medical treatment rooms, emergency signals, and switches and controls shall be made accessible or adaptable in accordance with the requirements of these standards.*

9.2* Post Office Lobbies. *Where writing desks or tables are provided, a minimum of at least one writing desk or table that complies with 4.32 must be provided. Clear passageways in front of customer service counters shall be not less than 48 in (1220 mm) clear width to permit maneuvering of a wheelchair. Letter drops shall be mounted at heights that comply with 4.2.*

(1) All fixed partitions must be installed to withstand a 250-pound force applied at any point and from any direction. Avoid designs that call for, or may necessitate, non-fixed partitions in circulation routes of handicapped people.

(2) Walls where handrails are provided for handicapped people must be capable of supporting handrails designed to support a 250-pound pull force in any direction.

9.3 Self-Service Postal Centers. *Parcel post depositories, stamp vending machines, multi-commodity vending machines, and currency-coin changing machines shall be installed so that the operating mechanisms of all machines comply with 4.2 and 4.27. All mechanisms must be installed to permit close parallel approach by a wheelchair user.*

9.4 Post Office Boxes. *At least 5 percent of the post office boxes in a facility shall be accessible to wheelchair users. The total number of accessible post office boxes provided shall include a representative number of each of the standard USPS boxes currently being installed. Accessible post office boxes shall be located in the second or third set of modules from the floor, approximately 12 in to 36 in (305 mm to 915 mm) above the finished floor. Aisles between post office boxes shall be a minimum of 66 in (1675 mm) clear width.*

9.5 Locker Rooms. *Lockers in easily accessible areas must be provided for use by handicapped people. When double-tier lockers are used, only the bottom row of lockers may be assigned for use by wheelchair users. When full length lockers are used, all hooks, shelves, etc., intended for use by people in wheelchairs shall be located no higher than 48 in (1220 mm) above the finished floor. Lockers intended for use by handicapped people shall be equipped with latches and latch handles that comply with 4.27. Unobstructed aisle space in front of lockers used by handicapped people shall be a minimum of 42 in (1065 mm) clear width.*

9.6 Attendance-Recording Equipment. *Time clocks, card racks, log books, and other work assignment or attendance-recording equipment used by people in wheelchairs must be installed at a height no more than 48 in (1220 mm) above the finished floor. Counter space at check-in areas must be no more than 36 in (915 mm) above the finished floor.*

APPENDIX

This appendix contains additional information that should help the designer to understand the minimum requirements of the standard or to design buildings or facilities for greater accessibility. The paragraph numbers correspond to the sections or paragraphs of the standard to which the material relates and are therefore not consecutive (for example, A4.2.1 contains additional information relevant to 4.2.1). Sections for which additional material appears in this appendix have been indicated by an asterisk.

A4.2 Space Allowances and Reach Ranges.

A4.2.1 Wheelchair Passage Width.

(1) Space Requirements for Wheelchairs. Most wheelchair users need a 30 in (760 mm) clear opening width for doorways, gates, and the like, when the latter are entered head-on. If the wheelchair user is unfamiliar with a building, if competing traffic is heavy, if sudden or frequent movements are needed, or if the wheelchair must be turned at an opening, then greater clear widths are needed. For most situations, the addition of an inch of leeway on either side is sufficient. Thus, a minimum clear width of 32 in (815 mm) will provide adequate clearance. However, when an opening or a restriction in a passageway is more than 24 in (610 mm) long, it is essentially a passageway and must be at least 36 in (915 mm) wide.

(2) Space Requirements for Use of Walking Aids. Although people who use walking aids can maneuver through clear width openings of 32 in (815 mm), they need 36 in (915 mm) wide passageways and walks for comfortable gaits. Crutch tips, often extending down at a wide angle, are a hazard in narrow passageways where they might not be seen by other pedestrians. Thus, the 36 in (915 mm) width provides a safety allowance both for the disabled person and for others.

(3) Space Requirements for Passing. Able-bodied people in winter clothing, walking straight ahead with arms swinging, need 32 in (815 mm) of width, which includes 2 in (50 mm) on either side for sway, and another 1 in (25 mm) tolerance on either side for clearing nearby objects or other pedestrians. Almost all wheelchair users and those who use walking aids can also manage within this 32 in (815 mm) width for short distances. Thus, two streams of traffic can pass in 64 in (1625 mm) in a comfortable flow. Sixty inches (1525 mm) provide a minimum width for a somewhat more restricted flow. If the clear width is less than 60 in (1525 mm), two wheelchair users will not be able to pass but will have to seek a wider place for passing. Forty-eight inches (1220 mm) is the minimum width needed for an ambulatory person to pass a nonambulatory or semiambulatory person. Within this 48 in (1220 mm) width, the ambulatory person will have to twist to pass a wheelchair user, a person with a

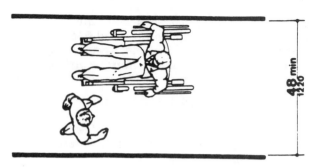

**Fig. A1
Minimum Passage Width for One Wheelchair
and One Ambulatory Person**

seeing eye dog, or a semiambulatory person. There will be little leeway for swaying or missteps (see Fig. A1).

A4.2.3 Wheelchair Turning Space. This standard specifies a minimum space of 60 in (1525 mm) diameter for a pivoting 180-degree turn of a wheelchair. This space is usually satisfactory for turning around, but many people will not be able to turn without repeated tries and bumping into surrounding objects. The space shown in Fig. A2 will allow most wheelchair users to complete U-turns without difficulty.

A4.2.4 Clear Floor or Ground Space for Wheelchairs. The wheelchair and user shown in Fig. A3 represent typical dimensions for a large adult male. The space requirements in this standard are based upon maneuvering clearances that will accommodate most larger wheelchairs. Fig. A3 provides a uniform reference for design not covered by this standard.

A4.2.5 & A4.2.6 Reach. *Reach ranges for persons seated in wheelchairs may be further clarified by Fig. A3(a). These drawings approximate in the plan view information shown in Fig. 4, 5, and 6 in other views.*

A4.3 Accessible Route.

A4.3.1 General.

(1) Travel Distances. Many disabled people can move at only very slow speeds; for many, traveling 200 ft (61 m) could take about 2 minutes. This assumes a rate of about 1.5 ft/s (455 mm/s) on level ground. It also assumes that the traveler would move continuously. However, on trips over 100 ft (30 m), disabled people are apt to rest frequently, which substantially increases their trip times. Resting periods of 2 minutes for every 100 ft (30 m) can be used to estimate travel times for people with severely limited stamina. In

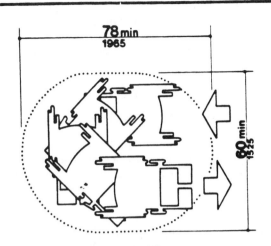

Fig. A2
Space Needed for Smooth U-Turn in a Wheelchair

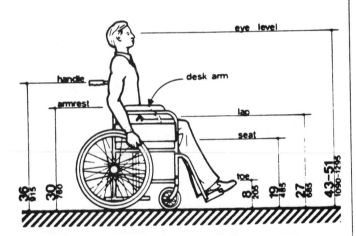

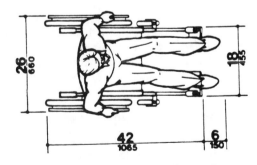

NOTE: Footrests may extend further for very large people.

Fig. A3
Dimensions of Adult-Sized Wheelchairs

inclement weather, slow progress and resting can greatly increase a disabled person's exposure to the elements.

(2) Sites. Level, indirect routes or those with running slopes lower than 1:20 can sometimes provide more convenience than direct routes with maximum allow-able slopes or with ramps.

A4.3.10 Egress. In buildings where physically handicapped people are regularly employed or are residents, an emergency management plan for their evacuation also plays an essential role in fire safety.

A4.4 Protruding Objects.

A4.4.1 General. Guide dogs are trained to recognize and avoid hazards. However, most people with severe impairments of vision use the long cane as an aid to mobility. The two principal cane techniques are the touch technique, where the cane arcs from side to side and touches points outside both shoulders; and the diagonal technique, where the cane is held in a stationary position diagonally across the body with the cane tip touching or just above the

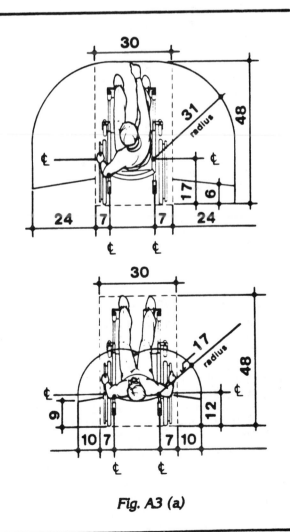

Fig. A3 (a)

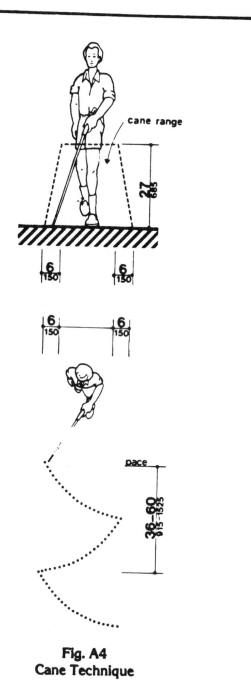

Fig. A4
Cane Technique

ground at a point outside one shoulder and the handle or grip extending to a point outside the other shoulder. The touch technique is used primarily in uncontrolled areas, while the diagonal technique is used primarily in certain limited, controlled, and familiar environments. Cane users are often trained to use both techniques.

Potential hazardous objects are noticed only if they fall within the detection range of canes (see Fig. A4). Visually impaired people walking toward an object can detect an overhang if its lowest surface is not higher than 27 in (685 mm). When walking alongside project-

ing objects, they cannot detect overhangs. Since proper cane and guide dog techniques keep people away from the edge of a path or from walks, a slight overhang of no more than 4 in (100 mm) is not hazardous.

A4.5 Ground and Floor Surfaces.

A4.5.1 General. Ambulant and semiambulant people who have difficulty maintaining balance and those with restricted gaits are particularly sensitive to slipping and tripping hazards. For such people, a stable and regular surface is necessary for safe walking, particularly on stairs. Wheelchairs can be propelled most easily on surfaces that are hard, stable, and regular. Soft, loose surfaces such as shag carpet, loose sand, and wet clay, and irregular surfaces, such as cobblestones, can significantly impede wheelchair movement.

Slip resistance is based on the frictional force necessary to keep a shoe heel or crutch tip from slipping on a walking surface under the conditions of use likely to be found on the surface. Although it is known that the static coefficient of friction is the basis of slip resistance, there is not as yet a generally accepted method to evaluate the slip resistance of walking surfaces.

Cross slopes on walks and ground or floor surfaces can cause considerable difficulty in propelling a wheelchair in a straight line.

A4.5.3 Carpet. Much more needs to be done in developing both quantitative and qualitative criteria for carpeting. However, certain functional characteristics are well established. When both carpet and padding are used, it is desirable to have minimum movement (preferably none) between the floor and the pad and the pad and the carpet, which would allow the carpet to hump or warp. In heavily trafficked areas, a thick, soft (plush) pad or cushion, particularly in combination with long carpet pile, makes it difficult for individuals in wheelchairs and those with other ambulatory disabilities to get about. This should not preclude their use in specific areas where traffic is light. Firm carpeting can be achieved through proper selection and combination of pad and carpet, sometimes with the elimination of the pad or cushion, and with proper installation.

A4.6 Parking and Passenger Loading Zones.

A4.6.3 Parking Spaces. High-top vans, which disabled people or transportation services often use, require higher clearances in parking garages than automobiles. When optional van spaces are provided within a garage, only the spaces themselves and a vehicle route to them require the specified clearances.

A4.6.4 Signage. Signs designating parking places for disabled people can be seen from a driver's seat if the signs are mounted high enough above the ground and located at the front of a parking space.

A4.8 Ramps.

A4.8.1 General. Ramps are essential for wheelchair users if elevators or lifts are not available to connect different levels. However, some people who use walk-ing aids have difficulty with ramps and prefer stairs.

A4.8.2 Slope and Rise. The ability to manage an incline is related to both its slope and its length. Wheelchair users with disabilities affecting arms or with low stamina have serious difficulty using inclines. Most ambulatory people and most people who use wheelchairs can manage a slope of 1:16. Many people cannot manage a slope of 1:12 for 30 ft (9 m). Many people who have difficulty negotiating very long ramps at relatively shallow slopes can manage very short ramps at steeper slopes.

A4.8.5 Handrails. The requirements for stair and ramp handrails in this standard are for adults. When children are principal users in a building or facility, a second set of handrails at an appropriate height can assist them and aid in preventing accidents.

A4.10 Elevators.

A4.10.6 Door Protective and Reopening Device. The required door reopening device would hold the door open for 20 seconds if the doorway remains unobstructed. After 20 seconds, the door may begin to close. However, if designed in accordance with ANSI A17.1-1978, the door closing movement could still be stopped if a person or object exerts sufficient force at any point on the door edge.

A4.10.7 Door and Signal Timing for Hall Calls. This paragraph allows variation in the location of call buttons, advance time for warning signals, and the door-holding period used to meet the time requirement.

A4.10.12 Car Controls. Industry-wide standardiza-tion of elevator control panel design would make all elevators significantly more convenient for use by people with severe visual impairments.

In many cases, it will be possible to locate the highest control on elevator panels within 48 in (1220 mm) from the floor.

A4.10.13 Car Position Indicators. A special but-ton may be provided that would activate the audible signal within the given elevator only for the desired trip, rather than maintaining the audible signal in constant operation.

A4.10.14 Emergency Communications. A device that requires no handset is easier to use by people who have difficulty reaching.

A4.11 Platform Lifts.

Platform lifts include porch lifts and other devices used for short-distance, vertical transportation of people in wheelchairs. At the present time, generally recognized safety standards for such lifts have not been developed. Care should be taken in selecting and installing lifts to ensure that they are free from hazards to users or to other individuals who may be in the vicinity where they are being operated.

A4.13 Doors.

A4.13.8 Thresholds at Doorways. Thresholds and surface height changes in doorways are particularly inconvenient for wheelchair users who also have low stamina or restrictions in arm movement, because complex maneuvering is required to get over the level change while operating the door.

A4.13.9 Door Hardware. Some disabled persons must push against a door with their chair or walker to open it. Applied kickplates on doors with closers can reduce required maintenance by withstanding abuse from wheelchairs and canes. To be effective, they should cover the door width, less approximately 2 in (51 mm), up to a height of 16 in (405 mm) from its bottom edge and be centered across the top.

A4.13.10 Door Closers. Closers with delayed action features give a person more time to maneuver through doorways. They are particularly useful on fre-quently used interior doors such as entrances to toilet rooms.

A4.13.11 Door Opening Force. Although most people with disabilities can exert at least 5 lbf (22.2N), both pushing and pulling from a stationary position, a few people with severe disabilities cannot exert even 3 lbf (13.3N). Although some people cannot manage the allowable forces in this standard and many others have difficulty, door closers must have certain minimum closing forces to close doors satisfactorily. Forces for pushing or pulling doors open are measured with a push-pull scale under the following conditions:

(1) Hinged doors: Force applied perpendicular to the door at the door opener or 30 in (760 mm) from the hinged side, whichever is farther from the hinge.

(2) Sliding or folding doors: Force applied parallel to the door at the door pull or latch.

(3) Application of force: Apply force gradually so that the applied force does not exceed the resistance of the door.

In high-rise buildings, air-pressure differentials may require a modification of this specification in order to meet the functional intent.

A4.13.12 Automatic Doors and Power-Assisted Doors. Sliding automatic doors do not need guard rails and are more convenient for wheelchair users and visually impaired people to use. If slowly opening automatic doors can be reactuated before their closing cycle is completed, they will be more convenient in busy doorways.

A4.15 *Drinking Fountains and Water Coolers.*

A4.15.2 *Drinking fountains with two spouts can assist both handicapped people and those people who find it difficult to bend over.*

A4.16 Water Closets.

A4.16.3 Height. Preferences for toilet seat heights vary considerably among disabled people. Higher seat heights may be an advantage to some ambulatory disabled people but a disadvantage for wheelchair

users and others. Toilet seats 18 in (455 mm) high seem to be a reasonable compromise. Thick seats and filler rings are available to adapt standard fixtures to these requirements.

A4.16.4 Grab Bars. Fig. A5(a) and (b) show the diagonal and side approaches most commonly used to transfer from a wheelchair to a water closet. Some wheelchair users can transfer from the front of the toilet, while others use a 90-degree approach. Most people who use the two additional approaches can also use either the diagonal approach or the side approach.

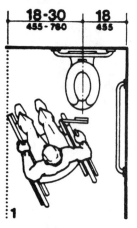 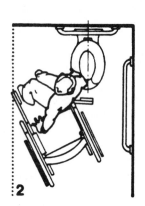 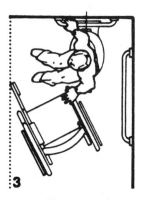 

1. Takes transfer position, swings footrest out of the way, sets brakes.

2. Removes armrest, transfers.

3. Moves wheelchair out of the way, changes position (some people fold chair or pivot it 90° to the toilet).

4. Positions on toilet, releases brake.

(a)
Diagonal Approach

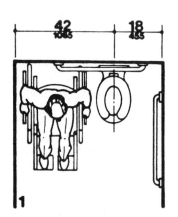 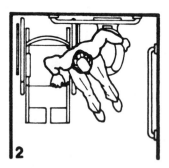 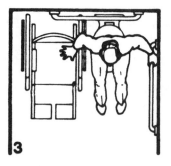

1. Takes transfer position, removes armrest, sets brakes.

2. Transfers.

3. Positions on toilet.

(b)
Side Approach

Fig. A5
Wheelchair Transfers

A4.16.5 Flush Controls. Flush valves and related plumbing can be located behind walls or to the side of the toilet, or a toilet seat lid can be provided if plumbing fittings are directly behind the toilet seat. Such designs reduce the chance of injury and imbalance caused by leaning back against the fittings. Flush controls for tank-type toilets have a standardized mounting location on the left side of the tank (facing the tank). Tanks can be obtained by special order with controls mounted on the right side. If administrative authorities require flush controls for flush valves to be located in a position that conflicts with the location of the rear grab bar, then that bar may be split or shifted toward the wide side of the toilet area.

A4.17 Toilet Stalls.

A4.17.5 Doors. To make it easier for wheelchair users to close toilet stall doors, doors can be provided with closers, spring hinges, or a pull bar mounted on the inside surface of the door near the hinge side.

A4.19 Lavatories and Mirrors.

A4.19.6 Mirrors. If mirrors are to be used by both ambulatory people and wheelchair users, then they must be at least 74 in (1880 mm) high at their topmost edge. A single full length mirror can accommodate all people, including children.

A4.21 Shower Stalls.

A4.21.1 General. Shower stalls that are 36 in by 36 in (915 mm by 915 mm) wide provide additional safety to people who have difficulty maintaining balance because all grab bars and walls are within easy reach. Seated people use the walls of 36 in by 36 in (915 mm by 915 mm) showers for back support. Shower stalls that are 60 in (1525 mm) wide and have no curb may increase usability of a bathroom by wheelchair users because the shower area provides additional maneuvering space.

A4.23 Bathrooms, Bathing Facilities, and Shower Rooms.

A4.23.9 Medicine Cabinets. Other alternatives for storing medical and personal care items are very useful to disabled people. Shelves, drawers, and floor-mounted cabinets can be provided within the reach ranges of disabled people.

A4.26 Handrails, Grab Bars, and Tub and Shower Seats.

A4.26.1 General. Many disabled people rely heavily upon grab bars and handrails to maintain balance and prevent serious falls. Many people brace their forearms between supports and walls to give them more leverage and stability in maintaining balance or for lifting. The maximum grab bar clearance of 1-1/2 in (38 mm) required in this standard is a safety clearance to prevent injuries from arms slipping through the opening. It also provides adequate gripping room.

A4.26.2 Size and Spacing of Grab Bars and Handrails. This specification allows for alternate shapes of handrails as long as they allow an opposing grip similar to that provided by a circular section of 1-1/4 in to 1-1/2 in (32 mm to 38 mm).

A4.27 Controls and Operating Mechanisms.

A4.27.3 Height. Fig. A6 further illustrates mandatory and advisory control mounting height provisions for typical equipment. Note distinction between built-in equipment (considered real property) and movable equipment (considered chattel, and not covered by the Architectural Barriers Act of 1968).

A4.28 Alarms.

A4.28.2 Audible Alarms. Audible emergency signals must have an intensity and frequency that can attract the attention of individuals who have partial hearing loss. People over 60 years of age generally have difficulty perceiving frequencies higher than 10,000 Hz.

A4.28.3 Visual Alarms. The specifications in this section do not preclude the use of zoned or coded alarm systems. In zoned systems, the emergency exit lights in an area will flash whenever an audible signal rings in the area.

A4.28.4 Auxiliary Alarms. Locating visual emergency alarms in rooms where deaf individuals may work or reside alone can ensure that they will always be warned when an emergency alarm is activated. To be effective, such devices must be located and oriented so that they will spread signals and reflections throughout a space or raise the overall light level sharply. The amount and type of light necessary to wake a deaf person from a sound sleep in a dark room will vary depending on a number of factors, including the size and configuration of the room, the distance between the source and the person, whether or not the light flashes, and the cycle of flashing. A 150-watt flashing bulb can be effective under some conditions. Certain devices currently available are designed specifically as visual alarms for deaf people. Deaf people may not need accessibility features other than the emergency alarm connections and communications devices. Thus, rooms in addition to those accessible for wheelchair users also should be equipped with emergency visual alarms or connections.

A4.29 Tactile Warnings.

A4.29.2 Tactile Warnings on Walking Surfaces. (Reserved).

A4.29.3 Tactile Warnings on Doors to Hazardous Areas. Tactile signals for hand reception are useful if it is certain that the signals will be touched.

A4.29.5 Tactile Warnings at Hazardous Vehicular Areas. (Reserved).

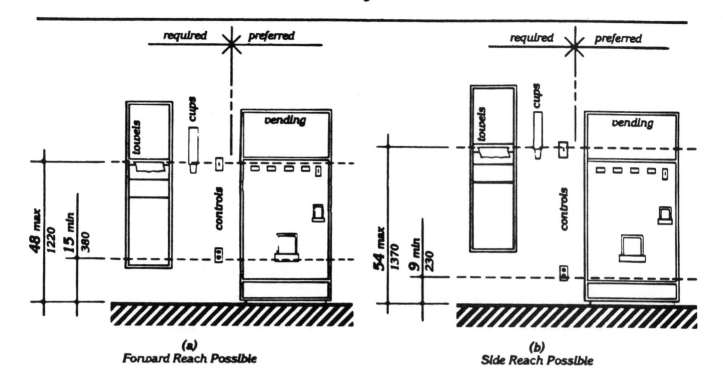

Fig. A6
Control Reach Limitations

A4.29.6 Tactile Warnings at Reflecting Pools.
(Reserved).

A4.29.7 Standardization. Too many tactile warnings or lack of standardization weakens their usefulness. Tactile signals can also be visual signals to guide dogs, since dogs can be trained to respond to a large variety of visual cues.

A4.30 Signage.

A4.30.1 General. In building complexes where finding locations independently on a routine basis may be a necessity (for example, college campuses), tactile maps or prerecorded instructions can be very helpful to visually impaired people. Several maps and auditory instructions have been developed and tested for specific applications. The type of map or instructions used must be based on the information to be communicated, which depends highly on the type of buildings or users.

Landmarks that can easily be distinguished by visually impaired individuals are useful as orientation cues. Such cues include changes in illumination level, bright colors, unique patterns, wall murals, location of special equipment, or other architectural features (for example, an exterior view).

Many people with disabilities have limitations in movement of their head and reduced peripheral vision. Thus, signage positioned perpendicular to the path of

travel is easiest for them to notice. People can generally distinguish signage within an angle of 30 degrees to either side of the centerline of their face without moving their head.

A4.30.2 Character Proportion. The legibility of printed characters is a function of the viewing distance, character height, the ratio of the stroke width to the height of the character, the contrast of color between character and background, and print font. The size of characters must be based upon the intended viewing distance. A severely nearsighted person may have to be much closer to see a character of a given size accurately than a person with normal visual acuity.

A4.30.3 Color Contrast. The greatest readability is usually achieved through the use of light-colored characters or symbols on a dark background.

A4.30.4 Raised or Indented Characters or Symbols. Signs with descriptive materials about public buildings, monuments, and objects of cultural interest can be raised or incised letters. However, a sighted guide or audio-tape device is often a more effective way to present such information. Raised characters are easier to feel at small sizes and are not susceptible to maintenance problems as are indented characters, which can fill with dirt, cleaning compounds, and the like.

Braille characters can be used in addition to standard alphabet characters and numbers. Placing braille characters to the left of standard characters makes them more convenient to read. Standard dot sizing and spacing as used in braille publications are acceptable. Raised borders around raised characters can make them confusing to read unless the border is set far away from the characters.

A4.31 Telephones.

A4.31.3 Mounting Height. In localities where the dial-tone first system is in operation, calls can be placed at a coin telephone through the operator without inserting coins. The operator button is located at a height of 46 in (1170 mm) if the coin slot of the telephone is at 54 in (1370 mm).

A generally available public telephone with a coin slot mounted lower on the equipment would allow universal installation of telephones at a height of 48 in (1220 mm) or less to all operable parts.

A4.31.5 Equipment for Hearing Impaired People. Other aids for people with hearing impairments are telephones, teleprinter, and other telephonic devices that can be used to transmit printed messages through telephone lines to a teletype printer or television monitor.

A4.32 Seating, Tables, and Work Surfaces.

A4.32.4 Height of Work Surfaces. Different types of work require different work surface heights for comfort and optimal performance. Light detailed work such as writing requires a work surface close to elbow height for a standing person. Heavy manual work such as rolling dough requires a work surface height about 10 in (255 mm) below elbow height for a standing person. The principle of a high work surface height for light detailed work and a low work surface for heavy manual work also applies for seated persons; however, the limiting condition for seated manual work is clearance under the work surface.

Table A1 shows convenient work surface heights for seated persons. The great variety of heights for comfort and optimal performance indicates a need for alternatives or a compromise in height if people who stand and people who sit will be using the same counter area.

A4.33 Assembly Areas.

A4.33.2 Size of Wheelchair Locations. Spaces large enough for two wheelchairs allow people who are coming to a performance together to sit together.

A4.33.3 Placement of Wheelchair Locations. The location of wheelchair areas can be planned so that a variety of positions within the seating area are provided. This will allow choice in viewing and price categories.

A4.33.6 Placement of Listening Systems. A distance of 50 ft (15 m) allows a person to distinguish performers' facial expressions.

Table A1
Convenient Heights of
Work Surfaces for Seated People*

Conditions of Use	Short Women		Tall Men	
	in	mm	in	mm
Seated in a wheelchair:				
Manual work:				
Desk or removable armrests	26	660	30	760
Fixed, full-size armrests†	32‡	815	32‡	815
Light, detailed work:				
Desk or removable armrests	29	735	34	865
Fixed, full-size armrests†	32‡	815	34	865
Seated in a 16-in (405-mm) -high chair:				
Manual work	26	660	27	685
Light, detailed work	28	710	31	785

*All dimensions are based on a work-surface thickness of 1-1/2 in (38 mm) and a clearance of 1-1/2 in (38 mm) between legs and the underside of a work surface.

† This type of wheelchair arm does not interfere with the positioning of a wheelchair under a work surface.

‡ This dimension is limited by the height of the armrests: a lower height would be preferable. Some people in this group prefer lower work surfaces, which require positioning the wheelchair back from the edge of the counter.

A4.33.7 Types of Listening Systems. A listening system that can be used from any seat in a seating area is the most flexible way to meet this specification. Earphone jacks with variable volume controls can benefit only people who have slight hearing losses and do not help people with hearing aids. At the present time, audio loops are the most feasible type of listening system for people who use hearing aids, but people without hearing aids or those with hearing aids not equipped with inductive pickups cannot use them. Loops can be portable and moved to various locations within a room. Moreover, for little cost, they can serve a large area within a seating area. Radio frequency systems can be extremely effective and inexpensive. People without hearing aids can use them, but people with hearing aids need custom-designed equipment to use them as they are presently designed. If hearing aids had a jack to allow a by-pass of microphones, then radio frequency systems would be suitable for people with and without hearing aids. Some listening systems may be subject to interference from other equipment and feedback from hearing aids of people who are using the systems. Such interference can be controlled by careful engineering design that anticipates feedback and sources of interference in the surrounding area.

A4.34 Dwelling Units.

A4.34.2 Minimum Requirements. Handicapped people who live in accessible dwelling units of multi-family buildings or housing projects will want to participate in all on-site social activities, including visiting neighbors in their dwelling units. Hence, any circulation paths among all dwelling units and among all on-site facilities should be as accessible as possible. An accessible second exit to dwelling units provides an extra margin of safety in a fire.

A4.34.5 Bathrooms. Although not required by these specifications, it is important to install grab bars at toilets, bathtubs, and showers if it is known that a dwelling unit will be occupied by elderly or severely disabled people.

A4.34.6 Kitchens.

A4.34.6.1 Clearance. The minimum clearances provide satisfactory maneuvering spaces for wheelchairs only if cabinets are removed at the sink.

A4.34.6.5 Sink. Installing a sink with a drain at the rear so that plumbing is as close to the wall as possible can provide additional clear knee space for wheelchair users.

A4.34.6.6 Ranges and Cooktops. Although not required for minimum accessibility, countertop range units in a counter with adjustable heights can be an added convenience for wheelchair users.

A4.34.6.7 Ovens. Countertop or wall-mounted ovens with side-opening doors are easier for people in wheelchairs to use. Clear spaces at least 30 in (760 mm) wide under counters at the side of ovens are an added convenience. The pullout board or fixed shelf under side-opening oven doors provides a resting place for heavy items being moved from the oven to a counter.

A4.34.6.8 Refrigerator/Freezers. Side-by-side refrigerator/freezers provide the most usable freezer compartments. Locating refrigerators so that their doors can swing back 180 degrees is more convenient for wheelchair users.

A4.34.6.10 Kitchen Storage. Full height cabinets or tall cabinets can be provided rather than cabinets mounted over work counters. Additional storage space located conveniently adjacent to kitchens can be provided to make up for space lost when cabinets under counters are removed.

A9. Postal Facilities.

A9.2 Post Office Lobbies. *Furniture as chattel is not covered under the Architectural Barriers Act of 1968, but the requirements for lobby furniture and equipment are imposed by the United States Postal Service for greater accessibility in its customer lobbies.*

Note: Unedited copies of the American National Standards Institute standard, A117.1-1980, "Specifications for Making Buildings and Facilities Accessible to and Usable by Physically Handicapped People," are available from the American National Standards Institute, Inc., 1430 Broadway, New York, New York 10018.

THE ARCHITECTURAL BARRIERS ACT (Public Law 90-480) of August 12, 1968
AS AMENDED THROUGH 1984
42 U.S.C. §§4151 *et seq.*

An Act to insure that certain buildings financed with Federal funds are so designed and constructed as to be accessible to the physically handicapped.

Be it enacted by the Senate and House of Representatives of the United States of America in Congress assembled, That, as used in this Act, the term "building" means any building or facility (other than (A) a privately owned residential structure not leased by the Government for subsidized housing programs and (B) any building or facility on a military installation designed and constructed primarily for use by able bodied military personnel) the intended use for which either will require that such building or facility be accessible to the public, or may result in employment or residence therein of physically handicapped persons, which building or facility is —

(1) to be constructed or altered by or on behalf of the United States;

(2) to be leased in whole or in part by the United States after August 12, 1968;*

(3) to be financed in whole or in part by a grant or a loan made by the United States after August 12, 1968, if such building or facility is subject to standards for design, construction, or alteration issued under authority of the law authorizing such grant or loan; or

(4) to be constructed under authority of the National Capital Transportation Act of 1960, the National Capital Transportation Act of 1965, or title III of the Washington Metropolitan Area Transit Regulation Compact.

Sec. 2 The Administrator of General Services, in consultation with the Secretary of Health and Human Services, shall prescribe standards for the design, construction, and alteration of buildings (other than residential structures subject to this Act and buildings, structures, and facilities of the Department of Defense and of the United States Postal Service subject to this Act) to insure whenever possible that physically handicapped persons will have ready access to, and use of, such buildings.

A 1976 amendment, Public Law 94-541, deleted the following words from the end of section 2: "after construction or alteration in accordance with plans and specifications of the United States." Section 202 of Public Law 94-541 states that the amendment applies to "every lease entered into on or after January 1, 1977, including any renewal of a lease entered into before such a date which renewal is on or after such date." Regulations at 43 Fed. Reg. 16478 (April 19, 1978) amending 41 C.F.R. §101-19.6.

Sec. 3 The Secretary of Housing and Urban Development, in consultation with the Secretary of Health and Human Services, shall prescribe standards for the design, construction, and alteration of buildings which are residential structures subject to this Act to insure whenever possible that physically handicapped persons will have ready access to, and use of, such buildings.

Sec. 4 The Secretary of Defense, in consultation with the Secretary of Health and Human Services, shall prescribe standards for the design, construction, and alteration of buildings, structures, and facilities of the Department of Defense subject to this Act to insure whenever possible that physically handicapped persons will have ready access to, and use of, such buildings.

Sec. 4a The United States Postal Service, in consultation with the Secretary of Health and Human Services, shall prescribe such standards for the design, construction, and alteration of its buildings to insure whenever possible that physically handicapped persons will have ready access to, and use of, such buildings.

Sec. 5 Every building designed, constructed, or altered after the effective date of a standard issued under this Act which is applicable to such building, shall be designed, constructed, or altered in accordance with such standard.

Sec. 6 The Administrator of General Services, with respect to standards issued under section 2 of this Act, and the Secretary of Housing and Urban Development, with respect to standards issued under section 3 of this Act, and the Secretary of Defense, with respect to standards issued under section 4 of this Act, and the United States Postal Service, with respect to standards issued under section 4a of this Act —

(1) is authorized to modify or waive any such standard, on a case-by-case basis, upon application made by the head of the department, agency, or instrumentality of the United States concerned, and upon a determination by the Administrator or Secretary, as the case may be, that such modification or waiver is clearly necessary, and

(2) shall establish a system of continuing surveys and investigations to insure compliance with such standards.

Sec. 7(a) The Administrator of General Services shall report to Congress during the first week of January of each year on his activities and those of other departments, agencies, and instrumentalities of the Federal Government under this Act during the preceding fiscal year including, but not limited to, standards issued, revised, amended, or repealed under this Act and all case-by-case modifications, and waivers of such standards during such year.

(b) The Architectural and Transportation Barriers Compliance Board established by section 502 of the Rehabilitation Act of 1973 (Public Law 93-112) shall report to the Public Works and Transportation Committee of the House of Representatives and the Public Works Committee of the Senate during the first week of January of each year on its activities and actions to insure compliance with the standards prescribed under this Act.

INDEX

*Bold denotes major sections of Uniform Federal Accessibility Standards

DWELLING UNITS (CONTINUED)

EDUCATIONAL OCCUPANCY

EGRESS (See also ENTRANCES; EXITS)

NOTE

This document was published originally in the Federal Register on August 7, 1984 (49 FR 31528) and includes corrections made subsequent to its printing.

APPENDIX D

SUMMARY CHART:
COVERAGE AND EFFECTIVE DATES

| Law's Effective Date | Regulations Due by Federal Agency | Enforcement |

EMPLOYMENT

Private employers, state and local governments, employment agencies, labor organizations, and labor-management committees.

July 26, 1992 for employers with twenty-five (25) or more employees; July 26, 1994 for employers with fifteen (15) or more employees.

July 26, 1991, regulations implementing title I were published in the Federal Register by the Equal Employment Opportunity Commission (EEOC).

Procedures and remedies identical to those under Title VII of the Civil Rights Act of 1964, which are EEOC enforcement, private right of action, and relief including, hiring, promotion, reinstatement, and back pay.

STATE AND LOCAL GOVERNMENT

All activities of local and state governments.

January 26, 1992

July 26, 1991, regulations implementing title II were published in the Federal Register by the Department of Justice (DOJ).

Remedies identical to those under the Rehabilitation Act of 1973 Section 505, which are private right of action, injunctive relief, and some damages.

PUBLIC ACCOMMODATIONS

All business and service providers.

January 26, 1992, generally; no lawsuit may be filed before July 26, 1992, against businesses with twenty-five (25) or fewer employees and revenue $1 million or less; or before January 26, 1993, for businesses with ten (10) or fewer employees and revenue $500,000 or less.

July 26, 1991, regulations implementing title III, including the ADA Accessibility Guidelines issued by the Architectural and Transportation Barriers Compliance Board, were published by the Department of Justice (DOJ) in the Federal Register.

For individuals, remedies identical to Title II of the Civil Rights Act of 1964, which are private right of action, injunctive relief: For Attorney General enforcement in pattern or practice cases or cases of general importance, with civil penalties and compensatory damages.

New construction / alteration to public accommodations and commercial facilities.

January 26, 1992, for alterations. January 26, 1993, for new construction.

Same as above.

Same as above.

Law's Effective Date	Regulations Due by Federal Agency	Enforcement

PUBLIC TRANSPORTATION

Public transportation (buses, light and rapid rail including fixed-route systems, paratransit, demand response system and transportation facilities).

August 26, 1990, all orders for purchases or leases of new vehicles must be for accessible vehicles; one-car-per-train must be accessible as soon as practicable, but no later than July 26, 1995; paratransit services must be provided after January 26, 1992; new stations built after January 26, 1992, must be accessible. Key stations must be retrofitted by July 26, 1993; with some exceptions allowed up to July 26, 2020.	July 26, 1991, all regulations due from Department of Transportation (DOT).	Remedies identical to those under the Rehabilitation Act of 1973, Section 505, which are private right of action, injunctive relief, and some damages.

Public transportation by intercity Amtrak and commuter rail (including transportation facilities).

By July 26, 2000, Amtrak passenger coaches must have same number of accessible seats as would have been available if every car were built accessible; half of such seats must be available by July 26, 1995. Same one-car-per-train rule and new stations rule as above. All existing Amtrak stations must be retrofitted by July 26, 2010; key commuter stations must be retrofitted by July 26, 1993, with some extensions allowed up to twenty (20) years.	July 26, 1991, all regulations due from Department of Transportation (DOT).	Same as above.

TELECOMMUNICATIONS

July 26, 1993, telecommunications relay services to operate twenty-four (24) hours per day.	Regulations implementing title IV were published by the Federal Communications Commission (FCC) in the Federal Register.	Private right of action and FCC enforcement.

2

ADA Handbook

Appendix E

Terms Defined in Statute and Regulations

Terms Defined in Statute and Regulations

TERM	STATUTE	PAGE	REGULATIONS	PAGE
General				
auxiliary aids and services	3(1)*	4	28 CFR 35.104 28 CFR 36.303	13(II) 78(III)
disability	3(2)	4	29 CFR 1630.2 (g) 28 CFR 35.104 28 CFR 36.104	25(I) 16(II) 16(III)
State	3(3)	4	29 CFR 1630.2 (d) 28 CFR 35.104 28 CFR 36.104	23(I) 29(II) 39(III)
Title I			**29 CFR**	
Commission	101(1)	4	1630.2 (a)	23
covered entity	101(2)	4	1630.2 (b)	23
direct threat	101(3)	5	1630.2 (r)	47
drug	-		1630.3 (a)(1)	49
employee	101(4)	5	1630.2 (f)	24
employer	101(5)	5	1630.2 (e)	23
essential functions	-		1630.2 (n)	38
has a record of such impairment	-		1630.2 (k)	33
illegal use of drugs	101(6)	5	1630.3 (a)(2)	49
is regarded as having such an impairment	-		1630.2 (l)	34
major life activities	-		1630.2 (i)	27
person, labor organization, employment agency, commerce and industry affecting commerce	101(7)	5	1630.2 (c)	23
physical or mental impairment	-		1630.2 (h)	26
qualified individual with a disability	101(8)	5	1630.2 (m)	37
reasonable accommodation	101(9)*	5	1630.2 (o)	41

*The terms "auxiliary aids and services" and "reasonable accommodation" are not defined in the statute. Sections 3(1) and 101(9) do, however, list examples of auxiliary aids and services, and reasonable accommodations, respectively.

TERM	STATUTE	PAGE	REGULATIONS	PAGE
			29 CFR	
subtantially limits	-		1630.2 (j)	28
qualification standards	-		1630.2 (q)	46
undue hardship	101(10)	5	1630.2 (p)	44
Title II			**28 CFR**	
Auxiliary Aids & Services	-		35.104	11
Complete Complaint	-		35.104	13
Current Illegal Use of Drugs	-		35.104	14
Designated Agency	-		35.104	14
Disability	-		35.104	14
Drug	-		35.104	22
Facility	-		35.104	22
Illegal Use of Drugs	-		35.104	23
Individual with a Disability	-		35.104	24
Public Entity	201 (1)	11	35.104	24
Qualified Individual with a Disability	201 (2)	11	35.104	24
Title III			**28 CFR**	
Commerce	301 (1)	26	36.104	14
Commercial Facilites	301 (2)	26	36.104	14
Current Illegal Use of Drugs			36.104	16
Demand Responsive System	301 (3)	26	-	

TERM	STATUTE	PAGE	REGULATIONS	PAGE
Disability	-		36.104	16
Drug	-		36.104	24
Facility	-		36.104	24
Fixed Route System	301 (4)	26	-	
Illegal Use of Drugs	-		36.104	26
Individual with a Disability	-		36.104	26
Over-the-Road Bus	301 (5)	26	-	
Place of Public Accommodation	-		36.104	33
Private Club	-		36.104	32
Private Entity	301 (6)	26	36.104	32
Public Accommodation	301 (7)	27	36.104	33
Rail & Railroad	301 (8)	27	-	
Readily Achievable	301 (9)	27	36.104	34
Religious Entity	-		36.104	37
Service Animal	-		36.104	38
Specified Public Transportation	301 (10)	27	-	
State	-		36.104	39
Undue Burden	-		36.104	39
Vehicle	301 (11)	27	-	

APPENDIX F

SUMMARY OF THE LEGISLATIVE HISTORY OF THE ADA AND RELATED INFORMATION

Summary of Legislative History of the ADA and Related Information

I. Hearings (held in Washington, D.C. unless otherwise noted)

A. Senate

Committee on Labor and Human Resources, Subcommittee on the Handicapped (*)

September 27, 1988 (joint hearing with House Subcommittee on Select Education)
May 9, 1989 (full Committee)
May 10, 1989
May 16, 1989
June 22, 1989 (full Committee)

B. House

1. Committee on Education and Labor, Subcommittee on Select Education

September 27, 1988 (joint hearing with Senate Committee on Labor and Human Resources)
October 24, 1988 (Boston, Massachusetts)
July 18, 1989 (joint hearing with House Subcommittee on Employment Opportunities)
August 28, 1989 (Houston, Texas)
September 13, 1989 (joint hearing with House Subcommittee on Employment Opportunities)
October 6, 1989 (Indianapolis, Indiana)

2. Committee on Energy and Commerce

a. Subcommittee on Telecommunications and Finance
September 27, 1989

b. Subcommittee on Transportation and Hazardous Waste
September 28, 1989

3. Committee on the Judiciary, Subcommittee on Civil and Constitutional Rights
August 3, 1989
October 11, 1989
October 12, 1989 (full Committee hearing)

4. Committee on Public Works and Transportation, Subcommittee on Surface Transportation
September 20, 1989
September 26, 1989

* The Senate Subcommittee on the Handicapped has since been renamed the Senate Subcommittee on Disability Policy to conform to currently accepted terminology.

II. Committee and Subcommittee "Mark-up" dates

  A. Senate

    Committee on Labor and Human Resources
        August 2, 1989

  B. House

    1. Committee on Education and Labor
        November 9 and 14, 1989

    2. Committee on Energy and Commerce

        a. Subcommittee on Telecommunications and Finance
            October 12, 1989

        b. Full Committee
            March 3, 1990

    3. Committee on the Judiciary

        a. Subcommittee on Civil and Constitutional Rights
            April 25, 1990

        b. Full Committee
            May 1 and 2, 1990

    4. Committee on Public Works and Transportation

        a. Subcommittee on Surface Transportation
            March 6, 1990

        b. Full committee
            April 3, 1990

III. Floor Action

  A. Senate
        September 7, 1989
        Passed 76-8

  B. House
        May 17 and 22, 1990
        Passed 403-20

ADA Handbook

C. 1st conference
June 25, 1990

D. Senate moves to recommit to conference
July 11, 1990

E. 2nd conference
July 12, 1990

F. House passes final version of ADA
July 12, 1990
Passed 377-28

G. Senate passes final version of ADA
July 13, 1990
Passed 91-6

IV. ADA signed into law by President Bush on the White House lawn, July 26, 1990

V. Legislative Documents

A. The ADA is Public Law 101-336.

B. Committee Reports

1. Senate Committee on Labor and Human Resources
Senate Report No. 101-116
2. House Committee on Education and Labor
House Report No. 101-485, Part 2
3. House Committee on Energy and Commerce
House Report No. 101-485, Part 4
4. House Committee on the Judiciary
House Report No. 101-485, Part 3
5. House Committee on Public Works and Transportation
House Report No. 101-485, Part 1
6. Conference Reports
1st conference: House Report No. 101-558
2nd conference: House Report No. 101-596

VI. How to Obtain Legislative Documents

A. House

You may obtain a copy of the ADA statute, the House Committee reports, or the conference reports by:

1. Ordering by telephone from the House Document Room, by document number, (as listed above under section V): (202) 225-3456 (voice only)

or;

2. Picking them up at the House Document Room between 9A.M. and 6P.M., Monday through Friday. The House Document Room is Room B18 of House Annex 2, located at 2nd and D streets, SW, in Washington, D.C., across the street from the Federal Center Southwest Metro station.

B. Senate

You may obtain copies of the ADA statute, the Senate Committee report, or the conference reports by:

1. Sending a written request identifying the document number (as listed above under section V) to:

    Senate Document Room
    Hart Senate Office Building
    Washington, D.C. 20510-7106

or;

2. Picking them up at the Senate Document Room between 9A.M. and 5:30P.M., Monday through Friday. The Senate Document Room is Room B 04 of the Hart Senate Office Building, located on Constitution Avenue between 1st and 2nd streets, NE, in Washington, D.C. The phone number is (202) 224-7860 (voice) or (202) 224-4300 (TDD).

APPENDIX G

DISABILITY-RELATED TAX PROVISIONS APPLICABLE TO BUSINESSES

Disability-Related Tax Provisions Applicable to Businesses

The three disability-related provisions in the Internal Revenue Code applicable to businesses described below are of particular interest to businesses and people with disabilities:

1) **Targeted Jobs Tax Credit** (Title 26, Internal Revenue Code, section 51)

> Employers are eligible to receive a tax credit in the amount of 40 percent of the first $6,000 of first-year wages of a new employee who has a disability. There is no credit after the first year of employment. For an employer to qualify for the credit, a worker must have been employed for at least 90 days or have completed at least 120 hours of work for the employer. The Revenue Reconciliation Act of 1990, Public Law 101-508, extended this tax credit through December 31, 1991.

2) **Tax Deduction to Remove Architectural and Transportation Barriers to People with Disabilities and Elderly Individuals** (Title 26, Internal Revenue Code, section 190)

> Allows a deduction for "qualified architectural and transportation barrier removal expenses." Only expenditures that are for the purpose of making any facility or public transportation vehicle owned or leased by the taxpayer for use in connection with his or her trade or business more accessible to, and usable by, handicapped and elderly individuals are eligible for the deduction. The taxpayer must establish, to the satisfaction of the Secretary of the Treasury, that the resulting removal of the barrier meets the standards promulgated by the Secretary with the concurrence of the U.S. Architectural and Transportation Barriers Compliance Board.

> For purposes of this section, a "handicapped individual" is any individual who has a physical or mental disability (including, but not limited to, deafness and blindness) which, for that individual, constitutes or results in a functional limitation to employment, or who has any physical or mental impairment that substantially limits one or more major life activities of that individual.

> The deduction may not exceed $15,000 for any taxable year. (The maximum deduction had been $35,000 prior to passage of Public Law 101-508 in 1990, which lowered the maximum deduction.)

3) **Disabled Access Tax Credit** (Title 26, Internal Revenue Code, section 44)

> This tax credit is available to "eligible small businesses" in the amount of 50 percent of "eligible access expenditures" for the taxable year that exceed $250 but do not exceed $10,250.

"Eligible small businesses" are those businesses with either:

a) $1 million or less in gross receipts for the preceding tax year

   OR

b) 30 or fewer full-time employees during the preceding tax year.

"Eligible access expenditures" means amounts paid or incurred by an eligible small business for the purpose of enabling the small business to comply with applicable requirements under ADA. Certain types of expenditures are listed as included under the meaning of the term "eligible access expenditures." These include amounts paid or incurred:

i) for the purpose of removing architectural, communication, physical, or transportation barriers that prevent a business from being accessible to, or usable by, individuals with disabilities;

ii) to provide qualified readers, taped texts, and other effective methods of making visually delivered materials available to people with visual impairments;

iii) to provide qualified interpreters or other effective methods of making aurally delivered materials available to individuals with hearing impairments;

iv) to acquire or modify equipment, or devices for individuals with disabilities, or

v) to provide other similar services, modifications, materials, or equipment.

Expenditures that are not necessary to accomplish the above mentioned purposes are not eligible. Expenses in connection with new construction are not eligible. "Disability" has the same meaning as it does in the ADA. Barrier removals or the provision of services, modifications, materials, or equipment must meet standards promulgated by the Secretary in order to be eligible.

Example: Company A purchases equipment to meet its reasonable accommodation obligation under ADA for $8,000. The amount by which $8,000 exceeds $250 is $7,750. Fifty percent of $7,750 is $3,875. The employer may take a tax credit in the amount of $3,875 on its next tax return.

Example: Company B removes a physical barrier in accordance with its reasonable accommodation obligation under ADA. The barrier removal meets standards promulgated by the Secretary.

The company expends $12,000 on this barrier removal. The amount by which $12,000 exceeds $250 but not $10,250 is a full $10,000. Fifty percent of $10,000 is $5,000. Company B is eligible for a $5,000 tax credit on its next tax return.

For further information on these provisions, contact the **Internal Revenue Service, Office of the Chief Counsel, P.O. Box 7604, Ben Franklin Station, Washington D.C. 20044 (202) 566-3292 (voice only).**

APPENDIX H

SUPREME COURT CASES RELATED TO SECTION 504

Supreme Court Cases Related to Section 504 of the Rehabilitation Act of 1973, as Amended

Alexander v. Choate, 469 U.S. 287 (1985).

Atascadero State Hospital v. Scanlon, 473 U.S. 234 (1985).

Bowen v. American Hospital Association, 476 U.S. 610 (1986).

City of Cleburne v. Cleburne Living Center, 473 U.S. 432 (1985).

Community Television of Southern California v. Gottfried, 459 U.S. 498 (1983).

Consolidated Rail Corporation v. Darrone, 465 U.S. 624 (1984).

Department of Transportation v. Paralyzed Veterans of America, 477 U.S. 597 (1986).

Hendrick Hudson Central School District Board of Education v. Rowley, 458 U.S. 176 (1982).

Honig v. Doe, 108 S.Ct. 592 (1988).

Irving Independent School District v. Tatro, 468 U.S. 883 (1984).

Pennhurst State School & Hospital v. Halderman, 451 U.S. 1 (1981).

School Board of Nassau County v. Arline, 107 S.Ct. 1123 (1987).

School Committee of the Town of Burlington v. Department of Education of Massachusetts, 471 U.S. 359 (1985).

Smith v. Robinson, 468 U.S. 992 (1984).

Southeastern Community College v. Davis, 442 U.S. 397 (1979).

Traynor v. Turnage, 108 S.Ct. 1372 (1988).

University of Texas v. Camenisch, 451 U.S. 390 (1981).

Appendix I

Agency Regulations Implementing Section 504 of the Rehabilitation Act of 1973, as amended, in Federally Assisted Programs

Agency Regulations Implementing Section 504 of the Rehabilitation Act of 1973, as Amended, in Federally Assisted Programs

Final Rules

ACTION 45 C.F.R. pt. 1232 (1990); 44 Fed. Reg. 31,018 (1979)

AID/IDCA 22 C.F.R. pt. 217 (1990); 45 Fed. Reg. 66,414 (1980)

USDA 7 C.F.R. pt. 15b (1991); 47 Fed. Reg. 25,458 (1982)

CAB 14 C.F.R. pt. 382 (1990); 47 Fed. Reg. 25,948 (1982)

Commerce 15 C.F.R. pt 8b (1990); 47 Fed. Reg. 17,744 (1982)

DOD 32 C.F.R. pt. 56 (1990); 47 Fed. Reg. 15,122 (1982)

ED 34 C.F.R. pt. 104 (1990); 45 Fed. Reg. 30,936 (1980)

Energy 10 C.F.R. §§1040.61-.74 (1990); 45 Fed. Reg. 40,514 (1980)

EPA 40 C.F.R. pt. 7 (1990); 49 Fed. Reg. 1656 (1984)

GSA 41 C.F.R. §§ 101-8.300 to .311 (1990); 47 Fed. Reg. 25,337 (1982)

HHS 45 C.F.R. pt. 84 (1990); 42 Fed. Reg. 22,676 (1977)

HUD 24 C.F.R. pt. 8 (1989); 53 Fed. Reg. 20,233 (1988)

Interior 43 C.F.R. §§ 17.200-.280 (1990); 47 Fed. Reg. 29,542 (1982)

Justice 28 C.F.R. §§ 42.501-.540 (1990); 45 Fed. Reg. 37,622 (1980); 49 Fed. Reg. 35,724 (1984)

Labor 29 C.F.R. pt. 32 (1990); 45 Fed. Reg. 66,709 (1980)

NASA 14 C.F.R. pt. 1251 (1990); 44 Fed. Reg. 52,680 (1979)

NEA 45 C.F.R. pt. 1110 (1990); 44 Fed. Reg. 22,730 (1979)

NEH 45 C.F.R. pt. 1170 (1990); 46 Fed. Reg. 55,897 (1981)

NSF 45 C.F.R. pt. 605 (1990); 47 Fed. Reg. 8573 (1982)

NRC 10 C.F.R. §§ 4.101-.233 (1991); 45 Fed. Reg. 14,533 (1980)

OPM 5 C.F.R. §§ 900.701-.710 (1991); 45 Fed. Reg. 75,568 (1980)

SBA 13 C.F.R. pt. 113 (1991); 44 Fed. Reg. 20,068 (1979)

State 22 C.F.R. pt. 142 (1990); 45 Fed. Reg. 69,438 (1990)

TVA 18 C.F.R. pt. 1302 (1990); 49 Fed. Reg. 20,484 (1990)

DOT 49 C.F.R. pt. 27 (1990); 44 Fed. Reg. 31,442 (1979) as amended by 46 Fed. Reg. 37,488 (1981)

Treasury 31 C.F.R. § 51.55 (1990); 46 Fed. Reg. 48,034 (ORS) (1981) as amended by 48 Fed. Reg. 46,982 (1983)

VA 38 C.F.R. §§ 18.401-18b.95 (1990); 45 Fed. Reg. 63,268 (1980)

Appendix J

Opinions Related to Section 504 of the Rehabilitation Act of 1973, as Amended, of the Attorney General and the Office of Legal Counsel, U.S. Department of Justice

Opinions Related to Section 504 of the Rehabilitation Act of 1973, as Amended, of the Attorney General and the Office of Legal Counsel, U.S. Department of Justice

1. "Rehabilitation Act of 1973 -- Coverage of Alcoholics and Drug Addicts." Griffin B. Bell, Attorney General of the United States, to Joseph Califano, Secretary of Health, Education and Welfare, April 12, 1977.

2. "Opinion as to whether the term 'Federal financial assistance' as used in section 504 ..., includes Federal programs of guarantee or insurance." John M. Harmon, Assistant Attorney General, Office of Legal Counsel, to F. Peter Libassi, Esq., General Counsel, Department of Health, Education and Welfare, September 23, 1977.

3. "Architectural Barriers Act, § 1, 42 U.S.C. 4151," Leon Ulman, Deputy Assistant Attorney General, Office of Legal Counsel, to Drew S. Days III, Assistant Attorney General, Civil Rights Division, May 8, 1980.

4. "Applicability of Certain Cross-Cutting Statutes to Block Grants Under the Omnibus Reconciliation Act of 1981," Theodore B. Olson, Assistant Attorney General, Office of Legal Counsel to Michael Horowitz, Counsel to the Director, Office of Management and Budget, January 18, 1982.

5. "Application of Section 504 of the Rehabilitation Act to Persons with AIDS, AIDS-Related Complex, or Infection with the AIDS Virus," Charles J. Cooper, Assistant Attorney General, Office of Legal Counsel, to Ronald E. Robertson, General Counsel, Department of Health and Human Services, June 20, 1986.

6. "Application of Section 504 of the Rehabilitation Act to HIV-Infected Individuals," Douglas W. Kmiec, Acting Assistant Attorney General, Office of Legal Counsel, to Arthur B. Culvahouse, Jr., Counsel to the President, September 27, 1988.

APPENDIX K

LIST OF COMMON ACRONYMS

List of Common Acronyms

ABA	Architectural Barriers Act of 1968, P.L. 90-480, requires that all buildings and facilities, built or altered after 1968, that are leased from or owned by the Federal government be accessible to persons with disabilities.
ADA	Americans with Disabilities Act of 1990, P.L. 101-336
ADAAG	Americans with Disabilities Act Accessibility Guidelines
AIDS	Acquired Immunodeficiency Syndrome
ANPRM	Advance Notice of Proposed Rulemaking
ASCII	American Standard Code for Information Interchange
ATBCB	Architecture and Transportation Barriers Compliance Board
ATM	Automatic Teller Machine
CDC	Centers for Disease Control, agency within HHS
CIL	Centers for Independent Living
CFR	Code of Federal Regulations
CPA	Certified Public Accountant
DOC	Department of Commerce
DOT	Department of Transportation
DOJ	Department of Justice
ED	Department of Education
EEOC	Equal Employment Opportunity Commission
EHA	Education for All Handicapped Children Act, P.L. 94-142
ERISA	Employee Retirement Income Security Act
FCC	Federal Communications Commission
FHAA	Fair Housing Amendments Act of 1988
FR	Federal Register
GSA	General Services Administration
HAL	Handicapped Assistance Loans, administered by SBA
HEW	Department of Health, Education and Welfare (Restructured in 1979 into the present Department of Health and Human Services and Department of Education)
HHS	Department of Health and Human Services
HIV	Human Immunodeficiency Virus
HUD	Department of Housing and Urban Development
JAN	Job Accommodation Network, service of PCEPD
LEAA	Law Enforcement Assistance Administration, formerly an agency of DOJ
MGRAD	Minimum Guidelines and Requirements for Accessible Design, established by ATBCB
NARIC	National Rehabilitation Information Center, funded by NIDRR
NCD	National Council on Disability
NIDRR	National Institute on Disability and Rehabilitation Research, part of ED
NIH	National Institutes of Health, agency within HHS
NLS	National Library Service for the Blind and Physically Handicapped -- service of the Library of Congress
NPRM	Notice of Proposed Rulemaking
OCR	Office for Civil Rights, within various agencies including HHS and ED

OFCCP	Office of Federal Contract Compliance Programs, office within DOL
OMB	Office of Management and Budget
OPM	Office of Personnel Management
OSHA	Occupational Safety and Health Administration, division of DOL
OSERS	Office of Special Education and Rehabilitation Services, division of ED
PCEPD	President's Committee on the Employment of People with Disabilities
P.L.	Public Law
RFA	Regulatory Flexibility Analysis
RIA	Regulatory Impact Analysis
RSA	Rehabilitation Services Administration, division of ED
SBA	Small Business Administration
TDD	Telecommunications Device for the Deaf
UFAS	Uniform Federal Accessibility Standards
UGESP	Uniform Guidelines on Employee Selection Procedures
U.S.C.	United States Code
501	Section 501 of title V of the Rehabilitation Act of 1973, as amended, requires federal agencies to take affirmative action in the hiring, placement, and promotion of people with disabilities in federal employment.
502	Section 502 of title V of the Rehabilitation Act of 1973, as amended, established ATBCB as the agency responsible for the enforcement of the ABA and the establishment of minimum guidelines for accessible design.
503	Section 503 of title V of the Rehabilitation Act of 1973, as amended, requires affirmative action in the hiring, placement and promotion of persons with disabilities by federal contractors that receive federal contracts of more than $2,500.
504	Section 504 of title V of the Rehabilitation Act of 1973, as amended, prohibits discrimination against qualified persons with disabilities in the programs or activities (including hiring practices) of any federal Executive agency or any organization receiving federal financial assistance.
508	Section 508 of title V of the Rehabilitation Act of 1973, as amended, requires the Federal Government to establish guidelines for electronic equipment accessibility and to procure accessible electronic office equipment in order to ensure equivalent communications capabilities to disabled and non-disabled employees.
94-142	The Education for All Handicapped Children Act of 1975 established that free, appropriate education must be available through the public school system to children with disabilities. 94-142 also authorized federal appropriations for special education.

APPENDIX L

RELATED FEDERAL DISABILITY LAWS

Related Federal Disability Laws

There are dozens of federal statutes establishing programs or containing provisions that pertain specifically to individuals with disabilities. The Department of Education in August, 1988 published *Summary of Existing Legislation Affecting Persons with Disabilities*, a booklet which describes many federal laws and programs that affect people with disabilities. The Department is updating this publication and expects to have it ready for publication in the spring of 1992. Copies can at that time be obtained by contacting the **Clearinghouse on Disability Information, U.S. Department of Education, Room 3132 Switzer Building, Washington, D.C. 20202-2524, at (202) 732-1241 or (202) 732-1723 (both are voice and TDD numbers).**

Following are descriptions of selected federal disability statutes that are relevant to promoting the purposes of ADA's employment, public services, and public accommodations provisions.

In addition to these programs, there are several tax code provisions that provide businesses with financial incentives to hire people with disabilities or make employment and access-enhancing expenditures required by, or consistent with the purposes of, the ADA. For descriptions of these provisions, see Appendix item G, Disability Related Tax Provisions Applicable to Businesses.

I. Rehabilitation Act of 1973

Rehabilitation Services Administration and National Institute on Disability and Rehabilitation Research, Department of Education

The Rehabilitation Act of 1973 is the principal federal legislation establishing programs aimed at promoting the employment and independent living of people with disabilities. Programs authorized under this Act are administered within the U.S. Department of Education by the Rehabilitation Services Administration and the National Institute on Disability and Rehabilitation Research. Following are selected programs established under this Act to promote these purposes.

A. Programs administered by the Rehabilitation Services Administration

The Rehabilitation Services Administration administers the principal federal service programs designed to promtote the rehabilitatation, employment, and independent living of people with disabilities.

1) Centers for Independent Living (Title VII, Part B of the Act)

Centers for Independent Living are community based, nonresidential centers that provide independent living services to enable individuals with disabilities to live and function independently.

Services provided to individuals with severe disabilities include independent living skills training, counseling and personal advocacy services on income benefits and legal rights, information and referral, peer counseling, education and training necessary for living in the community and participation in community activities, housing assistance, transportation, equipment and adaptive aid loans, and personal care attendant training and referral.

Other services provided are outreach/community education, technical assistance to other community agencies, transitional services to assist youth in making the transition from school to the community, intake and assessment, service coordination, emergency intervention, social and recreation, and vocational/educational/employment services.

Independent living centers are often an excellent source of advice on an array of accessibility, attitudinal, and other issues of concern to people with disabilities. There are 202 centers for independent living across the country. For the location and/or telephone number of one nearest you contact either the **Independent Living Research Utilization Center at 2323 South Shephard Street, Suite 1000, Houston, Texas 77019, telephone (713) 520-0232 (voice) or (713) 520-5136 (TDD)** or the **National Council on Independent Living at Troy Atrium, Fourth Street and Broadway, Troy, New York 12180, telephone (518) 274-1979 (voice) or (518) 274-0701 (TDD).**

2) State Vocational Rehabilitation Agencies (Title I of the Act)

Eighty-four State vocational rehabilitation agencies are funded by the Federal Government. These agencies operate in each State, territory, and the District of Columbia to provide vocational rehabilitation services to individuals with physical or mental disabilities. Separate agencies service individuals who are blind or visually impaired in several States.

Services are provided based upon eligibility criteria that include the presence of a physical or mental disability; evidence that the disability results in a substantial handicap to employment; and the reasonable expectation that vocational rehabilitation services can benefit the individual in terms of employability.

State vocational rehabilitation agencies provide assessment and evaluation services, counseling, guidance and referral services, vocational training, physical and mental restoration services, job development and job placement services, among other types of services to assist individuals with disabilities to become gainfully employed.

State vocational rehabilitation agencies can assist employers by assessing the accommodations that may be necessary for an employee with a disability, provide technical assistance on the nature and functional limitation of a disability, and make referrals to appropriate resources for rehabilitation technology services.

State agencies administer several types of supported employment programs, including the Supported Employment State Formula Grant program, Community-Based Supported Employment Projects, and Supported Employment State-Change Grants. Supported employment is competitive work in an integrated setting for individuals with severe disabilities for whom competitive work has not traditionally occurred and who, because of their disability, need on-going support services to perform such work.

For further information, including information on how to contact the vocational rehabilitation office nearest you, contact the **Rehabilitation Services Administration, Mary E. Switzer Building, Room 3028, 330 C Street, SW, Washington, D.C. 20202, telephone (202) 732-1282 (voice) or (202) 732-1330 (TDD).**

3) Projects with Industry (PWI) (Title VI of the Act)

PWI is a Federal Government/private industry initiative, involving corporations, labor organizations, trade associations, foundations, and voluntary agencies, that operate through a partnership with the rehabilitation community. The program creates, as well as expands, job opportunities for people with disabilities in the competitive labor market. As part of this program, training is provided for jobs in realistic work settings, generally within commercial or industrial establishments, coupled with supportive services to enhance pre- and post-employment success of people with disabilities in the marketplace.

There are one hundred and twenty-five federally funded PWI's, affiliated with more than 4,000 private corporations. Each project is required by law to have a Business Advisory Council that provides the mechanism for private sector business participation in policy-making for the project. This affords business and industry the opportunity to provide input into the design and character of training programs that are geared to existing job openings.

PWI's can be a good starting point for meeting other business people in your locality who have experience in hiring, and a commitment to hiring, people with disabilities. To locate the closest PWI, contact the **Inter-National Association of Business, Industry and Rehabilitation (I-NABIR) at P.O. Box 15242, Washington, D.C. 20003, telephone (202) 543-6353 (voice only),** or the **Rehabilitation Services Administration, Mary E. Switzer Building, Room 3028, 330 C Street, SW, Washington, D.C. 20202, (202) 732-1282 (voice) or (202) 732-1330 (TDD).**

B. Programs administered by the National Institute on Disability and Rehabilitation Research

The National Institute on Disability and Rehabilitation Research administers the principal federal disability research programs, the Technology Related Assistance for Individuals with Disabilities Act, regional ADA technical assistance centers, and certain other ADA related activities described below.

Existing Programs

1) National Rehabilitation Information Center (NARIC)

NARIC is an information center and library on disability and rehabilitation. It collects and disseminates the results of federally funded research projects. Its collection includes commercially published books, journal articles, and audiovisual materials. It currently has more than 30,000 documents.

NARIC has information specialists who will perform searches for the inquirer. Information may be requested by calling **(800) 346-2742 (voice or TDD) or (301) 588-9284 (voice or TDD) between the hours of 8 A.M. and 6 P.M. Eastern Standard Time on Monday through Friday. NARIC's address is National Rehabilitation Information Center, 8455 Colesville Road, Suite 935, Silver Spring, Maryland 20910.**

2) Research and Training Centers

NIDRR funds 39 research and training centers specialized by subject matter and dispersed throughout the country. The R&T centers conduct applied research directed towards producing new knowledge in the disability and rehabilitation field that will improve rehabilitation services and promote the independent living of people with disabilities. Centers also develop and conduct related teaching and training programs to disseminate and speed the utilization of key findings.

Many of the centers focus on issues pertaining to particular disabilities. Other centers whose specialty areas may be of particular interest to the reader are:

Center on Enhancing Employability of Individuals with Handicaps

Center for Access to Rehabilitation and Economic Opportunity

Center on Rural Rehabilitation Services

Independent Living Research Utilization center

Center on Improving Supported Employment Outcomes for Individuals with Developmental and Other Severe Disabilities

Center on New Directions for Rehabilitation Facilities

Information on other R&T centers, as well as how to contact those listed above, may be obtained from the **National Institute on Disability and Rehabilitation Research, U.S. Department of Education, 400 Maryland Avenue, SW, Washington, D.C. 20202-2572 (202) 732-1134 (voice) or (202) 732-5079 (TDD).**

3) Technology Related Assistance for Individuals with Disabilities Act

NIDRR is funding the development of State programs and projects to provide technology-related assistance to persons with disabilities and to train service providers and people with disabilities in the application of assistive technology.

More information about these programs and projects may be obtained by contacting **NIDRR at the address listed above or at (202) 732-5066 (voice) or (202) 732-5079 (TDD).**

Proposed Programs Facilitating the Implementation of the ADA

Congress provided funds to NIDRR in 1991 to develop a technical assistance program to facilitate the implementation of the ADA. These funds will be used for the following three major programs, conducted under grants from NIDRR over a 5-year period, beginning in the fall of 1991;

4) Regional Disability and Business Accommodation Centers (RDBACs)

Ten regional centers will be established to provide a broad range of information, technical assistance, and training on the ADA to employers and other covered entities, people with disabilities, and other segments of the community. Technical assistance will focus on facilitating the effective implementation of the ADA, successful employment outcomes for individuals with disabilities, and greater accessibility in public accommodations.

5) National Peer Training Projects

These projects will be designed to enhance the capacity of persons with disabilities and their organizations to facilitate the implementation of the ADA. One project will provide training for local capacity-building in independent living centers providing services to individuals with disabilities. A second project will develop peer and family training networks.

6) Materials Development Projects

This project will develop, test, and distribute technical assistance and training materials to be used by individuals with disabilities, employers, service providers, the regional centers, and others who need to know about the ADA.

More information about these programs may be obtained by contacting the **National Institute on Disability and Rehabilitation Research, Department of Education, 400 Maryland Avenue, SW, Switzer Building, Washington, D.C. 20202-2601, (202) 732-1134 (voice) or (202) 732-5079 (TDD).**

II. Work Incentive Programs for People with Disabilities

Social Security Administration, Department of Health and Human Services

These programs are intended to provide individuals with disabilities who are beneficiaries of two programs---the Social Security Disability Insurance (SSDI) and Supplemental Security Income (SSI) programs---supports they need to move from benefit dependency to self sufficiency. Work incentives are intended to help beneficiaries enter or reenter the workforce by protecting their entitlement to cash payments and/or Medicaid or Medicare protection until they can support themselves.

Among the work incentives available to either SSDI or SSI recipients, or both, are:

- impairment-related work expenses
- trial work period
- extended period of eligibility
- continuation of Medicare coverage
- Medicare for people with disabilities who work
- earned income exclusion
- student earned income exclusion
- blind work expenses
- plan for achieving self-support
- property essential to self-support
- section 1619 work incentives

For more information about these programs, contact the **Program Management Branch, Social Security Administration, 3R1 Operations Building, 6401 Security Boulevard, Baltimore, Maryland 21235 (301) 965-9864 (voice only).**

III. Developmental Disabilities Assistance and Bill of Rights Act

Administration on Developmental Disabilities, Department of Health and Human Services

This legislation supports the development and coordination of programs and services promoting the independence, productivity, community integration, and protection of the rights of persons of all ages with developmental disabilities.

A developmental disability is defined as a severe, chronic disability attributable to a mental or physical impairment, or combination of both, that is manifested before age 22; is likely to continue indefinitely; results in substantial limitations in three or more of the following areas of major life activity: self-care, receptive and expressive language, learning, mobility, self-direction, capacity for independent living, and economic self-sufficiency; and results in the need for individually planned and coordinated services lifelong or over an extended period of time.

One program authorized under the Act is the Protection and Advocacy Program, which provides for the protection and advocacy of the individual rights of all persons with developmental disabilities who are, or may be, eligible for treatment, services or habilitation, or who are being considered for a change in living arrangments. The Protection and Advocacy agencies (P&A's) are also extensively involved in training and education activities for persons with developmental disabilities and their families, and in public information and awareness efforts. They will be involved in protecting the rights of individuals with developmental disabilities covered under the Americans with Disabilities Act.

For more information about Developmental Disabilities Act programs, including how to locate the nearest P&A agency, contact the **Administration on Developmental Disabilities, Program Operations Division, 200 Independence Avenue SW, Room 329D, Washington, D.C. 20201 (202) 245-2897 (voice) or (202) 245-2890 (TDD).**

IV. Job Training Partnership Act

Office of Employment and Training Programs, Department of Labor

The Job Training Partnership Act authorizes programs that train and place "economically disadvantaged" persons in the work force through joint public-private sector initiatives. Each State has a State Job Training Coordinating Council and one or more Private Industry Councils at the local level which administer the program. JTPA is the largest federal job placement and training program.

The program is not targeted specifically to individuals with disabilities, but individuals with disabilities who meet the income criteria are eligible for services. In addition, up to 10 percent of JTPA service recipients may be individuals who are not economically disadvantaged within the meaning of the statute but who have encountered barriers to employment; this group includes "individuals with handicaps." The Act defines a "handicapped individual" as any individual who has a mental or physical disability that contitutes or results in a substantial handicap to employment.

For the most part, JTPA funds benefiting persons with disabilities have been used to place persons with mild and moderate disabilities in community jobs.

For more information on this program, contact the **Office of Employment and Training Programs, Department of Labor, 200 Constitution Avenue NW, Room N4709, Washington, D.C. 20210, (202) 535-0580 (voice only).**

Appendix M

ADA Questions and Answers

EMPLOYMENT

Q. What employers are covered by the ADA, and when is the coverage effective?

A. The employment provisions of title I of the ADA apply to private employers, State and local governments, employment agencies, and labor unions. Employers with 25 or more employees will be covered starting July 26, 1992, when title I goes into effect. Employers with 15 or more employees will be covered two years later, beginning July 26, 1994.

In addition, the employment practices of State and local governments of any size are covered by title II of the ADA, which goes into effect on January 26, 1992. The standards to be used under title II for determining whether employment discrimination has occurred depend on whether the public entity at issue is also covered by title I. Beginning July 26, 1992, if the public entity is covered by title I, then title I standards will apply. If not, the standards of section 504 of the Rehabilitation Act will apply. From January 26, 1992, when title II goes into effect, until July 26, 1992, when title I goes into effect, public entities will be subject to the section 504 standards.

Q. What practices and activities are covered by the employment nondiscrimination requirements?

A. The ADA prohibits discrimination in all employment practices, including job application procedures, hiring, firing, advancement, compensation, training, and other terms, conditions, and privileges of employment. It applies to recruitment, advertising, tenure, layoff, leave, fringe benefits, and all other employment-related activities.

Q. Who is protected against employment discrimination?

A. Employment discrimination is prohibited against "qualified individuals with disabilities." Persons discriminated against because they have a known association or relationship with a disabled individual also are protected. The ADA defines an "individual with a disability" as a person who has a physical or mental impairment that substantially limits one or more major life activities, has a record of such an impairment, or is regarded as having such an impairment.

The first part of the definition makes clear that the ADA applies to persons who have substantial, as distinct from minor, impairments, and that these must be impairments that limit major life activities such as seeing, hearing, speaking, walking, breathing, performing manual tasks, learning, caring for oneself, and working. An individual with epilepsy, paralysis, a substantial hearing or visual impairment, mental retardation, or a learning disability would be covered, but an individual with a minor, nonchronic condition of short duration, such as a sprain, infection, or broken limb, generally would not be covered.

The second part of the definition would include, for example, a person with a history of cancer that is currently in remission or a person with a history of mental illness.

The third part of the definition protects individuals who are regarded and treated as though they have a substantially limiting disability, even though they may not have such an impairment. For example, this provision would protect a severely disfigured qualified individual from being denied employment because an employer feared the "negative reactions" of others.

Q. Who is a "qualified individual with a disability?"

A. A qualified individual with a disability is a person who meets legitimate skill, experience, education, or other requirements of an employment position that he or she holds or seeks, and who can perform the "essential functions" of the position with or without reasonable accommodation. Requiring the ability to perform "essential" functions assures that an individual will not be considered unqualified simply because of inability to perform marginal or incidental job functions. If the individual is qualified to perform essential job functions except for limitations caused by a disability, the employer must consider whether the individual could perform these functions with a reasonable accommodation. If a written job description has been prepared in advance of advertising or interviewing applicants for a job, this will be considered as evidence, although not necessarily conclusive evidence, of the essential functions of the job.

Q. Does an employer have to give preference to a qualified applicant with a disability over other applicants?

A. No. An employer is free to select the most qualified applicant available and to make decisions based on reasons unrelated to the existence or consequence of a disability. For example, if two persons apply for a job opening as a typist, one a person with a disability who accurately types 50 words per minute, the other a person without a disability who accurately types 75 words per minute, the employer may hire the applicant with the higher typing speed, if typing speed is needed for successful performance of the job.

Q. What is "reasonable accommodation?"

A. Reasonable accommodation is a modification or an adjustment to a job or the work environment that will enable a qualified applicant or employee with a disability to perform essential job functions. Reasonable accommodation also includes adjustments to assure that a qualified individual with a disability has rights and privileges in employment equal to those of nondisabled employees.

Q. What kinds of actions are required to reasonably accommodate applicants and employees?

A. Examples of reasonable accommodation include making existing facilities used by employees readily accessible to and usable by an individual with a disability; restructuring a job; modifying work schedules; acquiring or modifying equipment; providing qualified readers or interpreters; or appropriately modifying examinations, training, or other programs. Reasonable accommodation also may include reassigning a current employee to a vacant position for which the individual is qualified, if the person becomes disabled and is unable to do the original job. However, there is no obligation to find a position for an applicant who is not qualified for the position sought. Employers are not required to lower quality or quantity standards in order to make an accommodation, nor are they obligated to provide personal use items such as glasses or hearing aids.

The decision as to the appropriate accommodation must be based on the particular facts of each case. In selecting the particular type of reasonable accommodation to provide, the principal test is that of effectiveness, i.e., whether the accommodation will enable the person with a disability to do the job in question.

Q. Must employers be familiar with the many diverse types of disabilities to know whether or how to make a reasonable accommodation?

A. No. An employer is required to accommodate only a "known" disability of a qualified applicant or employee. The requirement generally will be triggered by a request from an individual with a disability, who frequently can suggest an appropriate accommodation. Accommodations must be made on an individual basis, because the nature and extent of a disabling condition and the requirements of the job will vary in each case. If the individual does not request an accommodation, the employer is not obligated to provide one. If a disabled person requests, but cannot suggest, an appropriate accommodation, the employer and the individual should work together to identify one. There are also many public and private resources that can provide assistance without cost.

Q. What are the limitations on the obligation to make a reasonable accommodation?

A. The disabled individual requiring the accommodation must be otherwise qualified, and the disability must be known to the employer. In addition, an employer is not required to make an accommodation if it would impose an "undue hardship" on the operation of the employer's business. "Undue hardship" is defined as "an action requiring significant difficulty or expense" when considered in light of a number of factors. These factors include the nature and cost of the accommodation in relation to the size, resources, nature, and structure of the employer's operation. Where the facility making the accommodation is part of a larger entity, the structure and overall resources of the larger organization would be considered, as well as the financial and administrative relationship of the facility to the larger organization. In general, a larger employer would be expected to make accommodations requiring greater effort or expense than would be required of a smaller employer.

Q. Must an employer modify existing facilities to make them accessible?

A. An employer may be required to modify facilities to enable an individual to perform essential job functions and to have equal opportunity to participate in other employment-related activities. For example, if an employee lounge is located in a place inaccessible to a person using a wheelchair, the lounge might be modified or relocated, or comparable facilities might be provided in a location that would enable the individual to take a break with co-workers.

Q. May an employer inquire as to whether a prospective employee is disabled?

A. An employer may not make a pre-employment inquiry on an application form or in an interview as to whether, or to what extent, an individual is disabled. The employer may ask a job applicant whether he or she can perform particular job functions. If the applicant has a disability known to the employer, the employer may ask how he or she can perform job functions that the employer considers difficult or impossible to perform because of the disability, and whether an accommodation would be needed. A job offer may be conditioned on the results of a medical examination, provided that the examination is required for all entering employees in the same job category regardless of disability, and that information obtained is handled according to confidentiality requirements specified in the Act. After an employee enters on duty, all medical examinations and inquiries must be job related and necessary for the conduct of the employer's business. These provisions of the law are intended to prevent the employer from basing hiring and employment decisions on unfounded assumptions about the effects of a disability.

Q. Does the ADA take safety issues into account?

A. Yes. The ADA expressly permits employers to establish qualification standards that will exclude individuals who pose a direct threat — i.e., a significant risk of substantial harm— to the health or safety of the individual or of others, if that risk cannot be lowered to an acceptable level by reasonable accommodation. However, an employer may not simply assume that a threat exists; the employer must establish through objective, medically supportable methods that there is genuine risk that substantial harm could occur in the workplace. By requiring employers to make individualized judgments based on reliable medical or other objective evidence rather than on generalizations, ignorance, fear, patronizing attitudes, or stereotypes, the ADA recognizes the need to balance the interests of people with disabilities against the legitimate interests of employers in maintaining a safe workplace.

Q. Can an employer refuse to hire an applicant or fire a current employee who is illegally using drugs?

A. Yes. Individuals who currently engage in the illegal use of drugs are specifically excluded from the definition of a "qualified individual with a disability" protected by the ADA when an action is taken on the basis of their drug use.

Q. Is testing for illegal drugs permissible under the ADA?

A. Yes. A test for illegal drugs is not considered a medical examination under the ADA; therefore, employers may conduct such testing of applicants or employees and make employment decisions based on the results. The ADA does not encourage, prohibit, or authorize drug tests.

Q. Are people with AIDS covered by the ADA?

A. Yes. The legislative history indicates that Congress intended the ADA to protect persons with AIDS and HIV disease from discrimination.

Q. How does the ADA recognize public health concerns?

A. No provision in the ADA is intended to supplant the role of public health authorities in protecting the community from legitimate health threats. The ADA recognizes the need to strike a balance between the right of a disabled person to be free from discrimination based on unfounded fear and the right of the public to be protected.

Q. What is discrimination based on "relationship or association?"

A. The ADA prohibits discrimination based on relationship or association in order to protect individuals from actions based on unfounded assumptions that their relationship to a person with a disability would affect their job performance, and from actions caused by bias or misinformation concerning certain disabilities. For example, this provision would protect a person with a disabled spouse from being denied employment because of an employer's unfounded assumption that the applicant would use excessive leave to care for the spouse. It also would protect an individual who does volunteer work for people with AIDS from a discriminatory employment action motivated by that relationship or association.

Q. Will the ADA increase litigation burdens on employers?

A. Some litigation is inevitable. However, employers who use the period prior to the effective date of employment coverage to adjust their policies and practices to conform to ADA requirements will be much less likely to have serious litigation concerns. In drafting the ADA, Congress relied heavily on the language of the Rehabilitation Act of 1973 and its implementing regulations. There is already an extensive body of law interpreting the requirements of that Act to which employers can turn for guidance on their ADA obligations. The Equal Employment Opportunity Commission, which has issued regulations implementing the ADA's employment provisions, will publish a technical assistance manual with guidance on how to comply and will provide other assistance to help employers meet ADA requirements. Equal employment opportunity for people with disabilities will be achieved most quickly and effectively through widespread voluntary compliance with the law, rather than through reliance on litigation to enforce compliance.

Q. How will the employment provisions be enforced?

A. The employment provisions of the ADA will be enforced under the same procedures now applicable to race, sex, national origin, and religious discrimination under title VII of the Civil Rights Act of 1964. Complaints regarding actions that occur after July 26, 1992, may be filed with the Equal Employment Opportunity Commission or designated State human rights agencies. Available remedies will include hiring, reinstatement, back pay, and court orders to stop discrimination.

PUBLIC ACCOMMODATIONS
Q. What are public accommodations?

A. Public accommodations are private entities that affect commerce. The ADA public accommodations requirements extend, therefore, to a wide range of entities, such as restaurants, hotels, theaters, doctors' offices, pharmacies, retail stores, museums, libraries, parks, private schools, and day care centers. Private clubs and religious organizations are exempt from the ADA's requirements for public accommodations.

Q. Will the ADA have any effect on the eligibility criteria used by public accommodations to determine who may receive services?

A. Yes. If a criterion screens out or tends to screen out individuals with disabilities, it may only be used if necessary for the provision of the services. For instance, it would be a violation for a retail store to have a rule excluding all deaf persons from entering the premises, or for a movie theater to exclude all individuals with cerebral palsy. More subtle forms of discrimination are also prohibited. For example, requiring presentation of a driver's license as the sole acceptable means of identification for purposes of paying by check could constitute discrimination against individuals with vision impairments. This would be true if such individuals are ineligible to receive licenses and the use of an alternative means of identification is feasible.

Q. Does the ADA allow public accommodations to take safety factors into consideration in providing services to individuals with disabilities?

A. The ADA expressly provides that a public accommodation may exclude an individual, if that individual poses a direct threat to the health or safety of others that cannot be mitigated by appropriate modifications in the public accommodation's policies or procedures, or by the provision of auxiliary aids. A public accommodation will be permitted to establish objective safety criteria for the operation of its business; however, any safety standard must be based on objective requirements rather than stereotypes or generalizations about the ability of persons with disabilities to participate in an activity.

Q. Are there any limits on the kinds of modifications in policies, practices, and procedures required by the ADA?

A. Yes. The ADA does not require modifications that would fundamentally alter the nature of the services provided by the public accommodation. For example, it would not be discriminatory for a physician specialist who treats only burn patients to refer a deaf individual to another physician for treatment of a broken limb or respiratory ailment. To require a physician to accept patients outside of his or her specialty would fundamentally alter the nature of the medical practice.

Q. What kinds of auxiliary aids and services are required by the ADA to ensure effective communication with individuals with hearing or vision impairments?

A. Appropriate auxiliary aids and services may include services and devices such as qualified interpreters, assistive listening devices, notetakers, and written materials for individuals with hearing impairments; and qualified readers, taped texts, and brailled or large print materials for individuals with vision impairments.

Q. Are there any limitations on the ADA's auxiliary aids requirements?

A. Yes. The ADA does not require the provision of any auxiliary aid that would result in an undue burden or in a fundamental alteration in the nature of the goods or services provided by a public accommodation. However, the public accommodation is not relieved from the duty to furnish an alternative auxiliary aid, if available, that would not result in a fundamental alteration or undue burden. Both of these limitations are derived from existing regulations and caselaw under section 504 and are to be determined on a case-by-case basis.

Q. Will restaurants be required to have brailled menus?

A. No, not if waiters or other employees are made available to read the menu to a blind customer.

Q. Will a clothing store be required to have brailled price tags?

A. No. Sales personnel could provide price information orally upon request.

Q. Will a bookstore be required to maintain a sign language interpreter on its staff in order to communicate with deaf customers?

A. No, not if employees communicate by pen and notepad when necessary.

Q.   **Are there any limitations on the ADA's barrier removal requirements for existing facilities?**

A.   Yes. Barrier removal need be accomplished only when it is "readily achievable" to do so.

Q.   **What does the term "readily achievable" mean?**

A.   It means "easily accomplishable and able to be carried out without much difficulty or expense."

Q.   **What are examples of the types of modifications that would be readily achievable in most cases?**

A.   Examples include the simple ramping of a few steps, the installation of grab bars where only routine reinforcement of the wall is required, the lowering of telephones, and similar modest adjustments.

Q.   **Will businesses need to rearrange furniture and display racks?**

A.   Possibly. For example, restaurants may need to rearrange tables and department stores may need to adjust their layout of racks and shelves in order to permit wheelchair access.

Q.   **Will businesses need to install elevators?**

A.   Businesses are not required to retrofit their facilities to install elevators unless such installation is readily achievable, which is unlikely in most cases.

Q.   **When barrier removal is not readily achievable, what kinds of alternative steps are required by the ADA?**

A.   Alternatives may include such measures as in-store assistance for removing articles from high shelves, home delivery of groceries, or coming to the door to receive or return dry cleaning.

Q.   **Must alternative steps be taken without regard to cost?**

A.   No, only readily achievable alternative steps must be undertaken.

Q.   **How is "readily achievable" determined in a multisite business?**

A.   In determining whether an action to make a public accommodation accessible would be "readily achievable," the overall size of the parent corporation or entity is only one factor to be considered. The ADA also permits consideration of the financial resources of the particular facility or facilities involved and the administrative or fiscal relationship of the facility or facilities to the parent entity.

Q.   **Who has responsibility for removing barriers in a shopping mall, the landlord who owns the mall or the tenant who leases the store?**

A.   Legal responsibility for removing barriers depends upon who has legal authority to make alterations, which is generally determined by the contractual agreement between the landlord and tenant. In most cases the landlord will have full control over common areas.

Q. What does the ADA require in new construction?

A. The ADA requires that all new construction of places of public accommodation, as well as of "commercial facilities" such as office buildings, be accessible. Elevators are generally not required in facilities under three stories or with fewer than 3,000 square feet per floor, unless the building is a shopping center, mall, or professional office of a health care provider.

Q. Is it expensive to make all newly constructed public accommodations and commercial facilities accessible?

A. The cost of incorporating accessibility features in new construction is less than one percent of construction costs. This is a small price in relation to the economic benefits to be derived from full accessibility in the future, such as increased employment and consumer spending and decreased welfare dependency.

Q. Must every feature of a new facility be accessible?

A. No, only a reasonable number of elements such as parking spaces and bathrooms must be made accessible in order for a facility to be "readily accessible." Moreover, mechanical areas, such as catwalks and fan rooms, to which access is required only for purposes of maintenance and repairs, might not need to be physically accessible if the essential functions of the work performed in those areas require physical mobility.

Q. What are the ADA requirements for altering facilities?

A. All alterations that could affect the usability of a facility must be made in an accessible manner to the maximum extent feasible. For example, if during renovations a doorway is being relocated, the new doorway must be wide enough to meet the new construction standard for accessibility. When alterations are made to a primary function area, such as the lobby of a bank or the dining area of a cafeteria, an accessible path of travel to the altered area must also be provided. The bathrooms, telephones, and drinking fountains serving that area must also be made accessible. These additional accessibility alterations are only required to the extent that the added accessibility costs are not disproportionate to the overall cost of the alterations. Elevators are generally not required in facilities under three stories or with fewer than 3000 square feet per floor, unless the building is a shopping center, mall, or professional office of a health care provider.

Q. Does the ADA permit a disabled person to sue a business when that individual believes that discrimination is about to occur, or must the individual wait for the discrimination to occur?

A. The ADA public accommodations provisions permit an individual to allege discrimination based on a disabled person's reasonable belief that discrimination is about to occur. This provision allows a person who uses a wheelchair to challenge the planned construction of a new place of public accommodation, such as a shopping mall, that would not be accessible to wheelchair users. The resolution of such challenges prior to the construction of an inaccessible facility would enable any necessary remedial measures to be incorporated in the building at the planning stage, when such changes would be relatively inexpensive.

Q.   How does the ADA affect existing State and local building codes?

A.   Existing codes remain in effect. The ADA allows the Attorney General to certify that a State law, local building code, or similar ordinance that establishes accessibility requirements meets or exceeds the minimum accessibility requirements for public accommodations and commercial facilities. Any State or local government may apply for certification of its code or ordinance. The Attorney General can certify a code or ordinance only after prior notice and a public hearing at which interested people, including individuals with disabilities, are provided an opportunity to testify against the certification.

Q.   What is the effect of certification of a State or local code or ordinance?

A.   Certification can be advantageous if an entity has constructed or altered a facility according to a certified code or ordinance. If someone later brings an enforcement proceeding against the entity, the certification is considered "rebuttable evidence" that the State law or local ordinance meets or exceeds the minimum requirements of the ADA. In other words, the entity can argue that the construction or alteration met the requirements of the ADA because it was done in compliance with the State or local code that had been certified.

Q.   When are the public accommodations provisions effective?

A.   In general, they become effective on January 26, 1992.

Q.   How will the public accommodations provisions be enforced?

A.   Private individuals may bring lawsuits in which they can obtain court orders to stop discrimination. Individuals may also file complaints with the Attorney General, who is authorized to bring lawsuits in cases of general public importance or where a "pattern or practice" of discrimination is alleged. In these cases, the Attorney General may seek monetary damages and civil penalties. Civil penalties may not exceed $50,000 for a first violation or $100,000 for any subsequent violation.

MISCELLANEOUS

Q.   Is the Federal government covered by the ADA?

A.   The ADA does not cover the executive branch of the Federal Government. The executive branch continues to be covered by title V of the Rehabilitation Act of 1973, which prohibits discrimination in services and employment on the basis of handicap and which is a model for the requirements of the ADA. The ADA, however, does cover Congress and other entities in the legislative branch of the Federal Government.

Q.   What requirements, other than those mandating nondiscrimination in employment, does the ADA place on State and local governments?

A.   All government facilities, services, and communications must be accessible consistent with the requirements of section 504 of the Rehabilitation Act of 1973. Individuals may file complaints with Federal agencies to be designated by the Attorney General or bring private lawsuits.

Q. Does the ADA cover private apartments and private homes?

A. The ADA generally does not cover private residential facilities. These facilities are addressed in the Fair Housing Amendments Act of 1988, which prohibits discrimination on the basis of disability in selling or renting housing. If a building contains both residential and nonresidential portions, only the nonresidential portions are covered by the ADA. For example, in a large hotel that has a residential apartment wing, the residential wing would be covered by the Fair Housing Act and the other rooms would be covered by the ADA.

Q. Does the ADA cover air transportation?

A. Discrimination by air carriers is not covered by the ADA but rather by the Air Carrier Access Act (49 U.S.C. 1374 (c)).

Q. What are the ADA's requirements for public transit buses?

A. The ADA requires the Department of Transportation to issue regulations mandating accessible public transit vehicles and facilities. The regulations must include a requirement that all new fixed-route, public transit buses be accessible and that supplementary paratransit services be provided for those individuals with disabilities who cannot use fixed-route bus service. For information on how to contact the Department of Transportation, see page 19.

Q. How will the ADA make telecommunications accessible?

A. The ADA requires the establishment of telephone relay services for individuals who use telecommunications devices for the deaf (TDD's) or similar devices. The Federal Communications Commission will issue regulations specifying standards for the operation of these services.

Q. Are businesses entitled to any tax benefit to help pay for the cost of compliance?

A. As amended in 1990, the Internal Revenue Code allows a deduction of up to $15,000 per year for expenses associated with the removal of qualified architectural and transportation barriers.

The 1990 amendment also permits eligible small businesses to receive a tax credit for certain costs of compliance with the ADA. An eligible small business is one whose gross receipts do not exceed $1,000,000 or whose workforce does not consist of more than 30 full-time workers. Qualifying businesses may claim a credit of up to 50 percent of eligible access expenditures that exceed $250 but do not exceed $10,250. Examples of eligible access expenditures include the necessary and reasonable costs of removing architectural, physical, communications, and transportation barriers; providing readers, interpreters, and other auxiliary aids; and acquiring or modifying equipment or devices.

For more specific information about ADA requirements affecting Public Services and Public Accommodations contact:

Office on the Americans with Disabilities Act
Civil Rights Division
U.S. Department of Justice
P.O. Box 66118
Washington, D.C. 20035-6118
(202) 514-0301 (Voice)
(202) 514-0383 (TDD)

For more specific information about ADA requirements affecting employment contact:

Equal Employment Opportunity Commission
1801 L Street NW
Washington, DC 20507
800-669-EEOC (Voice)
800-800-3302 (TDD)

For more specific information about ADA requirements affecting transportation contact:

Department of Transportation
400 Seventh Street SW
Washington, DC 20590
(202) 366-9305 (Voice)
(202) 755-7687 (TDD)

For more specific information about requirements for accessible design in new construction and alterations contact:

Architectural and Transportation Barriers
Compliance Board
1111 18th Street NW
Suite 501
Washington, DC 20036
800-USA-ABLE (Voice)
800-USA-ABLE (TDD)

For more specific information about ADA requirements affecting telecommunications contact:

Federal Communications Commission
1919 M Street NW
Washington, DC 20554
(202) 632-7260 (Voice)
(202) 632-6999 (TDD)

APPENDIX N

ADA HIGHLIGHTS -- TITLE II
STATE AND LOCAL GOVERNMENT SERVICES

Title II Highlights

I. Who is Covered by Title II of the ADA

➤ The title II regulation covers "public entities."

➤ "Public entities" include any State or local government and any of its departments, agencies, or other instrumentalities.

➤ All activities, services, and programs of public entities are covered, including activities of State legislatures and courts, town meetings, police and fire departments, motor vehicle licensing, and employment.

- Unlike section 504 of the Rehabilitation Act of 1973, which only covers programs receiving Federal financial assistance, title II extends to all the activities of State and local governments whether or not they receive Federal funds.

➤ Private entities that operate public accommodations, such as hotels, restaurants, theaters, retail stores, dry cleaners, doctors' offices, amusement parks, and bowling alleys, are not covered by title II but are covered by title III of the ADA and the Department's regulation implementing title III.

➤ Public transportation services operated by State and local governments are covered by regulations of the Department of Transportation.

- DOT's regulations establish specific requirements for transportation vehicles and facilities, including a requirement that all new busses must be equipped to provide services to people who use wheelchairs.

II. Overview of Requirements

➤ State and local governments --

- May not refuse to allow a person with a disability to participate in a service, program, or activity simply because the person has a disability.

  - For example, a city may not refuse to allow a person with epilepsy to use parks and recreational facilities.

- Must provide programs and services in an integrated setting, unless separate or different measures are necessary to ensure equal opportunity.

- Must eliminate unnecessary eligibility standards or rules that deny individuals with disabilities an equal opportunity to enjoy their services, programs or activities unless "necessary" for the provisions of the service, program or activity.

  - Requirements that tend to screen out individuals with disabilities, such as requiring a driver's license as the only acceptable means of identification, are also prohibited.

- Safety requirements that are necessary for the safe operation of the program in question, such as requirements for eligibility for drivers' licenses, may be imposed if they are based on actual risks and not on mere speculation, stereotypes, or generalizations about individuals with disabilities.

- Are required to make reasonable modifications in policies, practices, and procedures that deny equal access to individuals with disabilities, unless a fundamental alteration in the program would result.

  - For example, a city office building would be required to make an exception to a rule prohibiting animals in public areas in order to admit guide dogs and other service animals assisting individuals with disabilities.

- Must furnish auxiliary aids and services when necessary to ensure effective communication, unless an undue burden or fundamental alteration would result.

- May provide special benefits, beyond those required by the regulation, to individuals with disabilities.

- May not place special charges on individuals with disabilities to cover the costs of measures necessary to ensure nondiscriminatory treatment, such as making modifications required to provide program accessibility or providing qualified interpreters.

- Shall operate their programs so that, when viewed in their entirety, they are readily accessible to and usable by individuals with disabilities.

III. "Qualified Individuals with Disabilities"

➤ Title II of the Americans with Disabilities Act provides comprehensive civil rights protections for "qualified individuals with disabilities."

➤ An "individual with a disability" is a person who --

- Has a physical or mental impairment that substantially limits a "major life activity," or

- Has a record of such an impairment, or

- Is regarded as having such an impairment.

➤ Examples of physical or mental impairments include, but are not limited to, such contagious and noncontagious diseases and conditions as orthopedic, visual, speech, and hearing impairments; cerebral palsy, epilepsy, muscular dystrophy, multiple sclerosis, cancer, heart disease, diabetes, mental retardation, emotional illness, specific learning disabilities, HIV disease (whether symptomatic or asymptomatic), tuberculosis, drug addiction, and alcoholism. Homosexuality and bisexuality are not physical or mental impairments under the ADA.

➤ "Major life activities" include functions such as caring for oneself, performing manual tasks, walking, seeing, hearing, speaking, breathing, learning, and working.

➤ Individuals who currently engage in the illegal use of drugs are not protected by the ADA when an action is taken on the basis of their current illegal use of drugs.

➤ "Qualified" individuals.

   • A "qualified" individual with a disability is one who meets the essential eligibility requirements for the program or activity offered by a public entity.

   • The "essential eligibility requirements" will depend on the type of service or activity involved.

      • For some activities, such as State licensing programs, the ability to meet specific skill and performance requirements may be "essential."

      • For other activities, such as where the public entity provides information to anyone who requests it, the "essential eligibility requirements" would be minimal.

IV. Program Access

➤ State and local governments--

   • Must ensure that individuals with disabilities are not excluded from services, programs, and activities because buildings are inaccessible.

   • Need not remove physical barriers, such as stairs, in all existing buildings, as long as they make their programs accessible to individuals who are unable to use an inaccessible existing facility.

   • Can provide the services, programs, and activities offered in the facility to individuals with disabilities through alternative methods, if physical barriers are not removed, such as --

      • Relocating a service to an accessible facility, e.g., moving a public information office from the third floor to the first floor of a building.

      • Providing an aide or personal assistant to enable an individual with a disability to obtain the service.

      • Providing benefits or services at an individual's home, or at an alternative accessible site.

   • May not carry an individual with a disability as a method of providing program access, except in "manifestly exceptional" circumstances.

- Are not required to take any action that would result in a fundamental alteration in the nature of the service, program, or activity or in undue financial and administrative burdens. However, public entities must take any other action, if available, that would not result in a fundamental alteration or undue burdens but would ensure that individuals with disabilities receive the benefits or services.

V. Integrated Programs

➤ Integration of individuals with disabilities into the mainstream of society is fundamental to the purposes of the Americans with Disabilities Act.

➤ Public entities may not provide services or benefits to individuals with disabilities through programs that are separate or different, unless the separate programs are necessary to ensure that the benefits and services are equally effective.

➤ Even when separate programs are permitted, an individual with a disability still has the right to choose to participate in the regular program.

- For example, it would not be a violation for a city to offer recreational programs specially designed for children with mobility impairments, but it would be a violation if the city refused to allow children with disabilities to participate in its other recreational programs.

➤ State and local governments may not require an individual with a disability to accept a special accommodation or benefit if the individual chooses not to accept it.

VI. Communications

➤ State and local governments must ensure effective communication with individuals with disabilities.

➤ Where necessary to ensure that communications with individuals with hearing, vision, or speech impairments are as effective as communications with others, the public entity must provide appropriate auxiliary aids.

- "Auxiliary aids" include such services or devices as qualified interpreters, assistive listening headsets, television captioning and decoders, telecommunications devices for deaf persons (TDD's), videotext displays, readers, taped texts, Brailled materials, and large print materials.

- A public entity may not charge an individual with a disability for the use of an auxiliary aid.

➤ Telephone emergency services, including 911 services, must provide direct access to individuals with speech or hearing impairments.

➤ Public entities are not required to provide auxiliary aids that would result in a fundamental alteration in the nature of a service, program, or activity or in undue financial and administrative burdens. However, public entities must still furnish another auxiliary aid, if available, that does not result in a fundamental alteration or undue burdens.

VII. New Construction and Alterations

➤ Public entities must ensure that newly constructed buildings and facilities are free of architectural and communication barriers that restrict access or use by individuals with disabilities.

➤ When a public entity undertakes alterations to an existing building, it must also ensure that the altered portions are accessible.

➤ The ADA does not require retrofitting of existing buildings to eliminate barriers, but does establish a high standard of accessibility for new buildings.

   • Public entities may choose between two technical standards for accessible design: The Uniform Federal Accessibility Standard (UFAS), established under the Architectural Barriers Act, or the Americans with Disability Act Accessibility Guidelines, adopted by the Department of Justice for places of public accommodation and commercial facilities covered by title III of the ADA.

   • The elevator exemption for small buildings under ADA Accessibility Guidelines would not apply to public entities covered by title II.

VIII. Enforcement

➤ Private parties may bring lawsuits to enforce their rights under title II of the ADA. The remedies available are the same as those provided under section 504 of the Rehabilitation Act of 1973. A reasonable attorney's fee may be awarded to the prevailing party.

➤ Individuals may also file complaints with appropriate administrative agencies.

   • The regulation designates eight Federal agencies to handle complaints filed under title II.

   • Complaints may also be filed with any Federal agency that provides financial assistance to the program in question, or with the Department of Justice, which will refer the complaint to the appropriate agency.

IX. Complaints

➤ Any individual who believes that he or she is a victim of discrimination prohibited by the regulation may file a complaint. Complaints on behalf of classes of individuals are also permitted.

➤ Complaints should be in writing, signed by the complainant or an authorized representative, and should contain the complainant's name and address and describe the public entity's alleged discriminatory action.

➤ Complaints may be sent to --

Coordination and Review Section
Civil Rights Division
U.S. Department of Justice
P.O. Box 66118
Washington, D.C. 20035-6118.

➤ Complaints may also be sent to agencies designated to process complaints under the regulation, or to agencies that provide Federal financial assistance to the program in question.

X. Designated Agencies

The following agencies are designated for enforcement of title II for components of State and local governments that exercise responsibilities, regulate, or administer services, programs, or activities in the following functional areas --

(1) <u>Department of Agriculture</u>: Farming and the raising of livestock, including extension services.

(2) <u>Department of Education</u>: Education systems and institutions (other than health-related schools), and libraries.

(3) <u>Department of Health and Human Services</u>: Schools of medicine, dentistry, nursing, and other health-related schools; health care and social service providers and institutions, including "grass-roots" and community services organizations and programs; and preschool and daycare programs.

(4) <u>Department of Housing and Urban Development</u>: State and local public housing, and housing assistance and referral.

(5) <u>Department of Interior</u>: Lands and natural resources, including parks and recreation, water and waste management, environmental protection, energy, historic and cultural preservation, and museums.

(6) <u>Department of Justice</u>: Public safety, law enforcement, and the administration of justice, including courts and correctional institutions; commerce and industry, including banking and finance, consumer protection, and insurance; planning, development, and regulation (unless otherwise assigned); State and local government support services; and all other government functions not assigned to other designated agencies.

(7) <u>Department of Labor</u>: Labor and the work force.

(8) <u>Department of Transportation</u>: Transportation, including highways, public transportation, traffic management (non-law enforcement), automobile licensing and inspection, and driver licensing.

XI. Technical Assistance

➤ The ADA requires that the Federal agencies responsible for issuing ADA regulations provide "technical assistance."

➤ Technical assistance is the dissemination of information (either directly by the Department or through grants and contracts) to assist the public, including individuals protected by the ADA and entities covered by the ADA, in understanding the new law.

➤ Methods of providing information include, for example, audio-visual materials, pamphlets, manuals, electronic bulletin boards, checklists, and training.

➤ The Department issued for public comment on December 5, 1990, a government-wide plan for the provision of technical assistance.

The Department's efforts focus on raising public awareness of the ADA by providing--

- Fact sheets and pamphlets in accessible formats,

- Speakers for workshops, seminars, classes, and conferences,

- An ADA telephone information line, and

- Access to ADA documents through an electronic bulletin board for users of personal computers.

➤ The Department has established a comprehensive program of technical assistance relating to public accommodations and State and local governments.

- Grants will be awarded for projects to inform individuals with disabilities and covered entities about their rights and responsibilities under the ADA and to facilitate voluntary compliance.

- The Department will issue a technical assistance manual by January 26, 1992, for individuals or entities with rights or duties under the ADA.

For additional information, contact:

Office on the Americans with Disabilities Act
Civil Rights Division
U.S. Department of Justice
P.O. Box 66118
Washington, D.C 20035-6118
(202) 514-0301 (Voice)
(202) 514-0383 (TDD)
(202) 514-6193 (Electronic Bulletin Board).

Appendix O

ADA Highlights -- Title III
Public Accommodations
and Commercial Facilities

Title III Highlights

I. Who is Covered by title III of the ADA

II. Overview of Requirements

III. "Individuals with Disabilities"

IV. Eligibility for Goods and Services

V. Modifications in Policies, Practices, and Procedures

VI. Auxiliary Aids

VII. Existing Facilities: Removal of Barriers

VIII. Existing Facilities: Alternatives to Barrier Removal

IX. New Construction

X. Alterations

XI. Overview of Americans with Disabilities Act Accessibility Guidelines for New Construction and Alterations

XII. Examinations and Courses

XIII. Enforcement of the ADA and its Regulations

XIV. Technical Assistance

I. Who is Covered by Title III of the ADA

➤ The title III regulation covers --

- Public accommodations (i.e., private entities that own, operate, lease, or lease to places of public accommodation),

- Commercial facilities, and

- Private entities that offer certain examinations and courses related to educational and occupational certification.

➤ Places of public accommodation include over five million private establishments, such as restaurants, hotels, theaters, convention centers, retail stores, shopping centers, dry cleaners, laundromats, pharmacies, doctors' offices, hospitals, museums, libraries, parks, zoos, amusement parks, private schools, day care centers, health spas, and bowling alleys.

➤ Commercial facilities are nonresidential facilities, including office buildings, factories, and warehouses, whose operations affect commerce.

➤ Entities controlled by religious organizations, including places of worship, are not covered.

➤ Private clubs are not covered, except to the extent that the facilities of the private club are made available to customers or patrons of a place of public accommodation.

➤ State and local governments are not covered by the title III regulation, but rather by the Department of Justice's title II regulation.

II. Overview of Requirements

➤ Public accommodations must --

- Provide goods and services in an integrated setting, unless separate or different measures are necessary to ensure equal opportunity.

- Eliminate unnecessary eligibility standards or rules that deny individuals with disabilities an equal opportunity to enjoy the goods and services of a place of public accommodation.

- Make reasonable modifications in policies, practices, and procedures that deny equal access to individuals with disabilities, unless a fundamental alteration would result in the nature of the goods and services provided.

- Furnish auxiliary aids when necessary to ensure effective communication, unless an undue burden or fundamental alteration would result.

- Remove architectural and structural communication barriers in existing facilities where readily achievable.

- Provide readily achievable alternative measures when removal of barriers is not readily achievable.

- Provide equivalent transportation services and purchase accessible vehicles in certain circumstances.

- Maintain accessible features of facilities and equipment.

- Design and construct new facilities and, when undertaking alterations, alter existing facilities in accordance with the Americans with Disabilities Act Accessibility Guidelines issued by the Architectural and Transportation Barriers Compliance Board and incorporated in the final Department of Justice title III regulation.

➤ A public accommodation is not required to provide personal devices such as wheelchairs; individually prescribed devices (e.g., prescription eyeglasses or hearing aids); or services of a personal nature including assistance in eating, toileting, or dressing.

➤ A public accommodation may not discriminate against an individual or entity because of the known disability of a person with whom the individual or entity is known to associate.

➤ Commercial facilities are only subject to the requirement that new construction and alterations conform to the ADA Accessibility Guidelines. The other requirements applicable to public accommodations listed above do not apply to commercial facilities.

➤ Private entities offering certain examinations or courses (i.e., those related to applications, licensing, certification, or credentialing for secondary or postsecondary education, professional, or trade purposes) must offer them in an accessible place and manner or offer alternative accessible arrangements.

III. "Individuals with Disabilities"

➤ The Americans with Disabilities Act provides comprehensive civil rights protections for "individuals with disabilities."

➤ An individual with a disability is a person who --

- Has a physical or mental impairment that substantially limits one or more "major life activities," or

- Has a record of such an impairment, or

- Is regarded as having such an impairment.

➤ Examples of physical or mental impairments include, but are not limited to, such contagious and noncontagious diseases and conditions as orthopedic, visual, speech, and hearing impairments; cerebral palsy, epilepsy, muscular dystrophy, multiple sclerosis, cancer, heart disease, diabetes, mental retardation, emotional illness, specific learning disabilities, HIV disease (whether symptomatic or asymptomatic), tuberculosis, drug addiction, and alcoholism. Homosexuality and bisexuality are not physical or mental impairments under the ADA.

➤ "Major life activities" include functions such as caring for oneself, performing manual tasks, walking, seeing, hearing, speaking, breathing, learning, and working.

➤ Individuals who currently engage in the illegal use of drugs are not protected by the ADA when an action is taken on the basis of their current illegal use of drugs.

IV. Eligibility for Goods and Services

➤ In providing goods and services, a public accommodation may not use eligibility requirements that exclude or segregate individuals with disabilities, unless the requirements are "necessary" for the operation of the public accommodation.

• For example, excluding individuals with cerebral palsy from a movie theater or restricting individuals with Down's Syndrome to only certain areas of a restaurant would violate the regulation.

➤ Requirements that tend to screen out individuals with disabilities, such as requiring a blind person to produce a driver's license as the sole means of identification for cashing a check, are also prohibited.

➤ Safety requirements may be imposed only if they are necessary for the safe operation of a place of public accommodation. They must be based on actual risks and not on mere speculation, stereotypes, or generalizations about individuals with disabilities.

• For example, an amusement park may impose height requirements for certain rides when required for safety.

➤ Extra charges may not be imposed on individuals with disabilities to cover the costs of measures necessary to ensure nondiscriminatory treatment, such as removing barriers or providing qualified interpreters.

V. Modifications in Policies, Practices, and Procedures

➤ A public accommodation must make reasonable modifications in its policies, practices, and procedures in order to accommodate individuals with disabilities.

➤ A modification is not required if it would "fundamentally alter" the goods, services, or operations of the public accommodation.

4